B. NATHAN

Uncovering the One-Story Home

P ractical in design, the one-story home is a mainstay of popularity in America—from shore to shore and border to border. Its appeal, however, is on many levels: its unique ability to accommodate any number of floor plan configurations, its diverse nature—from sprawling to diminutive—and its convenience and affordability.

The homes offered in this volume are among the best you'll find for quality design. Conceived by an elite and well-recognized group of professionals, known as the Blue Ribbon Network of Designers, the plans are well-executed, efficient and focus on livability. The sizes of the homes range from palatial to petite and all variations of volume in between. There are estate-quality mansions, horizon-hovering ranch homes, mid-sized move-ups, comfortable family homes, quaint cottages and even some vacation getaways. All are designed with the care and attention to detail you'd expect from award-winning residential designers, and there's one or more to fit your lifestyle and budget perfectly.

Styles of the homes cover the gamut: traditional homes (over 139 pages of plans in a huge range of sizes), period homes (contemporary, Tudor and European), country designs (with porches and rural charm), cottages (in smaller square footages), luxury estates (filled with amenities), sun-country beauties (for sun-belt regions) and vacation retreats (for a second home or retirement option). There are even some expandable styles that allow you to build on a single level and expand to an upper or lower level when the time is right.

Discover the possibilities of one-story living between these pages. And when you've made your favorite choice, call Home Planners to guide you in purchasing the complete blueprint package to make your one-story dream a reality. Whatever your needs, whatever your budget, we're helping to plan what America builds.

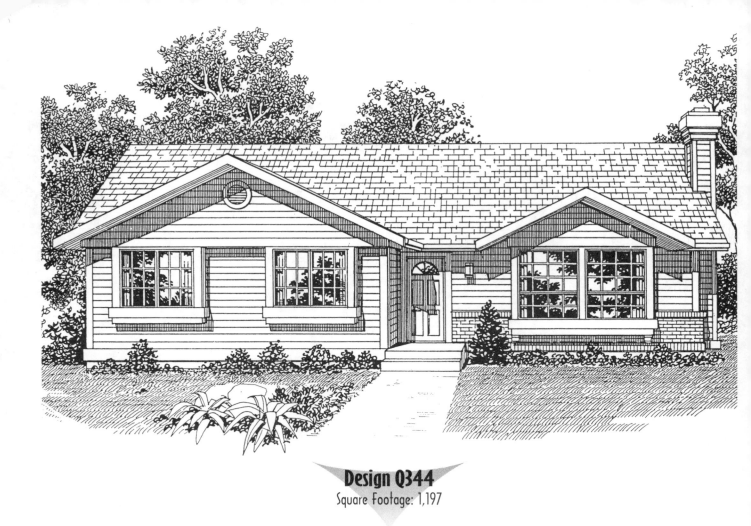

Design Q344
Square Footage: 1,197

◆ This compact, three-bedroom design is ideal as a starter or retirement home. Its siding and brick combination and lovely bumped-out windows give it a cozy, rustic feeling. The bedrooms are positioned along the rear of the home for maximum privacy. Each bedroom has a large window overlooking the rear yard; the master bedroom is especially spacious. The entry opens directly onto a large living area with box-bay window and fireplace. The country kitchen contains long, roomy counters, a convenient serving bar and a breakfast nook with box-bay window. The side door provides quick, easy access to the kitchen and to the basement. If needed, the basement may be finished for additional living space or bedrooms.

— DESIGN BY —
SELECT HOME DESIGNS

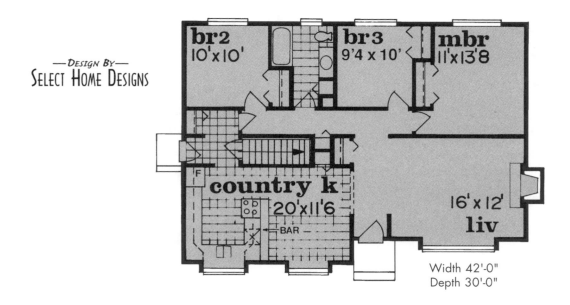

br2
10'x10'

br3
9'4 x 10'

mbr
11'x13'8

F

country k
20'x11'6

BAR

16'x12'
liv

Width 42'-0"
Depth 30'-0"

Traditional One-Story Homes under 1,500 square feet

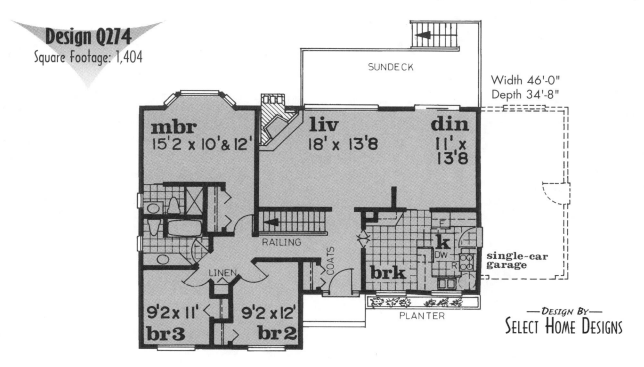

Width 46'-0"
Depth 34'-8"

SUNDECK

mbr
15'2 x 10' & 12'

liv
18' x 13'8

din
11' x 13'8

RAILING

LINEN

COATS

brk

k

single-car
garage

9'2 x 11'
br3

9'2 x 12'
br2

PLANTER

—DESIGN BY—
SELECT HOME DESIGNS

◆ Taking advantage of a rear view, this tidy three-bedroom home features great indoor/outdoor spaces. The large living room/dining room area has a corner fireplace. The living room has a wonderful picture window while the dining area has sliding glass doors to the rear sundeck. A bay window in the master suite serves as a bright accent. The master suite also has a private bath with shower. Family bedrooms share a full bath with a handy linen closet nearby. For casual meals, the breakfast area connects to the kitchen which is appointed with abundant counter space and a side door to the single-car garage (optional). A full basement may be developed later for additional space.

Design Q440
Square Footage: 1,092

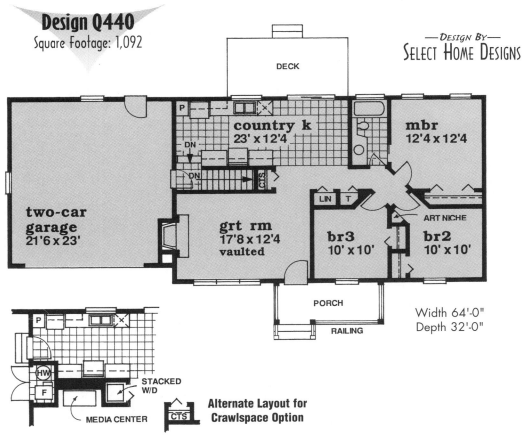

DECK

P

country k
23' x 12'4

DN

DN

CTS

two-car
garage
21'6 x 23'

grt rm
17'8 x 12'4
vaulted

mbr
12'4 x 12'4

LIN   T

ART NICHE

br3
10' x 10'

br2
10' x 10'

PORCH

RAILING

Width 64'-0"
Depth 32'-0"

P

HW

F

STACKED
W/D

MEDIA CENTER

CTS

**Alternate Layout for
Crawlspace Option**

◆ Compact, yet efficient, this one-story home opens with a quaint covered porch to a convenient floor plan. The great room has a vaulted ceiling and warming hearth for cozy winter blazes. The step-saving galley kitchen is pure country with space for a family-sized dining area and sliding glass doors to the rear deck. The master bedroom has an angled entry and windows overlooking the rear yard. It shares a full bath that has a split entry with two family bedrooms (note the art niche at the entry to Bedroom 2). If you choose the crawlspace option, you'll gain space for a washer and dryer and a spot for a built-in media center. The two-car garage is reached through a side door in the kitchen.

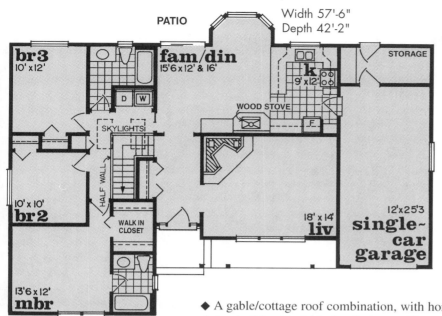

PATIO

Width 57'-6"
Depth 42'-2"

br3
10' x 12'

fam/din
15'6 12' & 16'

STORAGE

k
9' x 12'

D W

WOOD STOVE

SKYLIGHTS

F

10' x 10'
br2

HALF WALL

WALK IN CLOSET

18' x 14'
liv

12'x25'3
single-car garage

13'6 x 12'
mbr

─ DESIGN BY ─
SELECT HOME DESIGNS

Design Q251
Square Footage: 1,471

◆ A gable/cottage roof combination, with horizontal siding and multi-pane windows, lend charm to this affordable family home. The covered entry opens directly to an expansive living room featuring a corner fireplace. The kitchen, dining room and family room are warmed by a rustic wood stove. Sliding glass doors in the family room area lead out back to a patio and the rear yard beyond. The dining room rests in a bay windowed area and provides a view to the back. Lovely skylights brighten the hallway and the staircase to the basement (finish the basement later as the family grows). Three bedrooms include a master suite with private, full bath and a walk-in closet. Family bedrooms share a full bath. The laundry alcove is nearby for convenience.

◆ Horizontal siding and quaint window boxes lend a country appeal to the exterior of this design. If you choose this cute one-story home, you'll have the option of a powder room or a main-floor laundry room layout. The central foyer leads to a roomy living room with masonry fireplace and box-bay window. The nearby country kitchen has a long, L-shaped counter and a bay-window dining area. A rear door leads to the patio (basement stairs are directly opposite this door). Three bedrooms angle off the central hall. The master has a large window overlooking the rear yard and His and Hers wall closets. Family bedrooms face to the front of the house.

Design Q500
Square Footage: 1,253

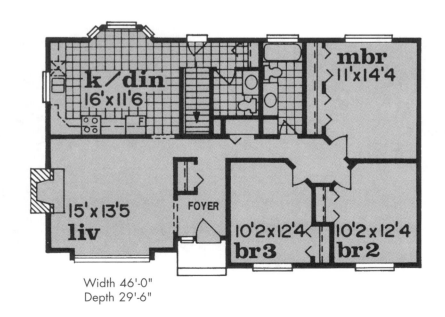

k/din
16'x11'6

mbr
11'x14'4

15'x13'5
liv

FOYER

10'2x12'4
br3

10'2x12'4
br2

Width 46'-0"
Depth 29'-6"

Optional Laundry

—DESIGN BY—
SELECT HOME DESIGNS

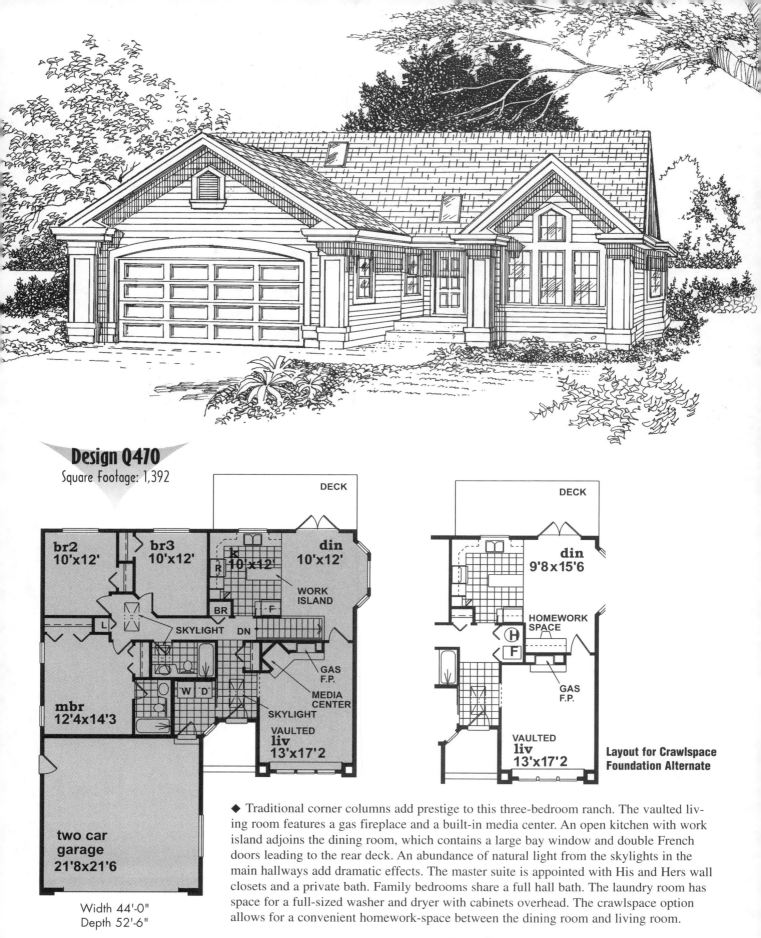

Design Q470
Square Footage: 1,392

DECK

br2 10'x12'

br3 10'x12'

k 10'x12'

din 10'x12'

R

WORK ISLAND

BR

F

L

SKYLIGHT   DN

mbr 12'4x14'3

W   D

GAS F.P.

MEDIA CENTER

SKYLIGHT

VAULTED liv 13'x17'2

two car garage 21'8x21'6

Width 44'-0"
Depth 52'-6"

DECK

din 9'8x15'6

HOMEWORK SPACE

H

F

GAS F.P.

VAULTED liv 13'x17'2

Layout for Crawlspace Foundation Alternate

◆ Traditional corner columns add prestige to this three-bedroom ranch. The vaulted living room features a gas fireplace and a built-in media center. An open kitchen with work island adjoins the dining room, which contains a large bay window and double French doors leading to the rear deck. An abundance of natural light from the skylights in the main hallways add dramatic effects. The master suite is appointed with His and Hers wall closets and a private bath. Family bedrooms share a full hall bath. The laundry room has space for a full-sized washer and dryer with cabinets overhead. The crawlspace option allows for a convenient homework-space between the dining room and living room.

—DESIGN BY—
SELECT HOME DESIGNS

9

Design 2165
Square Footage: 880

—DESIGN BY—
HOME PLANNERS

TABLE SPACE

KIT.
9⁰ x 11⁰

DINING

DN.

REFG. RANGE

SLIDING DOOR

STUDY
BED RM.
9⁰ x 9⁸

BED RM.
13⁴ x 10⁰

SLIDING DOOR

BOOKS

CL.

LIN. CL.

CL.

LIVING RM.
16⁸ x 14⁰

COATS

LIN.

BATH

BED RM.
10⁰ x 10⁸

Width 36'-0"
Depth 26'-0"

◆ Though not for everyone, this cozy ranch design will be the perfect plan for those who are looking for a small footprint. It may serve as either a two- or three-bedroom design depending on how you choose to use the extra room to the rear. The living room is large and contains windowed dining space that leads directly to a galley-style kitchen. There is also table space here for more casual meals. Sliding doors allow the kitchen area to be closed off from both the living room and the study/bedroom. The bedrooms have ample closet space and share a full bath with two linen closets. A coat closet in the hallway is a handy feature. The basement could be finished at a later time if additional room is needed.

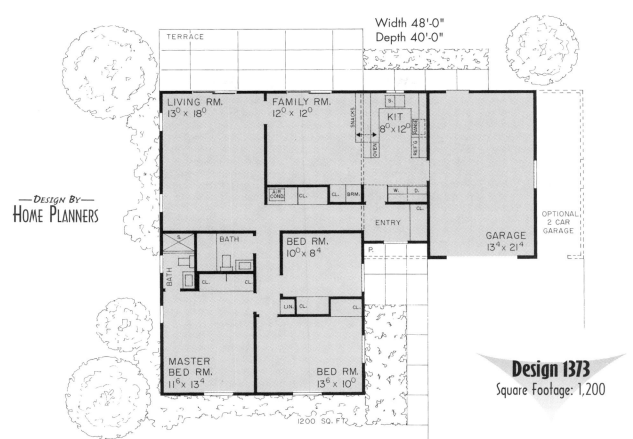

TERRACE

LIVING RM.
13⁰ x 18⁰

FAMILY RM.
12⁰ x 12⁰

KIT
8⁰ x 12⁰

S.

SNACKS

OVEN

REF'G

RANGE

—DESIGN BY—
HOME PLANNERS

AIR COND.

CL.

CL.

BRM.

W.

D.

CL.

ENTRY

GARAGE
13⁴ x 21⁴

OPTIONAL
2 CAR
GARAGE

BATH

S

BATH

CL.

CL.

BED RM.
10⁰ x 8⁴

P.

LIN.

CL.

CL.

MASTER
BED RM.
11⁶ x 13⁴

BED RM.
13⁶ x 10⁰

Design 1373
Square Footage: 1,200

1200 SQ. FT.

◆ This traditional, L-shaped home has an attractive recessed front entrance that leads to a convenient floor plan. The entry directs traffic into the U-shaped kitchen and the family room beyond or down the hall to the large living area and then the bedrooms. Two closets—one at the entry and one farther down the hall—secure ample storage space. The kitchen is separated from the family room by a pass-through counter for casual dining. Sliding glass doors in the family room and the living room open to a long terrace at the back. The master suite has a full bath with shower and double-wide closet. Family bedrooms share a full bath with hall linen closet. The single-car garage may be expanded to a two-car garage if you wish.

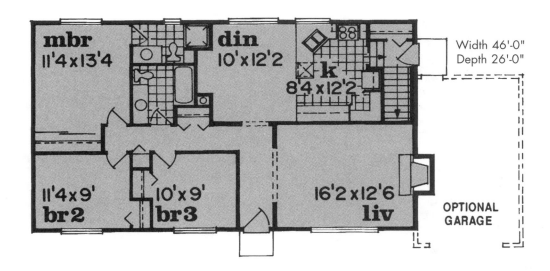

Design Q343
Square Footage: 1,196

mbr
11'4 x 13'4

din
10' x 12'2

k
8'4 x 12'2

Width 46'-0"
Depth 26'-0"

11'4 x 9'
br2

10' x 9'
br3

16'2 x 12'6
liv

OPTIONAL
GARAGE

◆ Offering unique design features, this cozy bungalow is charming with horizontal siding, shuttered windows and multi-pane glass. The foyer leads to a spacious living room with warming fireplace and huge picture window. The dining room has a buffet alcove, providing extra space for entertaining. The kitchen is nearby and is well appointed with an angled sink and walk-in pantry. A short flight of stairs leads to a landing with side-door access and then on to the basement. If you wish, you may build a single-car garage for which plans are included. The master bedroom includes a full wall closet and private bath. Two additional bedrooms share the main bathroom with soaking tub.

—Design By—
Select Home Designs

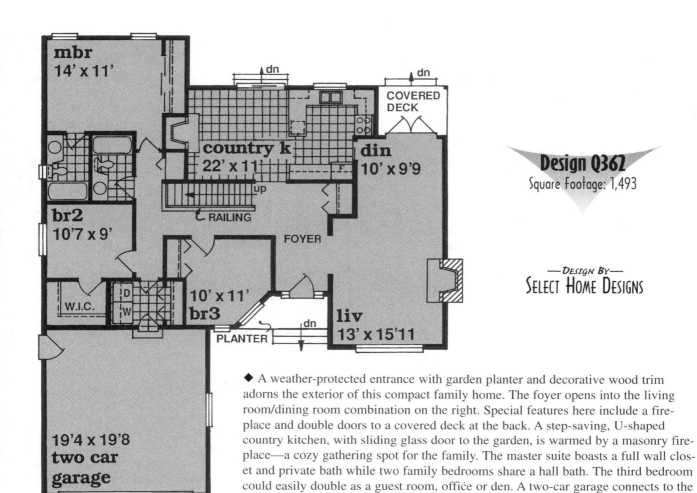

mbr
14' x 11'

br2
10'7 x 9'

W.I.C.

D
W

10' x 11'
br3

PLANTER

19'4 x 19'8
two car
garage

Width 48'-0"
Depth 56'-0"

dn

country k
22' x 11'

RAILING

up

dn

COVERED
DECK

din
10' x 9'9

F

FOYER

dn

liv
13' x 15'11

Design Q362
Square Footage: 1,493

—DESIGN BY—
SELECT HOME DESIGNS

◆ A weather-protected entrance with garden planter and decorative wood trim adorns the exterior of this compact family home. The foyer opens into the living room/dining room combination on the right. Special features here include a fireplace and double doors to a covered deck at the back. A step-saving, U-shaped country kitchen, with sliding glass door to the garden, is warmed by a masonry fireplace—a cozy gathering spot for the family. The master suite boasts a full wall closet and private bath while two family bedrooms share a hall bath. The third bedroom could easily double as a guest room, office or den. A two-car garage connects to the main house at a laundry room with washer/dryer space.

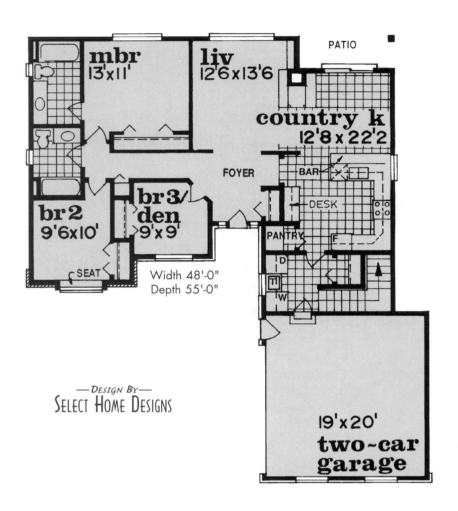

mbr
13'x11'

liv
12'6x13'6

PATIO

country k
12'8 x 22'2

FOYER

BAR

DESK

br2
9'6x10'

br3/
den
9'x9'

PANTRY

F

D

W

SEAT

Width 48'-0"
Depth 55'-0"

— Design By —
Select Home Designs

19'x20'
two~car
garage

◆ This affordable three-bedroom is not only attractive, but offers all the conveniences. The country kitchen, for example, offers abundant U-shaped counters, a desk/organizer area, a pantry and an eating bar. Sliding glass doors in the country kitchen open to a covered patio—ideal for outdoor entertaining. The living room shares the see-through fireplace with the kitchen and also offers a large window overlooking the rear yard. Direct access from the two-car garage through the laundry room and on to the kitchen is convenient for the family shopper. A master suite offers a full wall closet and private bath with soaking tub. Two additional bedrooms include one that might make the perfect office or guest room.

Design Q495
Square Footage: 1,332

Rear Elevation

—DESIGN BY—
SELECT HOME DESIGNS

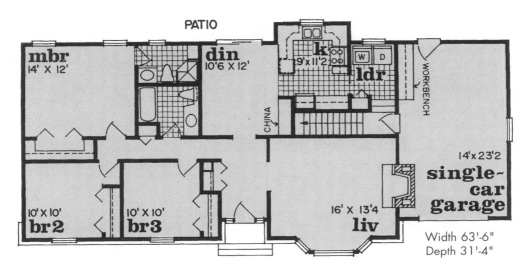

PATIO

mbr
14' X 12'

din
10'6 X 12'

k
9' x 11'2

ldr

W D

WORKBENCH

CHINA

14'x 23'2
single-
car
garage

10' X 10'
br2

10' X 10'
br3

16' X 13'4
liv

Width 63'-6"
Depth 31'-4"

◆ Brick veneer and siding provide an attractive, low-maintenance option for this ranch home. A weather-protected entry opens to a spacious foyer with a living room on the right and the dining room straight ahead. The living room sports a fireplace and bay window, while the dining room has built-in china cabinet space. The kitchen easily serves the dining room and is U-shaped with ample counters. Sliding glass doors in the dining room lead to a rear patio and the yard beyond. The master bedroom has a walk-in closet and private bath with corner shower. Two additional bedrooms share a hall bath. The single-car garage allows room for a work bench. The laundry area leads to the garage.

15

Design Q363
Square Footage: 1,489

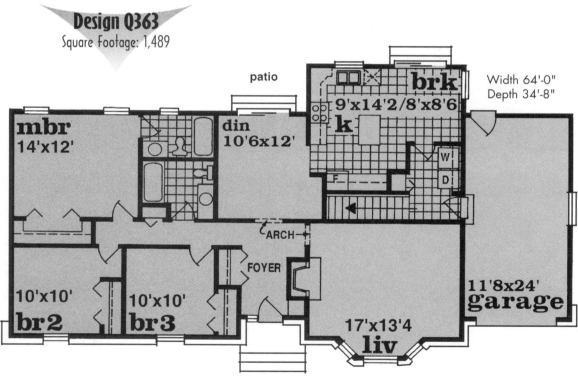

patio

brk

din
10'6x12'

9'x14'2/8'x8'6

k

Width 64'-0"
Depth 34'-8"

mbr
14'12'

W

F

D

ARCH

FOYER

br2
10'10'

br3
10'10'

11'8x24'
garage

17'x13'4
liv

◆ This tidy design is accented with brick veneer and a lovely bay window at the living room. The foyer opens to a hallway that leads, through an arch, to the dining room, or through another arch to the living room. The kitchen is located just beyond the dining room and is large enough for a breakfast nook and island work space. Sliding glass doors in the dining room open to a rear patio and the yard; additional sliding glass doors in the breakfast area do the same. The master bedroom is graced with a walk-in closet and a full bath. Two family bedrooms share a hall bath. If you choose, make one of these bedrooms a den or home office. A single-car garage has access to the house through the laundry area.

—DESIGN BY—
SELECT HOME DESIGNS

Design Q359
Square Footage: 1,432

◆ This comfortable home functions as either a three-bedroom home or a two-bedroom with den design. The living room, with fireplace, rests in a prominent carousel bay and is warmed by a fireplace. The dining room is open to the living room and is decorated with a bumped out area flanked by windows. The spacious country kitchen, with abundant counter space, conveniently serves the dining room. Access the rear patio through a door in the kitchen. The main hall has a feeling of spaciousness due to an open-railed staircase leading to the basement. The master suite features a walk-in closet and bath with His and Hers vanities. Family bedrooms share a main bath with soaking tub. An alcove laundry is on the main level near the bedrooms for convenience.

— DESIGN BY —
SELECT HOME DESIGNS

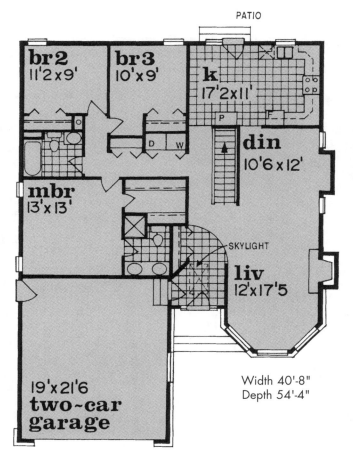

PATIO

br2
11'2 x 9'

br3
10' x 9'

k
17'2 x 11'

din
10'6 x 12'

mbr
13' x 13'

SKYLIGHT

liv
12' x 17'5

19' x 21'6
two-car garage

Width 40'-8"
Depth 54'-4"

Design 3355

Square Footage: 1,387

LD

◆ Though modest in size, this fetching one-story home offers a great deal of livability with three bedrooms (or two with study) and a spacious gathering room with a fireplace and a sloped ceiling. The galley kitchen, designed to save steps, provides a pass-through snack bar and has a planning desk and attached breakfast room. In addition to two secondary bedrooms with a full bath, there's a private master bedroom that enjoys views and access to the backyard. The master bath features a large dressing area, a corner vanity and a raised whirlpool tub. Indoor/outdoor living relationships are strengthened by easy access from the dining room, study/bedroom and master bedroom to the rear terrace.

Quote One®

Cost to build? See page 436 to order complete cost estimate to build this house in your area!

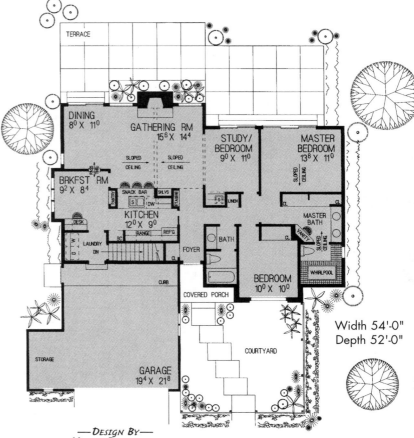

Width 54'-0"
Depth 52'-0"

— DESIGN BY —
HOME PLANNERS

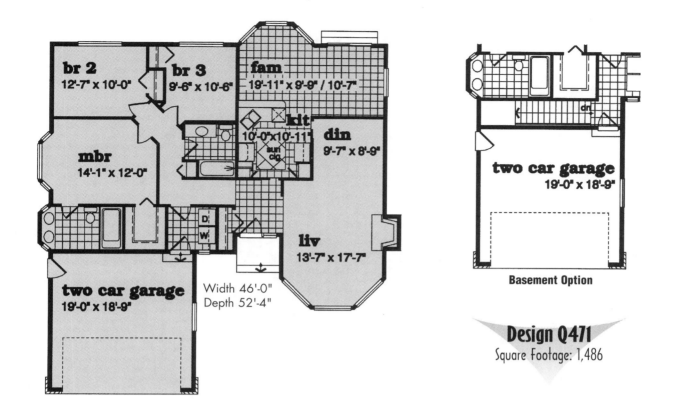

br 2
12'-7" x 10'-0"

br 3
9'-6" x 10'-6"

fam
19'-11" x 9'-9" / 10'-7"

mbr
14'-1" x 12'-0"

kit
10'-0" x 10'-11"

din
9'-7" x 8'-9"

liv
13'-7" x 17'-7"

two car garage
19'-0" x 18'-9"

Width 46'-0"
Depth 52'-4"

two car garage
19'-0" x 18'-9"

Basement Option

Design Q471
Square Footage: 1,486

◆ This ranch design with board-and-batten siding and brick accents has great curb appeal. This is further enhanced by the carousel living room with fireplace and attached dining area. A step-saving galley kitchen has a sunshine ceiling and adjoins the rear-facing family room with breakfast bay. Sliding glass doors here lead to the rear yard. Three bedrooms include a master suite with a large walk-in closet, charming bay window and bath with His and Hers vanities. The main bath is shared by the two additional rear-facing bedrooms. A two-car garage connects to the house at a service entry which also contains a laundry alcove. The basement option for this home is 1,566 square feet.

— DESIGN BY —
SELECT HOME DESIGNS

Design Q425
Square Footage: 1,296

◆ Perfect for a starter or empty-nester home, this economical-to-build one-story is as delightful on the inside as it is appealing on the outside. Fishscale siding, a covered porch and window boxes adorn the exterior. Inside, the foyer spills over to a spacious living room with corner fireplace. The country kitchen is across the hall and offers a unique U-shaped counter and ample space for a large dining table. Sliding glass doors lead to the rear yard and a handy service entrance leads past the laundry alcove to the single-car garage. The three bedrooms (or make it two and a den) revolve around the central bath with soaking tub. The master bedroom has His and Hers entries to the wall closet.

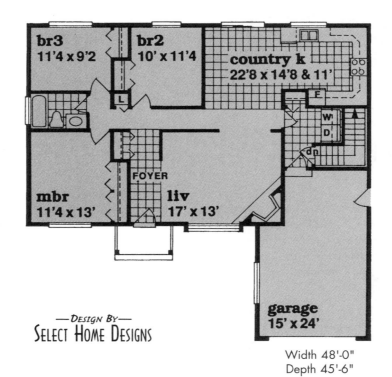

br3
11'4 x 9'2

br2
10' x 11'4

country k
22'8 x 14'8 & 11'

L

mbr
11'4 x 13'

FOYER

liv
17' x 13'

W
D

dn

garage
15' x 24'

— DESIGN BY —
SELECT HOME DESIGNS

Width 48'-0"
Depth 45'-6"

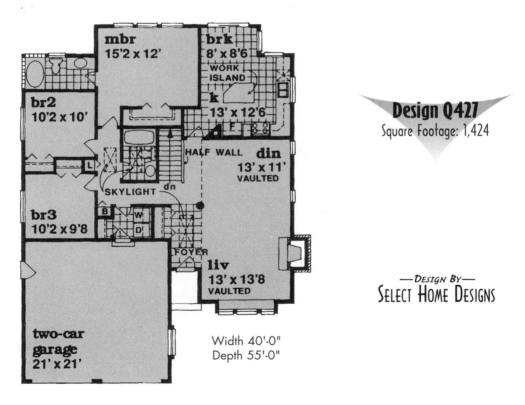

mbr
15'2 x 12'

brk
8' x 8'6

WORK ISLAND

k
13' x 12'6

br2
10'2 x 10'

HALF WALL

din
13' x 11'
VAULTED

L

SKYLIGHT

dn

br3
10'2 x 9'8

B

W
D

FOYER

liv
13' x 13'8
VAULTED

two-car garage
21' x 21'

Width 40'-0"
Depth 55'-0"

Design Q427
Square Footage: 1,424

—DESIGN BY—
SELECT HOME DESIGNS

◆ This affordable three-bedroom starter or empty-nester home offers an efficient floor plan and maximizes square footage. The skylit foyer spills into a vaulted living room, warmed by a hearth and graced with a box-bay window. Just beyond is a vaulted dining room, near the country kitchen. The gourmet will delight in the appointments in the kitchen: a center work island, abundant counter space and a sunny breakfast area with sliding glass doors to the rear garden. The master bedroom boasts a walk-in closet and bath with whirlpool spa. Two additional bedrooms share a bath with skylight. The two-car garage can be reached through a service entrance at the laundry alcove.

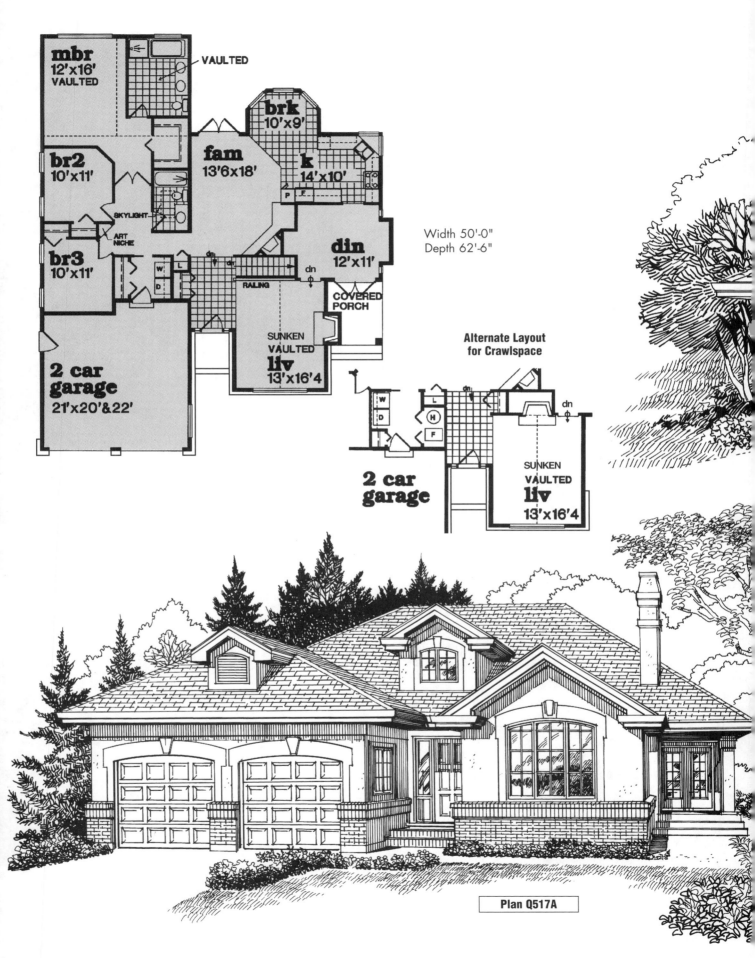

mbr
12'x16'
VAULTED

VAULTED

br2
10'x11'

br3
10'x11'

SKYLIGHT

ART NICHE

2 car garage
21'x20'&22'

fam
13'6x18'

brk
10'x9'

k
14'x10'

P   F

W L

D

RAILING

dn

dn

din
12'x11'

dn

COVERED PORCH

SUNKEN
VAULTED
liv
13'x16'4

Width 50'-0"
Depth 62'-6"

Alternate Layout for Crawlspace

W
D

L

H
F

dn

dn

2 car garage

SUNKEN
VAULTED
liv
13'x16'4

Plan Q517A

22

Plan Q517B

Design Q517A/Q517B
Square Footage: 1,784

◆ The same floor plan offers two exterior elevations—each perfect in its own way. One is a contemporary stucco version with keystone and brick detailing. The other is traditional brick throughout. Please specify either Q517A or Q517B when ordering to indicate which you'd prefer. The floor plan is identical for both exteriors. It begins with a welcoming foyer, brightly lit by abundant natural light from gabled windows above. Vaulted ceilings throughout the foyer and living room add to the openness of the plan. The living room has a cozy fireplace; the dining room is graced by double doors to the side porch. A modified U-shaped work center in the kitchen contains a corner sink with window and is adjacent to a carousel-bay breakfast room. The adjoining family room has a corner fireplace and a media center, plus double doors to the rear patio. The master bedroom offers a walk-in closet and vaulted bath with His and Hers vanities, a whirlpool spa and separate shower. Two additional bedrooms—or make it one and a den—share a skylit hall bath. Choose a basement or crawlspace foundation. Plans include details for both.

—DESIGN BY—
SELECT HOME DESIGNS

23

◆ A low-budget home can be a showplace, too. Exquisite site proportion, fine detailing, projected wings and interesting rooflines help provide the appeal of this modest one-story plan. Both bedrooms have excellent wall space and wardrobe storage. The master bath features a vanity, twin lavatories, a stall shower and a whirlpool tub. Another full bath is strategi- cally located to service the second bedroom as well as other areas of the house. Open planning results in a spacious liv- ing/dining area with fireplace and access to the outdoor ter- races. An angled snack bar separates the living area from the convenient kitchen. Or if you prefer a more traditional lay- out, choose the optional kitchen design.

Design 2911
Square Footage: 1,233

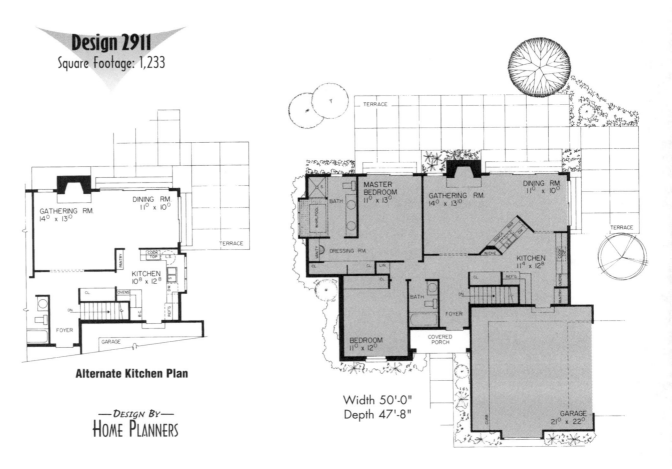

Alternate Kitchen Plan

—DESIGN BY—
HOME PLANNERS

Width 50'-0"
Depth 47'-8"

Design 7224
Square Footage: 1,339

◆ An arched entry complements the brick-and-siding facade of this cute one-story home. The entry foyer leads directly into the great room with ten-foot ceiling and fireplace flanked by windows. To the left is an L-shaped kitchen with snack bar counter separating the work area from the breakfast nook. A wall of windows overlooks the rear yard and a door gains access to it. On the right are three bedrooms, including a master suite with His and Hers vanities, a whirlpool tub, a separate shower and a huge walk-in closet. The master bedroom is appointed with a tray ceiling. Two family bedrooms have windows facing front and share a full bath. A convenient laundry area has built-in cabinets and access to the two-car garage.

— Design By —
Design Basics, Inc.

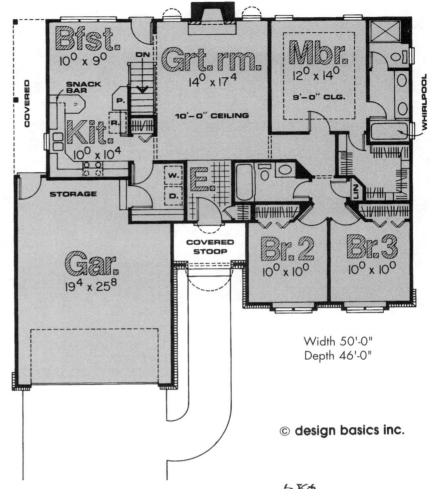

Bfst.
10⁰ x 9⁰

SNACK BAR

Kit.
10⁰ x 10⁴

STORAGE

Grt. rm.
14⁰ x 17⁴

10'–0" CEILING

Mbr.
12⁰ x 14⁰

9'–0" CLG.

WHIRLPOOL

Gar.
19⁴ x 25⁸

COVERED STOOP

Br. 2
10⁰ x 10⁰

Br. 3
10⁰ x 10⁰

Width 50'-0"
Depth 46'-0"

© design basics inc.

G. MacDonald

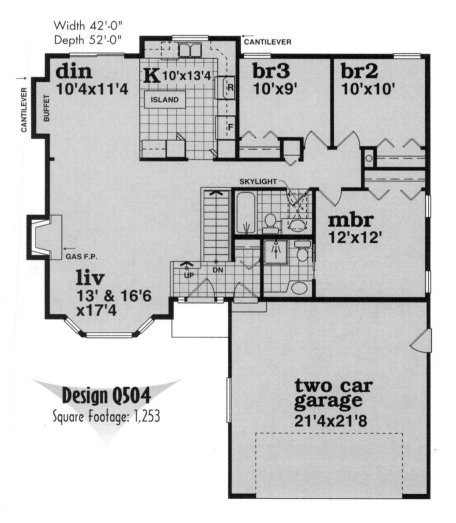

Width 42'-0"
Depth 52'-0"

CANTILEVER

CANTILEVER

din
10'4x11'4

BUFFET

K 10'x13'4

ISLAND

R

F

br3
10'x9'

br2
10'x10'

SKYLIGHT

GAS F.P.

liv
13' & 16'6
x17'4

UP

DN

mbr
12'x12'

Design Q504
Square Footage: 1,253

two car garage
21'4x21'8

◆ A multi-pane bay window, nestled in a gabled roof, adds charm to this bungalow and gives it a touch of elegance. The covered front entry shares a foyer with access from the two-car garage. A coat closet here is handy. The stairway to the basement is also found here. A large living/dining area is to the left. The living room has a fireplace and bay window; the dining room has a buffet alcove. The kitchen is conveniently located to serve the dining room and enjoys a view over the sink to the rear yard. A master bedroom and two family bedrooms are on the right side of the plan. The master has a private bath, while the family bedrooms share a full bath with skylight. A two-car garage sits to the front of the plan to help shield the bedrooms from street noise.

— DESIGN BY —
HOME PLANNERS

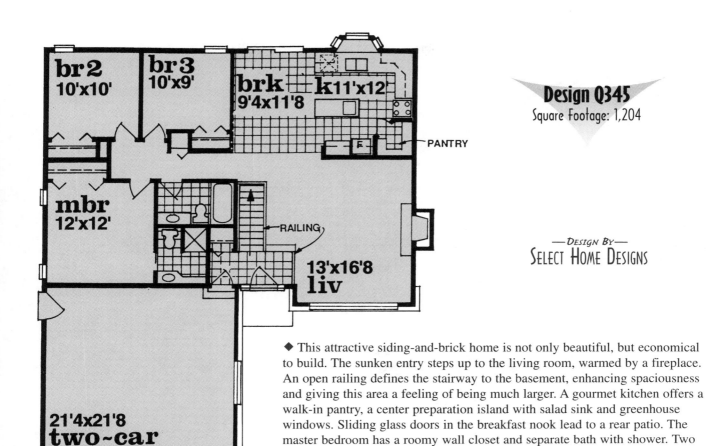

br2
10'x10'

br3
10'x9'

brk
9'4x11'8

k11'x12

PANTRY

mbr
12'x12'

RAILING

13'x16'8
liv

21'4x21'8
**two-car
garage**

Width 42'-8"
Depth 50'-4"

Design Q345
Square Footage: 1,204

—Design By—
SELECT HOME DESIGNS

◆ This attractive siding-and-brick home is not only beautiful, but economical to build. The sunken entry steps up to the living room, warmed by a fireplace. An open railing defines the stairway to the basement, enhancing spaciousness and giving this area a feeling of being much larger. A gourmet kitchen offers a walk-in pantry, a center preparation island with salad sink and greenhouse windows. Sliding glass doors in the breakfast nook lead to a rear patio. The master bedroom has a roomy wall closet and separate bath with shower. Two secondary bedrooms share a bath with soaking tub. A two-car garage sits to the front of the plan, creating privacy and quiet for the bedrooms.

Design Q515
Square Footage: 1,064

— DESIGN BY —
SELECT HOME DESIGNS

◆ This farmhouse design squeezes space-efficient features into its compact design. A cozy front porch opens into a vaulted great room and its adjoining dining room. Twin dormer windows above flood this area with natural light and accentuate the high ceilings. A warm hearth in the great room adds to its coziness. The U-shaped kitchen has a breakfast bar open to the dining room and a sink overlooking a flower box . A nearby side-door access is found in the handy laundry room. Vaulted bedrooms are positioned along the back of the plan. They contain wall closets and share a full bath with soaking tub. An open-rail staircase leads to the basement, which can be developed into living or sleeping space at a later time, if needed. Plans include details for both basement and crawlspace foundations.

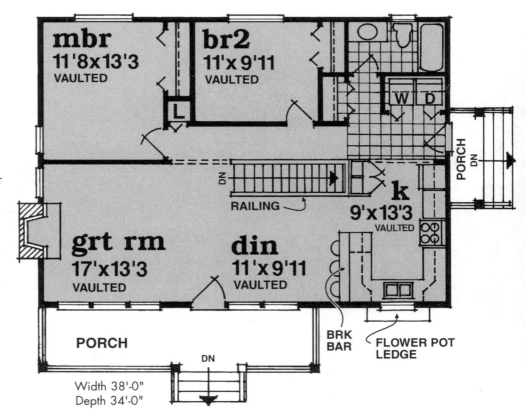

mbr
11'8x13'3
VAULTED

br2
11' x 9'11
VAULTED

W D

L

DN

RAILING

PORCH
DN

k
9'x13'3
VAULTED

grt rm
17'x13'3
VAULTED

din
11' x 9'11
VAULTED

PORCH

DN

BRK BAR

FLOWER POT LEDGE

Width 38'-0"
Depth 34'-0"

Design Q444
Square Footage: 1,357

◆ Victorian appointments enhance the facade of this one-story home: horizontal siding, fishscale details in the gable fronts and simple millwork pieces. The main living area is graced by a vaulted ceiling, a built-in media center and a three-sided fireplace that separates the living area from the country kitchen. The work area of the kitchen is L-shaped and has an island work counter for convenience. The dining space features sliding glass doors to the rear deck. A service entry at the side has space for a washer and dryer and a laundry tub. A stairway to the basement is also found here. The center hallway has a skylight and plant ledge above and leads to the three bedrooms. Family bedrooms share a full hall bath with skylight; the master bedroom has a private bath. If you choose the crawlspace option, you'll gain buffet space in the country kitchen and extra storage beyond the laundry room.

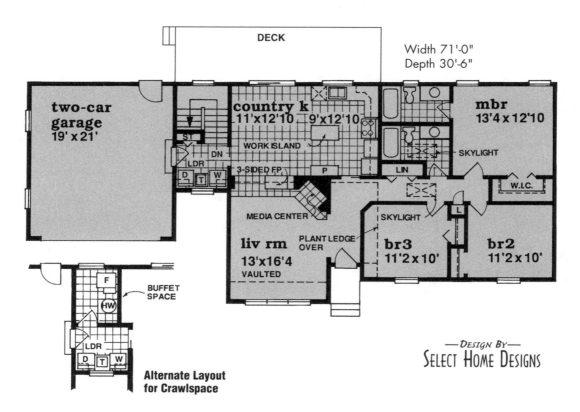

Width 71'-0"
Depth 30'-6"

DECK

two-car garage
19' x 21'

country k
11'x12'10   9'x12'10

mbr
13'4 x 12'10

SKYLIGHT

WORK ISLAND

DN

LDR

D   T   W

3-SIDED FP.

LIN

P

W.I.C.

MEDIA CENTER

SKYLIGHT

L

liv rm
13'x16'4

PLANT LEDGE OVER

br3
11'2 x 10'

br2
11'2 x 10'

VAULTED

F

HW

BUFFET SPACE

LDR

D   T   W

Alternate Layout for Crawlspace

— DESIGN BY —
SELECT HOME DESIGNS

Design 9187
Square Footage
(Basic Plan): 1,462

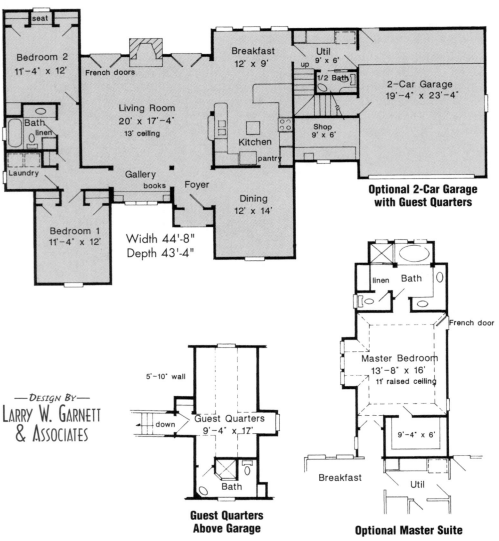

Bedroom 2
11'-4" x 12'

French doors

Bath
linen

Laundry

Bedroom 1
11'-4" x 12'

seat

Living Room
20' x 17'-4"
13' ceiling

Gallery
books

Foyer

Breakfast
12' x 9'

Kitchen

pantry

Dining
12' x 14'

Util
9' x 6'
up

1/2 Bath

Shop
9' x 6'

2-Car Garage
19'-4" x 23'-4"

**Optional 2-Car Garage
with Guest Quarters**

Width 44'-8"
Depth 43'-4"

—DESIGN BY—
LARRY W. GARNETT
& ASSOCIATES

5'-10" wall

down

Guest Quarters
9'-4" x 17'

Bath

**Guest Quarters
Above Garage**

linen   Bath

French door

Master Bedroom
13'-8" x 16'
11' raised ceiling

9'-4" x 6'

Breakfast

Util

Optional Master Suite

◆ Start small with this charming cottage and grow as you go! The basic design offers amenities often found in homes twice the size. Special features include French doors flanking the charming fireplace in the living room, a window seat bordered by twin closets in Bedroom 2, a laundry room conveniently located to the bedrooms and bath, and an efficient kitchen nestled between the formal dining room and breakfast nook. When you're ready, enlarging the plan is simple, and designed to finish in stages. A sumptuous master suite with a large walk-in closet and pampering bath may be added as the need for additional space arises. A two-car garage with a large shop area, utility room and ½ bath may be completed in the next phase. Completing the expansion of this terrific plan are the guest quarters located above the garage.

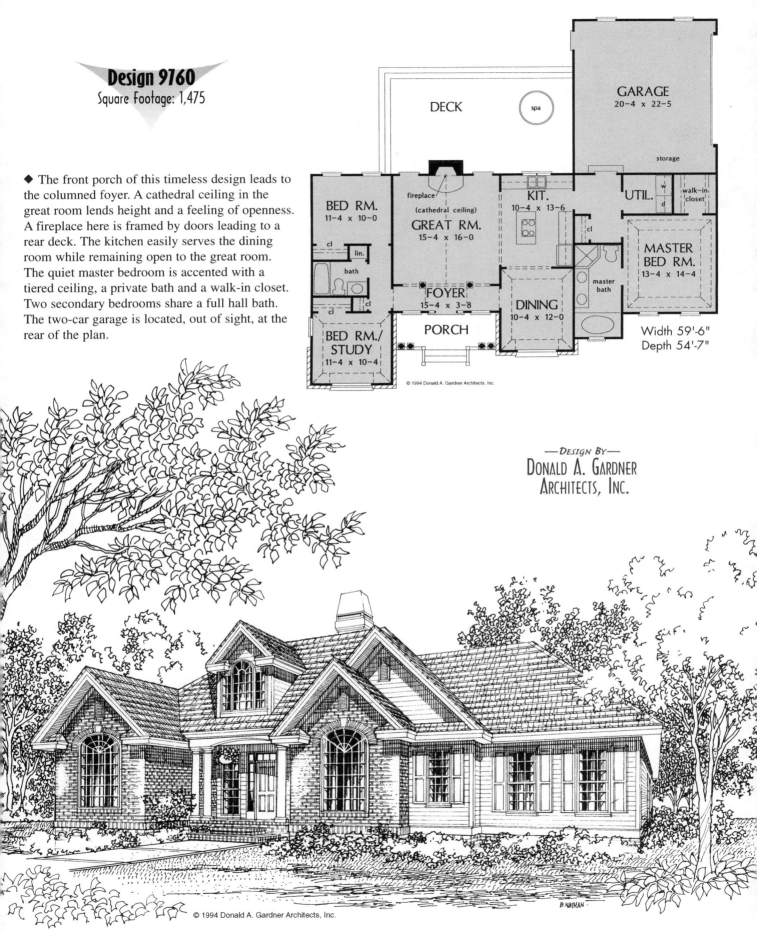

Design 9760

Square Footage: 1,475

◆ The front porch of this timeless design leads to the columned foyer. A cathedral ceiling in the great room lends height and a feeling of openness. A fireplace here is framed by doors leading to a rear deck. The kitchen easily serves the dining room while remaining open to the great room. The quiet master bedroom is accented with a tiered ceiling, a private bath and a walk-in closet. Two secondary bedrooms share a full hall bath. The two-car garage is located, out of sight, at the rear of the plan.

DECK

spa

GARAGE
20-4 x 22-5

storage

BED RM.
11-4 x 10-0

fireplace

(cathedral ceiling)

GREAT RM.
15-4 x 16-0

KIT.
10-4 x 13-6

UTIL.

w
d

walk-in closet

cl

lin.

bath

cl

FOYER
15-4 x 3-8

cl

master bath

MASTER BED RM.
13-4 x 14-4

DINING
10-4 x 12-0

cl

BED RM./
STUDY
11-4 x 10-4

PORCH

Width 59'-6"
Depth 54'-7"

© 1994 Donald A. Gardner Architects, Inc.

—DESIGN BY—
DONALD A. GARDNER
ARCHITECTS, INC.

B. NATHAN

© 1994 Donald A. Gardner Architects, Inc.

31

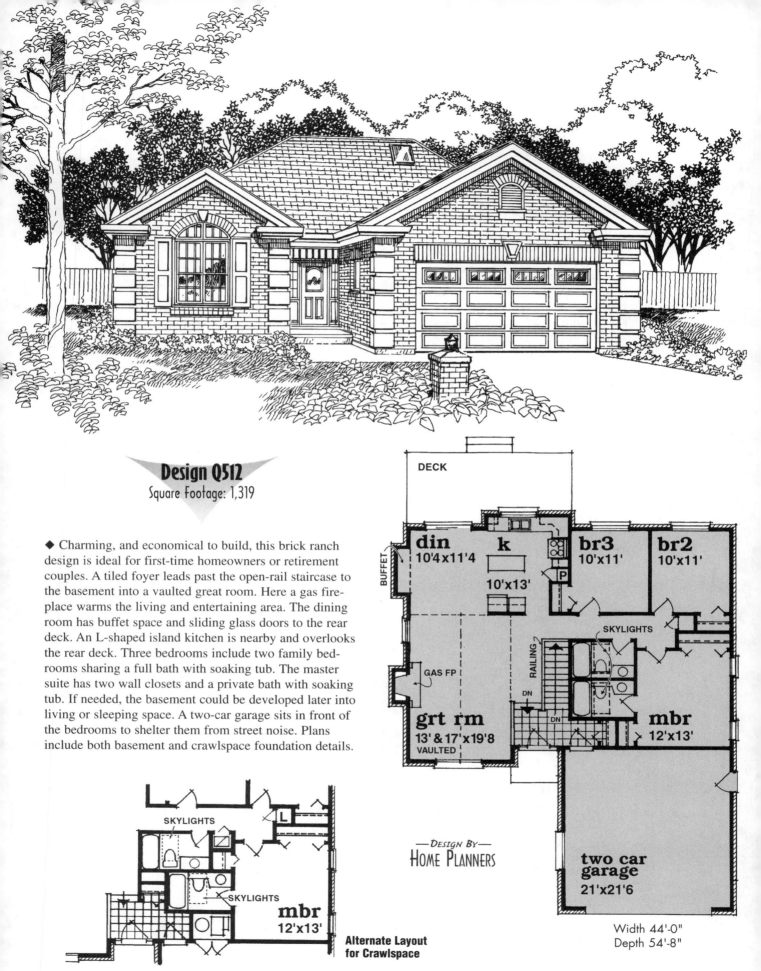

Design Q512
Square Footage: 1,319

◆ Charming, and economical to build, this brick ranch design is ideal for first-time homeowners or retirement couples. A tiled foyer leads past the open-rail staircase to the basement into a vaulted great room. Here a gas fireplace warms the living and entertaining area. The dining room has buffet space and sliding glass doors to the rear deck. An L-shaped island kitchen is nearby and overlooks the rear deck. Three bedrooms include two family bedrooms sharing a full bath with soaking tub. The master suite has two wall closets and a private bath with soaking tub. If needed, the basement could be developed later into living or sleeping space. A two-car garage sits in front of the bedrooms to shelter them from street noise. Plans include both basement and crawlspace foundation details.

DECK

din
10'4x11'4

BUFFET

k
10'x13'

br3
10'x11'

br2
10'x11'

SKYLIGHTS

GAS FP

RAILING

DN

DN

mbr
12'x13'

grt rm
13' & 17'x19'8
VAULTED

two car garage
21'x21'6

Width 44'-0"
Depth 54'-8"

— DESIGN BY —
HOME PLANNERS

SKYLIGHTS

SKYLIGHTS

mbr
12'x13'

Alternate Layout for Crawlspace

32

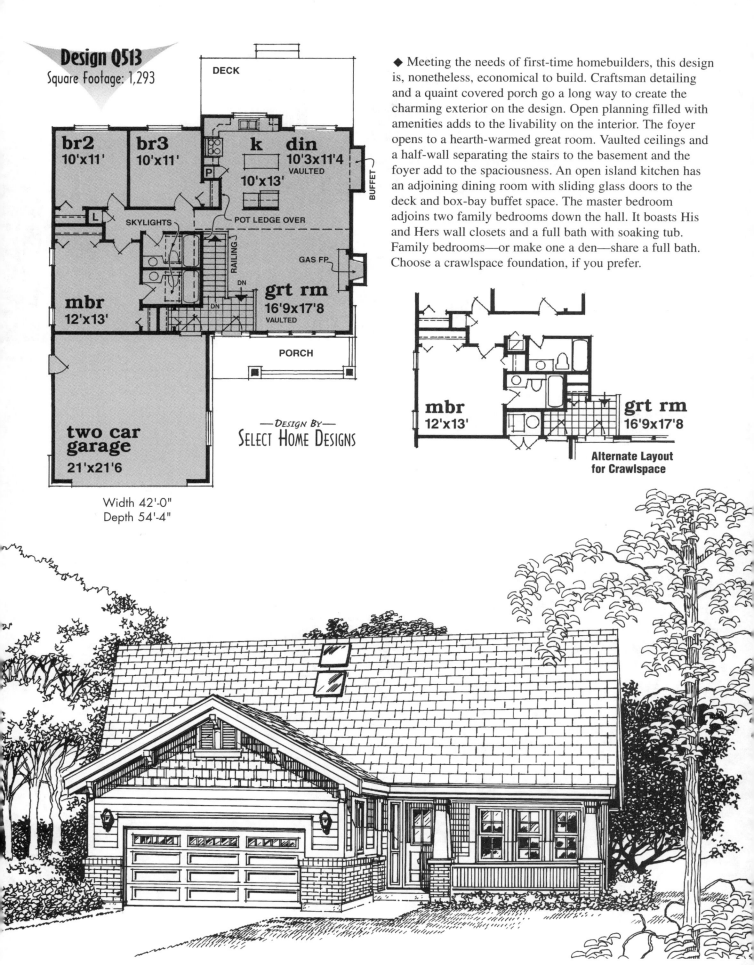

Design Q513
Square Footage: 1,293

DECK

br2 10'x11'

br3 10'x11'

k 10'x13'

din 10'3x11'4 VAULTED

BUFFET

SKYLIGHTS

POT LEDGE OVER

RAILING

GAS FP.

mbr 12'x13'

DN

DN

grt rm 16'9x17'8 VAULTED

PORCH

two car garage 21'x21'6

— DESIGN BY —
SELECT HOME DESIGNS

Width 42'-0"
Depth 54'-4"

◆ Meeting the needs of first-time homebuilders, this design is, nonetheless, economical to build. Craftsman detailing and a quaint covered porch go a long way to create the charming exterior on the design. Open planning filled with amenities adds to the livability on the interior. The foyer opens to a hearth-warmed great room. Vaulted ceilings and a half-wall separating the stairs to the basement and the foyer add to the spaciousness. An open island kitchen has an adjoining dining room with sliding glass doors to the deck and box-bay buffet space. The master bedroom adjoins two family bedrooms down the hall. It boasts His and Hers wall closets and a full bath with soaking tub. Family bedrooms—or make one a den—share a full bath. Choose a crawlspace foundation, if you prefer.

mbr 12'x13'

grt rm 16'9x17'8

Alternate Layout for Crawlspace

33

QUIET TERRACE · SCREEN · LIVING TERRACE

Width 68'-0"
Depth 28'-0"

MASTER
BED RM.
13⁰ x 13⁶

BATH

CL.

BATH

CL.

FAMILY RM
10⁶ x 13⁶

S · D.W. · W. · D.

KIT.
10⁶ x 8⁰

RANGE

REF'G

LAUNDRY

CL.

DINING

AIR
COND.

CHINA

STORAGE
16⁰ x 8⁰

CARPORT-GARAGE
20⁰ x 20⁰

CL.

LIN
CL.

CL.

BED RM.
10⁰ x 13⁶

CL.

BED RM.
10⁸ x 10⁰

ENTRY

CL.

LIVING RM.
18⁰ x 19⁶

R

FENCE

—Design By—
Home Planners

QUOTE ONE®

Cost to build? See page 436
to order complete cost estimate
to build this house in your area!

Design 1323
Square Footage: 1,344

L D

◆ Incorporated into the set of blueprints for this design are details for building each of three charming, traditional exteriors. A study of the floor plan reveals fine livability. There are two full baths, a fine family room, an efficient work center, a formal dining area, bulk storage facilities and sliding glass doors to the two rear terraces. The laundry room is strategically located near the kitchen. Three bedrooms include a master bedroom with double closets and a full, private bath. The two secondary bedrooms share a full hall bath. Each of the facades has its special charm. Choose the ranch with a covered porch and horizontal siding or the more traditional facade with horizontal siding and a carport. Or you may prefer the elegant brick option with a semi-enclosed carport.

◆ This design offers you a choice of three distinctively different exteriors, and the blueprints show details for all three optional elevations. In less than 1,400 square feet there are features galore. In addition to the two eating areas and the open planning of the gathering room, the indoor-outdoor relationships are of great interest. The basement may be developed at a later date for recreational activities. Be sure to note the storage potential, particularly the linen closet, the pantry, the china cabinet and the broom closet. Depending on your tastes, you may choose one of the three delightful exteriors shown here. Two are somewhat contemporary with vertical siding; one has a shed roof and privacy wall. The third is more traditional in nature and features multi-pane, shuttered windows and coach lamps at the garage.

—DESIGN BY—
HOME PLANNERS

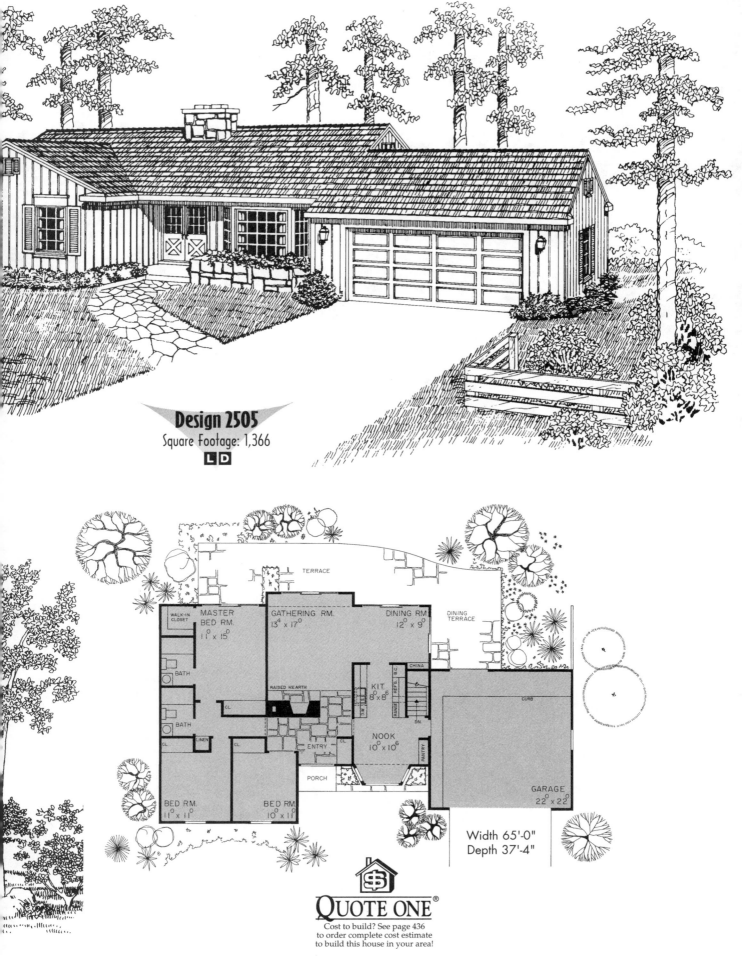

Design 2505
Square Footage: 1,366
L **D**

TERRACE

WALK-IN CLOSET

MASTER BED RM.
11⁰ x 15⁰

GATHERING RM.
13⁴ x 17⁰

DINING RM.
12⁰ x 9⁰

DINING TERRACE

BATH

RAISED HEARTH

KIT.
8⁰ x 8⁶

CHINA

BATH

CL

LINEN

CL

CL

ENTRY

NOOK
10⁰ x 10⁶

PANTRY

RANGE

REFG. B.C.

DN.

CURB

BED RM.
11⁰ x 11⁰

BED RM
10⁰ x 11⁰

PORCH

GARAGE
22⁰ x 22⁰

Width 65'-0"
Depth 37'-4"

QUOTE ONE®
Cost to build? See page 436
to order complete cost estimate
to build this house in your area!

Design 1107
Square Footage: 1,416

L D

◆ This smart-looking traditional adaptation will be economical to build because of its perfectly rectangular shape. The low-pitched roof has a wide overhang which accentuates its low-slung qualities. The attached two-car garage is oversized to permit the location of extra bulk storage space. Further, its access to the house is through the handy separate laundry area. This house functions as either a four-bedroom or three-bedroom design. Make the fourth bedroom a study, if you choose. Features include a fireplace in the living room, built-in china cabinet in the breakfast room, sizable vanities in the main bath and a beautiful terrace reached through sliding glass doors in the breakfast room.

—DESIGN BY—
HOME PLANNERS

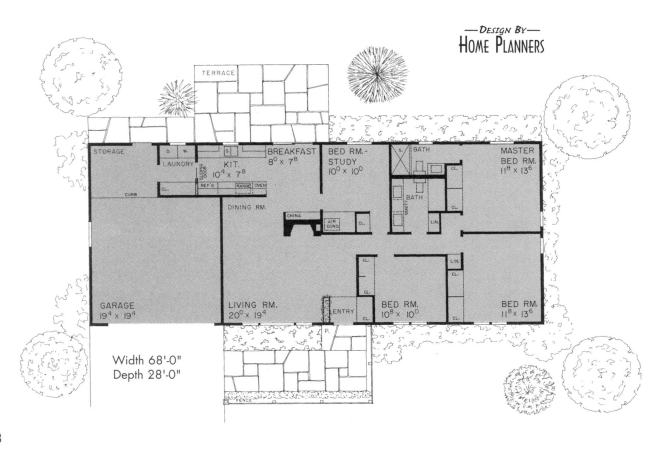

Design 1025
Square Footage: 1,426

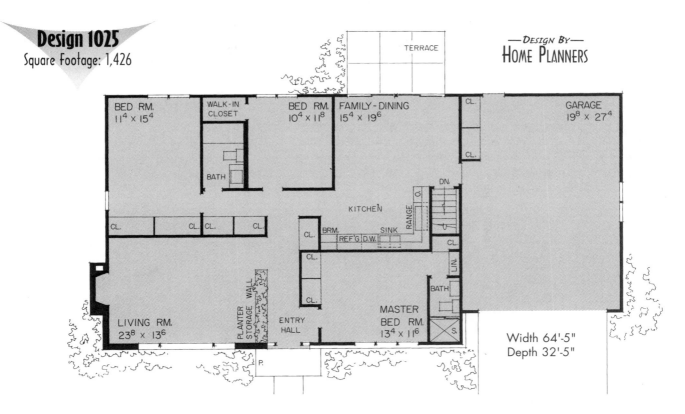

BED RM.
11^4 x 15^4

WALK-IN CLOSET

BED RM.
10^4 x 11^8

FAMILY-DINING
15^4 x 19^6

TERRACE

CL.

GARAGE
19^8 x 27^4

—DESIGN BY—
HOME PLANNERS

BATH

CL.

DN.

KITCHEN

CL. CL. CL.

CL.

BRM.

RANGE

O.

SINK

REF'G D.W.

CL.

CL.

LIN.

BATH

PLANTER STORAGE WALL

CL.

S.

LIVING RM.
23^8 x 13^6

ENTRY HALL

MASTER BED RM.
13^4 x 11^6

Width 64'-5"
Depth 32'-5"

P.

◆ With brick veneer and vertical siding, this home is a real charmer. The master bedroom is located to the front of the home—away from family bedrooms for privacy—and contains three closets and a private bath. The living room is defined from the entry by a planter wall and has a center fireplace for interest. A family room/dining area adjoins the L-shaped kitchen and has sliding glass doors to the rear terrace. Family bedrooms—one with walk-in closet—share the use of a hall bath. The garage is located to the side and features extra storage space for bulk items. You may decide to finish the basement space later for additional bedrooms, a recreation room or hobby space.

◆ In less than 1,400 square feet, you'll find three bedrooms, two full baths, a separate dining room with large window, a formal living room, a galley-style kitchen overlooking the rear yard and an informal family room. Sliding glass doors in the family room gain access to a wonderful rear terrace; a laundry alcove here is convenient and saves space. In addition, there is the attached two-car garage. Note the location of the stairs when this plan is built with a basement. The exterior is predominantly brick—the front features both stone and vertical boards and battens, with brick on the other three sides. Multi-pane windows, a covered porch and shutters add to the charm.

Design 1305
Square Footage: 1,382

D

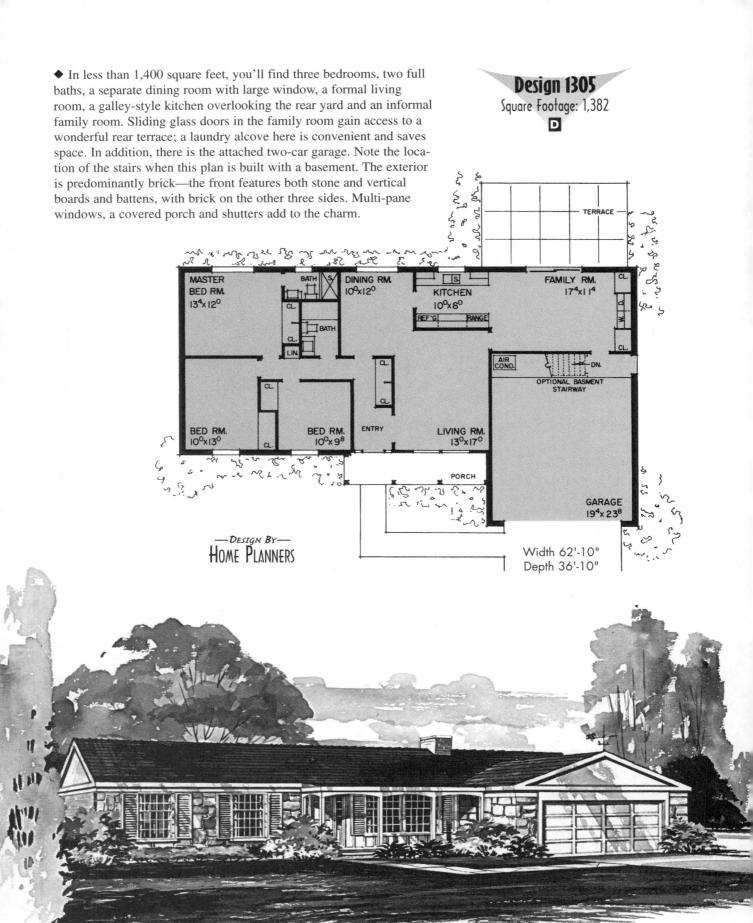

TERRACE

MASTER BED RM. 13⁴x12⁰

BATH

DINING RM. 10⁰x12⁰

KITCHEN 10⁰x8⁰

REF'G   RANGE

FAMILY RM. 17⁴x11⁴

CL.

BATH

LIN.

CL.

AIR COND.

OPTIONAL BASEMENT STAIRWAY

DN.

BED RM. 10⁰x13⁰

CL.

BED RM. 10⁰x9⁸

ENTRY

LIVING RM. 13⁰x17⁰

PORCH

GARAGE 19⁴x23⁸

—DESIGN BY—
HOME PLANNERS

Width 62'-10"
Depth 36'-10"

Design 1075
Square Footage: 1,232
L D

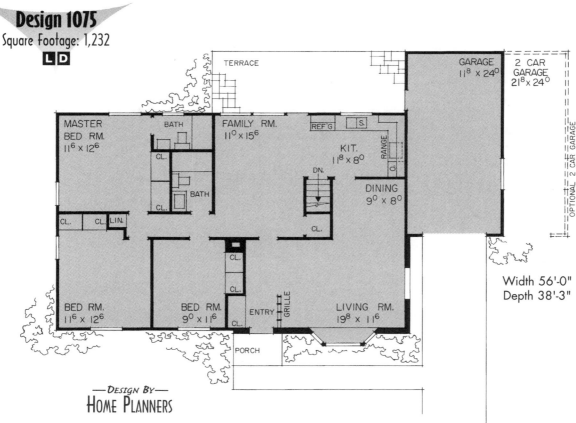

TERRACE

GARAGE
11⁸ x 24⁰

2 CAR GARAGE
21⁸ x 24⁰

MASTER BED RM.
11⁶ x 12⁶

BATH

FAMILY RM.
11⁰ x 15⁶

REF'G   S.

KIT.
11⁸ x 8⁰

RANGE

CL.

DN.

DINING
9⁰ x 8⁰

BATH

CL.

CL.

CL. LIN.

CL.

OPTIONAL 2 CAR GARAGE

Width 56'-0"
Depth 38'-3"

BED RM.
11⁶ x 12⁶

BED RM.
9⁰ x 11⁶

CL.

CL.

ENTRY

GRILLE

LIVING RM.
19⁸ x 11⁶

PORCH

—DESIGN BY—
HOME PLANNERS

◆ This picturesque one-story home has much to offer small families. Because of its rectangular shape and its predominantly frame exterior, construction costs will be reasonable. Long on livability, the floor plan offers a living room with bay window and grille separating it from the entry and open to the formal dining room. A family room opens to the L-shaped kitchen and features sliding glass doors to the rear terrace. The master suite has a private bath and large wall closets. Family bedrooms share the use of the main bath. The one-car garage may be expanded if needed. One of the bedrooms might make a perfect den or home office.

Design 1367
Square Footage: 1,432

—DESIGN BY—
HOME PLANNERS

MASTER BED RM. 12⁸ x 10⁸

BATH

STUDY-DINING RM. 10⁴ x 10⁸

KIT. 11⁸ x 10⁸

FAMILY RM. 20⁰ x 11⁸

TERRACE

BATH

STOR.

PANTRY

REF'G

SNACK BAR

RANGE

BED RM. 10⁰ x 12⁴

BED RM. 10⁰ x 9⁰

ENTRY

AIR COND.

LIVING RM. 16⁰ x 12⁴

OPTIONAL BASEMENT STAIRS

CURB

WINDOW SEAT

FENCE

GARAGE 19⁸ x 23⁴

Width 66'-10"
Depth 36'-10"

◆ Brick veneer, a projecting two-car garage with a gabled end, wood shutters, attractive window treatment, a paneled front door and a wood fence with lamp post are among the features that make this traditional house so charming. The formal living room with loads of blank wall space is just right for effective furniture placement and sized for quiet conversation. The family room serves for informal activities and features a snack bar and pass-through to the kitchen. Adjacent to the kitchen is an optional room that could become a formal dining room or a den, as you choose. Bedrooms include a master suite with private bath and double-wall closets, and two family bedrooms sharing a full bath with linen closet.

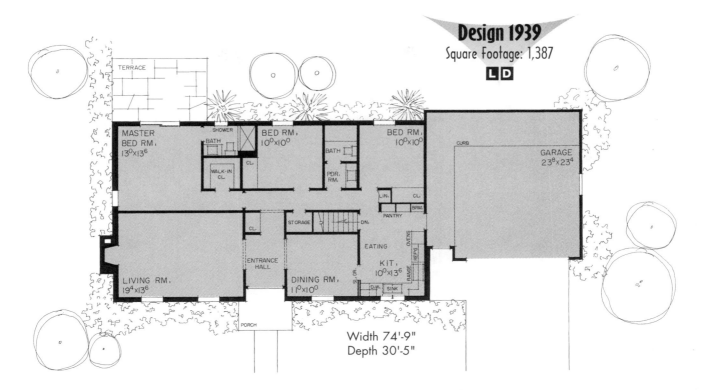

Design 1939
Square Footage: 1,387

L D

TERRACE

MASTER
BED RM.
13⁰x13⁶

SHOWER

BATH

WALK-IN
CL.

CL.

BED RM.
10⁰x10⁰

BATH

PDR.
RM.

BED RM.
10⁰x10⁰

LIN.

CL.

BRM.

PANTRY

CURB

GARAGE
23⁸x23⁴

CL.

STORAGE

DN.

EATING

OVENS

REF'G.

LIVING RM.
19⁴x13⁶

ENTRANCE
HALL

DINING RM.
11⁰x10⁰

KIT.
10⁰x13⁶

RANGE

D.W.

SINK

PORCH

Width 74'-9"
Depth 30'-5"

◆ This finely proportioned house has more than its share of charm. The brick veneer exterior contrasts nicely with the narrow horizontal siding of the oversized attached two-car garage. The focal point of the exterior, however, is the recessed front entry with double Colonial-style doors. The secondary service entrance through the garage is handy to the kitchen area. The plan features three bedrooms—one a master suite with private bath and sliding glass doors leading to a private rear terrace. Family bedrooms share a full bath with linen closet. A living room with fireplace, a front kitchen with eating area and a formal dining room round out the remainder of the floor plan. Storage abounds, plus the basement can be developed later for additional bedrooms or recreation space if needed.

— DESIGN BY —
HOME PLANNERS

Design 1311
Square Footage: 1,050
L

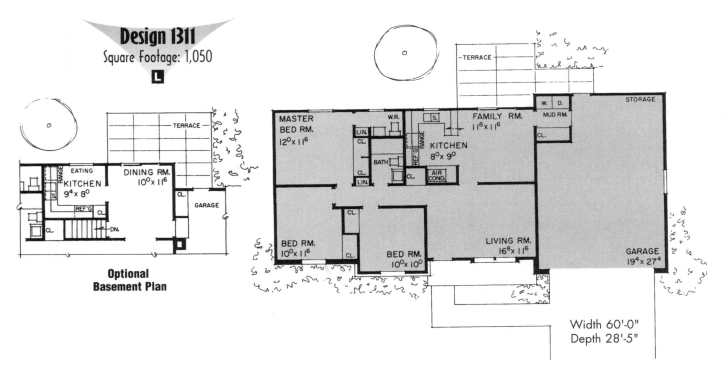

Optional Basement Plan

KITCHEN	9⁴ x 8⁰
DINING RM.	10⁰ x 11⁶
MASTER BED RM.	12⁰ x 11⁶
FAMILY RM.	11⁸ x 11⁶
KITCHEN	8⁰ x 9⁰
BED RM.	10⁰ x 11⁶
BED RM.	10⁰ x 10⁰
LIVING RM.	16⁸ x 11⁶
GARAGE	19⁴ x 27⁴

Width 60'-0"
Depth 28'-5"

◆ Delightful design and effective, flexible planning come in small packages, too! This fine traditional exterior, with its covered front entrance, features an alternate basement plan. Note how the non-basement layout provides a family room and mud room, while the basement option shows kitchen eating and a dining room. In both versions, sliding glass doors lead from the dining or family room space to a rear terrace. The kitchen is U-shaped and features a sink with window overlooking the rear yard. Three bedrooms include two family bedrooms sharing a full bath and a master bedroom with half-bath. The garage has extra storage space and connects to the main house through a service entrance with mud room.

— DESIGN BY —
HOME PLANNERS

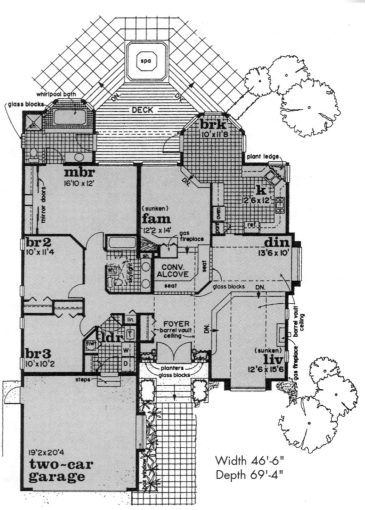

Rear Elevation

Design Q296
Square Footage: 1,939

Traditional One-Story Homes 1,500 to 2,000 Square Feet

◆ This unique design begins with a double-door entry into a barrel-vaulted foyer accented by two round-top windows and an arched glass block wall. Curved ceilings and open-plan design enhance both the living and dining rooms. The living room is sunken and features a fireplace and box-bay window. The dining room also has a box-bay. Beyond is the U-shaped kitchen, connecting directly to an octagonal breakfast nook. The nook has access to the rear deck and spa beyond. The family room is up just a step or two and is graced by a gas fireplace and conversation alcove with built-in seats. The master bedroom also has access to the rear deck via a luxurious bath with spa tub, separate shower and compartmented toilet. Two additional bedrooms share the use of a full bath with twin vanities. Plans include details for both basement and crawlspace foundations.

—DESIGN BY—
SELECT HOME DESIGNS

Width 46'-6"
Depth 69'-4"

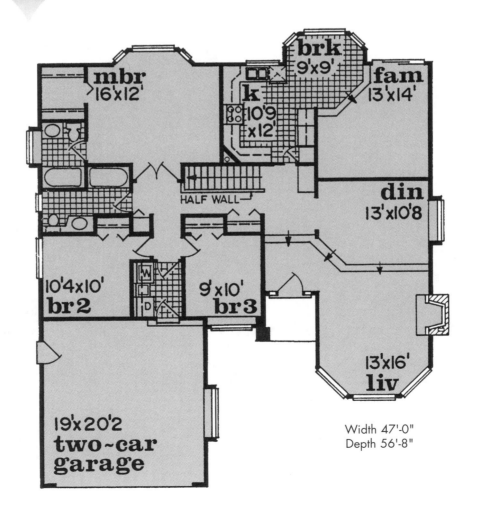

Design Q282
Square Footage: 1,662

mbr
16'x12'

brk
9'x9'

fam
13'x14'

k
10'9
x12

din
13'x10'8

HALF WALL

10'4x10'
br2

W
D

9'x10'
br3

13'x16'
liv

19'x20'2
**two-car
garage**

Width 47'-0"
Depth 56'-8"

46

Rear Elevation

◆ This elegant design offers a choice of exteriors—brick or horizontal siding. The plans include details for both. The focal point of the exterior is the large windowed bay, complemented by a hip roof. The recessed entry flows into the sunken living room with fireplace and then on to the formal dining room (note the box-bay window). The breakfast bay, with greenhouse windows, connects the kitchen and sunken family room. The kitchen is U-shaped for convenience and has abundant counter space. Sliding glass doors in the family room open to a rear patio. In the master bedroom is another bay window with cozy window seat, a walk-in closet and full, private bath with soaking tub. Additional bedrooms share a full bath. Choose basement or crawlspace foundation. Plans include both.

—DESIGN BY—
SELECT HOME DESIGNS

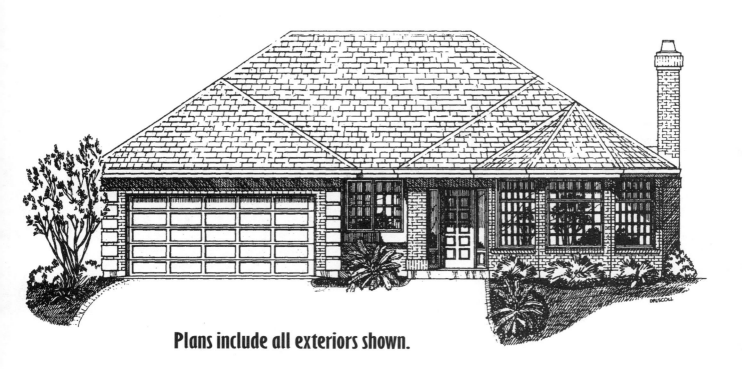

Plans include all exteriors shown.

Design Q366
Square Footage: 1,538

◆ This compact three-bedroom offers a wealth of amenities—and you can make one of the bedrooms into a den or home office, if you choose! A skylit foyer spills into a vaulted living room with a bay-window seat and corner fireplace. The dining room is open to the living room and connects directly to the kitchen where there is another bay-window seat. An angled snack bar separates the kitchen from the family room; double doors open onto the patio at the back of the house. The master bedroom offers still another bay window with window seat and has a walk-in closet and private bath. The family bedrooms—one with walk-in closet—share a full bath. Note the laundry room space in the service entrance to the two-car garage. Plans include details for both basement and crawlspace foundations.

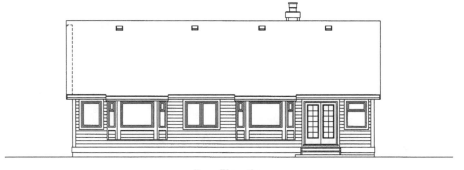

Rear Elevation

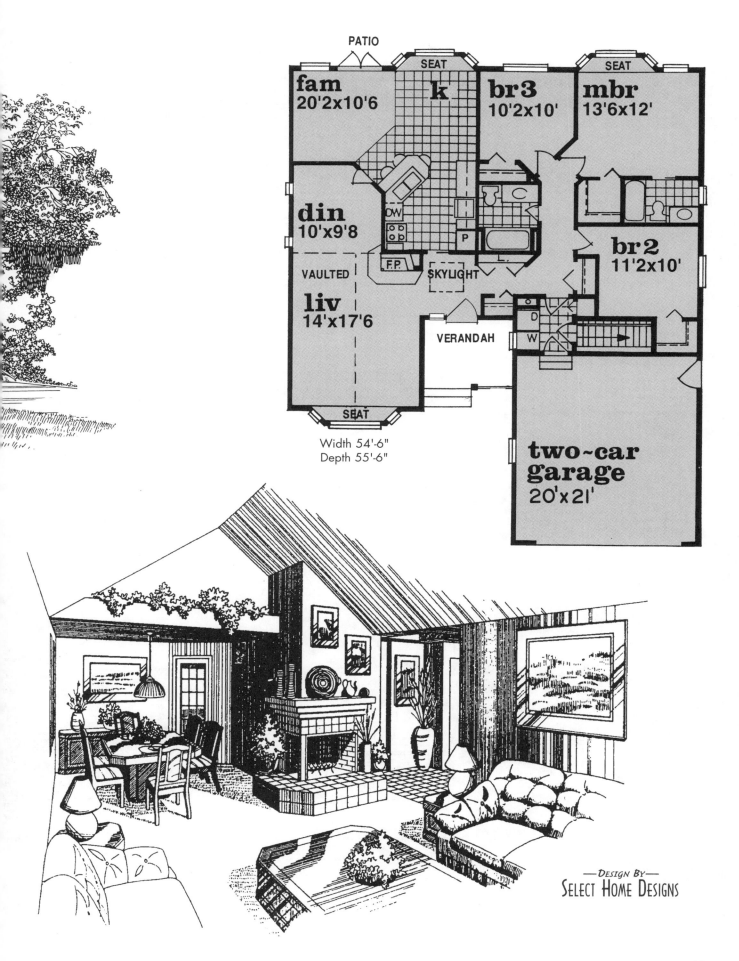

PATIO

fam
20'2x10'6

SEAT

k

br3
10'2x10'

SEAT

mbr
13'6x12'

din
10'x9'8

DW

F.P.

P

SKYLIGHT

VAULTED

liv
14'x17'6

br2
11'2x10'

D

W

VERANDAH

SEAT

Width 54'-6"
Depth 55'-6"

**two-car
garage**
20'x21'

DESIGN BY
SELECT HOME DESIGNS

Design Q450

Square Footage: 1,588

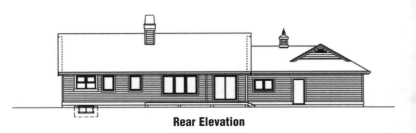

Rear Elevation

◆ Gables enhance the exterior of this three-bedroom country-style home. The columned front porch conceals a recessed entry that opens to a foyer leading directly into the vaulted great room and dining room. Amenities here include a built-in audio/video center, a pot ledge, a fireplace and sliding glass doors to the rear covered porch and deck. The country kitchen is easily accessed from all main areas of the home. It features a work island and vaulted ceiling. A service entrance just beyond the kitchen holds a pantry, a laundry area and access to the two-car garage with workshop space. The bedrooms are down a skylit hall and include a master suite with walk-in closet and bath with double vanity and soaking tub. The family bedrooms share the use of a full bath. Plans include details for both basement and crawlspace foundations.

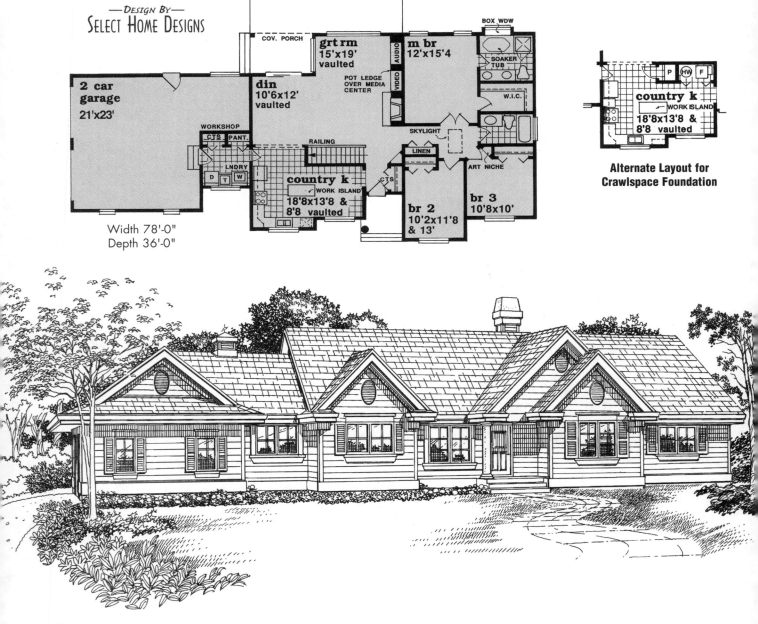

—DESIGN BY—
SELECT HOME DESIGNS

DECK

COV. PORCH

grt rm 15'x19' vaulted

AUDIO VIDEO

POT LEDGE OVER MEDIA CENTER

m br 12'x15'4

BOX WDW

SOAKER TUB

W.I.C.

SKYLIGHT

2 car garage 21'x23'

din 10'6x12' vaulted

WORKSHOP

CTS PANT.

LNDRY

D T W

RAILING

country k 18'8x13'8 & 8'8 vaulted

LINEN

CTS

ART NICHE

br 2 10'2x11'8 & 13'

br 3 10'8x10'

Width 78'-0"
Depth 36'-0"

P HW F

country k WORK ISLAND 18'8x13'8 & 8'8 vaulted

Alternate Layout for Crawlspace Foundation

Design Q240
Square Footage: 1,608

◆ The plans for this cute bungalow offer choices of exterior finishes. The recessed entry is weather-protected and opens to a skylit, tiled foyer. The living room is sunken a few steps and enjoys a bay window and focal-point fireplace. Adjoining is the formal dining room, separated from the living room by an open railing. The kitchen takes on a modified U-shape and has a bright window box over the sink. The connecting breakfast bay and family room has a corner fireplace and sliding glass door to the patio. Bedrooms are positioned away from noisy traffic areas and include a master suite with full bath (note the plant shelf and skylight). Two family bedrooms and a shared bath are nearby. The laundry room connects the main house to the two-car garage. Plans include details for both basement and crawlspace foundations.

— Design by —
Select Home Designs

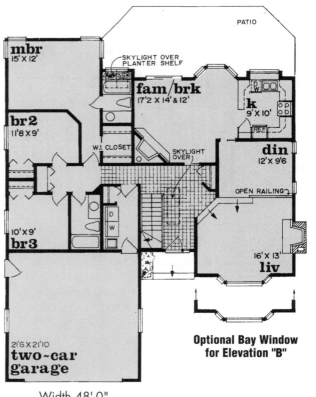

**Optional Bay Window
for Elevation "B"**

Width 48'-0"
Depth 58'-10"

Design Q254
Square Footage: 1,553

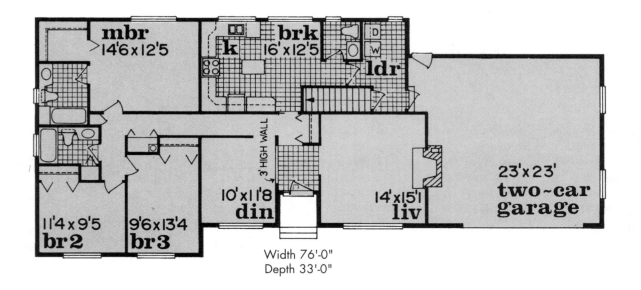

mbr
14'6 x 12'5

brk
16' x 12'5

k

ldr

br2
11'4 x 9'5

br3
9'6 x 13'4

din
10' x 11'8

3' HIGH WALL

liv
14' x 15'1

23' x 23'
two-car
garage

Width 76'-0"
Depth 33'-0"

◆ Traditional in every respect, this one-story features shutters, a covered entry and horizontal siding on the exterior. Its interior is introduced by a tiled entry leading to a formal living room with fireplace on the right and a formal dining room—separated from the entry by a three-foot wall—on the left. Ahead is a convenient coat closet and the large U-shaped kitchen with work island and ample counter space. An attached breakfast nook overlooks the rear yard. The laundry area holds a half bath and access to the two-car garage. The master bedroom is gigantic and has a walk-in closet and bath with soaking tub. Family bedrooms feature wall closets and share the use of a full main bath.

—DESIGN BY—
SELECT HOME DESIGNS

Design Q321

Square Footage: 1,666

◆ A courtyard with planter box leads up a few steps to the double-door entry of this ranch home. Open-plan design minimizes hallways and floor area. For instance, the bright, skylit entry opens directly to the living room which features a corner fireplace and sliding glass doors to the rear yard. The breakfast area has a bay window and is convenient to the U-shaped kitchen with island work center. A service entry with mud/laundry room and half bath connect the kitchen to the two-car garage which leads out to a porch at the side door. The master bedroom at the other end of the plan features His and Hers wall closets and a private bath with soaking tub. Two additional bedrooms—one can serve as a den—share a main bath. Choose the crawlspace option if you prefer.

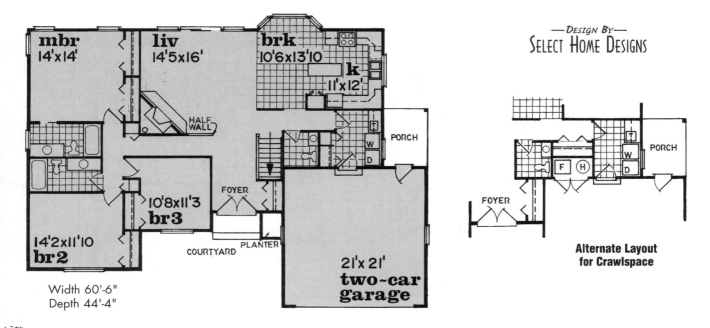

— DESIGN BY —
SELECT HOME DESIGNS

mbr 14'x14'

liv 14'5x16'

brk 10'6x13'10

k 11'x12'

HALF WALL

PORCH

W D

br3 10'8x11'3

FOYER

br2 14'2x11'10

COURTYARD   PLANTER

two-car garage 21'x 21'

Width 60'-6"
Depth 44'-4"

T   W
F   H   D

PORCH

FOYER

Alternate Layout for Crawlspace

Design Q320

Square Footage: 1,566
Bonus Room: 149 sq. ft.

◆ This simple country one-story has decorative touches at its entry including a planter box and columned front porch. The foyer introduces additional touches such as a coat closet with plant ledge above and a plant ledge in the hall. The living room is vaulted and contains a warming fireplace. Both the kitchen and dining area are also vaulted—the dining room has sliding glass doors to the rear yard. Note the U-shape of the kitchen for efficiency. The main-floor laundry room has three-way access from the workshop, the backyard and the two-car garage. The stairway to the basement is also found here. A roomy wall closet appoints the master bedroom, which also boasts a private bath. Family bedrooms share a bath with linen closet. Plans include details for both basement and crawlspace foundations.

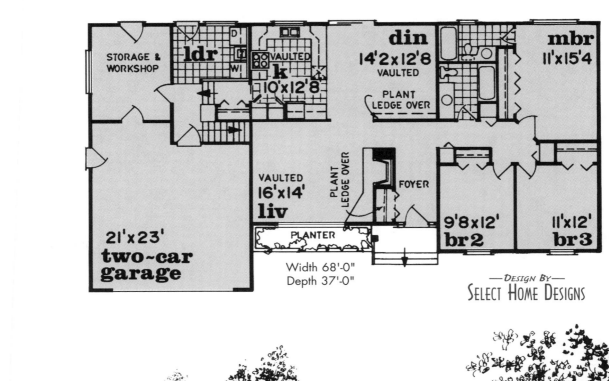

STORAGE & WORKSHOP

ldr

D
W

VAULTED
k
10'x12'8

din
14'2x12'8
VAULTED

PLANT LEDGE OVER

mbr
11'x15'4

VAULTED
16'x14'
liv

PLANT LEDGE OVER

FOYER

9'8x12'
br2

11'x12'
br3

21'x23'
two-car garage

PLANTER

Width 68'-0"
Depth 37'-0"

—DESIGN BY—
SELECT HOME DESIGNS

Design Q448
Square Footage: 1,577

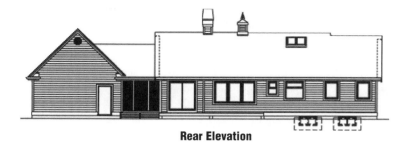

Rear Elevation

◆ Circle-head windows lend character to the exterior of this country-style three-bedroom home. Inside, it is well designed and well appointed. The entry foyer is skylit and leads to a vaulted great room with a centrally located fireplace open to the kitchen and breakfast nook. The formal dining room is also vaulted and has sliding glass doors to the rear deck and to a side screened porch. Both entries to the kitchen/breakfast

area are accented—one by an arch; one with a plant ledge. The laundry is located in a service entrance to the two-car garage. The master bedroom is all you might want with three wall closets and a private bath with separate tub and shower and double vanities. Family bedrooms have the use of a full bath with skylight. Choose the crawlspace option if you wish. Plans include both versions.

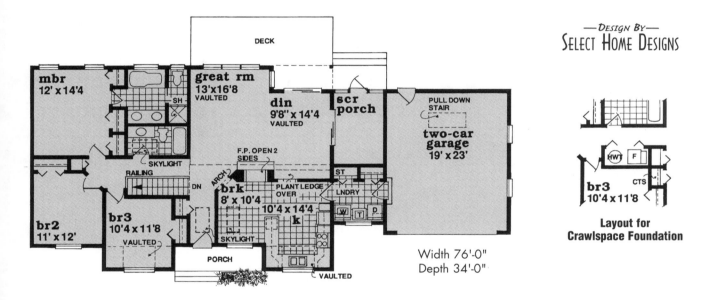

— DESIGN BY —
SELECT HOME DESIGNS

Width 76'-0"
Depth 34'-0"

br3
10'4 x 11'8

**Layout for
Crawlspace Foundation**

Design 3376
Square Footage: 1,999
L D

◆ Small families will appreciate the layout of this traditional ranch. The foyer opens to the gathering room with fireplace and sloped ceiling. The dining room opens to the gathering room for entertaining ease and offers sliding glass doors to a rear terrace. The breakfast room also provides access to a covered porch for dining outdoors. The media room to the left of the home offers a bay window and a wet bar, or it can double as a third bedroom.

— DESIGN BY —
HOME PLANNERS

Quote One®
Cost to build? See page 436 to order complete cost estimate to build this house in your area!

MASTER BED RM.
12⁰ x 15⁴ + BAY

WHIRLPOOL

BATH

VANITY

DRSG.

CL.

CL.

BATH

LINEN

CL.

BED RM.
12⁰ x 13⁴

BAR

SLOPED CEILING

MEDIA RM./B.R.
11⁰ x 11⁸ + BAY

GATHERING RM.
17⁰ x 21⁸

SLOPED   CEILING

FOYER

CL.

DN

SER. ENT.

PDR. RM.

PORCH

DINING RM.
9⁸ x 13⁴

PORCH

BUTLER PANTRY

P'TRY

BRKFST. RM.
11⁰ x 10⁰ + BAY

REF'G.

KITCHEN
11⁰ x 9²

RANGE

CURB

GARAGE
20⁴ x 20⁰

Width 60'-0"
Depth 55'-0"

56

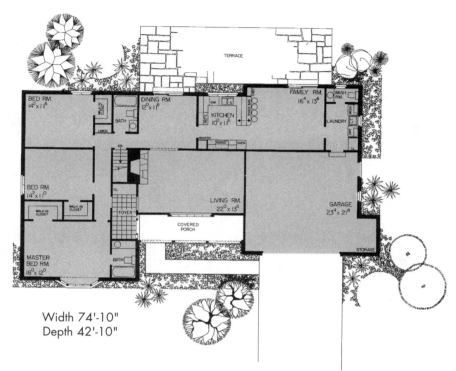

Design 2603

Square Footage: 1,949

LD

QUOTE ONE®

Cost to build? See page 436
to order complete cost estimate
to build this house in your area!

Width 74'-10"
Depth 42'-10"

◆ It would be difficult to beat the appeal of this traditional one-story home. Its slightly modified U-shape with two front-facing gables and covered front porch add to the exterior charm. Inside, there are three large bedrooms serviced by two full baths and three walk-in closets. The efficient U-shaped kitchen is flanked by the formal dining room and the informal family room with sliding glass doors to the rear terrace. A pantry, a built-in oven and a pass-through snack bar further enhance the livability of this area. A formal living room has a focal-point fireplace and huge, multi-pane windows overlooking the covered front porch. Extra storage space in the garage will add to the appeal of this plan.

—DESIGN BY—
HOME PLANNERS

Design 2802

Square Footage: 1,729

LD

Width 68'-2"
Depth 48'-10"

◆ The three exteriors shown on these pages house the same efficient floor plan. Please specify which you prefer when ordering. The Tudor version of this plan displays an effective use of half-timbered stucco and brick as well as an authentic bay window to create an elegant elevation. The Spanish-inspired design has stuccoed arches, multi-pane windows and a gracefully sloped roof. The contemporary version has a mix of fieldstone and vertical wood siding with an absence of posts or columns for a modern look. Window placement and roof configurations are different for each.

Design 2803

Square Footage: 1,679

LD

Width 68'-0"
Depth 48'-0"

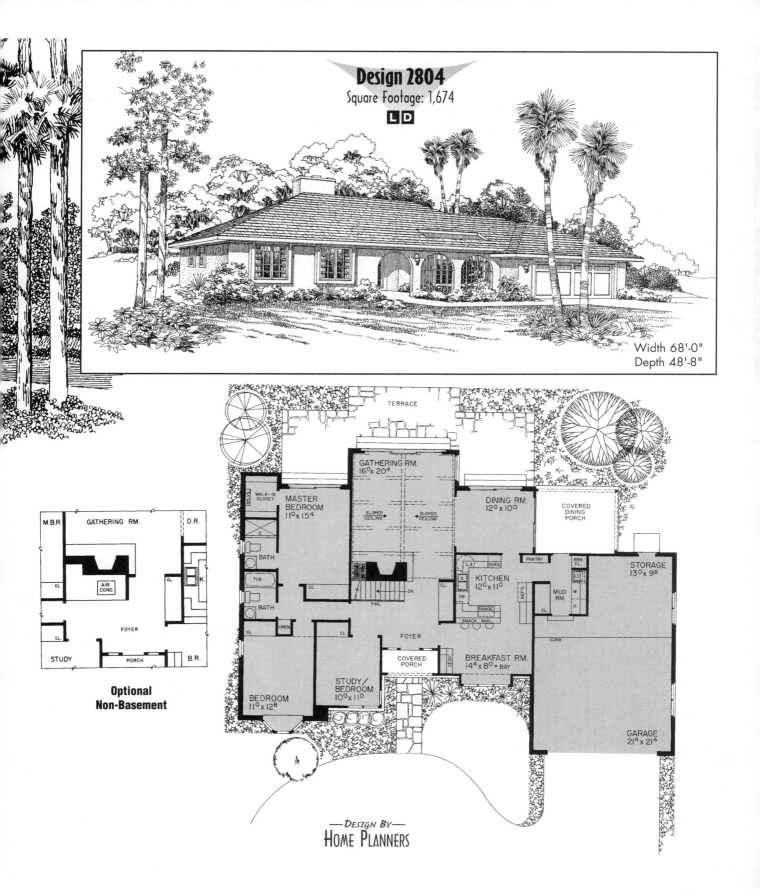

Design 2804
Square Footage: 1,674
L D

Width 68'-0"
Depth 48'-8"

TERRACE

GATHERING RM.
16⁰ x 20⁴

MASTER
BEDROOM
11⁰ x 15⁴

WALK-IN
CLOSET

BATH

TUB

BATH

SLOPED
CEILING

SLOPED
CEILING

DINING RM.
12⁰ x 10⁰

COVERED
DINING
PORCH

PANTRY

KITCHEN
12⁰ x 11⁰

STORAGE
13⁰ x 9⁸

OVEN

RANGE

MUD
RM.

CURB

LINEN

RAIL

DN

SNACK BAR

FOYER

COVERED
PORCH

BREAKFAST RM.
14⁴ x 8⁰ + BAY

BEDROOM
11⁰ x 12⁸

STUDY/
BEDROOM
10⁰ x 11⁰

GARAGE
21⁴ x 21⁴

Optional
Non-Basement

M.B.R.   GATHERING RM.   D.R.

CL.   AIR COND.   CL.   K.

CL.   FOYER

STUDY   PORCH   B.R.

— DESIGN BY —
Home Planners

On the inside, a great floor plan is found. The gathering room will be a favorite place for friends and family, offering rustic appeal and rear terrace doors. A full-sized kitchen with snack bar and breakfast room is well suited for the gourmet. The master bedroom has a large walk-in closet, private bath and doors to the terrace. Two additional bedrooms—or make one a study—share a hall bath. A large storage area or shop space is available in the two-car garage. Blueprints include details for an optional non-basement plan. The Quote One® custom price quote system is available for Design 2802 only.

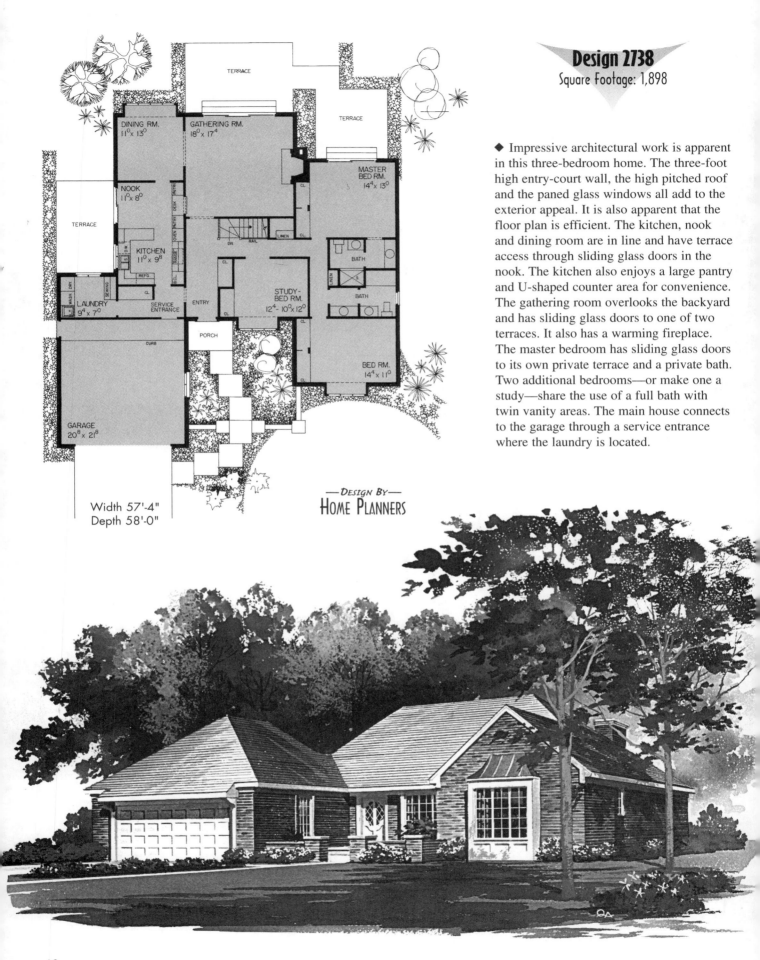

Design 2738
Square Footage: 1,898

DINING RM.
11⁰ x 13⁰

GATHERING RM.
18⁰ x 17⁴

TERRACE

TERRACE

MASTER BED RM.
14⁴ x 13⁰

NOOK
11⁰ x 8⁰

TERRACE

KITCHEN
11⁰ x 9⁸

LINEN

BATH

LAUNDRY
9⁴ x 7⁰

SERVICE ENTRANCE

ENTRY

STUDY-BED RM.
12⁴ x 10⁰ x 12⁰

LINEN

BATH

CURB

PORCH

GARAGE
20⁸ x 21⁸

BED RM.
14⁴ x 11⁰

Width 57'-4"
Depth 58'-0"

— DESIGN BY —
HOME PLANNERS

◆ Impressive architectural work is apparent in this three-bedroom home. The three-foot high entry-court wall, the high pitched roof and the paned glass windows all add to the exterior appeal. It is also apparent that the floor plan is efficient. The kitchen, nook and dining room are in line and have terrace access through sliding glass doors in the nook. The kitchen also enjoys a large pantry and U-shaped counter area for convenience. The gathering room overlooks the backyard and has sliding glass doors to one of two terraces. It also has a warming fireplace. The master bedroom has sliding glass doors to its own private terrace and a private bath. Two additional bedrooms—or make one a study—share the use of a full bath with twin vanity areas. The main house connects to the garage through a service entrance where the laundry is located.

Design 2806
Square Footage: 1,584

L **D**

Width 58'-10"
Depth 50'-10"

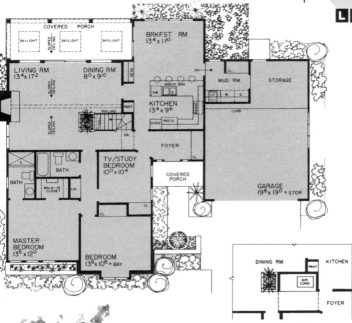

Optional Non-Basement

◆ Two exterior facades share one, compact floor plan in this design. Please specify which you prefer when ordering. The appealing Tudor home offers half-timbering and stone accents on its exterior, while the stone-and-shingle cottage has more classic accents. Inside, they both contain the same great floor plan. The living/dining room at the rear of the plan has direct access to the covered porch. Notice the built-in planter adjacent to the open staircase leading to the basement. A breakfast room overlooks the covered porch. A desk, snack bar and mud room with laundry facilities are near the U-shaped kitchen. The master bedroom features a private bath and a walk-in closet. The large front bedroom has a bay window, while a third bedroom may serve as a study. The Quote One® custom price quote system is available for Design 2805 only.

—DESIGN BY—
HOME PLANNERS

Design 2805
Square Footage: 1,547

L **D**

Width 58'-0"
Depth 51'-5"

◆ This bountiful bungalow is an owner's paradise with a luxurious master suite that far exceeds its Craftsman-style roots. The large gathering room is joined to the dining room and is accented with a large brick fireplace. The galley kitchen has an abundance of cabinet space, a walk-in pantry and a full-sized snack bar from the sunny breakfast room. A lovely screened porch that is accessed from both the dining room and the breakfast room adds an extra measure of charm to casual living. Two secondary bedrooms include one that can double as a den with a foyer entrance and another that is romanced with an expanse of corner windows and a wrap-around flower box.

Design 3314
Square Footage: 1,959

L

— DESIGN BY —
HOME PLANNERS

QUOTE ONE®
Cost to build? See page 436
to order complete cost estimate
to build this house in your area!

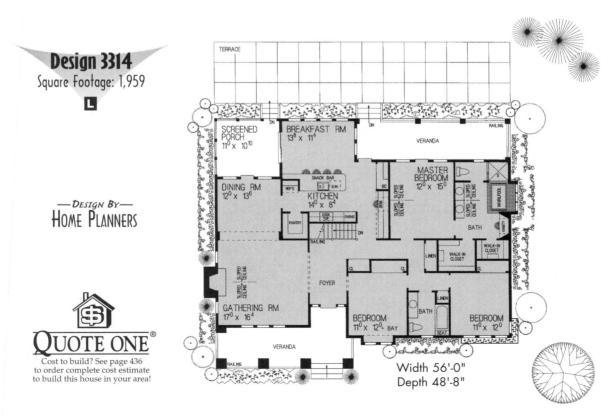

Width 56'-0"
Depth 48'-8"

Design Q239
Square Footage: 1,548

◆ A low-maintenance brick exterior with quoining and shutters adorns this compact home. The skylit foyer opens to a sunken living room with fireplace and entry to the formal dining room. The kitchen has a sunshine ceiling, spacious counters and is convenient to both the dining room and breakfast/family room area (look for sliding glass doors to the rear deck). A laundry area is located in an alcove in the kitchen. The bedroom hallway is brightened by a skylight and leads to two family bedrooms with shared bath and the master suite. Appointments in the master suite include a walk-in closet and full, private bath. The two-car garage sits to the front of the plan and protects the bedrooms from street noise.

— DESIGN BY —
SELECT HOME DESIGNS

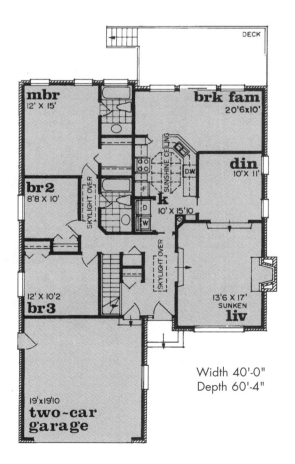

Width 40'-0"
Depth 60'-4"

Design 2565
Square Footage: 1,540
L D

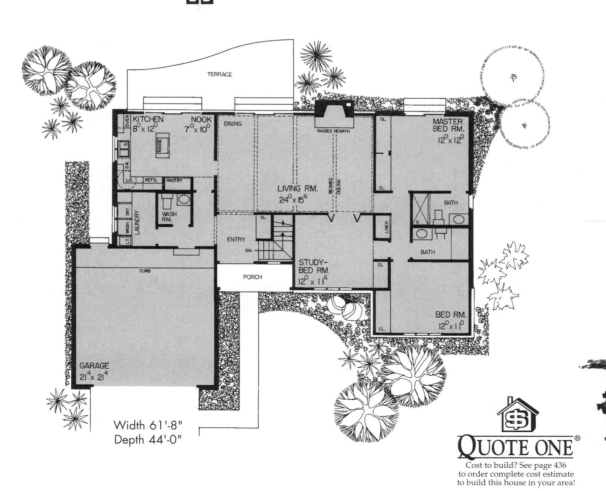

TERRACE

KITCHEN 8⁰ x 12⁰

NOOK 7⁰ x 10⁰

DINING

RAISED HEARTH

MASTER BED RM. 12⁰ x 12⁰

OVEN

RANGE

REFG.

PANTRY

LIVING RM. 24⁰ x 15⁶

BEAMED CEILING

CL.

CL.

BATH

DW

LS

WASH RM.

LAUNDRY

DRY

WASH

LT

ENTRY

DN.

LINEN

S.

BATH

CURB

PORCH

STUDY-BED RM. 12⁰ x 11⁶

CL.

CL.

GARAGE 21⁴ x 21⁴

BED RM. 12⁰ x 11⁰

Width 61'-8"
Depth 44'-0"

Cost to build? See page 436
to order complete cost estimate
to build this house in your area!

QUOTE ONE®

◆ This modest-sized design has much to offer in livability. It may function as either a three-bedroom home or a two-bedroom home with a study. The spacious living room features a raised-hearth fireplace, sliding doors to the terrace and a beam ceiling. The U-shaped kitchen has an island work center and includes a breakfast nook with sliding glass doors to the rear terrace. The stairway to the basement leads to a possible future recreation area. In addition to the two full baths serving the bedrooms, there is an extra washroom near the laundry room and service area. Blueprints for this design show details for three elevations: the Tudor, the Colonial and the contemporary.

—DESIGN BY—
HOME PLANNERS

Design 2878
Square Footage: 1,521

LD

—DESIGN BY—
HOME PLANNERS

◆ This charming, compact design combines traditional styling with sensational commodities and modern livability. Thoughtful zoning places sleeping areas to one side, apart from household activity. The plan includes a spacious gathering room with sloped ceiling and centered fireplace, and a formal dining room overlooking a rear terrace. A handy pass-through connects the breakfast room and an efficient kitchen. The laundry is strategically positioned nearby for handy access. An impressive master suite enjoys access to a private rear terrace and offers a separate dressing area with walk-in closet. Two family bedrooms, or one and a study, are nearby and share a full bath.

QUOTE ONE®
Cost to build? See page 436
to order complete cost estimate
to build this house in your area!

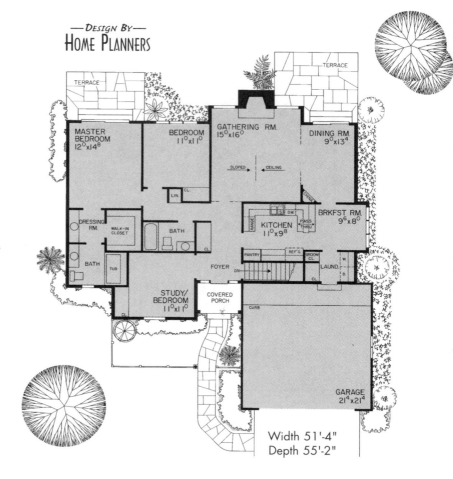

Width 51'-4"
Depth 55'-2"

This home, as shown in the photograph, may differ from the actual blueprints. For more detailed information, please check the floor plans carefully.

Photo by Andrew D. Lautman

Design 3340
Square Footage: 1,689

L

◆ A charming cupola over the garage and delightful fan windows set the tone for this cozy cottage. A central fireplace and a sloped ceiling highlight the living room's comfortable design, complete with sliding patio doors and an adjoining dining room. The large eat-in kitchen has a snack bar, planning desk and patio doors from the breakfast room. An angular hallway leads to the master bedroom featuring a large walk-in closet, twin-sink vanity and a compartmented bath. A secondary bedroom features a lovely window seat. A third bedroom is perfectly situated to be a study. The two-car garage has a separate storage area with a utility entrance where there is space for a washer and dryer.

— DESIGN BY —
HOME PLANNERS

Quote One®
Cost to build? See page 436 to order complete cost estimate to build this house in your area!

Width 58'-0"
Depth 52'-6"

Design 2810
Square Footage: 1,536

L D

—DESIGN BY—
HOME PLANNERS

◆ This design is particularly energy efficient. All exterior walls employ 2x6 studs to permit the installation of thick insulation. The high cornice design also allows for more ceiling insulation. According to many experts, the use of 2x6's spaced 24" O.C. results in the need for less lumber and saves construction time. However, the energy-efficient features of this design does not end with the basic framing members.

Efficiency begins right at the front door where the vestibule acts as an airlock restricting the flow of cold air to the interior. The basic rectangular shape of the house spells efficiency, without sacrificing exterior appeal. Economy is also embodied in such features as back-to back plumbing, centrally located furnace, minimal window and door openings and, most important of all, size.

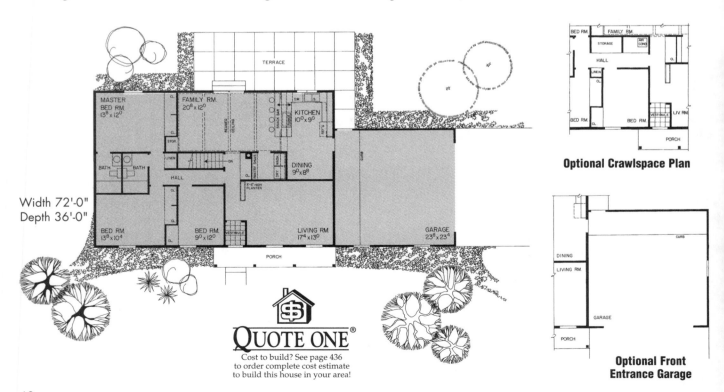

Width 72'-0"
Depth 36'-0"

Optional Crawlspace Plan

Optional Front Entrance Garage

QUOTE ONE®
Cost to build? See page 436
to order complete cost estimate
to build this house in your area!

Design 1890

Square Footage: 1,628

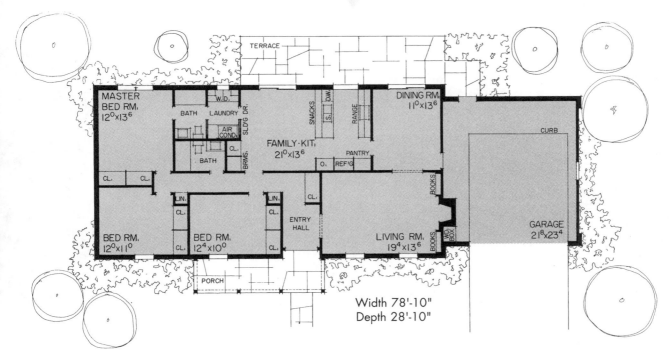

TERRACE

MASTER BED RM. 12⁰x13⁶

BATH

W.D.

LAUNDRY

AIR COND.

CL.

BATH

SLDG. DR.

BRMS.

SNACKS

D.W.

RANGE

DINING RM. 11⁰x13⁶

FAMILY·KIT. 21⁰x13⁶

PANTRY

REFIG.

O.

CURB

CL.

CL.

BED RM. 12⁰x11⁰

LIN.

CL.

BED RM. 12⁴x10⁰

LIN.

CL.

CL.

CL.

ENTRY HALL

BOOKS

LIVING RM. 19⁴x13⁶

BOOKS

W.D. BOX

GARAGE 21⁸x23⁴

PORCH

Width 78'-10"
Depth 28'-10"

◆ The pedimented gable and columns at the front porch set the tone for this modestly sized traditional home. The pleasant symmetry of the windows and the double front doors complete the picture. Inside, each square foot is wisely planned for efficient livability. Note the formal living room with a fireplace flanked by built-in bookshelves. The formal dining room is attached and accesses the rear terrace through sliding glass doors. The family room area of the kitchen also has sliding glass doors to the terrace and gives way to the laundry area and shared bath with the master bedroom. Two family bedrooms share a full bath in the hallway. Note the two linen closets, the utility and broom closets and the coat closet.

—DESIGN BY—
HOME PLANNERS

Design 1896
Square Footage: 1,690

—DESIGN BY—
HOME PLANNERS

◆ Complete family livability is provided by this exceptional floor plan. Further, this design has a truly delightful traditional exterior. The fine layout features a center entrance hall with a storage closet in addition to the coat closet. Then, there is the formal, front living room and the adjacent, separate dining room. The U-shaped kitchen has plenty of counter and cupboard space; there is even a pantry. The family room functions with the kitchen and is but a step away from the outdoor terrace. The mud room has space for storage and laundry equipment. An extra wash room is nearby. The large family will find those four bedrooms and two full baths just the answer for sleeping and bath accommodations.

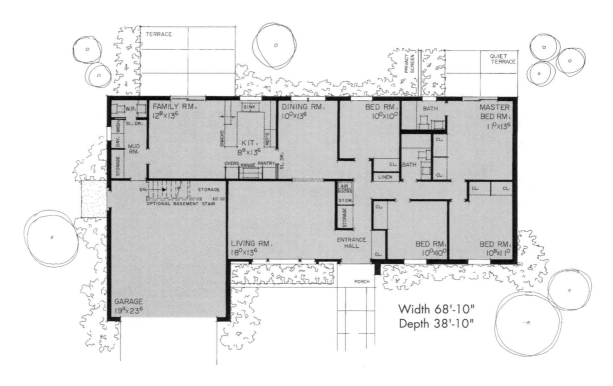

Width 68'-10"
Depth 38'-10"

Design 1346

Square Footage: 1,644

◆ Brick veneer, a covered front porch and shuttered windows add to the enchantment of this traditional one-story home. The entry foyer holds a coat closet and leads to the left into the formal living room and ahead to the dining room, which has sliding glass doors to the rear terrace. The galley-style kitchen separates the formal areas from the informal family room, which also has sliding glass doors to the terrace and a warming fireplace. The bedrooms are to the right of the plan and include a master suite with private bath and two family bedrooms sharing a full bath with linen closet. The two-car garage connects to the main house via a mud/laundry room with wash room.

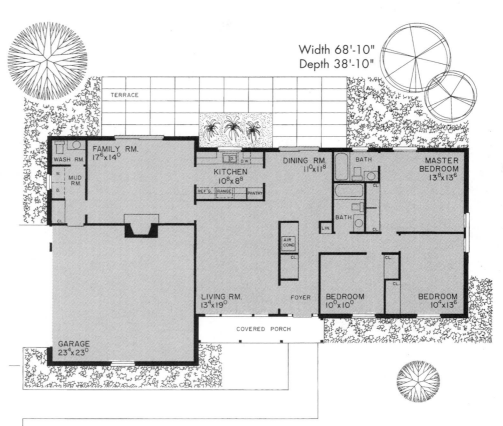

Width 68'-10"
Depth 38'-10"

TERRACE

FAMILY RM.
17⁶x14⁰

WASH RM.

MUD RM.

KITCHEN
10⁸x8⁸

REF'G. RANGE

PANTRY

DINING RM.
11⁰x11⁸

BATH

BATH

MASTER BEDROOM
13⁸x13⁶

LIN.

AIR COND

CL.

LIVING RM.
13⁴x19⁰

FOYER

BEDROOM
10⁰x10⁰

BEDROOM
10⁴x13⁶

COVERED PORCH

GARAGE
23⁴x23⁰

— DESIGN BY —
HOME PLANNERS

Design 1186
Square Footage: 1,872

◆ This appealing home has an interesting and practical floor plan that caters to both the adults and the children in your family. The children's wing projects to the back and includes three bedrooms and a shared full bath with double vanities. The master bedroom is on the opposite side of the home and has a private bath with make-up vanity. In between are the formal and informal living areas, including a living room/dining room combination and a family room with fireplace and sliding glass doors to the terrace with pool. The dining room also has access to the terrace area. The galley kitchen has a pass-through counter to the family room for convenience. The two-car garage has extra storage space and an access door at the mud/laundry room to the main house.

—DESIGN BY—
Home Planners

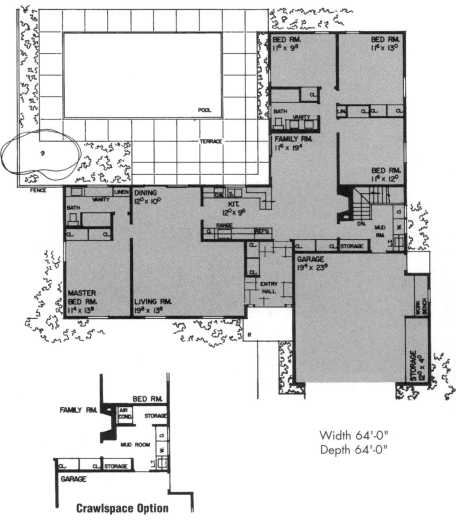

Width 64'-0"
Depth 64'-0"

Crawlspace Option

Design 3144
Square Footage: 1,760

◆ If you are short on space and searching for a home that is long on both good looks and livability, search no more! This impressive L-shaped home measures only 56'-5" in width and, therefore, works well on a somewhat narrow building site. It loses nothing in the way of great floor planning. From the covered entry, the plan is zoned into formal and informal spaces. The formal living room is to the back and features a fireplace and large window overlooking the rear yard. The family room/dining area is close to the kitchen and its attached breakfast nook and has access to a side terrace as does the breakfast nook. The kitchen is U-shaped and shares a snack-bar counter with the breakfast nook. To reach the two-car garage with massive storage space, enter the service area with laundry and washroom. Bedrooms are at the other side of the plan and include a master suite with private bath and two family bedrooms.

— DESIGN BY —
HOME PLANNERS

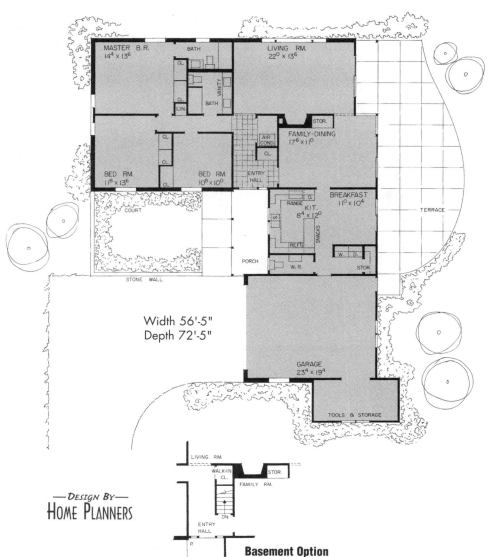

Width 56'-5"
Depth 72'-5"

Basement Option

◆ This unique series of homes contains two different floor plans that work with one of three different exteriors. Order either floor plan and details for all three exteriors will be included. If you prefer the floor plan with the 26-foot keeping room, order Design 2611. If you would rather have a living room, dining room and family room, choose Design 2612. The remainder of the floor plans are quite similar. Each features three bedrooms including a master suite with private bath. The kitchen and eating area are to the front of both plans; yet Design 2612 has an L-shaped kitchen, while Design 2611 has a U-shaped kitchen. Design 2611 has its basement stairway at the service entrance near the laundry; Design 2612 puts its basement stairway in the hallway at the entrance. Each has a two-car garage and half-bath besides the main and master baths.

—Design By—
Home Planners

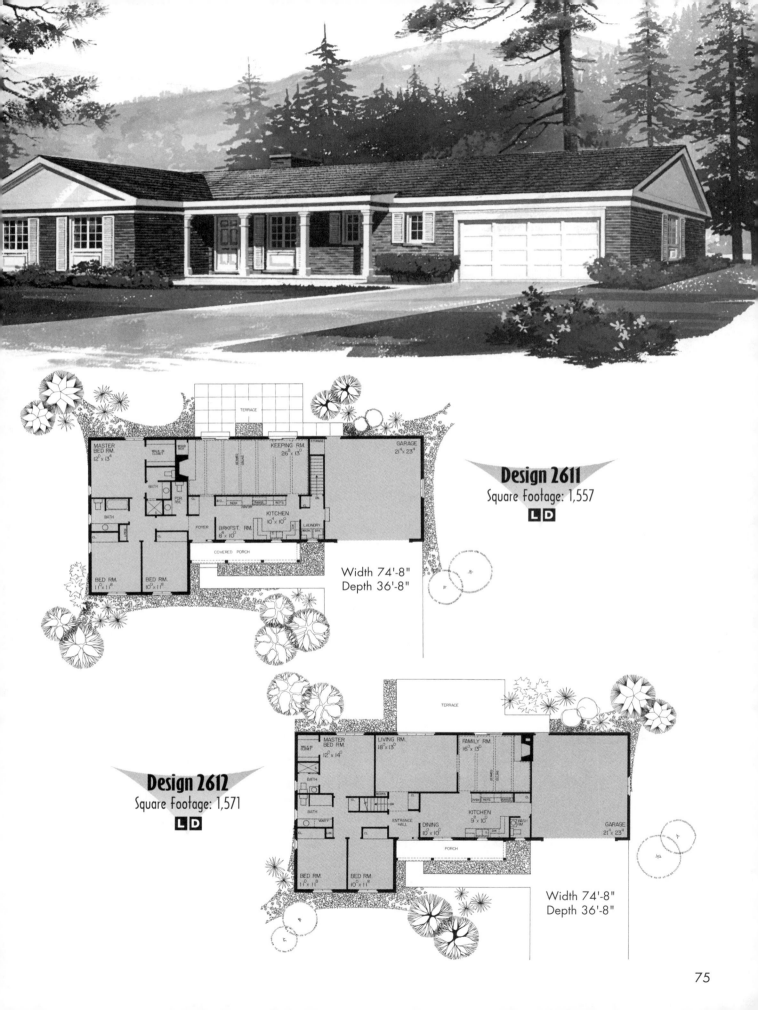

Design 2611
Square Footage: 1,557

L D

Width 74'-8"
Depth 36'-8"

Design 2612
Square Footage: 1,571

L D

Width 74'-8"
Depth 36'-8"

Design Q497
Square Footage: 1,746

◆ Special detailing, low-maintenance brick and shuttered windows add a traditional touch to this home. The skylit foyer opens to a sunken living room with sliding glass doors to the rear yard. The dining room shares a through-fireplace with the living room and has bayed windows for a view. The U-shaped kitchen is just beyond and has a large breakfast room for casual meals. The laundry room/mud room is gigan-

tic and connects the house to the two-car garage. The master suite is the picture of luxury with loads of windows and a bath with raised whirlpool tub, separate shower and double vanities. Family bedrooms share a full hall bath. Stairs to the basement are contained with an open railing with a planter ledge over. Plans include details for both a basement and a crawlspace foundation.

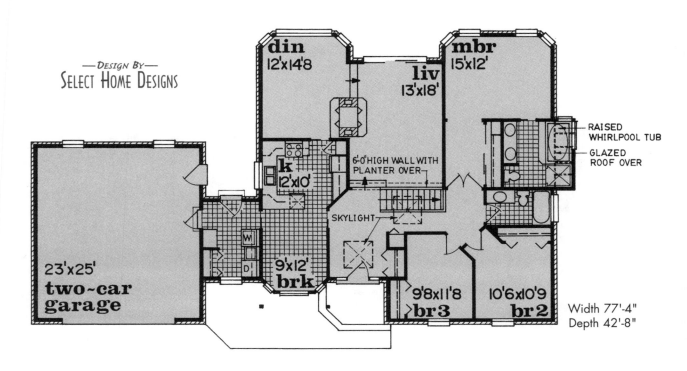

— DESIGN BY —
SELECT HOME DESIGNS

din 12'x14'8

mbr 15'x12'

liv 13'x18'

RAISED WHIRLPOOL TUB

GLAZED ROOF OVER

k 12'x10'

6'-0" HIGH WALL WITH PLANTER OVER

SKYLIGHT

23'x25'
two-car garage

W
D

9'x12'
brk

9'8x11'8
br3

10'6x10'9
br2

Width 77'-4"
Depth 42'-8"

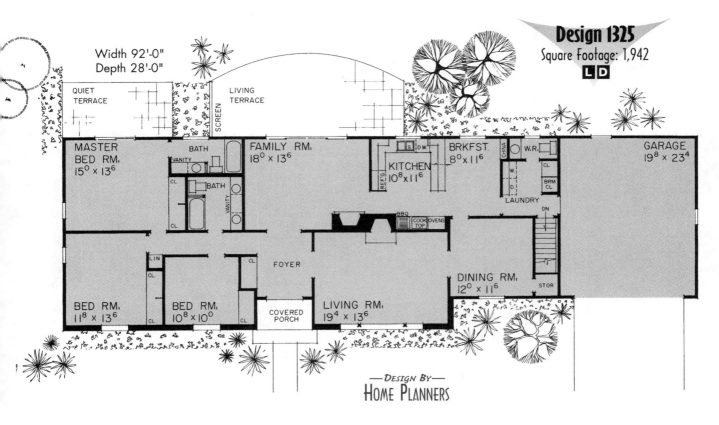

Width 92'-0"
Depth 28'-0"

QUIET TERRACE

LIVING TERRACE

SCREEN

MASTER BED RM. 15⁰ x 13⁶

BATH

VANITY

CL

BATH

VANITY

CL

FAMILY RM. 18 x 13⁶

KITCHEN 10⁸ x 11⁶

REF'G

S DW

BBQ

COOK TOP

OVENS

BRKFST. 8⁰ x 11⁶

CHINA

W.R.

CL

W D

BRM CL

LAUNDRY

DN

GARAGE 19⁸ x 23⁴

LIN

CL

CL

BED RM. 11⁸ x 13⁶

CL

BED RM. 10⁸ x 10⁰

CL

FOYER

COVERED PORCH

LIVING RM. 19⁴ x 13⁶

DINING RM. 12⁰ x 11⁶

STOR

—DESIGN BY—
HOME PLANNERS

◆ Brick veneer, multi-paned windows and quaint shutters come together in a classic one-story rendition. Double doors introduce the large front entry hall, which permits direct access to the formal living room on the right and the family room ahead. Both living spaces boast fireplaces; the family room has sliding glass doors to the living terrace at the rear. The dining room is to the right of the living room and also has an entry to the central hall for kitchen access. A small storage closet is located in the dining room—perfect for linens and special occasion tableware. The U-shaped kitchen has a pass-through counter to the breakfast room, which sports a built-in china hutch. Beyond is the service entrance with laundry room, broom closets and a wash room. The two-car garage connects to the house at this point. Bedrooms are at the opposite end of the house and include a master suite with private bath and two family bedrooms sharing a full bath.

Design 2941
Square Footage: 1,842

Design 2943
Square Footage: 1,834

◆ The classic design of this floor plan works for either of the two exteriors shown here. Please specify which you'd prefer when ordering. The Early American exterior is charming with its horizontal siding, stone accents and window boxes. A dovecote, a picket fence and a garden court enhance its appeal. The contemporary option features vertical siding and a wide overhanging roof with exposed rafter ends. Both exterior choices open from a covered entrance to a spacious foyer with a dramatic open staircase to the basement. This area can be finished later with recreation space or additional bedrooms. The large gathering room beyond features a fireplace flanked by windows, a sloped ceiling and sliding glass doors to the rear terrace. The dining room nearby also enjoys access to the terrace. The breakfast room and kitchen share space and include a box-bay window, a planning desk and a snack-bar counter. The laundry is found in the service entrance to the garage and holds a handy broom closet. At the opposite end of the plan are two bedrooms and a well-defined media room. Built-ins in the media room make it convenient. The master suite has sliding glass doors to the terrace and a truly luxurious bath with whirlpool tub and double sinks. The walk-in closet in the master suite has built-in shelves. Look for extra storage in the two-car garage. The Quote One® custom price quote system is available for Design 2943 only.

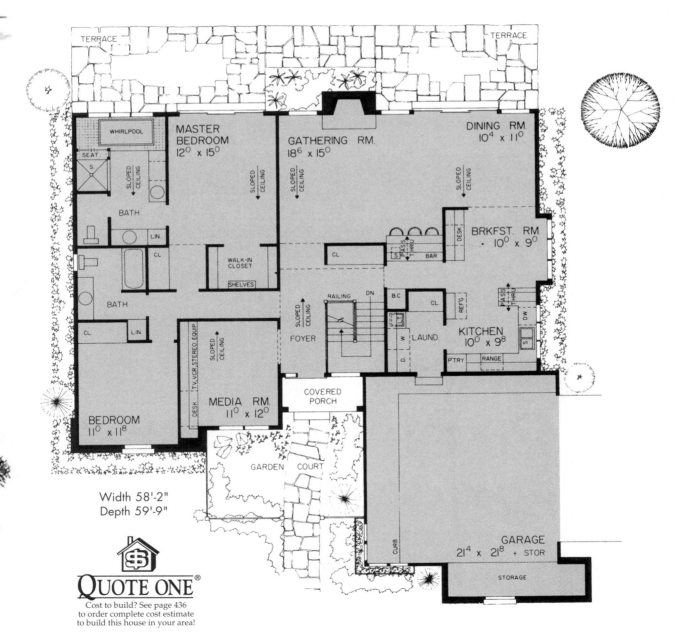

Width 58'-2"
Depth 59'-9"

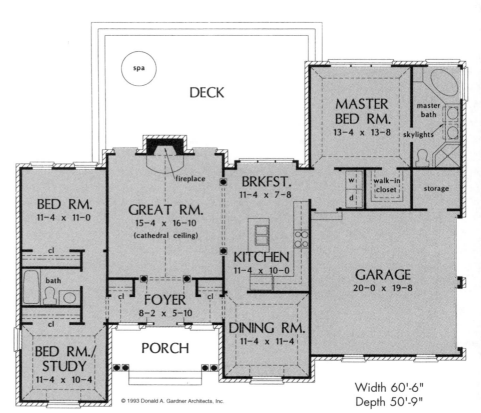

Design 9728
Square Footage: 1,576

◆ This stately, three-bedroom, one-story home exhibits sheer elegance with its large, arched windows, round columns, covered porch, and brick veneer. In the foyer, natural light enters through arched windows in clerestory dormers. In the great room, a dramatic cathedral ceiling and a fireplace set the mood. Through gracious, round columns, the kitchen and breakfast room open up. For sleeping, turn to the master bedroom. Here, a large, walk-in closet and a well-planned master bath with a double-bowl vanity, a garden tub and a shower will pamper. Two additional bedrooms are located at the opposite end of the house for privacy.

DECK

spa

MASTER BED RM.
13-4 x 13-8

master bath

skylights

walk-in closet

storage

BED RM.
11-4 x 11-0

cl

bath

cl

GREAT RM.
15-4 x 16-10
(cathedral ceiling)

fireplace

BRKFST.
11-4 x 7-8

KITCHEN
11-4 x 10-0

w d

GARAGE
20-0 x 19-8

BED RM./
STUDY
11-4 x 10-4

cl

FOYER
8-2 x 5-10

cl

PORCH

DINING RM.
11-4 x 11-4

Width 60'-6"
Depth 50'-9"

—DESIGN BY—
DONALD A. GARDNER
ARCHITECTS, INC.

B. NATHAN.

B. NATHAN

Design 9765
Square Footage: 1,537

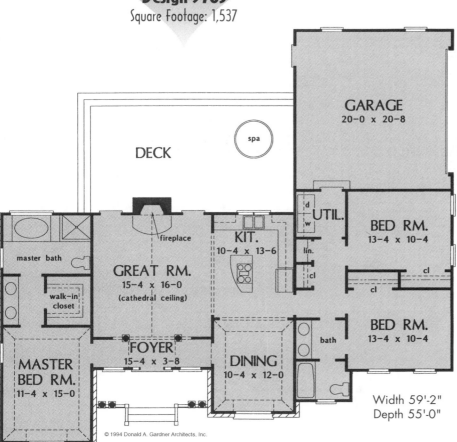

GARAGE
20-0 x 20-8

DECK

spa

fireplace

KIT.
10-4 x 13-6

master bath

GREAT RM.
15-4 x 16-0
(cathedral ceiling)

walk-in
closet

UTIL.

d
w

lin.

cl

cl

BED RM.
13-4 x 10-4

cl

FOYER
15-4 x 3-8

DINING
10-4 x 12-0

bath

BED RM.
13-4 x 10-4

MASTER
BED RM.
11-4 x 15-0

Width 59'-2"
Depth 55'-0"

◆ The intricate window treatment and stately columns give this home magnificent curb appeal. Inside, the columns continue from the foyer into the spacious great room with its cathedral ceiling and raised-hearth fireplace. The fireplace is flanked by windows with a view to the rear deck and the spa. The great room opens to the large island kitchen and the formal dining room with its dramatic tray ceiling. Another tray ceiling can be found in the master bedroom. It also includes a large bath with dual vanities, a whirlpool tub, a separate shower and a walk-in closet. The remaining bedrooms, a shared full bath and a conveniently placed utility room are located in the right wing of the house.

—DESIGN BY—
DONALD A. GARDNER
ARCHITECTS, INC.

Design 9427

Square Footage: 1,687

◆ Intriguing rooflines create a dynamic exterior for this home. It is even further enhanced by a tasteful accenting of brick. The interior floor plan is equally attractive. Towards the rear, a wide archway forms the entrance to the spacious family living area with its centrally placed fireplace and bay-windowed nook area. An island and a walk-in pantry complete the efficient kitchen (note the corner window treatment overlooking the yard). This home also boasts a terrific master suite complete with walk-in wardrobe, spa tub with corner windows and a compartmented shower and toilet area.

—DESIGN BY—

ALAN MASCORD
DESIGN ASSOCIATES, INC.

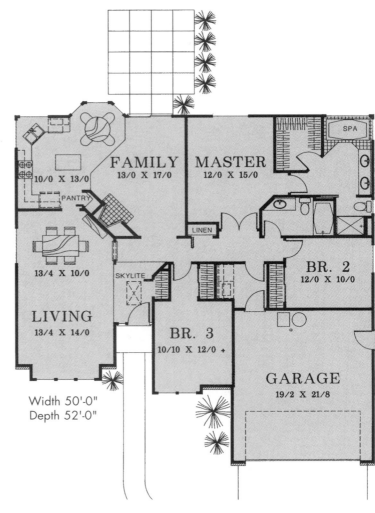

FAMILY 13/0 X 17/0

MASTER 12/0 X 15/0

SPA

10/0 X 13/0

PANTRY

LINEN

BR. 2 12/0 X 10/0

LIVING 13/4 X 14/0

SKYLITE

BR. 3 10/10 X 12/0 +

GARAGE 19/2 X 21/8

Width 50'-0"
Depth 52'-0"

©1996 Donald A. Gardner Architects, Inc.

B. NATHAN.

◆ The arches of the covered porch make an attractive contrast to the pointed gables and dormer of this lovely home. Inside, spaciousness is the key word, as decorative pillars mark the boundaries of the foyer and formal dining room, and lead into the great room with cathedral ceiling and fireplace. In the kitchen, the cook will enjoy the glow from the fireplace as well as the large walk-in pantry and island work area. A cheerful breakfast nook offers lots of sunshine and access to the back porch. The master suite also has access to the porch and a sumptuous master bath. A full hall bath is shared by two bedrooms, one of which could serve as a study. Stairs off the kitchen lead to attic storage and a bonus room with a skylight.

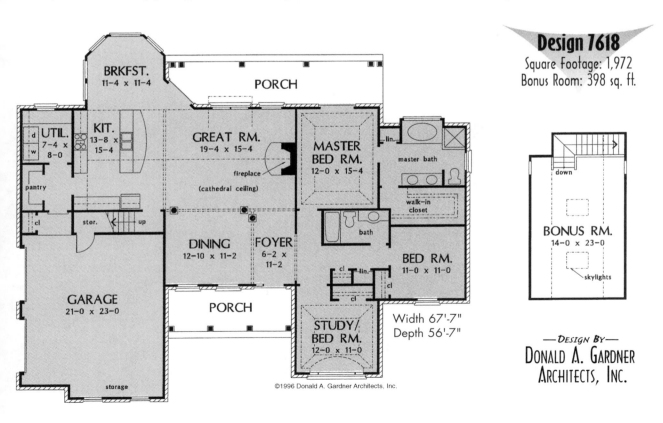

©1996 Donald A. Gardner Architects, Inc.

Width 67'-7"
Depth 56'-7"

Design 7618
Square Footage: 1,972
Bonus Room: 398 sq. ft.

—Design By—
Donald A. Gardner
Architects, Inc.

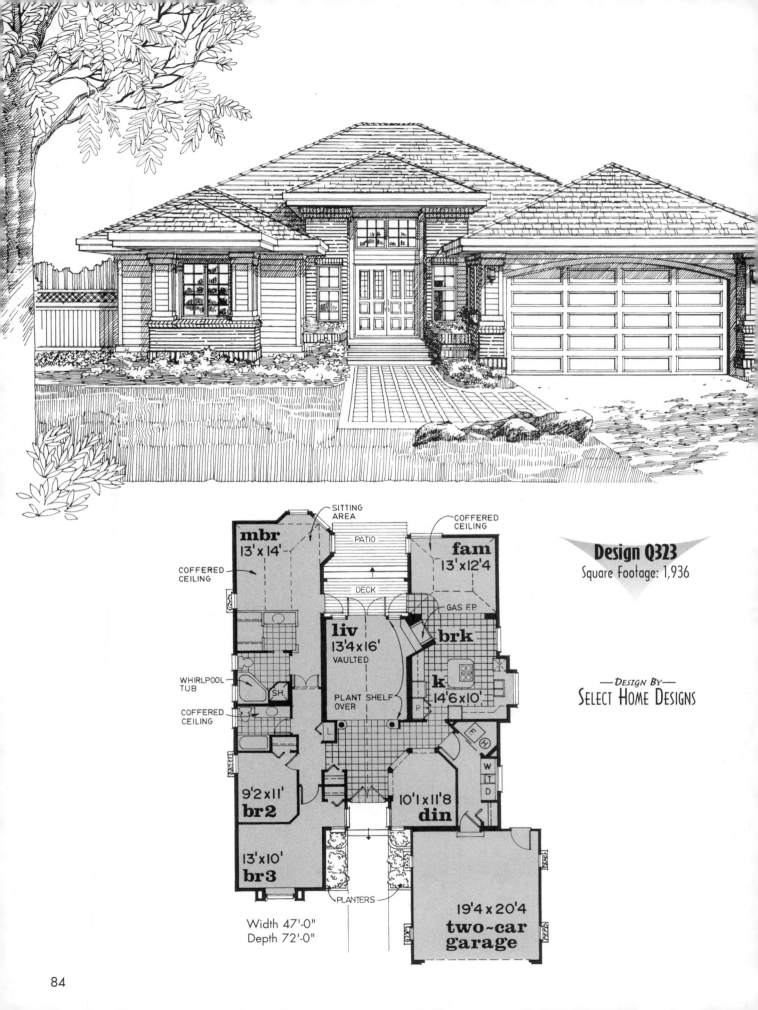

mbr
13' x 14'

COFFERED
CEILING

SITTING
AREA

PATIO

DECK

COFFERED CEILING

fam
13'x12'4

Design Q323
Square Footage: 1,936

GAS F.P.

WHIRLPOOL
TUB

SH.

liv
13'4x16'
VAULTED

PLANT SHELF
OVER

brk

k
14'6x10'

— DESIGN BY —
SELECT HOME DESIGNS

COFFERED
CEILING

L

F

H

W
D

9'2x11'
br2

10'1x11'8
din

13'x10'
br3

PLANTERS

Width 47'-0"
Depth 72'-0"

19'4 x 20'4
**two~car
garage**

Alternate Elevation

◆ Choose from one of two exteriors for this lovely home—details for both are included in the blueprints. The traditional version has brick veneer with horizontal wood siding as accents. The stucco version has the same general style but rendered completely in cool white. Both surround a livable, light-filled floor plan. A transom window over the entry and the living room accentuates the vaulted ceiling which stretches throughout the foyer and living room. A fireplace shares space with both the living room and the breakfast room, and is easily enjoyed even in the family room. Note the lovely coffered ceiling in this casual living area. The kitchen is L-shaped and features a large pantry and island cooktop. Nearby is the service area with laundry and access to the two-car garage. Bedrooms are in-line at the left of the plan and include a lovely master suite with coffered ceiling, bay-windowed sitting area, deck access, walk-in closet and very thoughtfully appointed bath. Two family bedrooms and a full bath are to the front of the home. Bedroom 3 has a box-bay window.

Rear Elevation

Design Q365
Square Footage: 1,624

Plans include all exteriors shown.

◆ This affordable ranch home offers a choice of exteriors—a contemporary California stucco or a traditional version with horizontal siding and brick detailing. The entry is graced by light-giving transom windows—perfect for the plant ledge over decorative columns leading to the living room. The living room also has a vaulted ceiling, a fireplace and rear-yard access. The formal dining room is also vaulted with tall, arched windows at the front and has entry from the foyer and from the central hall to access the kitchen more conveniently.

—DESIGN BY—
SELECT HOME DESIGNS

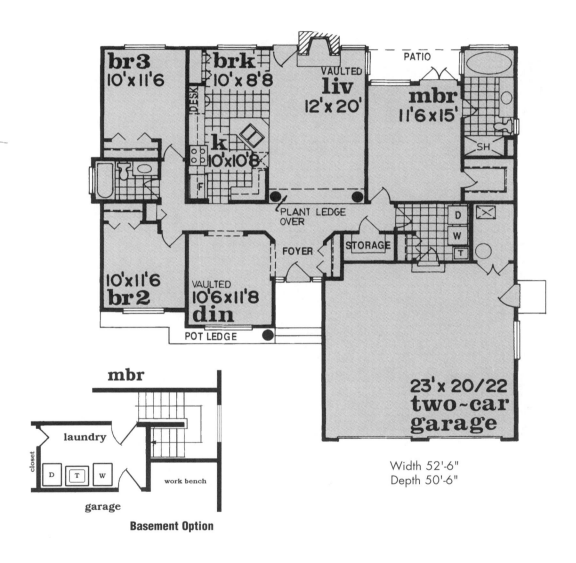

Width 52'-6"
Depth 50'-6"

Basement Option

An attached breakfast room features a planning desk and allows space for casual dining. The master bedroom boasts French door access to the patio and features a walk-in closet and bath with whirlpool tub. Two additional bedrooms share a main bath with soaking tub. A large laundry area leads to a two-car garage. Note the storage space in the hall near the service entrance. Plans include details for both a basement and a crawlspace option.

Design 9202
Square Footage: 1,808

◆ Discriminating buyers will love the refined yet inviting look of this three-bedroom ranch plan. A tiled entry with ten-foot ceilings leads into the spacious great room with large bay window. An open-hearth fireplace warms both the great room and kitchen. The sleeping area features a large master suite with a dramatic arched window and a bath with whirlpool, His and Hers vanities and a walk-in closet. Don't miss the storage space in the oversized garage.

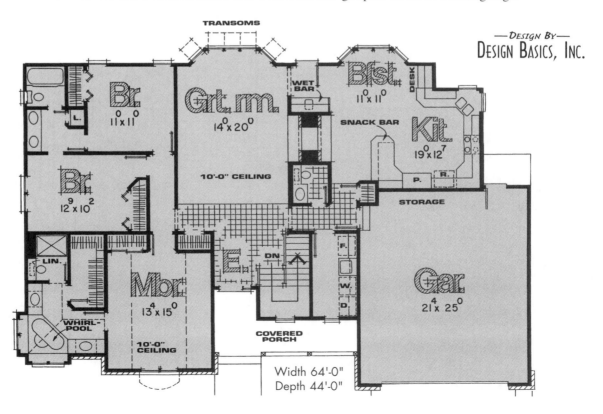

—DESIGN BY—
DESIGN BASICS, INC.

TRANSOMS

Br. 11 x 11

Grt. rm. 14⁰ x 20⁰

WET BAR

Bfst. 11⁰ x 11⁰

DESK

SNACK BAR

Kit. 19⁰ x 12⁷

P.   R.

Br. 12 x 10²

10'-0" CEILING

STORAGE

LIN.

Mbr. 13⁴ x 15⁰

DN

F.

W.

D.

Gar. 21⁴ x 25⁰

WHIRL-POOL

10'-0" CEILING

COVERED PORCH

Width 64'-0"
Depth 44'-0"

Design 9734

Square Footage: 1,977
Bonus Room: 430 sq. ft.

—Design By—
Donald A. Gardner
Architects, Inc.

◆ A two-story foyer with a Palladian window above sets the tone for this sunlit home. Columns mark the passage from the foyer to the great room, which features a centered fireplace and built-in cabinets. This room offers views and access to a rear screen porch with four skylights and a wet bar—and just a few steps away is a deck with spa. The nearby breakfast room offers a separate entrance to the rear deck and shares light from outdoor areas with the kitchen. The formal dining room offers a coffered ceiling and a Palladian window with views to the front property. A secluded master suite offers comfort and style to spare, with a skylit bath, corner whirlpool tub, generous walk-in closet and private access to the rear deck and spa. On the opposite side of the plan, a front bedroom with coffered ceiling and Palladian window could be a study. This room shares a hall bath with a secondary bedroom. Please specify basement or crawlspace foundation when ordering.

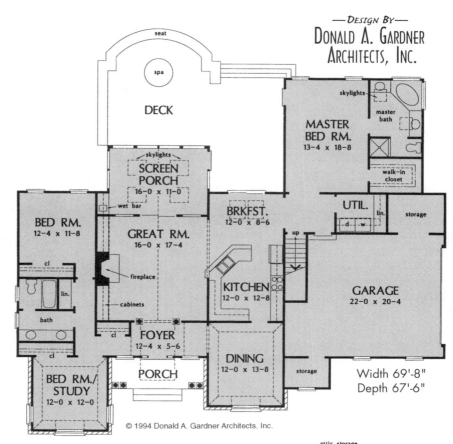

© 1994 Donald A. Gardner Architects, Inc.

Width 69'-8"
Depth 67'-6"

Quote One®
Cost to build? See page 436
to order complete cost estimate
to build this house in your area!

BONUS RM.
18-0 x 19-0

© 1994 Donald A. Gardner Architects, Inc.

◆ Wood frame, weatherboard siding and stacked stone give this home its country cottage appeal. The concept is reinforced by the double elliptical arched front porch, the Colonial balustrade and the roof-vent dormer. Inside, the foyer leads to the great room and the dining room. The well-planned kitchen easily serves the breakfast room. A rear deck makes outdoor living extra enjoyable. Three bedrooms include a master suite with a tray ceiling and a luxurious bath. The two secondary bedrooms share a compartmented bath. This home is designed with a basement foundation.

—DESIGN BY—
DESIGN TRADITIONS

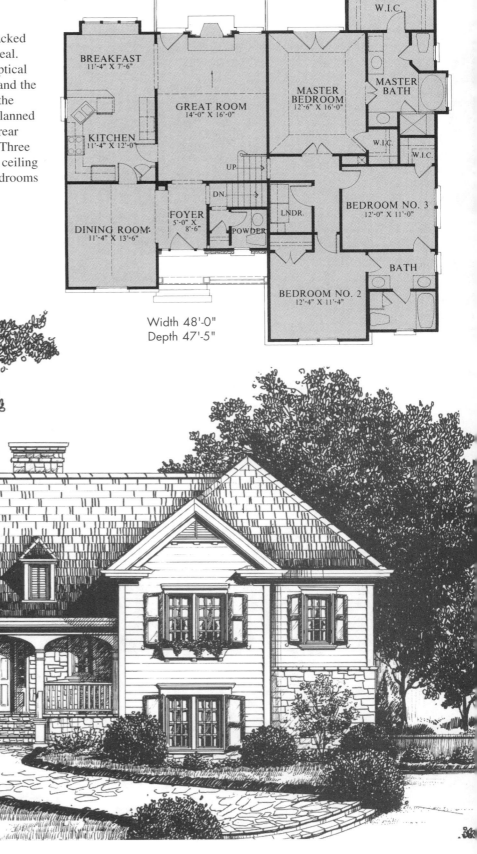

Width 48'-0"
Depth 47'-5"

© American Home Gallery, Ltd.

Design 7221
Square Footage: 1,580

◆ Brick wing walls give a visually expansive front elevation to this charming home. From the entry, traffic flows into the bright great room that has an impressive two-sided fireplace. The dining room opens to the great room, offering a view of the fireplace. French doors off the entry lead to the kitchen. Here, a large pantry, a planning desk and a snack bar are appreciated amenities. The breakfast nook accesses a large, comfortable screened porch. The laundry room is strategically located off the kitchen and provides direct access to the garage. The master suite features a formal ceiling, French doors and a pampering bath. Two secondary bedrooms and a full hall bath complete the sleeping wing.

— DESIGN BY —
DESIGN BASICS, INC.

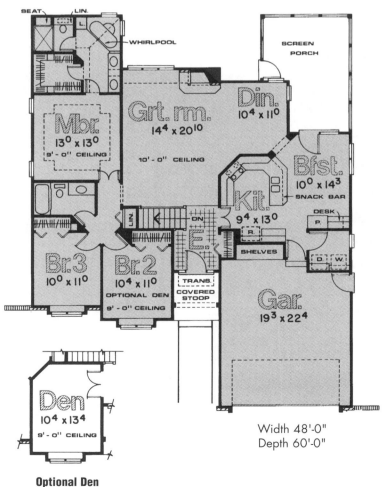

SEAT   LIN.

WHIRLPOOL

SCREEN
PORCH

Mbr.
13⁰ x 13⁰
9'-0" CEILING

Grt. rm.
14⁴ x 20¹⁰
10'-0" CEILING

Din.
10⁴ x 11⁰

Bfst.
10⁰ x 14³
SNACK BAR

Kit.
9⁴ x 13⁰

DESK
P.

LIN.

DN

SHELVES

D W

Br.3
10⁰ x 11⁰

Br.2
10⁴ x 11⁰
OPTIONAL DEN
9'-0" CEILING

TRANS.
COVERED
STOOP

Gar.
19³ x 22⁴

Den
10⁴ x 13⁴
9'-0" CEILING

Width 48'-0"
Depth 60'-0"

Optional Den

Design Q431
Square Footage: 1,911

◆ Horizontal wood siding graces the exterior of this quaint one-story home. Enter through double doors to an entry where a skylight spills its brightness into the living and dining area. The living space has a vaulted ceiling over a full-height window wall and a warming fireplace. The open plan kitchen and its attached family room are ideal for a casual gathering spot. The kitchen features a spacious work island, a pantry and a breakfast nook. A large rear deck extends beyond the family room. In the master suite are a walk-in closet and bath with His and Hers vanities, corner shower and whirlpool spa. The family bedrooms share a skylit main bath. The service entrance to the garage holds an alcove for a washer and dryer and the stairway to the basement. Plans include details for both basement and crawlspace foundations.

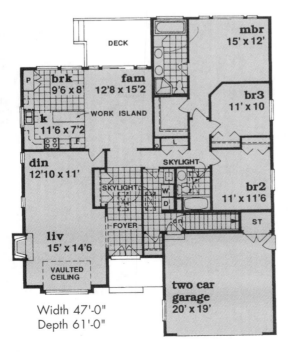

DECK

brk
9'6 x 8'

fam
12'8 x 15'2

P

WORK ISLAND

k
11'6 x 7'2

din
12'10 x 11'

SKYLIGHT

W
D

FOYER

liv
15' x 14'6

VAULTED CEILING

mbr
15' x 12'

br3
11' x 10

SKYLIGHT

br2
11' x 11'6

ST

two car garage
20' x 19'

Width 47'-0"
Depth 61'-0"

— DESIGN BY —
SELECT HOME DESIGNS

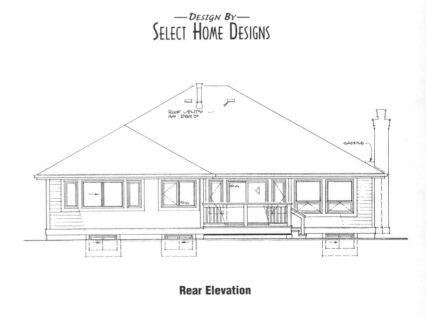

ROOF VENTS AS REQ'D

SADDLE

Rear Elevation

Design 3600
Square Footage: 2,258

L

Width 68'-0"
Depth 64'-0"

Traditional One-Story Homes
2,000 to 2,500 Square Feet

◆ This unique one-story plan seems tailor-made for empty-nesters or for a small family. A grand, tiled foyer opens to formal and informal living areas: to the left, an elegant formal dining room with raised ceiling and bay window, and to the right, a living room with sloped ceiling and view to the front property through triple windows. Ahead, the foyer leads to an open living area: a family room with vaulted ceiling, centered fireplace with tiled hearth, and access to the rear deck. The morning room bay adjoins a roomy well-equipped kitchen with a food preparation island, and offers separate access to the wood deck. The master suite is secluded to the rear of the plan and offers a sumptuous bath with a whirlpool tub, dual lavatories, a separate shower and walk-in closet. An adjoining office/den boasts a private porch. One family bedroom or guest room with a private, full bath is positioned for privacy on the opposite side of the plan.

QUOTE ONE®

Cost to build? See page 436
to order complete cost estimate
to build this house in your area!

Rear Elevation

—DESIGN BY—
HOME PLANNERS

Design 3601
Square Footage: 2,424

L

◆ This unique one-story plan seems tailor-made for a small family or for empty-nesters. Formal areas are situated well for entertaining—living room to the right and formal dining room to the left. A large family room is found to the rear. It has access to a rear wood deck and is warmed in the cold months by a welcome hearth. The U-shaped kitchen features an attached morning room for casual meals. It is near the laundry and a washroom. Bedrooms are split. The master suite sits to the right of the plan and has a walk-in closet and fine bath. A nearby study has a private porch. Two family bedrooms are on the other side of the home and share a bath.

—DESIGN BY—
HOME PLANNERS

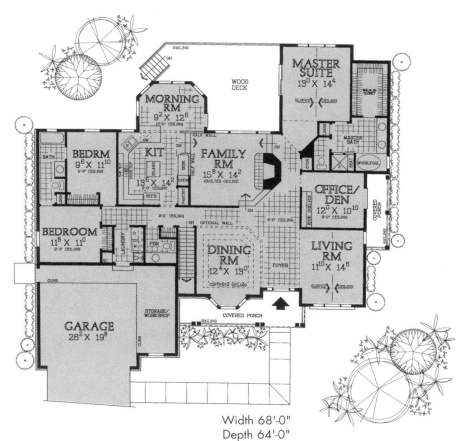

Width 68'-0"
Depth 64'-0"

QUOTE ONE®
Cost to build? See page 436
to order complete cost estimate
to build this house in your area!

94

◆ A projecting portico with an archway supported by two sets of twin columns provides shelter, as well as an appealing front entrance. The dramatic central foyer has a high ceiling and an abundance of natural light. At the center of the plan is the family room with its sloped ceiling. It has a raised-hearth fireplace and an entertainment center. It looks over a low wall into the kitchen. The snack bar is nearby. French doors open to the covered patio. This plan offers the increasingly popular feature of the split sleeping facilities. There are two bedrooms and a bath for the children. At the opposite end of the plan is the master suite, where the focal point is the raised-hearth fireplace, which can be enjoyed on three sides—even from the whirlpool!

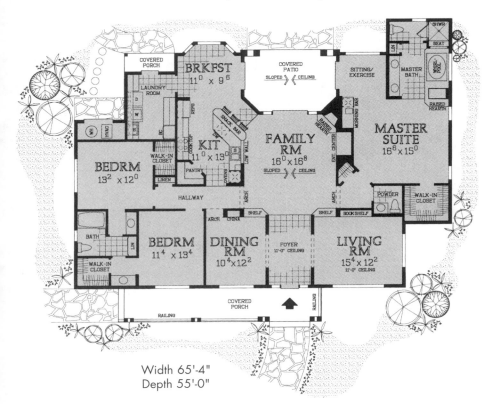

Width 65'-4"
Depth 55'-0"

Design 3613
Square Footage: 2,407

L

—DESIGN BY—
HOME PLANNERS

Cost to build? See page 436 to order complete cost estimate to build this house in your area!

© American Home Gallery, Ltd.

Design T052
Square Footage: 2,090

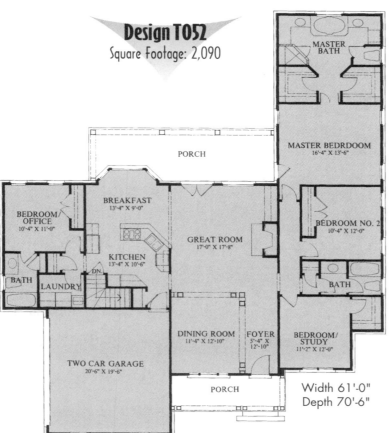

PORCH

MASTER BATH

MASTER BEDRDOOM
16'-4" X 13'-6"

BREAKFAST
13'-4" X 9'-0"

BEDROOM/
OFFICE
10'-4" X 11'-0"

GREAT ROOM
17'-0" X 17'-8"

BEDROOM NO. 2
10'-4" X 12'-0"

KITCHEN
13'-4" X 10'-6"

DN.

BATH

LAUNDRY

BATH

DINING ROOM
11'-4" X 12'-10"

FOYER
5'-4" X
12'-10"

BEDROOM/
STUDY
11'-2" X 12'-0"

TWO CAR GARAGE
20'-6" X 19'-6"

PORCH

Width 61'-0"
Depth 70'-6"

◆ This traditional home features board-and-batten and cedar shingles in a well-proportioned exterior. The foyer opens to the dining room and leads to the great room, which offers French doors to the rear columned porch. An additional bedroom, or study, shares a full bath with a family bedroom, while the lavish master suite enjoys a private bath with two walk-in closets, two vanities, a whirlpool tub and a compartmented toilet. The kitchen overlooks a bayed breakfast area and shares views of the outdoors with the great room. A fourth bedroom, home office or guest suite nestles to the rear of the plan and is handy to the laundry. This home is designed with a basement foundation.

— DESIGN BY —
DESIGN TRADITIONS

Quote One®
Cost to build? See page 436
to order complete cost estimate
to build this house in your area!

BATH

BEDROOM NO. 3
11'-6" X 11'-0"

BEDROOM NO. 2
11'-4" X 11'-0"

SUN ROOM
12'-0" X 13'-8"

PORCH

Width 62'-4"
Depth 62'-2"

MASTER BATH

W.I.C.

MASTER BEDROOM
13'-4" X 15'-6"

PORCH

BREAKFAST
10'-0" X 9'-0"

FAMILY ROOM
18'-0" X 14'-0"

LAUNDRY

KITCHEN
12'-0" X 13'-2"

BATH

STORAGE

DN

TWO CAR GARAGE
20'-4" X 19'-8"

DINING ROOM
11'-4" X 11'-4"

FOYER
6'-8" X 11'-10"

DEN/GUEST BEDROOM
11'-4" X 14'-0"

PORCH

—DESIGN BY—
DESIGN TRADITIONS

Design T061
Square Footage: 2,170

◆ This classic cottage boasts a stone-and-wood exterior with a welcoming arch-top entry that leads to a columned foyer. An extended-hearth fireplace is the focal point for the family room, while a near-by sunroom with covered porch access opens up the living area to the outdoors. The gourmet island kitchen opens through double doors from the living area, and the breakfast area hugs a private porch. Sleeping quarters include a master wing with a spacious, angled bath and a sitting room or den which has its own full bath—perfect for a guest suite. On the opposite side of the plan, two family bedrooms share a full bath. This home is designed with a basement foundation.

QUOTE ONE®
Cost to build? See page 436
to order complete cost estimate
to build this house in your area!

© American Home Gallery, Ltd.

Alternate Elevation

Design 9323
Square Footage: 2,276

— Design By —
Design Basics, Inc.

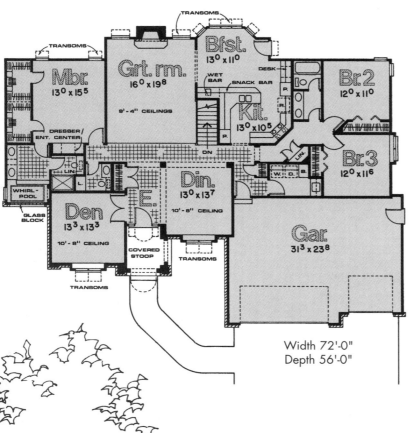

Mbr.
13⁰ x 15⁵

Grt. rm.
16⁰ x 19⁶

9'-4" CEILINGS

Bfst.
13⁰ x 11⁰

TRANSOMS

TRANSOMS

DRESSER/
ENT. CENTER

WHIRL-
POOL

GLASS
BLOCK

WET
BAR

DESK

SNACK BAR

Kit.
13⁰ x 10⁵

Br 2
12⁰ x 11⁰

Br. 3
12⁰ x 11⁶

DN

LIN

W.D.

Den
13³ x 13³

10'-8" CEILING

Din.
13⁰ x 13⁷

10'-8" CEILING

E.

COVERED
STOOP

TRANSOMS

Gar.
31³ x 23⁸

Width 72'-0"
Depth 56'-0"

TRANSOMS

◆ Drama and harmony are expressed by utilizing a variety of elegant exterior materials. An expansive entry views the private den with French doors and an open dining room (both rooms have extra-high ceilings). The great room with a window-framed fireplace is conveniently located next to the eat-in kitchen with bayed breakfast area. Special amenities include a wet bar/servery, two pantries, planning desk and snack bar. Two secluded secondary bedrooms enjoy easy access to a compartmented bath with a twin vanity. His and Hers closets and a built-in armoire that could be an entertainment center or a dresser, grace the master bedroom. A luxurious master bath features glass blocks over the whirlpool, double sinks and an extra linen storage cabinet. An alternate elevation is provided at no extra cost.

Design 7231

Square Footage: 2,047

◆ This handsome ranch home features brick siding and wood railings on a lovely covered porch. Inside, the plan allows for a private den off the entry to be converted to a third bedroom, if preferred. Ten-foot ceilings in the dining room and the great room add depth and sophistication. The great room features a fireplace flanked by transom windows; the dining room has hutch space. The U-shaped kitchen is made for the gourmet cook, with a pantry and loads of counter space. Accessed by French doors, the master bedrooms is indulgent with a walk-in closet and bath with corner whirlpool, double vanity and separate shower with seat. A full bath in the hall serves the second bedroom and the den.

— DESIGN BY —
DESIGN BASICS, INC.

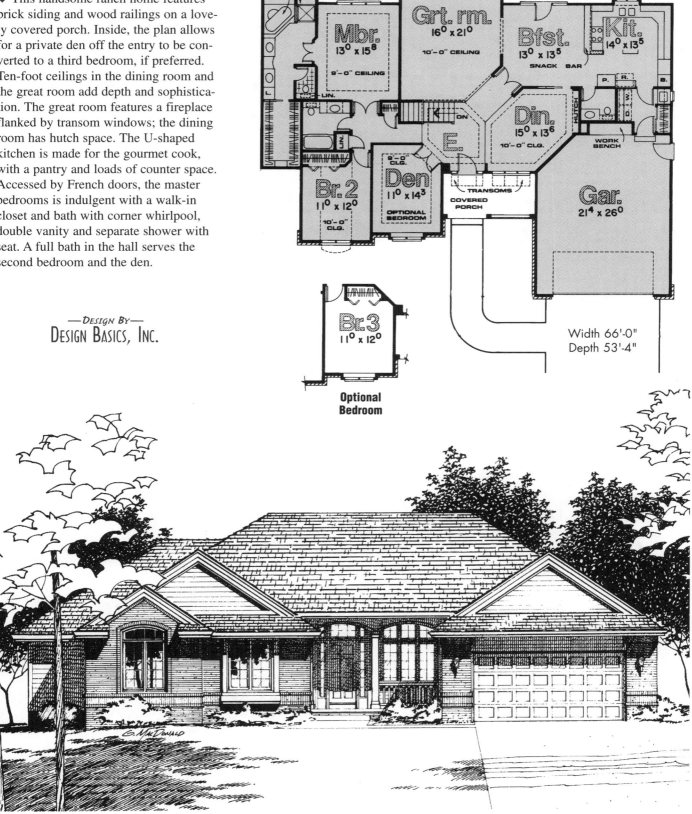

TRANSOMS

WHIRLPOOL   **SEAT**

Mbr.
$13^0 \times 15^8$
$9'-0''$ CEILING

Grt. rm.
$16^0 \times 21^0$
$10'-0''$ CEILING

Bfst.
$13^0 \times 13^5$
SNACK BAR

Kit.
$14^0 \times 13^5$

LIN.

DN

Din.
$15^0 \times 13^6$
$10'-0''$ CLG.

HUTCH

P.   R.
D.   W.

WORK BENCH

Br. 2
$11^0 \times 12^0$
$10'-0''$ CLG.

Den
$11^0 \times 14^3$
OPTIONAL BEDROOM
$9'-0''$ CLG.

E.

COVERED PORCH

TRANSOMS

Gar.
$21^4 \times 26^0$

Br. 3
$11^0 \times 12^0$

Optional Bedroom

Width 66'-0"
Depth 53'-4"

Design Q404

Square Footage: 2,404

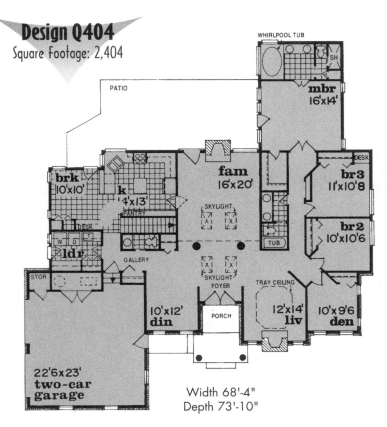

WHIRLPOOL TUB

PATIO

mbr
16'x14'

brk
10'x10'

k
14'x13'

PANTRY

DESK

br3
11'x10'8

DESK

fam
16'x20'

SKYLIGHT

br2
10'x10'6

W D

ldr

DESK

TUB

GALLERY

SKYLIGHT

FOYER

STOR

TRAY CEILING

10'x12'
din

PORCH

12'x14'
liv

10'x9'6
den

22'6x23'
two-car garage

Width 68'-4"
Depth 73'-10"

◆ Low-maintenance brick finish, shuttered windows and a covered porch surrounded by decorative pillars provide a fine welcoming exterior for this three-bedroom ranch design. Directly in view of the skylit foyer is a spacious family room with matching twin skylights. A plant shelf and decorative columns visually zone the entry and family room. The living room with tray ceiling and fireplace sits to the right of the foyer while the dining room sits to the left. A gourmet kitchen features a center prep island, long pantry, breakfast room and built-in desk. The spacious rear deck allows space for outdoor relaxation and extends the indoor living spaces. Bedrooms are positioned away from the living areas for privacy. The master bedroom boasts a walk-in closet, access to the rear deck and a lavish bath with His and Hers vanities and whirlpool spa. Plans include details for both a basement and a crawlspace foundation.

—DESIGN BY—
SELECT HOME DESIGNS

Design 9634
Square Footage: 2,099

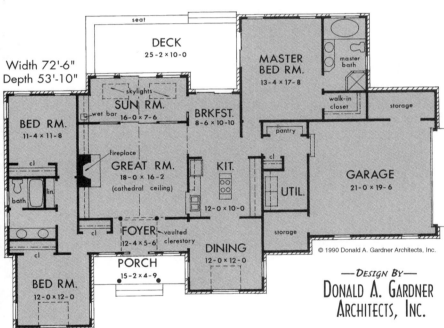

Width 72'-6"
Depth 53'-10"

DECK 25-2 × 10-0

seat

MASTER BED RM. 13-4 × 17-8

master bath

walk-in closet

storage

skylights

SUN RM. 16-0 × 7-6

wet bar

BED RM. 11-4 × 11-8

BRKFST. 8-6 × 10-10

pantry

fireplace

GREAT RM. 18-0 × 16-2 (cathedral ceiling)

KIT. 12-0 × 10-0

cl

UTIL.

GARAGE 21-0 × 19-6

bath

lin

cl

cl

FOYER 12-4 × 5-6

vaulted clerestory

storage

BED RM. 12-0 × 12-0

PORCH 15-2 × 4-9

DINING 12-0 × 12-0

© 1990 Donald A. Gardner Architects, Inc.

—Design By—
Donald A. Gardner Architects, Inc.

◆ This enchanting design incorporates the best in floor planning all on one level. The central great room is the hub of the plan from which all other rooms radiate. It is highlighted with a fireplace and cathedral ceiling. Nearby is a skylit sunroom with sliding glass doors to the rear deck and a built-in wet bar. The galley-style kitchen adjoins an attached breakfast room that also connects to the sunroom. The master suite is split from the family bedrooms and contains access to the rear deck. Its bathroom contains such special amenities as a large walk-in closet and double vanity. Family bedrooms share a full bath also with double vanity. Extra storage space is contained in the garage. Please specify basement or crawlspace foundation when ordering.

pantry

cl

down

kitchen

garage

storage

Alternate Plan for Basement

Rear Elevation

101

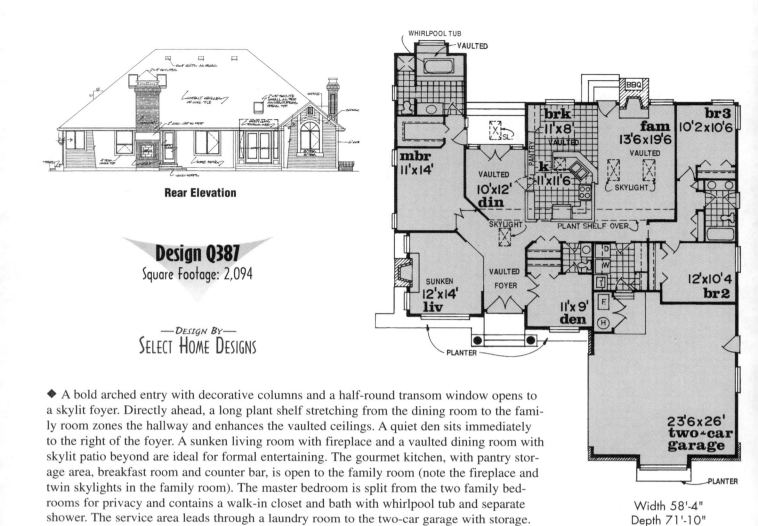

Rear Elevation

Design Q387
Square Footage: 2,094

— DESIGN BY —
SELECT HOME DESIGNS

◆ A bold arched entry with decorative columns and a half-round transom window opens to a skylit foyer. Directly ahead, a long plant shelf stretching from the dining room to the family room zones the hallway and enhances the vaulted ceilings. A quiet den sits immediately to the right of the foyer. A sunken living room with fireplace and a vaulted dining room with skylit patio beyond are ideal for formal entertaining. The gourmet kitchen, with pantry storage area, breakfast room and counter bar, is open to the family room (note the fireplace and twin skylights in the family room). The master bedroom is split from the two family bedrooms for privacy and contains a walk-in closet and bath with whirlpool tub and separate shower. The service area leads through a laundry room to the two-car garage with storage. Plans include details for both a basement and a crawlspace foundation.

Width 58'-4"
Depth 71'-10"

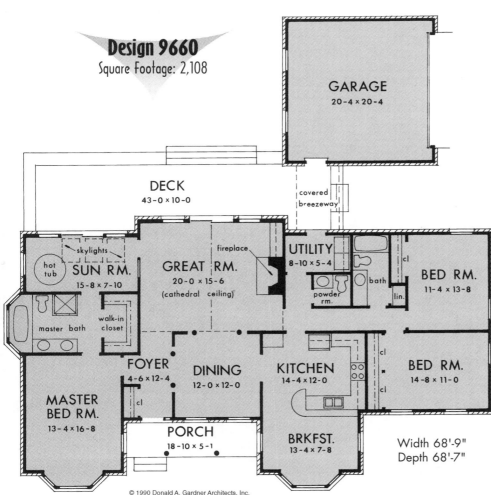

Design 9660
Square Footage: 2,108

GARAGE
20-4 × 20-4

DECK
43-0 × 10-0

covered breezeway

skylights

hot tub

SUN RM.
15-8 × 7-10

fireplace

GREAT RM.
20-0 × 15-6
(cathedral ceiling)

UTILITY
8-10 × 5-4

bath

cl

BED RM.
11-4 × 13-8

powder rm.

lin.

cl

master bath

walk-in closet

FOYER
4-6 × 12-4

DINING
12-0 × 12-0

KITCHEN
14-4 × 12-0

cl

BED RM.
14-8 × 11-0

cl

MASTER BED RM.
13-4 × 16-8

cl

PORCH
18-10 × 5-1

BRKFST.
13-4 × 7-8

Width 68'-9"
Depth 68'-7"

◆ Multi-pane windows, dormers, copper-covered bay windows, a covered porch with round columns and brick siding help to emphasize the sophisticated appearance of this three-bedroom home. An added special feature to this plan is the sunroom with hot tub that's accessible to both the master bath and great room. The great room has a fireplace, cathedral ceiling and sliding glass door with arched window above to allow plenty of natural light. The spacious master bedroom contains a walk-in closet and a bath with double-bowl vanity, shower and garden tub. Two family bedrooms are located at the opposite end of the house for privacy.

—DESIGN BY—
DONALD A. GARDNER
ARCHITECTS, INC.

—DESIGN BY—

DONALD A. GARDNER
ARCHITECTS, INC.

◆ This home is built for entertaining. The foyer opens to a central hall that has columns to define the entry to the great room. The large great room is perfect for parties and the kitchen, with sunny skylights and an adjoining dining room, creates a cozy breakfast buffet. Access from both rooms to the expansive deck completes the entertaining picture. The location of the kingly master bedroom and the family bedrooms allows for quiet comfort. The master suite has deck access, a walk-in closet and a bath with corner whirlpool, double sinks and skylights. Family bedrooms share a full bath with double vanities. A bonus room over the garage can be developed at a later date for office space, a guest room or hobby area.

Design 9739
Square Footage: 2,211
Bonus Room: 408 sq. ft.

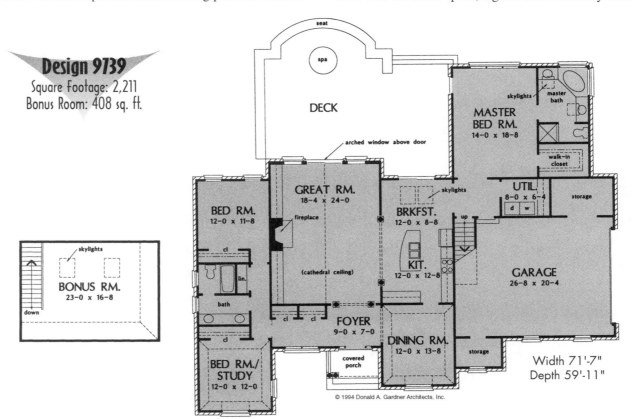

Width 71'-7"
Depth 59'-11"

COPYRIGHT LARRY E. BELK

Design 8126
Square Footage: 2,127
Bonus Room: 338 sq. ft.

— DESIGN BY —
LARRY E. BELK DESIGNS

FUTURE GAME ROOM
19-0 X 13-0
8 FT CLG

EXPANDABLE AREA
13-0 X 26-0

↑4 FT KNEE WALL↑ ↑8 FT CLG LINE↑ ↑8 FT CLG LINE↑ ↑4 FT KNEE WALL↑

BRKFST ROOM
11-0 X 10-0
10 FT CLG

COVERED PATIO

PAN

42" LEDGE

HIS   HERS

10 FT CLG

BEDROOM 3
11-6 X 12-6
8 FT CLG

LIN

FP

K.S.

MASTER BATH
11 FT CLG

LIN

KITCHEN
13-0 X 14-0
10 FT CLG

GREAT ROOM
17-6 X 18-6
10 FT CLG

BATH 2

MASTER BEDRM
13-4 X 15-0
10 FT CLG

BEDROOM 2
12-0 X 11-0
8 FT CLG

UTIL
6-6 X 11-0

DINING ROOM
13-0 X 12-0
10 FT CLG

FOYER
10 FT CLG

PORCH

GARAGE

COPYRIGHT LARRY E. BELK

Width 62'-0"
Depth 62'-6"

◆ Three arched windows, shutters and a brick facade provide just the right touch of elegance and give this home a picturesque appeal. Ten-foot ceilings in the living areas lend an open spaciousness inside. A corner fireplace in the great room offers warmth and light to the main living areas. Guests and family alike will enjoy the rear covered patio with access to a sunny breakfast area and adjoining kitchen with snack counter. The formal dining room sits just off the foyer and opens to the great room through decorative columns. Luxurious accomodations abound in the master suite: a bath with coffered ceiling, large His and Hers closets, a whirlpool tub, a shower with a seat and knee-space vanity. Bedrooms 2 and 3 on the opposite side of the plan share a hall bath. Stairs at the front of the plan lead to an expandable area on the second floor. Please specify crawlspace or slab foundation when ordering.

Rear Elevation

— DESIGN BY —
SELECT HOME DESIGNS

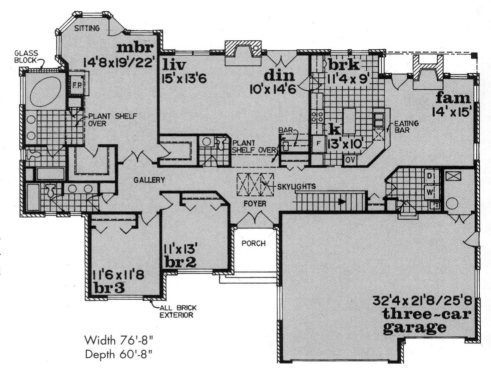

mbr 14'8x19/22'

liv 15'x13'6

din 10'x14'6

brk 11'4 x 9'

fam 14'x15'

GLASS BLOCK

F.P.

PLANT SHELF OVER

GALLERY

PLANT SHELF OVER

k 13'x10'

EATING BAR

BAR

F

OV

SKYLIGHTS

FOYER

11'x13' br2

11'6x11'8 br3

PORCH

D W

ALL BRICK EXTERIOR

32'4 x 21'8/25'8 three-car garage

Width 76'-8"
Depth 60'-8"

◆ This sprawling ranch has a floor plan designed to capture a view to the rear of the lot. The skylit foyer introduces the living and dining rooms; a plant ledge visually separates the entry from these rooms. A wet bar, fireplace and French doors adorn the dining room. The efficient kitchen, with a long center preparation island, built-in desk and snack bar, is open to both the breakfast room and the family room. A masonry barbecue is back-to-back with the fireplace in the family room. A lavish master bath adorns the master suite. It contains a whirlpool spa under a glass block wall, a double vanity and separate shower. The family bedrooms share a main bath with twin vanity and soaking tub. The three-car garage is accessed through the service entrance at the laundry room. Plans include details for both a basement and a crawlspace foundation.

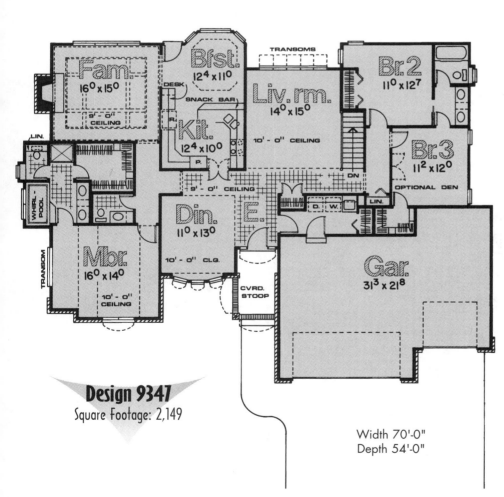

Fam.
16⁰ x 15⁰
9' - 0"
CEILING

Bfst.
12⁴ x 11⁰

DESK

SNACK BAR

TRANSOMS

Br.2
11⁰ x 12⁷

Liv. rm.
14⁰ x 15⁰

10' - 0" CEILING

Kit.
12⁴ x 10⁰

P.

Br.3
11² x 12⁰

OPTIONAL DEN

LIN.

WHIRL-POOL

9' - 0" CEILING

DN

D. W.

LIN.

TRANSOM

Din.
11⁰ x 13⁰

10' - 0" CLG.

E

Mbr.
16⁰ x 14⁰

10' - 0"
CEILING

CVRD.
STOOP

Gar.
31³ x 21⁸

Design 9347
Square Footage: 2,149

Width 70'-0"
Depth 54'-0"

◆ Beautiful and accommodating, this ranch home features open entry views into formal rooms and volume ceilings in major living spaces. The family room has a spider-beamed ceiling and cozy fireplace. In the kitchen are a snack bar through to the octagonal breakfast area, a built-in desk and pantry. An open staircase leads to a basement that can be finished later as needs arise. Sleeping areas are comprised of three bedrooms including a master with walk-in closet, double vanity and whirlpool. Bedroom 3 may be used as a den with French doors to the hall. A Hollywood bath serves both secondary bedrooms. Note the three-car garage with storage or workbench space, accessed through the laundry area.

Design by
Design Basics, Inc.

◆ This beautiful design is enhanced by brick siding and decorative wood columns at the entry. Plant ledges, which encompass the colonnaded foyer, and high vaulted ceilings throughout adorn the interior. Directly in view of the foyer is a vaulted family room which opens to a large railed deck beyond. The fireplace in the family room also warms the breakfast nook as the two are separated only by a low railing. A gourmet kitchen offers a center preparation island, a long pantry and a built-in desk. A formal dining room is also defined by columns and sits just across the hall from the family room. The master suite has double doors opening to the rear deck, a large walk-in closet, a whirlpool spa, His and Hers vanities and a separate shower. Family bedrooms share the use of a main bath in the hall. The two-car garage features extra storage space. Plans include details for both a basement and a crawlspace foundation.

Design Q380
Square Footage: 2,021

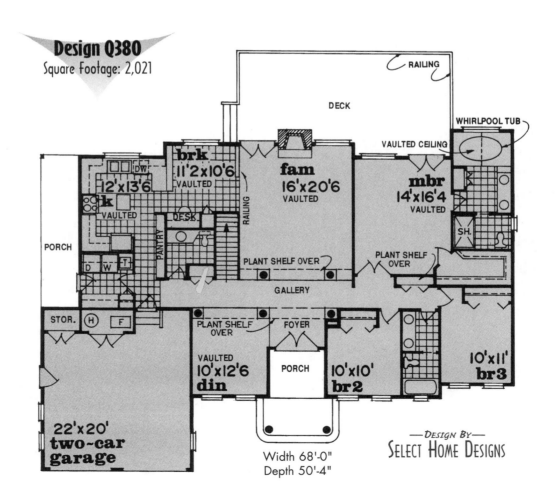

Width 68'-0"
Depth 50'-4"

— DESIGN BY —
SELECT HOME DESIGNS

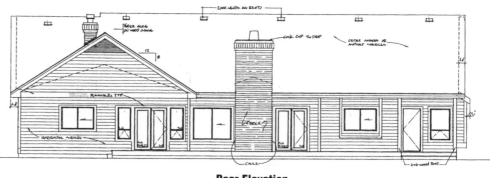

Rear Elevation

Design Q391
Square Footage: 2,211

—Design By—
Select Home Designs

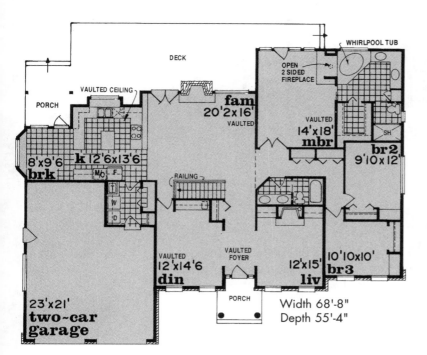

PORCH

VAULTED CEILING

DECK

WHIRLPOOL TUB

OPEN 2 SIDED FIREPLACE

fam 20'2x16'
VAULTED

VAULTED 14'x18' **mbr**

SH

br2 9'10x12'

8'x9'6 **brk**

k 12'6x13'6

M/o F.

RAILING

W/D

VAULTED 12'x14'6 **din**

VAULTED FOYER

12'x15' **liv**

10'10x10' **br3**

23'x21' **two-car garage**

PORCH

Width 68'-8"
Depth 55'-4"

◆ A high roofline on the exterior of this home allows for a vaulted ceiling extending from the foyer to the family room on the inside. Formal living and dining rooms open to either side of the foyer. The fireplace in the living room is flanked by shelves, while the fireplace in the family room has a door on one side that leads to the rear deck. A wet bar in the dining room allows easy entertaining. Abundant windows and high vaulted ceilings create a bright and spacious atmosphere in the bayed breakfast room and kitchen. The kitchen is U-shaped and has a center preparation island. At the opposite end of the plan, the master bedroom features a private access to the deck and a cozy two-sided fireplace. The bath in this suite offers His and Hers basins, a whirlpool tub and a large shower. Two family bedrooms share a full hall bath with dual sinks. Plans include details for both a basement and a crawlspace foundation.

Design Q244
Square Footage: 2,419

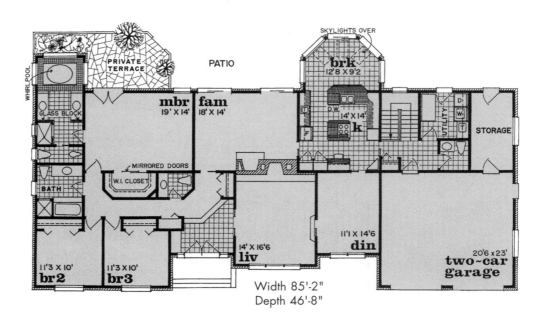

PATIO

SKYLIGHTS OVER

PRIVATE TERRACE

WHIRLPOOL

GLASS BLOCK

brk
12'8 X 9'2

mbr
19' X 14'

fam
18' X 14'

D.W.

k
14' X 14'

UTILITY

STORAGE

BATH

MIRRORED DOORS

W.I. CLOSET

11'3 X 10'
br2

11'3 X 10'
br3

14' X 16'6
liv

11'1 X 14'6
din

20'6 x 23'
two-car
garage

Width 85'-2"
Depth 46'-8"

◆ Long and low, with brick siding and multi-paned shuttered windows, this ranch home is the picture of elegance. Enter through double doors to a sunken foyer and sunken living room with fireplace. The dining room is beyond the living room and a step up. It also accesses the kitchen. The family room is to the rear of the plan and features a fireplace and sliding glass doors to the rear patio. The island kitchen has counter and cabinet space to suit any gourmet. Its attached breakfast nook is sunny due to skylights above. The master bedroom is huge and has a private terrace and bath with double sinks, whirlpool tub and separate shower. Family bedrooms are to the front of the plan. The two-car garage has well-appreciated storage space. Plans include details for both a basement and a crawlspace foundation.

— Design By —
Select Home Designs

◆ Many years of delightful living will surely be enjoyed in this one-story traditional. The covered front porch adds charm to the exterior as do the paned windows. Easy living centers around the large gathering room with a raised-hearth fireplace and sliding doors to the rear terrace. The dining room is set off just enough to accommodate more formal dinners and is easily accessible from the eat-in kitchen. The kitchen ameni-ties include a cooktop island, an abundance of cabinet and counter space along with an adjoining utility room. The master bedroom has private patio access, a large walk-in closet and a compartmented bath. A study, a secondary bedroom and a full hall bath complete the plan. Note the large linen closet and powder room in the central hall. Extra storage space is available in the two-car garage.

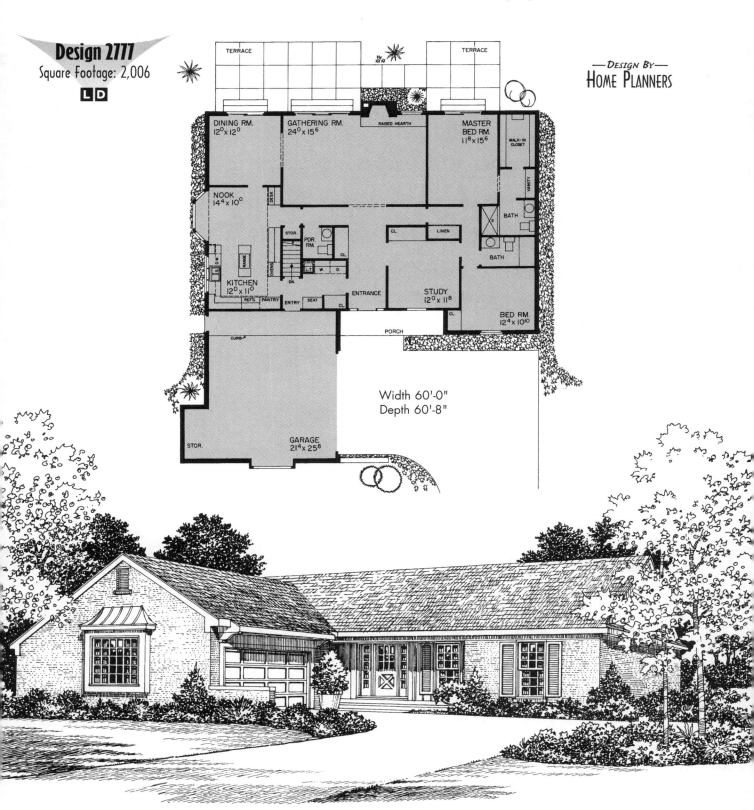

Design 2777
Square Footage: 2,006
L D

—DESIGN BY—
HOME PLANNERS

TERRACE

TERRACE

DINING RM.
12⁰ x 12⁰

GATHERING RM.
24⁰ x 15⁶

RAISED HEARTH

MASTER
BED RM.
11⁸ x 15⁶

WALK-IN
CLOSET

VANITY

NOOK
14⁴ x 10⁰

DESK

STOR.

PDR.
RM.

CL.

LINEN

BATH

BATH

RANGE

OVENS

D.

W.

CL.

KITCHEN
12⁰ x 11⁶

REFG.

PANTRY

ENTRY

SEAT

ENTRANCE

CL.

STUDY
12⁰ x 11⁸

DN.

PORCH

BED RM.
12⁴ x 10¹⁰

CL.

CURB

Width 60'-0"
Depth 60'-8"

STOR.

GARAGE
21⁴ x 25⁸

Design 9655
Square Footage: 2,032

© 1990 Donald A. Gardner Architects, Inc.

Design 9619
Square Footage: 2,021

© 1985 Donald A. Gardner Architects, Inc.

Rear Elevation

◆ Two different plans, but on the outside only—inside they share floor plans that are almost identical. The great room has a fireplace, a cathedral ceiling and sliding glass doors with an arched window above to allow for natural illumination of the room. A sunroom with a hot tub leads to an adjacent deck. This space can also be reached from the master bath. The spacious master bedroom has a walk-in closet and bath with double-bowl vanity, separate shower and garden tub. Two family bedrooms are located at the other end of the house for privacy. The two-car garage is connected to the main house by a breezeway. For Design 9619, please specify basement or crawlspace foundation when ordering.

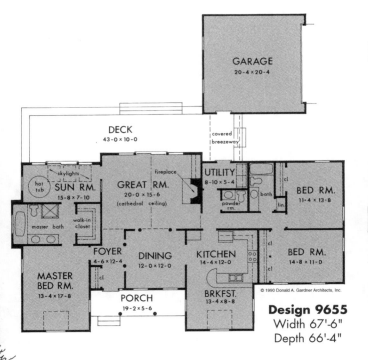

Design 9655
Width 67'-6"
Depth 66'-4"

—DESIGN BY—
DONALD A. GARDNER
ARCHITECTS, INC.

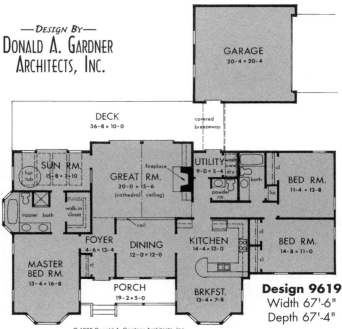

Design 9619
Width 67'-6"
Depth 67'-4"

© 1985 Donald A. Gardner Architects, Inc.

Rear Elevation

113

Design 2550
Square Footage: 1,892

D

◆ Stone and vertical siding provide a pleasing contrast on this charming one-story traditional. Diamond lite windows, a fence with lamp post and dovecote above the carriage lamp add interest to the exterior. Inside is a plan for all seasons. The entry leads to a massive gathering room with fireplace and wood box, plus sliding glass doors to the rear terrace. The attached dining room also has sliding glass doors to the terrace. The island kitchen and breakfast nook are nearby and have access to a side terrace for outdoor dining. Four bedrooms—or three and a study—sit on the left side of the plan. The master suite is well appointed with a walk-in closet and sumptuous bath. Note the built-in bookcase near the family bedrooms. A two-car garage with storage is reached through a service entry in the laundry room.

—DESIGN BY—
HOME PLANNERS

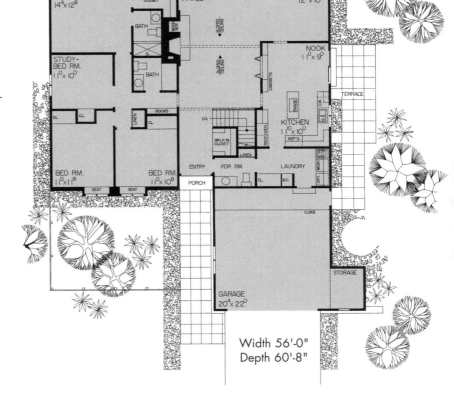

Width 56'-0"
Depth 60'-8"

Design 2204
Square Footage: 2,016

◆ This is a design to enjoy for years to come. The exterior boasts fieldstone detailing in a horizontal wood siding facade. On the inside, family and friends alike will enjoy the family room's beam ceiling and the living room's bowed window and fireplace. The U-shaped kitchen easily serves the nearby breakfast nook and the formal dining room. The sleeping zone includes two family bedrooms and a master bedroom with a private bath. Family bedrooms share a full hall bath. Sliding glass doors provide access to the full-width rear terrace from the master bedroom, family room and breakfast nook. The two-car garage is accessed through a service entry at the laundry room where there is also a wash room.

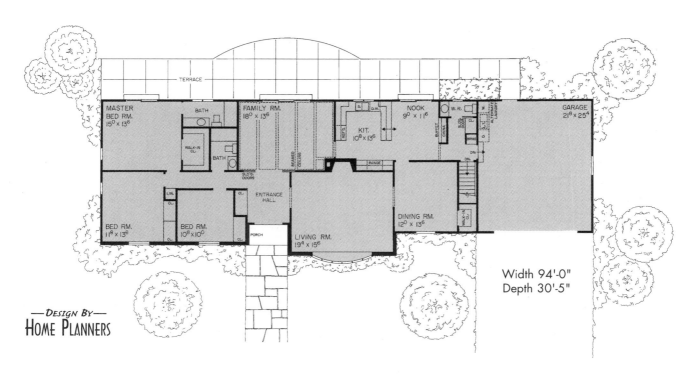

Width 94'-0"
Depth 30'-5"

— DESIGN BY —
Home Planners

Design 1788
Square Footage: 2,218
L D

◆ "Charm" is one of the many words which may be used to describe this fine design. The pedimented front porch, brick veneer and shuttered multi-pane windows are all exceptional details. But in addition to its exterior appeal, it has a practical and functional floor plan. The focal point of the interior is the sunken formal living room with its bay window overlooking the backyard and built-in bookcase. It is complemented by a formal dining room just across the hall. For informal occasions, the family room features a fireplace and terrace access. The U-shaped kitchen has sufficient room for a table, but also sports a planning desk and walk-in pantry. Bedrooms have ample closet space. Family bedrooms share a bath; the master suite has a private bath. Note the work shop and storage area in the two-car garage.

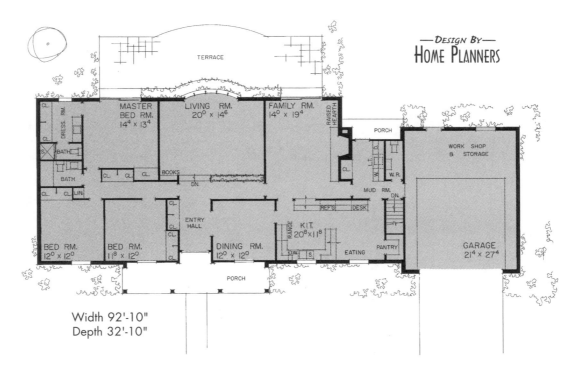

— DESIGN BY —
HOME PLANNERS

Width 92'-10"
Depth 32'-10"

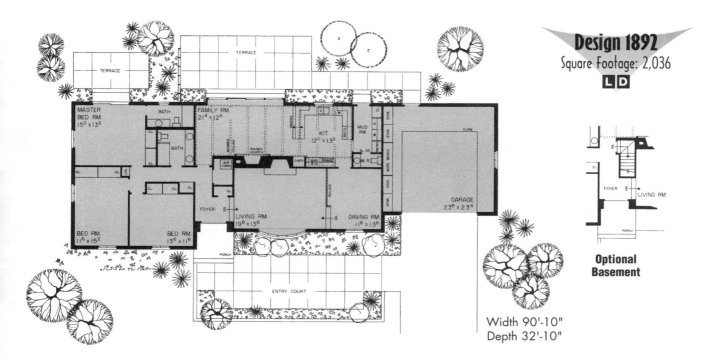

Optional Basement

Width 90'-10"
Depth 32'-10"

◆ The romance of French Provincial architecture is captured here by the hip roofs, the charm of the window detailing, the brick quoins at the corners, the delicate dentil work at the cornices, the massive centered chimney and the recessed double front doors. The slightly raised entry court completes the picture. The basic floor plan is a favorite of many. And little wonder, for all the areas work well together, while still maintaining a fine degree of separation of functions. The highlight of the interior, perhaps, will be the sunken living room. The family room, with its beam ceiling, will not be far behind in popularity. The separate dining room, mud room and efficient kitchen complete the livability.

— DESIGN BY —
HOME PLANNERS

Design 2931
Square Footage: 2,032

TERRACE

STUDY
12⁶ x 16⁰

GATHERING RM.
16⁶ x 16⁰

MASTER BEDROOM
14⁰ x 16⁰

SLOPED CEILING

SLOPED CEILING

CL

LINEN

DINING RM.
11⁸ x 10⁸

BAR

BRKFST. RM.
11⁸ x 10⁸

TERRACE

DRESSING RM.

WALK-IN CLOSET

BATH

SLOPED CEILING

CL

CL

FOYER

PANTRY DESK

OVEN

KITCHEN
11⁸ x 10⁰

BATH

WHIRLPOOL

BEDROOM
12⁴ x 12⁶

COVERED PORCH

LAUND.

REF'G

COOK TOP

DW

COURTYARD

GARAGE
21⁴ x 21⁴

STORAGE

Width 63'-0"
Depth 64'-4"

◆ Little details make the difference in this charming showplace: picket-fenced courtyard, carriage lamp, window boxes, shutters, muntined windows, multi-gabled roof, cornice returns, vertical and horizontal siding with corner board, front door with glass side lites, etc. Inside this appealing exterior there is a truly outstanding floor plan for the small family or empty-nesters. The master bedroom suite is long on luxury with a separate dressing room, private vanities and whirlpool bath. An adjacent study is just the right retreat. There's room to move and what a warm touch! It has its own fireplace. Other attractions: roomy kitchen and breakfast area, spacious gathering room, rear and side terraces and an attached two-car garage with storage.

— DESIGN BY —
HOME PLANNERS

Design 3332
Square Footage: 2,203

◆ Nothing completes a traditional-style home quite as well as a country kitchen with a fireplace and built-in wood box. Notice also the second fireplace (with raised hearth) and the sloped ceiling in the living room. The nearby dining room has an attached porch and separate dining terrace. Besides two family bedrooms with a shared full bath, there is also a marvelous master suite with rear terrace access, walk-in closet, whirlpool tub and double vanities. A handy washroom is near the laundry, just off the two-car garage.

Width 77'-2"
Depth 46'-6"

— DESIGN BY —
HOME PLANNERS

QUOTE ONE®
Cost to build? See page 436
to order complete cost estimate
to build this house in your area!

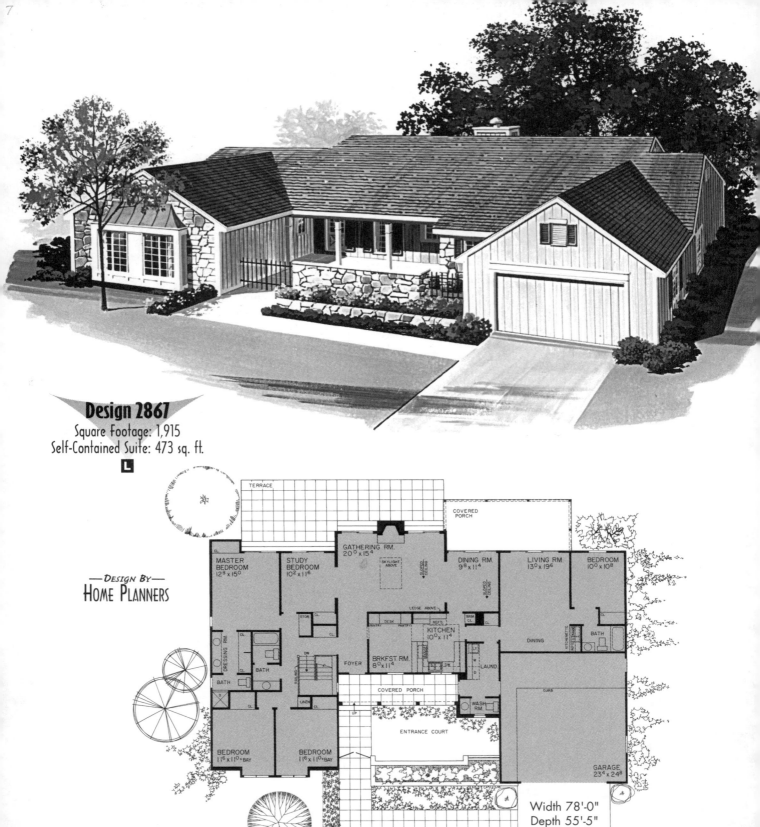

Design 2867
Square Footage: 1,915
Self-Contained Suite: 473 sq. ft.

L

—DESIGN BY—
Home Planners

TERRACE

COVERED PORCH

GATHERING RM.
20⁰ x 15⁴

MASTER BEDROOM
12⁸ x 15⁰

STUDY BEDROOM
10² x 11⁶

DINING RM.
9⁸ x 11⁴

LIVING RM.
13⁰ x 19⁶

BEDROOM
10⁰ x 10⁸

KITCHEN
10⁰ x 11⁴

DINING

BATH

DRESSING RM.

BATH

BATH

BRKFST RM.
8⁰ x 11⁴

FOYER

COVERED PORCH

LAUND.

WASH RM.

BEDROOM
11⁶ x 11⁰+BAY

BEDROOM
11⁶ x 11⁰+BAY

ENTRANCE COURT

GARAGE
23⁴ x 24⁸

Width 78'-0"
Depth 55'-5"

◆ This design features a self-contained suite (473 square feet) consisting of a bedroom, a bath, a living room and a kitchenette with a dining area. The remainder of the this traditional, one-story home, faced with fieldstone and vertical wood siding, is also very livable. One wing houses the four family bedrooms and two full baths. The center of the plan has a front-facing, U-shaped kitchen and breakfast room. The formal dining room and large gathering room enjoy access and views of the terrace and rear yard. Note the covered porch at the dining room, which it shares with the living room of the self-contained suite. A two-car garage is reached through a handy laundry with wash room.

Design 2916
Square Footage: 2,129

L

◆ Vertical wood siding and field-stone accent the facade of this Early American home. The covered front porch provides a shelter for the inviting paneled front door with its flanking side lites. Designed for fine family living, this three-bedroom home offers wonderful formal and informal living patterns. The 27' country kitchen features a beam ceiling, a fireplace and an efficient U-shaped work center. It is but a step from the mud room area with its laundry equipment, closets, cupboards, counter space and washroom. There are two dining areas—an informal eating space and a formal, separate dining room. The more formal gathering room is spacious with a sloping ceiling and two sets of sliding glass doors to the rear terrace.

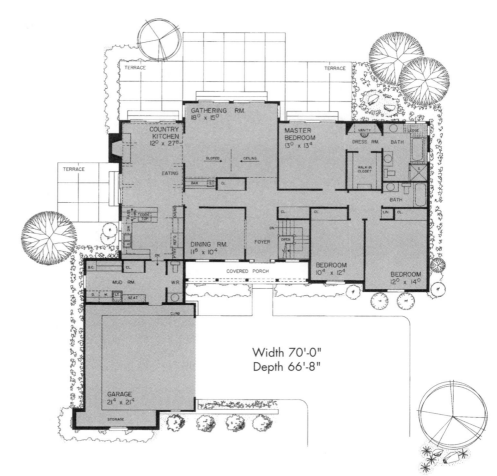

Width 70'-0"
Depth 66'-8"

—DESIGN BY—
HOME PLANNERS

QUOTE ONE®
Cost to build? See page 436
to order complete cost estimate
to build this house in your area!

121

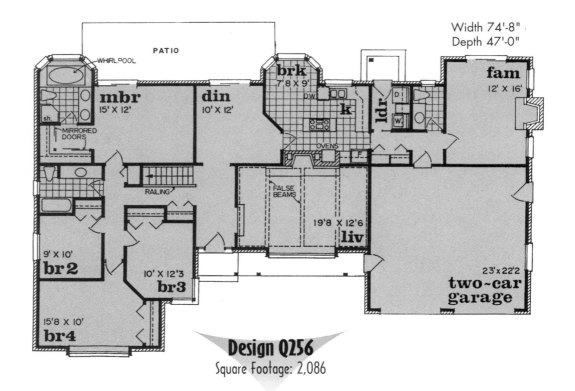

Width 74'-8"
Depth 47'-0"

PATIO

WHIRLPOOL

mbr
15' X 12'

MIRRORED
DOORS

sh.

br2
9' X 10'

br4
15'8 X 10'

br3
10' X 12'3

RAILING

din
10' X 12'

brk
7'8 X 9'

DW

k

OVENS

FALSE
BEAMS

liv
19'8 X 12'6

ldr

D

W

fam
12' X 16'

two-car
garage
23'x 22'2

Design Q256
Square Footage: 2,086

◆ Though a traditional ranch, this one-story has some of the quaint detailing shown in Tudor design. The covered entrance walkway, brick exterior with quoining and the large box windows add to its appeal. Inside, the sunken living room hosts a beam ceiling and oversized masonry fireplace. The dining room is across the hall and connects to the breakfast bay and kitchen with built-in oven and center cook island. A convenient laundry/mud room and adjacent powder room separate the kitchen from the family room. Sliding glass doors in the family room, dining room and master bedroom all lead to the rear yard. The family room also has a fireplace. Note the amenities in the master suite: a dressing room with mirrored wall closet and a bath with twin vanities and whirlpool tucked into a windowed bay. Two additional bedrooms—one of which may serve as a den—share a full bath. A two-car garage features three separate access points.

— DESIGN BY —
SELECT HOME DESIGNS

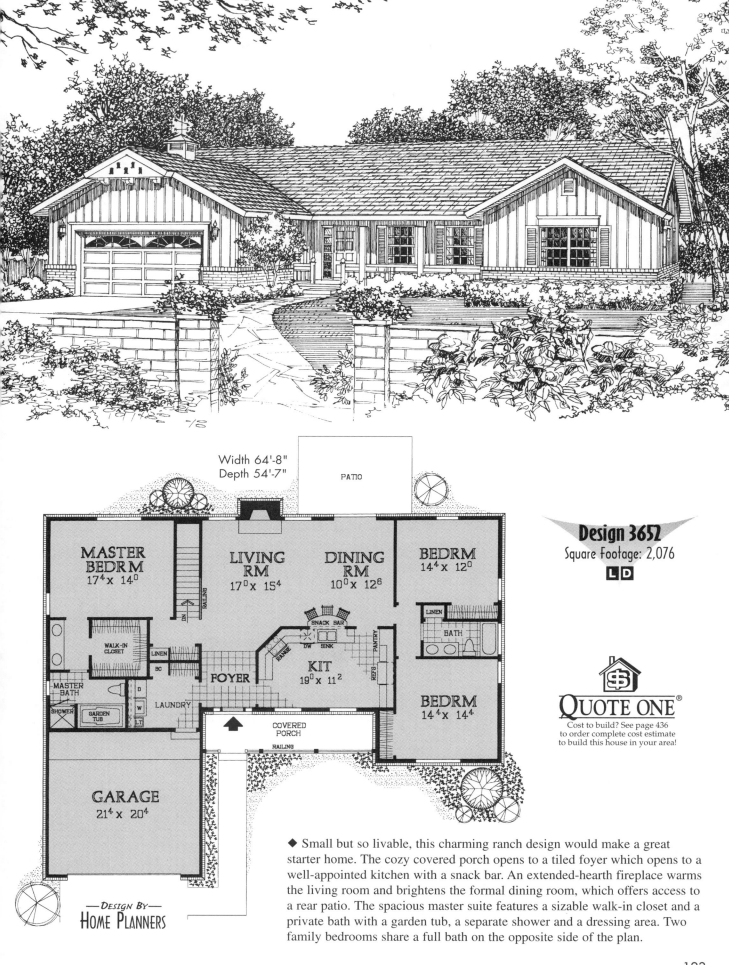

Width 64'-8"
Depth 54'-7"

PATIO

MASTER BEDRM
17⁴ x 14⁰

LIVING RM
17⁰ x 15⁴

DINING RM
10⁰ x 12⁶

BEDRM
14⁴ x 12⁰

WALK-IN CLOSET

LINEN

BC

LINEN

BATH

MASTER BATH

SHOWER

GARDEN TUB

D

W

LT

LAUNDRY

FOYER

SNACK BAR

DW

SINK

RANGE

KIT
19⁰ x 11²

REFG

PANTRY

BEDRM
14⁴ x 14⁴

COVERED PORCH

RAILING

RAILING

DN

GARAGE
21⁴ x 20⁴

— DESIGN BY —
HOME PLANNERS

Design 3652
Square Footage: 2,076

LD

QUOTE ONE®
Cost to build? See page 436
to order complete cost estimate
to build this house in your area!

◆ Small but so livable, this charming ranch design would make a great starter home. The cozy covered porch opens to a tiled foyer which opens to a well-appointed kitchen with a snack bar. An extended-hearth fireplace warms the living room and brightens the formal dining room, which offers access to a rear patio. The spacious master suite features a sizable walk-in closet and a private bath with a garden tub, a separate shower and a dressing area. Two family bedrooms share a full bath on the opposite side of the plan.

Design 3336
Square Footage: 2,022
L

— DESIGN BY —
HOME PLANNERS

◆ Compact and comfortable, you'll love this three-bedroom plan! It is a good building candidate for a small family or for empty-nester retirees. Of special interest are the covered eating porch and the sloped ceilings in the gathering room and the master bedroom. The kitchen offers new angles on your favorite amenities and also enjoys the companionship of an attached breakfast room. In the master suite, a full bath with a whirlpool tub, dual lavatories and a compartmented commode is sure to delight. A hall bath services the secondary bedrooms.

QUOTE ONE®
Cost to build? See page 436
to order complete cost estimate
to build this house in your area!

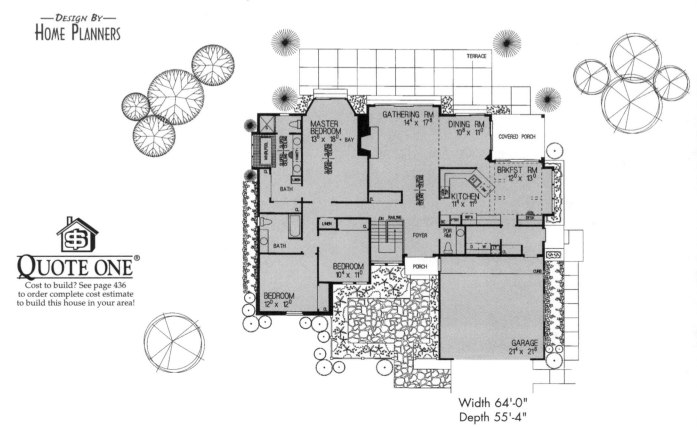

Width 64'-0"
Depth 55'-4"

Design 3327
Square Footage: 2,881
L D

◆ The high, massive hip roof of this home creates an imposing facade while varying roof planes and projecting gables enhance appeal. A central, high-ceilinged foyer routes traffic efficiently to the sleeping, formal and informal zones of the house. Note the sliding glass doors that provide access to outdoor living facilities. The built-in china cabinet and planter unit are fine features. In the angular kitchen, a high ceiling and efficient work patterning set the pace. The conversation room may act as a multi-purpose room. For TV time, a media room caters to audio-visual activities. Sleeping quarters include a spacious master bedroom; here you'll find a tray ceiling and sliding doors to the rear yard. An abundance of wall space for effective and flexible furniture arrangement further characterizes the room. Two sizable bedrooms serve the children.

— DESIGN BY —
HOME PLANNERS

QUOTE ONE®
Cost to build? See page 436
to order complete cost estimate
to build this house in your area!

Design Q408
Square Footage: 2,547

◆ A brick exterior, with traditional arch details and elegant rooflines, defines this stately ranch home. Formal dining and living rooms open through arches from the front entry foyer. Additional arches define the center hall leading to the master suite. Chefs can utilize their talents in the spacious kitchen with center cooktop, abundant counter space and light-filled breakfast nook. The family room is separated from the kitchen by a snack counter. It also features a corner fireplace and double doors to the rear patio. The private master suite is separated from family bedrooms and offers a walk-in closet and luxurious bath with whirlpool spa, oversized shower, twin vanity and compartmented toilet. Three additional bedrooms allow design flexibility—use one as a guest room, den or home office. The two-car garage is reached through handy access at the laundry room. The plans include both basement and crawlspace foundations.

— DESIGN BY —
SELECT HOME DESIGNS

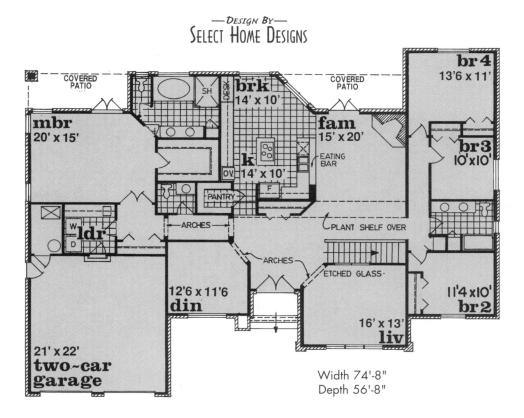

Width 74'-8"
Depth 56'-8"

Design 9709
Square Footage: 2,663
Bonus Room: 653 sq. ft.

© 1993 Donald A. Gardner Architects, Inc.

B. NATHAN

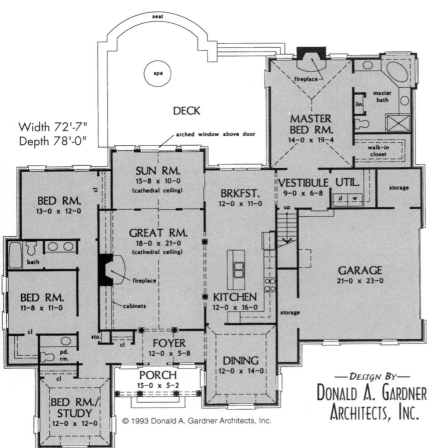

Width 72'-7"
Depth 78'-0"

seat

spa

DECK

arched window above door

SUN RM.
15-8 x 10-0
(cathedral ceiling)

BED RM.
13-0 x 12-0

GREAT RM.
18-0 x 21-0
(cathedral ceiling)

bath

fireplace

cabinets

BED RM.
11-8 x 11-0

cl

pd. rm.

sto.

cl

FOYER
12-0 x 5-8

BED RM./ STUDY
12-0 x 12-0

PORCH
15-0 x 5-2

© 1993 Donald A. Gardner Architects, Inc.

fireplace

MASTER BED RM.
14-0 x 19-4

master bath

lin

walk-in closet

BRKFST.
12-0 x 11-0

VESTIBULE

UTIL.
9-0 x 6-8

storage

d   w

up

KITCHEN
12-0 x 16-0

storage

GARAGE
21-0 x 23-0

DINING
12-0 x 14-0

—DESIGN BY—
DONALD A. GARDNER
ARCHITECTS, INC.

◆ This home features large arched windows, round columns, a covered porch, and brick veneer siding. The arched window in the clerestory above the entrance provides natural light to the interior. The great room boasts a cathedral ceiling, a fireplace, built-in cabinets and bookshelves. Sliding glass doors lead to the sun room. The L-shaped kitchen services the dining room, the breakfast area, and the great room. The master bedroom suite, with a fireplace, uses private passage to the deck and its spa. Three additional bedrooms—one could serve as a study—are at the other end of the house for privacy

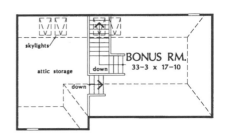

skylights

attic storage

down

down

BONUS RM.
33-3 x 17-10

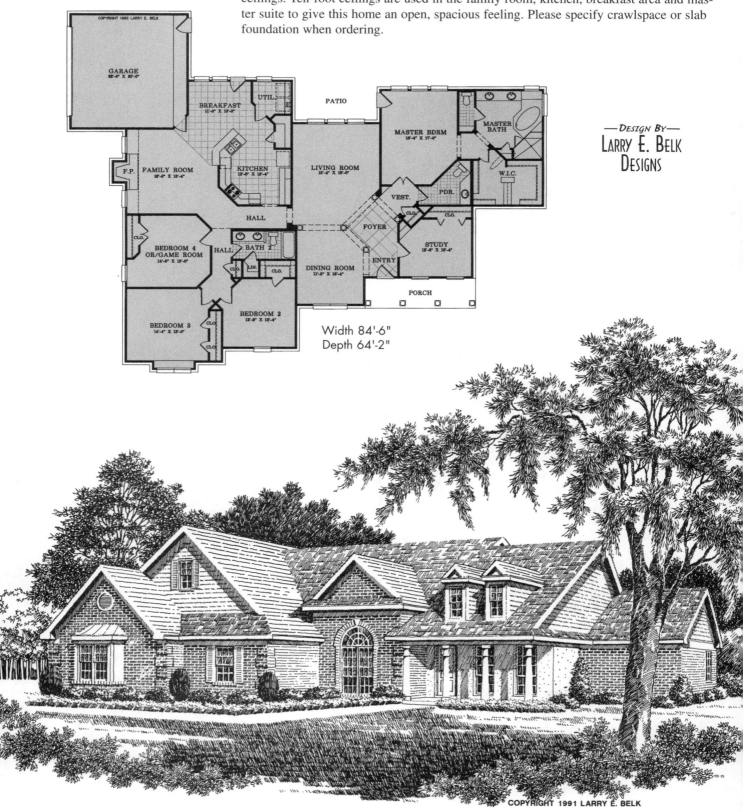

Design 8018
Square Footage: 2,846

◆ This Southern Colonial home is distinguished by its columned porch and double dormer. Inside, the angled foyer is defined by columns and connecting arches. The master suite is located away from the other bedrooms for privacy and includes a large master bath and a walk-in closet. Three additional bedrooms are located adjacent to the family room. The kitchen, breakfast area and family room are open—perfect for informal entertaining and family gatherings. The foyer, living room and dining room have twelve-foot ceilings. Ten-foot ceilings are used in the family room, kitchen, breakfast area and master suite to give this home an open, spacious feeling. Please specify crawlspace or slab foundation when ordering.

GARAGE

BREAKFAST

UTIL.

PATIO

MASTER BDRM

MASTER BATH

—DESIGN BY—
LARRY E. BELK
DESIGNS

FAMILY ROOM

KITCHEN

LIVING ROOM

W.I.C.

F.P.

VEST.

PDR.

CLO.

HALL

CLO.

FOYER

CLO.

STUDY

BEDROOM 4 OR/GAME ROOM

HALL

BATH 2

LIN.

CLO.

DINING ROOM

ENTRY

CLO.

CLO.

BEDROOM 3

CLO.

BEDROOM 2

PORCH

Width 84'-6"
Depth 64'-2"

© American Home Gallery, Ltd.

Design T053
Square Footage: 2,770

◆ This English cottage with cedar shake exterior displays the best qualities of a traditional design. With the bay window and recessed entry, visitors will feel warmly welcomed. The foyer opens to both the dining room and the great room with its fireplace and built-in cabinetry. Surrounded by windows, the breakfast room opens to a gourmet kitchen and a laundry room conveniently located near the garage entrance. To the right of the foyer is a hall powder room. Two bedrooms with large closets are joined by a full bath with individual vanities and a window seat. Through double doors at the end of a short hall, the master suite awaits with a tray ceiling and an adjoining sunlit sitting room. The master bath has His and Hers closets, separate vanities, an individual shower and a garden tub with bay window. This home is designed with a basement foundation.

— DESIGN BY —
DESIGN TRADITIONS

Width 73'-6"
Depth 78'-0"

Design 8000
Square Footage: 2,540

Width 70'-0"
Depth 65'-0"

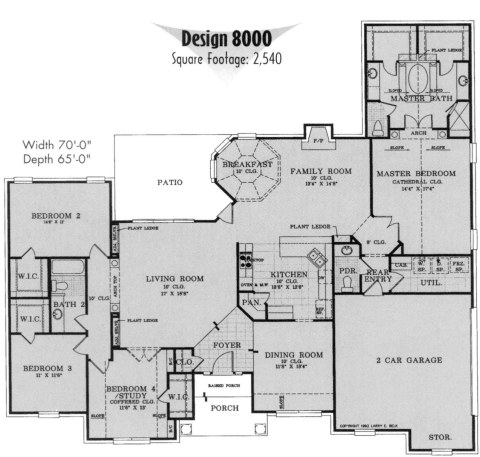

◆ A gabled stucco entry with over-sized columns emphasizes the arched glass entry of this winsome one-story brick home. Arched windows on either side of the front door add symmetry and style to this pleasing exterior. An arched passage, which leads to the three family bedrooms, flanked by twin bookcases and a plant ledge, provides focal interest to the living room. Bedroom 4 may also be a study, and can be entered from double French doors off the living room. A large, efficient kitchen shares space with an octagonal breakfast area and a family room with a fireplace. The master bedroom is entered through angled double doors and features a cathedral ceiling. Attention centers immediately on the arched entry to the relaxing master bath and its central whirlpool tub. Please specify crawlspace or slab foundation when ordering.

— Design By —
Larry E. Belk
Designs

—DESIGN BY—
LARRY E. BELK
DESIGNS

◆ This Southern-raised elevation looks cozy but lives large, with an interior layout and amenities preferred by today's homeowners. Inside, twelve-foot ceilings and graceful columns and arches lend an aura of hospitality throughout the formal rooms and the family's living space, the great room. Double doors open to the gourmet kitchen, which offers a built-in desk, a snack counter for easy meals and a breakfast room with a picture window. The secluded master suite features His and Hers walk-in closets, a whirlpool tub and a knee-space vanity. Each of two family bedrooms enjoys separate access to a shared bath and a private vanity. Please specify crawlspace or slab foundation when ordering.

Design 8143
Square Footage: 2,648
Bonus Room: 266 sq. ft.

BONUS ROOM
21-4 X 12-6

Width 68'-10"
Depth 77'-10"

Design Q278
Square Footage: 2,796

◆ This sprawling ranch has a brick exterior with quoins and sweeping roof accents. Double doors open to a sunken foyer which opens on the right to a coffered living room with corner fireplace. The dining room is nearby and features a pocket door to the convenient kitchen with cooktop island, walk-in pantry and bayed breakfast nook. The large family room has a masonry fireplace flanked by French doors to the rear yard. A

private den has double-door access and a lovely box-bay window. Three bedrooms include two family bedrooms and the master suite. Nothing is left to chance in the master bedroom. It features a dressing room and private terrace, plus a vaulted bath with spa, twin vanity and shower. The two-car garage is made even more useful with a workshop area. Choose a basement or crawlspace foundation—plans include details for both.

— DESIGN BY —
SELECT HOME DESIGNS

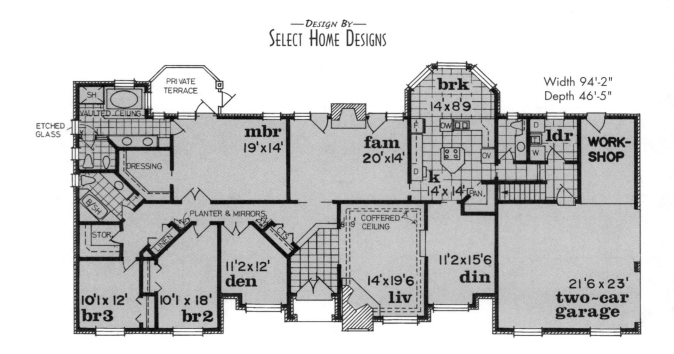

132

◆ This spacious one-story home has a classic Country French hip roof. Beyond the covered porch is an octagonal foyer. All of the living areas overlook the rear yard. Features include a fireplace in the living room, a skylight in the dining room and a second set of sliding glass doors in the family room leading to a covered porch. An island cooktop and other built-ins are featured in the roomy kitchen. Adjacent is the breakfast room which can be used for informal dining. The four bedrooms and the baths are clustered in one wing. Bay windows brighten the master bedroom, the breakfast room and the three-car garage.

Design 2851
Square Footage: 2,739

L

QUOTE ONE®
Cost to build? See page 436
to order complete cost estimate
to build this house in your area!

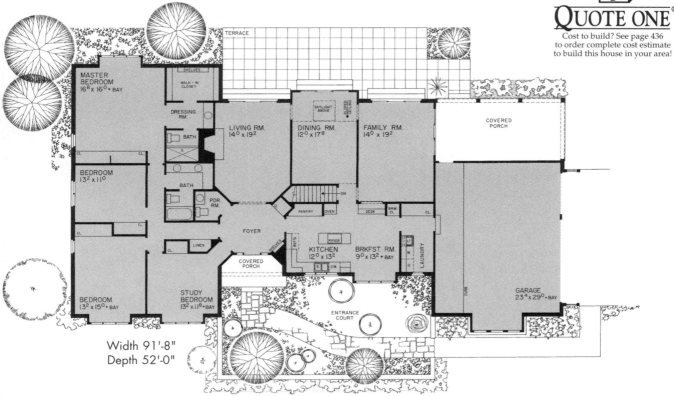

TERRACE

MASTER BEDROOM
16⁸ x 16⁰ + BAY

SHELVES

WALK - IN CLOSET

DRESSING RM.

BATH

LIVING RM.
14⁰ x 19²

SKYLIGHT ABOVE

DINING RM.
12⁰ x 17⁸

FAMILY RM.
14⁰ x 19²

COVERED PORCH

BEDROOM
13² x 11⁰

BATH

PDR. RM.

PANTRY   OVEN

DESK   BRM. CL.

CL.

CL.

CL.

LINEN

FOYER

RANGE

KITCHEN
12⁰ x 13²

BRKFST. RM.
9⁰ x 13² + BAY

LAUNDRY

COVERED PORCH

BEDROOM
13² x 15⁰ + BAY

STUDY BEDROOM
13² x 11⁸ + BAY

ENTRANCE COURT

GARAGE
23⁴ x 29⁰ + BAY

Width 91'-8"
Depth 52'-0"

—DESIGN BY—
HOME PLANNERS

133

◆ A graceful stucco arch supported by columns gives this home instant curb appeal. Stucco quoins are used to further accent its traditional brick finish. Inside, the angled foyer steps down into the living room and draws the eye to a duplicate of the exterior arch with columns. Built-in display shelves on either side provide plenty of room for books or treasures. Step down again to enter the formal dining room. The kitchen features a coffered ceiling and is conveniently grouped with a sunny bayed breakfast room and the family room, the perfect place for informal gatherings. Upon entering the master suite, the master bath becomes the focal point. Columns flank the entry to this luxurious bath with a whirlpool tub as its centerpiece, plus His and Hers walk-in closets, a separate shower and double-bowl vanities. This plan is available with either a crawlspace or slab foundation. Please specify when ordering.

— DESIGN BY —
LARRY E. BELK
DESIGNS

Design 8071
Square Footage: 2,517

Width 69'-0"
Depth 63'-6"

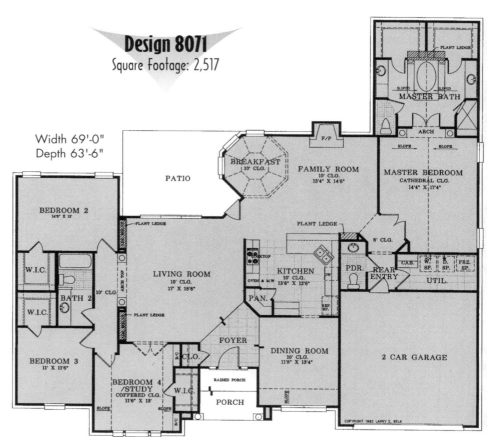

© 1992 Donald A. Gardner Architects, Inc.

Design 9695
Square Footage: 2,526

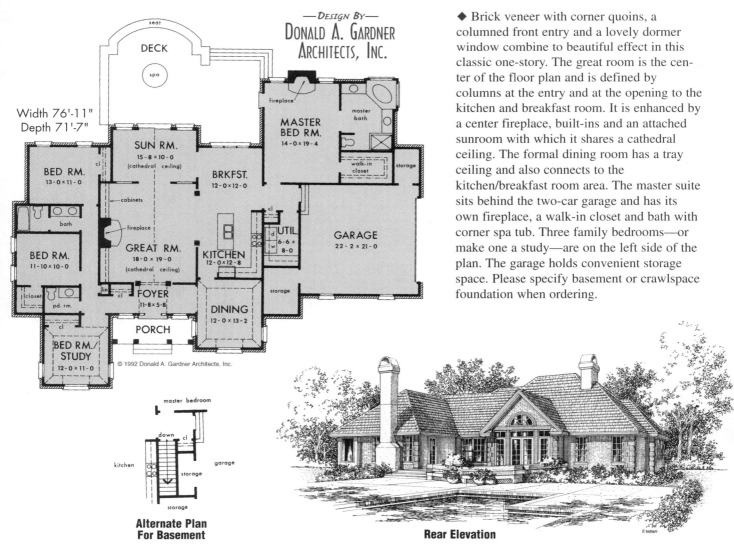

—DESIGN BY—
DONALD A. GARDNER
ARCHITECTS, INC.

Width 76'-11"
Depth 71'-7"

DECK

seat

spa

fireplace

MASTER
BED RM.
14-0 × 19-4

master
bath

walk-in
closet

storage

SUN RM.
15-8 × 10-0
(cathedral ceiling)

BRKFST.
12-0 × 12-0

BED RM.
13-0 × 11-0

cabinets

bath

fireplace

GREAT RM.
18-0 × 19-0
(cathedral ceiling)

KITCHEN
12-0 × 12-8

UTIL.
6-6 ×
8-0

GARAGE
22-2 × 21-0

BED RM.
11-10 × 10-0

closet

pd. rm.

lin

FOYER
11-8 × 5-8

DINING
12-0 × 13-2

storage

storage

BED RM./
STUDY
12-0 × 11-0

PORCH

© 1992 Donald A. Gardner Architects, Inc.

master bedroom

down   cl

kitchen   garage

storage

storage

**Alternate Plan
For Basement**

◆ Brick veneer with corner quoins, a columned front entry and a lovely dormer window combine to beautiful effect in this classic one-story. The great room is the center of the floor plan and is defined by columns at the entry and at the opening to the kitchen and breakfast room. It is enhanced by a center fireplace, built-ins and an attached sunroom with which it shares a cathedral ceiling. The formal dining room has a tray ceiling and also connects to the kitchen/breakfast room area. The master suite sits behind the two-car garage and has its own fireplace, a walk-in closet and bath with corner spa tub. Three family bedrooms—or make one a study—are on the left side of the plan. The garage holds convenient storage space. Please specify basement or crawlspace foundation when ordering.

Rear Elevation

135

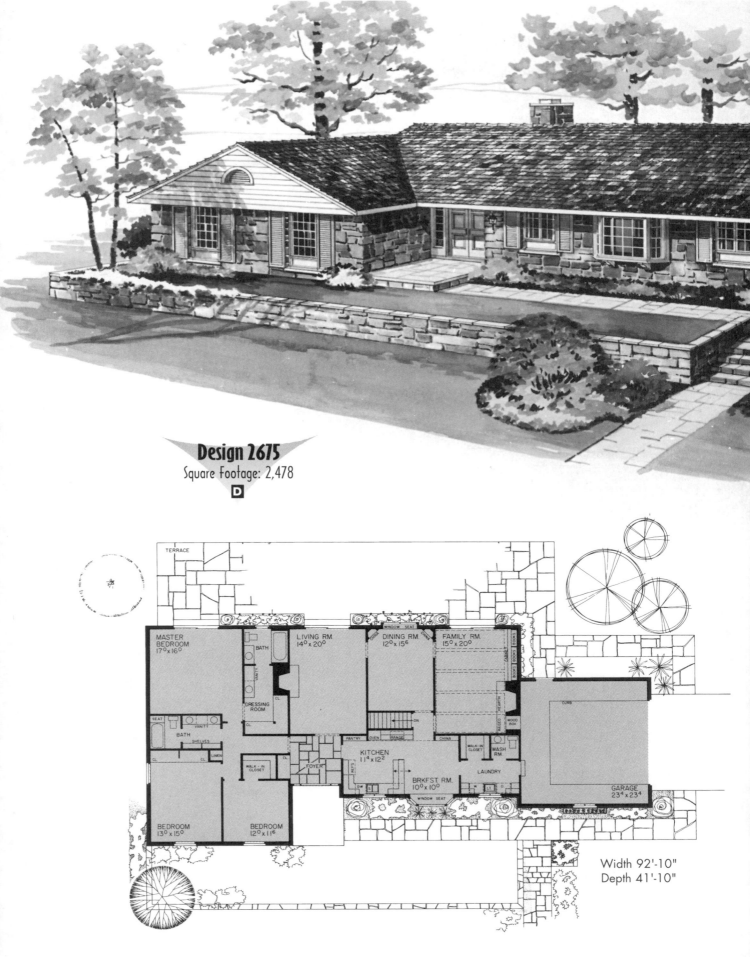

Design 2675
Square Footage: 2,478

D

TERRACE

MASTER BEDROOM
17⁰ x 16⁰

BATH

DRESSING ROOM

SEAT

BATH
VANITY

SHELVES

LINEN

CL

WALK-IN CLOSET

CL

FOYER

BEDROOM
13⁰ x 15⁰

BEDROOM
12⁰ x 11⁶

LIVING RM.
14⁰ x 20⁰

WINDOW SEAT

DINING RM.
12⁰ x 15⁶

FAMILY RM.
15⁰ x 20⁰

BOOKS

CABINET
BOOKS

HEARTH

WOOD BOX

PANTRY

OVEN

RANGE

CHINA

WALK-IN CLOSET

WASH RM.

KITCHEN
11⁴ x 12²

BRKFST. RM.
10⁰ x 10⁰

LAUNDRY

WINDOW SEAT

CURB

GARAGE
23⁴ x 23⁴

Width 92'-10"
Depth 41'-10"

◆ One beautiful stone facade; two great floor plans—the choice is yours. If you prefer a three-bedroom home, order Design 2675. If you need four bedrooms, order Design 2181. Either way, you'll find a floor plan that is well thought out. The fieldstone entry opens directly into the living room with fireplace and sliding glass doors to the rear terrace. The kitchen and breakfast nook are at the front of the plan, across the hall from the formal dining room (note corner china hutches). The family room is tucked away behind the service entrance to the two-car garage and is enhanced by a beam ceiling, a fireplace and built-ins. It also has access to the terrace. Bedrooms sit to the far left side of the plan. The master suite in each version is truly luxurious with terrace access and a bath with double vanity and a dressing area. Other extras in the plan: a bay window seat in the breakfast room, a large walk-in closet and a washroom in the laundry area, a linen closet in the hall and a window seat in the dining room.

Design 2181
Square Footage: 2,612

L D

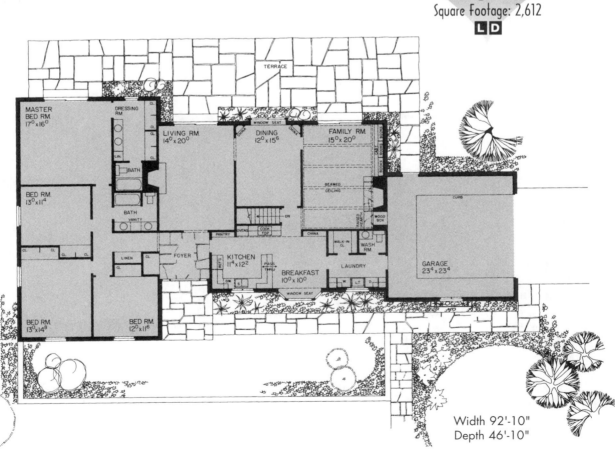

Width 92'-10"
Depth 46'-10"

◆ Low, strong rooflines and the solid, enduring qualities of brick give this house a permanent, here-to-stay appearance. The entry hall, with tray ceiling, introduces a very livable floor plan with both formal and informal living spaces. A large living room with fireplace is adjacent to the formal dining room, just across the hall from a U-shaped kitchen. Amenities here include a barbecue, a large pantry and a pass-through counter to the breakfast nook. The family room has a beam ceiling and its own fireplace, plus sliding glass doors to the rear terrace. There are four bedrooms in the plan; one of the secondary bedrooms could be used as a den. The master suite features access to the terrace and a bath with dressing room, makeup vanity and double wall closets. The two-car garage contains a large work shop area for the handyman.

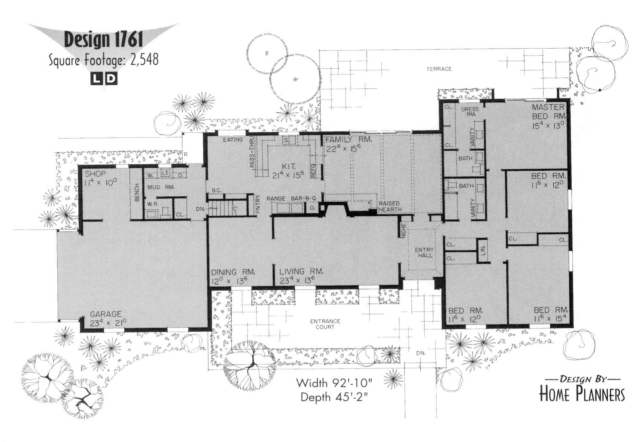

Design 1761
Square Footage: 2,548
L D

Width 92'-10"
Depth 45'-2"

—DESIGN BY—
HOME PLANNERS

Design 2778
Square Footage: 2,761

Width 80'-0"
Depth 64'-8"

— DESIGN BY —
Home Planners

◆ No matter what the occasion, family and friends will enjoy the sizable gathering room featured in this plan. A spacious 20' x 23', this room has a through-fireplace to the study, a sloped ceiling and two sets of sliding glass doors to the large rear terrace. Indoor-outdoor living can also be enjoyed in the dining room, study and master bedroom—all located to face the rear yard. There is also a covered dining porch, accessible through sliding glass doors in the dining and breakfast rooms. Note the light-filled bay in the breakfast room. A total of three bedrooms include two family bedrooms, sharing a full bath with double vanity, and a master suite with walk-in closet, exercise room and bath with separate tub and shower.

139

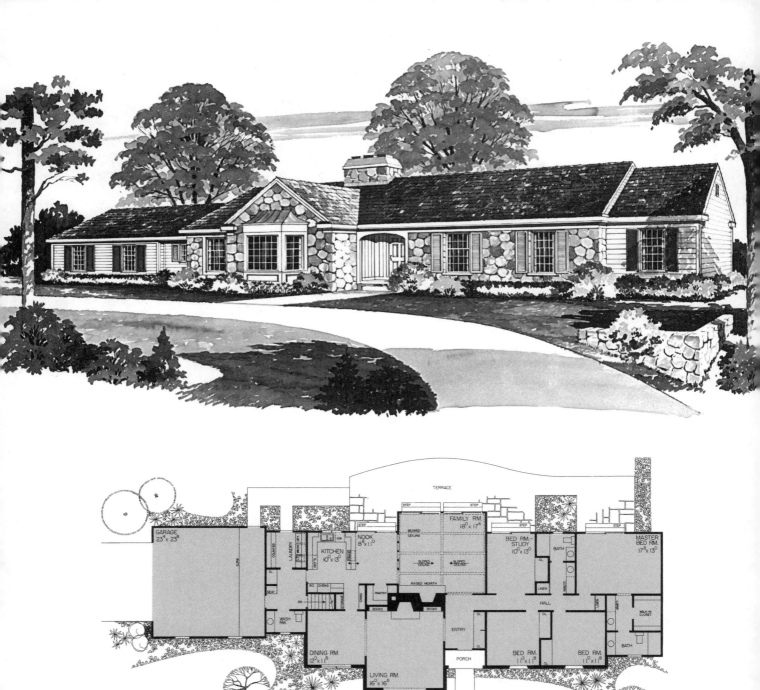

Width 106'-8"
Depth 41'-10"

Design 2544
Square Footage: 2,527

D

— DESIGN BY —
HOME PLANNERS

◆ A blend of exterior materials enhance the beauty of this fine home. Here, the masonry material used is fieldstone to contrast effectively with the horizontal siding. You may substitute brick or quarried stone if you wish. Adding appeal are the various projections and their roof planes, the window treatment and the recessed front entrance. Two large living areas highlight the interior. Each has a fireplace. Everyday chores will be easy and convenient with such features as the efficient kitchen, the walk-in pantry, the handy storage areas, the laundry and extra bedrooms, two baths with vanities and good closet accommodations. There's a basement for additional storage and recreation activities.

Design Q288
Square Footage: 2,559

Rear Elevation

◆ A low profile, accented with brick cladding, quoins and shuttered windows, enhances the front exterior of this one-story plan. The weather protected entry opens to a sunken living room with vaulted ceiling and fireplace. Double doors open to the formal dining room which also has direct access to the island kitchen. An octagonal breakfast bay overlooks the rear patio. The family room also has a warming fireplace and sliding glass doors to the patio. The master bedroom is a true retreat with a private patio, long wall closet and bath with vaulted ceiling over a whirlpool tub. The family bedrooms share a full hall bath. A three-car garage is reached through a door in the service area which also holds a washroom, stairs to the basement and the laundry. Plans include details for both a basement and a crawlspace foundation.

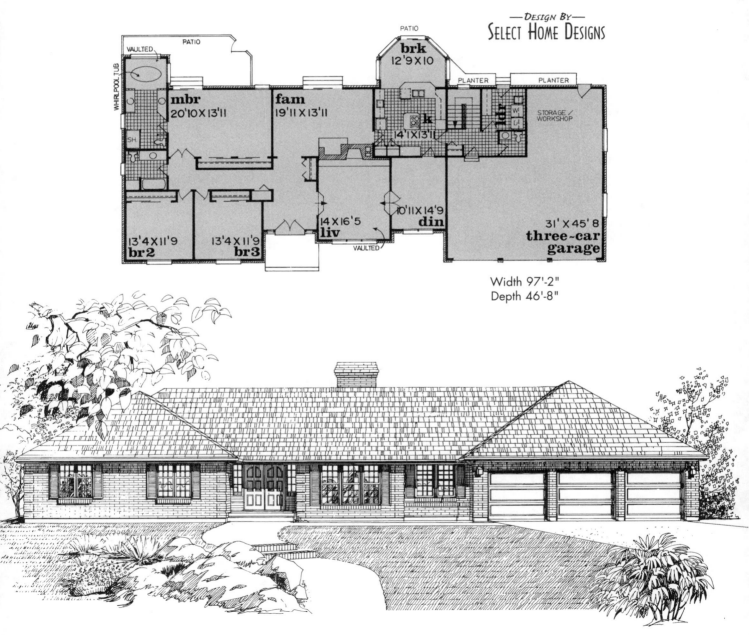

— DESIGN BY —
Select Home Designs

Width 97'-2"
Depth 46'-8"

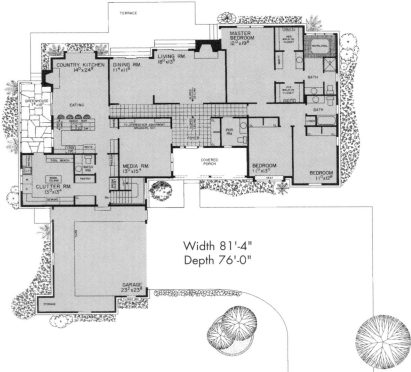

Width 81'-4"
Depth 76'-0"

—DESIGN BY—
HOME PLANNERS

QUOTE ONE®

Cost to build? See page 436
to order complete cost estimate
to build this house in your area!

Design 2880

Square Footage: 2,758
Greenhouse: 149 sq. ft.

L D

◆ This comfortable traditional home offers
plenty of modern livability. A clutter room off
the two-car garage is an ideal space for a workbench, sewing or hobbies. Across the hall one
finds a media room, the perfect place for
stereo, video and more. A spacious country
kitchen to the right of the greenhouse (great for
fresh herbs) is a cozy gathering place for family and friends, as well as a convenient work
area. Both the formal living room, with its
friendly fireplace, and the dining room provide
access to the rear grounds. A spacious, amenity-filled master suite features His and Hers
walk-in closets, a relaxing whirlpool tub and
access to the rear terrace. Two large secondary
bedrooms share a full bath.

Rear Elevation

Rear Elevation

Design 2832
Square Footage: 2,805
D

◆ The advantage of passive solar heating is a significant highlight of this contemporary design. The huge skylight over the atrium provides shelter during inclement weather, while permitting natural light to enter the atrium below and surrounding areas. Whether open to the sky, or sheltered by a glass or translucent covering, the atrium is a cheerful spot. The stone floor absorbs heat from the sun during the day and allows circulation of warm air to other areas at night. During the summer, shades provide protection from the sun without sacrificing natural light and the feeling of spaciousness. Sloping ceilings highlight each of the major rooms: three bedrooms, the formal living and dining rooms and the study. The conversation area between the two formal areas is a great spot for casual occasions. The broad expanses of roof can accommodate solar panels if an active system is installed to supplement the passive solar features of this design.

— DESIGN BY —
HOME PLANNERS

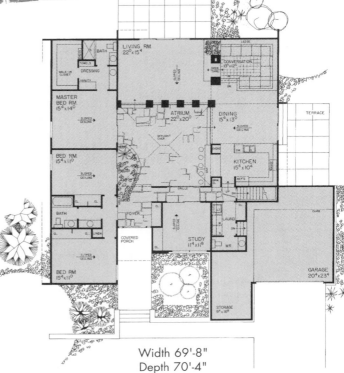

Width 69'-8"
Depth 70'-4"

Front Elevation

Design 2862
Square Footage: 3,238

—DESIGN BY—
Home Planners

◆ Earth shelters the interior of this house from both the cold of winter and the heat of summer. This three-bedroom design has passive solar capabilities. The sunroom, south facing for light, has a stone floor which will absorb heat. When needed, the heat will be circulated to the interior by opening the sliding glass doors or by mechanical means. Entrance to the home is through the vestibule or the garage. Both have a western exposure. A large, centrally located skylight creates an open feeling and lights up the interior of the plan where the formal and informal areas are located. The sunroom contains 425 square feet not included in the total. Note the separation of the master suite and the family bedrooms.

Width 95'-4"
Depth 51'-0"

Rear Elevation

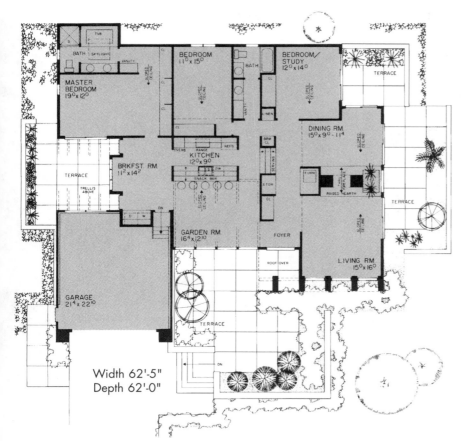

Design 2858
Square Footage: 2,231

MASTER BEDROOM 19⁰x12⁰

BEDROOM 11⁰x15⁰

BEDROOM/ STUDY 12⁰x14⁰

BATH SKYLIGHT

BATH

VANITY

TERRACE

TERRACE

BRKFST. RM. 11²x14⁹

KITCHEN 12⁰x9⁰

SNACK BAR

DINING RM. 15⁰x9⁰-11⁴

GARDEN RM. 16⁴x12¹⁰

FOYER

TERRACE

RAISED HEARTH

ROOF OVER

LIVING RM. 15⁰x16⁰

GARAGE 21⁴x22¹⁰

TERRACE

Width 62'-5"
Depth 62'-0"

◆ This sun-oriented design was created to face the south. Be doing so, it will have minimal northern exposure. It has been designed primarily for the more temperate U.S. latitudes using 2x6 wall construction. The morning sun will brighten the living and dining rooms, along with the adjacent terrace. Sun enters the garden room by way of the glass roof and walls. In the winter, the solar heat gain from the garden room should provide relief from high energy bills. Solar shades allow you to adjust the amount of light allowed to enter in the warmer months. The interior planning is efficient: a kitchen with snack bar and serving counter to the dining room, a breakfast room, three bedrooms (one could be a study) and a formal living room.

— DESIGN BY —
HOME PLANNERS

A. J. YOUNG
FUQUAY VARINA, N.C.

Design 3559
Square Footage: 2,916
L D

—DESIGN BY—
HOME PLANNERS

◆ Intricate details make the most of this
lovely one-story. The floor plan caters
to comfortable living. Besides the living
room/dining room area to the rear, there
is a large conversation area with fireplace and plenty of windows. The
kitchen is separated from living areas
by an angled snack-bar counter. A
media room to the front of the plan provides space for more private activities.
Three bedrooms grace the right side of
the plan. The master suite features a
tray vaulted ceiling and sliding glass
doors to the rear terrace. The dressing
area is graced by His and Hers walk-in
closets, double-bowl lavatory and a
compartmented commode.

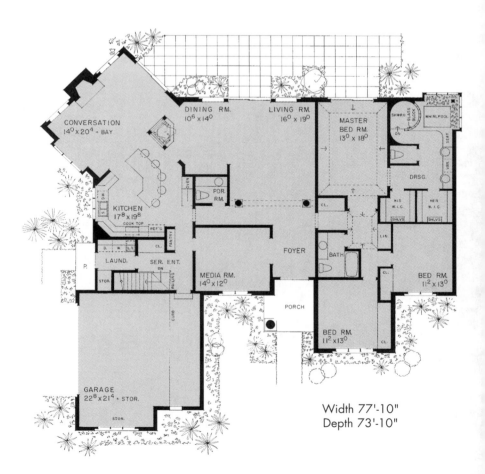

Width 77'-10"
Depth 73'-10"

QUOTE ONE®
Cost to build? See page 436
to order complete cost estimate
to build this house in your area!

146

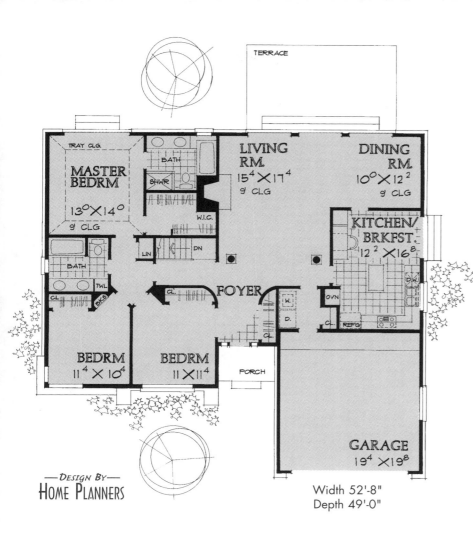

TERRACE

MASTER BEDRM
13⁰ X 14⁰
9' CLG

TRAY CLG.

BATH

SHWR

W.I.C.

LIVING RM.
15⁴ X 17⁴
9' CLG

DINING RM.
10⁰ X 12²
9' CLG

LIN | DN

BATH

TWL

CL

FOYER

CL

KITCHEN/ BRKFST.
12² X 16⁸

DW

OVN

W. D.

CL

REF'G

BEDRM
11⁴ X 10⁴

BEDRM
11 X 11⁴

PORCH

GARAGE
19⁴ X 19⁸

— DESIGN BY —
HOME PLANNERS

Width 52'-8"
Depth 49'-0"

Design 3454
Square Footage: 1,699
L D

◆ An efficient, spacious interior is part of this compact floor plan. Through a pair of columns, an open living and dining room area creates a comfortable space for entertaining, with sliding glass doors guaranteeing a bright, cheerful interior while providing easy access to outdoor living. A focal-point fireplace warms both areas. The L-shaped kitchen has an island work surface, a planing desk and an informal eating space. Sleeping quarters are highlighted by the master suite with tray ceiling and sliding glass doors to the yard. Its bath has a separate tub and shower and double sinks. Two family bedrooms share a hall bath. The garage is reached through a service entrance near the laundry alcove.

Quote One®

Cost to build? See page 436
to order complete cost estimate
to build this house in your area!

Design 2902
Square Footage: 1,632

L

◆ A sun space highlights this passive solar design. It features access from the kitchen, the dining room and the garage. It will be a great place to enjoy meals because of its location. Three skylights highlight the interior—in the kitchen, laundry and master bath. An air-locked vestibule helps this design's energy efficiency. Interior livability is excellent. The living/dining room rises with a sloped ceiling and enjoys a fireplace and two sets of sliding glass doors to the terrace. Three bedrooms are in the sleeping wing. The master bedroom will delight with its private bath with a luxurious whirlpool tub.

— DESIGN BY —
HOME PLANNERS

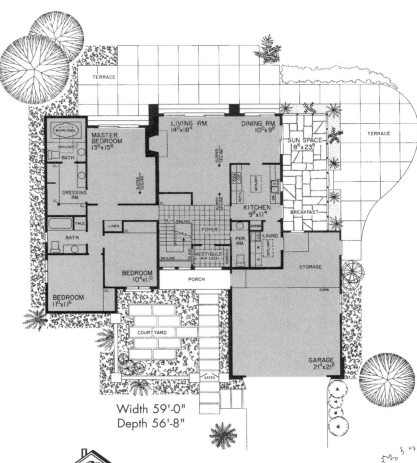

Width 59'-0"
Depth 56'-8"

QUOTE ONE®

Cost to build? See page 436
to order complete cost estimate
to build this house in your area!

148

Rear Elevation

Design 3560
Square Footage: 2,189
L

◆ Simplicity is the key to the stylish good looks of this home's facade. A walled garden entry and large window areas appeal to outdoor enthusiasts. Inside, the kitchen forms the hub of the plan. It opens directly off the foyer and contains an island cooktop and a work counter with eating space on the living area side. A sloped ceiling, a fireplace and sliding glass doors to a rear terrace are highlights in the living area. The master bedroom also sports sliding glass doors to the terrace. Its dressing area is enhanced with double walk-in closets, a whirlpool tub and a seated shower. Two family bedrooms are found on the opposite side of the house. They share a full bath with twin vanities.

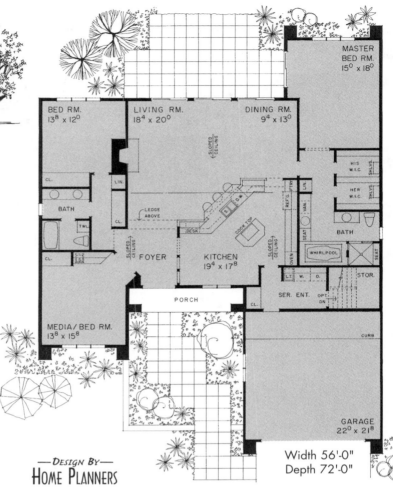

— DESIGN BY —
HOME PLANNERS

Width 56'-0"
Depth 72'-0"

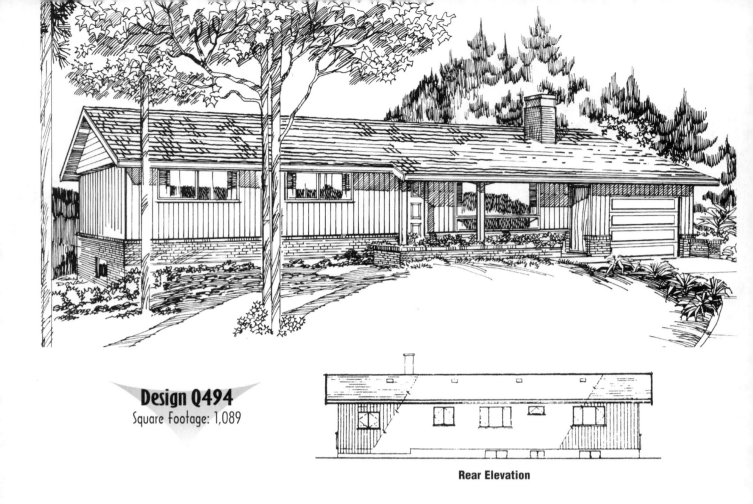

Design Q494
Square Footage: 1,089

Rear Elevation

◆ Brick and wood siding work in combination on the exterior of this cozy one-story home. The entry is protected by a covered porch and opens to a foyer with half-wall separating it from the living room, which features a large window overlooking the front porch. A fireplace warms this gathering space in cold weather. The U-shaped kitchen has abundant counter space and is adjacent to the dining room for convenience. Down a few steps is the handy laundry area with stairs to the basement and access to the single-car garage. Three bedrooms with wall closets share a main bath with soaking tub. The basement may be developed in the future to add more bedrooms or to create additional gathering space.

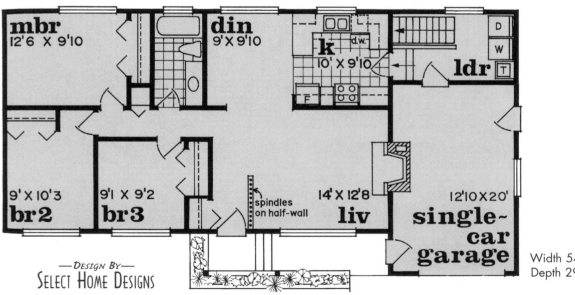

mbr
12'6 X 9'10

din
9' X 9'10

k
10' X 9'10

ldr

9' X 10'3
br2

9'1 X 9'2
br3

spindles
on half-wall

14' X 12'8
liv

12'10 X 20'
single-car garage

— DESIGN BY —
SELECT HOME DESIGNS

Width 54'-0"
Depth 29'-4"

Design 2864
Square Footage: 1,387
L D

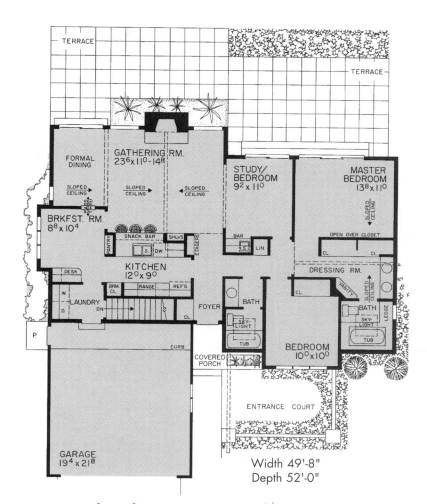

◆ Projecting the garage to the front of a house is very economical in two ways. One, it reduces the required lot size for building. And two, it protects the interior of the house from street noise. Many other characteristics of this home are worth mention, too. The foyer leads to a central hall with a galley kitchen on the left and the gathering room ahead. The gathering room has a sloped ceiling and fireplace flanked by windows overlooking the rear terrace. A small dining space in the left corner allows access to the terrace. The breakfast room is light filled and holds a planning desk. Two or three bedrooms sit to the right of the hall—use one as a study, if you wish. The master suite contains a dressing room, terrace access and bath with spa tub and skylight. The study also has terrace access.

QUOTE ONE®
Cost to build? See page 436
to order complete cost estimate
to build this house in your area!

— DESIGN BY —
HOME PLANNERS

Width 49'-8"
Depth 52'-0"

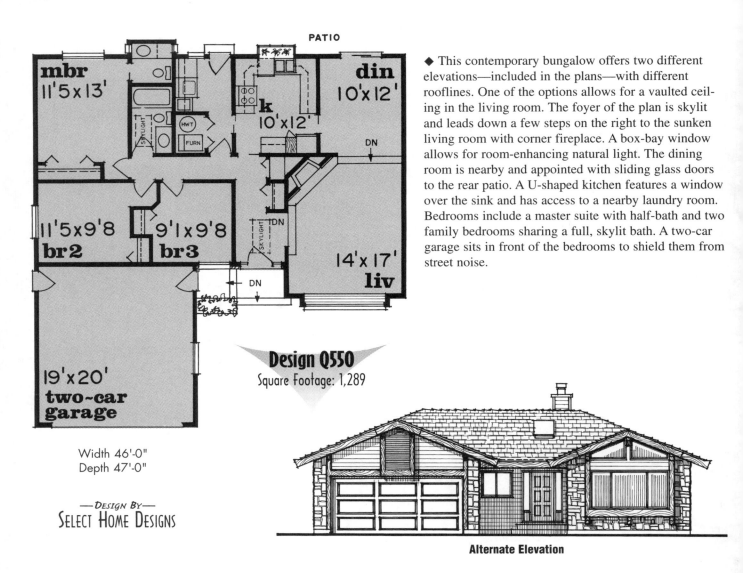

mbr
11'5 x 13'

br2
11'5 x 9'8

br3
9'1 x 9'8

k
10'12'

din
10' x 12'

PATIO

HWT

FURN

DN

DN

DN

SKYLIGHT

SKYLIGHT

liv
14' x 17'

two~car garage
19' x 20'

Width 46'-0"
Depth 47'-0"

— DESIGN BY —
SELECT HOME DESIGNS

Design Q550
Square Footage: 1,289

◆ This contemporary bungalow offers two different elevations—included in the plans—with different rooflines. One of the options allows for a vaulted ceiling in the living room. The foyer of the plan is skylit and leads down a few steps on the right to the sunken living room with corner fireplace. A box-bay window allows for room-enhancing natural light. The dining room is nearby and appointed with sliding glass doors to the rear patio. A U-shaped kitchen features a window over the sink and has access to a nearby laundry room. Bedrooms include a master suite with half-bath and two family bedrooms sharing a full, skylit bath. A two-car garage sits in front of the bedrooms to shield them from street noise.

Alternate Elevation

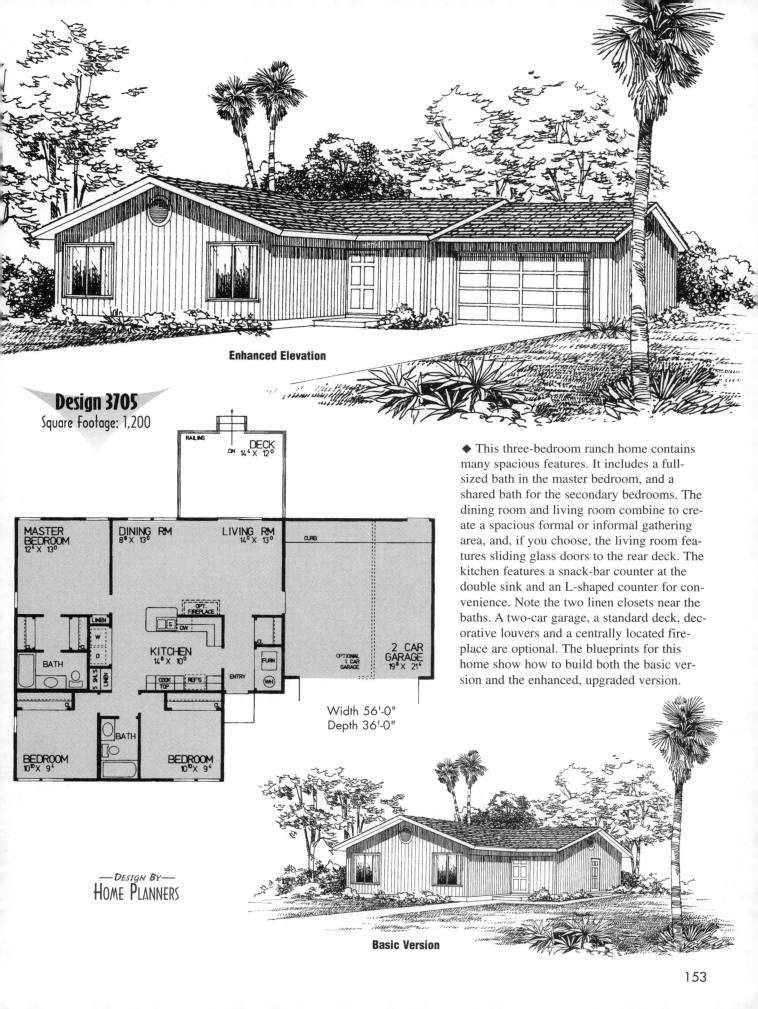

Enhanced Elevation

Design 3705
Square Footage: 1,200

DECK
14⁴ X 12⁰
RAILING
DN

MASTER BEDROOM
12⁰ X 13⁰

DINING RM
8⁸ X 13⁰

LIVING RM
14⁰ X 13⁰

CURB

LINEN

OPT. FIREPLACE

S
DW

BATH

W
D

KITCHEN
14⁸ X 10⁰

FURN

CL

2 CAR GARAGE
19⁸ X 21⁴

OPTIONAL 1 CAR GARAGE

COOK TOP

REF'G

ENTRY

WH

BEDROOM
10¹⁰ X 9⁴

BATH

BEDROOM
10¹⁰ X 9⁴

Width 56'-0"
Depth 36'-0"

— DESIGN BY —
HOME PLANNERS

◆ This three-bedroom ranch home contains many spacious features. It includes a full-sized bath in the master bedroom, and a shared bath for the secondary bedrooms. The dining room and living room combine to create a spacious formal or informal gathering area, and, if you choose, the living room features sliding glass doors to the rear deck. The kitchen features a snack-bar counter at the double sink and an L-shaped counter for convenience. Note the two linen closets near the baths. A two-car garage, a standard deck, decorative louvers and a centrally located fireplace are optional. The blueprints for this home show how to build both the basic version and the enhanced, upgraded version.

Basic Version

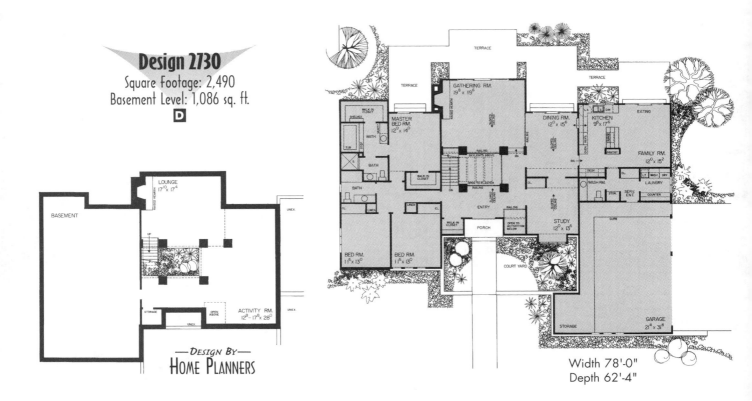

Design 2730

Square Footage: 2,490
Basement Level: 1,086 sq. ft.

D

—DESIGN BY—
HOME PLANNERS

Width 78'-0"
Depth 62'-4"

◆ This basic one-story is loaded with amenities and offers the option of finish-later space in its basement. The central living areas include the gathering room, the formal dining room and the study. All three areas have sloped ceilings; the gathering room and dining room offer sliding glass doors to the rear terrace. The family room combines with casual eating space, open to the L-shaped island kitchen. There is also terrace access at this point. The master suite accesses its own private area of the terrace and is further enhanced by two walk-in closets and a bath with whirlpool spa, separate shower and two vanities. Family bedrooms share a full bath in the hall. Note the large three-car garage with extra storage space.

154

◆ This smart design features a multi-gabled roof and vertical windows. It also offers efficient zoning by room functions and plenty of modern comforts for contemporary family living. A covered porch leads through a foyer to a large, central gathering room with a fireplace, a sloped ceiling and its own special view of the rear terrace. A modern kitchen with a snack bar features a pass-through to the breakfast room with a view of the terrace. There's also an adjacent dining room. A media room is privately situated along with the bedrooms from the rest of the house to offer a quiet, private area for enjoying music or surfing-the-net. A master bedroom suite includes its own dressing area with a whirlpool tub in the bath. A large garage includes an extra storage room and access to the main house via the laundry room.

Design 2913
Square footage: 1,835

D

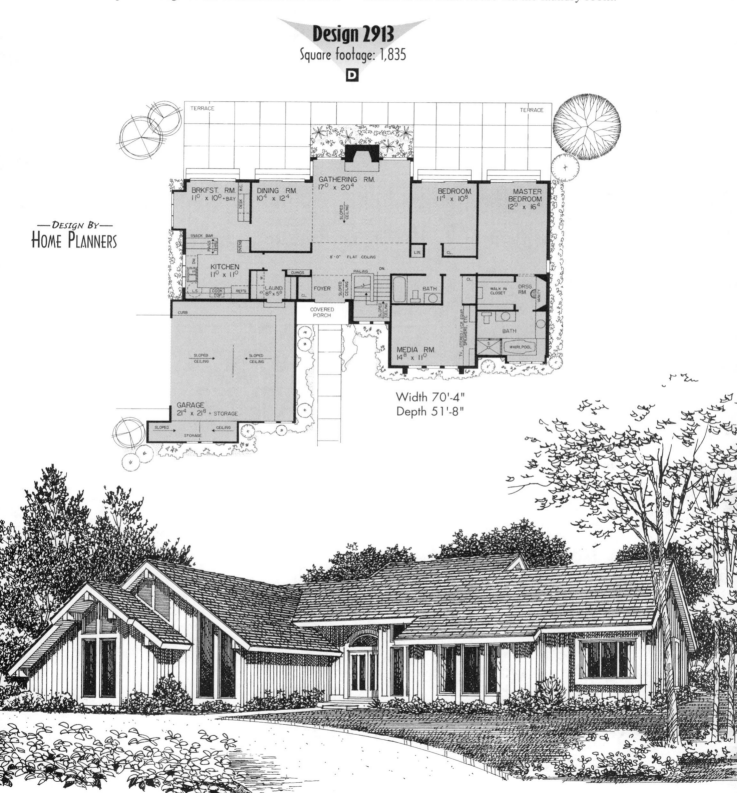

—Design By—
Home Planners

Width 70'-4"
Depth 51'-8"

Design 3708
Square Footage: 1,298

Enhanced Plan

◆ Traditional charm with an outstanding layout describes this low-cost, one-story ranch. A covered front porch welcomes visitors. Three bedrooms or two bedrooms and a study are accompanied by two full baths. An expansive living room, a formal dining room and an eat-in kitchen make up the living area of this home. The living room and master bedroom feature sliding glass doors to the deck, if you choose to build it. Access the two-car garage through a convenient laundry area just beyond the kitchen. Livability may be enhanced by the completion of an optional standard or double-sized deck, a fireplace in the living room and a two-car garage. Blueprints show how to build both the basic and the enhanced versions.

Width 52'-0"
Depth 44'-5"

RAILING · DN · RAILING

DECK
32⁰ X 12⁰

OPT. SINGLE DECK

OPT. FIREPLACE

BATH

MASTER BEDROOM
13⁰ X 11⁰

LIVING RM
18⁴ X 16⁰

DINING RM
13⁰ X 9⁴

KITCHEN
9⁰ X 11⁸

REF'G

DW

S

BATH

LINEN

BEDROOM
10⁸ X 10⁴

STUDY/ BEDROOM
10⁰ X 10⁴

ENTRY

COVERED PORCH

D

W

LAUNDRY
8¹⁰ X 5⁰

COOK TOP

FURN

WH

2 CAR GARAGE
19⁴ X 21⁸

—DESIGN BY—
HOME PLANNERS

Basic Plan

Design Q227
Square Footage: 1,404

— Design By —
Select Home Designs

◆ Traditional brick with wood accents characterizes this home. The entry is recessed and offset to the side of the main body of the house. A few steps up from the foyer takes you into the living and dining rooms—a bay window and fireplace highlight the long living room. The L-shaped kitchen completes the circle and offers space for a breakfast nook. The three bedrooms sit to the back of the plan and include two family bedrooms sharing a full bath and a master bedroom with private bath and walk-in closet. The two-car garage is accessed at an entry at the stairway landing to the basement. Finish basement space later, as needed, for a family room and extra bedrooms.

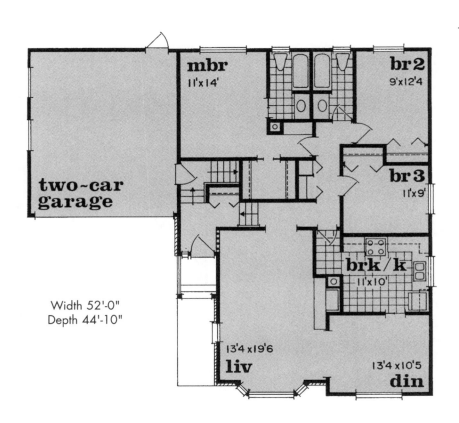

Width 52'-0"
Depth 44'-10"

◆ This elegant one-story contemporary is designed for sites that slope slightly to the front. As a consequence, the major rooms of the home are sunken just a few steps from the grand entry foyer. The large gathering room is in line with the entry doors and has sliding glass doors to the terrace and a through-fireplace to the study. The dining room is nearby, with sliding glass doors to a covered porch. The L-shaped kitchen and breakfast nook share the use of a patio just outside the nook. For real convenience, the study has built-ins and a powder room close at hand. Amenities in the master suite include a walk-in closet, spa tub and double sinks. Family bedrooms share a full bath with garden tub and double sinks.

Design 2789
Square Footage: 2,732
L D

— Design By —
Home Planners

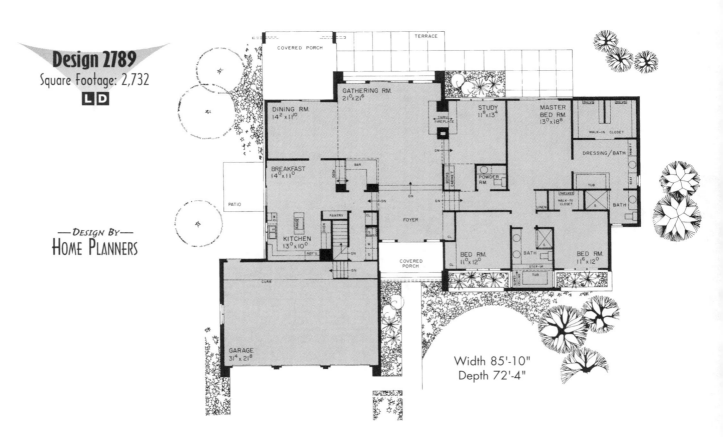

Width 85'-10"
Depth 72'-4"

◆ Clean, contemporary lines define this grand one-story home. Double doors open onto a sunlit foyer that leads to a sunken gathering room straight ahead. Thoughtful planning allows a see-through fireplace to share its warmth with the nearby study. Adjoining the gathering room is a dining room that opens onto a covered porch, perfect for dining alfresco. The master bedroom is located to the rear for privacy and opens to its own private terrace. Two walk-in closets, sized for frequent shoppers, share space with a master bath designed for pampering. Here, a bumped-out whirlpool tub invites relaxation. Other amenities include dual sinks, a separate shower and a compartmental toilet. Two family bedrooms located to the front of the plan share a full bath. A two-car garage has extra storage space.

Design 3359
Square Footage: 2,473
L D

QUOTE ONE®
Cost to build? See page 436 to order complete cost estimate to build this house in your area!

Width 82'-6"
Depth 81'-10"

ENTERTAINMENT TERRACE

COVERED PORCH

MASTER TERRACE

DINING ROOM
14⁴ x 12⁰

GATHERING ROOM
20² x 15¹⁰

STUDY
11⁸ x 13²

MASTER BEDRM
13⁰ x 18⁶

WALK-IN CLOSET

MASTER BATH

WHIRLPOOL

BRKFST ROOM
13¹⁰ x 11⁰

SNACK BAR

PDR

LINEN

WALK-IN CLOSET

KIT
12¹¹ x 10⁰

PANTRY

LAUNDRY

FOYER

BEDRM
10¹¹ x 12⁰

BATH

BEDRM
10¹¹ x 12⁰

COVERED PORCH

STEP-UP

TUB

GARAGE
26⁸ x 31⁸

—DESIGN BY—
HOME PLANNERS

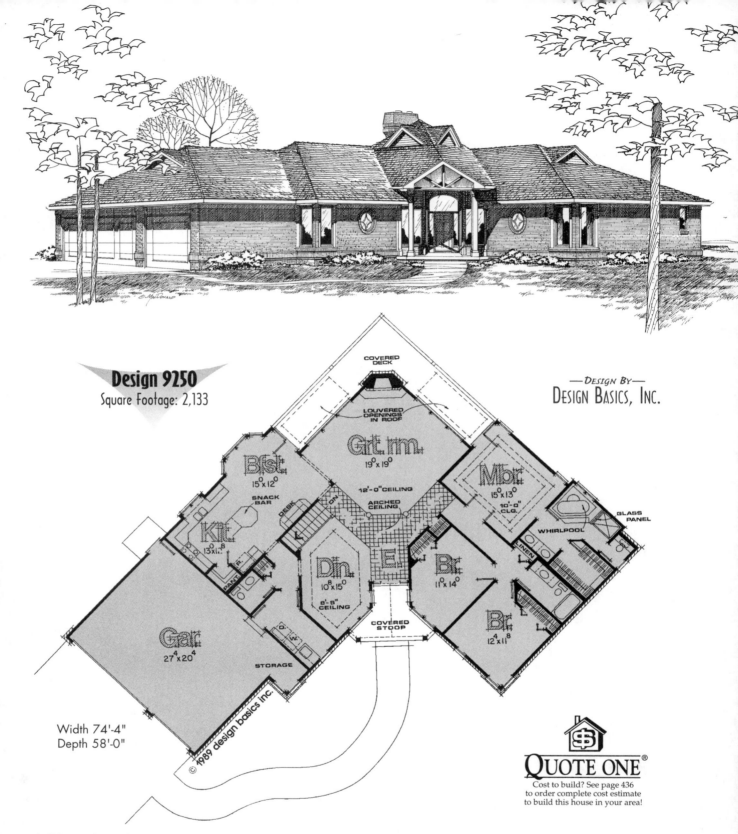

Design 9250
Square Footage: 2,133

—DESIGN BY—
DESIGN BASICS, INC.

COVERED DECK

LOUVERED OPENINGS IN ROOF

Grt. rm.
19⁰ x 19⁰

Bfst.
15⁰ x 12⁰

SNACK BAR

DESK

12'-0" CEILING

ARCHED CEILING

Mbr.
15⁰ x 13⁰

10'-0" CLG.

GLASS PANEL

WHIRLPOOL

Kit.
13 x 11⁸

LINEN

PANT.

Dn.
10⁸ x 15⁰

Br.
11⁰ x 14⁰

8'-8" CEILING

Gar.
27⁴ x 20⁴

STORAGE

COVERED STOOP

Br.
12⁴ x 11⁸

Width 74'-4"
Depth 58'-0"

© 1989 design basics inc.

QUOTE ONE®
Cost to build? See page 436
to order complete cost estimate
to build this house in your area!

◆ Diagonals used wisely in this contemporary design make it a versatile choice for a variety of lot arrangements. Open planning inside creates visual appeal—the entry offers interior vistas through decorative columns and graceful arches. A fabulous great room offers a corner fireplace framed by walls of windows, which allow stunning views to outdoor areas. An exquisite formal dining room with a coffered ceiling shares the natural light of the great room. An island kitchen with a snack bar, a planning desk and a walk-in pantry opens to a breakfast room with bayed nook. Homeowners will retreat to the restful master suite, which offers a coffered ceiling, corner whirlpool bath, a glass-enclosed shower, twin lavatories and a walk-in closet. Two family bedrooms share a nearby full bath. The three-car garage holds extra storage space and allows access to the house through the mud/laundry room. Note the half-bath and closet in the service hall.

Width 81'-4"
Depth 78'-0"

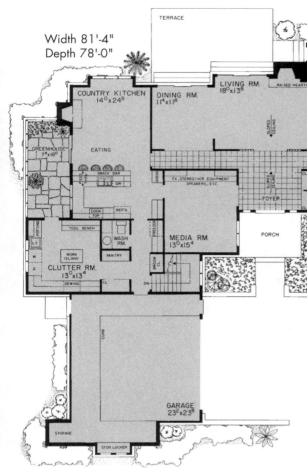

Design 2915
Square Footage: 2,758
Greenhouse: 149 sq. ft.

L D

Quote One®
Cost to build? See page 436
to order complete cost estimate
to build this house in your area!

◆ This grand plan excels in many ways. Start with the 340-square-foot country kitchen, which sports a fireplace, a snack bar and casual gathering space. A nearby clutter room allows space for hobbies. Across the hall, the media room contains a wall of built-ins. The combination living room/dining area features a sloped ceiling, raised-hearth fireplace and doors leading to the back terrace. The king-sized master suite offers all the extras with a pair of walk-in closets, a whirlpool made for two and loads of extra storage space. Two family bedrooms share a bath with handy linen closet. Of special note is the lovely greenhouse just outside the country kitchen—the perfect spot for an herb garden.

—DESIGN BY—
HOME PLANNERS

Design 2817
Square Footage: 1,536
L D

◆ Just under 1,600 square feet, this plan offers outstanding livability and options. The front facing living room allows space for formal occasions, while the beamed-ceiling family room serves for more casual affairs. Sliding glass doors in the family room lead to a terrace at the back. A pass-through counter between the kitchen and family room works well for quick meals-on-the-go, but for more elaborate dining use the dining space adjoining the kitchen. Four bedrooms are included. If you choose, make one of the secondary bedrooms an office or den. The three secondary bedrooms share a full bath, while the master bedroom has its own bath. A two-car garage faces to the side.

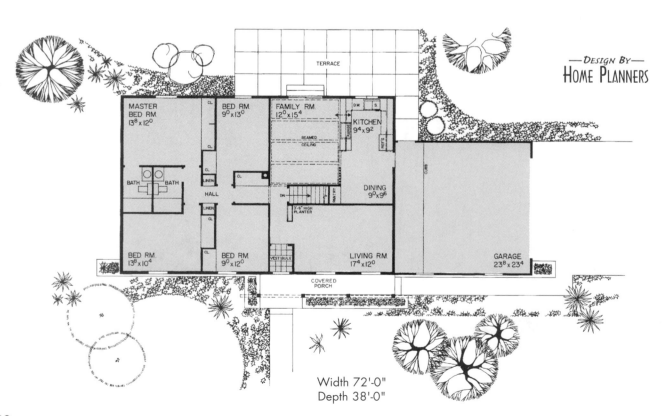

—Design by—
Home Planners

Width 72'-0"
Depth 38'-0"

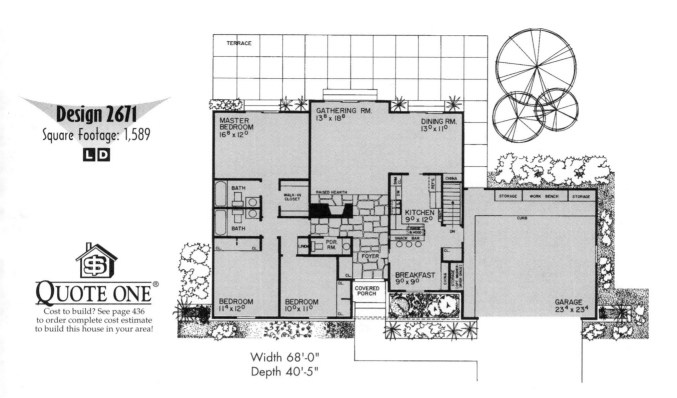

Design 2671
Square Footage: 1,589

L D

QUOTE ONE®
Cost to build? See page 436
to order complete cost estimate
to build this house in your area!

TERRACE

MASTER BEDROOM
16⁸ x 12⁰

GATHERING RM.
13⁸ x 18⁸

DINING RM.
13⁰ x 11⁰

BATH

WALK-IN CLOSET

RAISED HEARTH

KITCHEN
9⁰ x 12⁰

BATH

STORAGE   WORK BENCH   STORAGE

CURB

SNACK BAR

CL   CL

LIN

PDR. RM.

FOYER

BREAKFAST
9⁰ x 9⁰

CHINA

STORAGE
(OPT. WASHER-DRYER SPACE)

GARAGE
23⁴ x 23⁴

BEDROOM
11⁴ x 12⁰

BEDROOM
10⁰ x 11⁰

COVERED PORCH

Width 68'-0"
Depth 40'-5"

◆ The rustic exterior of this one-story home features vertical wood siding. The entry foyer is flooded with flagstone and leads to the three areas of the plan: the sleeping, living and work center. The sleeping area features three bedrooms. The master bedroom utilizes sliding glass doors to the rear terrace. The living area, consisting of gathering and dining rooms, also enjoys access to the terrace. The work center is efficiently planned. It houses the kitchen with a snack bar, the breakfast room with a built-in china cabinet and stairs to the basement. This is a very livable plan. Special amenities include a raised-hearth fireplace in the gathering room and a walk-in closet in the master bedroom.

—DESIGN BY—
HOME PLANNERS

Design 2351
Square Footage: 1,862

◆ The extension of the wide overhanging roof of this distinctive home provides shelter for the walkway to the front door. A raised brick planter adds appeal to the outstanding exterior design. The living patterns offered by this plan are delightfully different, yet extremely practical. Notice the separation of the master bedroom from the other two bedrooms. While assuring an extra measure of quiet privacy for the parents, this master bedroom location may be ideal for a live-in relative. Locating the kitchen in the middle of the plan frees up valuable outside wall space and leads to interesting planning. The front living room is sunken for dramatic appeal and need not have any cross-room traffic. The utility room houses the laundry and the heating and cooling equipment.

— DESIGN BY —
HOME PLANNERS

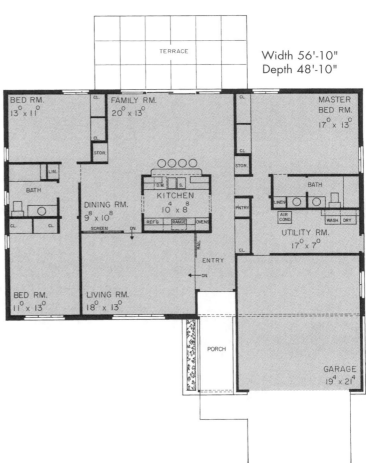

Width 56'-10"
Depth 48'-10"

HOME PLANNERS

Design 3368
Square Footage: 2,720
L D

◆ Rooflines are the key to the interesting exterior of this design. Their configuration allows for sloped ceilings in the gathering room and large foyer. Both the gathering room and the dining room offer access to the rear terrace via sliding glass doors. The master bedroom suite has a huge walk-in closet, garden whirlpool and separate shower. Two family bedrooms share a full bath. One of these bedrooms could be used as a media room with pass-through wet bar. Note the large kitchen with conversation bay and the wide terrace to the rear.

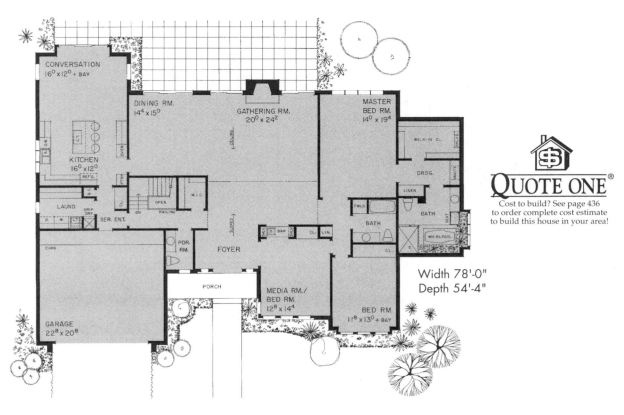

CONVERSATION 16⁰ x 12⁰ + BAY

DINING RM. 14⁴ x 15⁰

GATHERING RM. 20⁰ x 24²

MASTER BED RM. 14⁰ x 19⁴

KITCHEN 16⁰ x 12⁰

WALK-IN CL.

LAUND.

DRSG.

SER. ENT.

LINEN

FOYER

BATH

BATH

WHIRLPOOL

POR. RM.

GARAGE 22⁸ x 20⁸

PORCH

MEDIA RM./ BED RM. 12⁸ x 14⁰

BED RM. 11⁸ x 13⁰ + BAY

QUOTE ONE®
Cost to build? See page 436
to order complete cost estimate
to build this house in your area!

Width 78'-0"
Depth 54'-4"

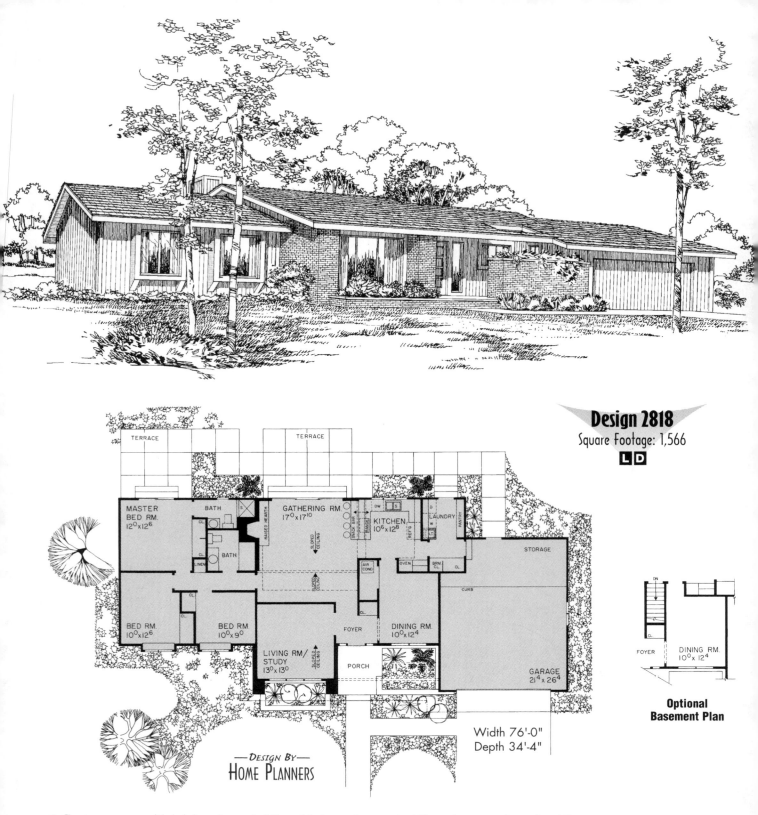

Design 2818
Square Footage: 1,566

L D

MASTER BED RM.
12⁰x12⁶

BATH

BATH

LINEN

GATHERING RM.
17⁰x17¹⁰

RAISED HEARTH

SLOPED CEILING

KITCHEN
10⁶x12⁸

SNACK BAR

DW

S

RANGE

REFG.

LAUNDRY

D

W

PANTRY

STORAGE

TERRACE

TERRACE

AIR COND.

OVEN

BRM CL.

CL.

SLOPED CEILING

CL.

CURB

BED RM.
10⁰x12⁶

CL.

BED RM.
10⁰x9⁰

LIVING RM./
STUDY
13⁰x13⁰

SLOPED CEILING

FOYER

PORCH

DINING RM.
10⁰x12⁴

GARAGE
21⁴x26⁴

Width 76'-0"
Depth 34'-4"

— DESIGN BY —
HOME PLANNERS

**Optional
Basement Plan**

DN

FOYER

CL.

DINING RM.
10⁰x 12⁴

◆ Contemporary, with brick and wood siding, this home has vertical lines that carry from the siding to the paned windows to the garage door. The front entry is recessed so the overhanging roof creates a covered porch. Beside the entry is a planter court with privacy wall. The floor plan is just as outstanding. The rear gathering room has a sloped ceiling, raised-hearth fireplace and sliding glass doors to the terrace. A snack bar separates the gathering room from the U-shaped kitchen. The formal living room—or make it a study—has a sloped ceiling and is accessed directly from the foyer. The formal dining room is convenient to the kitchen and overlooks the planter court. Three bedrooms and two closely placed baths are in the left wing of the house. Build on a crawlspace or basement foundation as you choose.

QUOTE ONE®
Cost to build? See page 436
to order complete cost estimate
to build this house in your area!

TERRACE

COUNTRY KITCHEN
14⁰ X 24⁸

GREEN HOUSE

EATING

SNACK BAR

LS   D   DW

LS   COOK REF'G
     TOP

D   W   LT

CLUTTER RM
14⁴ X 13⁴

WORK ISLAND

WASH RM

PANTRY/ STORAGE

SEWING

BC

DN

CURB

GARAGE
23⁸ X 23⁸

DINING RM
11⁰ X 11⁸

LIVING RM
18⁰ X 13⁸

RAISED HEARTH

LEDGE ABOVE

SLOPED CEILING

OVEN

LEDGE ABOVE

SLOPED CEILING

FOYER

MEDIA RM/ STUDY
13⁰ X 15⁴

FREEZER

PORCH

MASTER BEDROOM
13⁰ X 19⁸

CL

WALK-IN CLOSET

MASTER BATH

WHIRLPOOL

VANITY

S

BATH

PDR RM

STORAGE   LINEN

LIN

CL

BEDROOM
11⁰ X 15⁰

BEDROOM
11⁰ X 15⁰

Width 82'-8"
Depth 74'-0"

Design 3357
Square Footage: 2,913

L D

Quote One®
Cost to build? See page 436
to order complete cost estimate
to build this house in your area!

◆ One-story living never had it so good! From the formal living and dining rooms to a private media room, this house is designed to be enjoyed. Note the fireplace in the living room and sliding glass doors to the rear terrace in both the living and dining rooms. The greenhouse off the kitchen (note the second fireplace) adds 147 square feet to the plan. The clutter room is a use-all space where gardening or hobby activities can take place. At the opposite end of the house are a master bedroom with a generous bath containing two sinks, a whirlpool tub and a separate shower. The master bedroom has a door to the rear terrace. Notice the wealth of built-ins throughout the house.

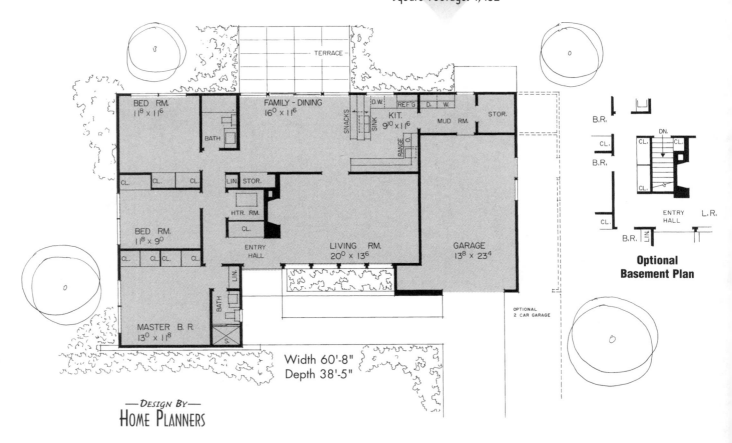

Design 1021
Square Footage: 1,432

TERRACE

BED RM.
11⁸ × 11⁶

FAMILY - DINING
16⁰ × 11⁶

D.W.

REF'G

D. W.

BATH

SNACKS

SINK

KIT.
9¹⁰ × 11⁶

MUD RM.

STOR.

CL.

CL.

CL.

LIN

STOR.

RANGE

O.

HTR. RM.

CL.

BED RM.
11⁸ × 9⁰

CL.

CL.

CL.

ENTRY
HALL

LIVING RM.
20⁰ × 13⁶

GARAGE
13⁸ × 23⁴

LIN.

BATH

MASTER B.R.
13⁰ × 11⁸

S.

OPTIONAL
2 CAR GARAGE

Width 60'-8"
Depth 38'-5"

Optional Basement Plan

B.R.

DN.

CL.

CL.

B.R.

CL.

CL.

ENTRY
HALL

L. R.

CL.

B.R.

LIN

—DESIGN BY—
HOME PLANNERS

◆ Designed in brick with wood siding accents, this straight-forward contemporary boasts great open living spaces. Double front doors open to a large living room with fireplace and continue to a family room-dining area with sliding glass doors to the rear terrace. The kitchen is configured in a double L-shape and has loads of counter space and a pass-through counter to the family room. The mud room has access to the single-car garage (or build as a two-car, if you wish) and a huge storage area. Three bedrooms grace the left side of the plan. The master has a private bath while the two family bedrooms share a full bath. Note the two linen closets and convenient hall coat closet.

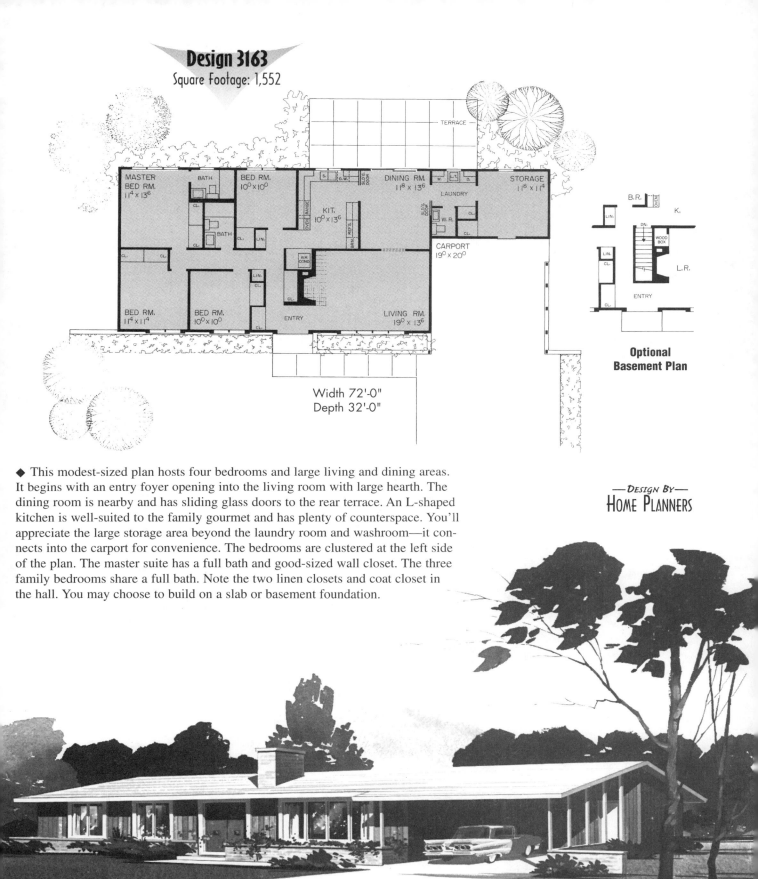

Design 3163
Square Footage: 1,552

TERRACE

MASTER BED RM. 11⁴ x 13⁶

BATH

BED RM. 10⁰ x 10⁰

DINING RM. 11⁸ x 13⁶

STORAGE 11⁸ x 11⁴

LAUNDRY

BATH

KIT. 10⁰ x 13⁶

CARPORT 19⁰ x 20⁰

BED RM. 11⁴ x 11⁴

BED RM. 10⁰ x 10⁰

ENTRY

AIR COND.

LIVING RM. 19⁰ x 13⁶

Width 72'-0"
Depth 32'-0"

Optional Basement Plan

B.R.

K.

L.R.

ENTRY

◆ This modest-sized plan hosts four bedrooms and large living and dining areas. It begins with an entry foyer opening into the living room with large hearth. The dining room is nearby and has sliding glass doors to the rear terrace. An L-shaped kitchen is well-suited to the family gourmet and has plenty of counterspace. You'll appreciate the large storage area beyond the laundry room and washroom—it connects into the carport for convenience. The bedrooms are clustered at the left side of the plan. The master suite has a full bath and good-sized wall closet. The three family bedrooms share a full bath. Note the two linen closets and coat closet in the hall. You may choose to build on a slab or basement foundation.

—DESIGN BY—
HOME PLANNERS

169

Design 2790
Square Footage: 2,075

— DESIGN BY —
HOME PLANNERS

Width 66'-0"
Depth 56'-4"

◆ Enter this contemporary, hip-roofed home through the double doors and you'll immediately appreciate the sloped ceilinged living room with fireplace. It has sliding glass doors to the covered porch at the rear, brightened by skylights above. The family room also has sliding glass doors—they lead to a rear terrace. A galley-style kitchen has a snack bar to share with the family room and its dining space. The laundry is adjacent to the service entrance and to stairs leading to the basement. Sleeping quarters consist of two family bedrooms and a master suite. The master bath features a walk-in closet and bath with dressing area. Family bedrooms share a full bath—note the walk-in linen closet. A two-car garage is accessed through the service area near the kitchen. Note the powder room and coat closet at the entry.

Design 2819
Square Footage: 2,459
D

◆ Indoor-outdoor living will be enjoyed to its fullest in this rambling one-story contemporary plan. Each of the rear rooms in this design, excluding the study, has access to a terrace or porch. Even the front breakfast room has access to a private dining patio. The covered porch off the living areas, family, dining and living rooms, has a sloped ceiling and sky-lights. A built-in barbecue and storage room are found on the second covered porch. Inside, there is exceptional livability. The master suite is especially nice, with a huge walk-in closet and grand bath. Note the through-fireplace that the living room shares with the study. A built-in etagere is nearby. There is even extra storage in the three-car garage.

—DESIGN BY—
HOME PLANNERS

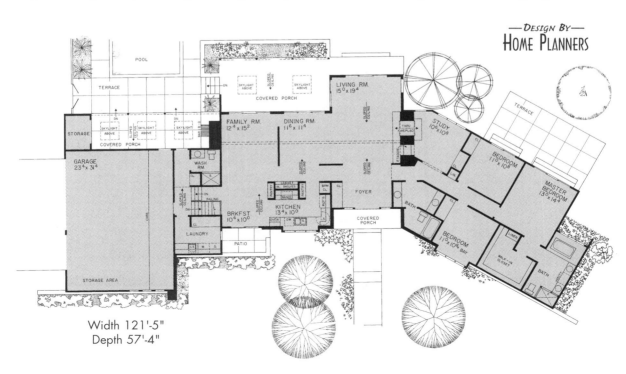

Width 121'-5"
Depth 57'-4"

Design 2756
Square Footage: 2,652
L D

◆ This impressive one-story design has numerous features that will assure the finest in contemporary living. For instance, the sunken gathering room and dining room share an impressive sloped ceiling; a series of three sliding glass doors provide access to the terrace. The family room, with a cozy fireplace, is ideal for informal entertaining. The kitchen features an efficient work island, pantry and built-in desk with a nearby sunny nook for morning coffee. The master bedroom opens to the rear terrace and its bath offers a separate step-up tub and a shower. Two additional bedrooms are located at the front of the home. The service entrance has a laundry area and wash room, plus access to the two-car garage.

— DESIGN BY —
HOME PLANNERS

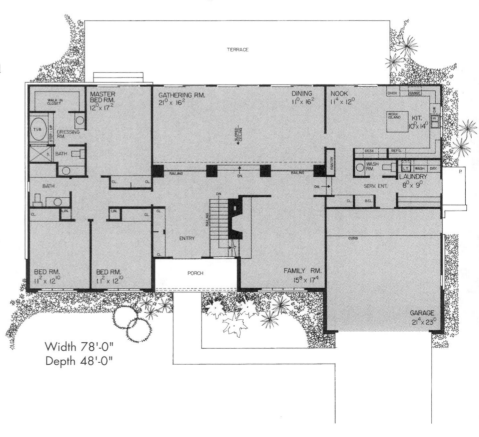

Width 78'-0"
Depth 48'-0"

Design 2866
Square Footage: 1,898
Mother-in-law Suite: 473 sq. ft.

◆ An extra living unit has been built into the design of this home. It would make an excellent mother-in-law suite. Should you choose not to develop this area as indicated, you might use it as two more bedrooms, a guest suite or even as hobby and game rooms. Whatever its final use, the suite will complement the main body of the house. The focal point of the main body is the large gathering room. Its features include a skylight, sloped ceiling, centered fireplace flanked on both sides by sliding glass doors, and an adjacent dining room on one side, a study on the other. The work center is clustered in the front of the plan. Sleeping quarters include three bedrooms and two baths. Outdoor areas are abundant: a court with privacy wall, two covered porches and a large terrace.

— DESIGN BY —
HOME PLANNERS

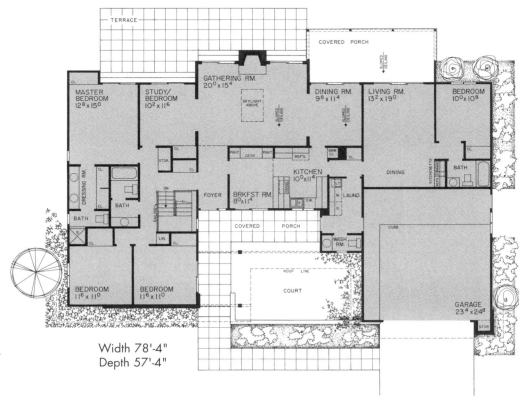

Width 78'-4"
Depth 57'-4"

Design 2871
Square Footage: 1,824
Greenhouse: 81 sq. ft.

◆ A greenhouse area off the dining room and living room provides a cheerful focal point for this comfortable three-bedroom home. The spacious living room features a cozy fireplace and a sloped ceiling. In addition to the dining room, there's a less formal breakfast room just off the modern kitchen. Both kitchen and breakfast areas look out onto a front terrace. Stairs just off the foyer lead down to a basement recreation room. The master bedroom suite opens to a terrace. A mud room and a wash room off the garage allow rear entry to the house during inclement weather.

—DESIGN BY—
HOME PLANNERS

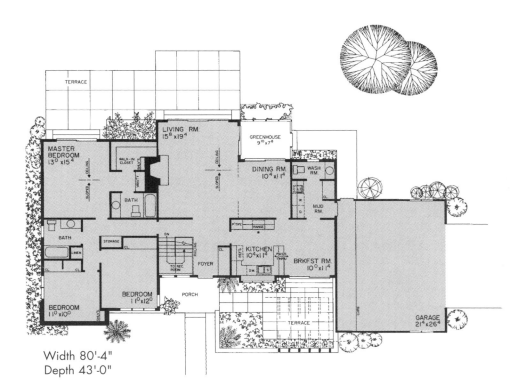

Width 80'-4"
Depth 43'-0"

Design 2918
Square footage: 1,693

D

◆ Alternating use of stone and wood gives a textured look to this striking contemporary home with wide overhanging rooflines and a built-in planter box. The design is just as exciting on the inside, with two bedrooms, including a master suite, a study (or optional third bedroom), a rear gathering room with a fireplace and a sloped ceiling, a rear dining room and an efficient U-shaped kitchen with a pass-through to an adjoining breakfast room. A mud room and washroom are located between the kitchen and the spacious two-car garage.

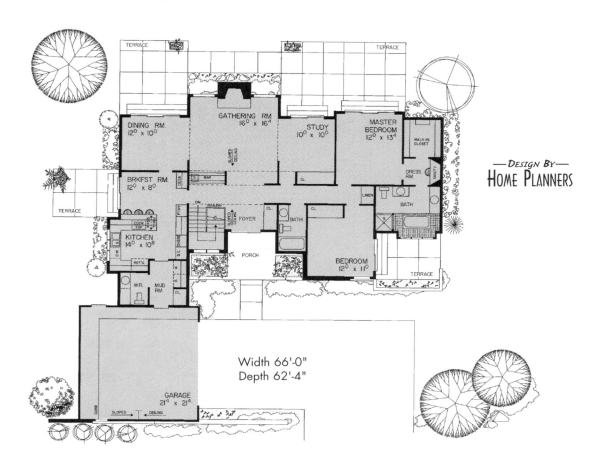

— DESIGN BY —
HOME PLANNERS

Width 66'-0"
Depth 62'-4"

Design 2877
Square Footage: 2,612
L D

◆ This dramatic Post-Modern design features a popular floor plan with an outstanding master bedroom suite. The bedroom itself is spacious, has a sloped ceiling, a large walk-in closet and sliding glass doors to the terrace. The bath contains two closets, twin vanities, a built-in seat and a corner tub. Three secondary bedrooms are served by a full bath. The living area of this one-story has the formal areas in the front and the informal areas to the rear. Both the living room and the family room have fireplaces. A U-shaped kitchen is graced with a pass-through counter to the breakfast room. A wide terrace enhances outdoor living. A handy mud room features a wash room and access to the two-car garage—note the large storage space.

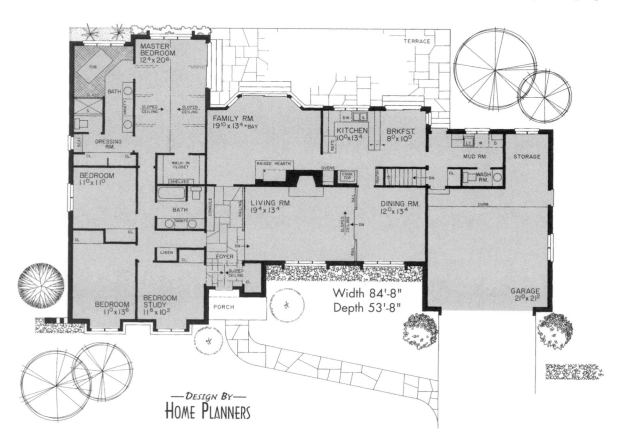

Width 84'-8"
Depth 53'-8"

— DESIGN BY —
Home Planners

Design 2528
Square Footage: 1,754

D

—DESIGN BY—
HOME PLANNERS

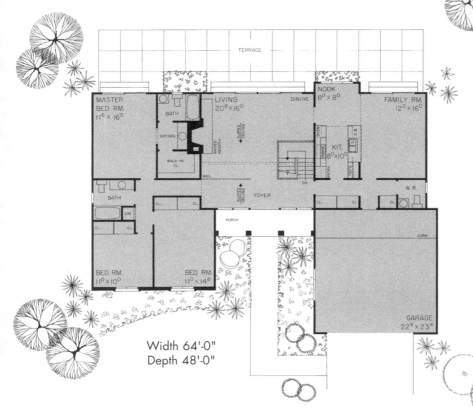

TERRACE

MASTER
BED RM.
11⁶ x 16⁰

BATH

DRESS

WALK-IN
CL.

LIVING
20⁸ x 16⁰

DINING

RAISED HEARTH

SLOPED CEILING

NOOK
8⁰ x 8⁰

OVEN

KIT.
8⁰ x 10⁰

REF.

FAMILY RM.
12⁰ x 16⁰

BATH

CL.

CL.

FOYER

DN.

RAIL

SLOPED CEILING

PORCH

CL.

CL.

W. R.

CL.

CURB

GARAGE
22⁴ x 23⁴

BED RM.
11⁰ x 10⁰

BED RM.
11⁰ x 14⁸

Width 64'-0"
Depth 48'-0"

◆ This inviting, U-shaped Western ranch adaptation offers outstanding living potential behind its double front doors and flanking glass panels. In under 1,800 square feet there are three bedrooms and 2½ baths. The master bath is luxurious with two sinks, a dressing area and a large walk-in closet. The formal living room is open to the dining room and offers a raised-hearth fireplace and a sloped ceiling. The functional kitchen features an adjacent breakfast nook and has easy access to the informal family room. A rear terrace stretches the width of the home and is accessible from the master bedroom, living room and family room. Stairs lead to a basement that may be developed at a later time.

— DESIGN BY —

HOME PLANNERS

Garage Plan G201

GARAGE
35⁰ x 23⁰

GUEST-
STUDIO
11⁸ x 11⁰

GARAGE
23² x 23⁰

BATH

HVAC

KITCHENETTE

CURB

CURB

Quote One®

Cost to build? See page 436
to order complete cost estimate
to build this house in your area!

◆ Frank Lloyd Wright had a knack for enhancing the environment with the homes he designed. These two adaptations reflect his purest Prairie style complemented by a brick exterior, a multitude of windows and a low-slung hip roof. The foyer introduces a gallery wall to display your artwork. To the right, an archway leads to a formal dining room lined with a wall of windows. Nearby, the spacious kitchen features an island snack bar. Centrally located, the two-story family/great room provides an ideal setting for formal or informal gatherings. If philosophical discussions heat up, they can be continued in the open courtyard. At this point, the two plans diverge. In 3637, the left wing contains the sleeping quarters and an office/den, plus a formal living room with the master suite on the right side of the plan. In 3636, the office/den and all bedrooms including the master are on the left and a two-car garage is on the right. Plans for a detached garage, Plan G201 are included with Design 3637.

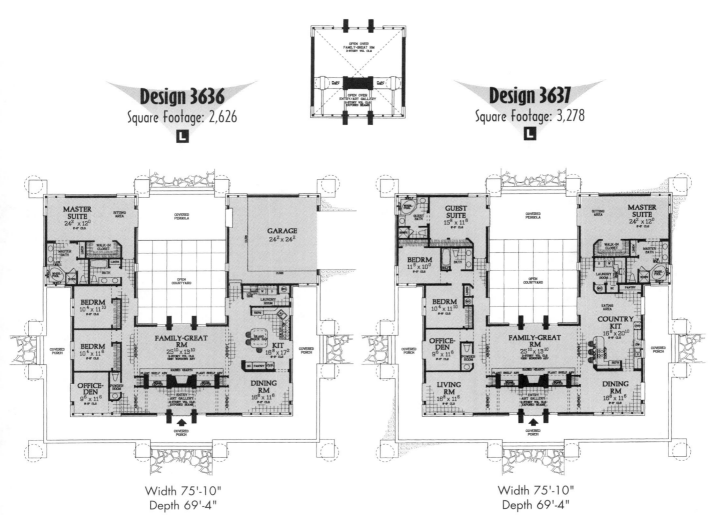

Design 3636
Square Footage: 2,626
L

Design 3637
Square Footage: 3,278
L

Width 75'-10"
Depth 69'-4"

Width 75'-10"
Depth 69'-4"

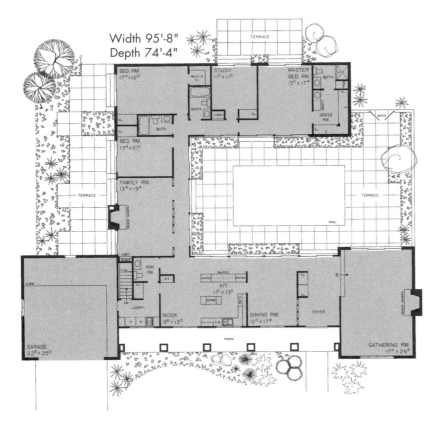

Width 95'-8"
Depth 74'-4"

TERRACE

BED RM.
17⁴x12⁰

STUDY
11⁰x11⁰

MASTER
BED RM.
13⁰x17⁴

BATH

WALK-IN
CL.

BATH

LINEN

DRESS
RM.

BED RM.
13⁴x10⁰

FAMILY RM.
13⁴x19⁴

TERRACE

POOL

TERRACE

PDR. RM.

LNDRY.

NOOK
9⁶x13⁰

KIT.
11⁰x13⁰

RANGE

OVENS PANTRY

SNACKS

DINING RM.
12⁰x17⁴

FOYER

PORCH

GARAGE
22⁸x25⁰

GATHERING RM.
17⁴x26⁸

◆ If you have a growing active family, the chances are good that they will want their new home to relate to the outdoors. This distinctive design puts a premium on private outdoor living. And you don't have to install a swimming pool to get the most enjoyment from this home. Developing this area as a garden court will provide the indoor living areas with a breathtaking awareness of nature's beauty. Notice the fine zoning of the plan and how each area has its own sliding glass doors to provide an unrestricted view. Three bedrooms plus study are serviced by three baths. The family and gathering rooms provide two great living areas and the kitchen is most efficient. Of special note is the master suite with dressing room, two sinks and linen closet.

Design 2343
Square Footage: 3,110

Width 55'-6"
Depth 57'-6"

DECK

BEDROOM NO. 3
11'-6" X 11'-0"

GREAT ROOM
14'-0" X 17'-6"

BREAKFAST
11'-4" X 8'-6"

KITCHEN
11'-4" X 10'-0"

MASTER
BEDROOM
12'-4" X 15'-6"

BATH

FOYER
6'-6" X 5'-0"

DN

HIS

MASTER
BATH

BEDROOM NO. 2
11'-0" X 12'-2"

STOOP

DINING ROOM
11'-4" X 10'-0"

PWDR.

LAUNDRY

HERS

TWO-CAR GARAGE
20'-4" X 19'-4"

QUOTE ONE®

Cost to build? See page 436
to order complete cost estimate
to build this house in your area!

WORKSHOP/
STORAGE

FUTURE
FAMILY ROOM
14'-0" X 17'-6"

FUTURE
GAME ROOM
11'-4" X 18'-6"

FUTURE
GUEST BEDROOM
11'-10" X 14'-6"

MECHANICAL

STOOP
ABOVE

UP.

FUTURE
BATH

STORAGE

SLAB ON GRADE

— DESIGN BY —
DESIGN TRADITIONS

One-Story Homes With European Influence

◆ Charmingly compact, this one-story home is as beautiful as it is practical. The impressive arch over the double front door is repeated with an arched window in the formal dining room. This room opens to a spacious great room with fireplace and is nearby the kitchen and bayed breakfast area. Split sleeping arrangements put the master suite with His and Hers walk-in closets at the right of the plan and two family bedrooms at the left. Additional space in the basement can later be developed as the family grows.

Design T039
Square Footage: 1,684

© American Home Gallery, Ltd.

Design P196
Square Footage: 2,193
Bonus Room: 400 sq. ft.

◆ Arched windows, corner quoins and stonework accent the facade on this attractive stucco home. Inside, the family room stretches from the foyer to the back of the house, where a fireplace is flanked by windows. The spacious island kitchen is handy to the formal dining room, which is defined by columns and lighted by a massive multi-paned window. Other features of the kitchen include a pass-through to the family room, a good-sized pantry and a sunny breakfast area with a French door to the backyard. To the left of the foyer, the formal living room could be used as a family bedroom, joining two others on that side of the house. The luxurious master suite is on the right and includes a sitting room and a pampering bath. Please specify basement or crawlspace foundation when ordering.

Floor plan labels:

Bedroom 2
12¹ x 11⁶

RADIUS WINDOW · FPL. · RADIUS WINDOW

FRENCH DOOR

PANTRY

Breakfast

DESK

TRAY CEILING

Sitting Room

Master Suite
15⁰ x 18⁰

Bath

LINEN

Family Room
16⁰ x 19⁶
13'-5" HIGH CEILING

ISLAND

DW.

PASS THRU

Kitchen

REF.

RANGE

PLANT SHELF ABOVE

FRENCH DOOR

Laund.

Vaulted M.Bath

SHWR.

Bedroom 3
10¹⁰ x 11⁰

PLANT SHELF ABOVE

COATS

OPT. DOOR

Foyer
13'-5" CEILING

W/D

K.S.

LINEN

W.i.c.

W.i.c.

Living Room / Opt. Bedroom 4
11⁰ x 12²

Dining Room
12¹ x 12⁰
13'-5" HIGH CEILING

STAIRS UP

STAIRS TO OPT. BSMT.

COVERED ENTRY

Storage

Garage
21⁰ x 21⁹

copyright © 1995 frank betz associates, inc.

W.i.c.

Bath

STAIRS DN.

Opt. Bonus
11⁰ x 20⁰

Width 64'-6"
Depth 59'-0"

—Design by—
Frank Betz
Associates, Inc.

182

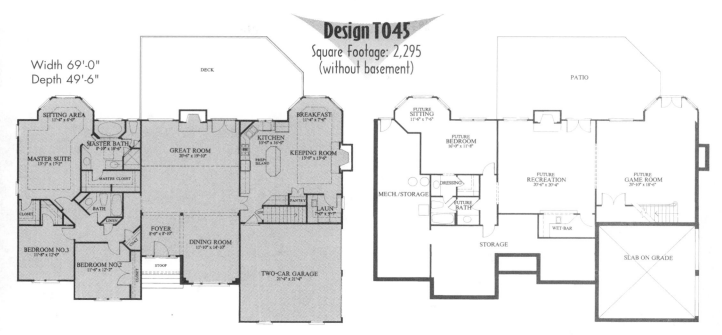

Width 69'-0"
Depth 49'-6"

Design T045
Square Footage: 2,295
(without basement)

First Floor Plan (left):
- SITTING AREA 11'-4" x 6'-0"
- MASTER SUITE 13'-2" x 19'-2"
- MASTER BATH 8'-10" x 10'-6"
- MASTER CLOSET
- BATH
- LINEN
- CLOSET
- BEDROOM NO.3 11'-8" x 12'-0"
- BEDROOM NO.2 11'-6" x 12'-2"
- CLOSET
- STOOP
- COAT
- FOYER 8'-9" x 8'-10"
- DINING ROOM 13'-10" x 14'-10"
- TWO-CAR GARAGE 21'-4" x 21'-4"
- DECK
- GREAT ROOM 20'-6" x 19'-10"
- PREP ISLAND
- KITCHEN 10'-0" x 16'-0"
- BREAKFAST 11'-4" x 7'-6"
- KEEPING ROOM 13'-0" x 13'-6"
- PANTRY
- LAUN 7'-0" x 9'-0"
- DN

Basement Plan (right):
- PATIO
- FUTURE SITTING 11'-6" x 7'-6"
- FUTURE BEDROOM 16'-0" x 11'-8"
- MECH./STORAGE
- DRESSING
- FUTURE BATH
- FUTURE RECREATION 20'-6" x 20'-4"
- FUTURE GAME ROOM 20'-10" x 18'-6"
- WET-BAR
- STORAGE
- SLAB ON GRADE

◆ The abundance of details in this plan make it the finest in one-story living. The great room and formal dining room are loosely defined by a simple column at the entry foyer, allowing for an open, dramatic sense of space. The kitchen with prep island shares the right side of the plan with a bayed breakfast area and keeping room with fireplace. Sleeping accommodations to the left of the plan include a master suite with sitting area, two closets and separate tub and shower. Two family bedrooms share a full bath. Additional living and sleeping space can be developed in the unfinished basement.

—DESIGN BY—
DESIGN TRADITIONS

© American Home Gallery, Ltd.

Design T011
Square Footage: 2,770

◆ The European-inspired excitement of this stucco home can be seen in its use of large, abundant windows. Inside, the spacious foyer leads directly to a large great room with a massive fireplace and French doors that lead outside. The banquet-sized dining room, just off the foyer, receives the brilliant light of the triple window, and features a dramatic, vaulted ceiling. The kitchen and breakfast room add another plus by providing openness. The spacious kitchen also offers all the amenities of a walk-in pantry, desk, breakfast bar and a large convenient laundry room. The master suite features a separate sitting area with a cathedral ceiling and access to the patio for a private owners' retreat. The two additional bedrooms have their own vanity within a shared bath. This home is designed with a basement foundation.

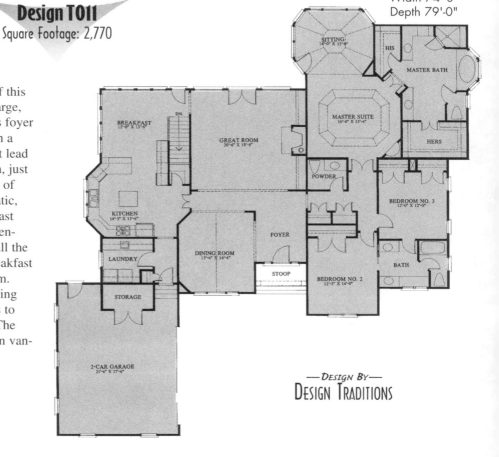

Width 74'-0"
Depth 79'-0"

—DESIGN BY—
DESIGN TRADITIONS

Design T099
Square Footage: 2,090

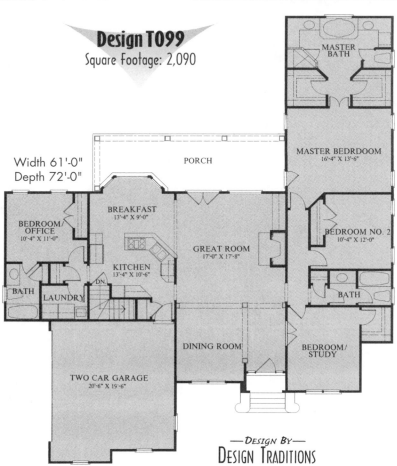

Width 61'-0"
Depth 72'-0"

MASTER BATH

MASTER BEDRDOOM
16'-4" X 13'-6"

PORCH

BREAKFAST
13'-4" X 9'-0"

BEDROOM/ OFFICE
10'-4" X 11'-0"

GREAT ROOM
17'-0" X 17'-8"

KITCHEN
13'-4" X 10'-6"

BEDROOM NO. 2
10'-4" X 12'-0"

BATH

LAUNDRY

DN.

BATH

DINING ROOM

BEDROOM/ STUDY

TWO CAR GARAGE
20'-6" X 19'-6"

— DESIGN BY —
DESIGN TRADITIONS

◆ People will surely stop to admire this exquisite house. Its European styling will work well in a variety of environments. As for livability, this plan has it all. Begin with the front door which opens into the dining and great rooms—the latter complete with fireplace and doors that open onto the back porch. The kitchen combines with the breakfast nook to create ample space for meals and quiet socializing—whatever your fancy. This plan incorporates four bedrooms; you may want to use one bedroom as an office and another as a study. The master bedroom houses a fabulous bath; be sure to check out the walk-in closets and spa tub. This home is designed with a basement foundation.

QUOTE ONE®
Cost to build? See page 436
to order complete cost estimate
to build this house in your area!

185

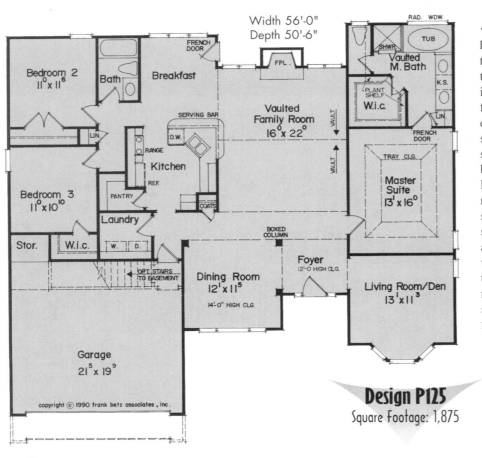

Width 56'-0"
Depth 50'-6"

Bedroom 2
11⁰ x 11⁶

Bath

Breakfast

FRENCH DOOR

RAD. WDW.

TUB

SHWR

Vaulted M. Bath

PLANT SHELF

W.i.c.

K.S.

LIN.

FRENCH DOOR

FPL.

Vaulted Family Room
16⁰ x 22⁰

VAULT

SERVING BAR

D.W.

RANGE

Kitchen

REF.

PANTRY

COATS

Bedroom 3
11⁰ x 10¹⁰

Laundry

Stor.

W.i.c.

W.

D.

OPT. STAIRS TO BASEMENT

BOXED COLUMN

Dining Room
12' x 11⁵
14'-0" HIGH CLG.

Foyer
12'-0" HIGH CLG.

TRAY CLG.

Master Suite
13' x 16⁰

Living Room/Den
13' x 11³

Garage
21⁵ x 19⁹

copyright © 1990 frank betz associates, inc.

Design P125
Square Footage: 1,875

—DESIGN BY—
FRANK BETZ ASSOCIATES, INC.

◆ The floor plan of this compact home offers several options for entertaining. Create a formal zone across the front of the house, or use the family room for guests and provide a den for quieter pursuits. For meals, choose either the formal dining room or the sunny breakfast area. A right-angled serving bar connects the kitchen with both the breakfast room and the family room. For privacy, two family bedrooms are separated from the master suite. Note the fine bath in the master suite: vaulted ceiling, garden tub, separate shower and double sinks, plus a walk-in closet. A two-car garage sits to the front of the plan to shield interior spaces from street noise. Please specify basement, crawlspace or slab foundation when ordering.

© American Home Gallery, Ltd.

2-CAR GARAGE
21'-3" x 26'-0"

— DESIGN BY —
DESIGN TRADITIONS

LAUN.

BREAKFAST
11'-6" x 12'-0"

KITCHEN
14'-0" x 16'-6"

DN

PAN

GREAT ROOM
16'-0" x 20'-6"

Width 72'-0"
Depth 73'-0"

M. BATH

SITTING

MASTER SUITE
15'-6" x 23'-3"

MASTER
CLOSET

BEDROOM No.3
12'-0" x 13'-6"

DINING ROOM
13'-0" x 13'-6"

FOYER

STUDY/
BEDROOM No.2
13'-0" x 13'-6"

GUEST ROOM/
CHILDRENS
DEN
13'-6" x 16'-9"

Design T008
Square Footage: 2,785

◆ The balance and symmetry of this European home have an inviting quality. An entry foyer allowing a grand view out of the back of the house leads directly to the great room. Just off the great room are a convenient and functional gourmet kitchen and a bright adjoining bay-windowed breakfast room. The master suite enjoys privacy in its position at the rear of the home. Three other bedrooms, one which might serve as a guest room or children's den and one that might work well as a study, round out the sleeping accommodations. This home is designed with a basement foundation.

Quote One®
Cost to build? See page 436
to order complete cost estimate
to build this house in your area!

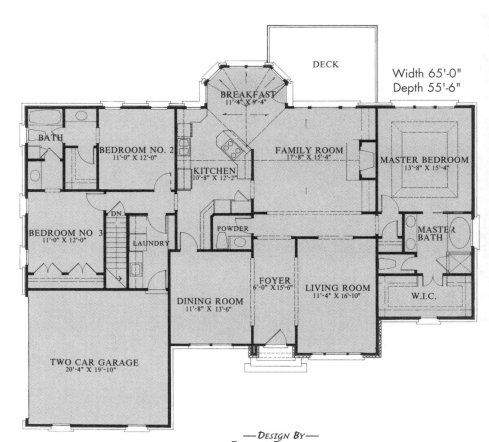

Design T138
Square Footage: 2,095

Width 65'-0"
Depth 55'-6"

DECK

BREAKFAST
11'-4" X 9'-4"

FAMILY ROOM
17'-8" X 15'-4"

MASTER BEDROOM
13'-8" X 15'-4"

BATH

BEDROOM NO. 2
11'-0" X 12'-0"

KITCHEN
10'-8" X 12'-2"

MASTER BATH

DN.

POWDER

BEDROOM NO 3
11'-0" X 12'-0"

LAUNDRY

W.I.C.

FOYER
6'-0" X 15'-6"

LIVING ROOM
11'-4" X 16'-10"

DINING ROOM
11'-8" X 13'-6"

TWO CAR GARAGE
20'-4" X 19'-10"

◆ This special cottage design carries a fully modern floor plan. The entry leads to open living areas with a dining room and a living room flanking the foyer. The family room—with a fireplace and built-in bookcases—is nearby the bright breakfast room with deck access. The efficiently patterned kitchen provides a helpful lead-in to the dining room. Two secondary bedrooms make up the left side of the plan. A full, compartmented bath connects them. In the master bedroom suite, a tiered ceiling and a bath with dual vanities, a whirlpool tub, a separate shower, a compartmented toilet and a walk-in closet are sure to please. The two-car, side-load garage opens to the laundry room. This home is designed with a basement foundation.

— DESIGN BY —
DESIGN TRADITIONS

© American Home Gallery, Ltd.

◆ Interesting rooflines, a stucco-and-stone facade and repeated arches at the entry give this home plenty of curb appeal. Inside, the formal dining and living rooms are separated by decorative columns. Large crowds can easily spill over into the vaulted family room, with its delightful fireplace, or to the backyard. A covered porch is reached from the breakfast nook that opens off the efficient kitchen. The sleeping zone includes a luxurious master suite and two family bedrooms. If you choose, you may develop space on a second level which could include an additional bedroom and bath and a bonus room to use as a bedroom or as home office space. Please specify basement or crawlspace foundation when ordering.

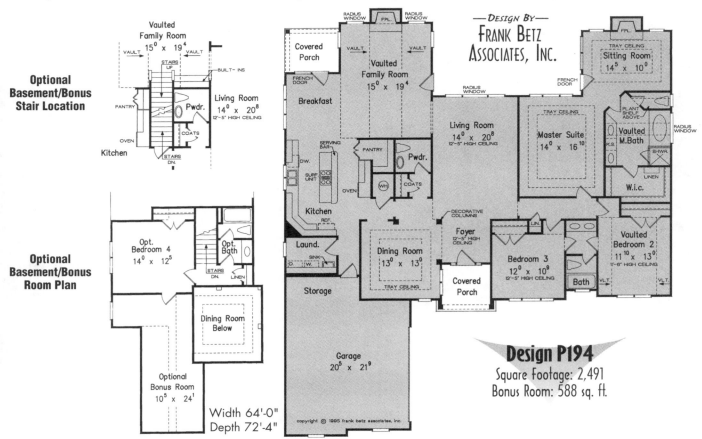

Optional Basement/Bonus Stair Location

Optional Basement/Bonus Room Plan

Width 64'-0"
Depth 72'-4"

— DESIGN BY —
FRANK BETZ
ASSOCIATES, INC.

Design P194
Square Footage: 2,491
Bonus Room: 588 sq. ft.

copyright © 1995 frank betz associates, inc.

189

Design P176
Square Footage: 2,403
Bonus Room: 285 sq. ft.

Width 60'-0"
Depth 67'-0"

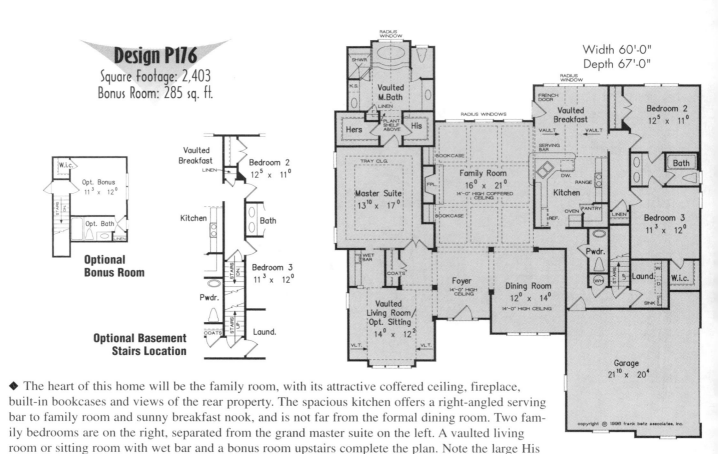

Optional Bonus Room

- W.i.c.
- Opt. Bonus 11³ x 12⁰
- Opt. Bath
- STAIRS DN
- LINEN

Optional Basement Stairs Location

- Vaulted Breakfast
- LINEN
- Bedroom 2 12⁵ x 11⁰
- Kitchen
- Bath
- Bedroom 3 11³ x 12⁰
- STAIRS DN
- Pwdr.
- STAIRS UP
- COATS
- Laund.

Floor plan labels:
- RADIUS WINDOW
- SHWR
- K.S.
- Vaulted M.Bath
- LINEN
- Hers
- PLANT SHELF ABOVE
- His
- TRAY CLG.
- BOOKCASE
- Master Suite 13¹⁰ x 17⁰
- FPL.
- Family Room 16⁰ x 21⁰ 14'-0" HIGH COFFERED CEILING
- BOOKCASE
- RADIUS WINDOWS
- FRENCH DOOR
- Vaulted Breakfast
- RADIUS WINDOW
- VAULT
- VAULT
- SERVING BAR
- Bedroom 2 12⁵ x 11⁰
- Bath
- DW.
- Kitchen
- RANGE
- OVEN
- PANTRY
- REF.
- LINEN
- Bedroom 3 11³ x 12⁰
- WET BAR
- COATS
- Foyer 14'-0" HIGH CEILING
- Dining Room 12⁰ x 14⁰ 14'-0" HIGH CEILING
- Pwdr.
- WH
- STAIRS
- Laund.
- W.i.c.
- SINK
- Vaulted Living Room/ Opt. Sitting 14⁰ x 12²
- VLT.
- VLT.
- Garage 21¹⁰ x 20⁴

copyright © 1998 frank betz associates, inc.

◆ The heart of this home will be the family room, with its attractive coffered ceiling, fireplace, built-in bookcases and views of the rear property. The spacious kitchen offers a right-angled serving bar to family room and sunny breakfast nook, and is not far from the formal dining room. Two family bedrooms are on the right, separated from the grand master suite on the left. A vaulted living room or sitting room with wet bar and a bonus room upstairs complete the plan. Note the large His and Hers walk in closets in the master bedroom, the walk-in closet in Bedroom 3 and the large corner shower in the master bath. Please specify basement or crawlspace foundation when ordering.

— DESIGN BY —
FRANK BETZ ASSOCIATES, INC.

190

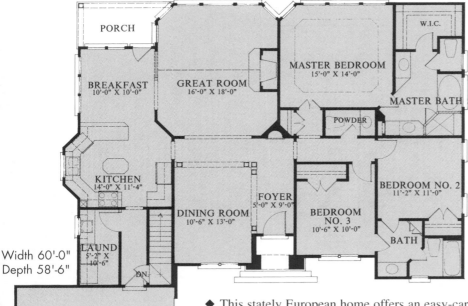

PORCH

BREAKFAST
10'-0" X 10'-0"

GREAT ROOM
16'-0" X 18'-0"

MASTER BEDROOM
15'-0" X 14'-0"

W.I.C.

MASTER BATH

POWDER

KITCHEN
14'-0" X 11'-4"

FOYER
5'-0" X 9'-0"

DINING ROOM
10'-6" X 13'-0"

BEDROOM NO. 2
11'-2" X 11'-0"

BEDROOM
NO. 3
10'-6" X 10'-0"

BATH

LAUND
5'-2" X
10'-6"

DN.

Width 60'-0"
Depth 58'-6"

TWO CAR GARAGE
20'-4" X 19'-4"

Design T071
Square Footage: 1,815

— DESIGN BY —
DESIGN TRADITIONS

Quote One®

Cost to build? See page 436
to order complete cost estimate
to build this house in your area!

◆ This stately European home offers an easy-care stucco exterior with finely detailed windows and a majestic front door that furthers a graceful presence. Inside, a grand, columned foyer opens to both the formal dining room and the great room with a vaulted ceiling and a fireplace. The spacious, well-appointed kitchen, open to a breakfast room and adjacent to the formal dining area, makes serving and entertaining easy and delightful work. Nestled away at the opposite end of the home, the master suite combines perfect solitude with elegant luxury. Features include a double-door entry, tray ceiling, niche detail and private rear deck. Two additional bedrooms, a full bath and a powder room accomodate other members of the family as well as guests. This home is designed with a basement foundation.

© American Home Gallery, Ltd.

Sitting Area

TRAY CEILING

Master Suite
16⁶ x 14⁰

FRENCH DOOR

ACTIVE DORMER W/ RAD. WDW.

RAD. WDW.

Breakfast
11'-0" HIGH CLG.

RAD. WDW.

RAD. WDW.

FRENCH DOOR

W.i.c.

SHWR.

Vaulted M.Bath

RAD. WDW.

VAULT

VAULT

Vaulted Family Room
15⁸ x 20²

FPL.

COATS

DBL. OVEN

Kitchen
11'-0" HIGH CLG.

RANGE

ISLAND

DW.

PANTRY

Bedroom 2
11⁰ x 13⁰

Bath

W.i.c.

LINEN

LINEN

FIREP.

VAULT

DECORATIVE COLUMNS

SINK

W.H.

W.

D.

Bedroom 3
12¹⁰ x 11⁶

PLANT SHELF ABOVE

W.i.c.

Pwdr.

ARCHED OPENINGS

Foyer
14'-0" HIGH CLG.

Dining Room
12⁰ x 14⁰
14'-0" HIGH CLG.

Laund.

OPT. STAIR TO BSMT.

FRENCH DOORS

Living Room
13⁵ x 14⁰

COVERED ENTRY

Garage
20⁵ x 20⁹

copyright © 1995 frank betz associates, inc.

GARAGE LOCATION WITH BASEMENT

—DESIGN BY—

FRANK BETZ
ASSOCIATES, INC.

Width 62'-0"
Depth 61'-0"

Design P127
Square Footage: 2,322

◆ Gables, arches and a stone-and-stucco exterior give this home plenty of curb appeal. Inside, you'll find a floor plan designed for easy entertaining. The dining room is close to the living room for formal occasions and opens into the spacious family room for informal gatherings. High ceilings and decorative columns are added attractions. The gourmet island kitchen offers a pantry, double ovens and a snack bar that serves both the family room and the sunny breakfast nook. The master suite is a homeowner's delight with a bayed sitting area, access to the backyard, a tray ceiling, huge walk-in closet and luxurious bath. Two family bedrooms and a full bath complete the plan. Please specify basement, crawlspace or slab foundation when ordering.

© American Home Gallery, Ltd.

Design T109
Square Footage: 1,770

Width 48'-0"
Depth 47'-5"

DECK

DN

BREAKFAST
11'-4" X 7'-4"

GREAT ROOM
14'-0" X 19'-6"

MASTER
BEDROOM
12'-6" X 16'-0"

W.I.C.

MASTER
BATH

KITCHEN
11'-4" X 12'-0"

W.I.C.

W.I.C.

UP

DN

FOYER
5'-0" X 8'-8"

DINING ROOM
11'-4" X 12'-6"

POWDER

LAUNDRY

BEDROOM NO. 3
12'-0" X 11'-0"

COAT

STOOP

BATH

BEDROOM NO. 2
12'-9" X 11'-9"

— DESIGN BY —
DESIGN TRADITIONS

◆ Perfect for a sloping lot, this European one-story plan offers privacy for the sleeping quarters by placing them a few steps up from the living area. The master suite is secluded off the central hallway, partitioned by double doors which are echoed by lovely French doors to the rear deck and by doors leading to a sumptuous bath with a windowed garden tub. Secondary bedrooms or guest quarters share a full bath with a double-bowl vanity. A spacious great room with centered fireplace offers rear deck access and opens to the breakfast room with a boxed window. The well-appointed U-shaped kitchen easily serves both formal and casual eating areas. The lower level offers bonus space that may be developed for recreational use. This home is designed with a basement foundation.

QUOTE ONE®
Cost to build? See page 436
to order complete cost estimate
to build this house in your area!

Design 7226
Square Footage: 1,479

◆ A covered porch and interesting window treatments add charisma to this cheerful ranch home. The entry opens onto a sunny great room warmed by a center fireplace framed with transom windows. Nearby, an efficient kitchen is highlighted by an island snack bar, a corner sink flanked with windows and access to the backyard. The spacious master suite features a walk-in closet and a pampering master bath with a whirlpool tub and compartmented toilet and shower area. Two secondary bedrooms—one an optional den designed with French doors—share a full hall bath.

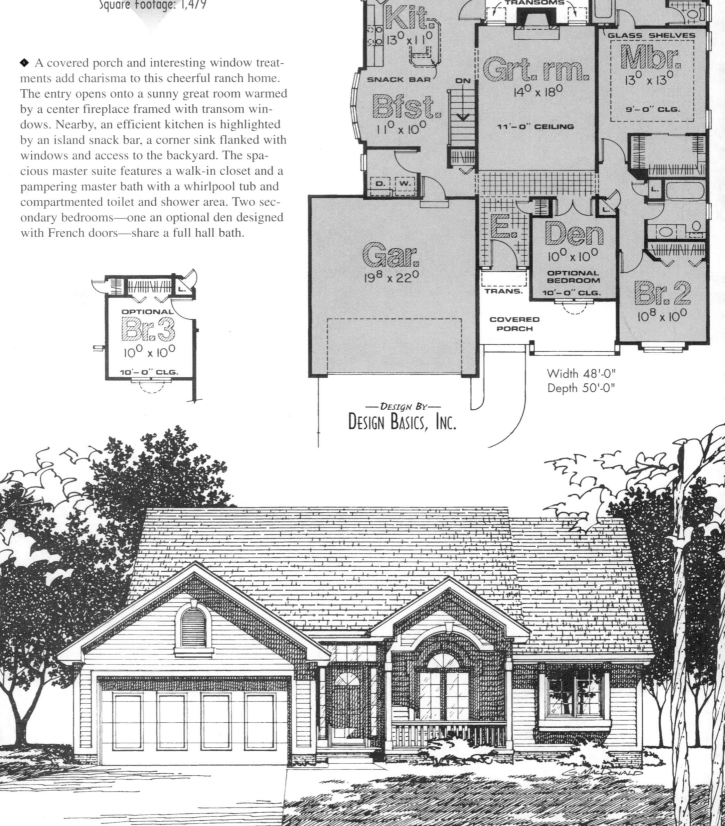

Kit. 13⁰ x 11⁰

SNACK BAR

Bfst. 11⁰ x 10⁰

D. W.

Grt. rm. 14⁰ x 18⁰

11'-0" CEILING

TRANSOMS

ON

Mbr. 13⁰ x 13⁰

9'-0" CLG.

WHIRLPOOL

GLASS SHELVES

P.

R.

L.

L.

Gar. 19⁸ x 22⁰

E.

TRANS.

Den 10⁰ x 10⁰

OPTIONAL BEDROOM 10'-0" CLG.

Br. 2 10⁸ x 10⁰

COVERED PORCH

Width 48'-0"
Depth 50'-0"

—DESIGN BY—
DESIGN BASICS, INC.

OPTIONAL **Br. 3** 10⁰ x 10⁰

10'-0" CLG.

L.

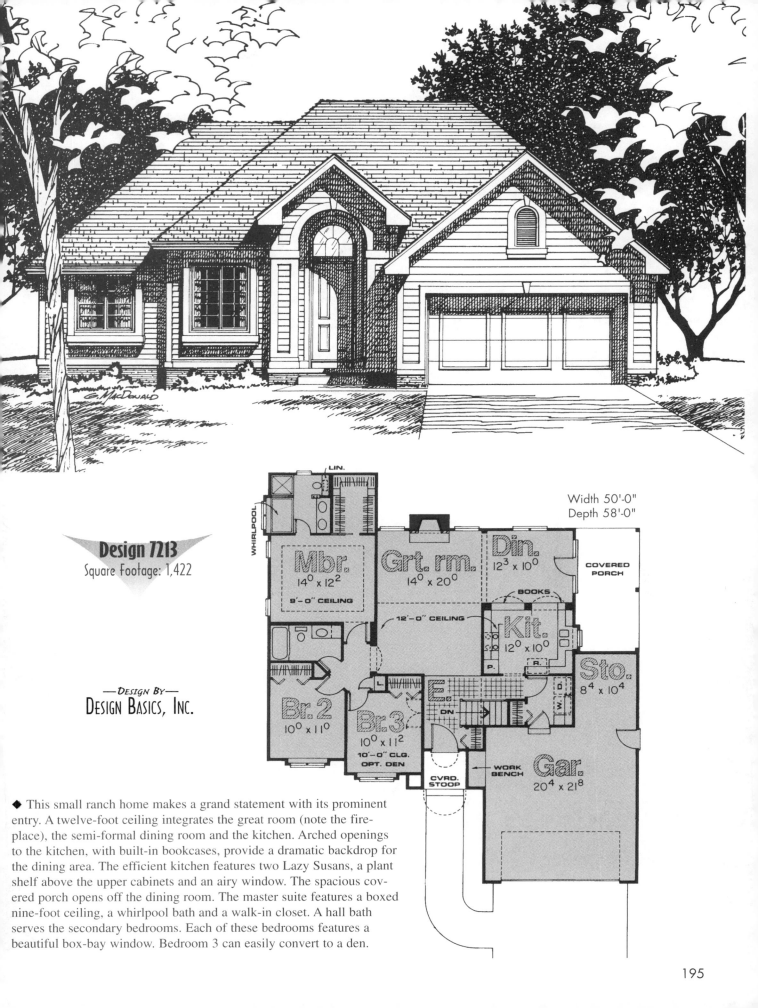

Design 7213
Square Footage: 1,422

—DESIGN BY—
DESIGN BASICS, INC.

Width 50'-0"
Depth 58'-0"

LIN.

WHIRLPOOL

Mbr.
14⁰ x 12²
9'-0" CEILING

Grt. rm.
14⁰ x 20⁰

Din.
12³ x 10⁰

COVERED
PORCH

12'-0" CEILING

BOOKS

Kit.
12⁰ x 10⁰

P.

R.

Sto.
8⁴ x 10⁴

Br. 2
10⁰ x 11⁰

Br. 3
10⁰ x 11²
10'-0" CLG.
OPT. DEN

L.

E

DN

W D

D

CVRD.
STOOP

WORK
BENCH

Gar.
20⁴ x 21⁸

◆ This small ranch home makes a grand statement with its prominent entry. A twelve-foot ceiling integrates the great room (note the fireplace), the semi-formal dining room and the kitchen. Arched openings to the kitchen, with built-in bookcases, provide a dramatic backdrop for the dining area. The efficient kitchen features two Lazy Susans, a plant shelf above the upper cabinets and an airy window. The spacious covered porch opens off the dining room. The master suite features a boxed nine-foot ceiling, a whirlpool bath and a walk-in closet. A hall bath serves the secondary bedrooms. Each of these bedrooms features a beautiful box-bay window. Bedroom 3 can easily convert to a den.

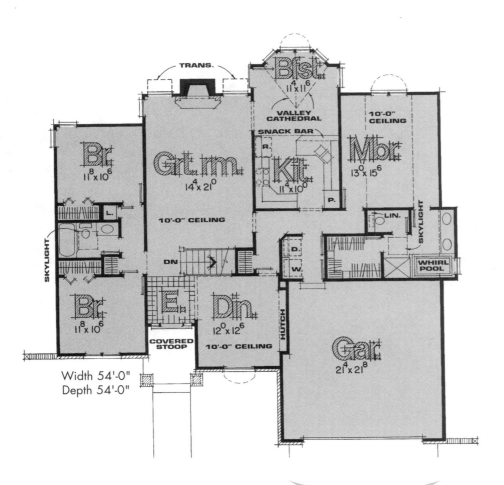

TRANS.

Bfst.
4 x 6
11 x 11

VALLEY CATHEDRAL

SNACK BAR

Br.
11⁸ x 10⁶

Grt. rm.
14⁴ x 21⁰

10'-0" CEILING

Kit.
11⁴ x 10⁰

R.

P.

**10'-0"
CEILING**

Mbr.
13⁰ x 15⁶

SKYLIGHT

L.

DN

D.

W.

LIN.

SKYLIGHT

**WHIRL
POOL**

Br.
11⁸ x 10⁶

E.

Dn.
12⁰ x 12⁶

HUTCH

**COVERED
STOOP**

10'-0" CEILING

Gar.
21⁴ x 21⁸

Width 54'-0"
Depth 54'-0"

◆ This volume-look home gives the impression of size and scope in just under 1,700 square feet. The large great room with fireplace is perfect for entertaining. The spacious kitchen has a snack bar and a breakfast room with a dramatic valley cathedral ceiling. Besides a large walk-in closet, other features in the master bedroom include a whirlpool tub, double vanity, skylit dressing area and convenient linen storage. Two family bedrooms share a full bath with a skylight and offer ample closet space.

—DESIGN BY—
DESIGN BASICS, INC.

Design 9237
Square Footage: 1,697

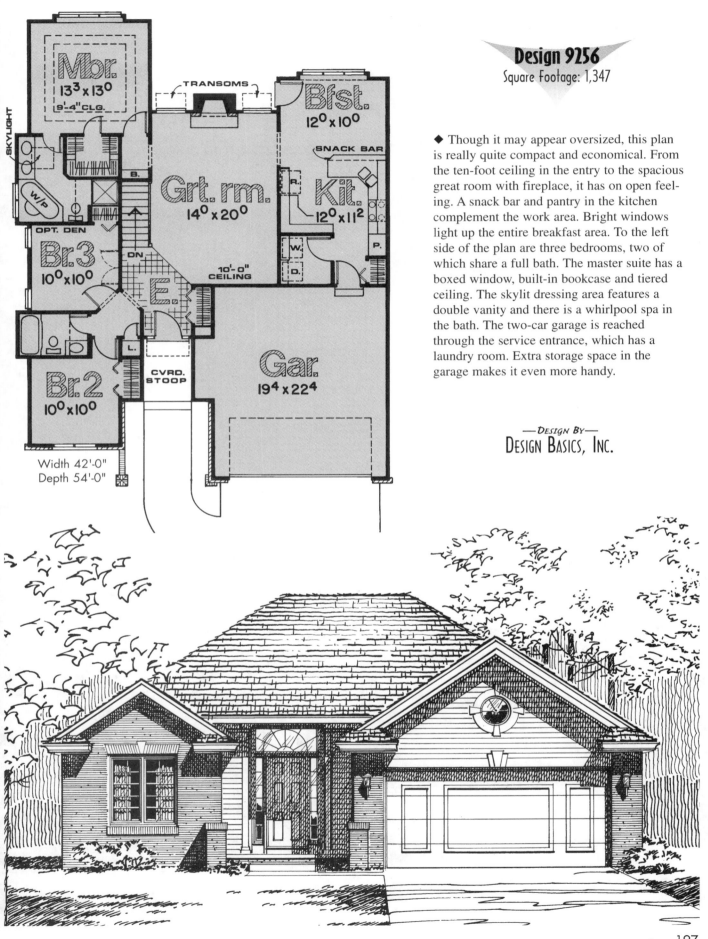

Design 9256
Square Footage: 1,347

Mbr.
13³ x 13⁰
9'-4" CLG.

SKYLIGHT

TRANSOMS

Bfst.
12⁰ x 10⁰

SNACK BAR

B.

Grt. rm.
14⁰ x 20⁰

R.

Kit.
12⁰ x 11²

OPT. DEN

DN

W.

Br.3
10⁰ x 10⁰

10'-0"
CEILING

E

D.

P.

L.

Br. 2
10⁰ x 10⁰

CVRD.
STOOP

Gar.
19⁴ x 22⁴

Width 42'-0"
Depth 54'-0"

◆ Though it may appear oversized, this plan is really quite compact and economical. From the ten-foot ceiling in the entry to the spacious great room with fireplace, it has on open feeling. A snack bar and pantry in the kitchen complement the work area. Bright windows light up the entire breakfast area. To the left side of the plan are three bedrooms, two of which share a full bath. The master suite has a boxed window, built-in bookcase and tiered ceiling. The skylit dressing area features a double vanity and there is a whirlpool spa in the bath. The two-car garage is reached through the service entrance, which has a laundry room. Extra storage space in the garage makes it even more handy.

—DESIGN BY—
DESIGN BASICS, INC.

Design 7230
Square Footage: 1,806

Br. 2
11⁰ x 11⁰

Br. 3
11⁰ x 11⁰

SHELVES

Bfst.
11⁴ x 11⁴

Kit.
12¹⁰ x 12⁰

Grt. rm.
15⁰ x 20⁰
10'-0" CEILING

LIN.

W.
D.

R.
P.
DN

Din.
11⁰ x 14⁰
10'-0" CLG.

E.

Mbr.
14⁰ x 15⁰
10'-0" CLG.

WHIRLPOOL

Gar.
23⁴ x 22⁴

COVERED PORCH

Width 55'-4"
Depth 56'-0"

—DESIGN BY—
DESIGN BASICS, INC.

◆ Beautiful columns and arched transoms are the focal points of this contemporary ranch home. The ten-foot entry opens to the formal dining room and the great room, which features a brick fireplace and arched windows. The large island kitchen offers an angled range, a multitude of cabinets and a sunny breakfast area with an atrium door to the backyard. Separate bedroom wings provide optimum privacy. The master wing to the right includes a whirlpool bath with a sloped ceiling, a plant shelf above dual lavatories and a large walk-in closet. The family bedrooms are at the opposite end of the house and share a full bath. The laundry room serves as a mudroom entry from the garage.

Design 9258
Square Footage: 2,498

◆ Elegant arches at the covered entry of this home give way to beautiful views of the formal dining room and living room inside. Ceilings in the main living areas and the master bedroom are vaulted. The gazebo dinette is open to the family room and to the gourmet kitchen, which includes an island cooktop and snack bar. Three bedrooms and a den are provided. One of these could become a sitting area for the master suite, if desired. A luxurious master bath provides twin vanities, a large walk-in closet and an oval whirlpool tub.

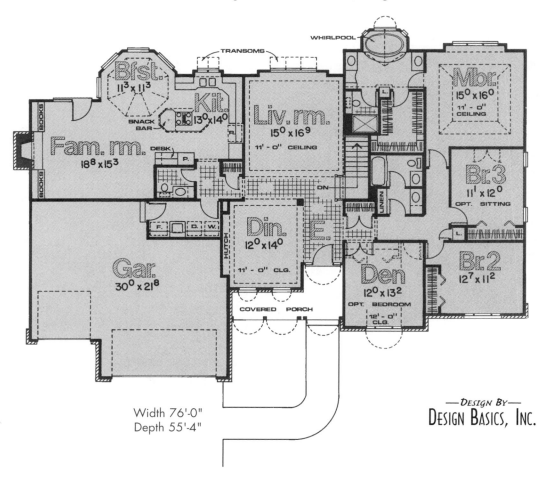

Bfst.
11³ x 11³

Kit.
13⁰ x 14⁰

Liv. rm.
15⁰ x 16⁹
11'-0" ceiling

Mbr.
15⁰ x 16⁰
11'-0" ceiling

Fam. rm.
18⁸ x 15³

Br.3
11' x 12⁰
OPT. SITTING

Gar.
30⁰ x 21⁸

Din.
12⁰ x 14⁰
11'-0" CLG.

Den
12⁰ x 13²
OPT. BEDROOM
11'-0" CLG.

Br.2
12⁷ x 11²

COVERED PORCH

Width 76'-0"
Depth 55'-4"

— DESIGN BY —
DESIGN BASICS, INC.

199

—DESIGN BY—
DESIGN BASICS, INC.

◆ This delightfully updated European plan has brick and stucco on the dramatic front elevation, showcased by sleek lines and decorative windows. An inviting entry has a view into the great room and is enhanced by an arched window and plant shelves above. The great room's fireplace is framed by sunny windows with transoms above. The bay-windowed dining room is nestled between the great room and the superb eat-in kitchen. The secluded master suite has a roomy walk-in closet and a luxurious bath with dual lavatories and whirlpool tub. Two additional bedrooms share a hall bath.

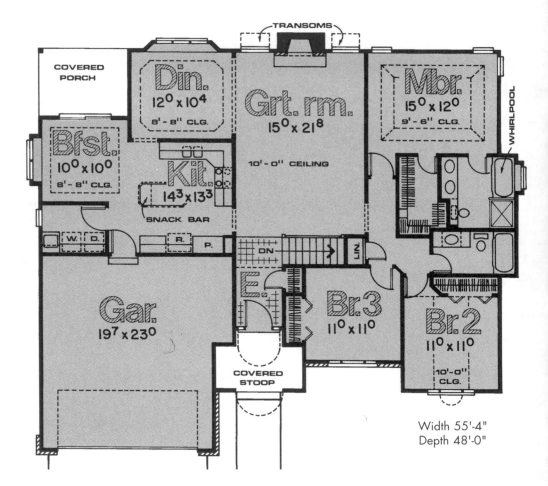

COVERED PORCH

Din.
$12^0 \times 10^4$
8'-8" CLG.

Grt. rm.
$15^0 \times 21^8$
10'-0" CEILING

TRANSOMS

Mbr.
$15^0 \times 12^0$
9'-6" CLG.

WHIRLPOOL

Bfst.
$10^0 \times 10^0$
8'-8" CLG.

Kit.
$14^3 \times 13^3$
SNACK BAR

W. D.   R.   P.

DN   LIN.

Gar.
$19^7 \times 23^0$

COVERED STOOP

Br.3
$11^0 \times 11^0$

Br.2
$11^0 \times 11^0$
10'-0" CLG.

Width 55'-4"
Depth 48'-0"

Design 9361
Square Footage: 1,666

© American Home Gallery, Ltd.

Design T030
Square Footage: 2,150

Quote One®
Cost to build? See page 436
to order complete cost estimate
to build this house in your area!

◆ This home draws its inspiration from both French and English country homes. From the foyer and across the spacious great room, French doors give a generous view of the covered rear porch. The adjoining dining room is subtly defined by the use of columns and a large triple window. The kitchen offers a large work island and adjoins the breakfast area and keeping room, which features a fireplace. The study to the front of the first floor could be a guest room. It shares a bath with the bedroom beside it. A secluded master suite with a coffered ceiling, angled bath and generous walk-in closet completes the plan. This home is designed with a basement foundation.

Width 64'-0"
Depth 64'-4"

— DESIGN BY —
DESIGN TRADITIONS

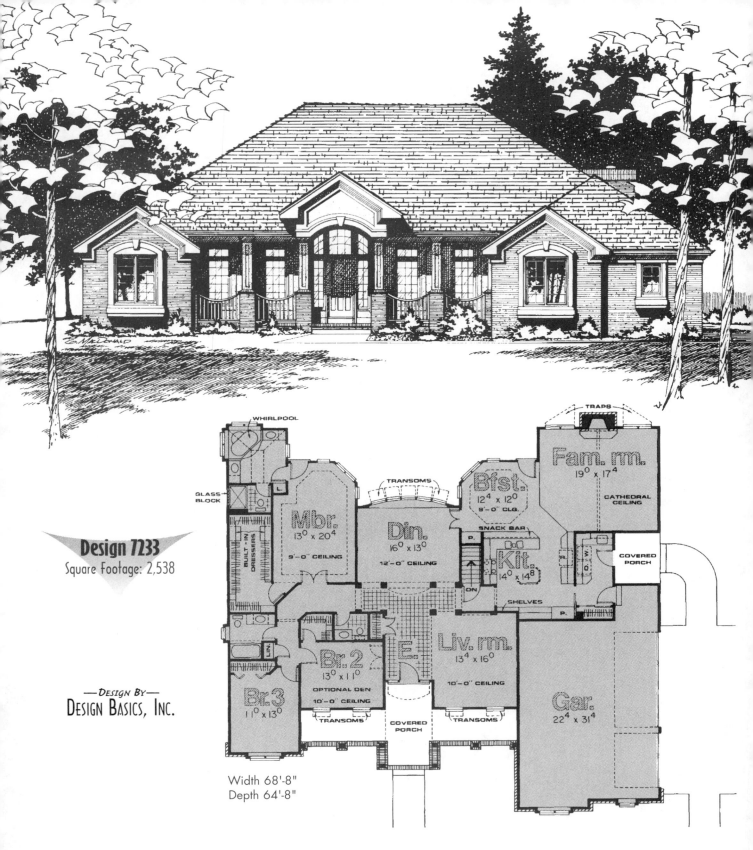

Design 7233
Square Footage: 2,538

— DESIGN BY —
DESIGN BASICS, INC.

Width 68'-8"
Depth 64'-8"

◆ The grand front porch gives this home a unique style and majestic curb appeal. Inside, the twelve-foot entry centers on the stately dining room with its bowed window. Both the living room and the second bedroom, which can be converted into a den, have ten-foot ceilings. The island kitchen features abundant pantries, a Lazy Susan and a snack bar. A sun filled breakfast area opens to the large family room with its cathe-dral ceiling and central fireplace. The private bedroom wing offers two secondary bedrooms and a luxurious master suite featuring a spacious walk-in closet with built-in dressers and private access to the backyard. It also includes a vaulted ceiling, a corner whirlpool tub and His and Hers vanities in the master bath. A three-car garage is reached through a service entrance in the laundry/mud room.

Kitchen

Design 9025
Square Footage: 2,481

Quote One®
Cost to build? See page 436
to order complete cost estimate
to build this house in your area!

◆ Multiple gables, bay windows and corner
windows with transoms above provide an
exterior reminiscent of English countryside
homes. A marble floor in the foyer extends
into the living room as an elegant fireplace
hearth. The formal dining room features an
eleven-foot ceiling, bay window and French
doors that open onto a private dining terrace. A spacious kitchen overlooks the breakfast area
and the family room which has a corner fireplace and
dramatic fourteen-foot ceiling with transom windows
above triple French doors. Another corner fireplace is
located in the master bedroom, which also contains a
built-in desk and triple French doors. The luxurious
master bath features mirrored doors at the large walk-in
closet, a dressing table and a whirlpool tub inset in a
bay window.

— DESIGN BY —
**LARRY W. GARNETT
& ASSOCIATES**

3-Car Garage

French Door   French Door

Bath
Linen
Mirrored
Doors

Master Bedroom
13'-4" x 22'-4"
10' Clg.

Family Room
14'-8" x 19'-4"
14' Clg.

Breakfast
10' x 10'

French Door

Courtyard

French Door

Desk

Kitchen
14' x 11'

Pantry

Dining
11' x 14'
11' Clg.

Desk

Util.

Bath 2

Living Room
15' x 19'-4"
11' Clg.

Foyer

Width 75'-4"
Depth 80'-8"

Bedroom 3
11'-4" x 13'

Bedroom 2
12' x 11'
11' Clg.

203

© American Home Gallery, Ltd.

Design T080
Square Footage: 2,120

BATH

BEDROOM NO. 3
11'-6" X 11'-0"

BEDROOM NO. 2
11'-4" X 11'-0"

SUN ROOM
12'-0" X 13'-9"

PORCH

MASTER BATH

W.I.C.

MASTER BEDROOM
13'-4" X 15'-8"

BREAKFAST
10'-0" X 9'-0"

FAMILY ROOM
18'-0" X 14'-0"

LAUNDRY

KITCHEN
12'-0" X 13'-9"

DN.

BATH

DINING ROOM
10'-6" X 13'-6"

FOYER

DEN
11'-4" X 12'-6"

TWO CAR GARAGE
20'-4" X 20'-8"

STOOP

Width 62'-0"
Depth 62'-6"

◆ Graceful arches accent this traditional facade and announce a floor plan that's just a little different than the rest. The foyer, formal dining room and an expansive family room, with a centered fireplace flanked by picture windows, are open to one another through columned archways. The master suite offers a coffered ceiling and a plush bath with a dressing area, as well as a private den. An island kitchen and breakfast room enjoy views through the spectacular sunroom. This home is designed with a basement foundation.

— DESIGN BY —
DESIGN TRADITIONS

QUOTE ONE®
Cost to build? See page 436
to order complete cost estimate
to build this house in your area!

Design 8923

Square Footage: 2,361
Storage Room: 214 sq. ft.

QUOTE ONE®

Cost to build? See page 436
to order complete cost estimate
to build this house in your area!

Rear Elevation

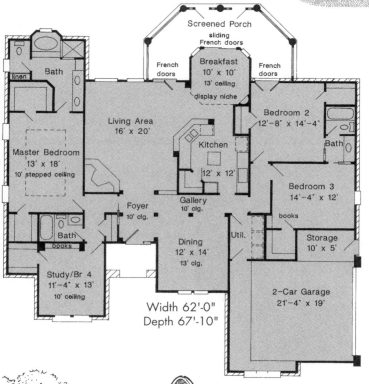

Screened Porch

sliding
French doors

French
doors

Breakfast
10' x 10'
13' ceiling

display niche

French
doors

Bath

linen

Living Area
16' x 20'

Bedroom 2
12'-8" x 14'-4"

Kitchen

Bath

12' x 12'

Master Bedroom
13' x 18'
10' stepped ceiling

Bedroom 3
14'-4" x 12'

Foyer
10' clg.

Gallery
10' clg.

Bath

books

books

Study/Br 4
11'-4" x 13'
10' ceiling

Dining
12' x 14'
13' clg.

Util.

Storage
10' x 5'

2-Car Garage
21'-4" x 19'

Width 62'-0"
Depth 67'-10"

◆ The combination of finely detailed brick and shingle siding recalls some of the distinctive architecture of the East Coast during the early part of this century. The foyer and gallery provide for a functional traffic pattern. The formal dining room to the front of the home is outlined by columns and features a thirteen-foot ceiling. The extensive living area offers a corner fireplace. A screened porch surrounding the breakfast room is an ideal entertainment area. The master suite features two spacious closets and a bath with a garden tub and an oversized shower. Bedroom 4 can serve as a study, nursery, guest room or home office.

—DESIGN BY—

LARRY W. GARNETT & ASSOCIATES

Design Q371

Square Footage: 1,794

◆ Details make the difference in this exquisite one-story home. A bold portico entry opens to a sunken foyer which boasts a multi-paned transom window over the high tray ceiling. High tray ceilings throughout the design add distinction and increase the sense of spaciousness. Stately decorative columns adorn the sunken living room and provide visual separation between the living room and dining rom. A warming fireplace acts as a focal point in the living room. The family room features a corner fireplace and French doors to the garden patio. It is also open to the efficient kitchen and sunny breakfast room with bay window. The master suite is filled with amenities: a cozy window seat, a walk-in closet and a bath with raised whirlpool spa and separate shower. Two family bedrooms share the use of a main bath in the hall. A laundry alcove leads the way to the service entrance to the two-car garage. Plans include details for both a basement and a crawlspace foundation.

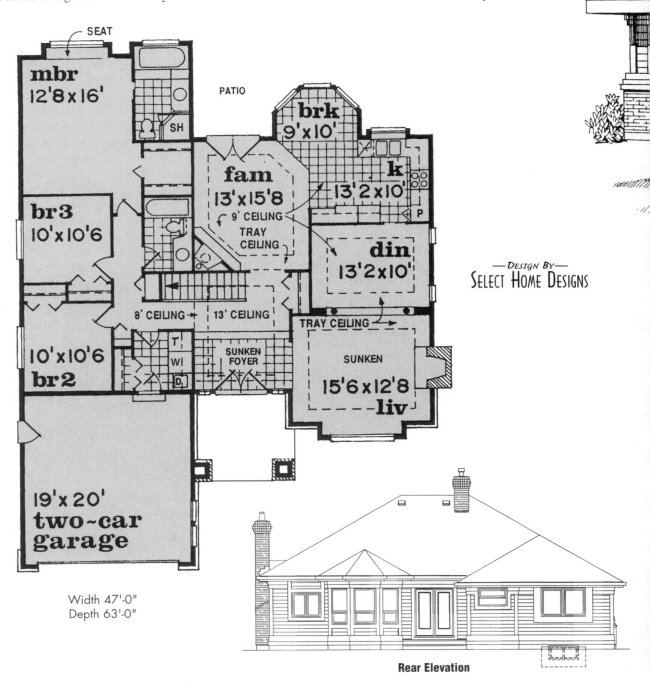

SEAT

mbr
12'8x16'

PATIO

brk
9'x10'

br3
10'x10'6

fam
13'x15'8

9' CEILING
TRAY CEILING

k
13'2x10'

P

din
13'2x10'

8' CEILING

13' CEILING

10'x10'6
br2

SUNKEN FOYER

TRAY CEILING

SUNKEN
15'6x12'8
liv

19'x20'
two-car garage

Width 47'-0"
Depth 63'-0"

—DESIGN BY—
SELECT HOME DESIGNS

Rear Elevation

View of Living Room

207

Design P100
Square Footage: 1,945

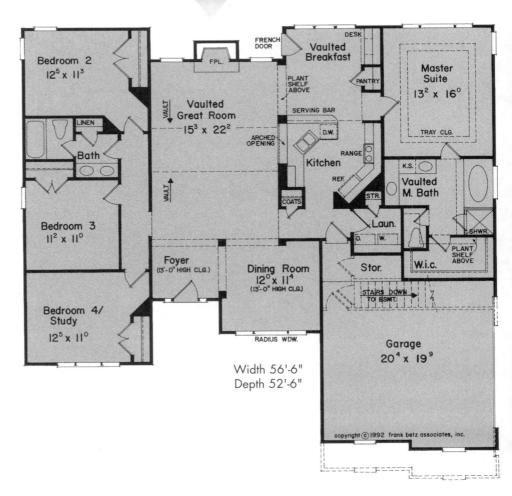

◆ Corner quoins and keystones above graceful windows decorate the exterior of this lovely home. The foyer is beautifully framed by columns marking the entrances to the dining room and vaulted great room. The great room features a fireplace with flanking windows overlooking the rear yard. The gourmet-style kitchen has angled counters and a serving bar that defines it from breakfast-room space. To the right of the combined kitchen and breakfast room, you will find a private master suite. A relaxing bath and large walk-in closet enhance this splendid retreat. It also features a tray ceiling and a plant shelf above the entry to the closet. Three family bedrooms—or make one a study—are separated from the master suite and share a full bath with secluded vanity area. Please specify basement or crawl-space foundation when ordering.

— DESIGN BY —

FRANK BETZ ASSOCIATES, INC.

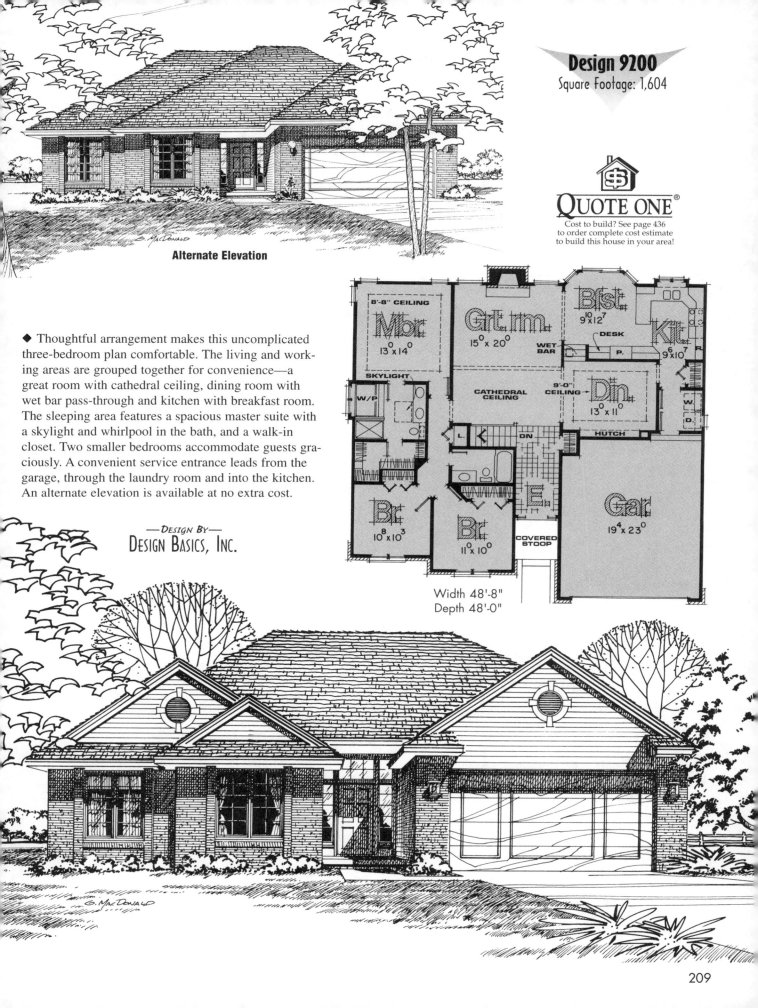

Design 9200
Square Footage: 1,604

Quote One®
Cost to build? See page 436
to order complete cost estimate
to build this house in your area!

Alternate Elevation

◆ Thoughtful arrangement makes this uncomplicated
three-bedroom plan comfortable. The living and working areas are grouped together for convenience—a
great room with cathedral ceiling, dining room with
wet bar pass-through and kitchen with breakfast room.
The sleeping area features a spacious master suite with
a skylight and whirlpool in the bath, and a walk-in
closet. Two smaller bedrooms accommodate guests gra-
ciously. A convenient service entrance leads from the
garage, through the laundry room and into the kitchen.
An alternate elevation is available at no extra cost.

— Design By —
Design Basics, Inc.

8'-8" CEILING

Mbr
13⁰ x 14⁰

SKYLIGHT

W/P

Br
10⁸ x 10³

Grt. rm.
15⁰ x 20⁰

CATHEDRAL
CEILING

DN

Br
11⁴ x 10⁰

COVERED
STOOP

Bfst
9¹⁰ x 12⁷

WET
BAR

DESK

9'-0"
CEILING

Dn
13⁰ x 11⁰

HUTCH

Kit
9 x 10

P.

Gar
19⁴ x 23⁰

W.
D.

Width 48'-8"
Depth 48'-0"

209

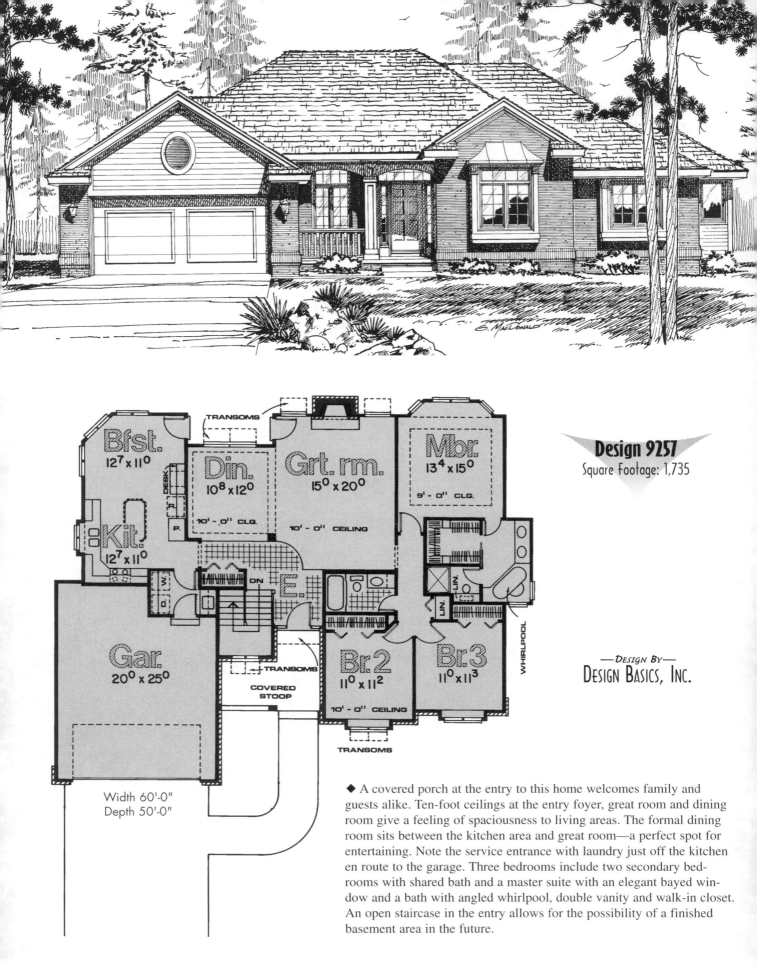

Bfst.
12⁷ x 11⁰

Din.
10⁸ x 12⁰

Grt. rm.
15⁰ x 20⁰

Mbr.
13⁴ x 15⁰

9' - 0" CLG.

Kit.
12⁷ x 11⁰

DESK

TRANSOMS

10' - 0" CLG.

10' - 0" CEILING

P.

DN

D.W.

Gar.
20⁰ x 25⁰

TRANSOMS

COVERED
STOOP

Br.2
11⁰ x 11²

10' - 0" CEILING

Br.3
11⁰ x 11³

LIN.

LIN.

WHIRLPOOL

TRANSOMS

Width 60'-0"
Depth 50'-0"

Design 9257
Square Footage: 1,735

—DESIGN BY—
DESIGN BASICS, INC.

◆ A covered porch at the entry to this home welcomes family and guests alike. Ten-foot ceilings at the entry foyer, great room and dining room give a feeling of spaciousness to living areas. The formal dining room sits between the kitchen area and great room—a perfect spot for entertaining. Note the service entrance with laundry just off the kitchen en route to the garage. Three bedrooms include two secondary bedrooms with shared bath and a master suite with an elegant bayed window and a bath with angled whirlpool, double vanity and walk-in closet. An open staircase in the entry allows for the possibility of a finished basement area in the future.

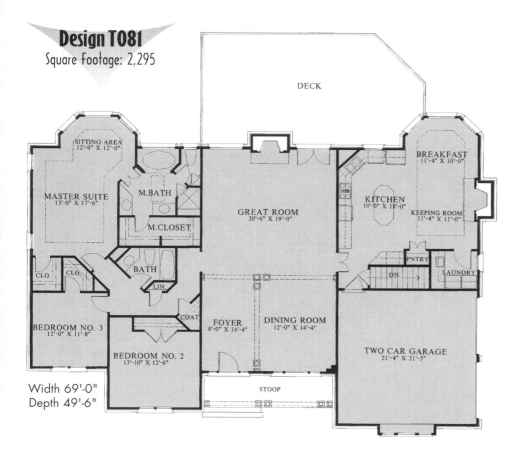

Design T081
Square Footage: 2,295

DECK

SITTING AREA
12'-0" X 12'-0"

MASTER SUITE
13'-0" X 17'-6"

M.BATH

M.CLOSET

BATH

LIN.

CLO. CLO.

GREAT ROOM
20'-6" X 19'-0"

BREAKFAST
11'-4" X 10'-0"

KITCHEN
10'-0" X 18'-0"

KEEPING ROOM
11'-4" X 11'-0"

PNTRY

DN.

LAUNDRY

BEDROOM NO. 3
12'-0" X 11'-8"

COAT

FOYER
8'-0" X 14'-4"

DINING ROOM
12'-0" X 14'-4"

BEDROOM NO. 2
13'-10" X 12'-6"

STOOP

TWO CAR GARAGE
21'-4" X 21'-5"

Width 69'-0"
Depth 49'-6"

◆ One-story living takes a lovely traditional turn in this brick one-story home. The foyer opens to the dining room through columned arches and to the great room, creating an extensive living area with a sense of spaciousness. To the right of the plan, this area opens to a second, more casual, living area through double doors. Gourmet cooks will fully appreciate this well-appointed kitchen with large food preparation counter and walk-in pantry. Family and friends will gather around the fireplace in the adjacent keeping room with beautiful bayed breakfast nook. To the left of the plan, two family bedrooms and a full bath share a central hall which leads to a sizable master suite with coffered ceiling, lovely bayed sitting area, and sumptuous bath with compartmented garden tub, dressing area and walk-in closet. This home is designed with a basement foundation.

QUOTE ONE®

Cost to build? See page 436
to order complete cost estimate
to build this house in your area!

—DESIGN BY—
DESIGN TRADITIONS

© American Home Gallery, Ltd.

Design 9375
Square Footage: 2,456

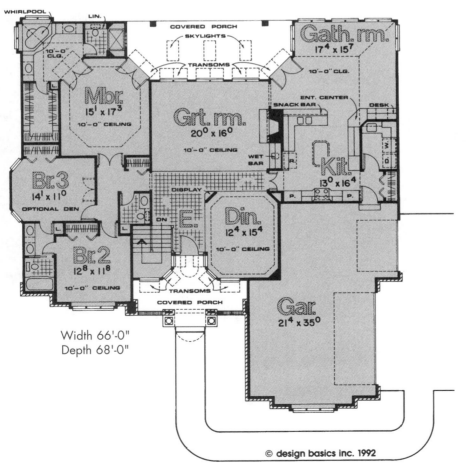

WHIRLPOOL
LIN.

Mbr.
15¹ x 17³
10'-0" CEILING

Br.3
14¹ x 11⁰
OPTIONAL DEN

Br.2
12⁸ x 11⁸
10'-0" CEILING

COVERED PORCH
SKYLIGHTS
TRANSOMS

Gath. rm.
17⁴ x 15⁷
10'-0" CLG.

Grt. rm.
20⁰ x 16⁰
10'-0" CEILING

WET BAR

ENT. CENTER
SNACK BAR

DESK

Kit.
13⁰ x 16⁴

DISPLAY

DN

Din.
12⁴ x 15⁴
10'-0" CEILING

TRANSOMS
COVERED PORCH

Gar.
21⁴ x 35⁰

Width 66'-0"
Depth 68'-0"

© design basics inc. 1992

— DESIGN BY —
DESIGN BASICS, INC.

◆ Tapered columns at the entry help to create a majestic front elevation. Inside, an open great room features a wet bar, a fireplace, tall windows and access to a covered porch with skylights. A wide kitchen features an ideally placed island, two pantries and easy laundry access. Double doors open to the master suite where attention is drawn to French doors leading to the master bath and the covered porch. The master bath provides beauty and convenience with a whirlpool, dual lavatories, plant shelves and a large walk-in closet. Two secondary bedrooms share a compartmented bath.

QUOTE ONE®
Cost to build? See page 436
to order complete cost estimate
to build this house in your area!

© American Home Gallery, Ltd.

Design T007
Square Footage: 2,697

◆ Dual chimneys (one a false chimney created to enhance the aesthetic effect) and a double stairway to the covered entry of this home create a balanced architectural statement. The sunlit foyer leads straight into the spacious great room, where French doors and large side windows provide a generous view of the covered veranda in back. The great room features a tray ceiling and a fireplace, bordered by twin bookcases. Another great view is offered from the spacious kitchen with breakfast bar and a roomy work island. The master suite provides a large balanced bath, a spacious closet and a glassed sitting area with access to the veranda. This home is designed with a basement foundation.

—DESIGN BY—
DESIGN TRADITIONS

QUOTE ONE®

Cost to build? See page 436 to order complete cost estimate to build this house in your area!

Width 65'-3"
Depth 67'-3"

Great Room Interior

DECK

— DESIGN BY —
DESIGN TRADITIONS

BREAKFAST
11'-4" X 8'-6"

Design T090

Square Footage: 1,733

BEDROOM NO. 3
11'-6" X 11'-0"

GREAT ROOM
14'-0" X 17'-6"

KITCHEN
11'-4" X 10'-0"

MASTER
BEDROOM
12'-4" X 15'-6"

BATH

Quote One®

Cost to build? See page 436
to order complete cost estimate
to build this house in your area!

BEDROOM NO. 2
11'-0" X 14'-8"

FOYER
6'-6" X 6'-6"

DINING ROOM
11'-4" X 10'-6"

DN.

HIS

PWDR.

MASTER
BATH

LAUNDRY

HERS

TWO-CAR GARAGE
20'-4" X 19'-4"

◆ Delightfully different, this brick one-story home has everything for the active family. The foyer opens to a formal dining room accented with decorative columns, and to a great room with warming fireplace and lovely French doors to the rear deck. The efficient kitchen adjoins a light-filled breakfast nook. A split bedroom plan offers a secluded master suite with coffered ceiling, His and Hers walk-in closets, double vanity and garden tub. Two family bedrooms, or one and a study, have separate access to a full bath on the left side of the plan. This home is designed with a basement foundation.

Width 55'-6"
Depth 57'-6"

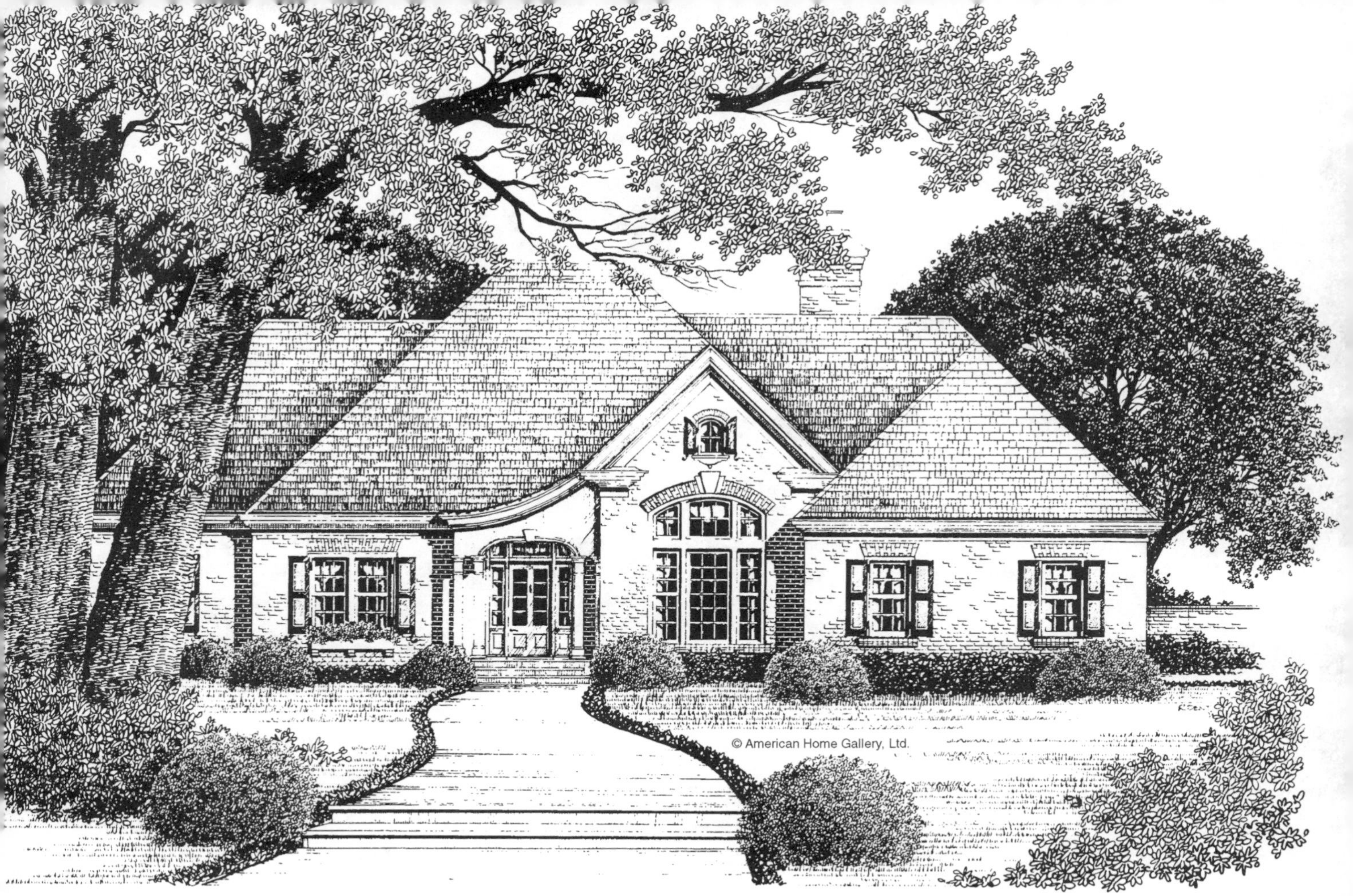
© American Home Gallery, Ltd.

Design T009

Square Footage: 2,902

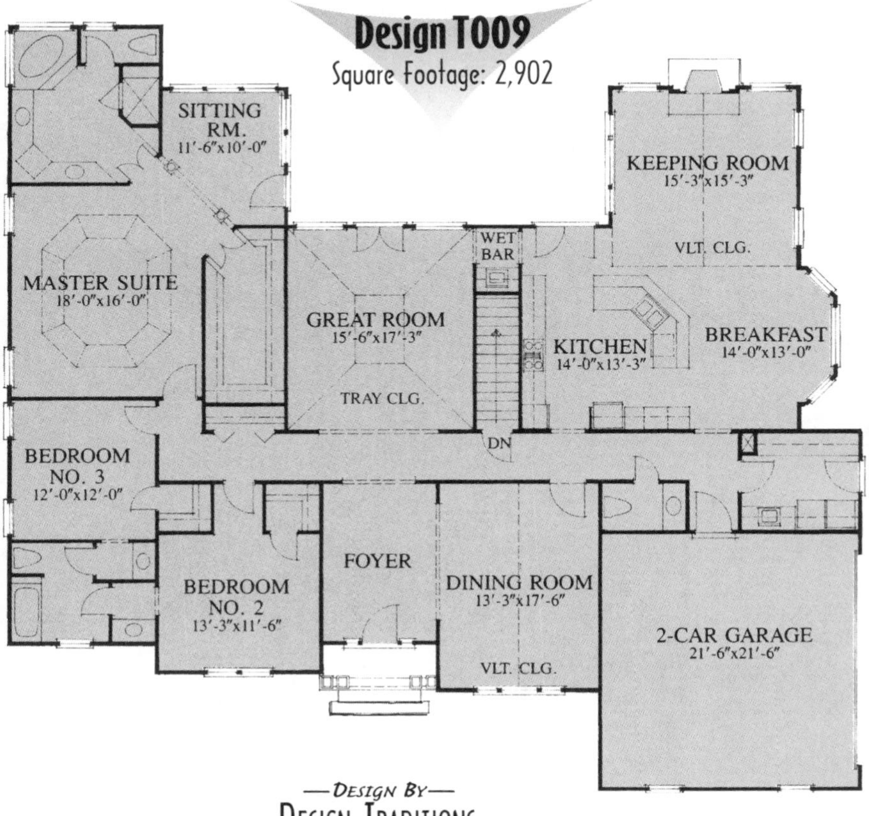
SITTING RM.
11'-6"x10'-0"
KEEPING ROOM
15'-3"x15'-3"
VLT. CLG.
WET BAR
MASTER SUITE
18'-0"x16'-0"
GREAT ROOM
15'-6"x17'-3"
TRAY CLG.
KITCHEN
14'-0"x13'-3"
BREAKFAST
14'-0"x13'-0"
DN
BEDROOM NO. 3
12'-0"x12'-0"
FOYER
DINING ROOM
13'-3"x17'-6"
VLT. CLG.
BEDROOM NO. 2
13'-3"x11'-6"
2-CAR GARAGE
21'-6"x21'-6"

—Design By—
Design Traditions

Width 71'-3"
Depth 66'-3"

◆ To highlight the exterior of this brick home, window jack arches have been artfully combined with arched transoms, gables and a sweeping roofline. The foyer opens into the formal dining room, which is highlighted by the vaulted ceiling treatment and the stunning triple window. Also open to the foyer is the great room with its dramatic tray ceiling. The accommodating kitchen, with a generous work island/breakfast bar, adjoins the breakfast area with its bright bay window and the keeping room with a fireplace, a vaulted ceiling and abundant windows. Two bedrooms and a connecting bath offering private vanities complete the rooms set along the front. The master suite, with its garden bath and glass sitting room, provides a quiet and peaceful retreat from the noise and pace of the day. This home is designed with a basement foundation.

QUOTE ONE®
Cost to build? See page 436 to order complete cost estimate to build this house in your area!

Design 9362
Square Footage: 2,172

◆ Beautiful arches and grand rooflines announce an interior that is both spectacular and convenient. The entry leads to a magnificent great room with centered fireplace and views to the rear grounds—a perfect complement to a front-facing formal living room. The dining room with tray ceiling and double arched windows opens from the entry and is just steps away from the kitchen—which features a food preparation island, pantry and access to a rear patio through the breakfast area. Bedroom 3 offers the possibility of a guest room at this end of the plan, with a nearby full bath. To the right of the plan, a glorious master suite, with raised ceiling and triple transoms, offers a relaxing bath with windowed whirlpool tub, twin lavatories and walk-in closet. A nearby family bedroom has access to a hall bath. The three-car garage offers extra storage space and a door to the rear patio. Note that major living areas all have eleven-foot ceilings.

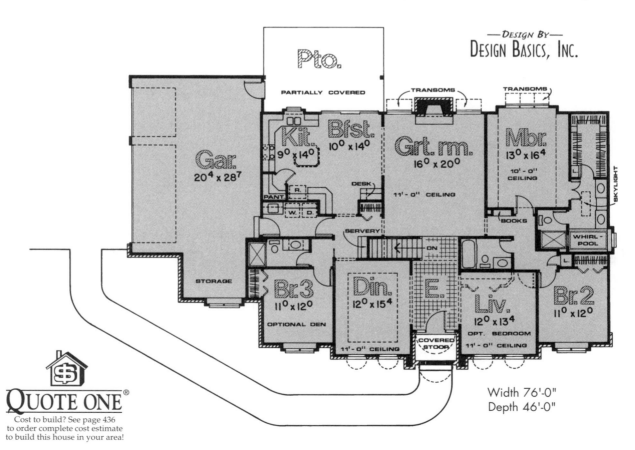

— DESIGN BY —
Design Basics, Inc.

Width 76'-0"
Depth 46'-0"

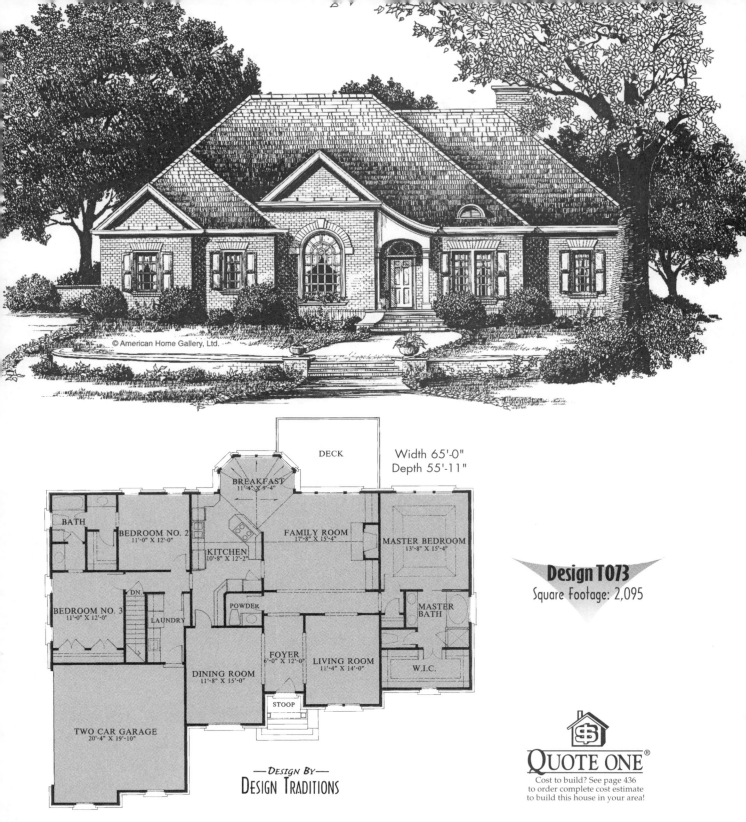

DECK

BREAKFAST
11'-4" X 9'-4"

Width 65'-0"
Depth 55'-11"

BATH

BEDROOM NO. 2
11'-0" X 12'-0"

KITCHEN
10'-8" X 12'-2"

FAMILY ROOM
17'-8" X 15'-4"

MASTER BEDROOM
13'-8" X 15'-4"

BEDROOM NO. 3
11'-0" X 12'-0"

DN.

LAUNDRY

POWDER

MASTER
BATH

FOYER
6'-0" X 12'-0"

LIVING ROOM
11'-4" X 14'-0"

W.I.C.

DINING ROOM
11'-8" X 15'-0"

STOOP

TWO CAR GARAGE
20'-4" X 19'-10"

—DESIGN BY—
DESIGN TRADITIONS

Design T073
Square Footage: 2,095

QUOTE ONE®
Cost to build? See page 436
to order complete cost estimate
to build this house in your area!

◆ The interesting shape of the flared eaves creates a natural cover for the front entry, establishing the focal point of this one-level brick traditional home. Inside, the foyer opens to the living room defined through the use of columns and the large dining room accented by dramatic window detail. A butler's pantry is strategically located just off the kitchen to provide ease of access when entertaining. The open family room displays a fireplace and built-in cabinetry for added storage. A wall of windows in the family room leads to the octagon-shaped breakfast area and deck outside. The right wing of this home features the master bedroom with bright window arrangement and tray ceiling detail. The large master bath with dual vanities, jacuzzi tub and shower is complete with a spacious walk-in closet. On the opposite side of the home are two additional bedrooms, each having its own vanity while sharing a tub area. This home is designed with a basement foundation.

217

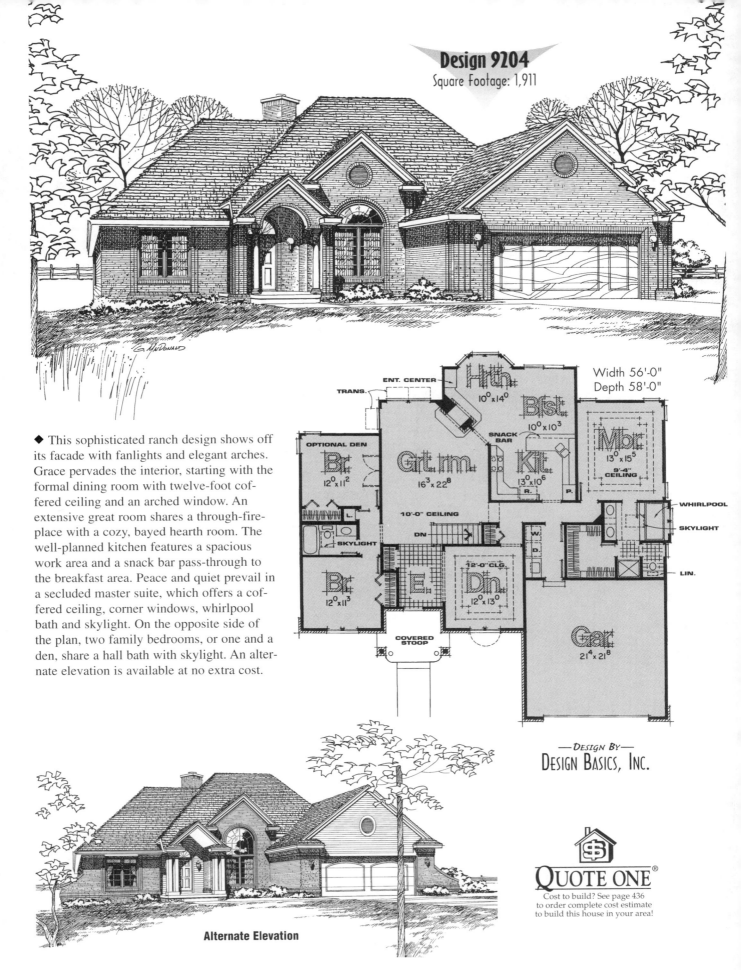

Design 9204
Square Footage: 1,911

Width 56'-0"
Depth 58'-0"

◆ This sophisticated ranch design shows off its facade with fanlights and elegant arches. Grace pervades the interior, starting with the formal dining room with twelve-foot coffered ceiling and an arched window. An extensive great room shares a through-fireplace with a cozy, bayed hearth room. The well-planned kitchen features a spacious work area and a snack bar pass-through to the breakfast area. Peace and quiet prevail in a secluded master suite, which offers a coffered ceiling, corner windows, whirlpool bath and skylight. On the opposite side of the plan, two family bedrooms, or one and a den, share a hall bath with skylight. An alternate elevation is available at no extra cost.

—DESIGN BY—
DESIGN BASICS, INC.

QUOTE ONE®
Cost to build? See page 436
to order complete cost estimate
to build this house in your area!

Alternate Elevation

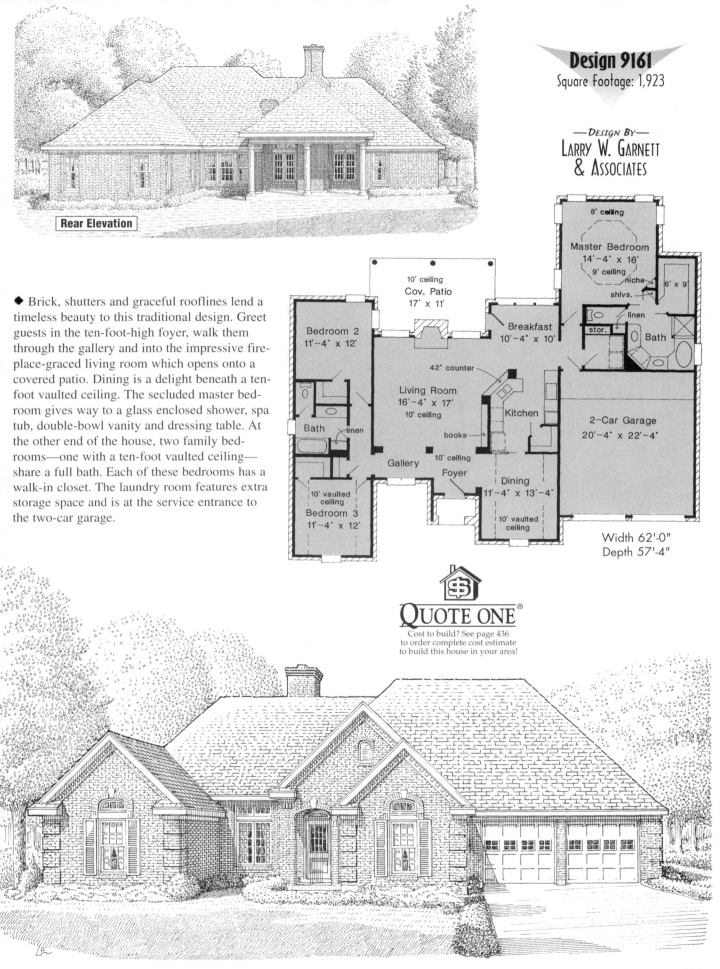

Design 9161

Square Footage: 1,923

—DESIGN BY—

LARRY W. GARNETT & ASSOCIATES

Rear Elevation

◆ Brick, shutters and graceful rooflines lend a timeless beauty to this traditional design. Greet guests in the ten-foot-high foyer, walk them through the gallery and into the impressive fireplace-graced living room which opens onto a covered patio. Dining is a delight beneath a ten-foot vaulted ceiling. The secluded master bedroom gives way to a glass enclosed shower, spa tub, double-bowl vanity and dressing table. At the other end of the house, two family bedrooms—one with a ten-foot vaulted ceiling—share a full bath. Each of these bedrooms has a walk-in closet. The laundry room features extra storage space and is at the service entrance to the two-car garage.

8' ceiling

Master Bedroom
14'-4" x 16'

9' ceiling

niche

6' x 9'

shlvs.

10' ceiling
Cov. Patio
17' x 11'

Breakfast
10'-4" x 10'

linen

stor.

Bath

Bedroom 2
11'-4" x 12'

42" counter

Living Room
16'-4" x 17'

10' ceiling

Kitchen

2-Car Garage
20'-4" x 22'-4"

Bath

linen

books

Gallery

10' ceiling

Foyer

Dining
11'-4" x 13'-4"

10' vaulted ceiling

Bedroom 3
11'-4" x 12'

10' vaulted ceiling

Width 62'-0"
Depth 57'-4"

QUOTE ONE®

Cost to build? See page 436
to order complete cost estimate
to build this house in your area!

219

Design 9201
Square Footage: 1,996

◆ Practical, yet equipped with a variety of popular amenities, this pleasant ranch home is an excellent choice for empty nesters or small families. The front living room can become a third bedroom if you choose. The great room with dramatic fireplace serves as the main living area. A luxurious master suite features a ten-foot tray ceiling and a large bath with whirlpool, skylight, plant ledge and twin vanities. The kitchen with breakfast room serves both the dining and great rooms. A tandem drive-through garage holds space for a third car or extra storage.

QUOTE ONE®
Cost to build? See page 436
to order complete cost estimate
to build this house in your area!

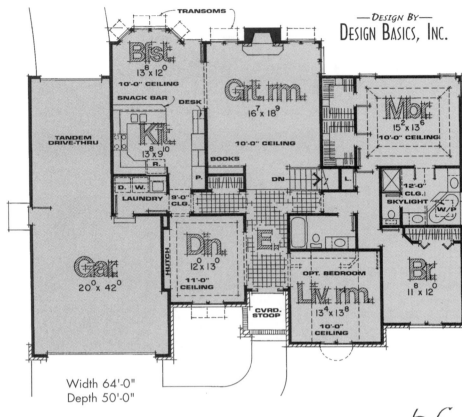

—DESIGN BY—
DESIGN BASICS, INC.

TRANSOMS

Bfst
13⁸ x 12⁰
10'-0" CEILING

SNACK BAR   DESK

Grt. rm.
16⁷ x 18⁹
10'-0" CEILING

Mbr
15² x 13⁶
10'-0" CEILING

Kit.
13⁸ x 9¹⁰
R.

BOOKS

D. W.

LAUNDRY

9'-0" CLG.

P.

DN

L.

12'-0" CLG.
SKYLIGHT
W/P

TANDEM
DRIVE-THRU

Gar
20⁰ x 42⁰

HUTCH

Dn
12 x 13⁰
11'-0" CEILING

E.

OPT. BEDROOM

Br
11 x 12

CVRD.
STOOP

Liv. rm.
13⁴ x 13⁸
10'-0" CEILING

Width 64'-0"
Depth 50'-0"

C. MacDONALD

220

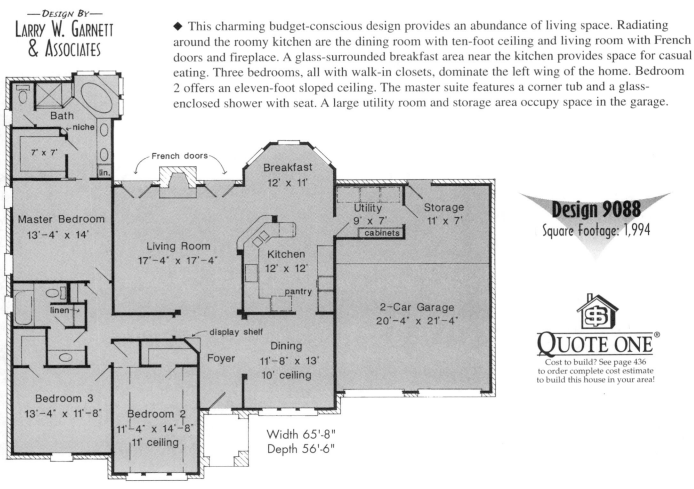

— DESIGN BY —
LARRY W. GARNETT & ASSOCIATES

◆ This charming budget-conscious design provides an abundance of living space. Radiating around the roomy kitchen are the dining room with ten-foot ceiling and living room with French doors and fireplace. A glass-surrounded breakfast area near the kitchen provides space for casual eating. Three bedrooms, all with walk-in closets, dominate the left wing of the home. Bedroom 2 offers an eleven-foot sloped ceiling. The master suite features a corner tub and a glass-enclosed shower with seat. A large utility room and storage area occupy space in the garage.

Bath

niche

7' x 7'

lin.

French doors

Breakfast
12' x 11'

Utility
9' x 7'

Storage
11' x 7'

cabinets

Design 9088
Square Footage: 1,994

Master Bedroom
13'-4" x 14'

Living Room
17'-4" x 17'-4"

Kitchen
12' x 12'

pantry

linen

2-Car Garage
20'-4" x 21'-4"

display shelf

Foyer

Dining
11'-8" x 13'
10' ceiling

Quote One®
Cost to build? See page 436
to order complete cost estimate
to build this house in your area!

Bedroom 3
13'-4" x 11'-8"

Bedroom 2
11'-4" x 14'-8"
11' ceiling

Width 65'-8"
Depth 56'-6"

221

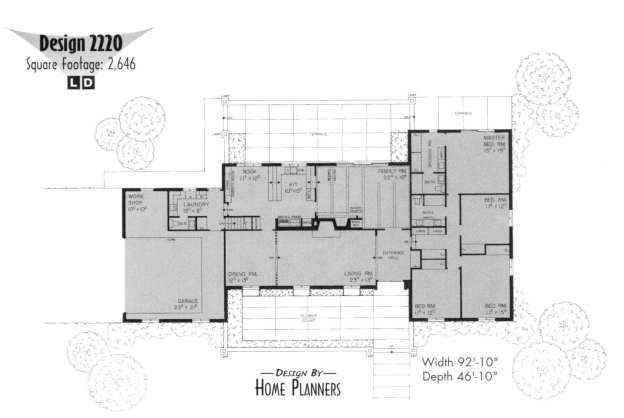

Design 2220
Square Footage: 2,646
L D

—DESIGN BY—
Home Planners

Width 92'-10"
Depth 46'-10"

◆ The gracious formality of this home is reminiscent of popular French styling. The hip roof, the brick quoins, the cornice details, the arched window heads, the distinctive shutters, the recessed double front doors, the massive center chimney and the delightful flower court are all features which set the dramatic appeal of this home. This floor plan is a favorite of many. The four-bedroom, two-bath sleeping wing is a zone by itself. Further, the formal living and dining rooms are ideally located—they function well together for entertaining and they look out upon the pleasant flower court. Overlooking the raised living terrace at the rear are the family and breakfast rooms and work center. Pass-through counters in the kitchen separate it from the nook and the family room. Don't miss the laundry, extra wash room and workshop in the garage.

Design 9028

Square Footage: 1,707

—DESIGN BY—
LARRY W. GARNETT & ASSOCIATES

◆ No slouch on amenities, this plan is a popular choice with those just starting out. High ceilings in the dining room and the master suite add a sense of space. A decorative front wall separates the formal dining area from the foyer while preserving the openness of the area. A bay-windowed breakfast room adjoins the kitchen area and opens to a rear porch for outdoor dining. Sleeping quarters include a master suite with vaulted ceiling, walk-in closet, glass-surrounded tub and separate shower, as well as two family bedrooms which share a full bath. The laundry area is conveniently located near the bedrooms.

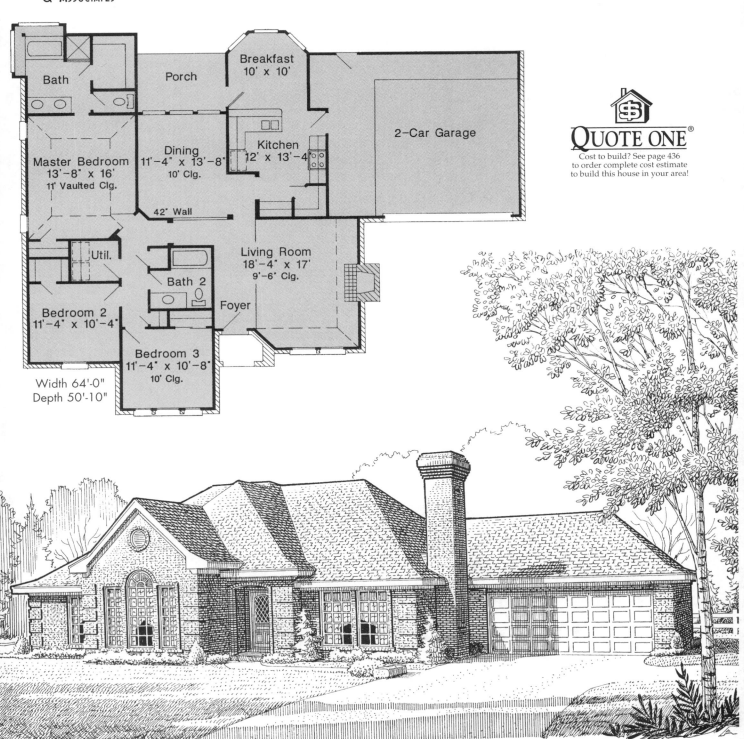

Bath

Porch

Breakfast
10' x 10'

2-Car Garage

Master Bedroom
13'-8" x 16'
11' Vaulted Clg.

Dining
11'-4" x 13'-8"
10' Clg.

Kitchen
12' x 13'-4"

42" Wall

Util.

Living Room
18'-4" x 17'
9'-6" Clg.

Bath 2

Bedroom 2
11'-4" x 10'-4"

Foyer

Bedroom 3
11'-4" x 10'-8"
10' Clg.

Width 64'-0"
Depth 50'-10"

Quote One®
Cost to build? See page 436
to order complete cost estimate
to build this house in your area!

Design 1989
Square Footage: 2,282
L D

◆ High style abounds in this picturesque ground-hugging design. The plan calls for a sunken living room and separate dining room. A fireplace in the living room keeps things cozy in the cold weather months. Overlooking the rear yard, and accessing it through sliding glass doors, the informal family room has a beamed ceiling and a fireplace of its own. The U-shaped kitchen and breakfast room are nearby; a snack bar counter separates them. A master suite is one of four bedrooms found to the left of the entry foyer. It has sliding glass doors to the terrace and a bath with built-in cabinets, double sinks and double wall closets. The family bedrooms share a full hall bath with double sinks. Access the two-car garage through the service area that holds a laundry and washroom. A large storage area in the garage enhances its usefulness.

—DESIGN BY—
HOME PLANNERS

Width 86'-10"
Depth 40'-10"

One-Story Tudor-Style Homes

Design 2606
Square Footage: 1,499

L

◆ This modest-sized house with its 1,499 square feet could hardly offer more in the way of exterior charm and interior livability. Measuring only 60 feet in width means it will not require a huge, expensive piece of property. The orientation of the garage and the front drive court are features that promote an economical use of property. In addition to the formal, separate living and dining rooms, there is the informal kitchen/family room area. Note the beamed ceiling, the fireplace, the sliding glass doors and the eating area in the family room.

TERRACE

FAMILY RM.
11⁴ x 16⁰

LIVING RM.
18⁰ x 12⁰

MASTER BED RM.
13⁰ x 11⁰

DRESSING RM.

BEAMED CEILING

BATH

EATING

RANGE

BATH

KITCHEN
11⁴ x 9⁸

ENTRANCE HALL

HALL

LINEN

DINING RM.
11⁸ x 11⁰

CL

BED RM.
10⁰ x 9⁴

BED RM.
11⁰ x 12⁰

DRY WASH

LAUNDRY

WASH RM.

GARAGE
23⁴ x 23⁴

Width 60'-0"
Depth 58'-0"

— DESIGN BY —
Home Planners

Quote One®
Cost to build? See page 436 to order complete cost estimate to build this house in your area!

MASTER BED RM.

LINEN

BATH

DN

ENT. HALL

HALL

CL

BED RM

BED RM

Optional Basement

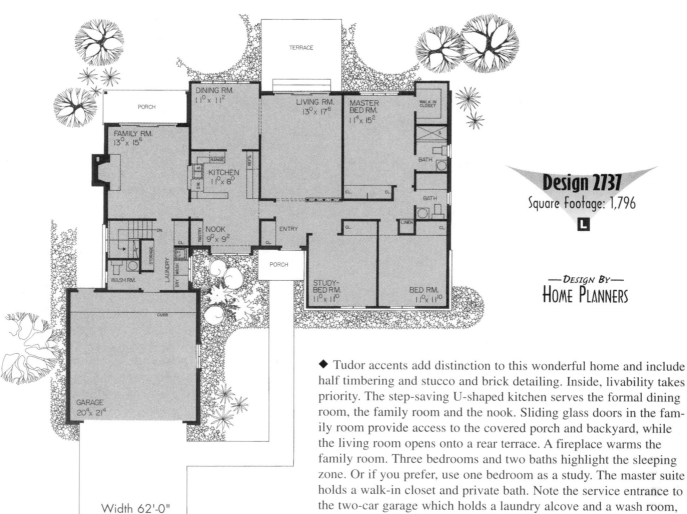

TERRACE

DINING RM.
11⁰ x 11²

LIVING RM.
13⁰ x 17⁶

MASTER BED RM.
11⁴ x 15²

WALK IN CLOSET

PORCH

FAMILY RM.
13⁰ x 15⁶

RANGE

KITCHEN
11' x 8⁰

REFG.

BATH

BATH

NOOK
9⁰ x 9²

ENTRY

LINEN

PANTRY

DN.

STORAGE

WASH RM.

LAUNDRY

PORCH

STUDY-BED RM.
11⁰ x 11⁰

BED RM.
11' x 11¹⁰

CURB

GARAGE
20⁴ x 21⁴

Width 62'-0"
Depth 57'-4"

Design 2737
Square Footage: 1,796

Ⓛ

—DESIGN BY—
HOME PLANNERS

◆ Tudor accents add distinction to this wonderful home and include half timbering and stucco and brick detailing. Inside, livability takes priority. The step-saving U-shaped kitchen serves the formal dining room, the family room and the nook. Sliding glass doors in the family room provide access to the covered porch and backyard, while the living room opens onto a rear terrace. A fireplace warms the family room. Three bedrooms and two baths highlight the sleeping zone. Or if you prefer, use one bedroom as a study. The master suite holds a walk-in closet and private bath. Note the service entrance to the two-car garage which holds a laundry alcove and a wash room, plus extra storage space.

Design 2929

Square Footage: 1,608

◆ This cozy Tudor features a very contemporary interior for convenience and practicality. The floor plan features a strategically located kitchen handy to the garage, dining room and dining terrace. The spacious living area has a dramatic fireplace that functions with the rear terrace. A favorite spot is the media room with space for a TV, VCR and stereo system. The master bedroom is large and has plenty of wardrobe storage. The extra guest room, or nursery, has a full bath.

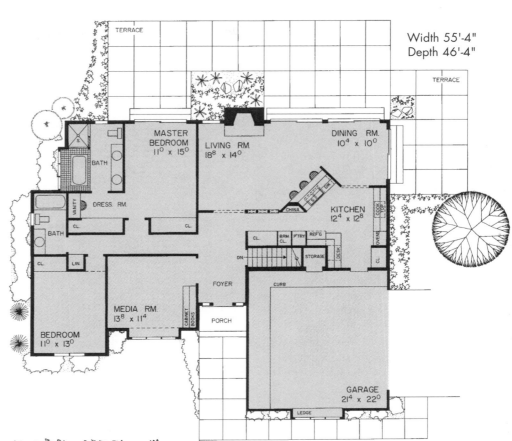

Width 55'-4"
Depth 46'-4"

TERRACE

MASTER BEDROOM
11⁰ x 15⁰

LIVING RM.
18⁸ x 14⁰

DINING RM.
10⁴ x 10⁰

TERRACE

BATH

VANITY

DRESS. RM.

CL.

CL.

BATH

CHINA

KITCHEN
12⁴ x 12⁸

CL.

COOK

OVENS

CL.

CL.

LIN.

CL.

BRM. CL.

P'TRY

REF'G

DESK

STORAGE

DN.

MEDIA RM.
13⁸ x 11⁴

CABINET BOOKS

FOYER

CURB

BEDROOM
11⁰ x 13⁰

PORCH

GARAGE
21⁴ x 22⁰

LEDGE

— DESIGN BY —
HOME PLANNERS

A.J. YOUNG
FUQUAY VARINA, N.C.

227

Design 2206
Square Footage: 1,769

L

◆ The charm of Tudor adaptations has become increasingly popular in recent years. And for good reason: its freshness of character adds a unique touch to any neighborhood. This interesting one-story home will be a standout wherever you choose to build it. The covered porch leads to the formal front entry—the foyer. From this point, the plans opens to the living areas, work areas and sleeping quarters. The formal living room features a beamed ceiling and fireplace and is open to the dining room. The family room shares a snack-bar counter with the U-shaped kitchen and also has sliding glass doors to the terrace. Each of the three bedrooms has a walk-in closet. The master suite is complete with a private bath. Note the powder room in the service area to the two-car garage.

—DESIGN BY—
HOME PLANNERS

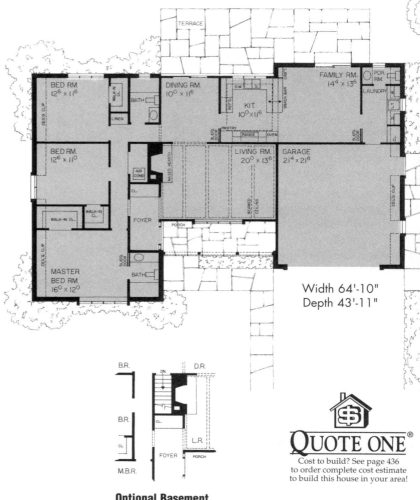

Width 64'-10"
Depth 43'-11"

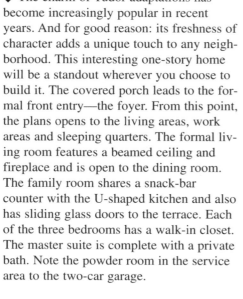

Optional Basement

QUOTE ONE®
Cost to build? See page 436 to order complete cost estimate to build this house in your area!

Design 2170
Square Footage: 1,646

L

◆ This L-shaped home is graced with an enchanting Olde English styling. The wavy-edged siding, the simulated beams, the diamond-lite windows, the unusual brick pattern and the interesting rooflines are all elements which set the character of authenticity. The center entry routes traffic directly to the formal living and the sleeping zones of the house. Between the kitchen/family room area and the attached two-car garage is the mud room. The family room is highlighted by the beam ceiling, a raised-hearth fireplace and the sliding glass doors to a rear terrace. Four bedrooms, two full baths and good closet space are features of the sleeping area. The master has its own private bath with a shower.

—DESIGN BY—
HOME PLANNERS

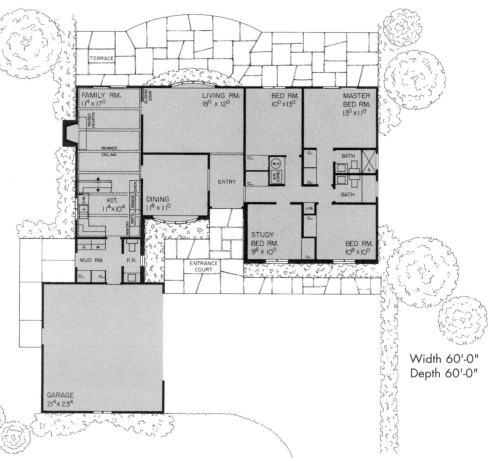

Width 60'-0"
Depth 60'-0"

Design 2728
Square Footage: 1,825

L D

◆ The curving front driveway produces an impressive approach to this delightful Tudor adaptation. A covered front porch shelters the centered entry hall which effectively routes traffic to all areas. The fireplace is the focal point of the spacious, formal living and dining areas. An efficient kitchen is conveniently located adjacent to the formal dining room and the informal family room. In addition to the two full baths in the sleeping zone, there is a handy washroom near the garage. Sliding glass doors opening from the dining room and family room provide easy access to the terrace and side porch.

— DESIGN BY —
HOME PLANNERS

Width 56'-0"
Depth 65'-8"

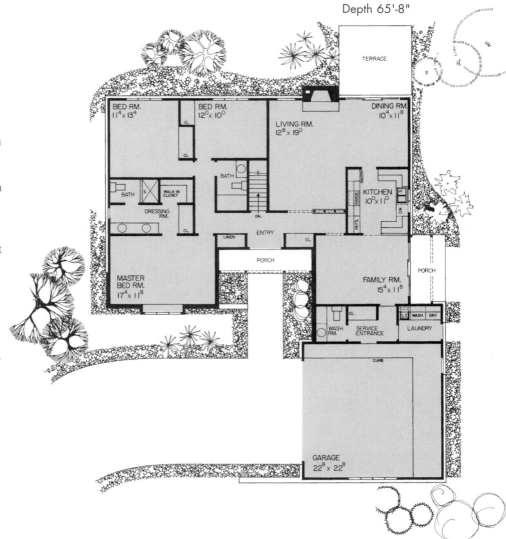

◆ If you've ever desired to have a large country kitchen in your home then this is the design for you. The features of this room are many: island range with snack bar, pantry and broom closets, eating area with sliding glass doors leading to a covered porch, adjacent mud room with laundry facilities and access to the garage, raised-hearth fireplace and conversation area with built-in desk on one side and shelves on the other. There are formal living and dining rooms, as well. The living room has sliding glass doors to the rear terrace. Bedrooms include a master suite with walk-in closet and private bath. Double vanities grace the bath that serves the two family bedrooms. One family bedroom features a walk-in closet.

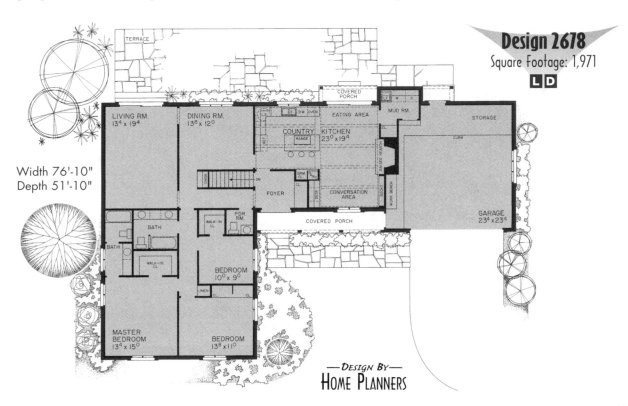

Design 2678
Square Footage: 1,971
L D

Width 76'-10"
Depth 51'-10"

TERRACE

LIVING RM.
13⁴ x 19⁴

DINING RM.
13⁸ x 12⁰

COVERED PORCH

EATING AREA

MUD RM.

STORAGE

COUNTRY KITCHEN
23⁰ x 19⁴

RANGE

FOYER

CONVERSATION AREA

GARAGE
23⁸ x 23⁴

BATH

BATH

WALK-IN CL.

PDR. RM.

WALK-IN

COVERED PORCH

BEDROOM
10⁰ x 9⁰

LINEN

MASTER BEDROOM
13⁴ x 15⁰

BEDROOM
13⁸ x 11⁰

DESIGN BY
Home Planners

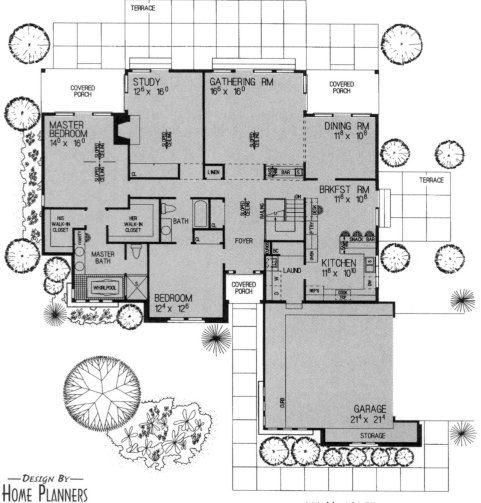

Design 3346
Square Footage: 2,032

L

◆ This home boasts a delightful Tudor exterior with a terrific interior floor plan. Though compact, there's plenty of living space: a large study with a fireplace, a gathering room, a formal dining room and a breakfast room. The master bedroom is enhanced with His and Hers walk-in closets and a relaxing, private bath with a soothing whirlpool tub. An additional bedroom with a full bath nearby completes the sleeping quarters.

Quote One®
Cost to build? See page 436 to order complete cost estimate to build this house in your area!

—DESIGN BY—
Home Planners

Width 63'-5"
Depth 64'-9"

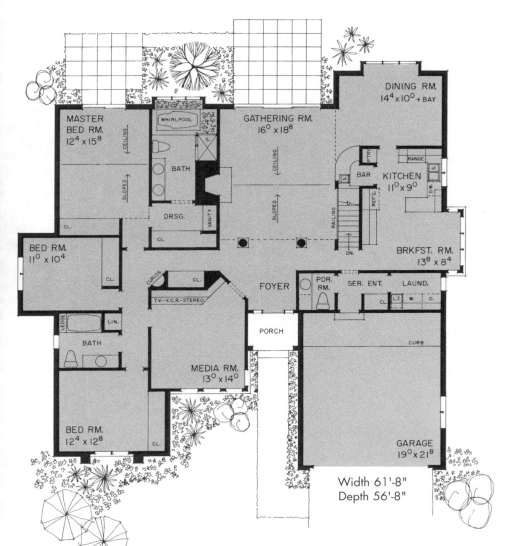

MASTER
BED RM.
12⁴ x 15⁸

BED RM.
11⁰ x 10⁴

BED RM.
12⁴ x 12⁸

WHIRLPOOL

BATH

DRSG.

CL.

CL.

VANITY

CL.

CURIOS

CL.

LEDGE

LIN.

BATH

T.V.-V.C.R.-STEREO

MEDIA RM.
13⁰ x 14⁰

GATHERING RM.
16⁰ x 18⁸

CEILING

CEILING

SLOPED

SLOPED

SLOPED

DINING RM.
14⁴ x 10⁰ + BAY

PTRY.

RANGE

S.

BAR

KITCHEN
11⁰ x 9⁰

D.W.

S.

REFG.

RAILING

DN.

BRKFST. RM.
13⁸ x 8⁴

FOYER

PDR.
RM.

SER. ENT.

LAUND.

L.T.

W.

D.

CL.

PORCH

CURB

GARAGE
19⁰ x 21⁸

Width 61'-8"
Depth 56'-8"

Design 3377
Square Footage: 2,217
L D

◆ This Tudor design provides a handsome exterior complemented by a spacious and modern floor plan. The sleeping area is positioned to the left side of the home. The master bedroom features an elegant bath with a whirlpool, a shower, dual lavs and a separate vanity area. Two family bedrooms share a full bath. A media room exhibits the TV, VCR and stereo. The enormous gathering room is set off by columns and contains a fireplace and sliding doors to the rear terrace. The dining room and breakfast room each feature a bay window.

QUOTE ONE®
Cost to build? See page 436
to order complete cost estimate
to build this house in your area!

— DESIGN BY —
HOME PLANNERS

Design 2847

Main Level: 1,874 sq. ft.
Finished Basement: 1,131 sq. ft.

L

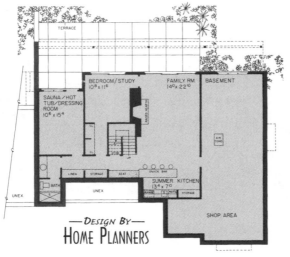

Width 78'-10"
Depth 43'-5"

◆ This magnificent Tudor design can be built as a one-story home to start, and expanded later in basement space as your family grows. The main level features a formal living room and dining room with a through-fireplace separating them. Both spaces have sliding glass doors to the rear deck, as does the breakfast room. The galley kitchen features an open counter with built-in range and access to the two-car garage. Bedrooms include two family bedrooms and a full bath, plus a master suite with private bath and access to the rear deck. Lower-level space contains a family room with fireplace, a shop area, an additional bedroom or study, a summer kitchen and a sauna or hot-tub room with dressing room space and full bath. A wide terrace graces the rooms in the basement.

Rear Elevation

Design 2962
Square Footage: 2,112

TERRACE   TERRACE

LIVING RM.
18² x21²

DINING RM.
9⁴ x13¹⁰

KITCHEN
10⁰ x13¹⁰

BRKFST. RM.
10⁰ x15¹⁰

RANGE

LAUNDRY

SLOPED CEILING

RAILING

CHINA BRM. CL.

DESK PANTRY

PDR. RM.

FOYER

BATH

WHIRLPOOL

BATH

WALK-IN CLOSET

LINEN LINEN VS.

STUDY
10⁰ x11⁰

COVERED PORCH

GARAGE
19⁶ x19⁶

MASTER BEDROOM
13² x16²

BEDROOM
13⁶ x11⁰

Width 63'-4"
Depth 54'-10"

QUOTE ONE®
Cost to build? See page 436
to order complete cost estimate
to build this house in your area!

◆ This home's English Tudor exterior houses a contemporary, well-planned interior. Each of the three main living areas—sleeping, living and working—are but a couple of steps from the foyer. Open planning, a sloped ceiling and plenty of glass create a nice environment for the living-dining area. Its appeal is further enhanced by the open staircase to the lower level recreation/hobby area. The L-shaped kitchen with its island range and work surface opens onto the large, sunny breakfast room. Nearby is the step-saving laundry room. The sleeping area has the flexibility of functioning as a two- or three-bedroom plan. Note the two-car garage with access to the large laundry room.

—DESIGN BY—
HOME PLANNERS

Design 2961
Square Footage: 2,919

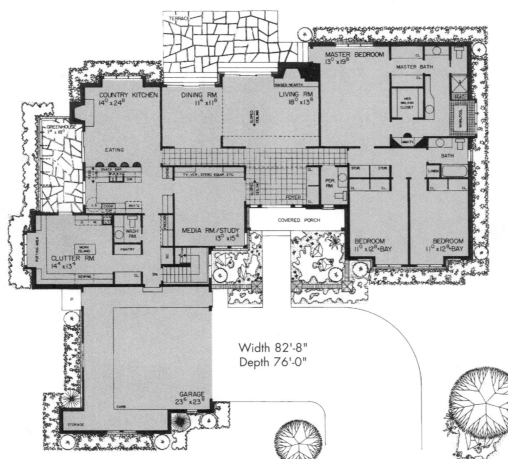

Width 82'-8"
Depth 76'-0"

◆ Cornice detailing and a brick exterior with stucco accents and beam work give this Tudor-style home its fashionable appeal. A brick wall forms the front court-yard. Inside, the spacious foyer with slate floor routes traffic to the living areas in the left wing or the sleeping zone in the right wing. Highlights include a media room, clutter room, country kitchen and 29-foot formal living/dining room area. The living room and country kitchen both have warming fire-places. The large master bedroom has a luxurious private bath. An added feature is the walled green-house located between the kitchen and clutter room. The two-car garage features an extra storage space area for hard to stow items.

— DESIGN BY —
HOME PLANNERS

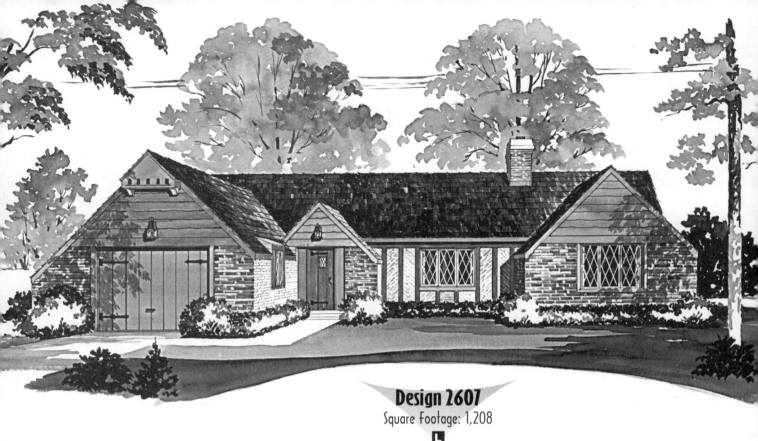

Design 2607
Square Footage: 1,208

L

◆ This English Tudor cottage is delightful, both inside and out. The front porch gives way to the main living area of the house. With a fireplace and windows that overlook both front and rear yards, the living room connects to the dining room with built-in china cabinet. The U-shaped kitchen is wonderfully efficient with a double sink, dishwasher, pantry and adjacent bay-windowed eating nook. A laundry area and half-bath also occupy this end of the house. At the opposite end are two bedrooms which share a full bath. The master features a double wall closet. The single-car garage has additional space for storage and connects to the main house at the service entrance. A wide terrace graces the rear of the home. You may choose to build this home on a basement or slab foundation—details are included for both.

—DESIGN BY—
Home Planners

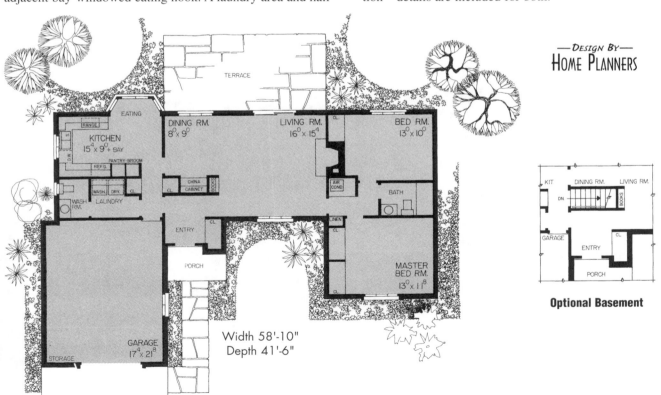

Width 58'-10"
Depth 41'-6"

Optional Basement

Design 2573
Square Footage: 2,747

L D

◆ A dapper Tudor ranch, this plan combines wood, brick and stucco to create an elegantly appealing exterior. Inside is a thoroughly contemporary floor plan. The open living room and dining area, with more than 410 square feet, features a fireplace, a wall of built-in shelves and a clear view to the outside through diagonally shaped windows. Other highlights include a family room with a raised-hearth fireplace, a U-shaped kitchen and adjacent breakfast nook, an optional bedroom/study or office and a four-bedroom sleeping wing including a master suite with access to a private terrace. The master also includes a walk-in closet, a dressing room with makeup vanity, an additional vanity and built-in towel storage. The service entrance holds a laundry room with built-ins and a half-bath, plus broom closet.

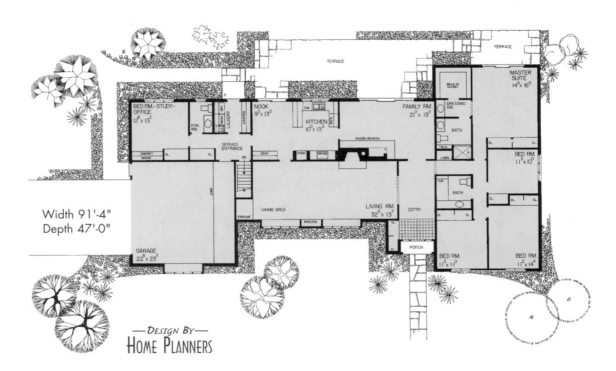

Width 91'-4"
Depth 47'-0"

— DESIGN BY —
HOME PLANNERS

—DESIGN BY—
Home Planners

Width 91'-4"
Depth 46'-4"

Design 2785
Square Footage: 2,375

LD

◆ Passersby will take second and third glances at this exceptional Tudor design. The floor plan offers a wealth of convenience and efficiency. One hall leads to each of the three bedrooms and the study in the sleeping wing; another leads to the living room, family room, kitchen and laundry with a washroom. A through-fireplace separates the living room and family room and there is terrace access convenient to both.

The formal dining room can be entered from both the foyer and the kitchen. The kitchen features a built-in desk, a pantry, an island snack bar with a sink and a pass-through to the family room. The master suite has a private terrace and walk-in closet, plus private bath. One family bedroom features a box-bay window. A three-car, side-load garage offers additional storage space.

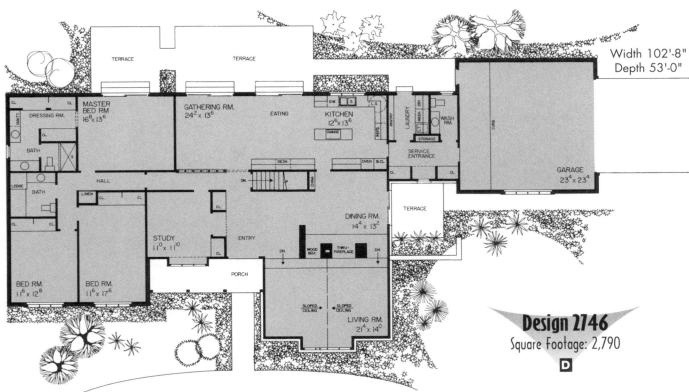

Width 102'-8"
Depth 53'-0"

TERRACE TERRACE

MASTER BED RM 16⁸ x 13⁶

DRESSING RM.

GATHERING RM. 24² x 13⁶

EATING

KITCHEN 12⁶ x 13⁶

RANGE

D.W. S

L.S.

REFS

PANTRY

LAUNDRY

WASH RM.

STORAGE

GARAGE 23⁴ x 23⁴

BATH

LEDGE

BATH

HALL

LINEN

CL

CL

DESK

DN

CHINA

OVEN B.CL

SERVICE ENTRANCE

TERRACE

STUDY 11⁰ x 11¹⁰

ENTRY

DINING RM. 14⁴ x 13²

BED RM. 11⁶ x 12⁸

BED RM. 11⁶ x 17⁶

PORCH

DN

WOOD BOX

THRU-FIREPLACE

DN

SLOPED CEILING

SLOPED CEILING

LIVING RM. 21⁴ x 14⁰

Design 2746
Square Footage: 2,790

D

◆ It's not surprising why this impressive Tudor is one of our most popular. Though encompassing Tudor style on the exterior, it houses a very up-to-date floor plan inside. The projecting sunken living room has stucco and simulated wood beams and a dramatic two-story-high window, complemented by a through-fireplace to the formal dining room. An island kitchen serves both the dining room and a more casual dining area that combines with the gathering room for one large informal space. Double sets of sliding glass doors in this area lead to a rear terrace. A study remains private near the entry and features a box-bay window. The master suite has sliding glass doors to its own private patio and has a private bath appointed in luxury. Two additional bedrooms share a full hall bath.

— DESIGN BY —
HOME PLANNERS

Rear Elevation

One-story Homes With A Country Flavor

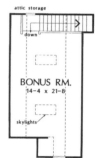

attic storage

down

BONUS RM.
14-4 x 21-8

skylights

Design 9782
Square Footage: 2,192

◆ Exciting volumes and nine-foot ceilings add elegance to a comfortable, open plan while secluded bedrooms are pleasant retreats in this home. Sunlight fills the airy foyer from a vaulted dormer and streams into the great room. A formal dining room, delineated from the foyer by columns, features a tray ceiling. Hosts whose guests always end up in the kitchen will enjoy entertaining here with only columns to separate them from the great room. Secondary bedrooms share a full bath complete with a linen closet. The front bedroom doubles as a study for extra flexibility and is accented by a tray ceiling. The master suite is highlighted by a tray ceiling and a spacious master bath with a walk-in closet.

—DESIGN BY—
DONALD A. GARDNER ARCHITECTS, INC.

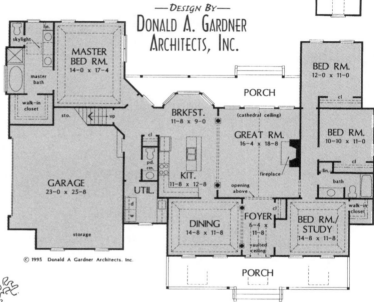

lin.

skylight

master bath

MASTER BED RM.
14-0 x 17-4

walk-in closet

sto.

up

GARAGE
23-0 x 25-8

storage

UTIL.

d w

pd. rm.

BRKFST.
11-8 x 9-0

KIT.
11-8 x 12-8

PORCH

(cathedral ceiling)

GREAT RM.
16-4 x 18-8

opening above

fireplace

BED RM.
12-0 x 11-0

cl

BED RM.
10-10 x 11-0

lin.

cl

bath

walk-in closet

DINING
14-8 x 11-8

FOYER
6-4 x 11-8

vaulted ceiling

BED RM./ STUDY
14-8 x 11-8

PORCH

© 1995   Donald A Gardner Architects. Inc.

Width 74'-10"
Depth 55'-8"

Width 60'-10"
Depth 51'-6"

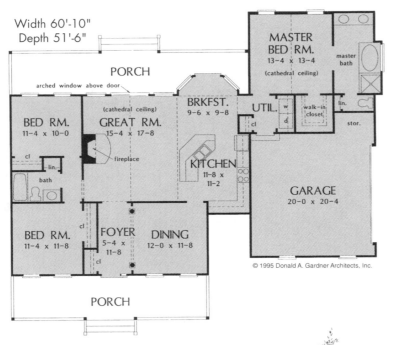

PORCH

arched window above door

BED RM.
11-4 x 10-0

(cathedral ceiling)
GREAT RM.
15-4 x 17-8

fireplace

cl

lin.

bath

BED RM.
11-4 x 11-8

cl

FOYER
5-4 x
11-8

cl

DINING
12-0 x 11-8

BRKFST.
9-6 x 9-8

UTIL.

KITCHEN
11-8 x
11-2

MASTER
BED RM.
13-4 x 13-4

(cathedral ceiling)

master
bath

cl

w

d

walk-in
closet

lin.

stor.

GARAGE
20-0 x 20-4

PORCH

© 1995 Donald A. Gardner Architects, Inc.

Design 9780
Square Footage: 1,561

— DESIGN BY —
DONALD A. GARDNER
ARCHITECTS, INC.

◆ Combining quaint country details with stunning modern elements, this lovely one-story home can really stretch a modest budget. The foyer opens to a formal dining room defined by columns, and leads to the great room which boasts a cathedral ceiling and a focal-point fireplace. The kitchen and breakfast room are open to the living area and offer access to the rear porch through the windowed bay. A quiet master suite nestles to the rear of the plan and includes a lavish bath with a garden tub and separate shower. Two family bedrooms share a full bath that opens from a gallery hall. The two-car garage adds space for storage.

Rear Elevation

B. NATHAN

Design 9749
Square Footage: 1,864
Bonus Room: 420 sq. ft.

◆ Quaint and cozy on the outside with front and rear porches, this three-bedroom country home surprises with an open floor plan featuring a large great room with a cathedral ceiling. Nine-foot ceilings add volume throughout the home. A central kitchen with an angled counter opens to the breakfast and great rooms for easy entertaining. The master bedroom is carefully positioned for privacy and offers a cathedral ceiling, garden tub with skylights, roomy walk-in closet and access to the rear deck. Two secondary bedrooms share a full hall bath. A bonus room with skylights may be developed later. Please specify basement or crawlspace foundation when ordering.

— DESIGN BY —

DONALD A. GARDNER ARCHITECTS, INC.

seat

spa

DECK

PORCH

arched window above door

(cathedral ceiling)

BRKFST.
11-4 x 8-0

(cathedral ceiling)
MASTER BED RM.
14-0 x 17-0

master bath

skylights

up   storage

walk-in closet

BED RM.
11-4 x 11-0

cl   lin.

fireplace

KITCHEN
11-4 x 12-9

cl
d
w
UTIL.

bath

GREAT RM.
15-4 x 18-8

pd. rm.

GARAGE
23-4 x 23-8

BED RM.
13-8 x 11-8

cl

FOYER
7-4 x 11-8

cl

DINING
14-8 x 11-8

© 1993 Donald A. Gardner Architects, Inc.

PORCH

Width 70'-4"
Depth 56'-4"

down

skylights

BONUS RM.
14-4 x 23-8

Rear Elevation

B. NATHAN

◆ This classic farmhouse enjoys a wraparound porch that's perfect for enjoyment of the outdoors. To the rear of the plan, a sun terrace with a spa opens from the master suite and the morning room. A grand great room offers a sloped ceiling and a corner fireplace with a raised hearth. The formal dining room is defined by a low wall and by graceful archways set off by decorative columns. The tiled kitchen has a centered island counter with a snack bar and adjoins a laundry area. Two family bedrooms reside to the side of the plan, and each enjoys private access to the covered porch. A secluded master suite nestles in its own wing and features a sitting area with access to the rear terrace and spa.

Design 3672
Square Footage: 2,090
L D

— DESIGN BY —
HOME PLANNERS

Width 84'-6"
Depth 64'-0"

© 1995 Donald A. Gardner Architects, Inc.

B. NATHAN

◆ This country home has more than just elegance, style and a host of amenities—it has heart. A cathedral ceiling highlights the great room, while a clerestory window and sliding glass doors really let in the light. Broad windows in the breakfast bay splash the L-shaped kitchen with natural light. The private master suite, with a tray ceiling and a walk-in closet, boasts luxurious amenities in the skylit master bath: a windowed whirlpool tub complements a separate shower. Two additional bedrooms share a full bath. The front bedroom features a walk-in closet and could also double as a study.

Width 62'-4"
Depth 55'-2"

PORCH

MASTER BED RM.
13-4 x 16-4

master bath

skylight

walk-in closet

BRKFST.
10-4 x 8-8

cl

lin.

w
d

storage

BED RM.
11-4 x 11-0

(cathedral ceiling)

GREAT RM.
15-4 x 18-6

cl

lin.

bath

fireplace

KIT.
11-4 x 12-10

UTIL.

walk-in closet

BED RM./ STUDY
11-0 x 11-8

FOYER
6-0 x 8-4

cl

DINING
11-0 x 11-8

GARAGE
21-0 x 21-8

storage

(optional door location)

PORCH

© 1995 Donald A. Gardner Architects, Inc.

Design 9779
Square Footage: 1,632

—DESIGN BY—
DONALD A. GARDNER
ARCHITECTS, INC.

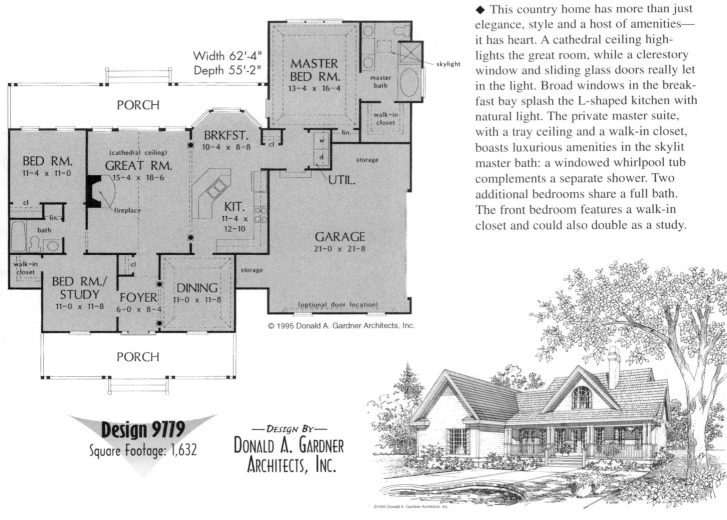

©1995 Donald A. Gardner Architects, Inc.

245

Design 9783
Square Footage: 1,832

BED RM.
12-8 x 11-0

cl
lin.
bath
walk-in
closet

BED RM./
STUDY
12-4 x 13-0

FOYER
6-4 x
9-8
vaulted
ceiling

DINING
12-4 x 13-0

GREAT RM.
16-4 x 18-8

fireplace

cl

(cathedral ceiling)

PORCH

Width 65'-4"
Depth 62'-0"

BRKFST.
11-4 x 9-2

KIT.
11-4 x 12-4

UTIL.

w d

up

cl

MASTER
BED RM.
14-0 x 16-4

skylight

master
bath

lin.

walk-in
closet

storage

GARAGE
21-8 x 22-4

storage

(optional door location)

PORCH

© 1995 Donald A. Gardner Architects, Inc.

attic
storage

storage

down

skylights

BONUS RM.
12-8 x 22-4

— Design By —
Donald A. Gardner
Architects, Inc.

◆ A traditional farmhouse look is combined with updated amenities to give
this home a warm, comfortable livability. The foyer is accented with a
clerestory window and vaulted ceiling
with columns defining the entrance to
the formal dining room. The great room
is crowned with a cathedral ceiling and
set off with a fireplace and columns
leading to the open kitchen. A gourmet
preparation island and a bayed breakfast
nook along with open views to the great
room make kitchen work a joy. A front
bedroom can be a study with a foyer
entrance. The master bedroom is privately situated at the rear of the plan
and is graced with a luxurious spa bathroom and walk-in closet.

© 1995 Donald A. Gardner Architects, Inc.   B. BATWAN

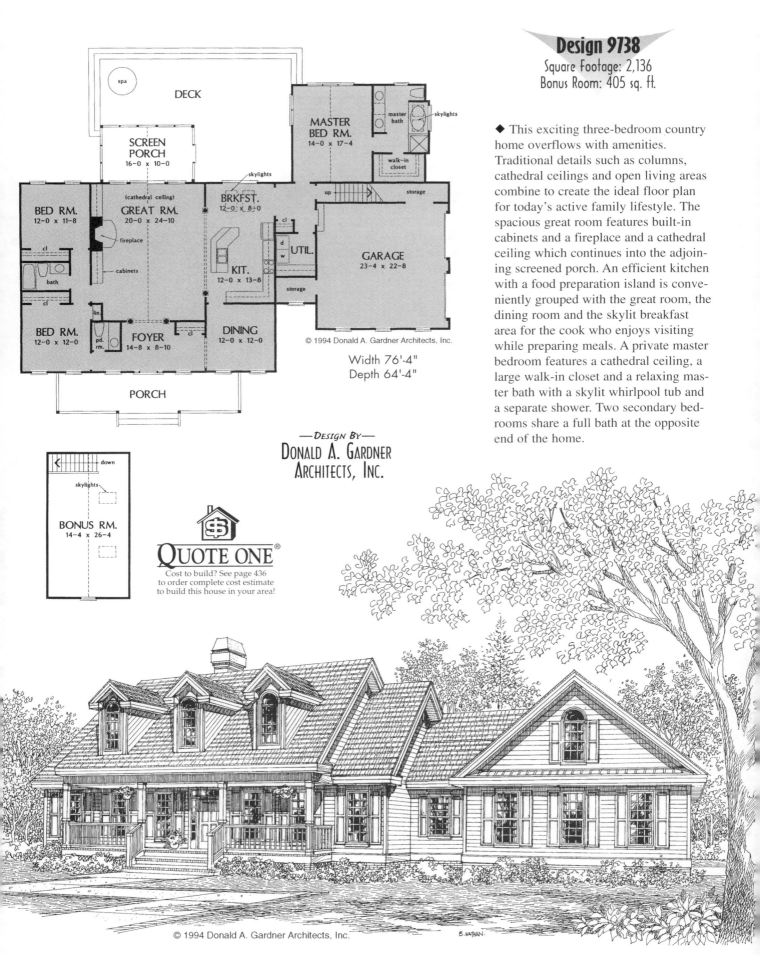

Design 9738

Square Footage: 2,136
Bonus Room: 405 sq. ft.

DECK

spa

SCREEN
PORCH
16-0 x 10-0

MASTER
BED RM.
14-0 x 17-4

master
bath

skylights

walk-in
closet

up

storage

BED RM.
12-0 x 11-8

GREAT RM.
20-0 x 24-10

(cathedral ceiling)

skylights

BRKFST.
12-0 x 8-0

cl

fireplace

cabinets

KIT.
12-0 x 13-8

d
w

UTIL.

GARAGE
23-4 x 22-8

bath

storage

BED RM.
12-0 x 12-0

lin.

pd.
rm.

FOYER
14-8 x 8-10

DINING
12-0 x 12-0

© 1994 Donald A. Gardner Architects, Inc.

Width 76'-4"
Depth 64'-4"

PORCH

—DESIGN BY—
DONALD A. GARDNER
ARCHITECTS, INC.

down

skylights

BONUS RM.
14-4 x 26-4

Quote One®
Cost to build? See page 436
to order complete cost estimate
to build this house in your area!

◆ This exciting three-bedroom country
home overflows with amenities.
Traditional details such as columns,
cathedral ceilings and open living areas
combine to create the ideal floor plan
for today's active family lifestyle. The
spacious great room features built-in
cabinets and a fireplace and a cathedral
ceiling which continues into the adjoining screened porch. An efficient kitchen
with a food preparation island is conveniently grouped with the great room, the
dining room and the skylit breakfast
area for the cook who enjoys visiting
while preparing meals. A private master
bedroom features a cathedral ceiling, a
large walk-in closet and a relaxing master bath with a skylit whirlpool tub and
a separate shower. Two secondary bedrooms share a full bath at the opposite
end of the home.

B. NATHAN.

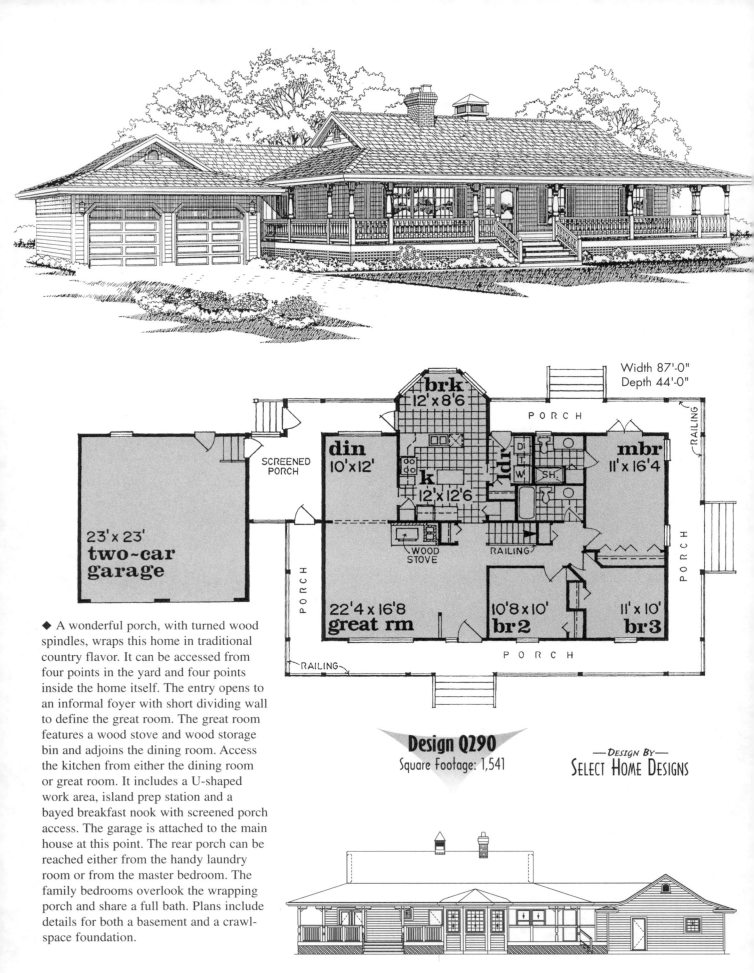

Width 87'-0"
Depth 44'-0"

SCREENED PORCH

PORCH

brk
12' x 8'6

din
10'x12'

k
12' x 12'6

ldr

DI
T
W
SH

mbr
11' x 16'4

23' x 23'
two-car garage

WOOD STOVE

RAILING

RAILING

PORCH

PORCH

22'4 x 16'8
great rm

10'8 x 10'
br2

11' x 10'
br3

PORCH

RAILING

◆ A wonderful porch, with turned wood spindles, wraps this home in traditional country flavor. It can be accessed from four points in the yard and four points inside the home itself. The entry opens to an informal foyer with short dividing wall to define the great room. The great room features a wood stove and wood storage bin and adjoins the dining room. Access the kitchen from either the dining room or great room. It includes a U-shaped work area, island prep station and a bayed breakfast nook with screened porch access. The garage is attached to the main house at this point. The rear porch can be reached either from the handy laundry room or from the master bedroom. The family bedrooms overlook the wrapping porch and share a full bath. Plans include details for both a basement and a crawl-space foundation.

Design Q290
Square Footage: 1,541

— DESIGN BY —
SELECT HOME DESIGNS

248

Design Q449
Square Footage: 1,578

◆ With a graceful pediment above and a sturdy, columned veranda below, this quaint home was made for country living. The veranda wraps slightly around on two sides of the facade and permits access to a central foyer with a den (or third bedroom) on the right and the country kitchen on the left. Look for an island work space in the kitchen and a plant ledge over the entry between the great room and the kitchen. A fireplace warms the great room and is flanked by windows overlooking the rear deck. A casually defined dining space has double-door access to this same deck. Bedrooms are clustered on the right side of the plan. The master suite offers an art niche at its entry and a bath with separate tub and shower. Family bedrooms share a skylit bath. Choose either a basement or crawlspace foundation for this design—both are included in the plans.

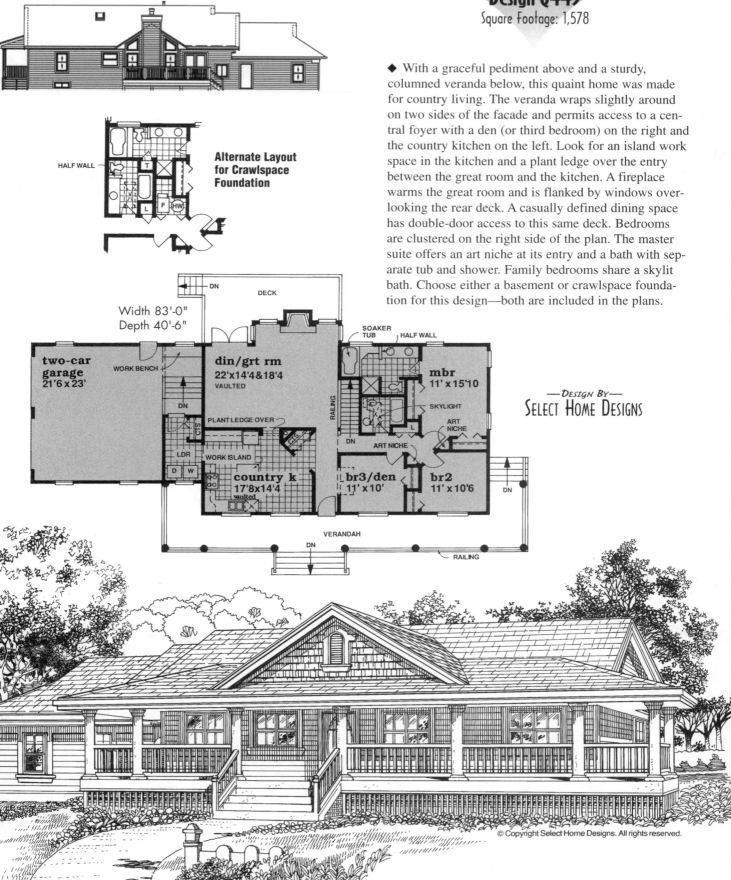

Alternate Layout for Crawlspace Foundation

HALF WALL

Width 83'-0"
Depth 40'-6"

DN
DECK

two-car garage
21'6 x 23'

WORK BENCH

DN

dinn/grt rm
22'x14'4 &18'4
VAULTED

PLANT LEDGE OVER

RAILING

LDR

WORK ISLAND

D W

country k
17'8x14'4
vaulted

SOAKER TUB
HALF WALL

mbr
11' x 15'10

SKYLIGHT

ART NICHE

DN

ART NICHE

br3/den
11' x 10'

br2
11' x 10'6

DN

VERANDAH
DN
RAILING

— DESIGN BY —
SELECT HOME DESIGNS

B. NATHAN · © 1995 Donald A. Gardner Architects, Inc.

Design 9788
Square Footage: 1,302

◆ Well designed for maximum efficiency and practical to build, this streamlined plan is big on popular innovations as well as curb appeal. A spacious cathedral ceiling expands the open great room, the dining room and the kitchen. A deck located next to the kitchen amplifies the living and entertaining space. The versatile bedroom/study features a cathedral ceiling and shares a full skylit bath with another bedroom. The master bedroom is highlighted by a cathedral ceiling for extra volume and light. Its private bath opens up with a skylight and includes a double-bowl vanity, a garden tub and a separately located toilet. A walk-in closet adjacent to the bedroom completes the suite.

—Design By—
Donald A. Gardner
Architects, Inc.

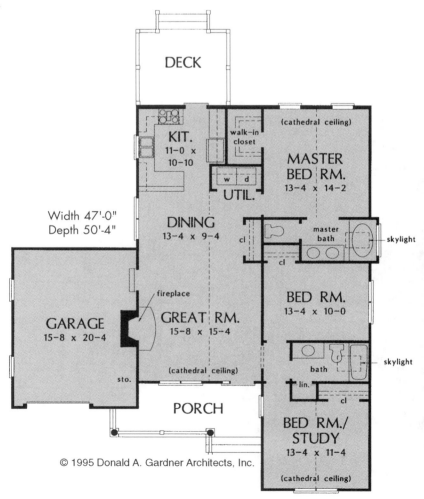

Width 47'-0"
Depth 50'-4"

© 1995 Donald A. Gardner Architects, Inc.

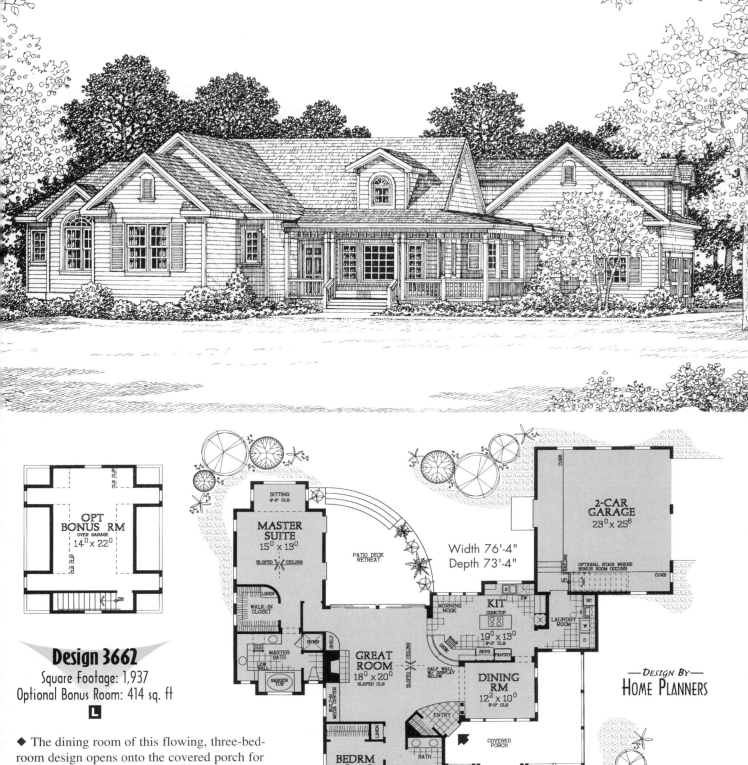

OPT
BONUS RM
OVER GARAGE
14⁰ x 22⁰

MASTER
SUITE
15⁰ x 13⁰
SLOPED CEILING

SITTING
9'-0" CLG

PATIO DECK
RETREAT

Width 76'-4"
Depth 73'-4"

2-CAR
GARAGE
23⁰ x 25⁸

OPTIONAL STAIR WHERE
BONUS ROOM OCCURS

MORNING
NOOK

KIT
19⁰ x 13⁰
9'-0" CLG
COOKTOP

LAUNDRY
ROOM

WALK-IN
CLOSET

LINEN

MASTER
BATH
LOW WALL

SHWR

SHELF

GARDEN
TUB

BUILT-IN
MEDIA CENTER

GREAT
ROOM
18⁰ x 20⁰
SLOPED CLG

HALF WALL
W/ DISPLAY
BELOW

PANTRY

REF.

DINING
RM
12² x 10⁰
9'-0" CLG

LINEN

BEDRM
10⁰ x 10⁰
9'-0" CLG

ENTRY

BATH

COVERED
PORCH

BEDRM
10⁰ x 10⁰
9'-0" CLG

—DESIGN BY—
HOME PLANNERS

Design 3662
Square Footage: 1,937
Optional Bonus Room: 414 sq. ft
Ⓛ

◆ The dining room of this flowing, three-bedroom design opens onto the covered porch for relaxing indoor-outdoor dining. The tiled entry foyer leads directly to the great room, with its built-in media center, corner shelves and access to the rear patio deck. A country kitchen with island cooktop, morning nook and built-in desk is open to the great room over a half wall. The master suite with sloped ceiling features an extended sitting area with windows on three sides. The walk-in closet has built-in linen shelves and the master bath has dual vanities and a garden tub.

Quote One®
Cost to build? See page 436
to order complete cost estimate
to build this house in your area!

251

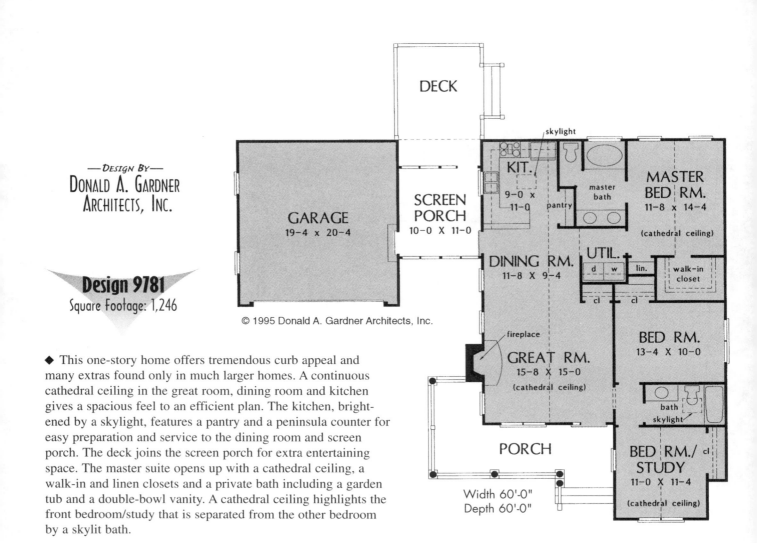

DECK

GARAGE
19-4 x 20-4

SCREEN
PORCH
10-0 X 11-0

skylight

KIT.
9-0 x
11-0

pantry

master
bath

MASTER
BED RM.
11-8 x 14-4

(cathedral ceiling)

UTIL.
d | w | lin.

walk-in
closet

cl | cl

DINING RM.
11-8 X 9-4

fireplace

GREAT RM.
15-8 X 15-0

(cathedral ceiling)

BED RM.
13-4 x 10-0

bath

skylight

PORCH

BED RM./
STUDY
11-0 X 11-4

(cathedral ceiling)

Width 60'-0"
Depth 60'-0"

—Design By—

Donald A. Gardner Architects, Inc.

Design 9781
Square Footage: 1,246

◆ This one-story home offers tremendous curb appeal and many extras found only in much larger homes. A continuous cathedral ceiling in the great room, dining room and kitchen gives a spacious feel to an efficient plan. The kitchen, brightened by a skylight, features a pantry and a peninsula counter for easy preparation and service to the dining room and screen porch. The deck joins the screen porch for extra entertaining space. The master suite opens up with a cathedral ceiling, a walk-in and linen closets and a private bath including a garden tub and a double-bowl vanity. A cathedral ceiling highlights the front bedroom/study that is separated from the other bedroom by a skylit bath.

© 1994 Donald A. Gardner Architects, Inc.

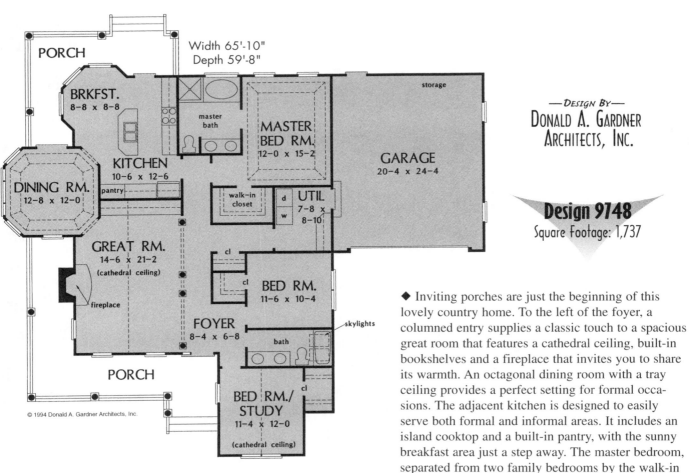

PORCH

Width 65'-10"
Depth 59'-8"

BRKFST.
8-8 x 8-8

storage

master
bath

MASTER
BED RM.
12-0 x 15-2

GARAGE
20-4 x 24-4

KITCHEN
10-6 x 12-6

DINING RM.
12-8 x 12-0

pantry

walk-in
closet

d
w

UTIL
7-8 x
8-10

GREAT RM.
14-6 x 21-2
(cathedral ceiling)

cl

fireplace

cl

cl

BED RM.
11-6 x 10-4

FOYER
8-4 x 6-8

skylights

bath

PORCH

BED RM./
STUDY
11-4 x 12-0

(cathedral ceiling)

© 1994 Donald A. Gardner Architects, Inc.

— DESIGN BY —
DONALD A. GARDNER
ARCHITECTS, INC.

Design 9748
Square Footage: 1,737

◆ Inviting porches are just the beginning of this lovely country home. To the left of the foyer, a columned entry supplies a classic touch to a spacious great room that features a cathedral ceiling, built-in bookshelves and a fireplace that invites you to share its warmth. An octagonal dining room with a tray ceiling provides a perfect setting for formal occasions. The adjacent kitchen is designed to easily serve both formal and informal areas. It includes an island cooktop and a built-in pantry, with the sunny breakfast area just a step away. The master bedroom, separated from two family bedrooms by the walk-in closet and utility room, offers privacy and comfort.

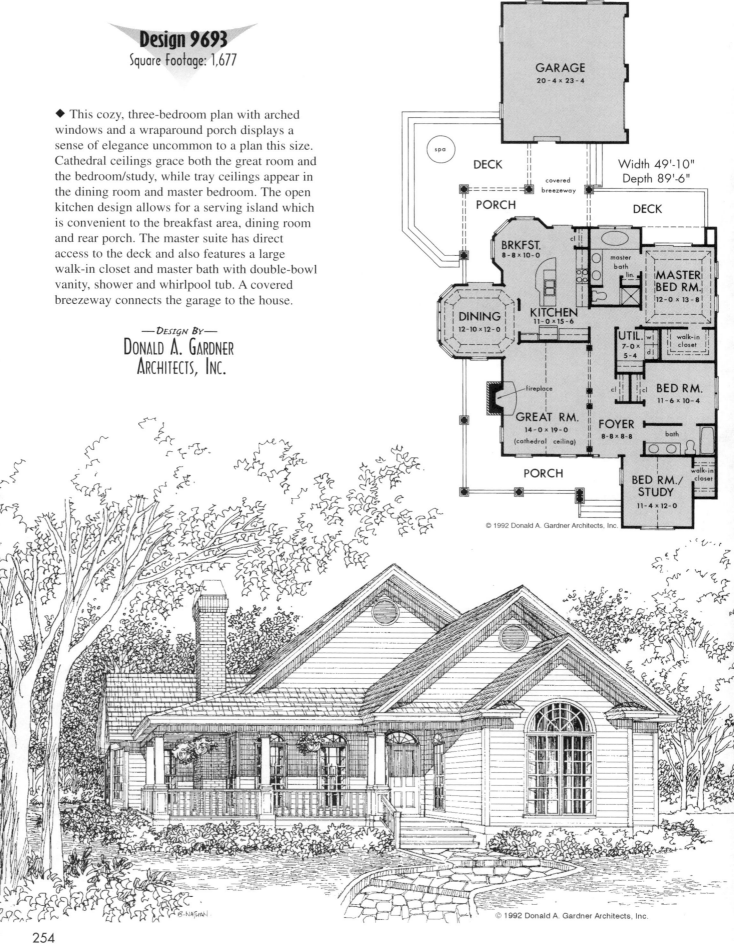

Design 9693
Square Footage: 1,677

◆ This cozy, three-bedroom plan with arched windows and a wraparound porch displays a sense of elegance uncommon to a plan this size. Cathedral ceilings grace both the great room and the bedroom/study, while tray ceilings appear in the dining room and master bedroom. The open kitchen design allows for a serving island which is convenient to the breakfast area, dining room and rear porch. The master suite has direct access to the deck and also features a large walk-in closet and master bath with double-bowl vanity, shower and whirlpool tub. A covered breezeway connects the garage to the house.

— DESIGN BY —
DONALD A. GARDNER
ARCHITECTS, INC.

GARAGE
20-4 x 23-4

spa

DECK

covered breezeway

PORCH

DECK

Width 49'-10"
Depth 89'-6"

BRKFST.
8-8 x 10-0

cl

master bath
lin.

MASTER BED RM.
12-0 x 13-8

DINING
12-10 x 12-0

KITCHEN
11-0 x 15-6

UTIL.
7-0 x 5-4

walk-in closet

fireplace

cl   cl

BED RM.
11-6 x 10-4

GREAT RM.
14-0 x 19-0
(cathedral ceiling)

FOYER
8-8 x 8-8

bath

PORCH

BED RM./ STUDY
11-4 x 12-0

walk-in closet

© 1992 Donald A. Gardner Architects, Inc.

B. NATHAN

© 1992 Donald A. Gardner Architects, Inc.

254

Design 9764
Square Footage: 1,815

◆ Dormers, arched windows and two covered porches lend gentle country appeal to this lovely home. Inside, the foyer opens to the dining room and leads through a columned archway to the great room, warmed by a fireplace. The covered, skylit back porch provides golden opportunities for outdoor entertaining. The open kitchen easily serves both the bayed breakfast room and the formal dining room. A cathedral ceiling graces the master suite, which also features a private bath with a double vanity and a whirlpool tub. A two-car garage with a skylit bonus room above is connected to the rear covered porch.

Width 70'-8"
Depth 70'-2"

GARAGE
21-0 x 21-4

storage

up

PORCH

skylights

MASTER BED RM.
14-8 x 15-4

BRKFST.
10-4 x 8-6

UTIL.
8-8 x 11-0

GREAT RM.
17-4 x 19-0

(cathedral ceiling)

KITCHEN
11-8 x 10-6

master bath

walk-in closet

fireplace

linen

bath

sto.

cl

FOYER
8-8 x 8-0

DINING
11-4 x 12-8

cl

BED RM.
12-2 x 12-4

BED RM.
10-10 x 12-4

cl

PORCH

©1994 Donald A. Gardner Architects, Inc.

— DESIGN BY —
DONALD A. GARDNER ARCHITECTS, INC.

attic stor.

skylights

down

BONUS RM.
24-8 x 11-10

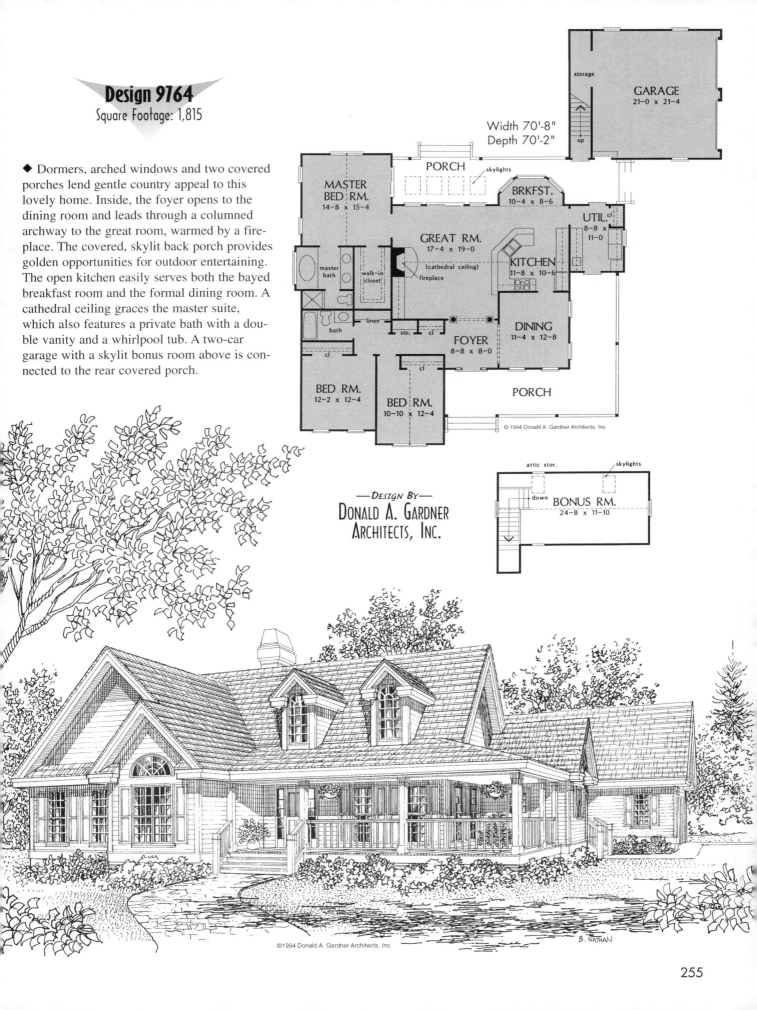

B. NATHAN

©1994 Donald A. Gardner Architects, Inc.

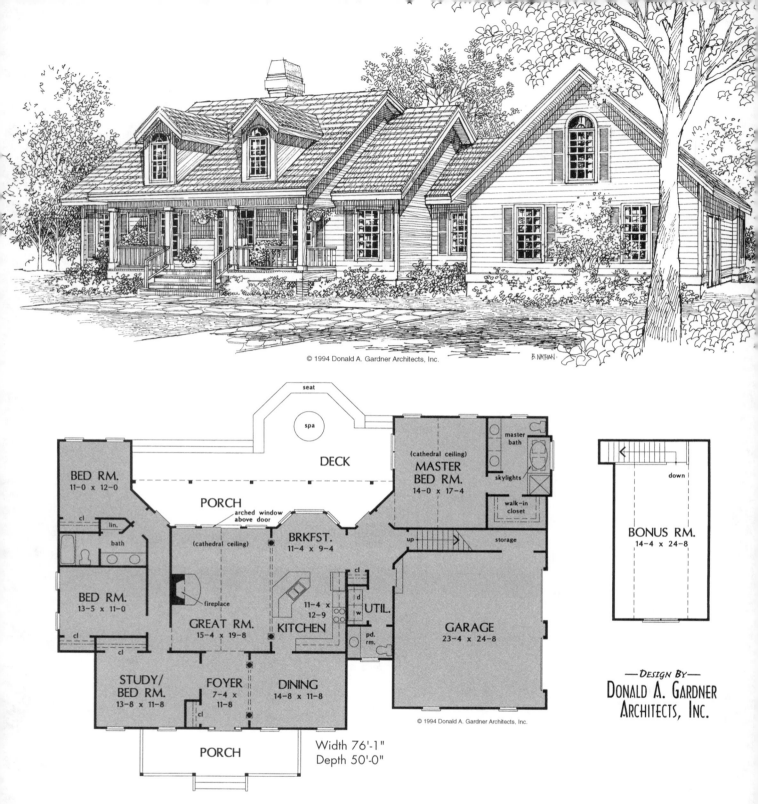

© 1994 Donald A. Gardner Architects, Inc.

B. NATHAN

seat

spa

DECK

BED RM.
11-0 x 12-0

cl

lin.

bath

PORCH

arched window
above door

(cathedral ceiling)

BRKFST.
11-4 x 9-4

MASTER
BED RM.
14-0 x 17-4

(cathedral ceiling)

master
bath

skylights

walk-in
closet

up

storage

BED RM.
13-5 x 11-0

cl

fireplace

GREAT RM.
15-4 x 19-8

KITCHEN

11-4 x
12-9

cl

d
w

UTIL.

GARAGE
23-4 x 24-8

cl

cl

STUDY/
BED RM.
13-8 x 11-8

cl

FOYER
7-4 x
11-8

DINING
14-8 x 11-8

pd.
rm.

© 1994 Donald A. Gardner Architects, Inc.

PORCH

Width 76'-1"
Depth 50'-0"

BONUS RM.
14-4 x 24-8

down

—DESIGN BY—
DONALD A. GARDNER
ARCHITECTS, INC.

Design 9756
Square Footage: 2,207
Bonus Room: 435 sq. ft.

◆ This quaint four-bedroom home with front and rear porches reinforces its beauty with arched windows and dormers. The pillared dining room opens on your right while a study that could double as a guest room is available on your left. Straight ahead lies the massive great room with its cathedral ceiling, enchanting fireplace and access to the private rear porch and the deck with a spa and seat. Within steps of the dining room is the efficient kitchen and the sunny breakfast nook. The master suite enjoys a cathedral ceiling, rear deck access and a master bath with a skylit whirlpool tub, a walk-in closet and a double vanity. Two additional bedrooms are located at the opposite end of the house and share a full bath with dual vanities.

—DESIGN BY—

DONALD A. GARDNER ARCHITECTS, INC.

Design 9778
Square Footage: 1,655

◆ Covered front porch dormers and arched windows welcome you to this modified version of one of our most popular country home plans. Interior columns dramatically open the foyer and the kitchen to the spacious great room. The drama is heightened by the great room's cathedral ceiling and centered fireplace. The kitchen, with its food preparation island, easily serves the breakfast area and the formal dining room. The master suite has a tray ceiling and access to the rear deck. Added luxuries include a walk-in closet and a skylit master bath with a double vanity, a garden tub and a shower. Two generous bedrooms share the second bath. Please specify basement or crawlspace foundation when ordering.

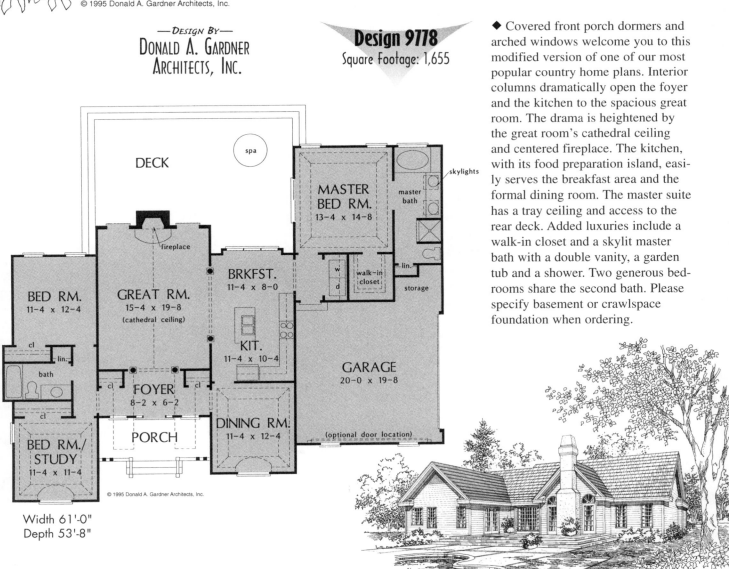

DECK

spa

MASTER BED RM.
13-4 x 14-8

skylights

master bath

fireplace

BRKFST.
11-4 x 8-0

w
d

walk-in closet

lin.

storage

GREAT RM.
15-4 x 19-8
(cathedral ceiling)

BED RM.
11-4 x 12-4

cl

lin.

bath

cl

KIT.
11-4 x 10-4

GARAGE
20-0 x 19-8

FOYER
8-2 x 6-2

cl

cl

BED RM./ STUDY
11-4 x 11-4

PORCH

DINING RM.
11-4 x 12-4

(optional door location)

Width 61'-0"
Depth 53'-8"

257

© 1995 Donald A. Gardner Architects, Inc.

B. NATHAN

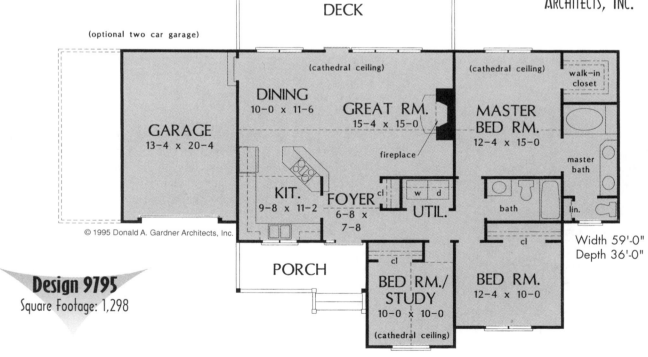

DECK

— DESIGN BY —
DONALD A. GARDNER
ARCHITECTS, INC.

(optional two car garage)

(cathedral ceiling)

GARAGE
13-4 x 20-4

DINING
10-0 x 11-6

GREAT RM.
15-4 x 15-0

fireplace

(cathedral ceiling)

MASTER
BED RM.
12-4 x 15-0

walk-in
closet

master
bath

KIT.
9-8 x 11-2

FOYER
6-8 x
7-8

cl

w   d

UTIL.

bath

lin.

cl

© 1995 Donald A. Gardner Architects, Inc.

Width 59'-0"
Depth 36'-0"

PORCH

BED RM./
STUDY
10-0 x 10-0

(cathedral ceiling)

BED RM.
12-4 x 10-0

Design 9795
Square Footage: 1,298

◆ Though smaller in square footage, this home is very livable and quite charming. A covered front porch gives it country detailing and leads into the central foyer where the main living areas dominate. A huge great room with fireplace, an adjoining dining room and the open, L-shaped island kitchen all center around a lovely rear deck. The dining room and living room share a cathedral ceiling that opens their space even more. To one side of the foyer is a study—or make it a third bedroom if needed. The master bedroom also has a cathedral ceiling and features a lovely bath with double sinks. A single-car garage, reached through a door in the dining area, can be expanded to a two-car if you choose.

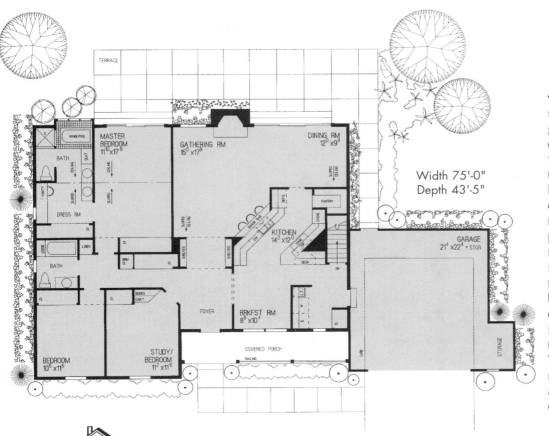

Width 75'-0"
Depth 43'-5"

◆ This charming, one-story traditional home greets visitors with a covered porch, decked out with columns and balusters. Inside, a galley-style kitchen shares a snack counter with the gathering room, which offers a fireplace and opens to the formal dining room. The lavish master suite nestles to the rear of the plan and boasts a sloped ceiling, a dressing room and a relaxing bath with a whirlpool tub and a separate shower. Two additional bedrooms—one could double as a study—enjoy views of the front property.

QUOTE ONE®

Cost to build? See page 436
to order complete cost estimate
to build this house in your area!

Design 2947
Square Footage: 1,830
L D

This home, as shown in the photograph, may differ from the actual blueprints.
For more detailed information, please check the floor plans carefully.

Photo by Andrew D. Lautman

— DESIGN BY —
HOME PLANNERS

SHOWER

WALK-IN CLOSET

MASTER SUITE
15¹⁰ x 12⁸
SLOPED CLG

MASTER BATH

ULTRA TUB

LIVING RM
15⁰ x 14⁰
SLOPED CLG

COVERED PATIO

BEDRM
9⁰ x 9⁸
SLOPED CLG

LINEN

BATH

REFG

RANGE

FOYER

9-SIDED FP

SLVS

CURIO

HVAC **WH**

D **W**

CURB

KITCHEN
8⁰ x 14⁶

DINING RM
9¹⁰ x 9⁴
COFFERED CLG

P **DW** **S**

GARAGE
19⁴ x 22¹⁰

COVERED PORCH

RAILING

RAILING

Width 44'-4"
Depth 47'-4"

Design 3659
Square Footage: 1,118

L

◆ Compact yet comfortable, this home has many appealing amenities. From the covered front porch, the entrance foyer opens onto the sunlit, octagonal dining room and the large living room. To the left of the foyer is the efficient kitchen that has the added bonus of no cross-room traffic. The master suite is luxurious and includes a lavish bath complete with a corner tub, a separate shower, a walk-in closet and twin vanities. A secondary bedroom has access to a full hall bath.

QUOTE ONE®
Cost to build? See page 436
to order complete cost estimate
to build this house in your area!

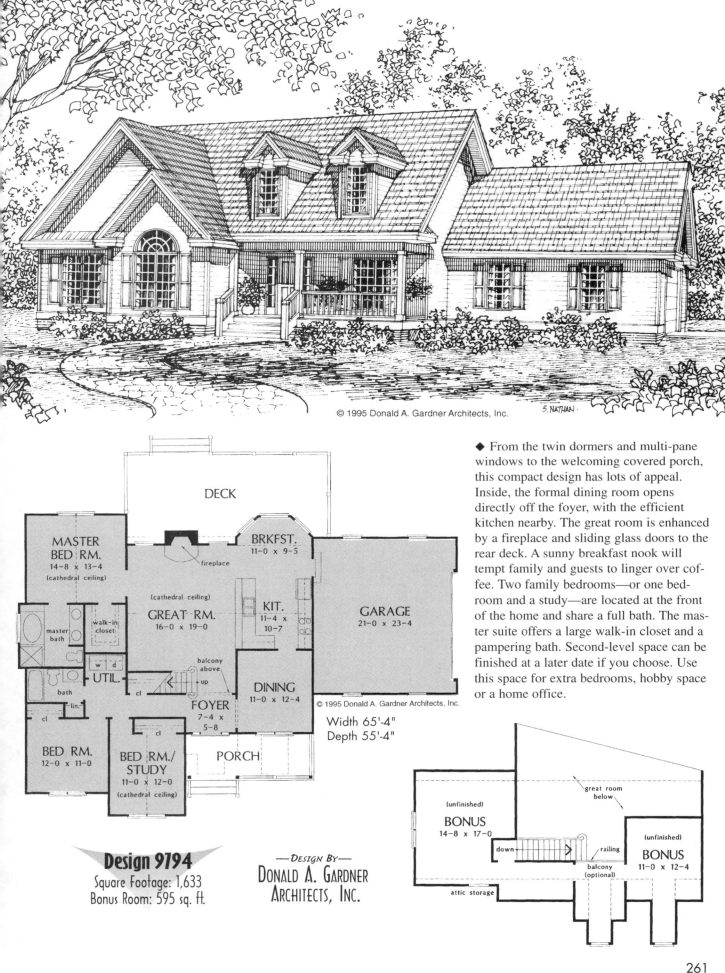

© 1995 Donald A. Gardner Architects, Inc.

S. NATHAN

DECK

MASTER BED RM.
14-8 x 13-4
(cathedral ceiling)

fireplace

BRKFST.
11-0 x 9-5

master bath

walk-in closet

(cathedral ceiling)

GREAT RM.
16-0 x 19-0

KIT.
11-4 x 10-7

GARAGE
21-0 x 23-4

w d

UTIL.

bath

balcony above

up

lin.

cl

FOYER
7-4 x 5-8

DINING
11-0 x 12-4

© 1995 Donald A. Gardner Architects, Inc.

cl

BED RM.
12-0 x 11-0

BED RM./ STUDY
11-0 x 12-0
(cathedral ceiling)

cl

PORCH

Width 65'-4"
Depth 55'-4"

Design 9794
Square Footage: 1,633
Bonus Room: 595 sq. ft.

—DESIGN BY—
DONALD A. GARDNER ARCHITECTS, INC.

◆ From the twin dormers and multi-pane windows to the welcoming covered porch, this compact design has lots of appeal. Inside, the formal dining room opens directly off the foyer, with the efficient kitchen nearby. The great room is enhanced by a fireplace and sliding glass doors to the rear deck. A sunny breakfast nook will tempt family and guests to linger over coffee. Two family bedrooms—or one bedroom and a study—are located at the front of the home and share a full bath. The master suite offers a large walk-in closet and a pampering bath. Second-level space can be finished at a later date if you choose. Use this space for extra bedrooms, hobby space or a home office.

(unfinished)

great room below

BONUS
14-8 x 17-0

down

railing

balcony (optional)

(unfinished)

BONUS
11-0 x 12-4

attic storage

261

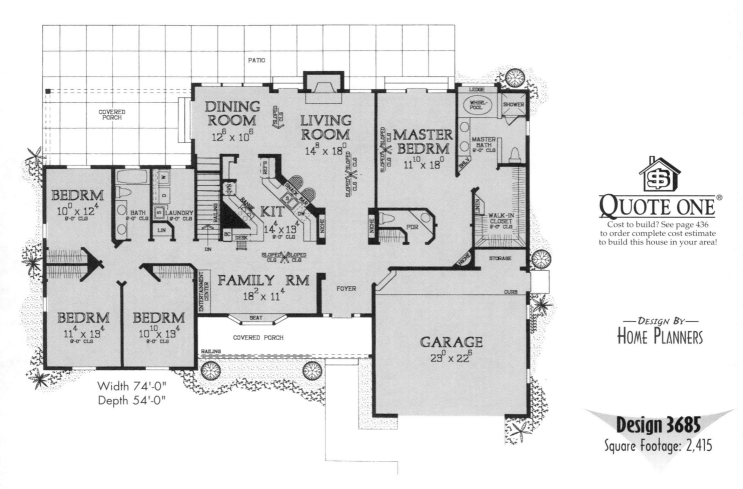

PATIO

COVERED PORCH

DINING ROOM
12⁶ x 10⁶

LIVING ROOM
14⁸ x 18⁰

SLOPED CLG

MASTER BEDRM
11¹⁰ x 18⁰

LEDGE

WHIRL-POOL

SHOWER

MASTER BATH
9'-0" CLG

BEDRM
10⁰ x 12⁴
9'-0" CLG

BATH
9'-0" CLG

LAUNDRY
9'-0" CLG

LIN

RANGE

REFG

SNACK BAR

KIT
14⁴ x 13⁰
9'-0" CLG

DW

NICHE

NICHE

PDR

LINEN

WALK-IN CLOSET
9'-0" CLG

RAILING

DN

BC

DESK

SLOPED CLG

SLOPED CLG

NICHE

STORAGE

ENTERTAINMENT CENTER

BEDRM
11⁴ x 13⁴
9'-0" CLG

BEDRM
10¹⁰ x 13⁴
9'-0" CLG

FAMILY RM
18² x 11⁴

FOYER

SEAT

COVERED PORCH

RAILING

CURB

GARAGE
23⁰ x 22⁶

Width 74'-0"
Depth 54'-0"

Quote One®
Cost to build? See page 436
to order complete cost estimate
to build this house in your area!

— DESIGN BY —
HOME PLANNERS

Design 3685
Square Footage: 2,415

◆ A quaint covered porch, country shutters and a clerestory dormer window decorate this traditional design with blue-ribbon style. The family room boasts a bay window with a seat, and a built-in entertainment center. An angled kitchen offers a snack bar which overlooks the living room and enjoys the glow of its hearth. The living area has a sloped ceiling and leads outdoors to a rear patio and, through the dining room, to a covered porch. Three sizable family bedrooms complement a sensational master suite, which features a whirlpool bath and an oversized walk-in closet.

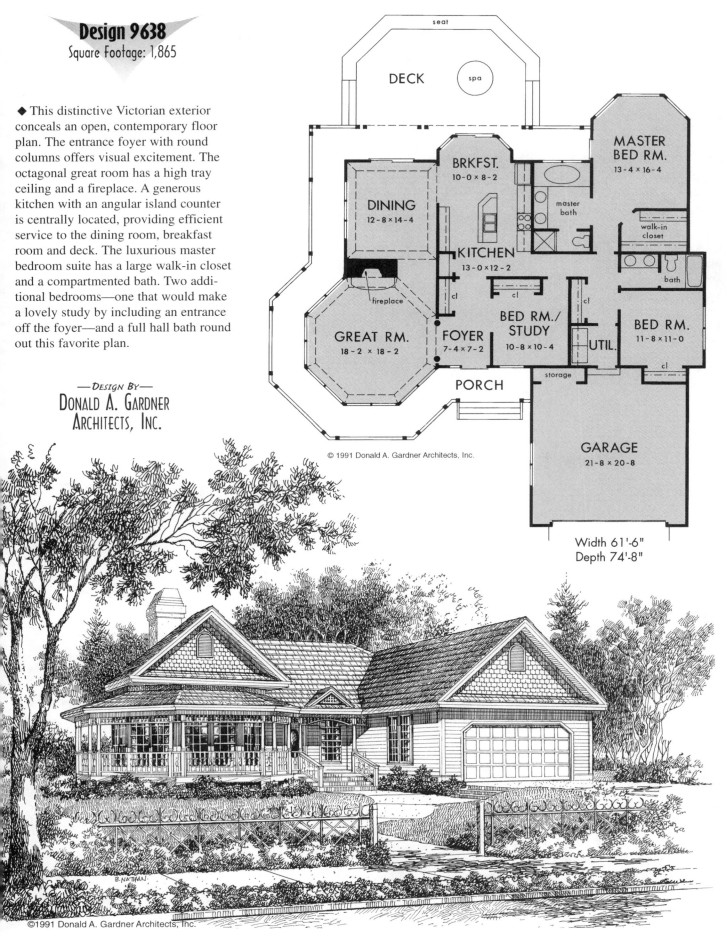

Design 9638

Square Footage: 1,865

◆ This distinctive Victorian exterior conceals an open, contemporary floor plan. The entrance foyer with round columns offers visual excitement. The octagonal great room has a high tray ceiling and a fireplace. A generous kitchen with an angular island counter is centrally located, providing efficient service to the dining room, breakfast room and deck. The luxurious master bedroom suite has a large walk-in closet and a compartmented bath. Two additional bedrooms—one that would make a lovely study by including an entrance off the foyer—and a full hall bath round out this favorite plan.

—Design By—

Donald A. Gardner
Architects, Inc.

seat

DECK

spa

BRKFST.
10-0 × 8-2

MASTER
BED RM.
13-4 × 16-4

DINING
12-8 × 14-4

master
bath

walk-in
closet

KITCHEN
13-0 × 12-2

bath

cl

cl

cl

fireplace

BED RM./
STUDY
10-8 × 10-4

cl

BED RM.
11-8 × 11-0

GREAT RM.
18-2 × 18-2

FOYER
7-4 × 7-2

UTIL.

cl

storage

PORCH

© 1991 Donald A. Gardner Architects, Inc.

GARAGE
21-8 × 20-8

Width 61'-6"
Depth 74'-8"

B. NATHAN.

263

Design 3718
Square Footage: 1,433

— DESIGN BY —
HOME PLANNERS

◆ This eye-catching three-bedroom ranch home is designed specifically for narrow lots. All the many features you've been looking for in a family home can be found. The master bedroom suite includes a full-sized bath and walk-in closet. A second bath is located between the two family bedrooms. The large great room offers plenty of space for all your family gatherings. Decorative louvers, two bay windows, a rear deck, a fireplace and a two-car garage are optional. Blueprints include details for both the basic and the enhanced version.

Enhanced Plan

Basic Plan

Width 35'-0"
Depth 78'-0"

RAILING

DECK
16⁰ X 12⁰

GREAT RM
13² X 33⁴

OPT. FIREPLACE

OPT. BAY WINDOW

OPT. BAY WINDOW

MASTER BEDROOM
12⁶ X 13⁴

WALK-IN CLOSET

BATH

LINEN

BEDROOM
11⁴ X 9⁴

KITCHEN
9⁰ X 16²

DW

BATH

LINEN

FOYER

DN

BEDROOM
11⁴ X 9⁸

COVERED PORCH

GARAGE
20¹⁰ X 21⁸

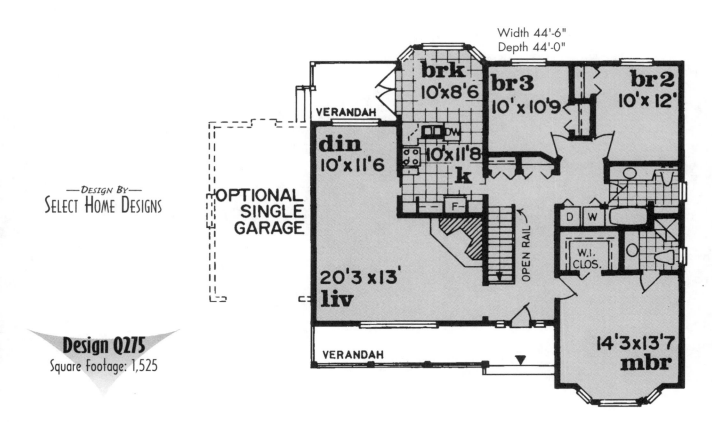

Width 44'-6"
Depth 44'-0"

brk
10'x8'6

br3
10' x 10'9

br2
10' x 12'

VERANDAH

din
10'x11'6

10'x11'8

k

OPTIONAL
SINGLE
GARAGE

F

OPEN RAIL

D W

W.I.
CLOS.

20'3 x13'
liv

VERANDAH

14'3x13'7
mbr

—Design by—
Select Home Designs

Design Q275
Square Footage: 1,525

◆ This charming country home is sized right for economy, but leaves out nothing in the way of livability. A bay window, front and rear verandas and a sweeping room all enrich its heritage design. The front veranda opens to the center hall which leads to the large living and dining areas. A corner fireplace in the living room warms the space in cold winter months. The kitchen and bayed breakfast nook sit to the rear and open to another veranda through double doors. Two family bedrooms are at the back of the plan and share a full hall bath. The master bedroom has a bay window, walk-in closet and private bath. Plans include a single-car option, so you can add on if you choose.

© 1993 Donald A. Gardner Architects, Inc.

Design 9726
Square Footage: 1,498
Optional Basement: 1,531 sq. ft.

◆ This charming country home utilizes multi-pane windows, columns, dormers and a covered porch to offer a welcoming front exterior. Inside, the great room with a dramatic cathedral ceiling commands attention; the kitchen and breakfast room are just beyond a set of columns. The tiered-ceiling dining room presents a delightfully formal atmosphere for dinner parties or family gatherings. A tray ceiling in the master bedroom contributes to its pleasant atmosphere, as do the large walk-in closet and the gracious master bath with a garden tub and a separate shower. The secondary bedrooms are located at the opposite end of the house for privacy. Please specify basement or crawlspace foundation when ordering.

—DESIGN BY—

DONALD A. GARDNER
ARCHITECTS, INC.

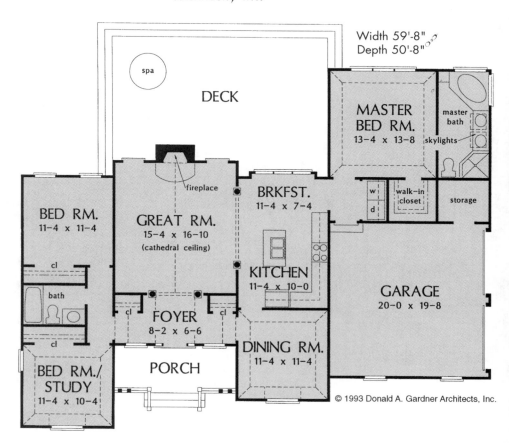

Width 59'-8"
Depth 50'-8"

© 1993 Donald A. Gardner Architects, Inc.

266

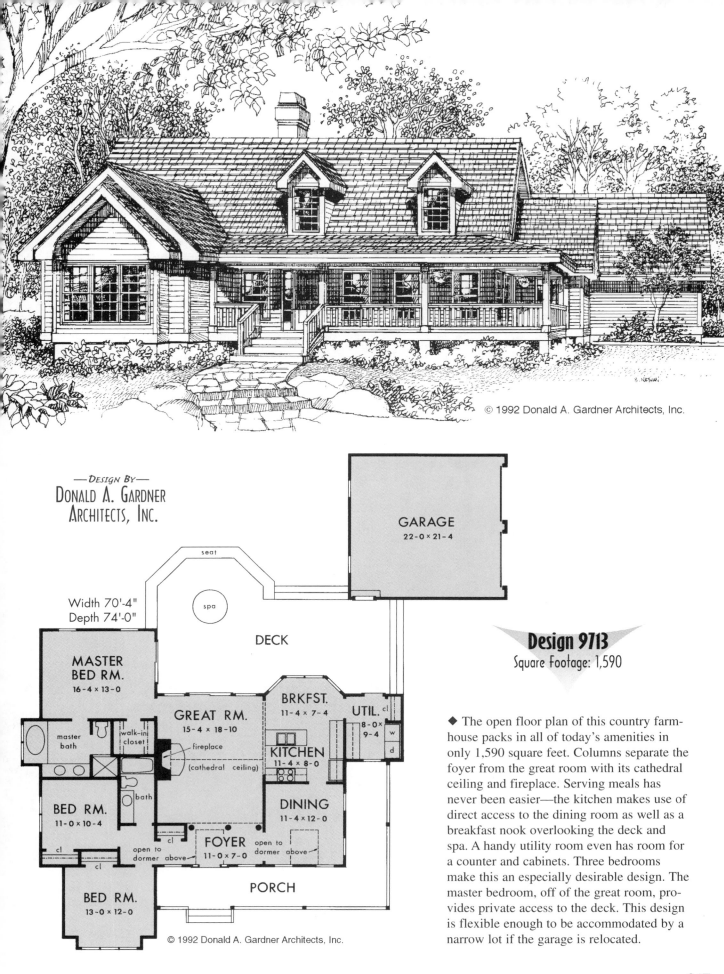

© 1992 Donald A. Gardner Architects, Inc.

—Design By—
Donald A. Gardner
Architects, Inc.

GARAGE
22-0 × 21-4

Width 70'-4"
Depth 74'-0"

seat

spa

DECK

MASTER
BED RM.
16-4 × 13-0

Design 9713
Square Footage: 1,590

master
bath

walk-in
closet

GREAT RM.
15-4 × 18-10

fireplace

(cathedral ceiling)

BRKFST.
11-4 × 7-4

UTIL.
8-0 ×
9-4

cl

w

d

KITCHEN
11-4 × 8-0

bath

BED RM.
11-0 × 10-4

DINING
11-4 × 12-0

cl

cl

cl

open to
dormer above

FOYER
11-0 × 7-0

open to
dormer above

BED RM.
13-0 × 12-0

PORCH

© 1992 Donald A. Gardner Architects, Inc.

◆ The open floor plan of this country farm-house packs in all of today's amenities in only 1,590 square feet. Columns separate the foyer from the great room with its cathedral ceiling and fireplace. Serving meals has never been easier—the kitchen makes use of direct access to the dining room as well as a breakfast nook overlooking the deck and spa. A handy utility room even has room for a counter and cabinets. Three bedrooms make this an especially desirable design. The master bedroom, off of the great room, provides private access to the deck. This design is flexible enough to be accommodated by a narrow lot if the garage is relocated.

267

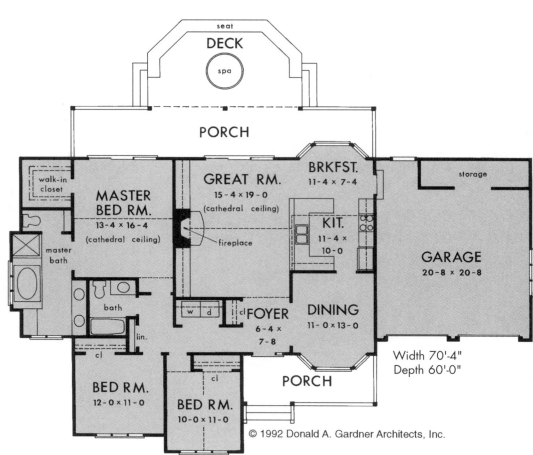

Design 9696
Square Footage: 1,625

◆ This family-pleasing design is thoughtful, indeed. Living areas include a kitchen with efficient work triangle, an adjoining breakfast room, a dining room with bay window, and of course, the great room with fireplace and access to a rear porch. The master bedroom also has porch access, along with a walk-in closet and a lavish bath. Two family bedrooms include one featuring a half-round transom window, adding appeal to the exterior and interior. The laundry room is convenient to all three bedrooms.

DECK
seat
spa

PORCH

walk-in closet

MASTER BED RM.
13-4 x 16-4
(cathedral ceiling)

master bath

bath

GREAT RM.
15-4 x 19-0
(cathedral ceiling)

fireplace

BRKFST.
11-4 x 7-4

storage

KIT.
11-4 x 10-0

GARAGE
20-8 x 20-8

lin.

cl

w d

cl

FOYER
6-4 x 7-8

DINING
11-0 x 13-0

BED RM.
12-0 x 11-0

cl

BED RM.
10-0 x 11-0

PORCH

Width 70'-4"
Depth 60'-0"

© 1992 Donald A. Gardner Architects, Inc.

—Design By—
DONALD A. GARDNER
ARCHITECTS, INC.

© 1992 Donald A. Gardner Architects, Inc.

B. NATHAN

Design 9727
Square Footage: 1,322

◆ Economical doesn't necessarily mean boring, as this country home will prove. It is well-proportioned and especially livable. A gracious foyer leads to the great room through a set of elegant columns. In this living area, a cathedral ceiling works well with a fireplace and skylights to bring the utmost in floor planning home. Outside, an expansive deck leaves room for a spa and built-in seating. A handsome master suite offers a tray ceiling and a private bath. Two additional bedrooms rest to the left of the plan. Each enjoys ample closet space as well as comfortable dimensions. A covered breezeway connects the main house to the two-car garage at the rear of the property.

—DESIGN BY—
DONALD A. GARDNER
ARCHITECTS, INC.

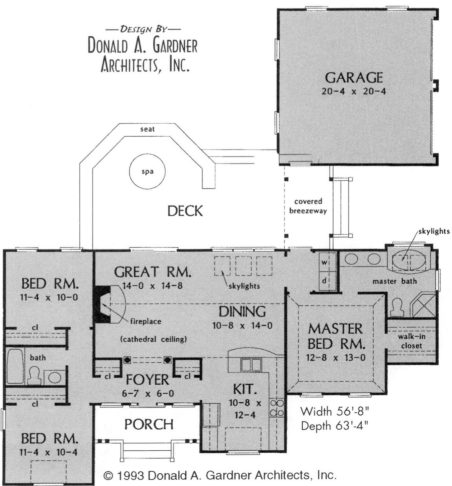

GARAGE
20-4 x 20-4

seat

spa

DECK

covered breezeway

skylights

BED RM.
11-4 x 10-0

cl

GREAT RM.
14-0 x 14-8

skylights

fireplace

(cathedral ceiling)

DINING
10-8 x 14-0

w
d

master bath

MASTER
BED RM.
12-8 x 13-0

walk-in closet

bath

cl

cl

FOYER
6-7 x 6-0

cl

KIT.
10-8 x 12-4

Width 56'-8"
Depth 63'-4"

BED RM.
11-4 x 10-4

PORCH

Design Q446

Square Footage: 1,408

Alternate Layout for Crawlspace Option

◆ Country details make the most of this delightful one-story home. Horizontal wood siding, shuttered windows and a covered veranda enhanced by turned spindles lend their magic. The entry opens into a vaulted great room, warmed by a focal-point fireplace. A charming pot ledge is found over the coat closet at the entry. The country kitchen is also vaulted and features a work island, walk-in pantry, open railing on the stairway to the basement and sliding glass doors to the rear deck. A service entrance connects the kitchen with the two-car garage and handy workshop and features space for a laundry. Bedrooms are to the right of the plan and include two family bedrooms that share a skylit main bath. The master bedroom is graced by two wall closets and a private bath with double vanity and soaking tub in a box-bay window. Plans for a basement or crawlspace foundation are included.

— DESIGN BY —

SELECT HOME DESIGNS

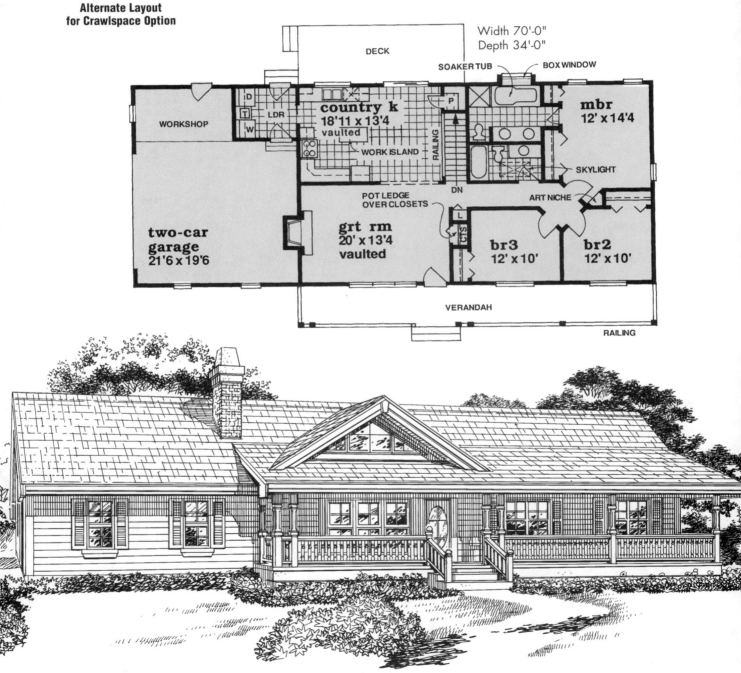

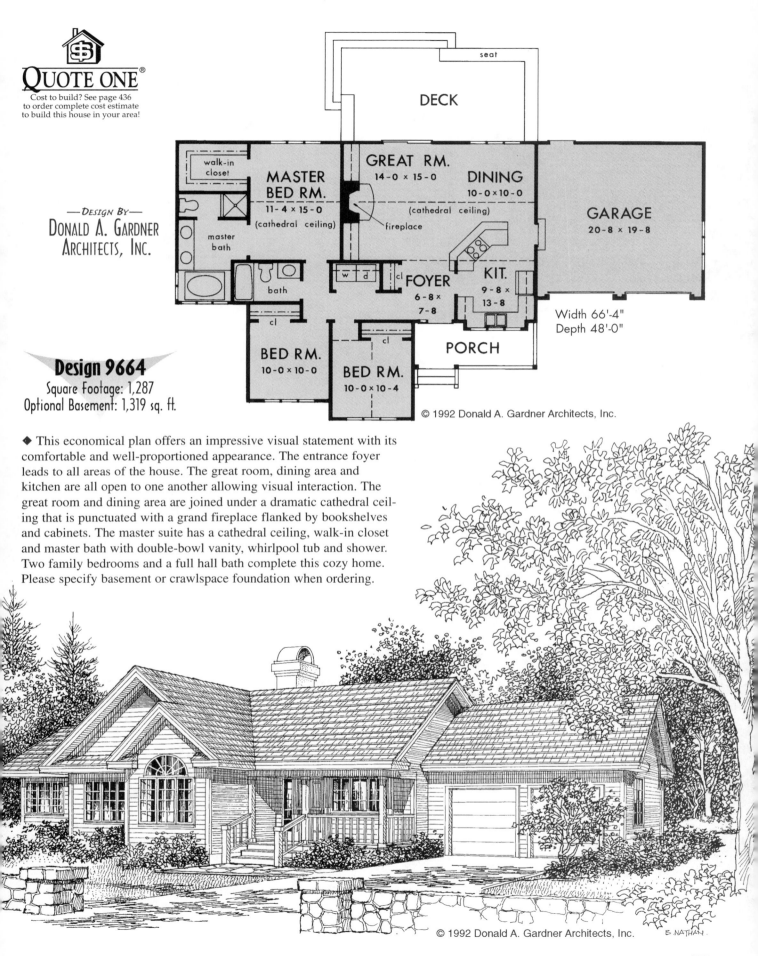

QUOTE ONE®

Cost to build? See page 436
to order complete cost estimate
to build this house in your area!

—DESIGN BY—
DONALD A. GARDNER
ARCHITECTS, INC.

DECK

seat

walk-in closet

MASTER BED RM.
11-4 × 15-0
(cathedral ceiling)

master bath

bath

w d cl

cl

GREAT RM.
14-0 × 15-0

fireplace

DINING
10-0 × 10-0
(cathedral ceiling)

FOYER
6-8 ×
7-8

KIT.
9-8 ×
13-8

GARAGE
20-8 × 19-8

Width 66'-4"
Depth 48'-0"

cl

BED RM.
10-0 × 10-0

BED RM.
10-0 × 10-4

cl

PORCH

© 1992 Donald A. Gardner Architects, Inc.

Design 9664
Square Footage: 1,287
Optional Basement: 1,319 sq. ft.

◆ This economical plan offers an impressive visual statement with its
comfortable and well-proportioned appearance. The entrance foyer
leads to all areas of the house. The great room, dining area and
kitchen are all open to one another allowing visual interaction. The
great room and dining area are joined under a dramatic cathedral ceiling that is punctuated with a grand fireplace flanked by bookshelves
and cabinets. The master suite has a cathedral ceiling, walk-in closet
and master bath with double-bowl vanity, whirlpool tub and shower.
Two family bedrooms and a full hall bath complete this cozy home.
Please specify basement or crawlspace foundation when ordering.

© 1992 Donald A. Gardner Architects, Inc.

B. NATHAN

271

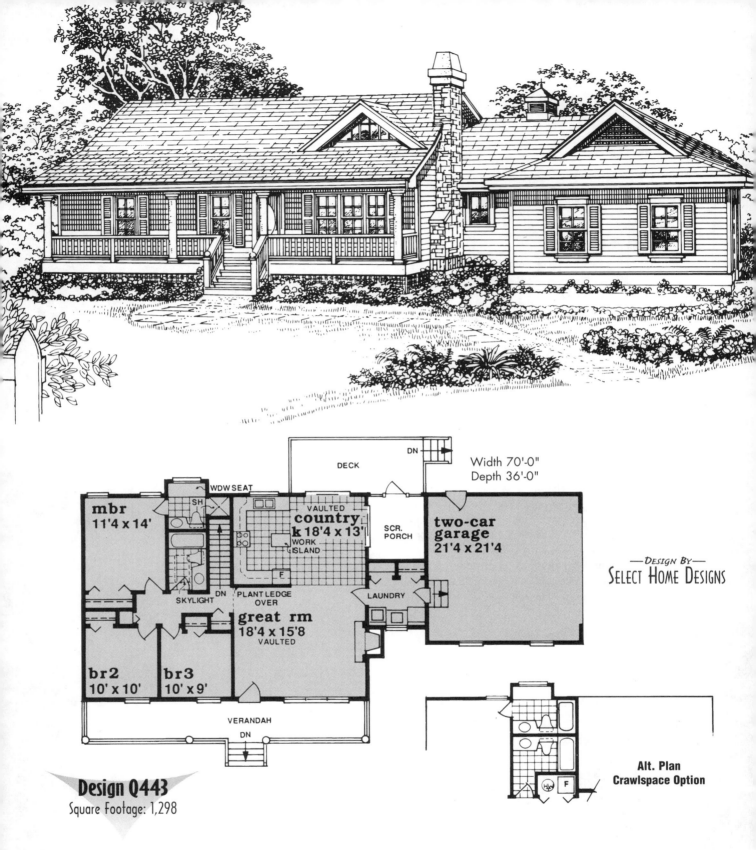

Width 70'-0"
Depth 36'-0"

DECK

DN

WDW SEAT

SH

mbr
11'4 x 14'

country
k 18'4 x 13'
VAULTED

WORK
ISLAND

SCR.
PORCH

two-car
garage
21'4 x 21'4

—DESIGN BY—
SELECT HOME DESIGNS

SKYLIGHT

DN

PLANT LEDGE
OVER

great rm
18'4 x 15'8
VAULTED

LAUNDRY

br2
10' x 10'

br3
10' x 9'

VERANDAH

DN

HW F

Alt. Plan
Crawlspace Option

Design Q443
Square Footage: 1,298

◆ A front veranda, cedar lattice and solid stone chimney enhance the appeal of this one-story country-style home. The open plan begins with the great room which has a fireplace and a plant ledge over the wall separating the living space from the country kitchen. The kitchen is U-shaped and has an island work counter and sliding glass doors to the rear deck and a screened porch. Vaulted ceilings in both the kitchen and great room add spaciousness. Look for three bedrooms, clustered together at the left of the plan. Family bedrooms feature wall closets and share the use of a skylit main bath. The master suite also has a wall closet and a private bath with window seat. The two-car garage is reached via the service entrance where there is a convenient laundry with utility closets. Plans for both a basement and a crawlspace foundation are included.

◆ This traditional three-bedroom home with front and side porches, arched windows and dormers projects the appearance of a much larger home. The great room features a cathedral ceiling, a fireplace and an arched window above the sliding glass door to the expansive rear deck. A spa here creates the perfect atmosphere for entertaining. Elegant round columns define the dining room. The master suite contains a pampering master bath with a whirlpool tub, a separate shower, a double-bowl vanity and a walk-in closet. Two other bedrooms share a full bath with a double-bowl vanity. Please specify basement or crawlspace foundation when ordering.

Design 9639
Square Footage: 1,541

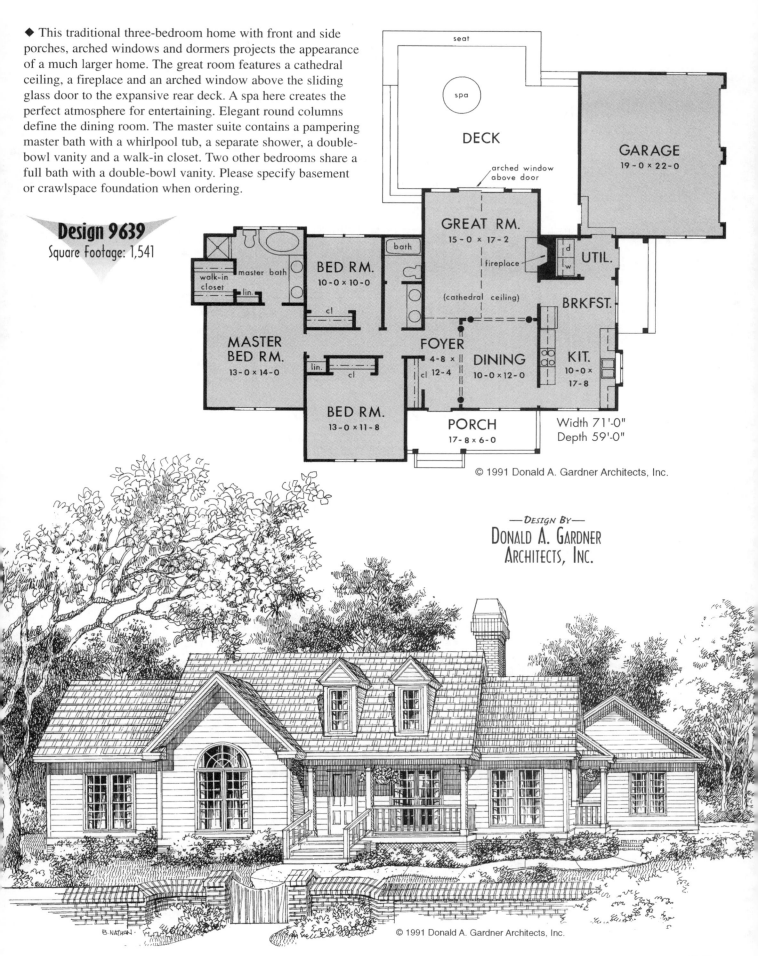

seat

DECK

spa

GARAGE
19-0 x 22-0

arched window above door

GREAT RM.
15-0 x 17-2

bath

UTIL.

fireplace

master bath

walk-in closet

lin.

BED RM.
10-0 x 10-0

(cathedral ceiling)

BRKFST.

MASTER BED RM.
13-0 x 14-0

cl

FOYER
4-8 x 12-4

DINING
10-0 x 12-0

KIT.
10-0 x 17-8

lin.

cl

BED RM.
13-0 x 11-8

cl

PORCH
17-8 x 6-0

Width 71'-0"
Depth 59'-0"

—DESIGN BY—
DONALD A. GARDNER
ARCHITECTS, INC.

B. NATHAN

Design Q447
Square Footage: 1,428

— DESIGN BY —
SELECT HOME DESIGNS

◆ This clever one-story ranch features a covered veranda at the front to enhance outdoor livability. The entry opens to a foyer that leads into a vaulted living room with fireplace on the left and a den or third bedroom on the right. The country kitchen is found to the back and is highlighted by a breakfast bar and sliding glass doors to the rear patio. The hallway con- tains an open-railed stairway to the basement and a laundry alcove, plus coat closet. Bedrooms are large and have ample closet space. The master bedroom features a walk-in closet and full, private bath. Family bedrooms share the use of a skylit main bath. Plans include details for both a basement and a crawlspace foundation.

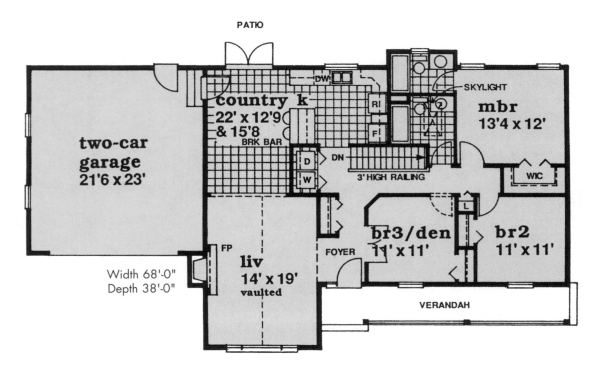

PATIO

country k
22' x 12'9
& 15'8
BRK BAR

DW

SKYLIGHT

mbr
13'4 x 12'

two-car
garage
21'6 x 23'

DN

3' HIGH RAILING

WIC

Width 68'-0"
Depth 38'-0"

FP

liv
14' x 19'
vaulted

FOYER

br3/den
11' x 11'

br2
11' x 11'

VERANDAH

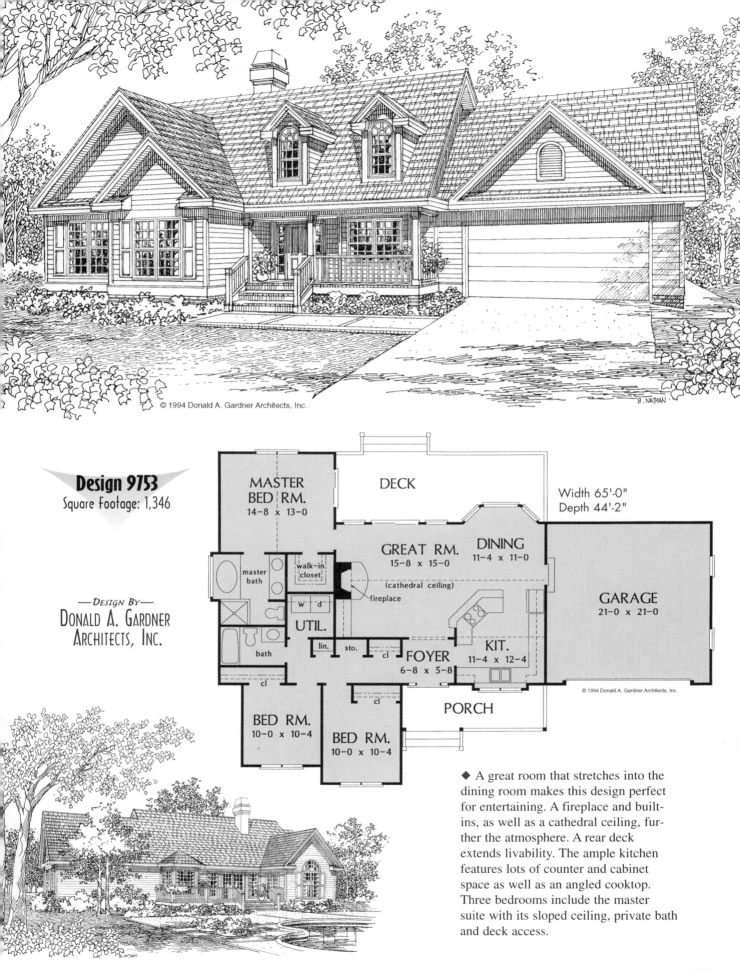

© 1994 Donald A. Gardner Architects, Inc.

B. NATHAN

Design 9753
Square Footage: 1,346

—DESIGN BY—
DONALD A. GARDNER
ARCHITECTS, INC.

MASTER
BED RM.
14-8 x 13-0

DECK

Width 65'-0"
Depth 44'-2"

master
bath

walk-in
closet

GREAT RM.
15-8 x 15-0

DINING
11-4 x 11-0

(cathedral ceiling)

fireplace

w   d

UTIL.

GARAGE
21-0 x 21-0

lin.   sto.   cl

bath

FOYER
6-8 x 5-8

KIT.
11-4 x 12-4

cl

© 1994 Donald A. Gardner Architects, Inc.

BED RM.
10-0 x 10-4

BED RM.
10-0 x 10-4

cl

PORCH

◆ A great room that stretches into the dining room makes this design perfect for entertaining. A fireplace and built-ins, as well as a cathedral ceiling, further the atmosphere. A rear deck extends livability. The ample kitchen features lots of counter and cabinet space as well as an angled cooktop. Three bedrooms include the master suite with its sloped ceiling, private bath and deck access.

275

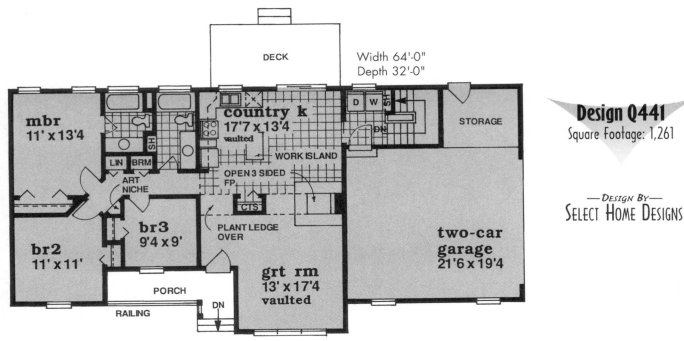

DECK

Width 64'-0"
Depth 32'-0"

mbr
11' x 13'4

country k
17'7 x 13'4
vaulted

D W

STORAGE

DN

Design Q441
Square Footage: 1,261

WORK ISLAND

OPEN 3 SIDED
FP

LIN BRM

ART
NICHE

CTS

br3
9'4 x 9'

PLANT LEDGE
OVER

br2
11' x 11'

two-car
garage
21'6 x 19'4

grt rm
13' x 17'4
vaulted

PORCH

RAILING

DN

—DESIGN BY—
SELECT HOME DESIGNS

◆ This compact, country home is perfect as a starter design or for empty nesters. Detailing on the outside includes a covered porch, shuttered windows and a Palladian-style window at the great room. The front entry opens directly into the great room, which is vaulted and features a three-sided fireplace which it shares with the country kitchen. A deck just beyond the kitchen will serve as an outdoor dining spot, accessed easily through sliding glass doors. The kitchen itself is L-shaped and has a handy work island. A nearby laundry area holds the stairway to the basement and access to the two-car garage with storage space. Three bedrooms include two family bedrooms and a full bath, plus a master bedroom with private bath. Plans include details for both a basement and a crawlspace foundation.

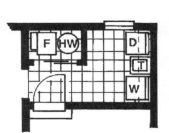

F HW

D

T

W

**Alternate Layout For
Crawlspace Option**

Enhanced Plan

BEDROOM
10⁴ x 10⁴

BEDROOM
10⁴ x 10⁴

RAILING   DN   DECK
13² x 9⁸

GREAT RM
13² X 33⁴

OPT. FIREPLACE

BEDROOM
11⁴ x 10⁴

LINEN

BATH

KITCHEN
9² x 17¹⁰

OPT. BAY WINDOW

DW

S

OPT. BAY WINDOW

BATH

COOK TOP

REF'G

WALK-IN CLOSET   LINEN

FOYER

MASTER BEDROOM
11⁴ x 16⁰

DN

RAILING

COVERED PORCH

Width 35'-0"
Depth 76'-0"

GARAGE
20¹⁰ x 21⁸

Design 3721
Square Footage: 1,648

◆ If you have a narrow lot to build your home on, then this compact ranch design is for you! It's only 35-feet wide, yet includes a super floor plan. The larger-than-expected great room has the option of two bay windows and a corner fireplace. The kitchen is long and narrow and has sufficient space for a table and chairs. Bedrooms include a master bedroom, with a walk-in closet, linen closet and full bath with double vanity and soaking tub. Three secondary bedrooms share a full bath. An open-railed stairway to the basement is found just to the left of the entry foyer. Begin with the basic plan, then add a two-car garage and rear deck as shown in this enhanced version.

— DESIGN BY —
Home Planners

Basic Plan

Design Q222
Square Footage: 1,356

◆ Charmingly compact, this easy-to-build design is ideal for first-time homeowners. The exterior is appealing with a brick facade, horizontal wood siding on the sides, a large brick chimney and a full-width covered veranda. The living room/dining room combination is warmed by a masonry fireplace and includes an optional spindle screen wall at the entry. A country kitchen has ample counter space, a U-shaped work area and dining space. Outdoor access can also be found here. Three bedrooms include a master suite with private bath and two family bedrooms sharing a full hall bath. Plans include details for both a basement and crawlspace foundation—the choice is yours.

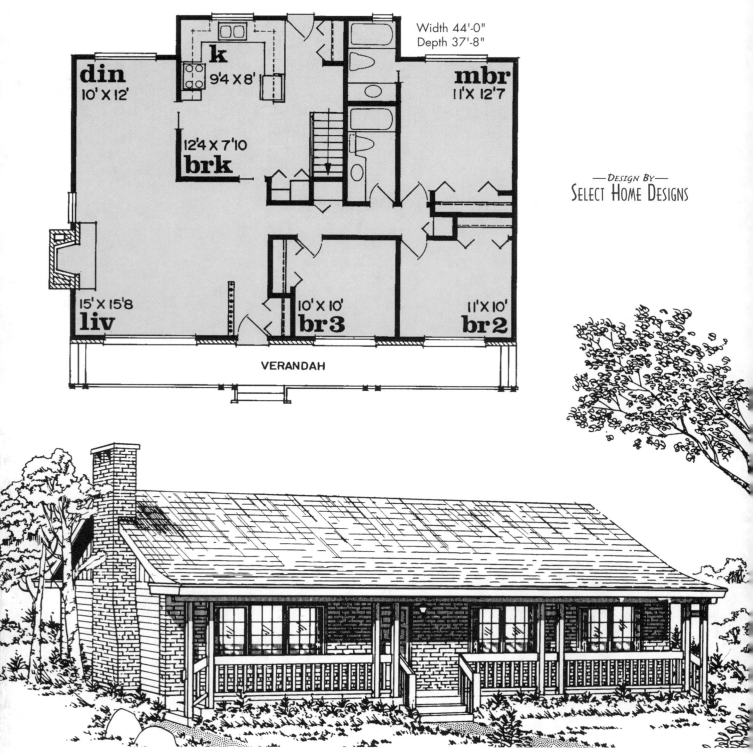

Width 44'-0"
Depth 37'-8"

din
10' X 12'

k
9'4 X 8'

12'4 X 7'10
brk

mbr
11'X 12'7

15' X 15'8
liv

10' X 10'
br3

11' X 10'
br2

VERANDAH

— DESIGN BY —
SELECT HOME DESIGNS

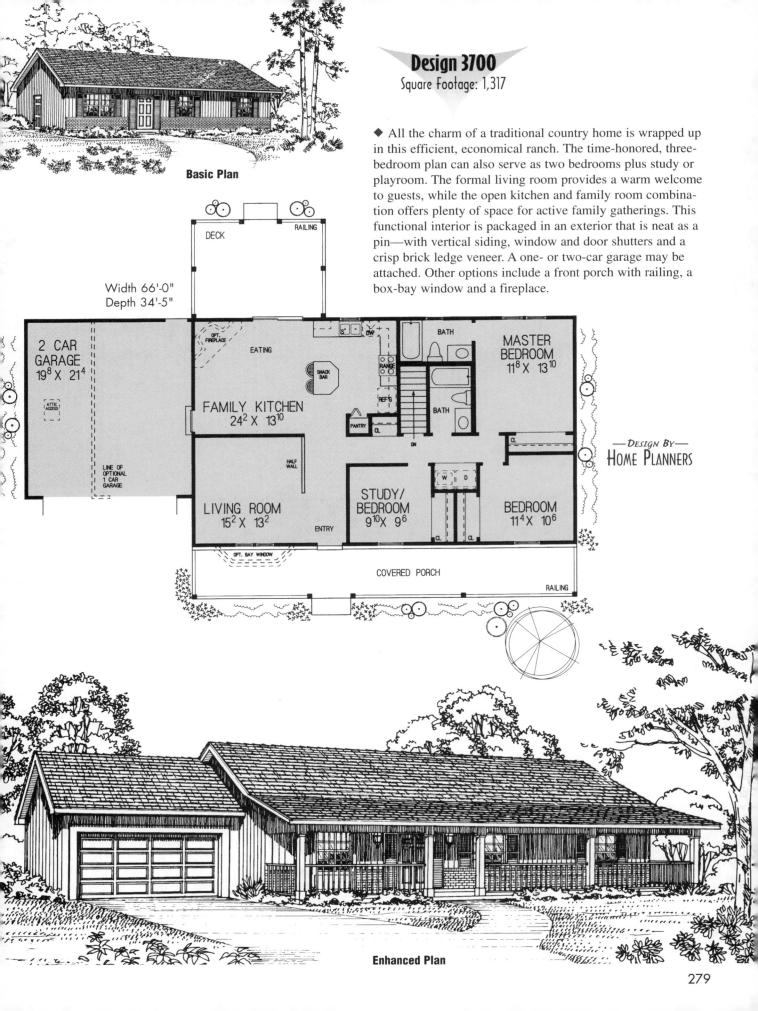

Basic Plan

Design 3700
Square Footage: 1,317

◆ All the charm of a traditional country home is wrapped up in this efficient, economical ranch. The time-honored, three-bedroom plan can also serve as two bedrooms plus study or playroom. The formal living room provides a warm welcome to guests, while the open kitchen and family room combination offers plenty of space for active family gatherings. This functional interior is packaged in an exterior that is neat as a pin—with vertical siding, window and door shutters and a crisp brick ledge veneer. A one- or two-car garage may be attached. Other options include a front porch with railing, a box-bay window and a fireplace.

Width 66'-0"
Depth 34'-5"

DECK

RAILING

2 CAR GARAGE
19⁸ X 21⁴

ATTIC ACCESS

LINE OF OPTIONAL 1 CAR GARAGE

OPT. FIREPLACE

EATING

SNACK BAR

FAMILY KITCHEN
24² X 13¹⁰

S DW

RANGE

REF'G

PANTRY

CL

BATH

BATH

DN

MASTER BEDROOM
11⁸ X 13¹⁰

—DESIGN BY—
Home Planners

CL

HALF WALL

LIVING ROOM
15² X 13²

ENTRY

STUDY/ BEDROOM
9¹⁰ X 9⁶

W D

CL CL

BEDROOM
11⁴ X 10⁶

OPT. BAY WINDOW

COVERED PORCH

RAILING

Enhanced Plan

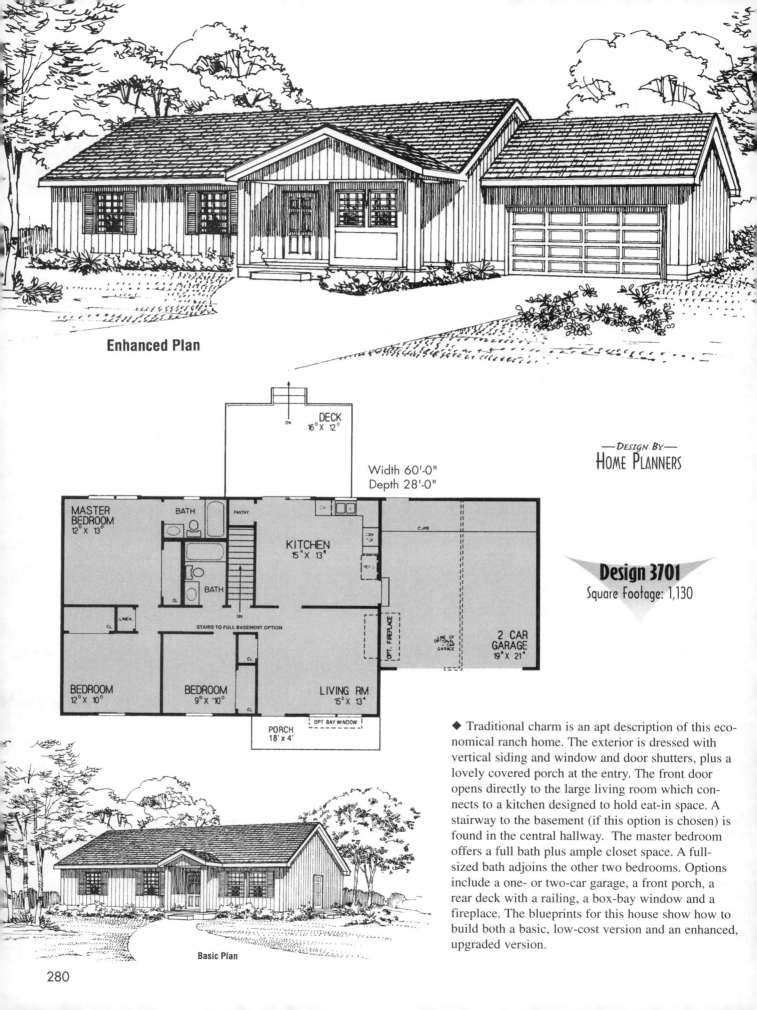

Enhanced Plan

DECK
16⁰ X 12⁰

Width 60'-0"
Depth 28'-0"

— DESIGN BY —
HOME PLANNERS

MASTER
BEDROOM
12⁰ X 13⁰

BATH

PANTRY

KITCHEN
15⁴ X 13⁰

Design 3701
Square Footage: 1,130

BATH

CL

LINEN

STAIRS TO FULL BASEMENT OPTION

OPT. FIREPLACE

LINE OF
OPTIONAL 1
CAR
GARAGE

2 CAR
GARAGE
19⁰ X 21⁴

BEDROOM
12⁰ X 10⁰

BEDROOM
9⁰ X 10⁰

CL

LIVING RM
15² X 13⁴

CL

PORCH
18' x 4'

OPT BAY WINDOW

◆ Traditional charm is an apt description of this economical ranch home. The exterior is dressed with
vertical siding and window and door shutters, plus a
lovely covered porch at the entry. The front door
opens directly to the large living room which connects to a kitchen designed to hold eat-in space. A
stairway to the basement (if this option is chosen) is
found in the central hallway. The master bedroom
offers a full bath plus ample closet space. A full-
sized bath adjoins the other two bedrooms. Options
include a one- or two-car garage, a front porch, a
rear deck with a railing, a box-bay window and a
fireplace. The blueprints for this house show how to
build both a basic, low-cost version and an enhanced,
upgraded version.

Basic Plan

Design 1113
Square Footage: 1,080

L D

◆ A cozy plan, but just right for a small family or empty-nesters. A covered front porch shelters visitors from inclement weather. An ample living room/dining room area leads the way to a rear kitchen overlooking a terrace. Two full baths serve three bedrooms—one a master suite. The kitchen includes informal eating space. Stairs lead to a full basement that may be developed as desired. Multi-lite windows with quaint shutters add a touch of charm to this design.

QUOTE ONE®

Cost to build? See page 436 to order complete cost estimate to build this house in your area!

—DESIGN BY—
HOME PLANNERS

MASTER BED RM. 12⁴ x 13⁶

BATH

RANGE   S

KIT. 12⁰ x 9⁰

CL.

DN.

BRM.
REFG

EATING

CL.

BATH

DINING

LIN.

CL.

CL.

CL.

BED RM 9⁰ x 13⁶

CL.

BED RM. 9⁰ x 10²

LIVING 14⁴ x 18⁴

P.

Width 36'-0"
Depth 34'-0"

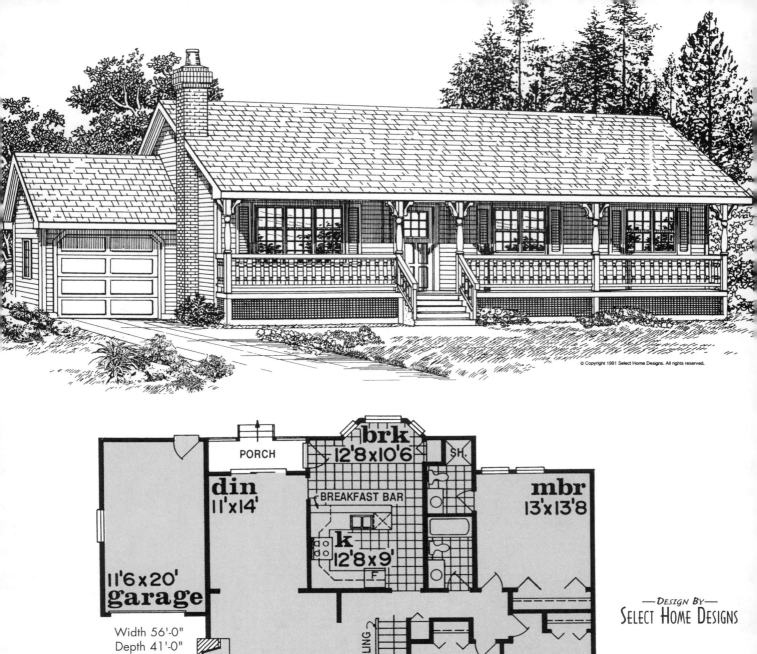

din
11'x14'

brk
12'8x10'6

SH.

mbr
13'x13'8

PORCH

BREAKFAST BAR

k
12'8x9'

F

11'6x20'
garage

Width 56'-0"
Depth 41'-0"

RAILING

—Design By—
Select Home Designs

13'6x16'
liv

FOYER

10'x10'
br3

10'x11'4
br2

RAILING

VERANDAH

Design Q361
Square Footage: 1,456

◆ A covered veranda, spanning the width of this three-bedroom home, is a graceful and charming exterior detail. It leads to an entry foyer and the large living and dining space beyond. Here a warming fireplace will act as a focal point. The dining room has a small covered porch beyond sliding glass doors. The U-shaped kitchen has a breakfast bar and serves the dining room and sunny breakfast bay easily. The master bedroom is one of three at the right of the plan and features a wall closet and full bath with shower. Two family bedrooms share use of a full hall bath. A full basement, with open-rail staircase, allows for future expansion. The single-car garage has rear-yard access.

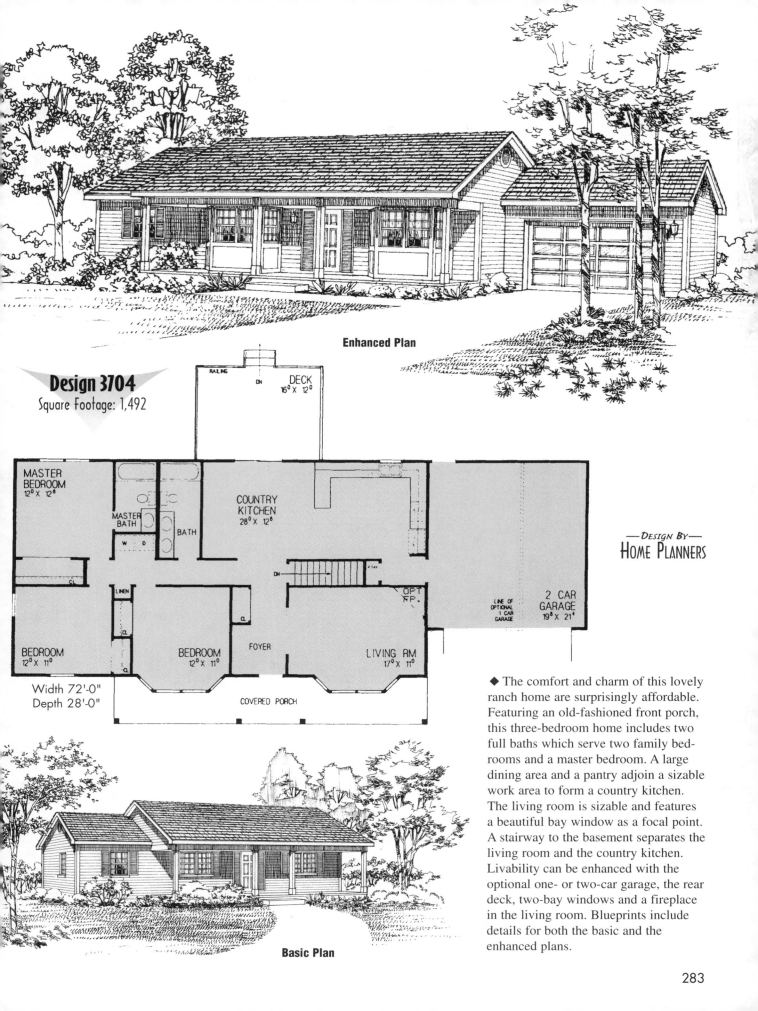

Enhanced Plan

Design 3704
Square Footage: 1,492

MASTER BEDROOM
12⁰ X 12⁸

MASTER BATH

BATH

W D

DECK
16⁰ X 12⁰

RAILING   DN

COUNTRY KITCHEN
28⁰ X 12⁸

DN

OPT FP.

LINE OF OPTIONAL 1 CAR GARAGE

2 CAR GARAGE
19⁸ X 21⁴

—DESIGN BY—
HOME PLANNERS

LINEN

CL

BEDROOM
12⁰ X 11⁰

BEDROOM
12⁰ X 11⁰

FOYER

LIVING RM
17⁰ X 11⁰

Width 72'-0"
Depth 28'-0"

COVERED PORCH

Basic Plan

◆ The comfort and charm of this lovely ranch home are surprisingly affordable. Featuring an old-fashioned front porch, this three-bedroom home includes two full baths which serve two family bedrooms and a master bedroom. A large dining area and a pantry adjoin a sizable work area to form a country kitchen. The living room is sizable and features a beautiful bay window as a focal point. A stairway to the basement separates the living room and the country kitchen. Livability can be enhanced with the optional one- or two-car garage, the rear deck, two-bay windows and a fireplace in the living room. Blueprints include details for both the basic and the enhanced plans.

Design 1920
Square Footage: 1,600

L

◆ This home offers a charming exterior with a truly great floor plan. The covered front porch at the entrance heralds outstanding features inside. The sleeping zone consists of three bedrooms and two full baths. Each of the bedrooms enjoys its own walk-in closet. You'll relish the efficient, U-shaped kitchen with the family room and the dining room to each side. There is also a laundry room with a wash room just off the garage.

QUOTE ONE®
Cost to build? See page 436
to order complete cost estimate
to build this house in your area!

—DESIGN BY—
HOME PLANNERS

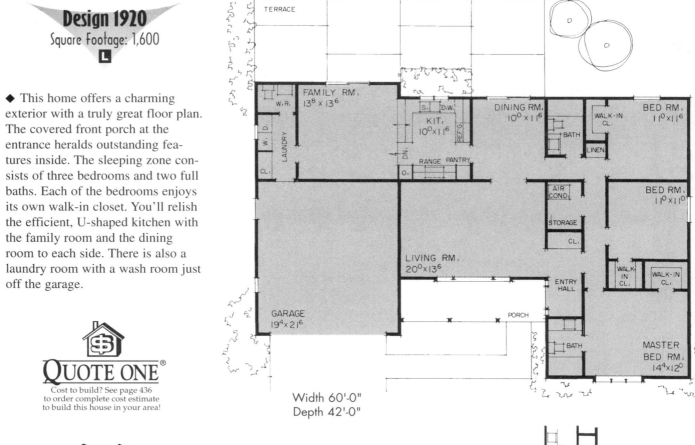

TERRACE

FAMILY RM.
13⁸ x 13⁶

W. R.

W. D.

LAUNDRY

CL.

KIT.
10⁰x11⁶

S. D.W.

REFG.

DN.

RANGE PANTRY

O.

DINING RM.
10⁰ x 11⁶

WALK-IN CL.

BATH

LINEN

BED RM.
11⁰x11⁶

AIR COND.

STORAGE

CL.

BED RM.
11⁰x11⁰

LIVING RM.
20⁰x13⁶

ENTRY HALL

WALK-IN CL.

WALK-IN CL.

GARAGE
19⁴x21⁶

PORCH

BATH

MASTER BED RM.
14⁴x12⁰

Width 60'-0"
Depth 42'-0"

DN.

LIVING RM.

LINEN

CL.

Optional Basement

284

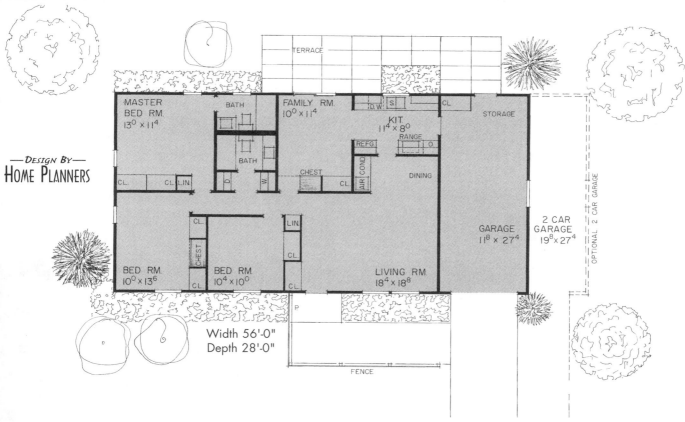

MASTER
BED RM.
$13^0 \times 11^4$

BATH

FAMILY RM.
$10^0 \times 11^4$

D.W. S

CL.

STORAGE

KIT
$11^4 \times 8^0$

REFG.

RANGE

O.

BATH

CHEST

CL.

AIR COND.

DINING

CL.

CL.

LIN.

D

W

CL.

LIN.

GARAGE
$11^8 \times 27^4$

2 CAR
GARAGE
$19^8 \times 27^4$

OPTIONAL 2 CAR GARAGE

CHEST

CL.

BED RM.
$10^0 \times 13^6$

BED RM.
$10^4 \times 10^0$

CL.

LIVING RM.
$18^4 \times 18^8$

P

TERRACE

—DESIGN BY—
HOME PLANNERS

Width 56'-0"
Depth 28'-0"

FENCE

◆ A careful study of the floor plan for this cozy traditional home reveals a fine combination of features. For instance, notice the wardrobe and storage facilities of the bedroom area—a built-in chest in one bedroom and also one in the family room. The master suite has a private bath, while family bedrooms share the use of the main bath. Note the laundry alcove at the entrance to the main bath. The living room is spacious and contains space for a dining area, plus a handy coat closet. The kitchen is designed for efficiency and features a window over the sink. A rear terrace can be reached through sliding glass doors in the family room and also from the single-car garage. The garage may be expanded to a two-car if needed and has storage space and a built-in closet.

Design 1191
Square Footage: 1,232
L D

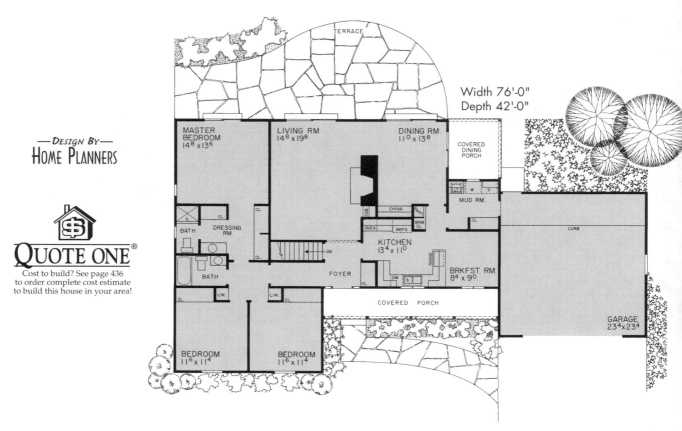

Width 76'-0"
Depth 42'-0"

TERRACE

MASTER BEDROOM 14⁸ x 13⁶

LIVING RM. 14⁸ x 19⁸

DINING RM. 11⁰ x 13⁸

COVERED DINING PORCH

CL.

CL.

MUD RM.

BATH

DRESSING RM.

CAB.

CHINA

CL.

CURB

OVEN

REF'G

BATH

DN

KITCHEN 13⁴ x 11⁰

BRKFST. RM. 8⁴ x 9⁰

RANGE

CL.

FOYER

DW

GARAGE 23⁴ x 23⁴

CL.

LIN.

LIN.

CL.

COVERED PORCH

BEDROOM 11⁶ x 11⁴

BEDROOM 11⁸ x 11⁴

—DESIGN BY—
Home Planners

Quote One®

Cost to build? See page 436
to order complete cost estimate
to build this house in your area!

Design 2672
Square Footage: 1,717
L D

◆ The traditional appearance of this one-story is emphasized by its covered porch, multi-pane windows, narrow clapboards and vertical wood siding. Not only is the exterior eye-appealing, but the interior has an efficient floor plan and is very livable. The front U-shaped kitchen has an attached breakfast room and is close to the mud room. Access to the two car garage is also found here. Both the large living room and the dining room have access to the rear terrace. The living room has a warming fireplace; the dining room has access to a covered dining porch. Bedrooms include two family bedrooms sharing a full hall bath. The master bedroom has access to the rear terrace and a private bath with dressing room.

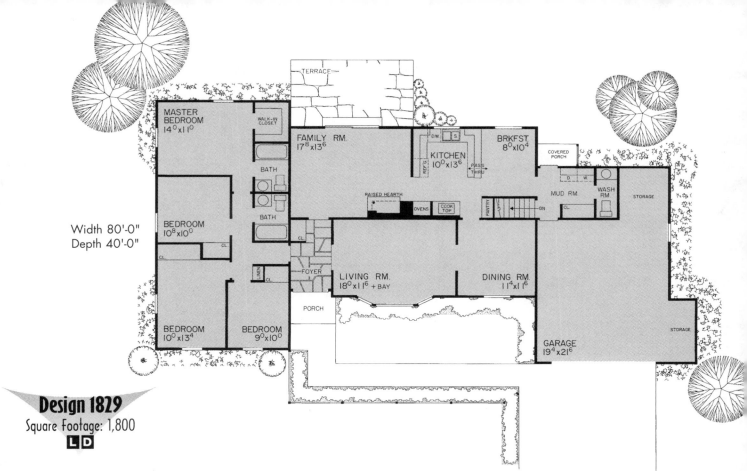

MASTER
BEDROOM
14⁰x11⁰

WALK-IN
CLOSET

TERRACE

FAMILY RM.
17⁸x13⁶

BRKFST
8⁰x10⁴

COVERED
PORCH

DW. S.

KITCHEN
10⁰x13⁶

BATH

REF'G

PASS
THRU

Width 80'-0"
Depth 40'-0"

BEDROOM
10⁸x10⁰

BATH

MUD RM.

WASH
RM.

STORAGE

RAISED HEARTH

OVENS

COOK
TOP

PANTRY

DN

CL.

CL.

LINEN

CL.

FOYER

LIVING RM.
18⁰x11⁶ + BAY

DINING RM.
11⁴x11⁶

BEDROOM
10⁰x13⁴

BEDROOM
9⁰x10⁰

PORCH

STORAGE

GARAGE
19⁴x21⁶

Design 1829
Square Footage: 1,800
L D

◆ The charm of a traditional heritage is apparent in this one-story home with its narrow, horizontal siding, delightful window treatment and high-pitched roof. Inside, the living potential is outstanding. A formal living room with bay window and dining room nearby handle entertaining easily. The sleeping wing is self-contained and has four bedrooms and two baths which include a master suite with private bath and walk-in closet. The family room features a raised-hearth fireplace and sliding glass doors to the rear terrace. The U-shaped kitchen shares its space with a breakfast room. A pass-through counter divides the two spaces. Through a handy mud room with attached wash room is access to the two-car garage (note the two storage areas!).

— DESIGN BY —
HOME PLANNERS

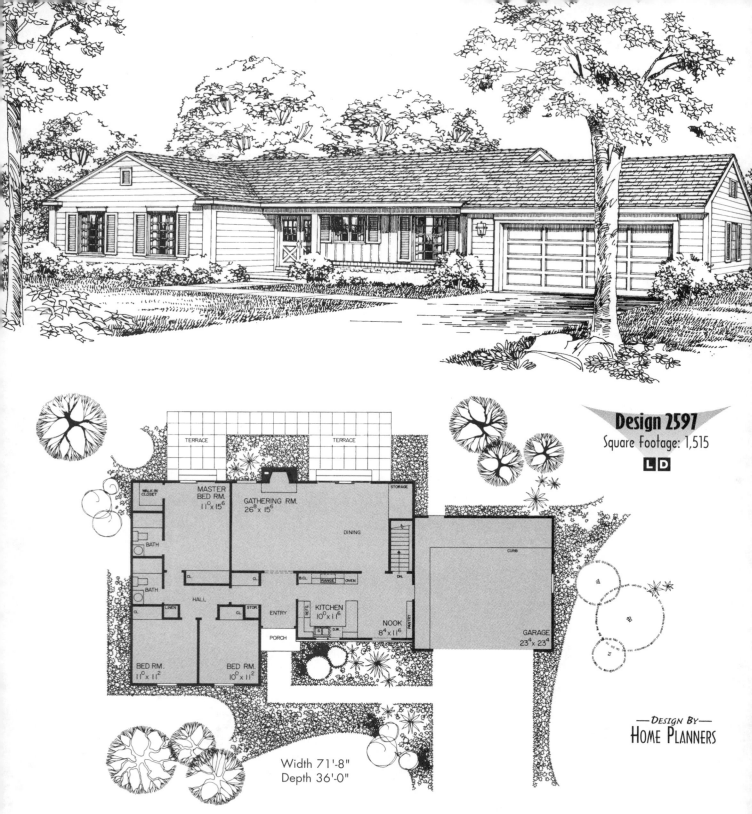

Design 2597

Square Footage: 1,515

LD

TERRACE

TERRACE

WALK IN CLOSET

MASTER BED RM.
11⁰ x 15⁶

GATHERING RM.
26⁸ x 15⁶

STORAGE

DINING

BATH

BATH

CL

CL

B.CL

RANGE

OVEN

DN

CURB

HALL

LINEN

CL

STOR

CL

ENTRY

KITCHEN
10⁰ x 11⁶

NOOK
8⁴ x 11⁶

PANTRY

GARAGE
23⁴ x 23⁴

BED RM.
11⁰ x 11²

BED RM.
10⁰ x 11²

PORCH

Width 71'-8"
Depth 36'-0"

—DESIGN BY—
HOME PLANNERS

QUOTE ONE®

Cost to build? See page 436
to order complete cost estimate
to build this house in your area!

◆ Whether it's a starter house you are after, or one in which to spend your retirement years, this pleasing farmhouse will provide a full measure of pride in ownership. The contrast of vertical and horizontal lines, the double front doors and the coach lamppost at the garage create an inviting exterior. The floor plan functions in an orderly and efficient manner. The spacious gathering room and dining room have a delightful view of the rear yard and make entertaining both family and friends a joy. The master bedroom has a private bath and a walk-in closet. Two additional bedrooms share a full hall bath. Extra amenities include plenty of storage facilities, two sets of glass doors to the terraces, a fireplace in the gathering room, a basement and an attached two-car garage.

— DESIGN BY —
HOME PLANNERS

Width 89'-0"
Depth 46'-2"

GARAGE
21⁸ x 21⁰

BEDRM
15⁰ x 13⁰
9'-0" CLG.

COVERED PATIO

MSTR BEDRM
19⁰ x 12⁰
SLOPED CEILING

MASTER BATH
WALK-IN CLOSET
SHWR
LINEN

LAUNDRY
WH HVAC D W
BC
LINEN
BATH

KIT
20⁶ x 10⁰
9'-0" CLG.
P
REF'G
R
SINK
DW

BREAKFAST NOOK

STORAGE

ENTERTAINMENT TERRACE

B-BQ GRILL

WET BAR
PLANT SHELF ABOVE

DINING RM
10² x 13⁶
SLOPED CLG

FOYER CLERESTORIES ABOVE

LIVING RM
18⁴ x 13⁶
SLOPED CLG

ENTERTAINMENT CENTER
PLANT SHELF ABOVE

TILE

COVERED PORCH

RAILING

RAILING

COVERED PORCH

RAILING

QUOTE ONE®
Cost to build? See page 436
to order complete cost estimate
to build this house in your area!

Design 3466
Square Footage: 1,800
L D

◆ Small but inviting, this one-story ranch-style farmhouse is the perfect choice for empty-nesters—and it's loaded with amenities to please the most particular homeowner. Step into a spectacular foyer, bathed in sunlight streaming through dual clerestories, front and rear. The foyer opens to formal living areas on the left and right and leads to split sleeping quarters toward the rear of the plan. Guests and family alike will enjoy the spacious living room, complete with sloped ceiling, warming fireplace, entertainment center and decorative plant shelves. The formal dining room offers a wet bar, sloped ceiling, built-in shelves and natural light from windows to the front and rear of the plan. A sumptuous master suite boasts a warming fireplace, sloped ceiling, whirlpool bath and separate shower. A family bedroom or guest suite offers a full bath on the opposite side of the plan. The kitchen is replete with popular amenities and shares light with a sunny breakfast nook with access to the entertainment terrace.

Design Q221
Square Footage: 1,360

◆ This economical-to-build family home features a low-maintenance exterior with stone and horizontal wood siding. A covered front veranda spans the full-width of the home and protects an entry leading to a center hall with living areas on the left and sleeping quarters on the right. The living room is enhanced by a fireplace and the dining room opens to the L-shaped kitchen with breakfast nook. Stairs to the basement are outside the kitchen and offer a landing entry to the single-car garage. The master bedroom is one of three to the right of the plan. It holds a separate entry to the bath shared with family bedrooms. Note the double sinks in this bath. One of the family bedrooms could serves as a den or home office.

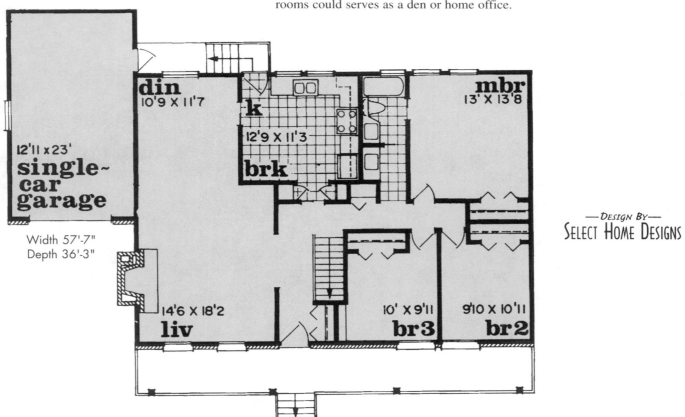

din
10'9 X 11'7

k

12'9 X 11'3

brk

mbr
13' X 13'8

12'11 x 23'
**single-
car
garage**

Width 57'-7"
Depth 36'-3"

14'6 X 18'2
liv

10' X 9'11
br3

9'10 X 10'11
br2

— DESIGN BY —
SELECT HOME DESIGNS

290

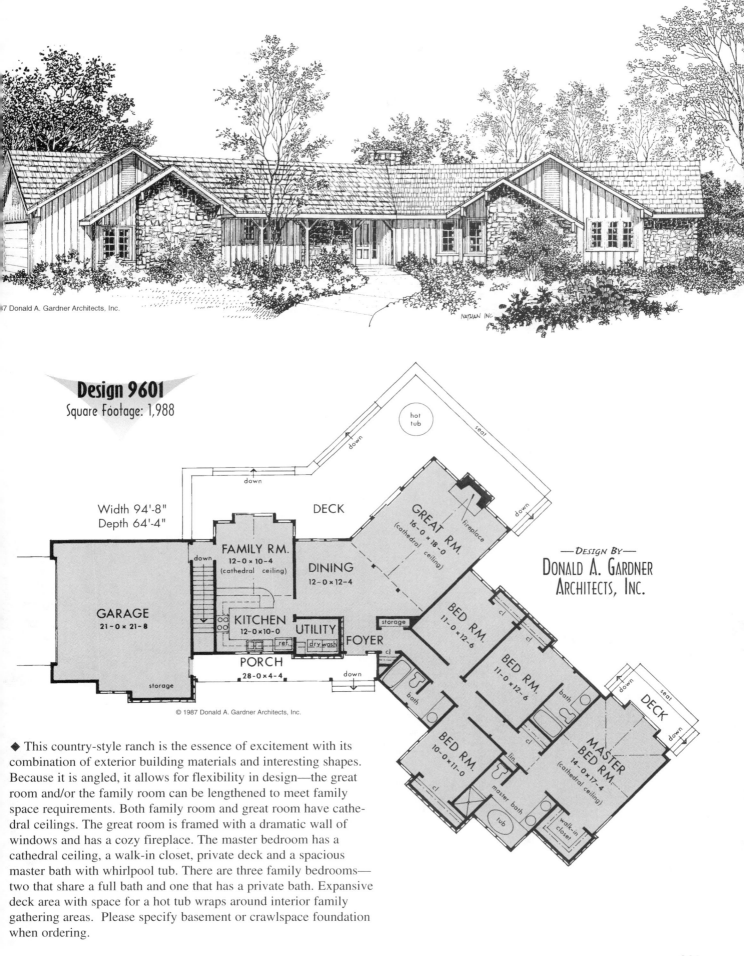

7 Donald A. Gardner Architects, Inc.

NATHAN INC

Design 9601
Square Footage: 1,988

Width 94'-8"
Depth 64'-4"

DECK

hot tub

seat

down

down

down

down

FAMILY RM.
12-0 x 10-4
(cathedral ceiling)

DINING
12-0x12-4

GREAT RM.
16-0 × 18-0
(cathedral ceiling)

fireplace

—DESIGN BY—
DONALD A. GARDNER
ARCHITECTS, INC.

GARAGE
21-0 x 21-8

KITCHEN
12-0×10-0

UTILITY

dry wash

ref.

storage

FOYER

cl

BED RM.
11-0 x 12-6

cl

cl

BED RM.
11-0 x 12-6

bath

storage

PORCH
28-0×4-4

down

bath

cl

DECK

seat

down

down

BED RM.
10-0×11-0

cl

lin.

master bath

tub

MASTER
BED RM.
14-0 x 17-4
(cathedral ceiling)

walk-in closet

© 1987 Donald A. Gardner Architects, Inc.

◆ This country-style ranch is the essence of excitement with its combination of exterior building materials and interesting shapes. Because it is angled, it allows for flexibility in design—the great room and/or the family room can be lengthened to meet family space requirements. Both family room and great room have cathedral ceilings. The great room is framed with a dramatic wall of windows and has a cozy fireplace. The master bedroom has a cathedral ceiling, a walk-in closet, private deck and a spacious master bath with whirlpool tub. There are three family bedrooms—two that share a full bath and one that has a private bath. Expansive deck area with space for a hot tub wraps around interior family gathering areas. Please specify basement or crawlspace foundation when ordering.

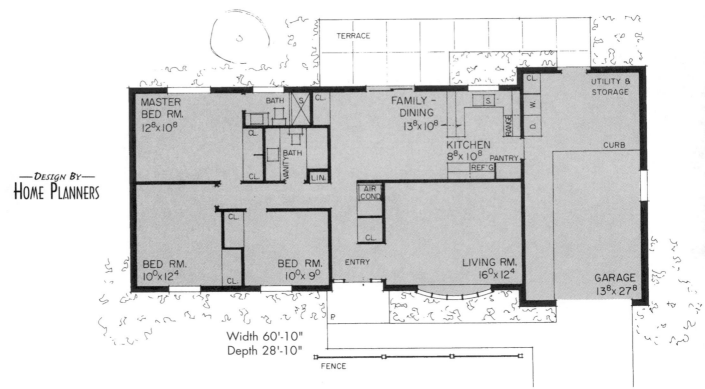

TERRACE

MASTER
BED RM.
12⁸x10⁸

BATH   CL.

CL.
BATH
VANITY

CL.   LIN.

FAMILY –
DINING
13⁸x10⁸

CL.   UTILITY &
STORAGE

S.

RANGE   W.

D.

KITCHEN
8⁸x10⁸   PANTRY

REF'G

CURB

— DESIGN BY —
HOME PLANNERS

AIR
COND

CL.

BED RM.
10⁰x12⁴

CL.

CL.

BED RM.
10⁰x9⁰

ENTRY

LIVING RM.
16⁰x12⁴

GARAGE
13⁸x27⁸

P

Width 60'-10"
Depth 28'-10"

FENCE

◆ The family working within the confines of a restricted building budget will find this eye-catching traditional ranch home the solution to its housing needs. The living room is free of cross-room traffic and lends itself to effective and flexible furniture place-ment. It is accented by a large bow window. The family-dining room is easily served by an efficient kitchen with a pass-through counter, and offers access to a terrace for out-door living. The kitchen leads on to a service entrance to the garage which has storage space and a laundry area with closet. The master bedroom has its own private bath, while two family bedrooms share a full bath with long vanity and linen closet.

Design 1364
Square Footage: 1,142
D

Design 3348
Square Footage: 2,549
L

◆ Covered porches front and rear will be the envy of the neighborhood when this house is built. The interior plan meets family needs perfectly in well-zoned areas: a sleeping wing with four bedrooms and two baths, a living zone with formal and informal gathering space and a work zone with U-shaped kitchen and laundry with washroom. The two-car garage has a huge storage area.

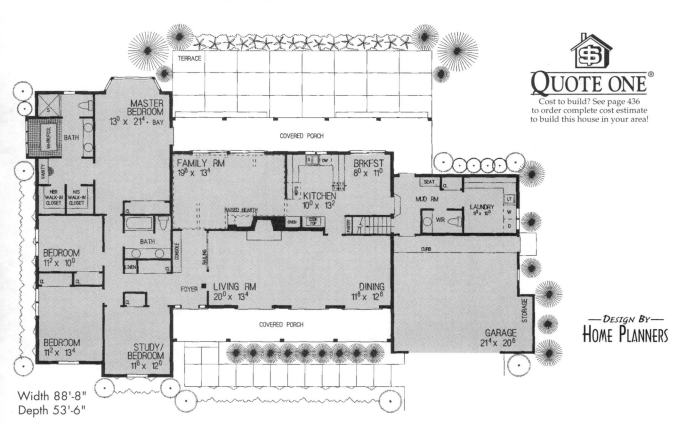

QUOTE ONE®
Cost to build? See page 436
to order complete cost estimate
to build this house in your area!

— DESIGN BY —
HOME PLANNERS

Width 88'-8"
Depth 53'-6"

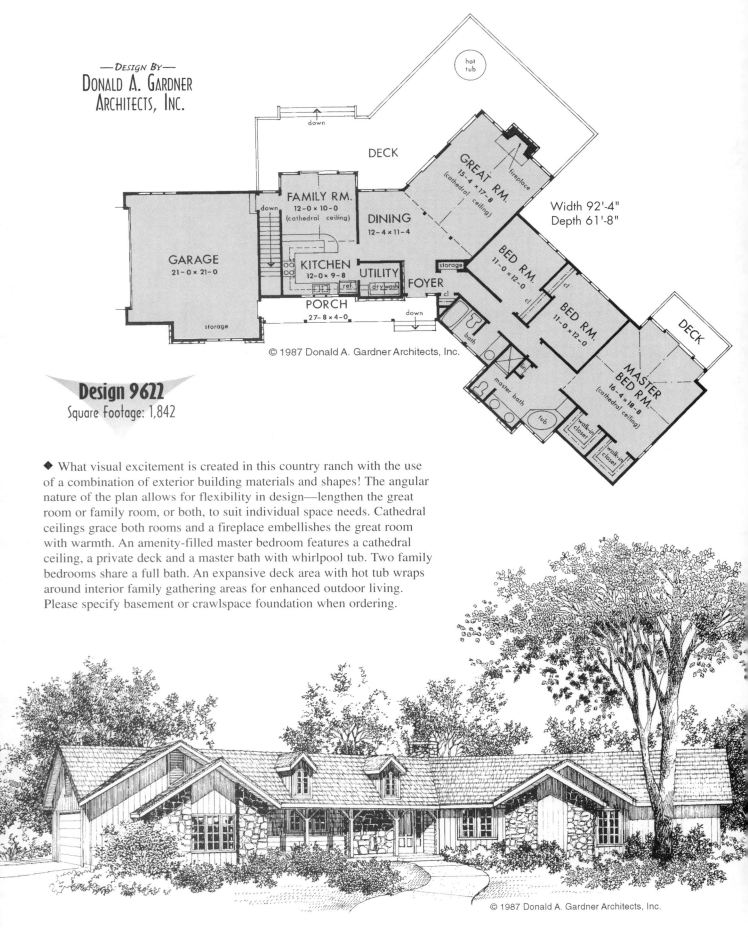

DECK

FAMILY RM.
12-0 × 10-0
(cathedral ceiling)

GREAT RM.
15-4 × 17-8
(cathedral ceiling)

hot tub

fireplace

DINING
12-4 × 11-4

Width 92'-4"
Depth 61'-8"

GARAGE
21-0 × 21-0

KITCHEN
12-0 × 9-8

UTILITY

storage

BED RM.
11-0 × 12-0

ref. dry wash

FOYER

BED RM.
11-0 × 12-0

DECK

down

PORCH
27-8 × 4-0

down

storage

cl

bath

master bath

tub

MASTER
BED RM.
16-4 × 18-8
(cathedral ceiling)

walk-in closet

walk-in closet

Design 9622
Square Footage: 1,842

◆ What visual excitement is created in this country ranch with the use of a combination of exterior building materials and shapes! The angular nature of the plan allows for flexibility in design—lengthen the great room or family room, or both, to suit individual space needs. Cathedral ceilings grace both rooms and a fireplace embellishes the great room with warmth. An amenity-filled master bedroom features a cathedral ceiling, a private deck and a master bath with whirlpool tub. Two family bedrooms share a full bath. An expansive deck area with hot tub wraps around interior family gathering areas for enhanced outdoor living. Please specify basement or crawlspace foundation when ordering.

Design Q442

Square Footage: 1,282

◆ Porch gables and fishscale siding bring back classic memories of yesteryear in this cozy one-story. The covered entry is vaulted and protects an entry to a vaulted living room with box-bay window and fireplace. The kitchen and dining area are to the front and feature an open railed stair to the basement and a U-shaped work area with pantry. The laundry area is nearby. It contains access to the two-car garage with workshop. Bedrooms line the rear of the plan. The master bedroom has a wall closet, a bayed window seat and private bath with box window. Two family bedrooms—one with walk-in closet—share access to a skylit main bath. Extra storage is available in a linen closet and coat closet in the center hall. Plans include details for both a basement and a crawl-space foundation.

— DESIGN BY —
SELECT HOME DESIGNS

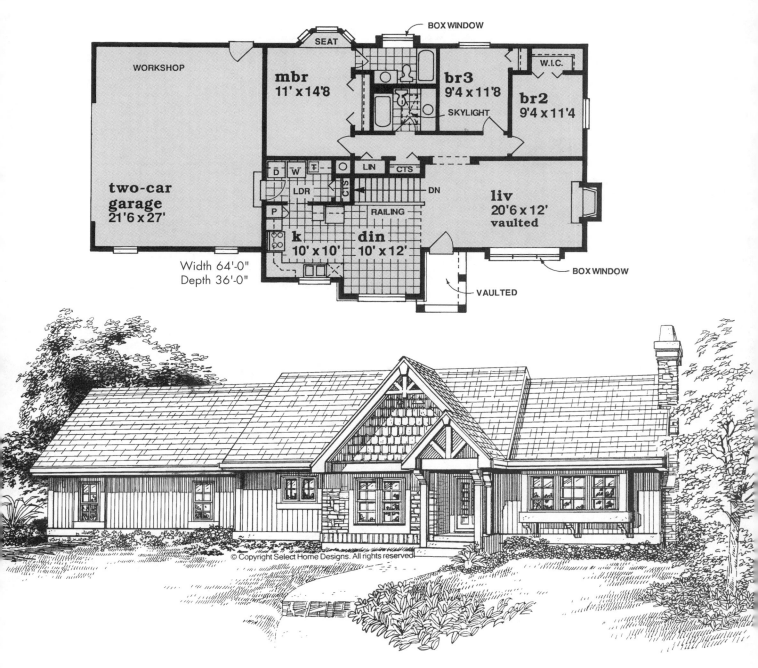

BOX WINDOW

WORKSHOP

SEAT

mbr
11' x 14'8

br3
9'4 x 11'8

SKYLIGHT

W.I.C.

br2
9'4 x 11'4

two-car garage
21'6 x 27'

D W T

LDR

P

LIN

CTS

C T S

DN

RAILING

liv
20'6 x 12'
vaulted

Width 64'-0"
Depth 36'-0"

k
10' x 10'

din
10' x 12'

VAULTED

BOX WINDOW

295

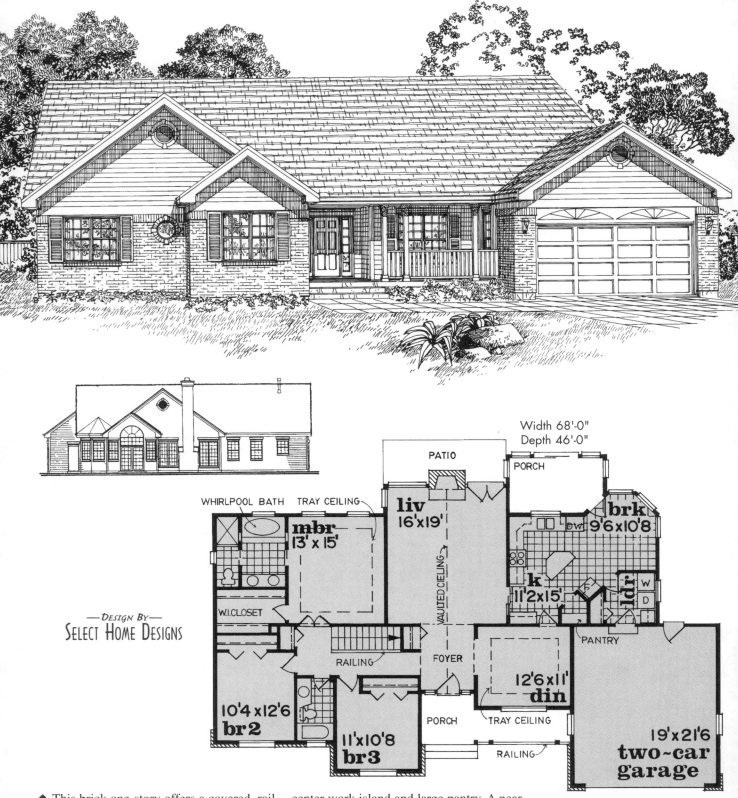

WHIRLPOOL BATH   TRAY CEILING

Width 68'-0"
Depth 46'-0"

PATIO

PORCH

liv
16'x19'

brk
9'6x10'8

mbr
13' x 15'

k
11'2x15'

ldr

W.I. CLOSET

VAULTED CEILING

PANTRY

— DESIGN BY —
SELECT HOME DESIGNS

RAILING

FOYER

12'6x11'
din

10'4 x12'6
br 2

11'x10'8
br3

TRAY CEILING

PORCH

RAILING

19'x21'6
**two-car
garage**

◆ This brick one-story offers a covered, rail porch that provides a weather-protected entry to the home. The vaulted foyer carries its ceiling detail into the living room where there is a fireplace and double-door access to the rear patio. The dining room has a tray ceiling and is found to the right of the entry. A screened porch decorates the breakfast room and allows for protected casual outdoor dining. The kitchen is U-shaped with a center work island and large pantry. A nearby laundry room has access to the two-car garage. Look no further than the master bedroom for true luxury. It boasts a tray ceiling and full bath with whirlpool spa, separate shower and double vanity. Family bedrooms have wall closets and share a full bath that separates them. Plans include details for both a basement and a crawl-space foundation—the choice is yours.

Design Q369
Square Footage: 1,760

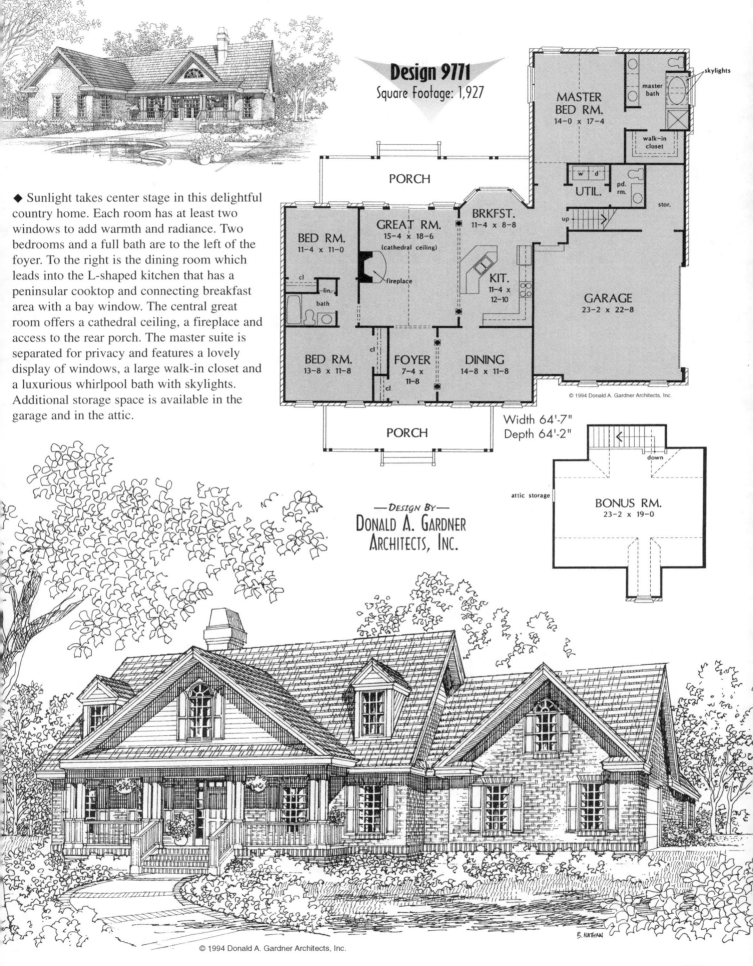

Design 9771
Square Footage: 1,927

◆ Sunlight takes center stage in this delightful country home. Each room has at least two windows to add warmth and radiance. Two bedrooms and a full bath are to the left of the foyer. To the right is the dining room which leads into the L-shaped kitchen that has a peninsular cooktop and connecting breakfast area with a bay window. The central great room offers a cathedral ceiling, a fireplace and access to the rear porch. The master suite is separated for privacy and features a lovely display of windows, a large walk-in closet and a luxurious whirlpool bath with skylights. Additional storage space is available in the garage and in the attic.

skylights

MASTER BED RM.
14-0 x 17-4

master bath

walk-in closet

PORCH

w d

UTIL.

pd. rm.

stor.

GREAT RM.
15-4 x 18-6
(cathedral ceiling)

BRKFST.
11-4 x 8-8

up

BED RM.
11-4 x 11-0

cl

lin.

bath

fireplace

KIT.
11-4 x 12-10

GARAGE
23-2 x 22-8

BED RM.
13-8 x 11-8

cl

FOYER
7-4 x 11-8

DINING
14-8 x 11-8

cl

© 1994 Donald A. Gardner Architects, Inc.

PORCH

Width 64'-7"
Depth 64'-2"

—DESIGN BY—
DONALD A. GARDNER
ARCHITECTS, INC.

attic storage

down

BONUS RM.
23-2 x 19-0

© 1994 Donald A. Gardner Architects, Inc.

B. NATHAN

©1994 Donald A. Gardner Architects, Inc.

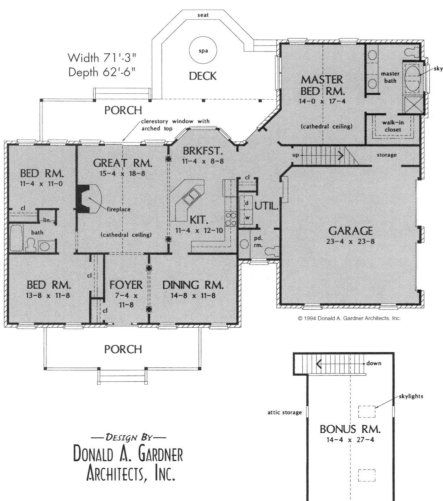

Width 71'-3"
Depth 62'-6"

seat

spa

DECK

PORCH

clerestory window with
arched top

BED RM.
11-4 x 11-0

GREAT RM.
15-4 x 18-8

BRKFST.
11-4 x 8-8

MASTER
BED RM.
14-0 x 17-4

master
bath

skylights

walk-in
closet

(cathedral ceiling)

storage

up

cl

fireplace

(cathedral ceiling)

cl

lin.

bath

KIT.
11-4 x 12-10

d

w

UTIL.

pd.
rm.

GARAGE
23-4 x 23-8

BED RM.
13-8 x 11-8

FOYER
7-4 x
11-8

DINING RM.
14-8 x 11-8

cl

cl

© 1994 Donald A. Gardner Architects, Inc.

PORCH

—DESIGN BY—
DONALD A. GARDNER
ARCHITECTS, INC.

down

attic storage

skylights

BONUS RM.
14-4 x 27-4

Design 9742
Square Footage: 1,954
Bonus Room: 436 sq. ft.

◆ This beautiful brick country
home offers style and comfort for
an active family. Two covered
porches and a rear deck with spa
invite enjoyment of the outdoors,
while a well-defined interior provides places to gather and entertain.
A cathedral ceiling soars above the
central great room, warmed by an
extended-hearth fireplace and by
sunlight through an arch-top
clerestory window. A splendid master suite enjoys its own secluded
wing, and offers a skylit whirlpool
bath, a cathedral ceiling and private
access to the deck. Two family bedrooms share a full bath on the opposite side of the plan.

One-Story Cottages

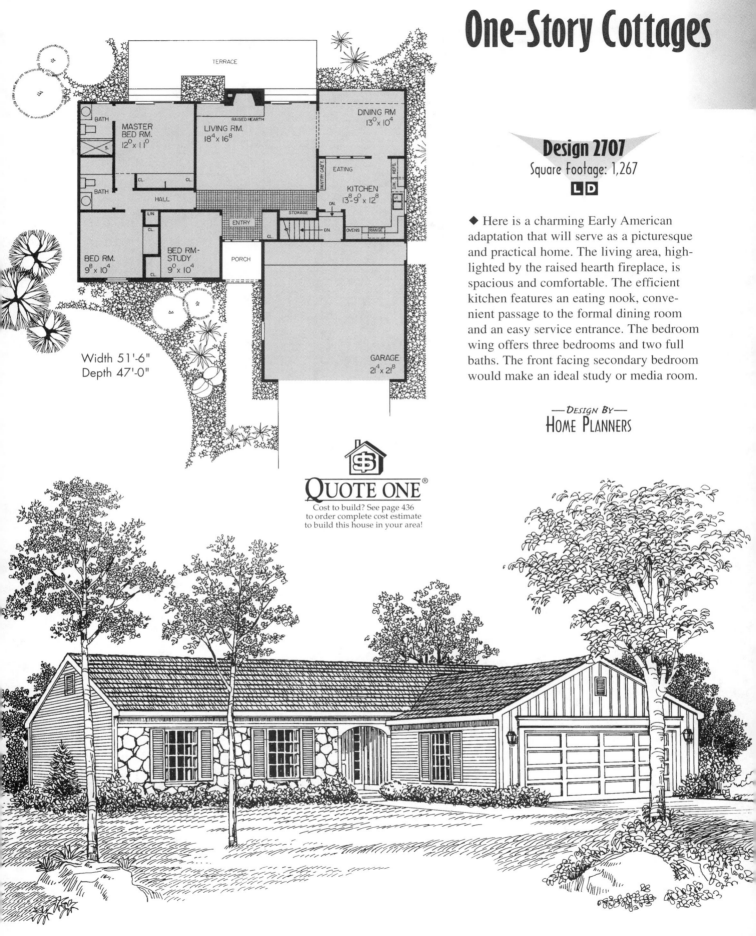

TERRACE

MASTER BED RM. 12⁰ x 11⁰

BATH

BATH

CL.

CL.

HALL

BED RM. 9⁸ x 10⁴

LIN

CL.

CL.

BED RM.- STUDY 9⁰ x 10⁴

CL.

PORCH

ENTRY

LIVING RM. 18⁴ x 16⁸

RAISED HEARTH

DINING RM 13⁰ x 10⁴

PANTRY CAB'T.

EATING

KITCHEN 13⁸-9⁰ x 12⁸

DW

S.

REFG.

STORAGE

DN.

DN

OVENS

RANGE

CL.

GARAGE 21⁴ x 21⁸

Width 51'-6"
Depth 47'-0"

Design 2707
Square Footage: 1,267

L D

◆ Here is a charming Early American adaptation that will serve as a picturesque and practical home. The living area, highlighted by the raised hearth fireplace, is spacious and comfortable. The efficient kitchen features an eating nook, convenient passage to the formal dining room and an easy service entrance. The bedroom wing offers three bedrooms and two full baths. The front facing secondary bedroom would make an ideal study or media room.

— DESIGN BY —
HOME PLANNERS

QUOTE ONE®
Cost to build? See page 436
to order complete cost estimate
to build this house in your area!

WHIRLPOOL

MASTER BEDROOM
13⁶ x 10⁶

MEDIA RM
12² x 10⁸

COVERED PORCH

BATH

CL

CL

AUDIO/VIDEO EQUIPMENT

LIVING RM
15⁰ x 15⁸

SLOPED CEILING

BEDROOM
9² x 10⁰

LINEN

BATH

REF'G

RANGE

KITCHEN
8⁰ x 11¹⁰

ENTRY

CL

DINING
10⁰ x 9⁴

P DW

S

W D

BATH

FURN

WH

GARAGE
19⁴ x 19⁸

CL

SLOPED CEILING   SLOPED CEILING

GUEST
14⁰ x 11⁰

Width 44'-0"
Depth 52'-4"

— DESIGN BY —
HOME PLANNERS

Design 3416
Square Footage: 1,375

L

◆ Here's a traditional design that will be economical to build and a pleasure to occupy. The front door opens into a spacious living room with sloped ceiling, corner fireplace and sliding glass doors to the covered porch and also to a dining room with coffered ceiling. The nearby L-shaped kitchen serves both easily. A few steps away is the cozy media room with built-in space for audio-visual equipment. Down the hall are two bedrooms and two baths; the master features a whirlpool and double vanity. The secondary bedroom has a full bath with linen closet. A guest room, completely separate from the main house, is found across the entry court. It includes a fireplace and sloped ceiling.

QUOTE ONE®
Cost to build? See page 436
to order complete cost estimate
to build this house in your area!

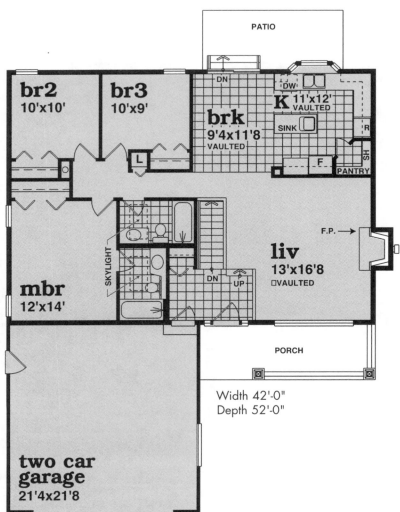

PATIO

DN

DW

K 11'x12'
VAULTED

br2
10'x10'

br3
10'x9'

brk
9'4x11'8
VAULTED

SINK

R

L

F

PANTRY

SH

SKYLIGHT

liv
13'x16'8
☐VAULTED

F.P. →

mbr
12'14'

DN

UP

DN

PORCH

two car
garage
21'4x21'8

Width 42'-0"
Depth 52'-0"

Design Q505
Square Footage: 1,260

◆ This economical-to-build bungalow
works well as a small family home or a
retirement cottage. It is available with a
basement foundation but could easily be
converted to a slab or crawlspace foundation. The covered porch leads to a
vaulted living room with fireplace.
Behind this living space is the U-shaped
kitchen with walk-in pantry and island
with utility sink. An attached breakfast
nook has sliding glass doors to a rear
patio. There are three bedrooms, each
with roomy wall closet. The master bedroom has a private full bath, while the
family bedrooms share a main bath.
Both baths have bright skylights. A two-
car garage sits to the front of the plan to
protect the bedrooms from street noise.

—— Design By ——
Select Home Designs

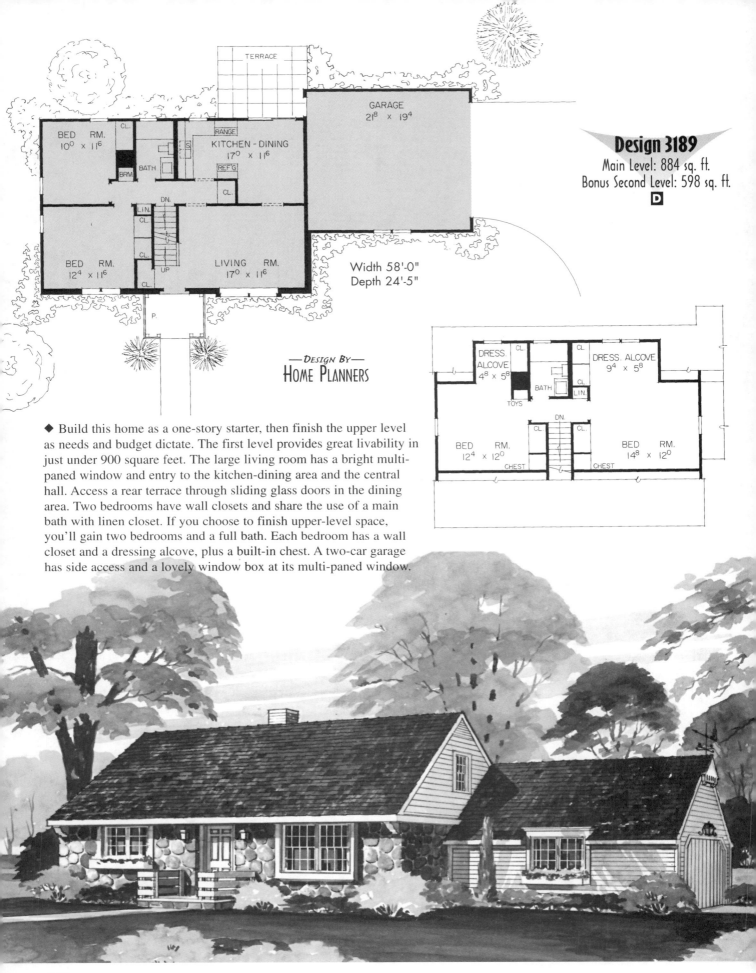

TERRACE

GARAGE
21⁸ x 19⁴

BED RM.
10⁰ x 11⁶

CL.

BATH

BRM.

RANGE

KITCHEN - DINING
17⁰ x 11⁶

REF'G

CL.

DN.

LIN.

CL.

CL.

UP

CL.

BED RM.
12⁴ x 11⁶

LIVING RM.
17⁰ x 11⁶

P.

Design 3189
Main Level: 884 sq. ft.
Bonus Second Level: 598 sq. ft.
D

Width 58'-0"
Depth 24'-5"

—DESIGN BY—
HOME PLANNERS

DRESS. ALCOVE
4⁸ x 5⁸

CL.

BATH

CL.

LIN.

CL.

DRESS. ALCOVE
9⁴ x 5⁸

TOYS

DN.

CL.

CL.

BED RM.
12⁴ x 12⁰

CHEST

BED RM.
14⁸ x 12⁰

CHEST

◆ Build this home as a one-story starter, then finish the upper level as needs and budget dictate. The first level provides great livability in just under 900 square feet. The large living room has a bright multi-paned window and entry to the kitchen-dining area and the central hall. Access a rear terrace through sliding glass doors in the dining area. Two bedrooms have wall closets and share the use of a main bath with linen closet. If you choose to finish upper-level space, you'll gain two bedrooms and a full bath. Each bedroom has a wall closet and a dressing alcove, plus a built-in chest. A two-car garage has side access and a lovely window box at its multi-paned window.

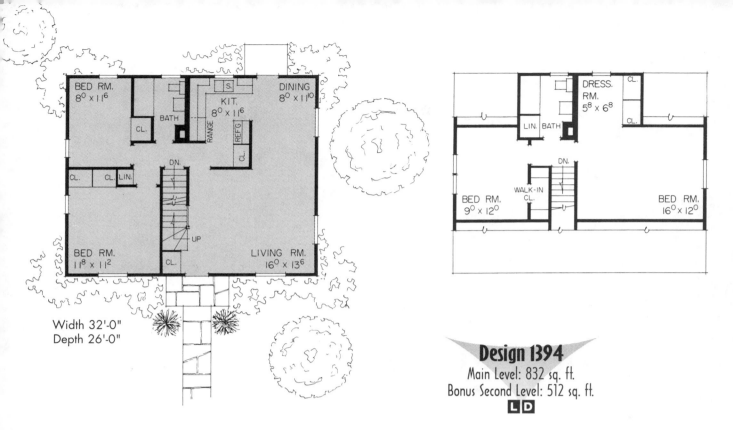

BED RM.
8⁰ x 11⁶

BATH

CL.

KIT.
8⁰ x 11⁶

S.

RANGE

REFG.

CL.

DINING
8⁰ x 11¹⁰

CL.   CL. LIN.

DN.

UP

CL.

BED RM.
11⁸ x 11²

LIVING RM.
16⁰ x 13⁶

Width 32'-0"
Depth 26'-0"

LIN. BATH

DRESS.
RM.
5⁸ x 6⁸

CL.

CL.

DN.

WALK-IN
CL.

BED RM.
9⁰ x 12⁰

BED RM.
16⁰ x 12⁰

Design 1394
Main Level: 832 sq. ft.
Bonus Second Level: 512 sq. ft.
L D

◆ Everything you need can be found on the main level of this home, but if you choose, you can develop the second level later to gain even more sleeping space. Exterior details include shuttered door and windows, a window box and an overhung roof at the entry. Inside, the main level holds a nice-sized living room and open dining area. Windows all around and a door to the rear yard open this area and keep it light-filled. The kitchen is L-shaped and convenient. The two bedrooms have wall closets and share the use of a full bath with linen closet. When finished, the upstairs holds two additional bedrooms and a full bath. One of the bedrooms holds a walk-in closet; the other has a dressing room and wall closet.

— DESIGN BY —
HOME PLANNERS

Design 1372
Main Level: 768 sq. ft.
Bonus Second Level: 432 sq. ft.

◆ Build as a one-story home—or expand later to the second floor for even more space. This classic Cape Cod cottage gives you the option and allows your floor plan to grow as your family does. The main level holds great livability with a large living room and a family kitchen with eat-in space. Side access to the carport resides in the kitchen. Two main-level bedrooms have wall closets and share a full bath. If you choose to finish the second level, plans call for two additional bedrooms and an optional full bath. Or you may decide to turn the entire second floor into a grand master suite with a sitting room and full bath. A full basement allows for even further expansion, if you wish.

— DESIGN BY —
HOME PLANNERS

Width 44'-0"
Depth 29'-0"

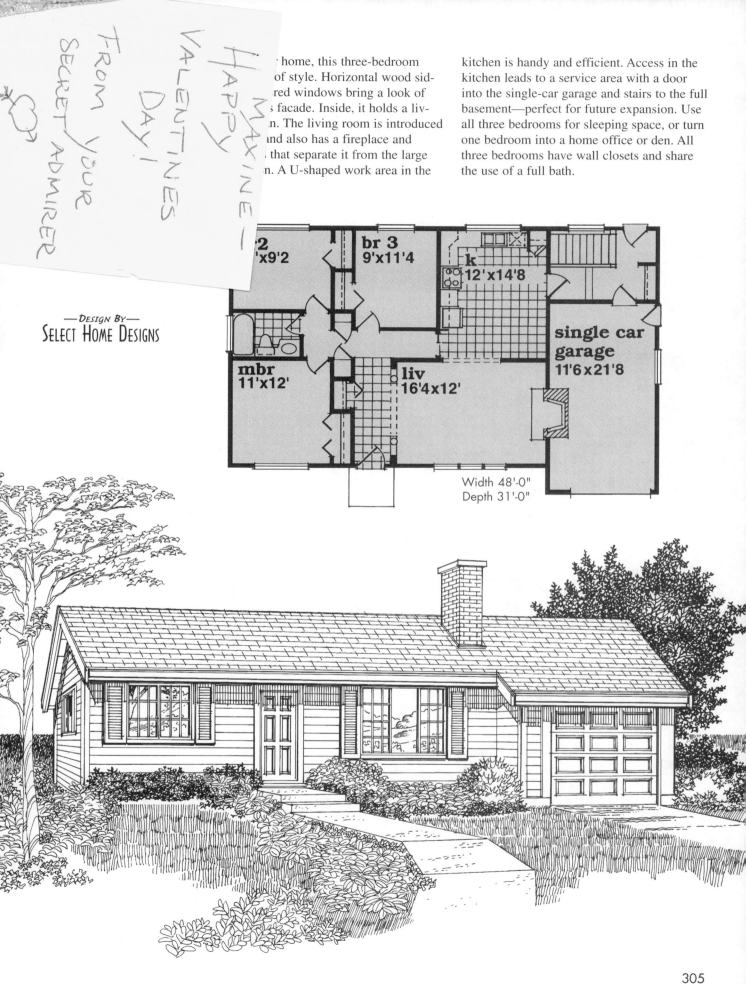

...r home, this three-bedroom ...of style. Horizontal wood sid-...red windows bring a look of ...s facade. Inside, it holds a liv-...n. The living room is introduced ...and also has a fireplace and ...that separate it from the large ...n. A U-shaped work area in the

kitchen is handy and efficient. Access in the kitchen leads to a service area with a door into the single-car garage and stairs to the full basement—perfect for future expansion. Use all three bedrooms for sleeping space, or turn one bedroom into a home office or den. All three bedrooms have wall closets and share the use of a full bath.

Hi MAXINE — Happy VALENTINES DAY! FROM YOUR SECRET ADMIRER

— DESIGN BY —
SELECT HOME DESIGNS

br 2
...'x9'2

br 3
9'x11'4

k
12'x14'8

single car garage
11'6 x 21'8

mbr
11'x12'

liv
16'4x12'

Width 48'-0"
Depth 31'-0"

Design 2153
Square Footage: 960
D

◆ This one distinct floor plan carries three exteriors for you to choose: one with horizontal siding and a box-bay window, one with a covered porch and one with a more formal traditional look. Plans include details for all three facades. The interior is the same for all three. Livability excels with multi-purpose living and dining areas. A walk-in closet graces the living room and will be appreciated for storing guests' coats. Three bedrooms share a hall bath; one also has access to a wash room off the kitchen. All bedrooms have wall closets. A single-car garage is accessed through a door in the dining area or from the backyard. A basement offers space for storage or future expansion, making this a perfect home for young families or empty-nesters.

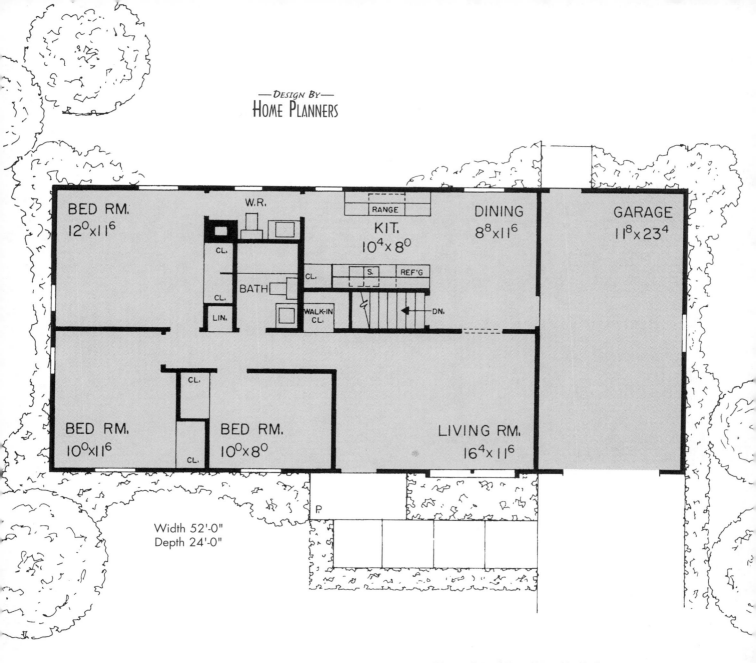

BED RM.
12⁰x11⁶

W.R.

CL.

BATH

CL.

CL.

LIN.

WALK-IN CL.

RANGE

KIT.
10⁴x8⁰

S. REF'G

DN.

DINING
8⁸x11⁶

GARAGE
11⁸x23⁴

BED RM.
10⁰x11⁶

CL.

CL.

BED RM.
10⁰x8⁰

LIVING RM.
16⁴x11⁶

P.

Width 52'-0"
Depth 24'-0"

Design Q237
Square Footage: 1,054

◆ This cottage is not only affordable, it offers a choice of two charming exteriors: a traditional brick or a wood-sided version. Details for both are included in the blueprints. The interior holds many amenities unusual for a plan of its size. The front porch protects the entry which opens directly to a large living room with masonry fireplace. It is complemented by a formal dining room open to the galley kitchen. Sliding doors open to a rear patio. A service entrance leads to the single-car garage (optional). Bedrooms share a full hall bath and have wall closets of ample size. The hallway is also graced by a storage closet with folding doors. If you choose, Bedroom 3 could double as a den or home office.

—Design By—
SELECT HOME DESIGNS

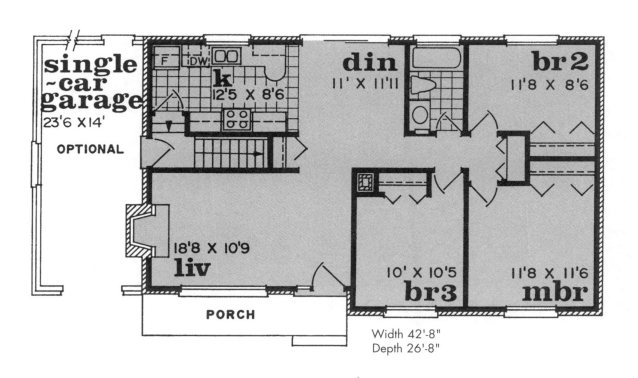

single ~car garage

23'6 X 14'

OPTIONAL

F DW

k

12'5 X 8'6

din

11' X 11'11

br 2

11'8 X 8'6

18'8 X 10'9

liv

10' X 10'5

br3

11'8 X 11'6

mbr

PORCH

Width 42'-8"
Depth 26'-8"

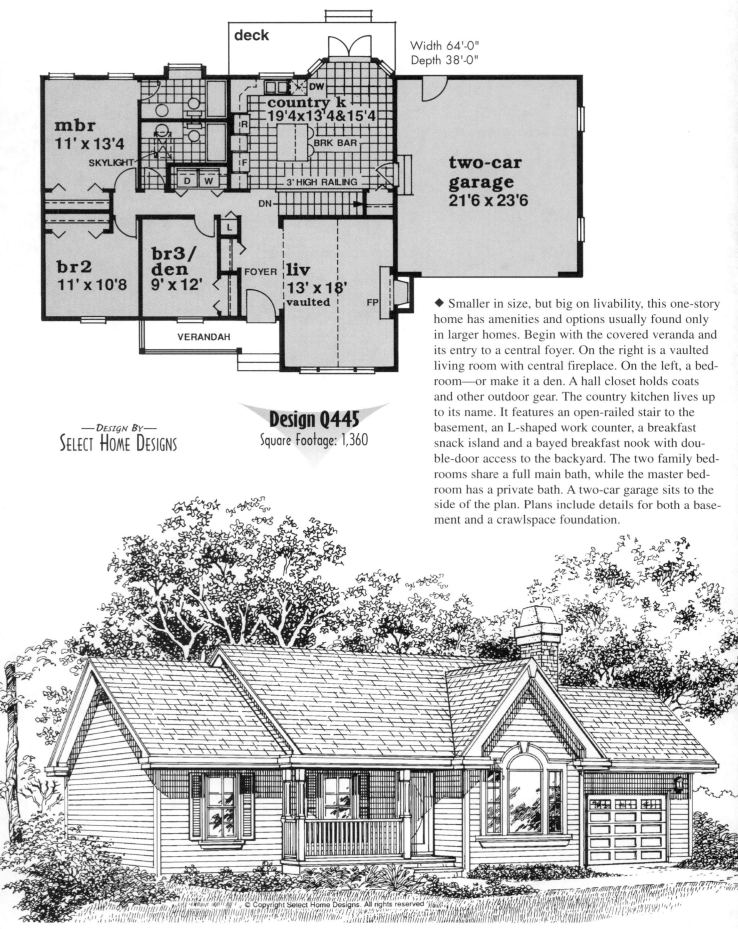

deck

Width 64'-0"
Depth 38'-0"

mbr
11' x 13'4

SKYLIGHT

country k
19'4 x 13'4 & 15'4

DW

R

F

BRK BAR

D W

3' HIGH RAILING

DN

two-car garage
21'6 x 23'6

br2
11' x 10'8

br3/ den
9' x 12'

L

FOYER

liv
13' x 18'
vaulted

FP

VERANDAH

— DESIGN BY —
SELECT HOME DESIGNS

Design Q445
Square Footage: 1,360

◆ Smaller in size, but big on livability, this one-story home has amenities and options usually found only in larger homes. Begin with the covered veranda and its entry to a central foyer. On the right is a vaulted living room with central fireplace. On the left, a bedroom—or make it a den. A hall closet holds coats and other outdoor gear. The country kitchen lives up to its name. It features an open-railed stair to the basement, an L-shaped work counter, a breakfast snack island and a bayed breakfast nook with double-door access to the backyard. The two family bedrooms share a full main bath, while the master bedroom has a private bath. A two-car garage sits to the side of the plan. Plans include details for both a basement and a crawlspace foundation.

—DESIGN BY—
SELECT HOME DESIGNS

Design Q250
Square Footage: 1,399

◆ Classic floor planning dominates this ideal one-story starter home, but, the exterior is worthy of consideration as well. It features a Palladian window, a covered veranda and multi-paned windows. The entry opens to a central foyer flanked by a living room with fireplace on the left and formal dining room on the right. Across the hall is the U-shaped kitchen and breakfast room with sliding glass doors to the rear terrace. A laundry area has access to the two-car garage and to the rear yard. There are three bedrooms and two full baths. The master bedroom has a large wall closet and private bath. Family bedrooms share a full bath. A full basement can be developed at a later time, if needed. Plans include details for both a basement and a crawlspace foundation.

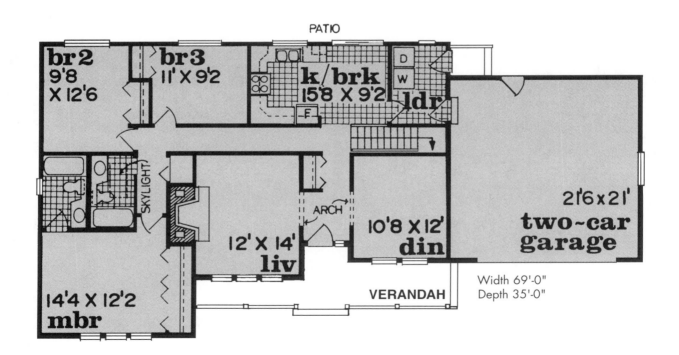

PATIO

br2 9'8 X 12'6

br3 11' X 9'2

k/brk 15'8 X 9'2

D
W

ldr

F

SKYLIGHT?

12' X 14' liv

ARCH

10'8 X 12' din

21'6 x 21' two-car garage

14'4 X 12'2 mbr

VERANDAH

Width 69'-0"
Depth 35'-0"

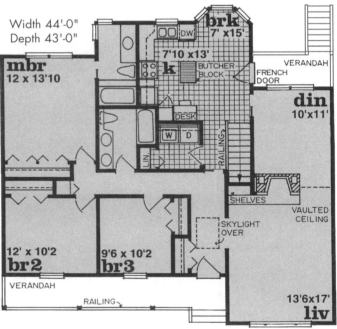

Width 44'-0"
Depth 43'-0"

mbr
12 x 13'10

brk
7' x15'

DW

7'10 x13'

k

BUTCHER BLOCK

FRENCH DOOR

VERANDAH

din
10'x11'

DESK

W   D

LIN.

RAILING

SHELVES

VAULTED CEILING

SKYLIGHT OVER

br2
12' x 10'2

br3
9'6 x 10'2

VERANDAH

RAILING

13'6x17'
liv

Design Q252
Square Footage: 1,475

— DESIGN BY —
SELECT HOME DESIGNS

◆ A railed veranda, turned posts and filigree in the corner and at the gable points complement a lovely Palladian window on the exterior of this home. The interior opens with a skylit foyer and living and dining rooms to the right. The living room is vaulted and features a fireplace and built-in book-shelves. The dining room overlooks a covered veranda accessed through a door in the breakfast room (note the bayed eating area). The kitchen takes advantage of this veranda access, as well. It is further enhanced by an L-shaped work area and butcher-block island. The bedrooms are clustered to the left of the plan. They include a master suite with full bath and two family bedrooms sharing a full bath with double vanity. Plans include details for both a basement and a crawlspace foundation.

Rear Elevation

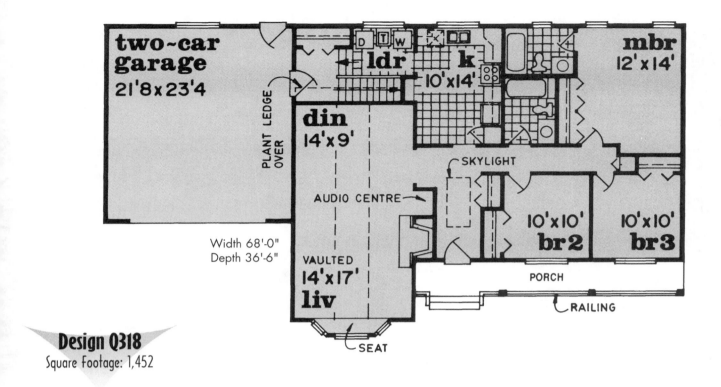

two-car garage 21'8 x 23'4

PLANT LEDGE OVER

D T W

ldr

k 10'x14'

mbr 12'x14'

din 14'x9'

AUDIO CENTRE

SKYLIGHT

Width 68'-0"
Depth 36'-6"

VAULTED 14'x17' **liv**

10'x10' **br2**

10'x10' **br3**

PORCH

RAILING

SEAT

Design Q318
Square Footage: 1,452

◆ This compact three-bedroom home is as economical to build as it is beautiful to behold. Its appeal begins right on the outside with a bay window, a half-circle window over the bay and a railed front porch. The entry foyer is skylit and leads to a hallway connecting the living areas with the sleeping quarters. The living room is vaulted and has a fireplace, a built-in audio-visual center and a window seat in the bay window.

The open dining room shares the vaulted ceiling. The kitchen, with ample work counters, has plenty of room for a breakfast table. It attaches to a laundry/mud room with storage closet and access to the two-car garage. Use all three bedrooms or convert Bedroom 2 to a handy den or home office. The master bedroom has a private bath. Choose a basement or crawl-space foundation—details for both are included.

— DESIGN BY —
SELECT HOME DESIGNS

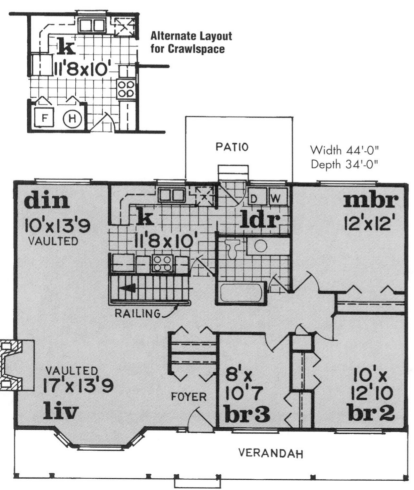

Alternate Layout for Crawlspace

k
11'8x10'

F   H

PATIO

Width 44'-0"
Depth 34'-0"

din
10'x13'9
VAULTED

k
11'8x10'

ldr

D W

mbr
12'12'

RAILING

VAULTED
17'x13'9

liv

FOYER

8'x
10'7

br3

10'x
12'10

br2

VERANDAH

Design Q313
Square Footage: 1,254

◆ Simple details make this starter home quite appealing. A posted front porch, with corner detail, a bay window and shuttered windows all lend a traditional flavor. The central foyer has a coat closet and opens on the left to a vaulted living room with fireplace. The dining room is also vaulted, but overlooks the backyard. An L-shaped kitchen and attached laundry share access to the back patio through a door between them. An additional hall closet sits at the beginning of a stretch to three bedrooms. Each of the bedrooms has a wall closet; two family bedrooms overlook the veranda. All three share the use of a full hall bath. Choose either a basement or crawlspace foundation—plans include details for both.

— DESIGN BY —
SELECT HOME DESIGNS

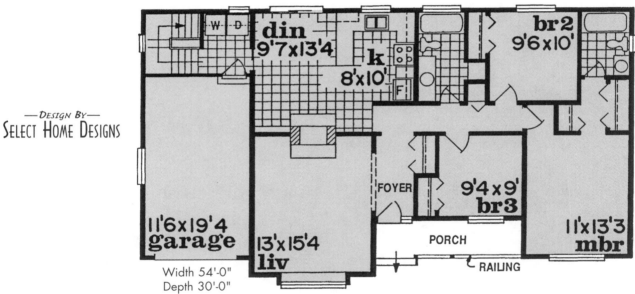

din
9'7x13'4

W D

k
8'x10'

F

br2
9'6x10'

—DESIGN BY—
SELECT HOME DESIGNS

11'6x19'4
garage

Width 54'-0"
Depth 30'-0"

13'x15'4
liv

FOYER

9'4x9'
br3

PORCH

RAILING

11'x13'3
mbr

Design Q346
Square Footage: 1,233

◆ A covered railed veranda, shuttered windows, siding and wood detailing and a Palladian window all lend their charm to this one-story ranch. The living room shares a through-fireplace with the dining area and also has a box-bay at the front. A U-shaped kitchen is efficient and pleasant with a window to the backyard over the sink. Garage access is through the laundry room, where you will also find stairs to the basement. The three bedrooms are on the right side of the plan. The master has two wall closets and a private bath. Family bedrooms share a full hall bath. A single-car garage sits to the side for convenience. If you choose, the basement can be developed later for additional space.

Design 5508
Square Footage: 1,676

Design 5509
Square Footage: 1,676

316

◆ The floor plan for each of these delightful cottages is virtually the same—only the exteriors are different. A wrapping covered porch sets the tone for two of the versions, while one has just a front covered porch, but includes a dormer window over the entry foyer. The porch conjures images of country life, where children play tag among the railed floor boards and grown-ups relax on swings or rocking chairs. Inside, bayed windows in the living/dining room combination and the family room offer great views to the porch beyond. Between these two rooms is a U-shaped kitchen with a large pantry and an adjacent utility room. The master bedroom features a large bath with a corner whirlpool tub, a separate shower and dual lavs and an equally large walk-in closet. Two additional bedrooms share a full bath. The two-car garage, built to protect the bedroom areas from street noise, completes this well-rounded plan.

Design 5507
Width 45'-0"
Depth 64'-0"

Design 5509
Width 45'-4"
Depth 64'-4"

Design 5508
Width 41'-0"
Depth 64'-0"

— DESIGN BY —
HOME PLANNERS

317

◆ This cozy cottage offers the choice of a three- (Design 3656) or four-bedroom (Design 3655) plan. Both designs feature a front-facing office/guest suite which provides privacy for the entry courtyard. With its separate entrance it offers the perfect haven for an in-home office or for those with live-in parents. The remainder of the house is designed with the same level of efficiency. It contains a large living area with access to a covered patio and a three-sided fireplace that shares its warmth with a dining room featuring built-ins. A unique kitchen provides garage access. The bedrooms include a comfortable master suite with a whirlpool tub, a double-bowl vanity and twin closets.

Width 44'-8"
Depth 54'-4"

Width 44'-8"
Depth 52'-4"

Quote One®
Cost to build? See page 436
to order complete cost estimate
to build this house in your area!

Design 3656
Square Footage: 1,414
L

Design 3655
Square Footage: 1,418
L

— DESIGN BY —
Home Planners

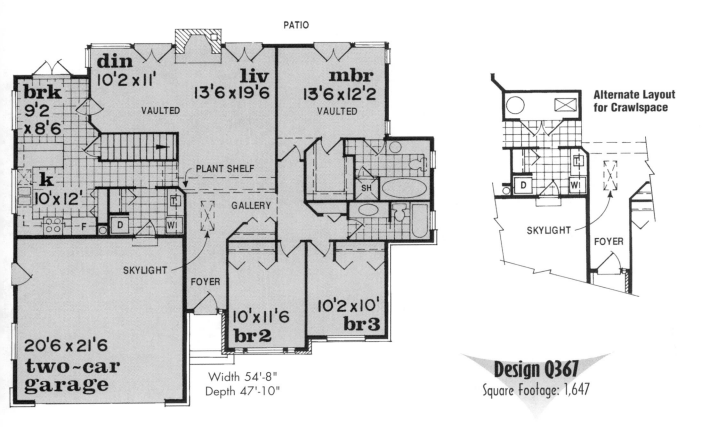

din
10'2 x 11'

brk
9'2 x 8'6

k
10'x12'

liv
13'6 x 19'6
VAULTED

mbr
13'6 x 12'2
VAULTED

PATIO

VAULTED

PLANT SHELF

GALLERY

SH

SKYLIGHT

FOYER

10'x11'6
br2

10'2 x10'
br3

20'6 x 21'6
two~car garage

Width 54'-8"
Depth 47'-10"

Alternate Layout for Crawlspace

SKYLIGHT

FOYER

Design Q367
Square Footage: 1,647

◆ This floor plan is designed for a home that captures a view to the rear of the lot. French doors in the dining room, living room, master bedroom and breakfast room all lead out to the patio in the back. In the front, a skylit patio is visually zoned from the living room by a plant shelf. Both the living room and dining room have vaulted ceilings and enjoy a warming fireplace set between them. A U-shaped kitchen has a breakfast bar to serve the sunny breakfast room. The bedrooms are to the right and include two family bedrooms sharing a full bath. The master suite is vaulted and has a walk in closet and private bath with separate tub and shower. Plans include details for both a basement and a crawlspace foundation.

— DESIGN BY —
SELECT HOME DESIGNS

Design 3689
Square Footage: 1,295

L D

◆ Equally gracious outside and inside, this one- or two-bedroom cottage has a post-and-rail covered porch hugging one wing, with convenient access through double doors or pass-through windows in the dining room and kitchen. The columned entry has a sloped ceiling and leads past a second bedroom or media room into a great room with sloped ceiling, fireplace and low wall along the staircase to the attic. The master suite fills the right wing and features a plant shelf in the bedroom and garden tub in the master bath, plus a large walk-in closet and laundry facilities.

Quote One®
Cost to build? See page 436 to order complete cost estimate to build this house in your area!

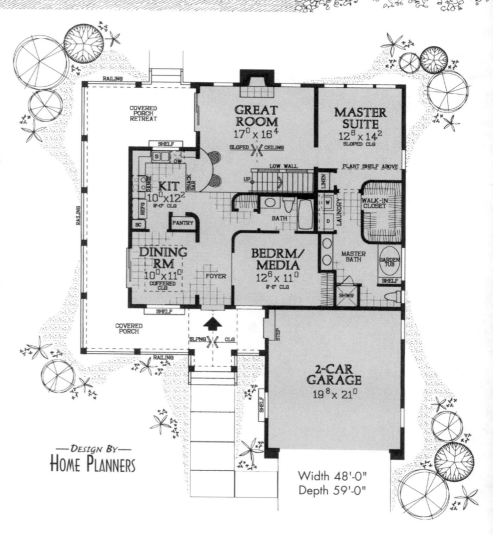

— DESIGN BY —
HOME PLANNERS

Width 48'-0"
Depth 59'-0"

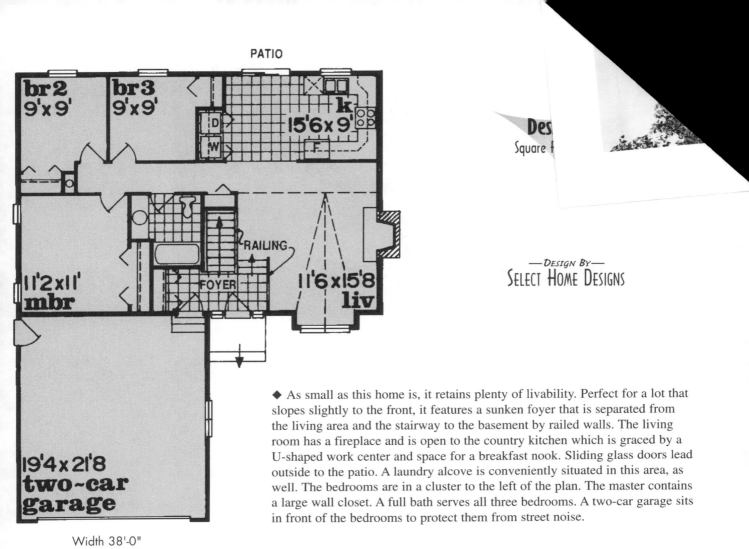

PATIO

br2
9'x9'

br3
9'x9'

k
15'6 x 9'

D

W

F

RAILING

FOYER

11'6 x 15'8
liv

11'2x11'
mbr

19'4 x 21'8
two-car garage

Width 38'-0"
Depth 48'-4"

—DESIGN BY—
SELECT HOME DESIGNS

◆ As small as this home is, it retains plenty of livability. Perfect for a lot that slopes slightly to the front, it features a sunken foyer that is separated from the living area and the stairway to the basement by railed walls. The living room has a fireplace and is open to the country kitchen which is graced by a U-shaped work center and space for a breakfast nook. Sliding glass doors lead outside to the patio. A laundry alcove is conveniently situated in this area, as well. The bedrooms are in a cluster to the left of the plan. The master contains a large wall closet. A full bath serves all three bedrooms. A two-car garage sits in front of the bedrooms to protect them from street noise.

Design 5531
Square Footage: 1,952

Design 5532
Square Footage: 1,968

Design 5533
Square Footage: 1,971

Width 42'-0"
Depth 65'-6"

Design 5531

◆ These three facades share a floor plan that is strikingly similar—the differences are in some of the window and ceiling details. Decide which facade you prefer, then order by the design number that corresponds to that facade. Every inch of space in this one-story home is designed to provide the ultimate in comfort and enjoyment. The front-facing great room offers either a coffered or a sloped ceiling and contains either a bay or box-bay window, an inviting fireplace and access to a formal dining area with a bay window. The U-shaped kitchen maximizes counter space and provides entry to both the dining area and the family room with its bayed breakfast area and rear-patio access. The master bedroom features another bay window—the perfect spot to wind down with a good book—and a master bath with a windowed whirlpool tub, dual sinks and a walk-in closet. Two additional bedrooms share a full hall bath with dual basins. Bedroom 3, with its French-door access, can be used as either a bedroom or a private den. A two-car garage and a convenient laundry room complete this amenity-filled plan.

Width 42'-8"
Depth 65'-10"

Design 5533

Width 42'-4"
Depth 65'-10"

Design 5532

—DESIGN BY—
HOME PLANNERS

323

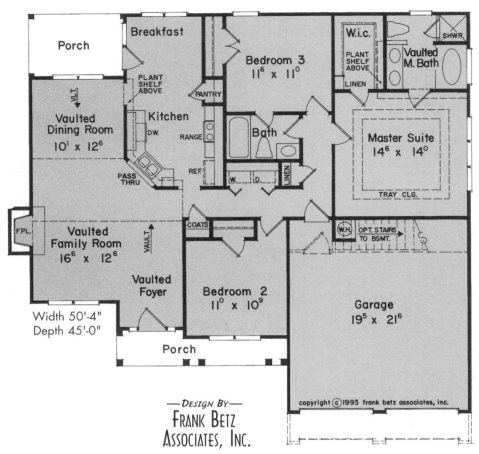

Porch

Breakfast

PLANT SHELF ABOVE

VLT

Vaulted Dining Room
10' x 12⁶

Kitchen
DW.

PANTRY

RANGE

PASS THRU

REF

W.i.c.

PLANT SHELF ABOVE

LINEN

SHWR.

Vaulted M. Bath

Bedroom 3
11⁶ x 11⁰

Bath

W. D. LINEN

Master Suite
14⁶ x 14⁰

TRAY CLG.

FPL.

Vaulted Family Room
16⁶ x 12⁶

VAULT

Vaulted Foyer

COATS

W.H. OPT. STAIRS TO BSMT.

Width 50'-4"
Depth 45'-0"

Bedroom 2
11⁰ x 10⁹

Garage
19⁵ x 21⁶

Porch

copyright © 1993 frank betz associates, inc.

—DESIGN BY—
FRANK BETZ
ASSOCIATES, INC.

Design P107
Square Footage: 1,373

◆ Columns add style as well as support to the covered front porch that dresses up this petite home. The foyer opens onto a family room that combines with the dining room to create a space sized to accommodate every occasion. The foyer, family room and dining room are all vaulted; the family room features a fireplace. An adjacent kitchen is designed for efficiency, uniting with the breakfast room for casual meals. A covered porch extends the dining area to the outside. Sleeping quarters include two family bedrooms and a spacious master suite. The master bedroom has a tray ceiling, a walk-in closet with plant ledge and bath with separate shower and tub and dual vanities. Please specify basement or crawlspace foundation when ordering.

Design Q273
Square Footage: 1,383

— DESIGN BY —
SELECT HOME DESIGNS

◆ Enhanced by farmhouse details—turned spindles on a covered porch and gable trim—this compact is as pleasing as it is affordable. The entry opens to a center hall with a living room on one side and dining room on the other. The living room features a box-bay window and warming fireplace. The dining room attaches to the U-shaped kitchen. A handy laundry area with access to the two-car garage (optional) is nearby. The three bedrooms stretch out along the rear width of the home. The master suite has a private bath and wall closet. Two family bedrooms also have wall closets and share the use of a full bath. The basement may be finished later for additional living or sleeping space.

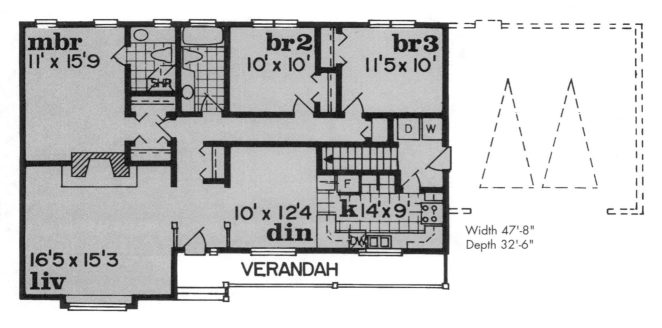

mbr
11' x 15'9

br2
10' x 10'

br3
11'5 x 10'

SHR

D W

F

10' x 12'4
din

k 14'x9'

16'5 x 15'3
liv

VERANDAH

Width 47'-8"
Depth 32'-6"

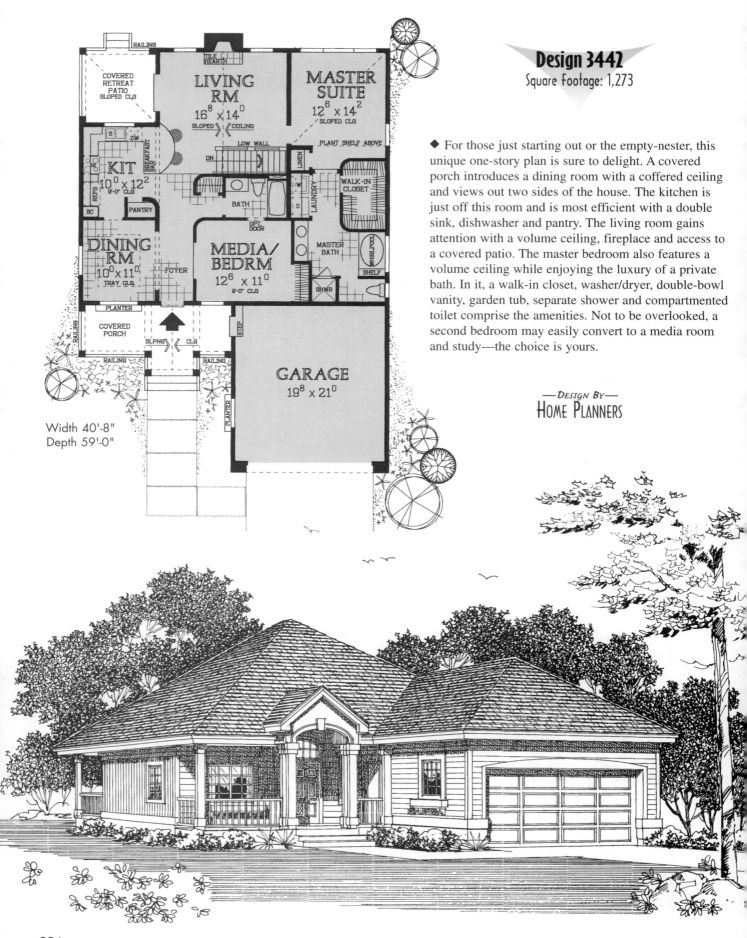

Design 3442
Square Footage: 1,273

COVERED RETREAT PATIO SLOPED CLG

LIVING RM
16⁸ x 14⁰
SLOPED CEILING

MASTER SUITE
12⁶ x 14²
SLOPED CLG

TILE HEARTH

LOW WALL

PLANT SHELF ABOVE

DN

LINEN

WALK-IN CLOSET

KIT
10⁰ x 12²
9'-0" CLG

BREAKFAST BAR

S DW

REFG

BC

PANTRY

BATH

OPT. DOOR

LAUNDRY

W D

MASTER BATH

WHIRLPOOL

SHELF

DINING RM
10⁰ x 11⁰
TRAY CLG

FOYER

MEDIA/ BEDRM
12⁶ x 11⁰
9'-0" CLG

SHWR

PLANTER

COVERED PORCH

SLPNG CLG

STEP

GARAGE
19⁸ x 21⁰

RAILING

PLANTER

Width 40'-8"
Depth 59'-0"

◆ For those just starting out or the empty-nester, this unique one-story plan is sure to delight. A covered porch introduces a dining room with a coffered ceiling and views out two sides of the house. The kitchen is just off this room and is most efficient with a double sink, dishwasher and pantry. The living room gains attention with a volume ceiling, fireplace and access to a covered patio. The master bedroom also features a volume ceiling while enjoying the luxury of a private bath. In it, a walk-in closet, washer/dryer, double-bowl vanity, garden tub, separate shower and compartmented toilet comprise the amenities. Not to be overlooked, a second bedroom may easily convert to a media room and study—the choice is yours.

—DESIGN BY—
HOME PLANNERS

PATIO

fam
13'6 x 10'

SEAT
brk
BAR

br2
10' x 10'4

mbr
11' x 14'

din
10' x 9'

k

F

liv
13'4 x 16'

FOYER

br3
12'6 x 9'6

D
W

SEAT

Width 45'-6"
Depth 54'-0"

19' x 20'6
two~car garage

Design Q364
Square Footage: 1,495

◆ This affordable, three-bedroom starter home has a practical layout and an appealing facade, which makes it an attractive choice in a smaller home. A bay window, horizontal siding and a covered entry with turned post and wood railings are the first details you'll notice. Inside, the floor plan minimizes hallways and maximizes floor area to encourage a sense of space. The living room/dining room combination features a window seat in the bay window and a warming fireplace. The kitchen has a breakfast bar, a bay-windowed eating area and attaches to a family room with sliding glass doors to the rear patio. Three bedrooms include two family bedrooms sharing a full bath and a master suite with walk-in closet and private bath. The two-car garage connects to the main house via a laundry area where stairs to the basement are also found.

—Design By—
Select Home Designs

327

◆ While relatively small in terms of square footage, this home has the design characteristics and fine craftsmanship of another era. Influenced by Shingle Style cottages, the exterior features a sloping gable with a gentle curve over the front porch. Shingle siding is accented by expansive windows surrounded with wide wood trim. Inside, the living area offers a fireplace and built-in media center. Decorative columns separate the living and dining areas. French doors open to a 6' x 17' rear porch from both the dining area and the master bedroom. The well-appointed master bath has ample linen storage, a private water closet and a garden tub with adjacent glass-enclosed shower. Family bedrooms have large wall closets and share access to a full bath.

Design 9023
Square Footage: 1,373

— DESIGN BY —
LARRY W. GARNETT
& ASSOCIATES

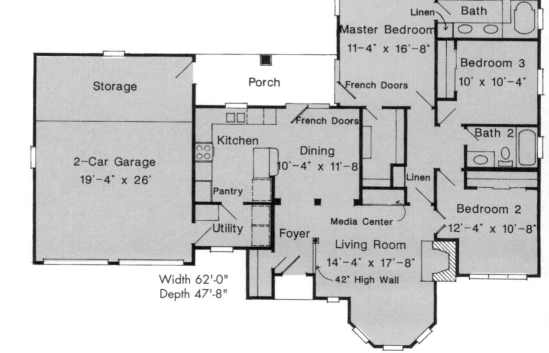

Storage

Porch

Linen   Bath

Master Bedroom
11'-4" x 16'-8"

French Doors

Bedroom 3
10' x 10'-4"

2-Car Garage
19'-4" x 26'

French Doors

Kitchen

Dining
10'-4" x 11'-8"

Bath 2

Pantry

Linen

Utility

Foyer

Media Center

Bedroom 2
12'-4" x 10'-8"

Living Room
14'-4" x 17'-8"

42" High Wall

Width 62'-0"
Depth 47'-8"

Luxury One-Story Homes

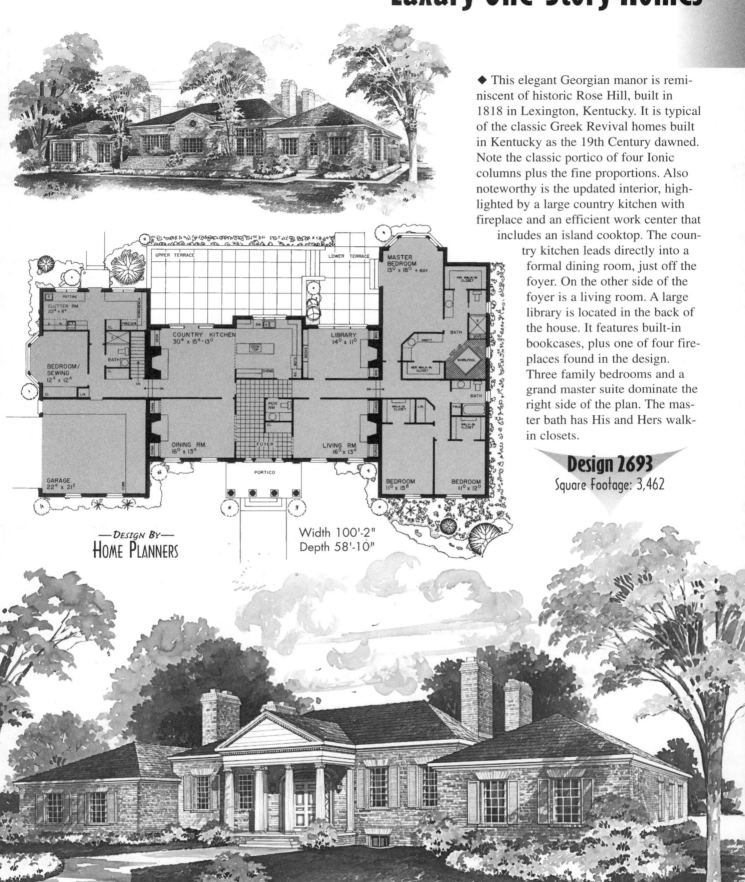

◆ This elegant Georgian manor is reminiscent of historic Rose Hill, built in 1818 in Lexington, Kentucky. It is typical of the classic Greek Revival homes built in Kentucky as the 19th Century dawned. Note the classic portico of four Ionic columns plus the fine proportions. Also noteworthy is the updated interior, highlighted by a large country kitchen with fireplace and an efficient work center that includes an island cooktop. The country kitchen leads directly into a formal dining room, just off the foyer. On the other side of the foyer is a living room. A large library is located in the back of the house. It features built-in bookcases, plus one of four fireplaces found in the design. Three family bedrooms and a grand master suite dominate the right side of the plan. The master bath has His and Hers walk-in closets.

Design 2693
Square Footage: 3,462

—DESIGN BY—
HOME PLANNERS

Width 100'-2"
Depth 58'-10"

Width 92'-8"
Depth 46'-8"

— DESIGN BY —
HOME PLANNERS

Quote One®
Cost to build? See page 436
to order complete cost estimate
to build this house in your area!

Design 2779
Square Footage: 3,225
LD

◆ A unique placement of rooms and efficient traffic flow characterize this French design. A formal dining room and the parlor flank the wide entry, which is also graced by double coat closets. The formal dining room is accessed by a butler's pantry to make serving that much easier. The parlor also has a doorway to the central hall. A huge gathering room contains a focal-point fireplace flanked by windows overlooking the backyard and connects to a study (or fourth bedroom) with which it shares a covered porch. The kitchen has an enormous work area for the gourmet—it is U-shaped and enhanced by an island range. Beyond is the service entrance containing a laundry room and wash room and access to the two-car garage. Basement stairs are also nearby. At the opposite end of the plan are three bedrooms—one a grand master suite. It features private terrace access, a walk-in closet and superb bath. One of two family bedrooms has a walk-in closet.

Design 9189
Square Footage: 2,908
Bonus: 479 sq. ft.

◆ The livability presented by
this house is outstanding. From a
large family gathering area to a
cozy study with a fireplace,
you're sure to find many pleasing attributes. The formal dining
room opens to the right of the
foyer. Conveniently accessed by
the kitchen, meals will take on a
special air when served here. A
gallery accentuates the family
room, which also sports a
twelve-foot ceiling, a fireplace,
built-ins and columns. Two bedrooms make up the right side of
the house. Both offer ample proportions and superb bath access.
In the master bedroom, a private
bath, an expansive walk-in closet
and outdoor passage create a true
retreat. A three-car garage with a
bonus room above and a pool
cabana complete the plan.

—DESIGN BY—
LARRY W. GARNETT & ASSOCIATES

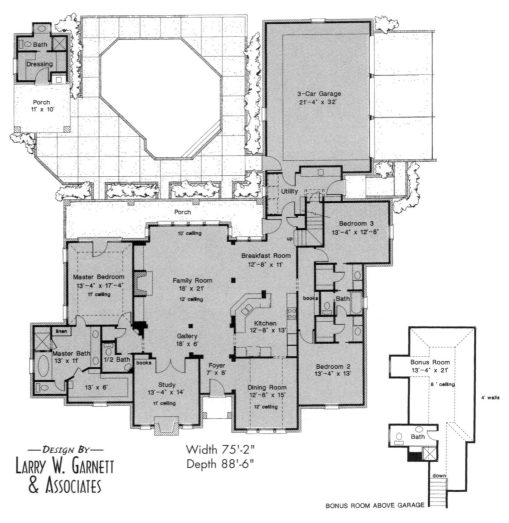

Width 75'-2"
Depth 88'-6"

331

DESIGN BY
Home Planners

BEDRM
12⁶ x 10⁰
10'-0" CLG

KIT
11⁶ x 14⁸
10'-0" CLG

MORNING RM
13⁰ x 18⁰
14'-6" CLG

FAMILY RM
SUNKEN
18⁰ x 12⁶
VOL CLG

MASTER SUITE
17⁰ x 13¹⁰
10'-0" CLG

MASTER BATH

WALK-IN CLOSET

BATH

OFFICE-DEN
12² x 12⁰

BEDRM
12⁶ x 10⁰
10'-0" CLG

LAUNDRY ROOM

BATH

DINING RM
11¹⁰ x 12⁰
12'-0" CLG

FOYER
14'-0" CLG

LIVING RM
14⁰ x 12¹⁰
14'-0" CLG

COVERED PORCH

GARAGE
29¹⁰ x 21⁶

GUEST RM
12⁰ x 10²
10'-0" CLG

ENTERTAINMENT PATIO

PRIVACY WALL

SPA

PRIVATE PATIO

Width 94'-1"
Depth 67'-4"

Design 3612
Square Footage: 2,946
L

◆ Varying hip roof planes complement a glass-paneled entry and divided-light transoms that reflect a well-articulated style and make a bold statement. The tiled foyer opens to formal and casual living areas, defined by arched colonnades and set off by an extended-hearth fireplace in the family room. The gourmet kitchen boasts a food preparation island, an angled snack bar and a walk-in pantry. A guest suite, or study, resides just off the living area. The secluded master suite enjoys a private patio with a spa, as well as a spacious bath with a box-bay whirlpool tub, twin lavatories and a knee-space vanity. A home office or den with a separate entry and porch, and two family bedrooms with a full bath complete the plan.

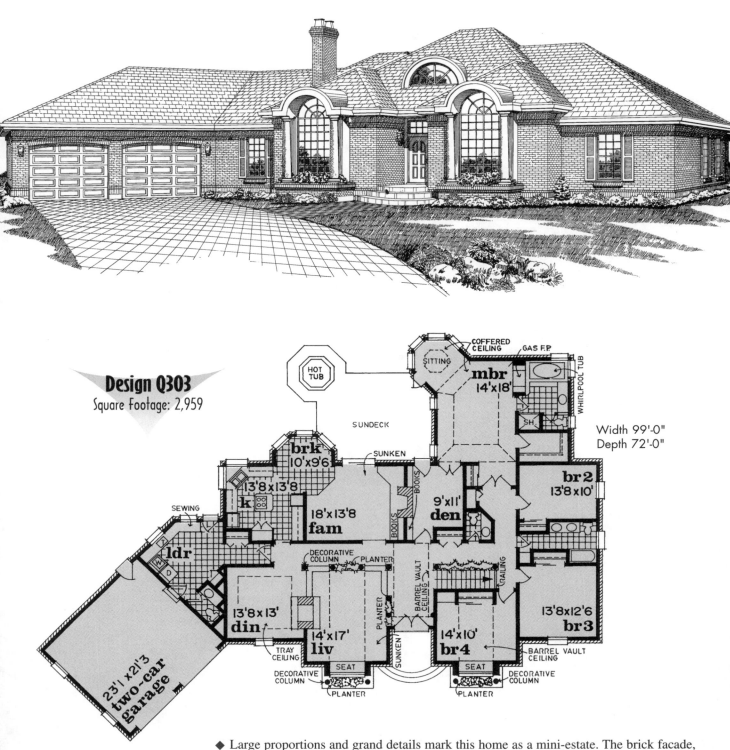

Design Q303
Square Footage: 2,959

Width 99'-0"
Depth 72'-0"

HOT TUB

SUNDECK

COFFERED CEILING

GAS F.P.

SITTING

WHIRLPOOL TUB

mbr
14'x18'

SH

brk
10'x9'6

SUNKEN

br2
13'8x10'

k

13'8x13'8

9'x11'
den

SEWING

18'x13'8
fam

BOOKS

ldr
W D

DECORATIVE COLUMN   PLANTER

BOOKS

BARREL VAULT CEILING

RAILING

13'8x13'
din

PLANTER

13'8x12'6
br3

TRAY CEILING

14'x17'
liv

SUNKEN

14'x10'
br4

BARREL VAULT CEILING

23'1 x 21'3
two-car
garage

DECORATIVE COLUMN

SEAT

SEAT

DECORATIVE COLUMN

PLANTER

PLANTER

— DESIGN BY —
SELECT HOME DESIGNS

◆ Large proportions and grand details mark this home as a mini-estate. The brick facade, two-story windows with circle-head tops and the double-door entry combine to good effect. The interior is no less elegant. Begin with a barrel-vaulted ceiling in the foyer, which opens directly to the sunken living and dining areas—separated from them only by decorative columns and planters. The living room is made for grand entertaining with a window seat, vaulted ceiling and through-fireplace to the dining room. The family room is just across the hall and is also sunken and warmed by a fireplace. Sliding glass doors to the sundeck and hot tub outside make this room special. A kitchen with octagonal breakfast nook is nearby. A cozy den can be accessed either from the hall or from the master bedroom. Details in the master suite include a gas fireplace, a light-filled sitting room, a walk-in closet and a wonderful bath. Three additional bedrooms share a full bath with double vanity. Choose either a basement or a crawlspace foundation—details for both are included.

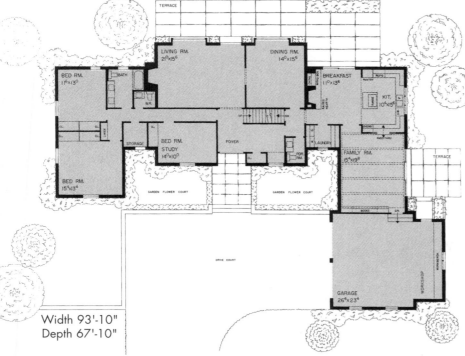

MASTER BED RM. 17⁵ x 19⁵

LINEN

WALK-IN CLOSET

CABINET

BATH

ATTIC STORAGE

WALK-IN CLOSET

WALK-IN CLOSET

DN

ROOF

ROOF

Design 1228
Main Level: 2,583 sq. ft.
Second Level Master Suite:
697 sq. ft.
L D

◆ This beautiful home has a wealth of detail taken from the rich traditions of French Regency design. The roof itself is a study in pleasant dormers, hips and valleys. The plan serves essentially as a one-story design—with a bonus on the upper level. If you choose to finish it, this level will yield a perfect private master suite. On the main level are spaces for both formal and casual gatherings. The living room and dining room have box-bay windows overlooking the rear terrace; the living room has a fireplace. The U-shaped kitchen with breakfast nook also has a fireplace and sliding glass doors to access the terrace. A nearby family room contains a beamed ceiling and accesses a private side terrace. Three bedrooms—or two and a study—sit at the opposite end of the plan. They share the use of a full bath—a powder room and huge storage area are nearby. Once completed, the upstairs master suite will have three walk-in closets, built-in linen and cabinet storage, four dormer windows and a full bath.

TERRACE

LIVING RM. 21⁶x15⁶

DINING RM. 14⁰x15⁶

BREAKFAST 11⁰x13⁶

PANTRY

REFG.

KIT. 10⁶x15⁰

BED RM. 17⁶x13⁰

BATH

W.R.

OVENS

PASS-THRU

BED RM. 14⁵x10⁰ STUDY

FOYER

LINEN

STORAGE

LAUNDRY

POR. RM.

FAMILY RM. 15⁵x19⁹

TERRACE

BED RM. 15⁵x13⁴

GARDEN FLOWER COURT

GARDEN FLOWER COURT

BOOKS

DRIVE COURT

WORKSHOP WORKBENCH

GARAGE 26⁴x23⁶

Width 93'-10"
Depth 67'-10"

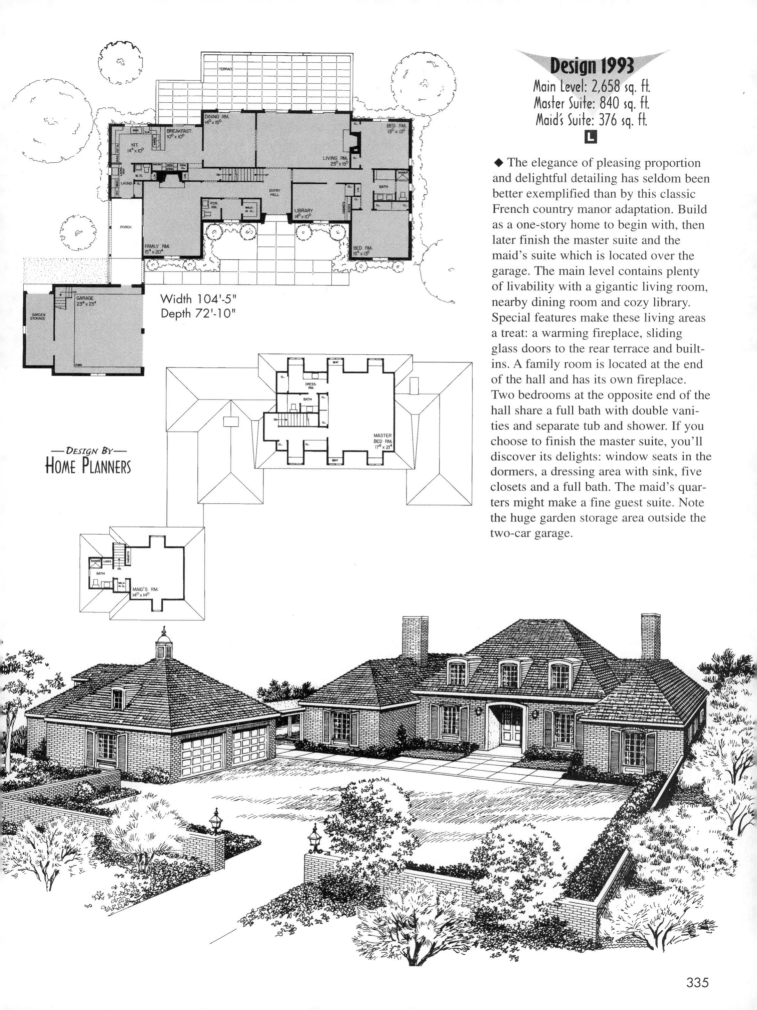

Design 1993

Main Level: 2,658 sq. ft.
Master Suite: 840 sq. ft.
Maid's Suite: 376 sq. ft.

L

◆ The elegance of pleasing proportion and delightful detailing has seldom been better exemplified than by this classic French country manor adaptation. Build as a one-story home to begin with, then later finish the master suite and the maid's suite which is located over the garage. The main level contains plenty of livability with a gigantic living room, nearby dining room and cozy library. Special features make these living areas a treat: a warming fireplace, sliding glass doors to the rear terrace and built-ins. A family room is located at the end of the hall and has its own fireplace. Two bedrooms at the opposite end of the hall share a full bath with double vanities and separate tub and shower. If you choose to finish the master suite, you'll discover its delights: window seats in the dormers, a dressing area with sink, five closets and a full bath. The maid's quarters might make a fine guest suite. Note the huge garden storage area outside the two-car garage.

Width 104'-5"
Depth 72'-10"

— DESIGN BY —
HOME PLANNERS

— DESIGN BY —
HOME PLANNERS

Width 86'-4"
Depth 80'-2"

QUOTE ONE®
Cost to build? See page 436
to order complete cost estimate
to build this house in your area!

Design 3664
Square Footage: 2,471

◆ Capstones, quoins and gentle arches lend an unpretentious spirit to this European-style plan. A vaulted entry introduces an unrestrained floor plan designed for comfort. The tiled gallery opens to a sizable great room that invites casual entertaining and features a handsome fireplace with an extended hearth, framed with decorative niches. The kitchen features a cooktop island and a built-in desk, and opens to a windowed breakfast bay which lets in natural light. For formal occasions, a great dining room permits quiet, unhurried evening meals. Relaxation awaits the homeowner in a sensational master suite, with an inner retreat and a private patio. Two family bedrooms share a private bath, and one room opens to a covered patio. A golf cart will easily fit into a side garage, which adjoins a roomy two-car garage that loads from the opposite side.

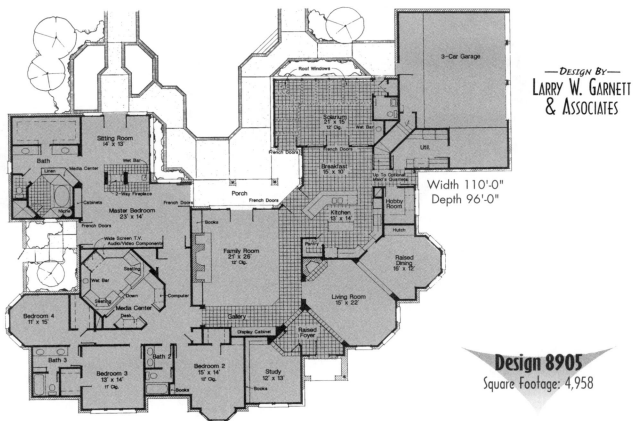

Design By
Larry W. Garnett & Associates

3-Car Garage

Roof Windows

Solarium
21' x 15'
12' Clg.

Wet Bar

Util.

Sitting Room
14' x 13'

Bath

Media Center

Linen

Cabinets

2-Way Fireplace

Wet Bar

Niche

French Doors

Master Bedroom
23' x 14'

French Doors

Breakfast
15' x 10'

French Doors

Kitchen
13' x 14'

Hobby Room

Up To Optional Maid's Quarters

Porch

French Doors

Wide Screen T.V.
Audio/Video Components

Books

Family Room
21' x 26'
12' Clg.

Pantry

Hutch

Seating

Wet Bar

Raised Dining
16' x 12'

Seating

Down

Computer

Media Center

Desk

Bedroom 4
11' x 15'

Gallery

Living Room
15' x 22'

Display Cabinet

Raised Foyer

Bath 3

Bath 2

Bedroom 3
13' x 14'
11' Clg.

Bedroom 2
15' x 14'
12' Clg.

Study
12' x 13'

Books

Books

Width 110'-0"
Depth 96'-0"

Design 8905
Square Footage: 4,958

◆ The amenities in this home are almost too numerous to mention them all. Three family bedrooms, one with a bay window, are accompanied by two full baths. The master suite, to the rear of the home, includes a two-way fireplace to the bedroom and the sitting room, easy access to three separate outdoor areas, a built-in media center and a bath with dual vanities and a separate shower and tub. A modern media center is sunken and features built-in seating and a wet bar. Fireplaces warm the spacious family and living rooms. A study to the left of the foyer provides built-in bookshelves. The kitchen, with a work island and a large pantry, serves the family room, the breakfast room and the raised dining room. French doors open to a commodious solarium. Maid's quarters may be built above the three-car garage.

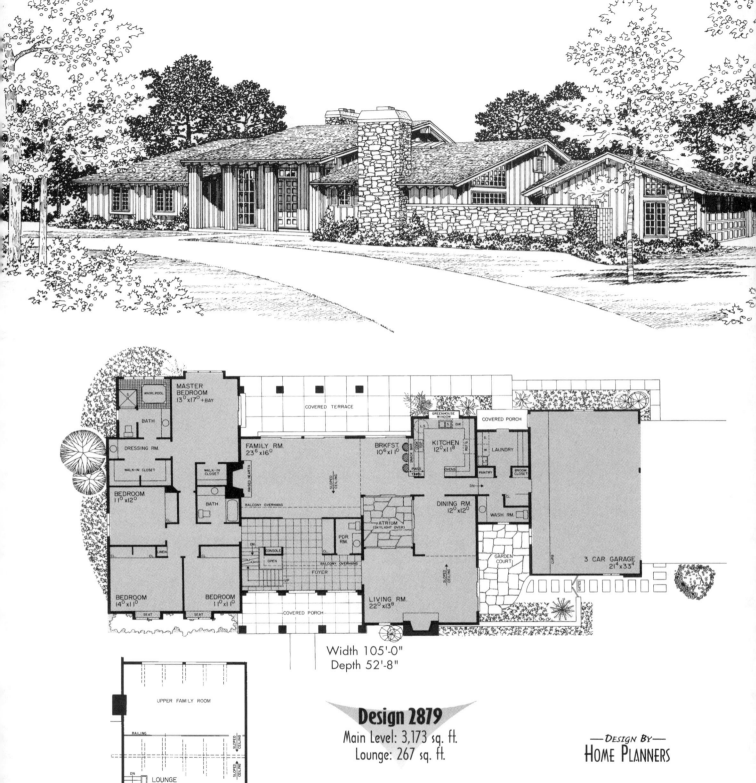

MASTER BEDROOM
13⁰x17⁰ +BAY

WHIRLPOOL

BATH

DRESSING RM.

WALK-IN CLOSET

BEDROOM
11⁰x12⁰

BATH

WALK-IN CLOSET

LINEN

BEDROOM
14⁰x11⁰

SEAT

BEDROOM
11⁰x11⁰

SEAT

COVERED TERRACE

FAMILY RM.
23⁶x16⁰

BRKFST.
10⁶x11⁰

GREENHOUSE WINDOW

KITCHEN
12⁰x11⁸

COVERED PORCH

LAUNDRY

PANTRY

BROOM CLOSET

OVENS

SLOPED CEILING

BALCONY OVERHANG

RAISED HEARTH

DN

CONSOLE

OPEN

UP

FOYER

BALCONY OVERHANG

ATRIUM
(SKYLIGHT OVER)

POR. RM.

CL.

DINING RM.
12⁰x12⁰

WASH RM.

GARDEN COURT

3 CAR GARAGE
21⁴x33⁴

CURB

GATES

LIVING RM.
22⁰x13⁸

SLOPED CEILING

COVERED PORCH

Width 105'-0"
Depth 52'-8"

UPPER FAMILY ROOM

RAILING

SLOPED CEILING

DN

LOUNGE
23⁶x12⁰

SLOPED CEILING

RAILING

UPPER FOYER

Quote One®

Cost to build? See page 436
to order complete cost estimate
to build this house in your area!

Design 2879

Main Level: 3,173 sq. ft.
Lounge: 267 sq. ft.

— DESIGN BY —
HOME PLANNERS

◆ This lavish modern design has it all, including an upper lounge, family room and foyer. A centrally located atrium with skylight provides focal interest downstairs. A large, efficient kitchen with snack bar service to the breakfast room enjoys its own greenhouse window. The spacious family room shares a warming fireplace and a view of the rear covered terrace. To the front, a living room with fireplace delights in a view of the garden court as well as the atrium. The deluxe master suite features a relaxing whirlpool, dressing area and an abundance of walk-in closets. Three secondary bedrooms, two with window seats, share a full bath.

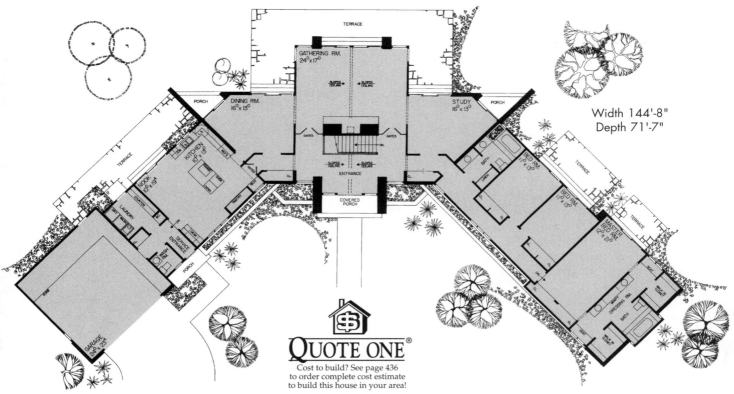

Width 144'-8"
Depth 71'-7"

Quote One®
Cost to build? See page 436
to order complete cost estimate
to build this house in your area!

Design 2534
Square Footage: 3,262

L

—DESIGN BY—
HOME PLANNERS

◆ Using the best of Western design with in-line floor planning, this grand ranch house is made for open spaces. The wings effectively balance a truly dramatic front entrance. Massive masonry walls support the wide overhanging roof with its exposed beams. The patterned double front doors are surrounded by a delightful expanse of glass. The raised planter and the masses of quarried stone (or brick if you prefer) enhance the exterior appeal. Inside, a distinctive and practical floor plan emerges. The entry is impressive and leads through gates to the grand gathering room. The right wing holds the three bedrooms, each of which has terrace access. The master has three closets (two are walk-in!) and a dressing area in the bath. The left wing holds the kitchen, dining room and service areas. Be sure to notice the many terraces and porches.

—DESIGN BY—
HOME PLANNERS

Design 1911
Square Footage: 3,107

◆ This solid brick country estate signals a plan filled with luxurious appointments. A recessed entry opens through double doors to an entrance hall at the center of the plan. It opens directly into the large living room that features sliding glass doors to the living terrace and a fireplace flanked by built-in bookshelves. Across the hall, and on either side of the entrance hall are the formal dining room with bay window and the library with bay window—or make it a fourth bedroom. A cozy family room is tucked in the corner. It is graced by sliding glass doors to the play terrace, a wet bar, a beamed ceiling and a fireplace. A pass-through counter connects it to the U-shaped kitchen and breakfast room beyond. All three bedrooms have walk-in closets. The master suite has a private bath with built-in chest, double vanities and an additional wall closet. Sliding glass doors in the master bedroom lead to its private terrace.

Width 80'-10"
Depth 74'-2"

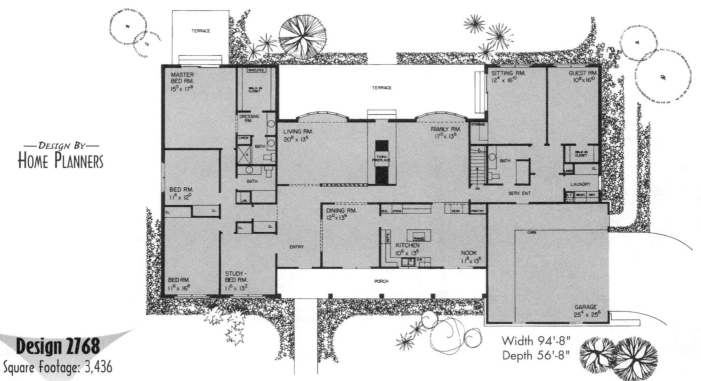

Width 94'-8"
Depth 56'-8"

Design 2768
Square Footage: 3,436

◆ Besides its elegant traditional exterior, with delightfully long covered front porch, this home has an exceptional interior. Four bedrooms and two full baths dominate the left side of the plan, while a complete guest suite with sitting room and full bath occupy the right side. The master suite features a bath with walk-in closet, double vanities and a dressing area. In the middle of the plan are living and dining spaces including a living room and family room, both with bow windows. A through-fireplace separates the two areas. A formal dining room is across the hall, near the L-shaped island kitchen and the breakfast nook. A service entrance holds a laundry and access to the two-car garage. Two rear terraces serve the living areas and the master suite.

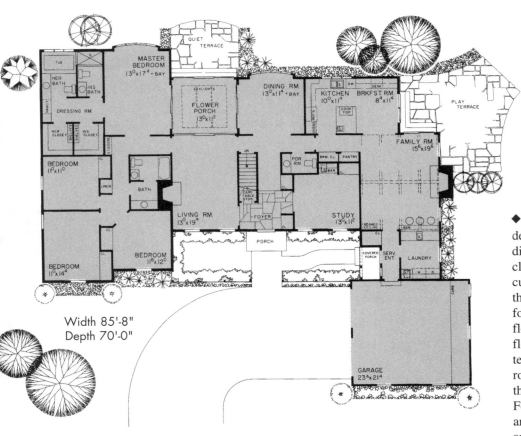

Width 85'-8"
Depth 70'-0"

— DESIGN BY —
HOME PLANNERS

Design 2888
Square Footage: 3,018

L

◆ An outstanding Early American design for the 20th-Century, this home displays exterior detailing with narrow clapboards, multi-paned windows and cupola. However, interior planning lets the active family spread out among the formal living room, family room, study, flower porch and two terraces. The flower porch is accessible from the master bedroom, living room and dining rooms. There's enough counter space in the kitchen for two or three helpers. Four bedrooms are in the sleeping zone area. The master bedroom features His and Hers bathrooms and two walk-in closets. Family bedrooms share a full bath with double vanities. A two-car garage is accessed through the service entrance where there is a laundry room.

—DESIGN BY—
HOME PLANNERS

Design 2921

Main Level: 3,215 sq. ft.
Second Floor Option: 711 sq. ft.
Sun Room: 296 sq. ft.

L D

◆ Organized zoning makes this traditional design a comfortable home for living. A central foyer facilitates flexible traffic patterns. Quiet areas of the house include a media room and luxurious master bedroom suite with fitness area, spacious closet space and bath, as well as a lounge or writing area. Informal living areas of the house include a sunroom, large country kitchen and an efficient food preparation area with an island. Formal living areas include a living area and formal dining room. The second floor holds two bedrooms and a lounge. Service areas include a room just off the garage for laundry, sewing or hobbies.

This home, as shown in the photographs, may differ from the actual blueprints. For more detailed information, please check the floor plans carefully.

Width 97'-8"
Depth 101'-4"

QUOTE ONE®

Cost to build? See page 436 to order complete cost estimate to build this house in your area!

Photos by Laszlo Regos

This home, as shown in the photograph, may differ from the actual blueprints.
For more detailed information, please check the floor plans carefully.

Photo by Andrew D. Lautman

Design 2615
Main Level: 2,563 sq. ft.
Bonus Second Level: 552 sq. ft.

L D

—DESIGN BY—
HOME PLANNERS

QUOTE ONE®
Cost to build? See page 436
to order complete cost estimate
to build this house in your area!

◆ It's easy to imagine this lovely New England home in a Norman Rockwell painting. Two arched entryways form covered porches, while the center front door conveys a special welcome. A warming fireplace greets you in the formal living room, where there is also passage to a solarium. The kitchen is situated to serve both formal and informal areas well, and the family room, featuring a corner bar, allows plenty of space for activities. The master bedroom, at the rear of the first floor, offers walk-in closets and a private bath with separate tub and shower and dual vanities. The second floor holds two family bedrooms, a full bath, dual linen storage and a built-in desk/vanity. A two-car garage is accessed through the service entrance.

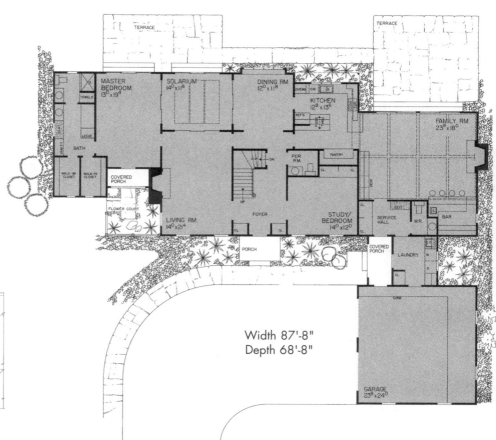

Width 87'-8"
Depth 68'-8"

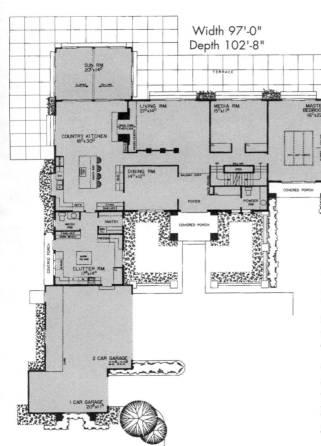

Width 97'-0"
Depth 102'-8"

SUN RM.
20'x14'

TERRACE

LIVING RM.
21'x14'

MEDIA RM.
15'x11'

MASTER
BEDROOM
16'x22'

BATH

COUNTRY KITCHEN
18'x30'

DINING RM.
14'x12'

DRESSING/
EXERCISE RM.
16'x12'

BALCONY OVER

FOYER

POWDER
RM.

COVERED PORCH

PANTRY

WASH
RM.

SHELVES
WORK BENCH

COVERED PORCH

WORK ISLAND

CLUTTER RM.
17'x14'

COVERED PORCH

2 CAR GARAGE
22'x22'

1 CAR GARAGE
20'x11'

Design 2920

Main Level: 3,067 sq. ft.
Second Floor Option: 648 sq. ft.
Sunroom: 296 sq. ft.

L D

—DESIGN BY—
HOME PLANNERS

◆ This contemporary design has a great deal to offer. A fireplace opens up to both the living room and country kitchen. The kitchen is a gourmets' delight, with a huge walk-in pantry, a deluxe work island which includes a snack bar, and easy access to the formal dining room. A media room has plenty of storage and offers access to the rear terrace. Privacy is the key word when describing the sleeping areas. The first-floor master bedroom is away from the traffic of the house and features a dressing/exercise room, a whirlpool tub and shower and a spacious walk-in closet. Two more bedrooms and a full bath are on the second floor. The three-car garage is arranged so that the owners have use of a double-garage with an attached single on reserve for guests. The cheerful sunroom adds 296 square feet to the total.

QUOTE ONE®

Cost to build? See page 436
to order complete cost estimate
to build this house in your area!

BEDROOM
13'x14'

BEDROOM
13'x14'

BATH

BALCONY

UPPER
FOYER

*This home, as shown in the photographs, may differ from the actual blueprints.
For more detailed information, please check the floor plans carefully.*

Photos by Bob Greenspan

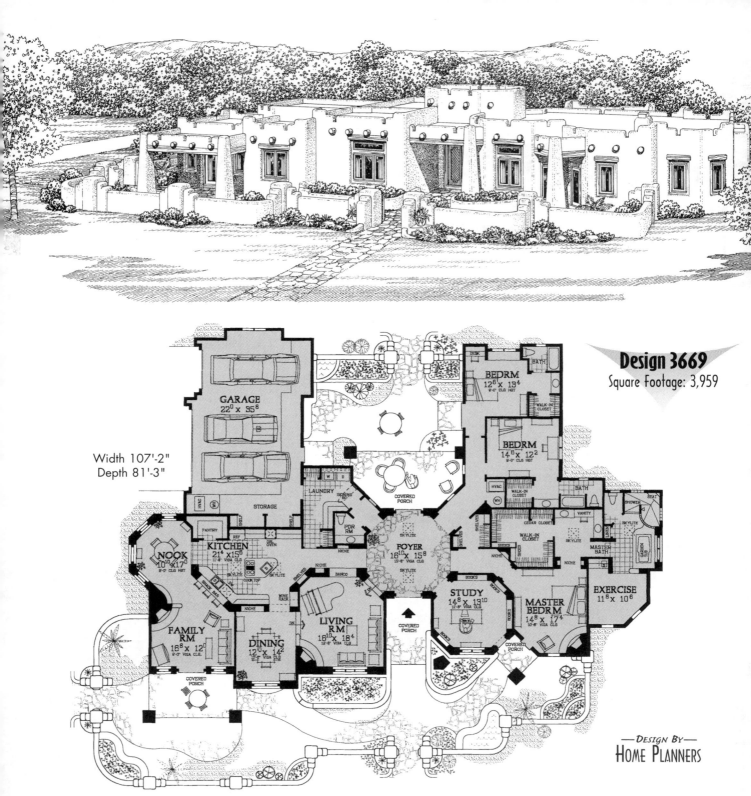

Design 3669
Square Footage: 3,959

Width 107'-2"
Depth 81'-3"

GARAGE
22⁰ x 35⁸

BEDRM
12⁶ x 13⁴

BEDRM
14⁸ x 12²

LAUNDRY

COVERED
PORCH

STORAGE

PANTRY

PDR
RM

KITCHEN
21⁴ x 15⁸

NOOK
10⁴ x 17⁰

FOYER
16¹⁰ x 15⁸

WALK-IN
CLOSET

CEDAR CLOSET

MASTER
BATH

FAMILY
RM
16⁸ x 12⁰

DINING
12⁰ x 14²

LIVING
RM
16⁸ x 18⁴

COVERED
PORCH

STUDY
14⁸ x 13¹⁰

MASTER
BEDRM
14⁸ x 17⁴

EXERCISE
11⁸ x 10⁶

COVERED
PORCH

COVERED
PORCH

—DESIGN BY—
Home Planners

◆ This spacious Santa Fe home radiates from the octagonal, skylit foyer, offering views of both the front and rear courtyards as well as passage to any part of the dwelling. A cozy study echoes the shape of the foyer and is enhanced by built-in bookcases and a separate entrance. The sunken formal living room is graced with a corner beehive fireplace and a built-in banco, or bench. The enormous kitchen will please the gourmet of the family with a cooktop work island, a huge walk-in pantry, a double oven, two skylights and a snack bar shared with the family room. An octagonal nook awaits for casual meals. The cozy family room is also filled with amenities: a corner beehive fireplace and access to a quiet covered porch. The sleeping zone is a wonder in itself: two secondary bedrooms with their own baths and walk-in closets and a lavish master bedroom suite designed to pamper. Luxuries include a corner beehive fireplace, an oversized walk-in closet, two separate vanities in a skylit dressing room, a sumptuous bath, a separate exercise room and private access to the front courtyard.

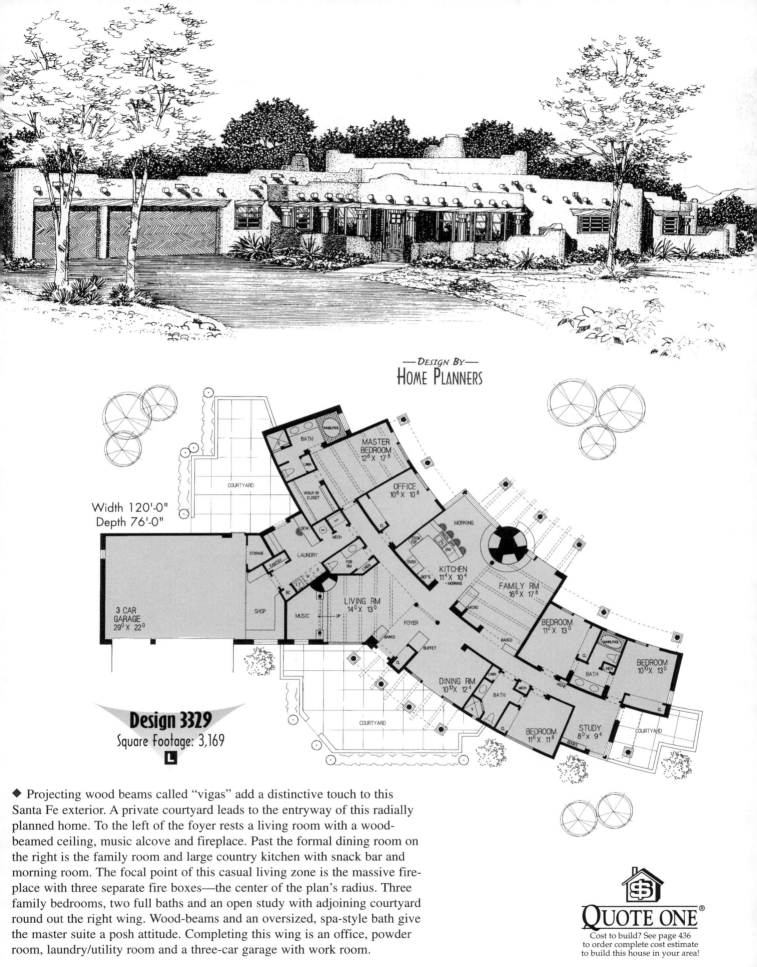

— DESIGN BY —
HOME PLANNERS

Width 120'-0"
Depth 76'-0"

COURTYARD

BATH
WHIRLPOOL

MASTER
BEDROOM
12⁶ X 17⁸

OFFICE
10⁶ X 10⁸

WALK-IN
CLOSET

LINEN

SEW

MECH

CL

MORNING

STORAGE

LAUNDRY

PANTRY

COOK TOP

OVEN

DW

KITCHEN
11⁴ X 10⁴
• MORNING

REF'G

FAMILY RM
16⁶ X 17⁸

SHOP

MUSIC

POR RM

LINEN

LIVING RM
14⁰ X 13⁰

UP

3 CAR
GARAGE
29⁰ X 22⁰

FOYER

BANCO

BEDROOM
11² X 13⁰

BANCO

BATH

LINEN

WHIRLPOOL

BEDROOM
10¹⁰ X 13⁰

BUFFET

DINING RM
10¹⁰ X 12⁴

MECH

BATH

NICHE

CL

CL

LINEN

COURTYARD

BEDROOM
11⁶ X 11⁸

STUDY
8⁰ X 9⁴

COURTYARD

ROCKS

Design 3329
Square Footage: 3,169

L

◆ Projecting wood beams called "vigas" add a distinctive touch to this Santa Fe exterior. A private courtyard leads to the entryway of this radially planned home. To the left of the foyer rests a living room with a wood-beamed ceiling, music alcove and fireplace. Past the formal dining room on the right is the family room and large country kitchen with snack bar and morning room. The focal point of this casual living zone is the massive fire-place with three separate fire boxes—the center of the plan's radius. Three family bedrooms, two full baths and an open study with adjoining courtyard round out the right wing. Wood-beams and an oversized, spa-style bath give the master suite a posh attitude. Completing this wing is an office, powder room, laundry/utility room and a three-car garage with work room.

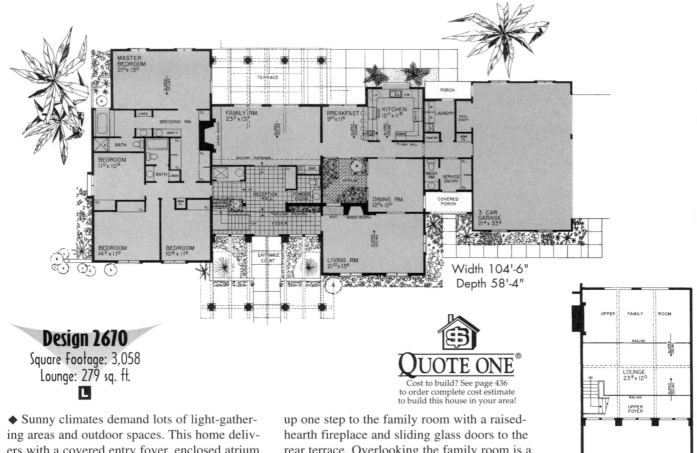

MASTER BEDROOM
21⁰ x 13⁰

TERRACE

FAMILY RM.
23² x 13⁴

BREAKFAST
9⁰ x 11⁶

KITCHEN
12⁰ x 11⁹

PORCH

LAUNDRY

LINEN

DRESSING RM.

VANITY

BATH

BEDROOM
11⁰ x 10⁸

BATH

LINEN

PANTRY

OVENS

WASH RM.

SERVICE ENTRY

ATRIUM

RECEPTION HALL

POWDER ROOM

BAR

DINING RM.
12⁰ x 12⁰

COVERED PORCH

FOYER

3 CAR GARAGE
21⁴ x 33⁴

BEDROOM
14³ x 11⁰

BEDROOM
10⁸ x 11⁶

ENTRANCE COURT

LIVING RM.
21¹⁰ x 13⁶

Width 104'-6"
Depth 58'-4"

Design 2670
Square Footage: 3,058
Lounge: 279 sq. ft.

L

Quote One®

Cost to build? See page 436
to order complete cost estimate
to build this house in your area!

UPPER FAMILY ROOM

RAILING

LOUNGE
23⁶ x 12⁰

RAILING

UPPER FOYER

◆ Sunny climates demand lots of light-gathering areas and outdoor spaces. This home delivers with a covered entry foyer, enclosed atrium, long rear terrace and plenty of windows. The atrium has a built-in seat and will bring light to the adjacent living room, dining room and breakfast room. Beyond the foyer, down a step, is the tiled reception hall that includes a powder room. This area leads to the sleeping wing and up one step to the family room with a raised-hearth fireplace and sliding glass doors to the rear terrace. Overlooking the family room is a railed lounge which can be used for a variety of activities. The sleeping area includes a master suite and three family bedrooms. The master features a sloped ceiling, a dressing room with a vanity sink, a separate tub and shower, and terrace access. Family bedrooms share a full bath.

—DESIGN BY—
HOME PLANNERS

One-Story Homes
For Sun Country

Width 72'-0"
Depth 57'-4"

COVERED PORCH

KITCHEN
14⁰ x 13²

BRKFST
9⁰ x 8⁶

MASTER
BEDROOM
13⁸ x 20⁶

WALK-IN
CLOSET

MASTER
BATH

WHIRLPOOL

DINING RM
12⁸ x 11⁸

WALK-IN
CLOSET

BAR

BEDROOM
12⁴ x 11⁶

FAMILY RM
21² x 15⁰

LAUND

FURN

PDR
RM

MECH RM

FOYER

LINEN

LIVING RM
15⁴ x 12⁸

BATH

COVERED PORCH

3 CAR
GARAGE
31⁴ x 21⁰

BEDROOM
12⁴ x 11⁸

BEDROOM
12⁴ x 11⁸

Design 3423
Square Footage: 2,577

◆ This spacious Southwestern home will be a pleasure to come home to. Immediately off the foyer are the dining room and step-down living room with bay window. The highlight of the four-bedroom sleeping area is the master suite with porch access and a whirlpool for soaking away the day's worries. The informal living area features an enormous family room with fireplace and bay-windowed kitchen and breakfast room. Notice the snack bar pass-through to the family room.

QUOTE ONE®

Cost to build? See page 436
to order complete cost estimate
to build this house in your area!

— DESIGN BY —
HOME PLANNERS

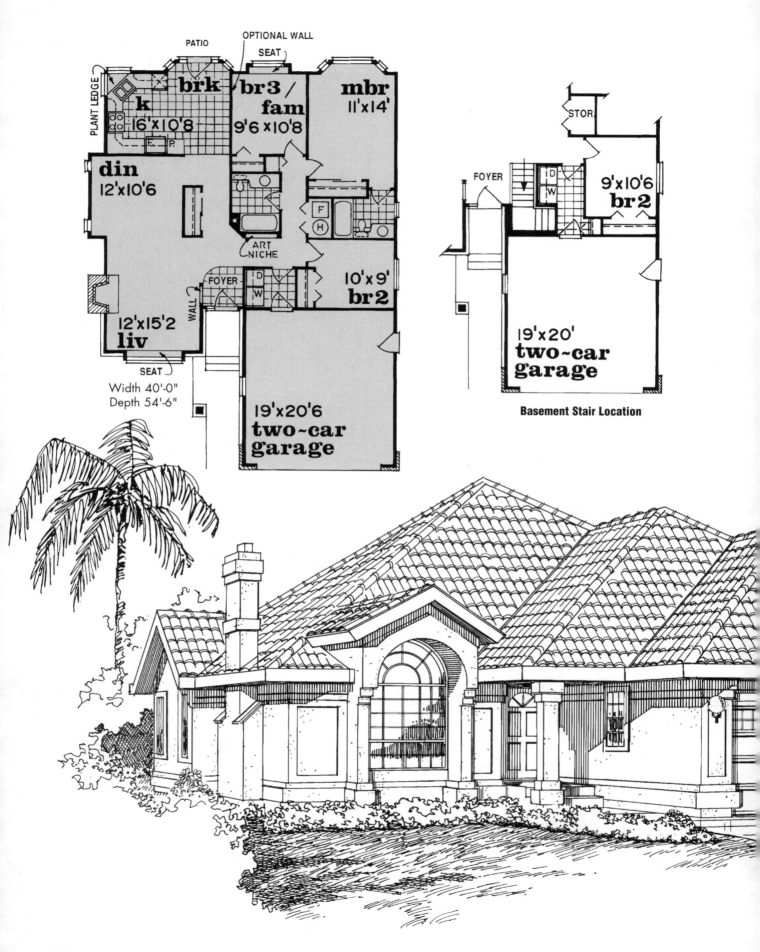

brk

k
16'x10'8

br3 / fam
9'6 x10'8

mbr
11'x14'

PATIO

OPTIONAL WALL

SEAT

PLANT LEDGE

do
do

F. P.

din
12'10'6

ART NICHE

F

H

FOYER

D
W

**10'x9'
br2**

WALL

SEAT

**12'15'2
liv**

Width 40'-0"
Depth 54'-6"

**19'x20'6
two-car
garage**

STOR.

FOYER

D
W

**9'x10'6
br2**

**19'x20'
two-car
garage**

Basement Stair Location

350

Alternate Elevation

Design Q354
Square Footage: 1,336

◆ This compact plan may be built with a
Floridian facade in stucco, or a more traditional siding-and-brick facade. Details for
both exteriors are included in the plans. You
also have the option of two or three bedrooms. One of the bedrooms could be used
as a family room. A half wall separates the
foyer from the living room, which is highlighted by a window seat in its box window,
a fireplace and an attached dining room. A
U-shaped kitchen features abundant counter
space, an angled sink under a corner plant
shelf and a sunny breakfast area with access
to the rear patio. The family room—or third
bedroom—has a bright window seat, also.
The master bedroom has no rival for luxury.
It has a bay-window seating area, large wall
closet and private bath. Access the two-car
garage through the service entrance at the
laundry alcove. Plans include optional basement foundation details.

— DESIGN BY —
SELECT HOME DESIGNS

Design 3440
Square Footage: 2,290
L

◆ There's plenty of room for everyone in this three- or optional four-bedroom home. The expansive gathering room welcomes family and guests with a through-fireplace to the dining room, an audio/visual center and a door to the outside. The kitchen includes a wide pantry, a snack bar and a separate eating area. It is open to the gathering room so the cook can enjoy the conversation. A quiet study or den has a box-bay window overlooking the front yard. Included in the master suite: two walk-in closets, a shower, a whirlpool tub and seat, dual vanities and linen storage. Two family bedrooms share a full bath with double vanities. A three-car garage can be accessed through the service entrance which has two handy closets and a laundry room with outdoor access.

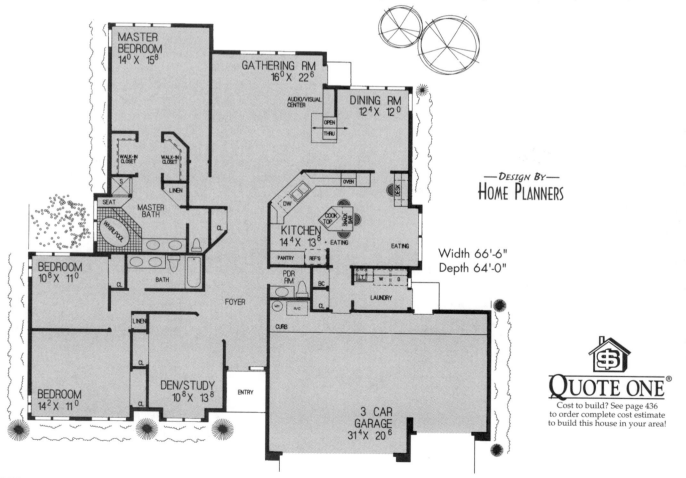

— DESIGN BY —
HOME PLANNERS

Width 66'-6"
Depth 64'-0"

Quote One®
Cost to build? See page 436 to order complete cost estimate to build this house in your area!

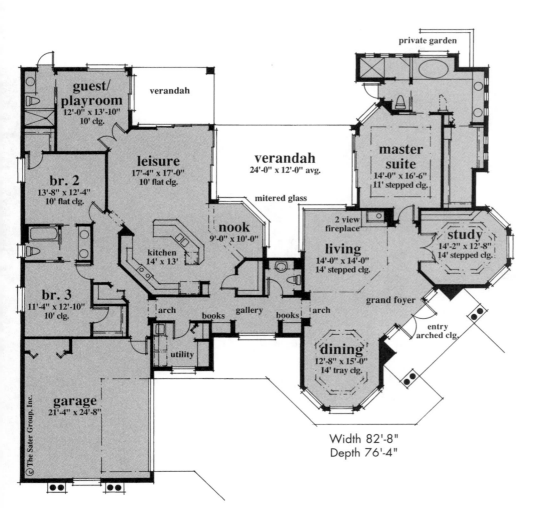

private garden

guest/
playroom
12'-0" x 13'-10"
10' clg.

verandah

master
suite
14'-0" x 16'-6"
11' stepped clg.

leisure
17'-4" x 17'-0"
10' flat clg.

verandah
24'-0" x 12'-0" avg.

br. 2
13'-8" x 12'-4"
10' flat clg.

mitered glass

nook
9'-0" x 10'-0"

2 view
fireplace

study
14'-2" x 12'-8"
14' stepped clg.

kitchen
14' x 13'

living
14'-0" x 14'-0"
14' stepped clg.

br. 3
11'-4" x 12'-10"
10' clg.

arch

books

gallery

books

arch

grand foyer

entry
arched clg.

utility

dining
12'-8" x 15'-0"
14' tray clg.

garage
21'-4" x 24'-8"

Width 82'-8"
Depth 76'-4"

© The Sater Group, Inc.

Design 6633
Square Footage: 2,986

◆ Tradition takes a bold step up with this Sun Country exterior—a bright introduction to the grand, unrestrained floor plan. Double doors lead to the formal rooms, which include an open living room with a two-view fireplace, a bayed dining room and a parlor or study with its own bay window. A secluded master suite with a compartmented bath complements family sleeping quarters, zoned for privacy.

—Design by—
The Sater
Design Collection

Bedroom 2
volume ceiling
11⁰ • 10⁰

Covered Patio

opt.
summer
kitchen

Master Bedroom
volume ceiling
15⁰ • 12⁰

Design 8630
Square Footage: 1,550

Bath

m opt. media center
or fireplace

sh

Family Room
volume ceiling
16⁸ • 14⁴

sh w.i.c.

Bath

lin

Bedroom 3
volume ceiling
11⁰ • 10⁰

pan

dw

ref

Kitchen
volume ceiling

w

d

ac

◆ Enjoy resort-style living in this striking sun-country home. Guests will always feel welcome when entertained in the formal living and dining areas, but the eat-in country kitchen overlooking the family room will be the center of attention. Casual living will be enjoyed in the large family room and out on the patio with the help of an optional summer kitchen and view of the fairway. Built-in shelves and an optional media center give you decorating options. The master suite features a volume ceiling and oversized master bath. Two secondary bedrooms accommodate guests or family and share a full hall bath. Plans for this home include a choice of two exterior elevations.

Living Room
13⁶ • 11⁰

volume ceiling

wh

Dining
11⁴ • 11⁰

ac

Foyer

Double Garage

Width 43'-0"
Depth 59'-0"

Entry

— DESIGN BY —
HOME DESIGN SERVICES

Alternate Elevation

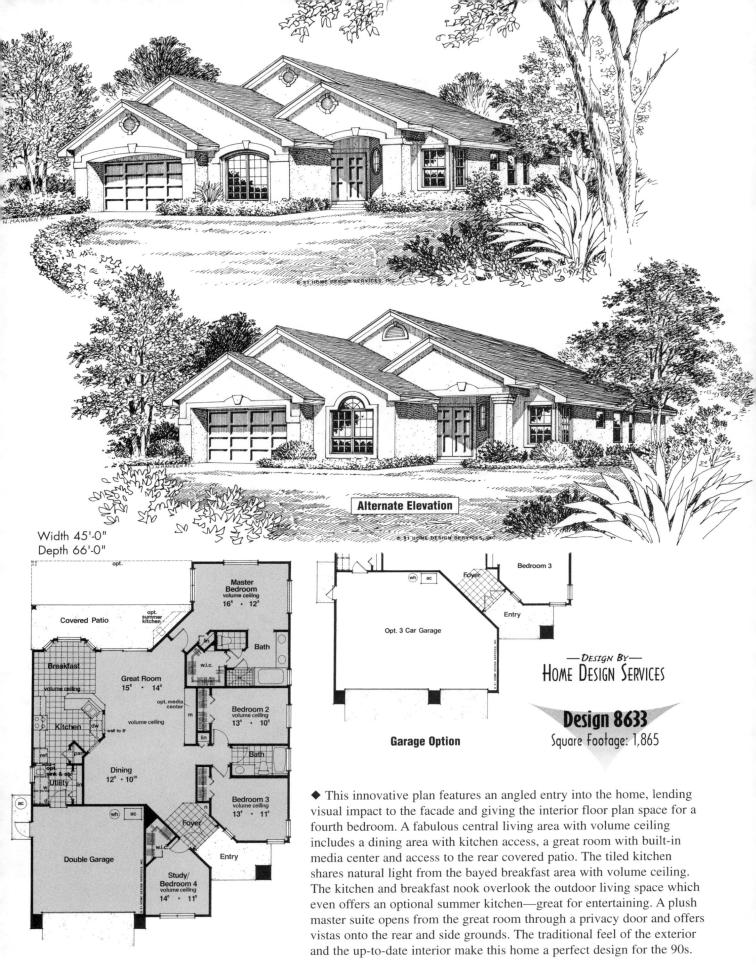

Width 45'-0"
Depth 66'-0"

Covered Patio

opt.
opt. summer kitchen

Master Bedroom
volume ceiling
16⁵ · 12²

Bath

w.i.c.

Breakfast
volume ceiling

Great Room
15⁵ · 14³

opt. media center

volume ceiling

Kitchen

dw

wall to 8'

ref

opt. sink & ap.

Utility

Dining
12⁹ · 10¹⁰

Bedroom 2
volume ceiling
13⁴ · 10⁶

Bath

lin

Double Garage

wh ac

Foyer

w.i.c.

Bedroom 3
volume ceiling
13⁴ · 11⁴

Entry

Study/ Bedroom 4
volume ceiling
14⁰ · 11⁰

wh ac

Foyer

Bedroom 3

Entry

Opt. 3 Car Garage

Garage Option

—Design By—
Home Design Services

Design 8633
Square Footage: 1,865

◆ This innovative plan features an angled entry into the home, lending visual impact to the facade and giving the interior floor plan space for a fourth bedroom. A fabulous central living area with volume ceiling includes a dining area with kitchen access, a great room with built-in media center and access to the rear covered patio. The tiled kitchen shares natural light from the bayed breakfast area with volume ceiling. The kitchen and breakfast nook overlook the outdoor living space which even offers an optional summer kitchen—great for entertaining. A plush master suite opens from the great room through a privacy door and offers vistas onto the rear and side grounds. The traditional feel of the exterior and the up-to-date interior make this home a perfect design for the 90s.

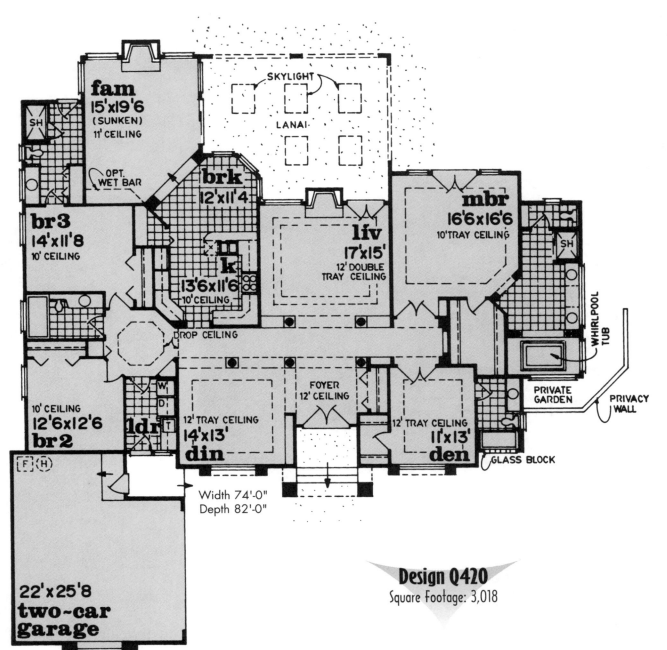

fam
15'x19'6
(SUNKEN)
11' CEILING

SH

OPT.
WET BAR

br3
14'x11'8
10' CEILING

brk
12'x11'4

k
13'6x11'6
10' CEILING

SKYLIGHT

LANAI

liv
17'x15'
12' DOUBLE
TRAY CEILING

mbr
16'6x16'6
10' TRAY CEILING

SH

DROP CEILING

WHIRLPOOL
TUB

10' CEILING
12'6x12'6
br2

W
D

1dr
T

12' TRAY CEILING
14'x13'
din

FOYER
12' CEILING

12' TRAY CEILING
11'x13'
den

PRIVATE
GARDEN

PRIVACY
WALL

GLASS BLOCK

F H

22'x25'8
**two-car
garage**

Width 74'-0"
Depth 82'-0"

Design Q420
Square Footage: 3,018

◆ Two distinct exteriors can be built from the details for this plan—both are perfect as sun-country designs. The entry is grand and allows for a twelve-foot ceiling in the entry foyer. Open planning calls for columns to separate the formal living room and the formal dining room from the foyer and central hall. Both rooms have tray ceilings, the living room has a fireplace and double-door access to the skylit lanai. The modified U-shaped kitchen has an attached breakfast room and steps down to the family room with fireplace and optional wet bar. A lovely octagonal foyer introduces family bedrooms and their private baths. A den with tray ceiling and full bath sits to the right of the foyer and doubles as guest room space when needed. The master suite is separated from family bedrooms. It has double-door access to the rear yard, a walk-in closet and a full bath with whirlpool tub, double vanity, compartmented toilet and separate shower. The whirlpool overlooks a private garden outside. Plans include details for both a basement and a crawlspace foundation.

DESIGN BY
SELECT HOME DESIGNS

Alternate Elevation

Rear Elevation

357

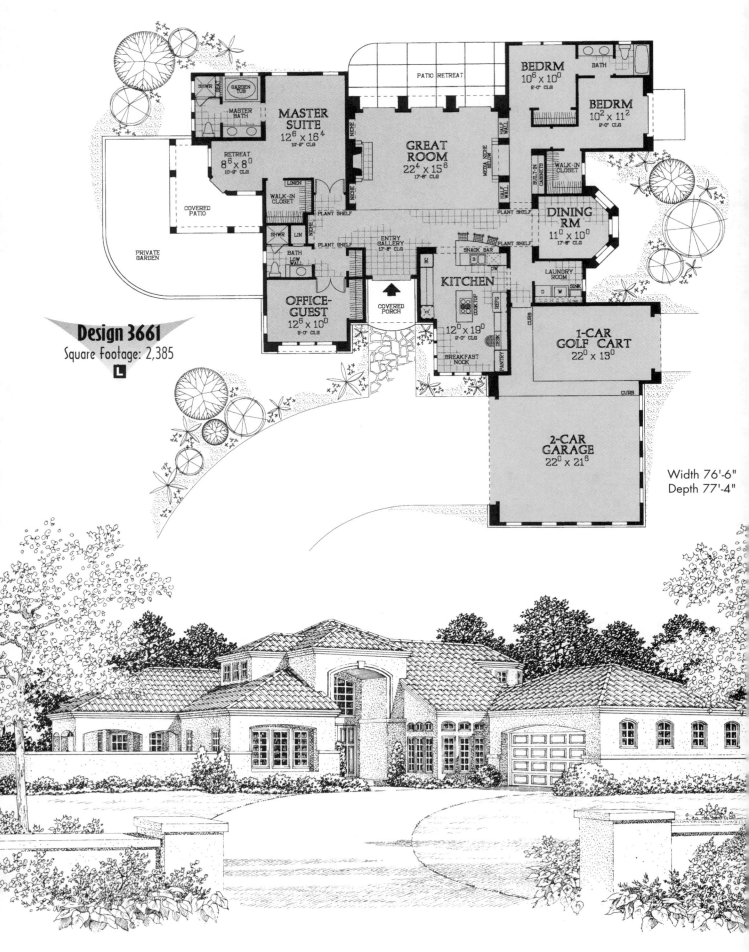

SHWR | GARDEN TUB

MASTER BATH

SEAT

BEDRM
10⁶ x 10⁰
9'-0" CLG

BATH

PATIO RETREAT

MASTER SUITE
12⁶ x 16⁴
10'-9" CLG

GREAT ROOM
22⁴ x 15⁶
17'-8" CLG

BEDRM
10² x 11²
9'-0" CLG

NICHE

HALF WALL

MEDIA NICHE BELOW

HALF WALL

RETREAT
8⁶ x 8⁰
10'-9" CLG

COVERED PATIO

LINEN

WALK-IN CLOSET

NICHE

NICHE

BUILT-IN CABINETS

WALK-IN CLOSET

DINING RM
11⁰ x 10⁰
17'-8" CLG

PRIVATE GARDEN

SHWR | LIN

BATH

LOW WALL

PLANT SHELF

ENTRY GALLERY
17'-8" CLG

PLANT SHELF

PLANT SHELF

PLANT SHELF

LAUNDRY ROOM

D | W | SINK

Design 3661
Square Footage: 2,385
L

OFFICE-GUEST
12⁶ x 10⁰
9'-0" CLG

COVERED PORCH

SNACK BAR
S
DW

KITCHEN
12⁰ x 19⁰
9'-0" CLG

REFG

PANTRY | DESK

BREAKFAST NOOK

CURB

1-CAR GOLF CART
22⁰ x 13⁰

Width 76'-6"
Depth 77'-4"

2-CAR GARAGE
22⁰ x 21⁶

CURB

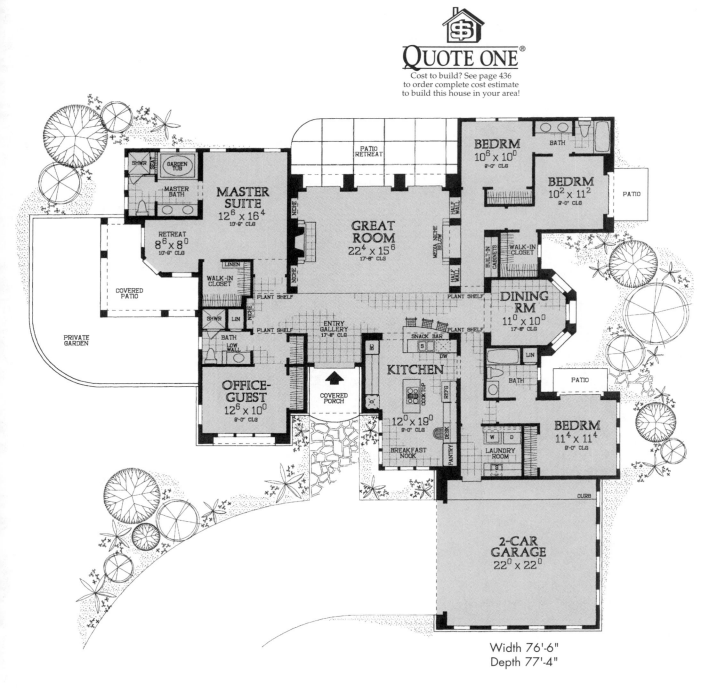

Design 3665
Square Footage: 2,678

L

—DESIGN BY—
HOME PLANNERS

◆ A vaulted entry and tall muntin windows complement a classic stucco exterior on this Floridian-style home, which offers a choice of two floor plans. Design 3665 replaces the golf-cart garage offered in Design 3661 with a fifth bedroom and full bath. In both plans, an entry gallery opens to the great room, with generous views to the rear property and columned access to a patio retreat. Niches, built-ins and half-walls decorate and help define this area. The island kitchen serves a convenient snack bar, while the nearby formal dining room offers privacy and natural light from a bay window. A secluded master wing soothes the homeowner with a sumptuous bath, a walk-in closet and an inner retreat with access to a covered patio.

QUOTE ONE®
Cost to build? See page 436
to order complete cost estimate
to build this house in your area!

PATIO RETREAT

BEDRM
10⁶ x 10⁰
8'-0" CLG

BATH

BEDRM
10² x 11²
9'-0" CLG

PATIO

MASTER SUITE
12⁶ x 16⁴
10'-9" CLG

SHWR

GARDEN TUB

MASTER BATH

GREAT ROOM
22⁴ x 15⁶
17'-8" CLG

NICHE

HALF WALL

MEDIA NICHE BELOW

HALF WALL

BUILT-IN CABINETS

WALK-IN CLOSET

RETREAT
8⁶ x 8⁰
10'-6" CLG

LINEN

WALK-IN CLOSET

NICHE

PLANT SHELF

PLANT SHELF

DINING RM
11⁰ x 10⁰
17'-8" CLG

COVERED PATIO

SHWR

LIN

NICHE

PLANT SHELF

ENTRY GALLERY
17'-8" CLG

SNACK BAR

PLANT SHELF

LIN

PRIVATE GARDEN

BATH

LOW WALL

PLANT SHELF

DW

BATH

PATIO

OFFICE-GUEST
12⁶ x 10⁰
9'-0" CLG

COVERED PORCH

KITCHEN
12⁰ x 19⁰
9'-0" CLG

COOKTOP

DESK

PANTRY

LAUNDRY ROOM

W D

BEDRM
11⁴ x 11⁴
9'-0" CLG

BREAKFAST NOOK

CURB

2-CAR GARAGE
22⁰ x 22⁰

Width 76'-6"
Depth 77'-4"

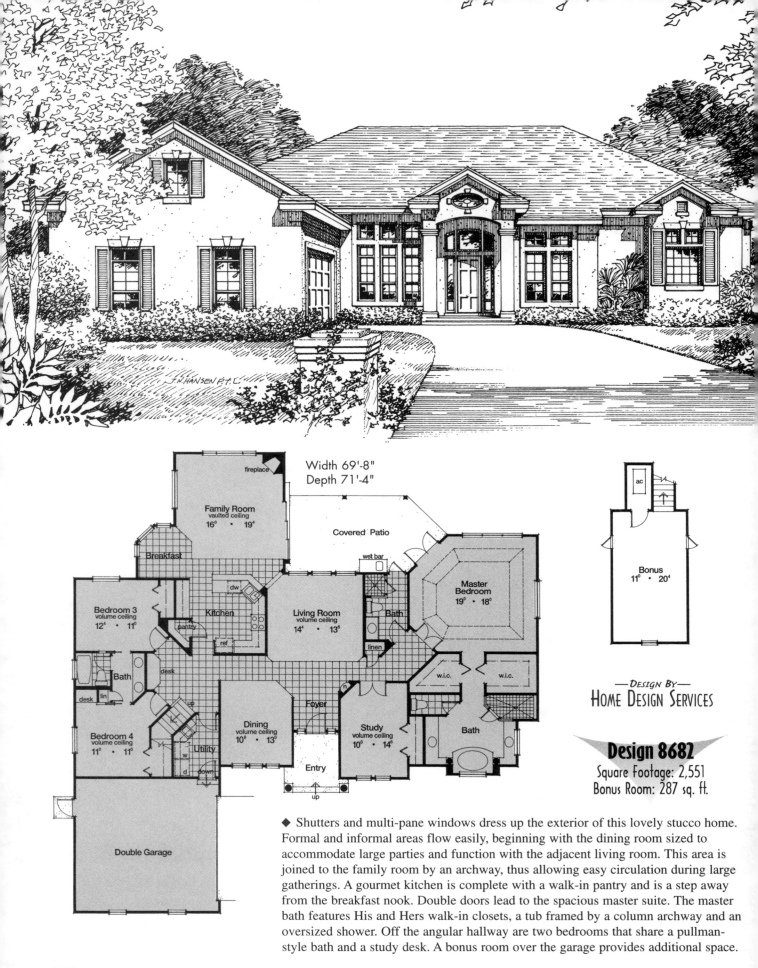

Width 69'-8"
Depth 71'-4"

fireplace

Family Room
vaulted ceiling
16⁰ • 19⁴

Covered Patio

wet bar

Master Bedroom
19⁰ • 18⁰

Breakfast

dw

Kitchen

Living Room
volume ceiling
14⁴ • 13⁶

Bath

ac

Bonus
11⁰ • 20⁴

Bedroom 3
volume ceiling
12⁴ • 11⁰

pantry

ref

linen

Bath

desk

w.i.c.

w.i.c.

desk   lin

up

Foyer

Bath

Bedroom 4
volume ceiling
11⁰ • 11⁰

w

Utility

d

down

Dining
volume ceiling
10⁸ • 13⁵

Study
volume ceiling
10⁰ • 14⁰

—DESIGN BY—
HOME DESIGN SERVICES

Entry

up

Design 8682
Square Footage: 2,551
Bonus Room: 287 sq. ft.

Double Garage

◆ Shutters and multi-pane windows dress up the exterior of this lovely stucco home. Formal and informal areas flow easily, beginning with the dining room sized to accommodate large parties and function with the adjacent living room. This area is joined to the family room by an archway, thus allowing easy circulation during large gatherings. A gourmet kitchen is complete with a walk-in pantry and is a step away from the breakfast nook. Double doors lead to the spacious master suite. The master bath features His and Hers walk-in closets, a tub framed by a column archway and an oversized shower. Off the angular hallway are two bedrooms that share a pullman-style bath and a study desk. A bonus room over the garage provides additional space.

Design Q418
Square Footage: 2,761

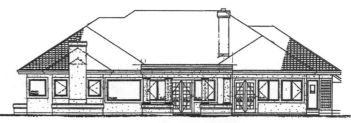

Rear Elevation

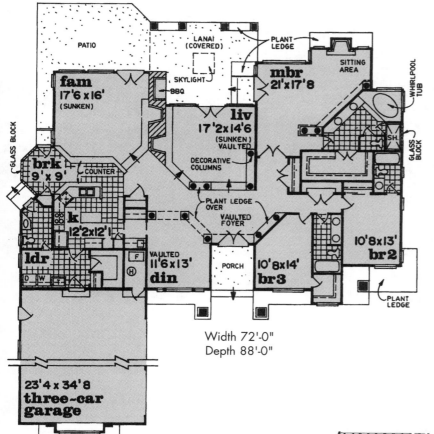

Width 72'-0"
Depth 88'-0"

fam 17'6 x 16' (SUNKEN)

PATIO

LANAI (COVERED)

PLANT LEDGE

SKYLIGHT

BBQ

mbr 21'x17'8

SITTING AREA

WHIRLPOOL TUB

liv 17'2x14'6 (SUNKEN) VAULTED

DECORATIVE COLUMNS

GLASS BLOCK

brk 9' x 9'

COUNTER

k 12'2x12'1

PLANT LEDGE OVER

VAULTED FOYER

SH.

GLASS BLOCK

ldr

VAULTED 11'6x13' din

PORCH

10'8x14' br3

10'8x13' br2

PLANT LEDGE

23'4 x 34'8 three-car garage

◆ Dramatic rooflines dominate this three-bedroom sun-country design. Interior space begins with a double-door entrance leading directly through the vaulted foyer to a sunken living room with vaulted ceiling and fireplace. A fully glazed wall at one end of the living room allows views to the covered, skylit lanai. A built-in barbecue adds to the fun on the lanai. Decorative columns separate the living room, dining room and Bedroom 3 from the foyer. If you choose, Bedroom 3 could be used as a den. The dining room reaches to the kitchen through a butler's pantry. In the kitchen are snack counters and an attached breakfast room with bay window. A sunken family room is just beyond. It is warmed by a fireplace and has double-door access to a rear patio. Bedrooms include a master suite with hearth-warmed sitting room, lanai access and bath with walk-in closet and whirlpool tub. Plans include details for both a basement and a crawlspace foundation.

— DESIGN BY —

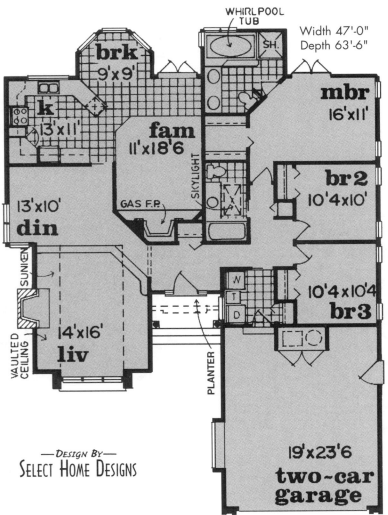

WHIRLPOOL TUB

brk 9'x9'

k 13'x11'

fam 11'x18'6

GAS F.P.

SKYLIGHT

SH.

13'x10' **din**

SUNKEN

VAULTED CEILING

14'x16' **liv**

PLANTER

mbr 16'x11'

br2 10'4x10'

W T D

10'4x10'4 **br3**

19'x23'6 **two-car garage**

Width 47'-0"
Depth 63'-6"

Design Q294
Square Footage: 1,692

◆ A dormer window brightens the foyer of this smaller Floridian home. A sunken living room to the left of the foyer takes advantage of a coffered ceiling and full-width window wall. The attached dining room connects to the U-shaped kitchen and bayed breakfast room. An open family room with gas fireplace completes the living spaces. Sleeping quarters are located to the right of the plan. The master suite has double doors to the rear yard and a pampering bath with separate whirlpool tub and shower and double vanities. Family bedrooms share a full hall bath. The two-car garage is accessed through a service entrance past the laundry alcove. Plans include details for a crawlspace and a basement foundation.

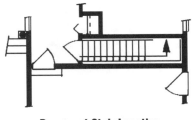

Basement Stair Location

Design Q417
Square Footage: 2,657

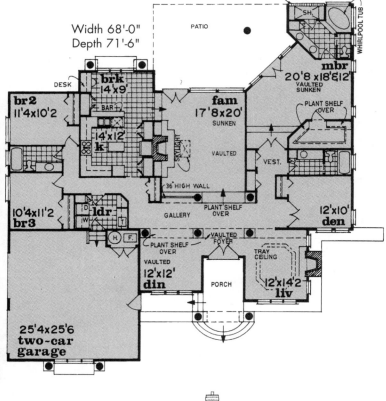

Width 68'-0"
Depth 71'-6"

PATIO

GLASS BLOCK

SH

WHIRLPOOL TUB

mbr
20'8 x18'8|12'
VAULTED
SUNKEN

PLANT SHELF OVER

DESK

brk
14'x9'

BAR

br2
11'4x10'2

fam
17'8x20'
SUNKEN

VAULTED

14'x12'

k

SKYLIGHT

VAULTED

VEST.

36' HIGH WALL

PLANT SHELF OVER

GALLERY

PLANT SHELF OVER

12'x10'
den

ldr

D
W

br3
10'4x11'2

H   F.

PLANT SHELF OVER

VAULTED FOYER

TRAY CEILING

VAULTED

12'x12'
din

PORCH

12'x14'2
liv

25'4x25'6
two-car garage

br2
10'4x10'

br3
10'4x10'

ldr
W
D

Alternate Bedroom Layout

◆ Elegant arched windows, a portico entry and low-maintenance stucco distinguish this California design. The interior is well-appointed and thoughtfully planned. Flanking the foyer are the formal living and dining rooms—defined by decorative columns and plant shelves. The living room boasts a tray ceiling and fireplace. A sunken family room sits in the center of the plan and is graced by double doors to the patio, a fireplace, a vaulted ceiling and a skylight. Two steps up is the U-shaped kitchen with island and attached breakfast room, separated by a snack-bar counter. Family bedrooms and a full bath are on the left side of the plan. The master suite and a den with full bath sit on the right. An alternate bedroom layout is included in the plans. Plans also include details for both a crawlspace and a slab foundation.

—Design By—
Select Home Designs

Rear Elevation

363

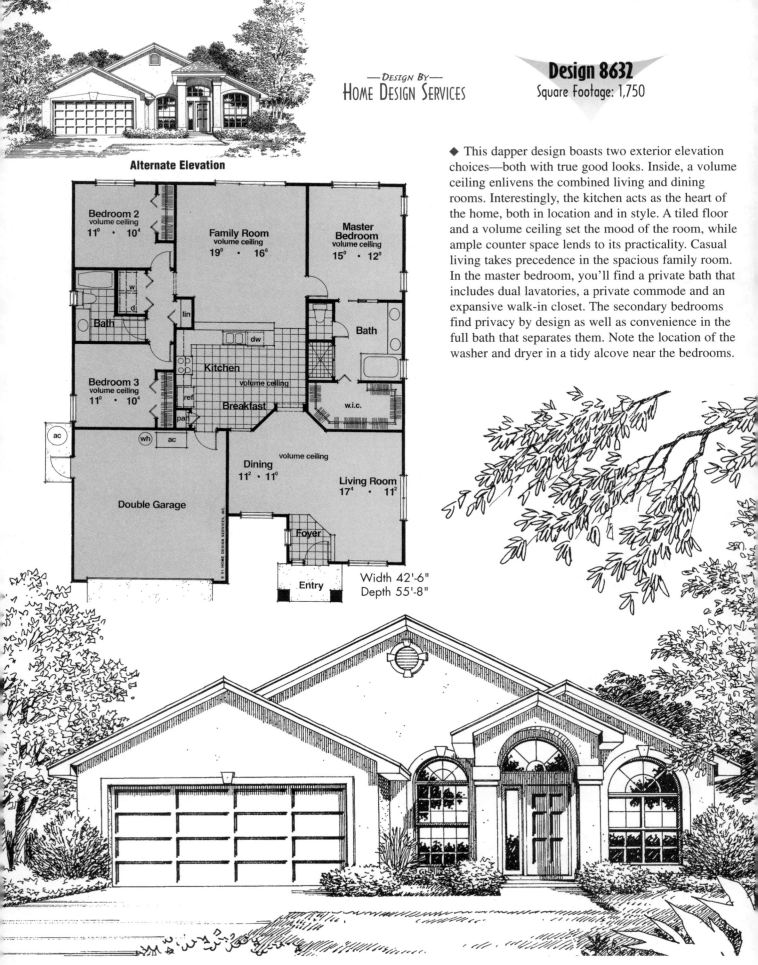

Alternate Elevation

—DESIGN BY—
HOME DESIGN SERVICES

Design 8632
Square Footage: 1,750

◆ This dapper design boasts two exterior elevation choices—both with true good looks. Inside, a volume ceiling enlivens the combined living and dining rooms. Interestingly, the kitchen acts as the heart of the home, both in location and in style. A tiled floor and a volume ceiling set the mood of the room, while ample counter space lends to its practicality. Casual living takes precedence in the spacious family room. In the master bedroom, you'll find a private bath that includes dual lavatories, a private commode and an expansive walk-in closet. The secondary bedrooms find privacy by design as well as convenience in the full bath that separates them. Note the location of the washer and dryer in a tidy alcove near the bedrooms.

Bedroom 2
volume ceiling
11⁰ · 10⁴

Family Room
volume ceiling
19⁰ · 16⁶

Master Bedroom
volume ceiling
15⁰ · 12⁰

Bath

w
d

lin

Kitchen
volume ceiling

dw

Bath

Bedroom 3
volume ceiling
11⁰ · 10⁴

ref

Breakfast

pan

w.i.c.

ac

wh

ac

Double Garage

Dining
11² · 11⁰

volume ceiling

Living Room
17⁴ · 11²

© '91 HOME DESIGN SERVICES, INC.

Foyer

Entry

Width 42'-6"
Depth 55'-8"

Bedroom 3
volume ceiling
11⁰ · 10¹⁰

Covered Patio
volume ceiling

Sitting

Bath

lin

Master
Bedroom
volume ceiling
23⁰ · 12⁴

Breakfast

volume ceiling

Family Room
volume ceiling
19⁰ · 13⁰

Bedroom 2
volume ceiling
11⁶ · 11⁰

fireplace

s

s

dw

Kitchen

Bath

ref

w.i.c.

Living Room
volume ceiling
11⁰ · 10⁶

Foyer

Dining
volume ceiling
12⁴ · 10⁰

w

Utility

d

ac

wh

Entry

Width 50'-0"
Depth 63'-0"

Double Garage

© HOME DESIGN SERVICES, INC.

Design 8661
Square Footage: 1,817

◆ First impressions make a grand statement in this volume-look home. A traditional split entry finds the living room on the left and the dining room on the right. The latter shares a large, open space with the family room, made more impressive with its volume ceiling. The tiled kitchen and breakfast room are the height of charm and efficiency. On one side of the plan, the master bedroom boasts a private sitting space and lavish bath with shutter doors at the soaking tub and a room-sized walk-in closet. At the other side of the house, two family bedrooms each afford ample closet space and room to grow. A "kid's" door leads to the covered patio at the rear of the plan. Note the handy laundry room leading to the two-car garage.

—DESIGN BY—
HOME DESIGN SERVICES

© HOME DESIGN SERVICES, INC.

J.N. HANSEN P.T.L.

365

◆ This modern home adds a contemporary twist to the typical ranch-style plan. The turret study and bayed dining room add a sensuous look from the streetscape. The main living areas open up to the lanai and offer broad views to the rear through large expanses of glass and doors. The family kitchen, nook and leisure room focus on the lanai, the entertainment center and an ale bar. The guest suites have separate baths and also access the lanai. The master bath features a curved glass shower, a whirlpool, and a private toilet and bidet room. Dual walk-in closets and an abundance of light further the appeal of this suite.

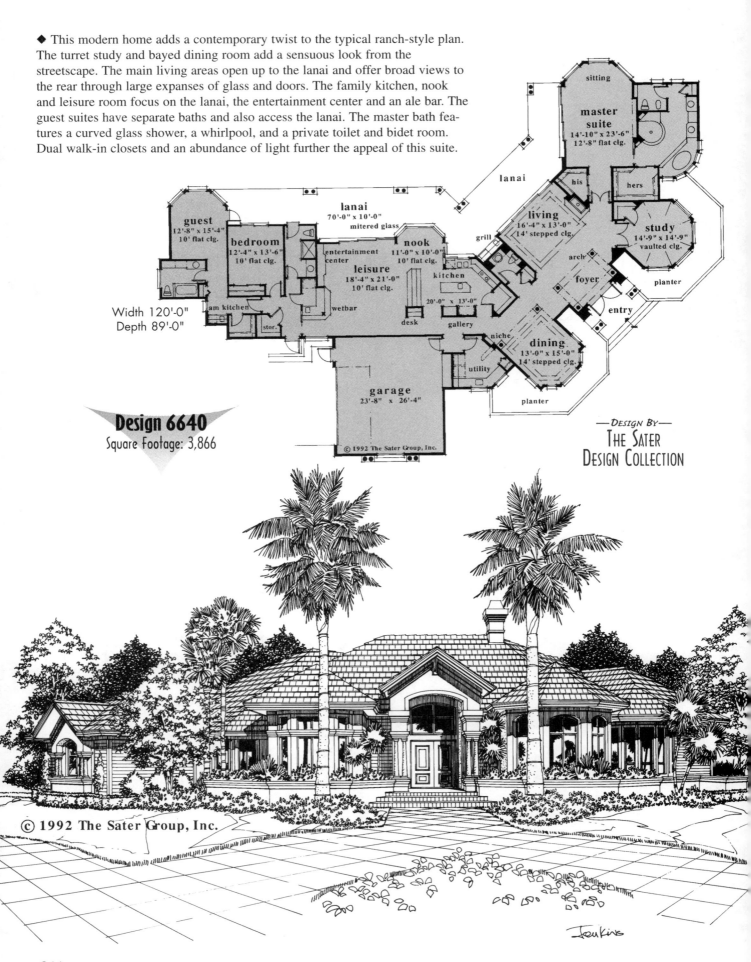

Width 120'-0"
Depth 89'-0"

Design 6640
Square Footage: 3,866

—DESIGN BY—
THE SATER
DESIGN COLLECTION

© 1992 The Sater Group, Inc.

—DESIGN BY—
HOME DESIGN SERVICES

◆ A graceful facade sets this charming home apart from the ordinary and transcends the commonplace. From the octagonal foyer, paved in granite, to the interesting breakfast nook, this well-executed plan incorporates rooms of various shapes but keeps its original concept of spaciousness intact. The living room is open and has a wall of windows overlooking the rear covered patio. A gigantic family room accesses the same patio, but also has built-ins and a fireplace. The nearby kitchen and nook are open to this casual area. For quieter pursuits, try the octagonal den/study, which opens off a foyer near the master suite. Filled with amenities, the master bedroom is warmed by its own hearth, has sliding glass doors to the patio and features a bath with two walk-in closets, a garden whirlpool and separate shower. Family bedrooms are at the opposite end of the design and share a full bath. A two-car garage opens to the rear.

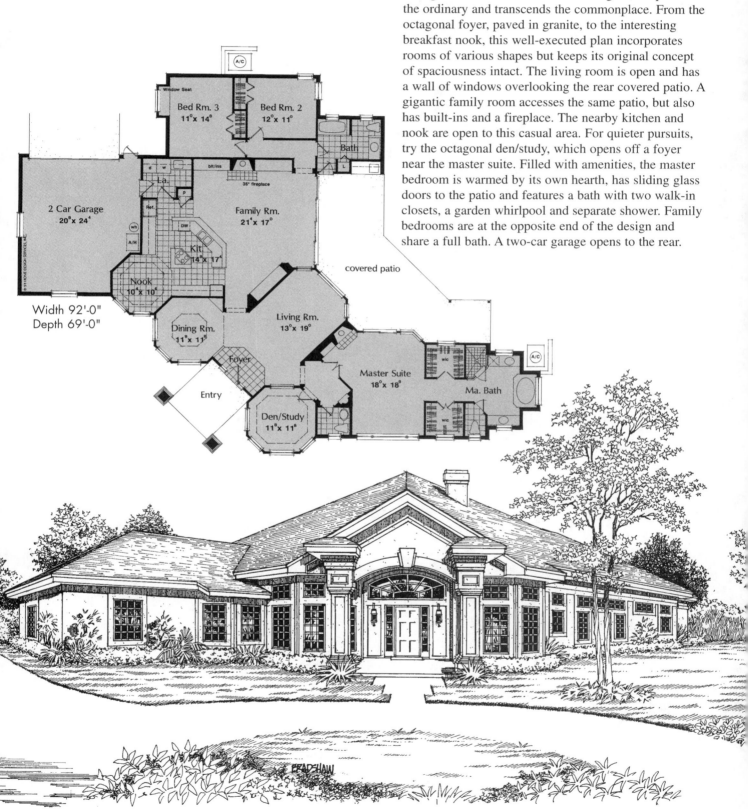

Width 92'-0"
Depth 69'-0"

© HOME DESIGN SERVICES, INC.

J. N. HANSEN P.T.L

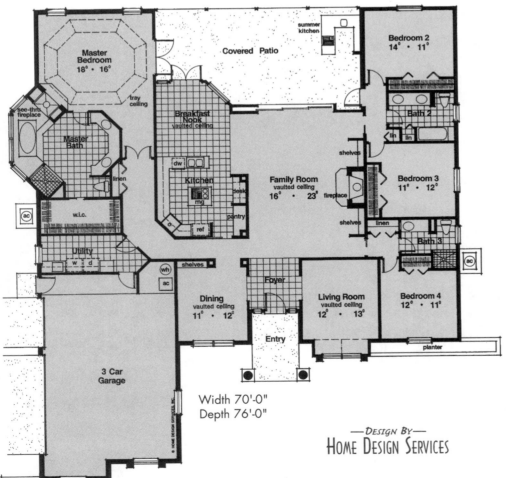

Master Bedroom 18⁰ · 16⁰

tray ceiling

see-thru fireplace

Master Bath

w.i.c.

Utility w d

Breakfast Nook vaulted ceiling

dw

Kitchen

rng

desk

ref

pantry

shelves

wh

ac

ac

Covered Patio

summer kitchen

Family Room vaulted ceiling 16⁰ · 23⁸ fireplace

shelves

shelves

Bedroom 2 14⁰ · 11⁰

Bath 2

lin lin

Bedroom 3 11⁸ · 12⁰

linen

Bath 3

Foyer

Dining vaulted ceiling 11⁰ · 12⁰

Living Room vaulted ceiling 12⁰ · 13⁰

Bedroom 4 12⁰ · 11⁰

planter

Entry

3 Car Garage

Width 70'-0"
Depth 76'-0"

planter

ac

— DESIGN BY —
HOME DESIGN SERVICES

Design 8653
Square Footage: 2,962

◆ Enter the formal foyer of this home and you are greeted with a traditional split living and dining room layout. The family room is where the real living takes place—whether gathered around the fireplace or expanding the space with the help of sliding glass, to include the outside patio and summer kitchen. The ultimate master suite contains coffered ceilings, a "boomerang" vanity and angular mirrors that reflect the bayed soaking tub and shower. Efficient use of space creates a huge closet with little dead center space. Two family bedrooms are situated to share a hall bath. Another bedroom has a semi-private bath, offering guests luxurious comfort.

PATIO
RETREAT

MASTER
SUITE
14⁴ x 15⁸
SLOPED CEILING

WALK-IN
CLOSET

COVERED
PATIO

MORNING
RM
11⁰ x 10⁴
13'-0" CLG

MASTER
BATH

WHIRLPOOL

SHOWER

BEDRM
10⁰ x 11¹⁰
9'-0" CLG

KIT

FAMILY
RM
15⁸ x 14⁰
13'-0" CLG

BATH

COOKTOP

ISLAND

OVN

REFG

PTRY

12¹⁰ x 14⁰
13'-0" CLG

HALF WALL

ARCHED OPNG

OFFICE/
DEN
10² x 10⁶
9'-0" CLG

BUILT-IN

COVERED
PORCH

HALF WALL

9'-0" CLG

BEDRM
12⁰ x 11²
9'-0" CLG

LAUNDRY

POWDER

BUILT-IN

D

W

L

BC

PLANT SHELVES ABOVE

HALF WALL

DINING
RM
14⁰ x 10⁴

HALF WALL

FOYER
13'-0" CLG

LIVING
RM
12⁴ x 14⁰
13'-0" CLG

CURB

WH

HVAC

9'-0" CLG

GARAGE
28⁴ x 22⁰

STORAGE/
WORKSHOP

CURB

COVERED
PORCH

RAILING

COVERED
PORCH

Width 70'-0"
Depth 67'-4"

◆ This well-planned stucco home is tailor-made for a small family or for empty-nesters. Formal areas are situated well for entertaining—living room to the right and formal dining room to the left of the foyer. A large family room in the rear has access to a covered patio and is warmed in the cold months by a welcome hearth. The efficient U-shaped kitchen features an attached morning room for casual meals and is near the laundry and a powder room. The master suite provides a private retreat and features a fine bath and large walk-in closet. A nearby office/den has a private porch. Two secondary bedrooms are located on the other side of the home and share a full bath. Note the large workshop/storage area in the two-car garage.

QUOTE ONE®

Cost to build? See page 436
to order complete cost estimate
to build this house in your area!

—DESIGN BY—
HOME PLANNERS

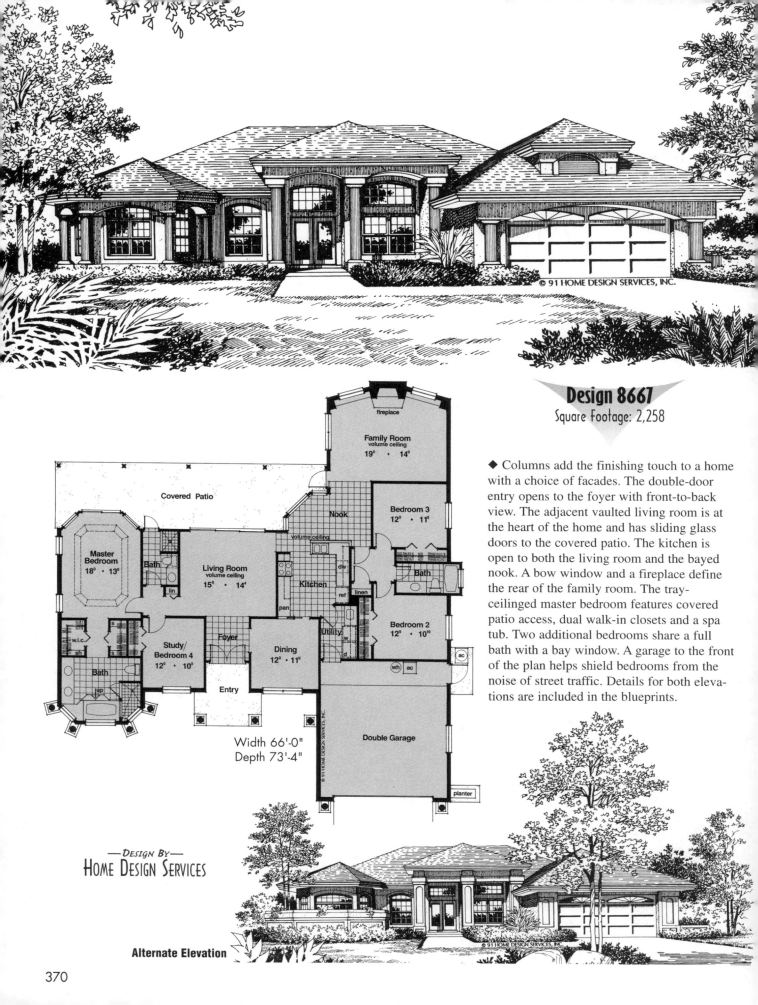

Design 8667
Square Footage: 2,258

◆ Columns add the finishing touch to a home with a choice of facades. The double-door entry opens to the foyer with front-to-back view. The adjacent vaulted living room is at the heart of the home and has sliding glass doors to the covered patio. The kitchen is open to both the living room and the bayed nook. A bow window and a fireplace define the rear of the family room. The tray-ceilinged master bedroom features covered patio access, dual walk-in closets and a spa tub. Two additional bedrooms share a full bath with a bay window. A garage to the front of the plan helps shield bedrooms from the noise of street traffic. Details for both elevations are included in the blueprints.

fireplace

Family Room
volume ceiling
19⁰ · 14⁰

Covered Patio

Nook

Bedroom 3
12⁰ · 11⁰

Master Bedroom
18⁰ · 13⁰

Bath

Living Room
volume ceiling
15⁸ · 14⁴

volume ceiling

Kitchen

dw

ref | linen

Bath

pan

w.i.c.

Bath

Study/ Bedroom 4
12⁰ · 10⁰

Foyer

Dining
12⁰ · 11⁰

Utility

w
d

Bedroom 2
12⁰ · 10¹⁰

wh | ac

ac

Entry

Width 66'-0"
Depth 73'-4"

Double Garage

planter

— DESIGN BY —
HOME DESIGN SERVICES

Alternate Elevation

370

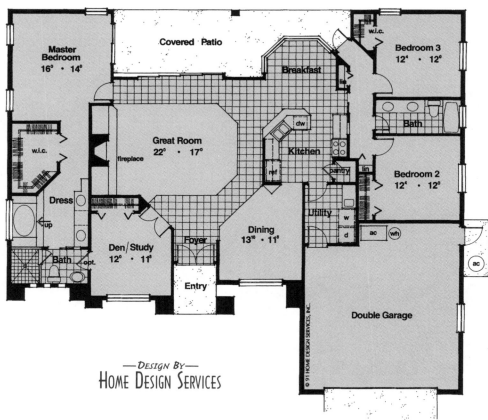

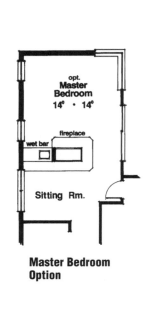

Master Bedroom Option

opt. **Master Bedroom** 14⁰ · 14⁰

wet bar   fireplace

Sitting Rm.

Covered Patio

Master Bedroom 16⁰ · 14⁰

w.i.c.

Great Room 22⁰ · 17⁰

fireplace

Dress

up

Bath   opt.

Den/Study 12⁰ · 11⁰

Foyer

Entry

Breakfast

lin

dw

Kitchen

ref

pantry   lin

Dining 13¹⁰ · 11⁰

Utility

w

d   ac   wh

w.i.c.

Bedroom 3 12⁴ · 12⁰

Bath

Bedroom 2 12⁴ · 12⁰

ac

Double Garage

— DESIGN BY —
HOME DESIGN SERVICES

Design 8601
Square Footage: 2,125

Width 65'-0"
Depth 56'-8"

◆ A luxurious master suite is yours with this lovely plan—and it comes with two different options—one has a wet bar and fireplace. An oversized great room with a grand fireplace is the heart of casual living in this relaxed plan. A formal dining room lies just off the foyer and offers easy access to the gourmet kitchen. Family bedrooms are split from the living area, perfect for a guest's comfort and privacy. A hall bath is shared by the two bedrooms as is a private door to the covered patio.

371

Design 8666
Square Footage: 2,931

Breakfast

Family Room
volume ceiling
17⁰ · 16⁸

shelf

fireplace

shelf

Covered Patio
vaulted ceiling

summer kitchen

dw

Master Bedroom
volume ceiling
24⁴ · 14⁸

Bath

Kitchen

ref

m

Bedroom 3
volume ceiling
12² · 11⁸

Living Room
vaulted ceiling
15⁸ · 14⁸

pantry

lin

Bath

w.i.c.   w.i.c.

Bath
volume ceiling

Den Study
volume ceiling
11⁴ · 10⁴

Foyer

Dining
volume ceiling
15¹⁰ · 11⁰

Utility
w
d
ac

Bedroom 2
volume ceiling
13³ · 12²

Entry

wh

Width 70'-8"
Depth 83'-0"

Garage

— DESIGN BY —
HOME DESIGN SERVICES

◆ The brick French-door entrance, corner quoins and keystone windows are just a few of this home's beautiful finishing touches. Inside, rich tile flows throughout for a beautiful decorating accent that starts from the ground up. The foyer opens to a large living room with a vaulted ceiling. The wonderfully equipped kitchen with a walk-in pantry opens up to the windowed breakfast area and an immense family room with built-in shelves and a fireplace. The large covered patio with a summer kitchen is perfect for cookouts and entertaining and is accessible through the breakfast area, living room or master suite. His and Hers walk-in closets, twin sinks, a compartmented toilet and a windowed tub make the master suite a study in elegance.

J.N. HANSEN P.T.L.

© HOME DESIGN SERVICES, INC

© The Sater Group, Inc.

Design 6663
Square Footage: 2,978

◆ The wonderfully balanced exterior of this Floridian design offers columns and circle-top windows at the covered entry. Inside, the formal living and dining rooms face the rear, with large glass doors providing excellent views to the veranda and beyond. The kitchen, nook and leisure room unite to provide a grand space for casual gatherings. The leisure room includes an optional wet bar. Bedrooms are planned for maximum privacy. The secondary bedrooms share a full bath; a separate lanai is available to Bedroom 2. The master wing includes a study that can serve as a reading room, a home office or a guest bedroom. It is conveniently located near the entry and has a powder room and coat closet. The master suite includes a bayed area and a master bath with garden tub, a large shower and His and Hers walk-in closets.

— DESIGN BY —
THE SATER DESIGN COLLECTION

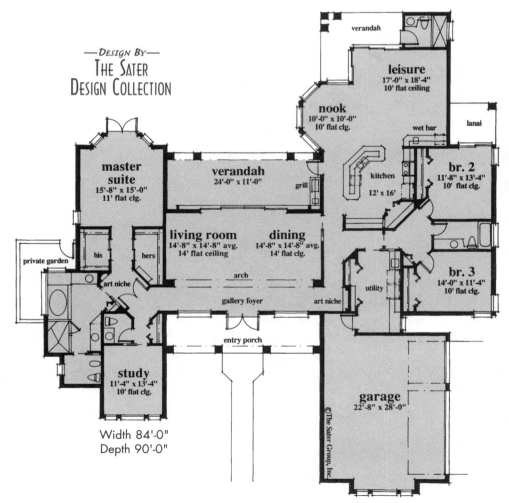

Width 84'-0"
Depth 90'-0"

373

Design 8672

Square footage: 2,397

◆ Low-slung, hipped rooflines and an abundance of glass enhance the unique exterior of this sunny, one-story home. Inside, the use of soffits and tray ceilings heighten the distinctive style of the floor plan. To the left, double doors lead to the private master suite which is bathed in natural light—compliments of an abundant use of glass—and enjoys a garden setting from the corner tub. Convenient planning of the gourmet kitchen places everything at minimum distances and serves the outdoor summer kitchen, breakfast nook and family room with equal ease. Completing the plan are two family bedrooms that share a full bath.

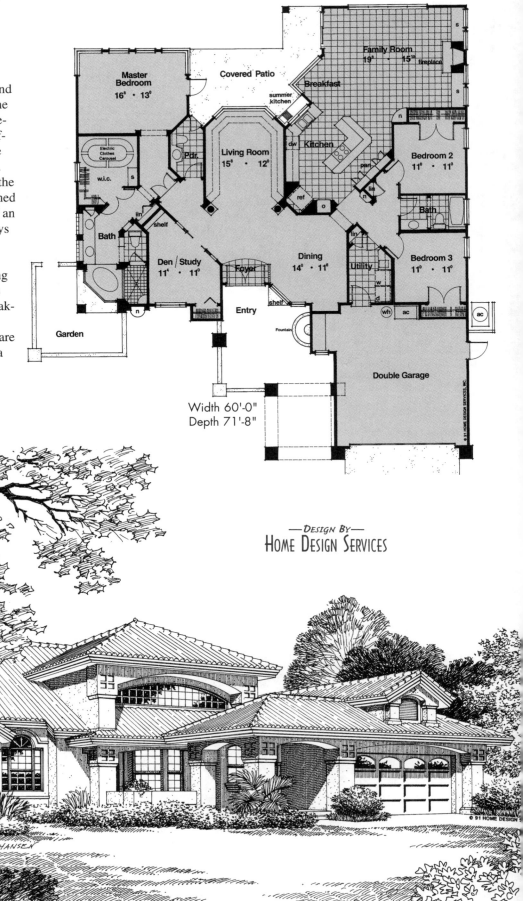

Width 60'-0"
Depth 71'-8"

— DESIGN BY —
HOME DESIGN SERVICES

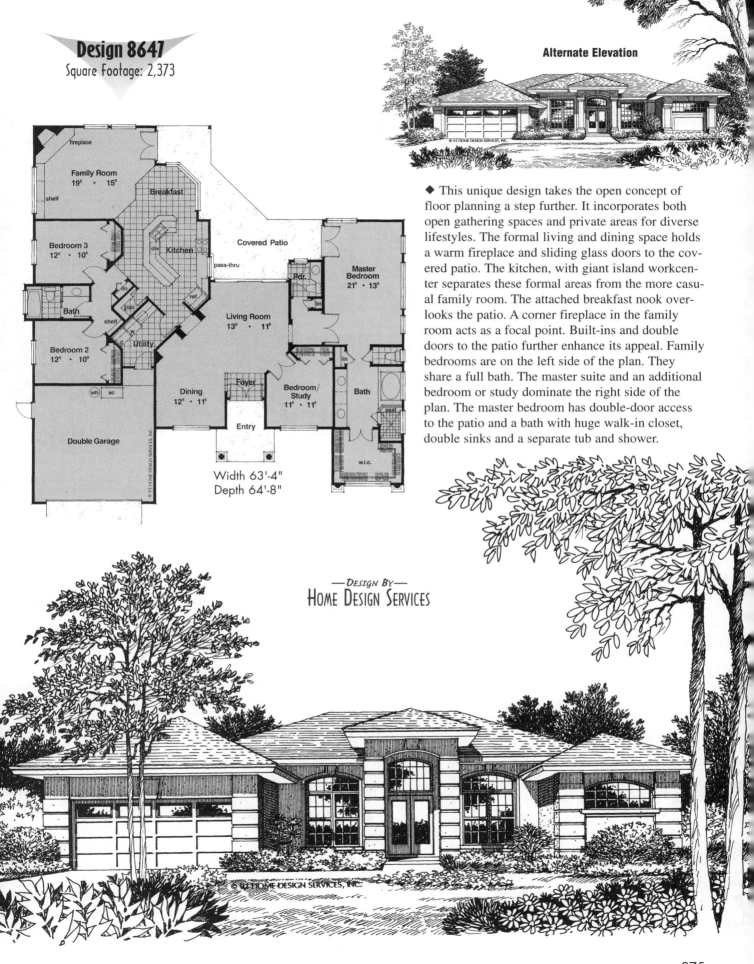

Design 8647
Square Footage: 2,373

Alternate Elevation

© 91 HOME DESIGN SERVICES, INC.

fireplace

Family Room
19⁸ · 15⁰

shelf

Breakfast

Bedroom 3
12⁰ · 10⁰

dw

Kitchen

Covered Patio

pass-thru

Bath

pan

Master Bedroom
21⁰ · 13⁰

Pdr.

ref

Living Room
13⁰ · 11⁸

shelf

Utility

w d

Bedroom 2
12⁰ · 10⁰

wh ac

Dining
12⁰ · 11⁸

Foyer

Bedroom/Study
11⁴ · 11⁰

Bath

seat

Double Garage

Entry

w.i.c.

© 91 HOME DESIGN SERVICES, INC

Width 63'-4"
Depth 64'-8"

◆ This unique design takes the open concept of floor planning a step further. It incorporates both open gathering spaces and private areas for diverse lifestyles. The formal living and dining space holds a warm fireplace and sliding glass doors to the covered patio. The kitchen, with giant island workcenter separates these formal areas from the more casual family room. The attached breakfast nook overlooks the patio. A corner fireplace in the family room acts as a focal point. Built-ins and double doors to the patio further enhance its appeal. Family bedrooms are on the left side of the plan. They share a full bath. The master suite and an additional bedroom or study dominate the right side of the plan. The master bedroom has double-door access to the patio and a bath with huge walk-in closet, double sinks and a separate tub and shower.

— DESIGN BY —
HOME DESIGN SERVICES

© 91 HOME DESIGN SERVICES, INC.

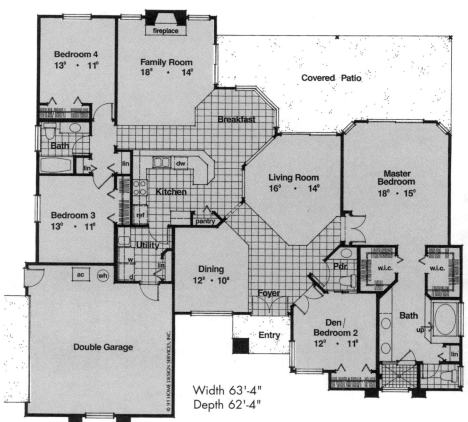

—Design By—
Home Design Services

Design 8669
Square Footage: 2,287

◆ This sunny home offers a wealth of livability in less than 2,300 square feet. The covered entry gives way to living and dining rooms. The living room is accented by columns and has sliding glass doors to the covered patio. The kitchen is well equipped with a pantry and a breakfast room, which has views of the patio. The family room is just a few steps away. It also accesses the patio and is warmed by a hearth. Two family bedrooms reside on this side of the plan. They share a full bath with two linen closets. The master bedroom offers large proportions and an expansive bath with dual walk-in closets, a double-bowl lavatory, a whirlpool, a separate shower and a compartmented toilet. A den is located off the entry and can also serve as another bedroom.

Width 63'-4"
Depth 62'-4"

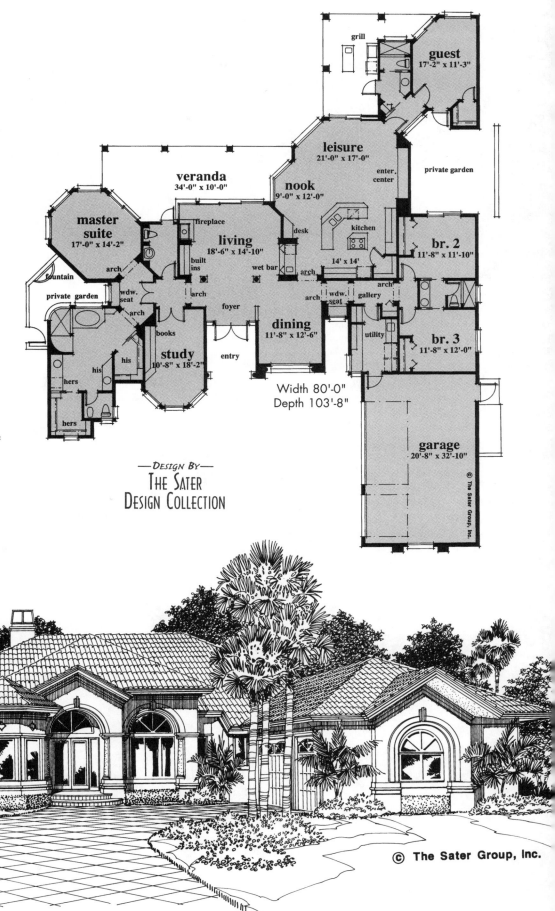

Design 6661

Square Footage: 3,265

◆ This dazzling Floridian home offers the best in formal and elegant living. A striking living room opens through sliding glass doors to the rear veranda and has built-in cabinetry, a fireplace and a wet bar for easy entertaining. The oversized kitchen is rich with amenities such as an angular snack bar, a cooktop island and walk-in pantry. Sunny windows frame the eating nook as it introduces the cozy leisure room that's complete with a built-in entertainment center. A smart guest room with a full cabana bath is just off the leisure room. Two family bedrooms are set against a gallery hall and are designed to share a compartmented bath. The master suite is stylishly set off with arches and a private garden visible from a lovely window seat and the luxurious bath. A multitude of windows makes the bedroom an elegant retreat.

—Design By—

The Sater Design Collection

guest 17'-2" x 11'-3"

grill

leisure 21'-0" x 17'-0"

enter. center

private garden

veranda 34'-0" x 10'-0"

nook 9'-0" x 12'-0"

master suite 17'-0" x 14'-2"

fireplace

living 18'-6" x 14'-10"

desk

kitchen

br. 2 11'-8" x 11'-10"

fountain

arch

private garden

wdw. seat

built ins

wet bar

14' x 14'

arch

arch

arch

gallery

arch

foyer

wdw. seat

his

hers

books

study 10'-8" x 18'-2"

dining 11'-8" x 12'-6"

utility

br. 3 11'-8" x 12'-0"

his

entry

hers

Width 80'-0"
Depth 103'-8"

garage 20'-8" x 32'-10"

© The Sater Group, Inc.

377

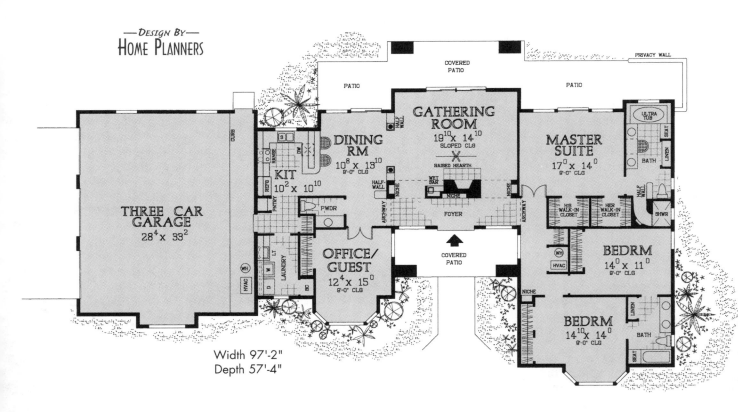

PRIVACY WALL

COVERED PATIO

PATIO

PATIO

ULTRA TUB

SEAT

GATHERING ROOM
19¹⁰ x 14¹⁰
SLOPED CLG

MASTER SUITE
17⁰ x 14⁰
9'-0" CLG

BATH

LINEN

DINING RM
10⁸ x 13¹⁰
9'-0" CLG

RAISED HEARTH

WET BAR

NICHE

THREE CAR GARAGE
28⁴ x 33²

KIT
10² x 10¹⁰

HALF WALL

NICHE

HIS WALK-IN CLOSET

HER WALK-IN CLOSET

SHWR

PNTRY

PWDR

HALF-WALL

FOYER

ARCHWAY

WH

HVAC

BEDRM
14⁰ x 11⁰
9'-0" CLG

HVAC

LAUNDRY

OFFICE/ GUEST
12⁴ x 15⁰
9'-0" CLG

COVERED PATIO

NICHE

BEDRM
14¹⁰ x 14⁰
9'-0" CLG

BATH

SEAT

Width 97'-2"
Depth 57'-4"

Design 3657
Square Footage: 2,319

◆ The grand style of this new design is reflected in divided-light windows and sunburst transoms that create a dazzling entry for this Mission-style country home. A Spanish-tile roof splashes the stately exterior with casual elegance, while the foyer lends dignity to a floor plan designed for active families. The heart of the home is the gathering room, with a raised-hearth fireplace, a wet bar and sliding-glass doors to the enter-

tainment patio. The formal dining room opens to a U-shaped kitchen, which offers a snack bar and leads to a tiled laundry. A home office or guest suite enjoys a nearby powder room. The right wing houses the family sleeping quarters which include a luxurious master suite with two walk-in closets, twin lavatories, a spa bath and doors to the covered patio. Two spacious secondary bedrooms share a private bath.

◆ Symmetry reigns supreme on the exterior of this Spanish-style design. A portico with three arches frames the entryway, while turrets on either side feature multi-pane windows with circle-head tops. The floor plan allows for the open lifestyle so enjoyed in the Southwest. Flanking the foyer are the formal living and dining rooms, each large enough for carefree entertaining. The rear of the home is wonderfully open—with a family room and U-shaped kitchen and easy access to a covered patio for indoor and outdoor casual living. To further pamper homeowners, the master suite offers a walk-in closet, a private office with covered porch, an exercise area and access to a deck with spa tub. Three family bedrooms—one with a private porch—share a full bath.

Design 3631
Square Footage: 2,831
L

—DESIGN BY—
HOME PLANNERS

Quote One®
Cost to build? See page 436 to order complete cost estimate to build this house in your area!

Width 84'-0"
Depth 77'-0"

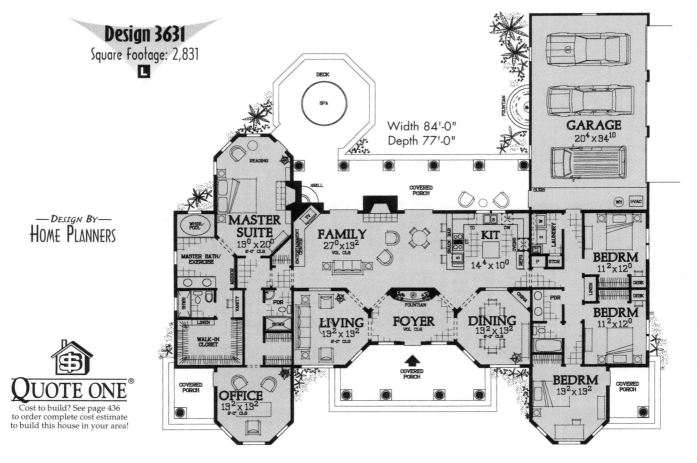

Design 9144
Square Footage: 2,090

◆ This exciting Southwestern design is enhanced by the use of arched windows and an inviting arched entrance. The large foyer opens to a massive great room with a fireplace and built-in cabinets. The kitchen features an island cooktop and a skylit breakfast area. The master suite has an impressive cathedral ceiling and a walk-in closet as well as a luxurious bath that boasts separate vanities, a corner whirlpool tub and a separate shower. Two additional bedrooms are located at the opposite end of the home for privacy and share a full bath. Please specify crawlspace or slab foundation when ordering.

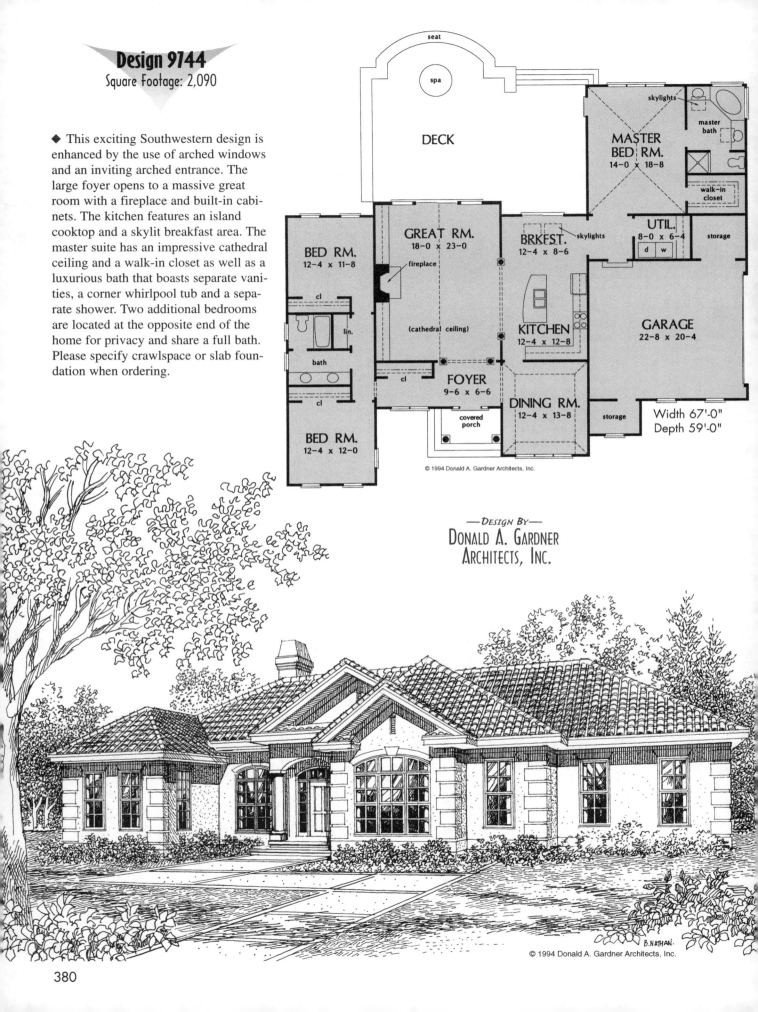

seat

spa

DECK

skylights

MASTER BED RM.
14-0 x 18-8

master bath

walk-in closet

GREAT RM.
18-0 x 23-0

BRKFST.
12-4 x 8-6

skylights

UTIL.
8-0 x 6-4

storage

fireplace

d   w

BED RM.
12-4 x 11-8

cl

lin.

bath

cl

(cathedral ceiling)

KITCHEN
12-4 x 12-8

GARAGE
22-8 x 20-4

FOYER
9-6 x 6-6

cl

BED RM.
12-4 x 12-0

covered porch

DINING RM.
12-4 x 13-8

storage

Width 67'-0"
Depth 59'-0"

© 1994 Donald A. Gardner Architects, Inc.

— DESIGN BY —
DONALD A. GARDNER
ARCHITECTS, INC.

B. NATHAN.

© 1994 Donald A. Gardner Architects, Inc.

380

— DESIGN BY —
HOME PLANNERS

TERRACE

COVERED
PORCH

GATHERING RM.
16⁸ x 19⁴

MASTER
BEDROOM
13⁰ x 13⁸

DRSG. RM.

VANITY

BATH

DINING RM.
12⁸ x 11⁰

SLOPED
CEILING

WALK-IN
CLOSET

8'-0" FLAT CEILING

TERRACE

BRKFST. RM.
10⁰ x 10⁸

OVENS

PASS THRU

REF'G F.TP.

DIN.

CL.

BATH

LIN

CL.

KITCHEN
13⁸ x 10⁸

SNACK BAR
COOK TOP

DW

SLOPED
CEILING

OPEN

CL.

FOYER

B.C. DESK

CL.

W

D

PORCH

BEDROOM
10⁸ x 11⁴

BEDROOM
11⁴ x 11⁴

W.R.

MUD RM.

PLANT LEDGE

SLOPED
CEILING

SLOPED
CEILING

GARAGE
21⁴ x 21⁴

CURB

PLANT LEDGE

Width 66'-0"
Depth 62'-0"

Design 2912
Square Footage: 1,864

◆ This contemporary design with smart Spanish styling incorporates careful zoning by room functions with lifestyle comfort. All three bedrooms, including a master bedroom suite with a large dressing area and lavish bath, are isolated at one end of the home. Entry to a breakfast room and kitchen is possible through a mud room off the garage. That's good news for carrying groceries from car to kitchen or slipping off muddy shoes. The efficient kitchen includes a snack bar and a convenient cooktop with easy service to the breakfast room, dining room and gathering room. A large rear gathering room features a sloped ceiling and a fireplace. A covered porch just off the dining room furthers living potential.

QUOTE ONE®
Cost to build? See page 436
to order complete cost estimate
to build this house in your area!

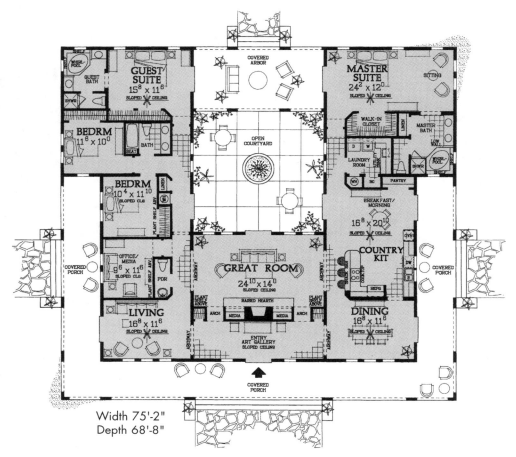

GUEST SUITE
15⁸ x 11⁸
SLOPED CEILING

GUEST BATH

SHWR

WHIRL-POOL

SHELF

BEDRM
11⁸ x 10⁰

BATH

SEAT

COVERED ARBOR

OPEN COURTYARD

MASTER SUITE
24² x 12⁰
SLOPED CEILING

SITTING

WALK-IN CLOSET

D W

LINEN

MASTER BATH

LAV WALL

WHIRL-POOL

SHWR

LAUNDRY ROOM

WH

BC

PANTRY

BEDRM
10⁴ x 11¹⁰
SLOPED CLG

COVERED PORCH

OFFICE/MEDIA
9⁶ x 11⁶
SLOPED CLG

PDR

BREAKFAST/MORNING
16⁸ x 20¹⁰
SLOPED CEILING

COUNTRY KIT

BRICK BAR

COVERED PORCH

REF

DW

GREAT ROOM
24¹⁰ x 14⁰
SLOPED CEILING

RAISED HEARTH

MEDIA

MEDIA

LIVING
16⁸ x 11⁶
SLOPED CEILING

DINING
16⁸ x 11⁶
SLOPED CEILING

ENTRY ART GALLERY
SLOPED CEILING

ARCH

COVERED PORCH

Width 75'-2"
Depth 68'-8"

◆ An open courtyard takes center-stage, providing a happy marriage of indoor-outdoor relationships. Art collectors will appreciate the gallery that enhances the entry and showcases their favorite works. The formal dining room accommodates special occasions with style, while casual mealtimes are enjoyed in the adjacent country kitchen conveniently designed with an island snack bar and a large pantry. The centrally located great room supplies the nucleus for formal and informal entertaining. A raised-hearth fireplace flanked by built-in media centers adds a special touch. A guest suite and two family bedrooms are on one side of the plan. On the other side, the master suite provides a private retreat where you may relax—try the sitting room or retire to the master bath for a pampering soak in the corner whirlpool.

—DESIGN BY—
HOME PLANNERS

QUOTE ONE®
Cost to build? See page 436
to order complete cost estimate
to build this house in your area!

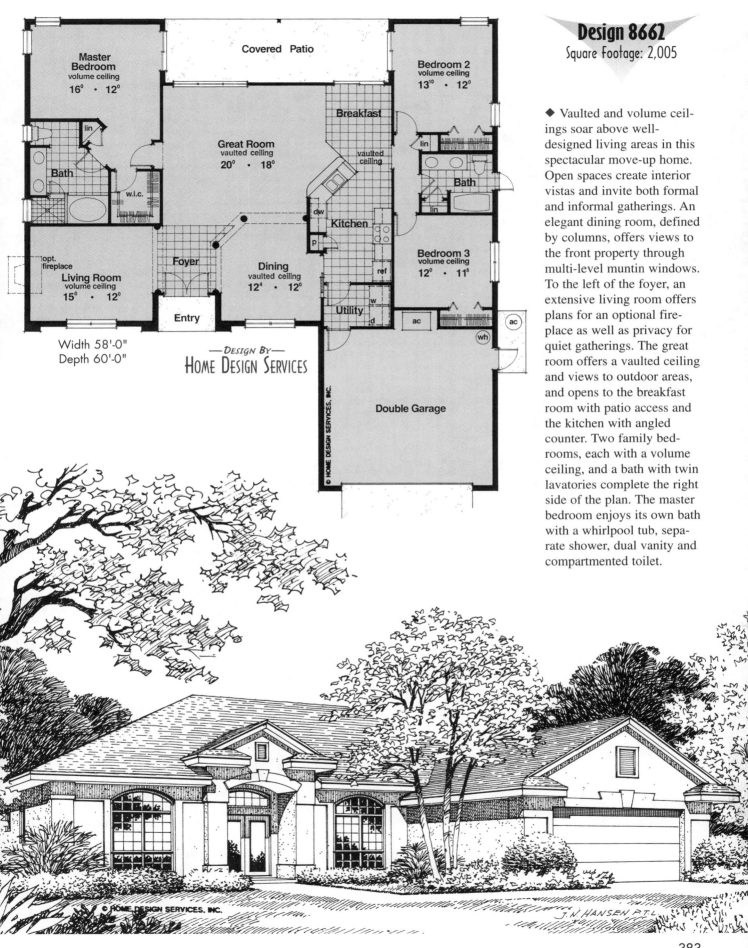

Master Bedroom
volume ceiling
16⁰ · 12⁰

Covered Patio

Design 8662
Square Footage: 2,005

Bedroom 2
volume ceiling
13¹⁰ · 12⁰

lin

Bath

Breakfast

Great Room
vaulted ceiling
20⁰ · 18⁰

vaulted ceiling

Bath

w.i.c.

lin

dw

Kitchen

p

opt. fireplace

Living Room
volume ceiling
15⁰ · 12⁰

Foyer

Dining
vaulted ceiling
12⁴ · 12⁰

Bedroom 3
volume ceiling
12⁰ · 11⁸

ref

Entry

Utility

w

Width 58'-0"
Depth 60'-0"

d

ac

ac

wh

— DESIGN BY —
HOME DESIGN SERVICES

Double Garage

© HOME DESIGN SERVICES, INC.

◆ Vaulted and volume ceilings soar above well-designed living areas in this spectacular move-up home. Open spaces create interior vistas and invite both formal and informal gatherings. An elegant dining room, defined by columns, offers views to the front property through multi-level muntin windows. To the left of the foyer, an extensive living room offers plans for an optional fireplace as well as privacy for quiet gatherings. The great room offers a vaulted ceiling and views to outdoor areas, and opens to the breakfast room with patio access and the kitchen with angled counter. Two family bedrooms, each with a volume ceiling, and a bath with twin lavatories complete the right side of the plan. The master bedroom enjoys its own bath with a whirlpool tub, separate shower, dual vanity and compartmented toilet.

© HOME DESIGN SERVICES, INC.

J. N. HANSEN P.T.L.

— Design By —
Home Planners

Quote One®
Cost to build? See page 436
to order complete cost estimate
to build this house in your area!

COVERED PORCH

BREAKFAST
9⁰ x 7²

BEDROOM
12⁸ x 11¹⁰

KITCHEN
10⁰ x 12¹⁰

FAMILY RM
16⁴ x 16⁶

MASTER
BEDROOM
14⁶ x 16²

WALK-IN
CLOSET

SNACK BAR

BATH

LINEN

SLOPED CEILING

BATH

WASH RM

WHIRLPOOL

RAISED HEARTH
CONVERSATION
PIT

SEAT

BEDROOM
12⁸ x 11⁸

LIVING RM
17¹⁰ x 20⁴

FOYER

CURB

COVERED
PORCH

CURB

3 CAR
GARAGE
29⁴ x 20²

Width 70'-0"
Depth 55'-10"

Design 3421
Square Footage: 2,145
L

◆ Split-bedroom planning makes the most of a one-story design. In this case the master suite is on the opposite side of the house from two family bedrooms. It is enhanced by a sloped ceiling, walk-in closet and sloped-ceiling bath with whirlpool, double vanities and separate shower. Gourmets can rejoice at the abundant work space in the U-shaped kitchen and will appreciate the natural light afforded by the large bay window in the breakfast room. The family room is open to the kitchen and graced with a sloped ceiling. The rear covered porch can be reached through sliding glass doors in the family room. A formal living room has a sunken conversation area with a cozy fireplace as its focus. A three-car garage shields the master suite from street noise.

Design 8649
Square Footage: 2,691

◆ Italianate lines add finesse to the formal facade of this home. Strong stucco symmetry, a soaring portico and gentle roofines are the prized hallmarks of a relaxed, yet formal Italianate design. A stepped fourteen-foot ceiling highlights the entry foyer. To the right, columns and a stepped twelve-foot ceiling grace the dining room. A plant soffit heralds the living room, which also has a twelve-foot ceiling. An angled cooktop counter adds flair to the kitchen. Look for a desk and walk-in pantry, plus a bright breakfast nook here. A corner fireplace, a ten-foot ceiling and a patio enhance the family room. An arch opens the entry to the lavish master suite. Two additional bedrooms come with separate entries to a full bath.

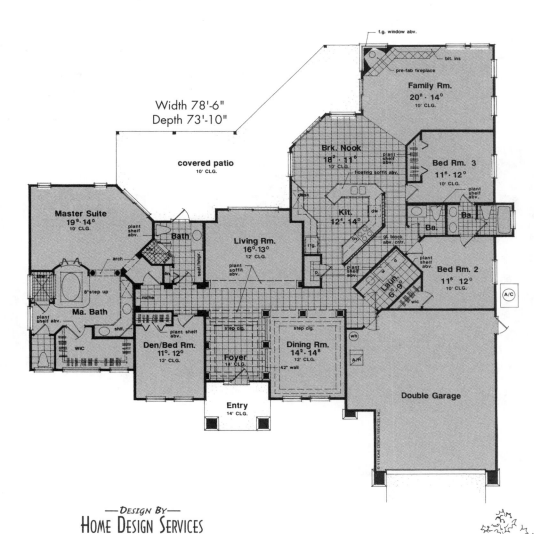

Width 78'-6"
Depth 73'-10"

covered patio
10' CLG.

f.g. window abv.

blt. ins
pre-fab fireplace

Family Rm.
20⁸ · 14⁰
10' CLG.

Brk. Nook
18² · 11⁰
10' CLG.

floating soffit abv.

desk

Kit.
12⁴ · 14⁰

dw

Bed Rm. 3
11⁸ · 12⁰
10' CLG.

plant shelf abv.

Ba.

Ba.

gl. block abv. cntr.

Master Suite
19⁶ · 14⁰
10' CLG.

plant shelf abv.

Bath

arch

Living Rm.
16⁰ · 13⁰
12' CLG.

plant soffit abv.

seat/hmpr.

frig.

plant shelf abv.

Laun.
6⁰ · 9⁰

wic

Bed Rm. 2
11⁸ · 12⁰
10' CLG.

A/C

8'step up

Ma. Bath

niche

plant shelf abv.

shlf.

plant shelf abv.

wic

Den/Bed Rm.
11⁰ · 12⁰
12' CLG.

step clg.

Foyer
14' CLG.

step clg.

Dining Rm.
14² · 14⁸
12' CLG.

42" wall

wh

Double Garage

Entry
14' CLG.

— DESIGN BY —
HOME DESIGN SERVICES

R. BRADSHAW

© 91 HOME DESIGN SERVICES, INC.

Design 8621
Square Footage: 2,480

◆ This Florida contemporary has been a best seller among families who insist on formal and casual living spaces. The master's retreat, with a bay sitting area, is secluded away from the family area for solitude. The master bath includes a sumptuous soaking tub, shower for two, His and Hers vanities and a huge walk-in closet. The secondary bedrooms share a split bath, designed for dual use as well as privacy. The kitchen, nook and family room all have magnificent views of the outdoor living space. A fireplace, flanked with built-in cabinets, warms the family room. A private den or study is accessed in the master-suite hallway, and, if needed, can serve as a guest bedroom because of the nearby pool bath (note the outside access here). A two-car garage protects family bedrooms from street noise.

Width 67'-4"
Depth 70'-8"

—DESIGN BY—
HOME DESIGN SERVICES

J.N. HANSEN P.T.L.

Width 60'-0"
Depth 76'-8"

fireplace

Family Room
vaulted ceiling
18⁰ · 16⁰

Breakfast
volume ceiling

Covered Patio

Master
Bedroom
volume ceiling
16⁰ · 19⁰

dw

Bedroom 2
volume ceiling
11⁰ · 10⁰

Kitchen

Living Room
volume ceiling
14⁰ · 12⁰

ref

pantry

w.i.c.   w.i.c.

Bath

up

Dining
volume ceiling
10⁴ · 15⁰

Foyer

Den Study
volume ceiling
10⁰ · 10⁰

Bath

storage

up

stor

Bedroom 3
11⁰ · 10⁰

Entry

d

Utility

w

wh

ac

Double Garage

down

Bonus Room
15⁸ · 23⁴

Design 8681

Square Footage: 2,322
Bonus Room: 370 sq. ft.

◆ Grand Palladian windows create a
classic look for this sensational stucco
home. A magnificent view from the living room provides unlimited vistas of
the rear grounds through a wall of glass.
The nearby dining room completes the
formal area. The kitchen, breakfast nook
and family room comprise the family
wing, coming together to form the perfect place for casual gatherings. Two
secondary bedrooms share a bath and
provide complete privacy to the master
suite located on the opposite side of the
plan. The master bedroom sets the
mood for relaxation and the lavish master bath pampers with a soaking tub
flanked by a step-down shower and a
compartmented toilet. Bonus space may
be completed at a later date to accommodate additional space requirements.

—DESIGN BY—
HOME DESIGN SERVICES

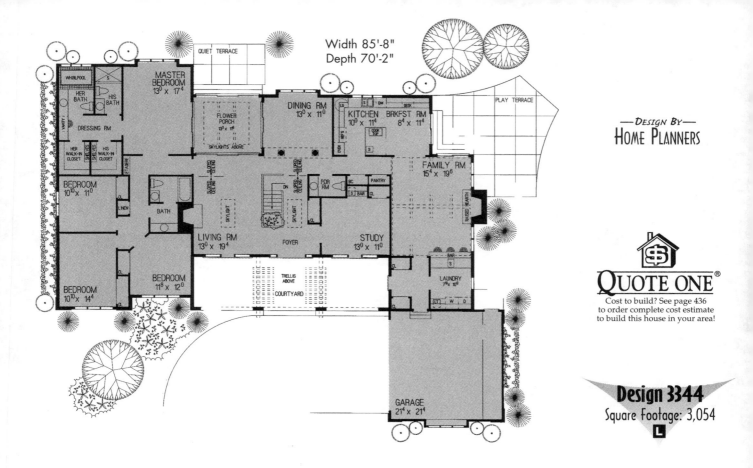

Width 85'-8"
Depth 70'-2"

QUOTE ONE®
Cost to build? See page 436
to order complete cost estimate
to build this house in your area!

Design 3344
Square Footage: 3,054
L

◆ This home features interior planning for today's active family. Informal areas include a living room with a fireplace, a family room with another fireplace and a wet bar and a study with a wet bar. A flower porch is shared by the dining room, living room and master bedroom and opens onto a rear terrace. Convenient to the kitchen is the formal dining room with an attractive bay window overlooking the backyard. The four-bedroom sleeping area contains a sumptuous master suite. It holds His and Hers walk-in closets, His and Hers baths, a whirlpool tub and a dressing area. Three family bedrooms share a full bath with a separate vanity area. The two-car garage can be reached through a service entrance that has a laundry room and courtyard access.

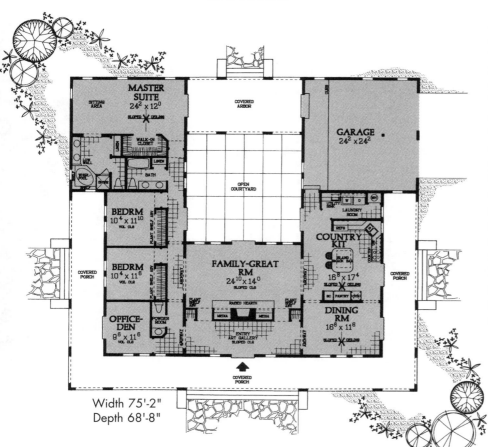

— DESIGN BY —
HOME PLANNERS

Width 75'-2"
Depth 68'-8"

MASTER SUITE 24² x 12⁰
SITTING AREA
SLOPED CEILING
WALK-IN CLOSET
LINEN
LINEN
BATH

BEDRM 10⁴ x 11¹⁰ VOL. CLG.

BEDRM 10⁴ x 11⁶ VOL. CLG.

OFFICE-DEN 9⁸ x 11⁶ VOL. CLG.

POWDER ROOM

COVERED PORCH

COVERED ARBOR

OPEN COURTYARD

FAMILY-GREAT RM 24¹⁰ x 14⁰ SLOPED CLG.

RAISED HEARTH

ENTRY ART GALLERY SLOPED CLG.

COVERED PORCH

GARAGE 24² x 24²

UTILITY
LAUNDRY ROOM

COUNTRY KIT 16⁸ x 17⁴ SLOPED CEILING
ISLAND BAR

PANTRY

DINING RM 16⁸ x 11⁶ SLOPED CEILING

COVERED PORCH

Design 3632
Square Footage: 2,539
L

◆ Exposed rafter tails, arched porch detailing, massive paneled front doors and stucco exterior walls enhance the western character of this U-shaped ranch house. Double doors open to a spacious, slope-ceilinged art gallery. The quiet sleeping zone is comprised of an entire wing. The extra room at the front of this wing may be used for a den or an office. The family dining and kitchen activities are located at the opposite end of the plan. Indoor-outdoor living relationships are outstanding. The large open courtyard is akin to the fabled Greek atrium. It is accessible from each of the zones and functions with a covered arbor which looks out over the rear landscape. The master suite has a generous sitting area, a walk-in closet, twin lavatories and a whirlpool plus a stall shower.

QUOTE ONE®
Cost to build? See page 436
to order complete cost estimate
to build this house in your area!

389

WHIRLPOOL S

MASTER BATH

COVERED PORCH

HIS WALK-IN CLOSET   HER WALK-IN CLOSET

BREAKFAST
11⁰ x 8²

FAMILY RM
12⁸ x 21⁰

STUDY
11² x 13⁸

BEDROOM
10² x 11⁴

MASTER BEDROOM
12⁸ x 20⁰

SLOPED CEILING

PTRY   OVENS

KITCHEN
11⁰ x 11⁰

DW

COOK TOP   REFG   CL

SLOPED CEILING   SLOPED CEILING

REFG   BAR   S

BATH

WALK-IN CLOSET

LAUN

WALK-IN CLOSET

SLOPED CEILING

DN

DN   DN

FOYER

SLOPED CEILING

PDR RM

W
D   LAUND

FURN   WH

BEDROOM
10² x 11⁶

SLOPED CEILING

LIVING RM
14⁰ x 18⁶

COVERED PORCH

DINING RM
10⁶ x 14⁶

CURB

3 CAR GARAGE
27² x 19¹⁰

Width 62'-0"
Depth 64'-0"

—DESIGN BY—
HOME PLANNERS

◆ Though distinctly Southwestern in design, this home has some features that are universally appealing. Note, for instance, the central gallery, perpendicular to the raised entry hall, and running almost the entire width of the house. An L-shaped, angled kitchen serves the breakfast room and family room in equal fashion. Sleeping areas are found in four bedrooms including an optional study and an exquisite master suite.

Design 3413
Square Footage: 2,517
L

QUOTE ONE®
Cost to build? See page 436 to order complete cost estimate to build this house in your area!

Width 93'-7"
Depth 74'-10"

BEDRM
12⁰ x 12⁴
9'-0" CLG

BEDRM
10⁴ x 13⁴
9'-0" CLG

BEDRM
10⁴ x 12⁰
9'-0" CLG

COVERED PATIO

COVERED PATIO

COVERED PATIO

—DESIGN BY—
HOME PLANNERS

MASTER
BEDRM
14⁸ x 14⁸
COFFERED CLG

SHOWER

MASTER
BATH

GARDEN
TUB

KIT
10⁰ x 14⁴
9'-0" CLG

FAMILY
RM
19⁰ x 17¹⁰
9'-0" CLG

WALK-IN
CLOSET

LINEN

BATH

LIN

RANGE

REF

PANT

SNACK BAR

DW

S

DESK

OVEN/
MICRO

STORAGE

LAUNDRY

DN

PDR
RM

DINING
13⁶ x 10⁸
COFFERED CLG

FOYER

MEDIA/
OFFICE
14⁸ x 14⁶
9'-0" CLG

BC STORAGE

COVERED
PORCH

Design 3640
Square Footage: 2,612

L

◆ Dramatic, interior angles provide for an immensely livable plan that is metered with elegance enough for any social occasion. The open passage to the living room and formal dining room from the foyer is perfect for entertaining, while casual areas are positioned to the rear of the plan. The spacious kitchen, with extra storage at every turn, has an eat-in nook and a door to the rear patio. Two family bedrooms share a hall bath to complete this wing. The master suite is split from the family area to ensure a private retreat. The large bedroom can easily accommodate a sitting area and has a luxurious bath, walk-in closet and sliding doors to a private patio.

GARAGE
21⁰ x 23⁶

QUOTE ONE®
Cost to build? See page 436
to order complete cost estimate
to build this house in your area!

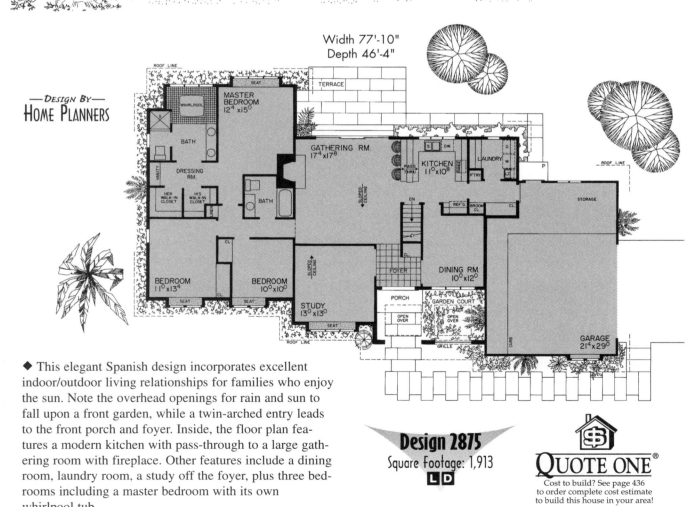

Width 77'-10"
Depth 46'-4"

— DESIGN BY —
HOME PLANNERS

ROOF LINE

TERRACE

SEAT

WHIRLPOOL

MASTER BEDROOM
12⁴ x15⁰

BATH

GATHERING RM.
17⁴ x17⁸

KITCHEN
11⁰ x10⁸

LAUNDRY

DRESSING RM.

VANITY

HER WALK-IN CLOSET

HIS WALK-IN CLOSET

BATH

SLOPED CEILING

PASS THRU

PTRY

ROOF LINE

REF'G

BROOM CL

CL

STORAGE

CL

DN

CL

BEDROOM
11⁰ x13⁴

SEAT

CL

BEDROOM
10⁰ x10⁰

SEAT

SLOPED CEILING

STUDY
13⁰ x13⁰

SEAT

FOYER

DINING RM.
10⁰ x12⁰

PORCH

OPEN OVER

GARDEN COURT
OPEN OVER

GARAGE
21⁴ x29⁰

ROOF LINE

GRILLE

CURB

◆ This elegant Spanish design incorporates excellent indoor/outdoor living relationships for families who enjoy the sun. Note the overhead openings for rain and sun to fall upon a front garden, while a twin-arched entry leads to the front porch and foyer. Inside, the floor plan features a modern kitchen with pass-through to a large gathering room with fireplace. Other features include a dining room, laundry room, a study off the foyer, plus three bedrooms including a master bedroom with its own whirlpool tub.

Design 2875
Square Footage: 1,913
L D

QUOTE ONE®
Cost to build? See page 436
to order complete cost estimate
to build this house in your area!

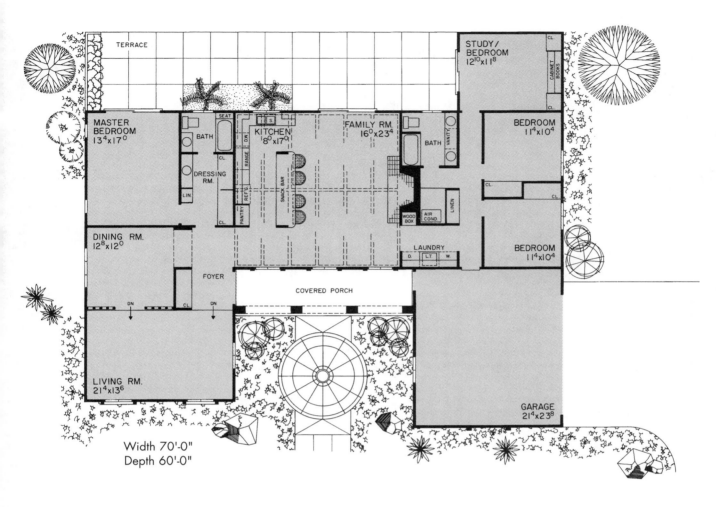

TERRACE

STUDY/
BEDROOM
12¹⁰x11⁸

CABINET
BOOKS

CL

CL

MASTER
BEDROOM
13⁴x17⁰

SEAT

BATH

KITCHEN
18⁰x17⁰

S

DW

RANGE

FAMILY RM.
16⁰x23⁴

BATH

VANITY

BEDROOM
11⁴x10⁴

CL

CL

CL

DRESSING
RM.

SNACK BAR

CL

LIN

DINING RM.
12⁸x12⁰

PANTRY

REF'G

WOOD
BOX

AIR
COND.

LINEN

BEDROOM
11⁴x10⁴

CL

FOYER

LAUNDRY
D. L.T. W.

DN

CL

DN

COVERED PORCH

LIVING RM.
21⁴x13⁶

GARAGE
21⁴x23⁸

Width 70'-0"
Depth 60'-0"

Design 2236
Square Footage: 2,307

◆ This delightful Spanish design will fit in well, regardless of your building location: mountains, endless prairie, farmland or suburbs. The hub of the plan is the kitchen/family room area. The beam ceiling and the raised-hearth fireplace contribute to the cozy, informal atmosphere. The separate dining room and the sunken living room function together formally. The master bedroom provides privacy from the three family bedrooms located at the opposite end of the plan. It features a magnificent view to the rear terrace and the landscape beyond.

—DESIGN BY—
HOME PLANNERS

◆ Originally styled for Southwest living, this home is a good choice in any region where casual elegance is desired. Easy living is the focus of the large gathering room, apparent in its open relationship to the dining room and kitchen via a snack bar. The long galley kitchen is designed for work efficiency and has a planning desk, service entrance and a beautiful breakfast room framed with windows. The master bedroom and bath have a dramatic sloped ceiling and are joined by a traditional dressing room. Two secondary bedrooms—the front facing one would make a nice study—share a hall bath.

Design 2948
Square Footage: 1,830

Quote One®

Cost to build? See page 436 to order complete cost estimate to build this house in your area!

— DESIGN BY —
Home Planners

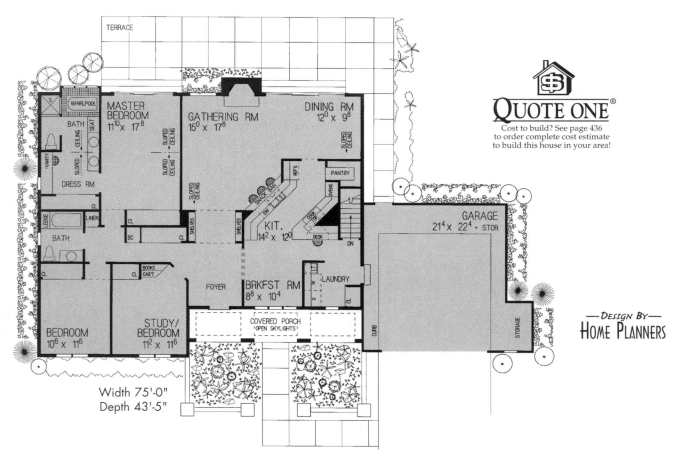

Width 75'-0"
Depth 43'-5"

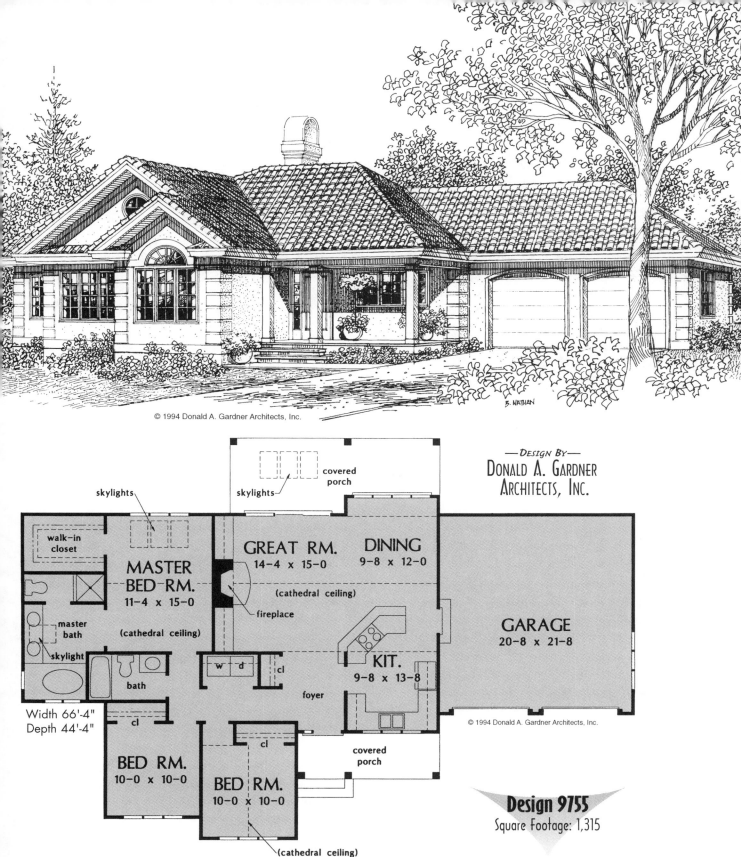

© 1994 Donald A. Gardner Architects, Inc.

B. NATHAN

skylights

skylights

covered
porch

— DESIGN BY —
DONALD A. GARDNER
ARCHITECTS, INC.

**walk-in
closet**

**MASTER
BED-RM.**
11-4 x 15-0

(cathedral ceiling)

**master
bath**

skylight

bath

GREAT RM.
14-4 x 15-0

(cathedral ceiling)

fireplace

w d   cl

foyer

DINING
9-8 x 12-0

KIT.
9-8 x 13-8

GARAGE
20-8 x 21-8

© 1994 Donald A. Gardner Architects, Inc.

Width 66'-4"
Depth 44'-4"

cl

BED RM.
10-0 x 10-0

cl

BED RM.
10-0 x 10-0

covered
porch

Design 9755
Square Footage: 1,315

(cathedral ceiling)

◆ Southwestern influences are evident in this design, from the tiled roof to the warm, stucco exterior. A covered porch leads indoors where the great room features a fireplace flanked by built-ins, a cathedral ceiling and sliding glass doors to the covered porch. The dining room is open to the great room and has a box-bay window overlooking the rear yard. In the kitchen, an island counter cooktop allows the cook to interact with family and friends. Three bedrooms include two family bedrooms—one with cathedral ceiling— that share a hall bath and a master suite with skylights, a walk-in closet and a private bath. A two-car garage is accessed through a side door in the kitchen.

395

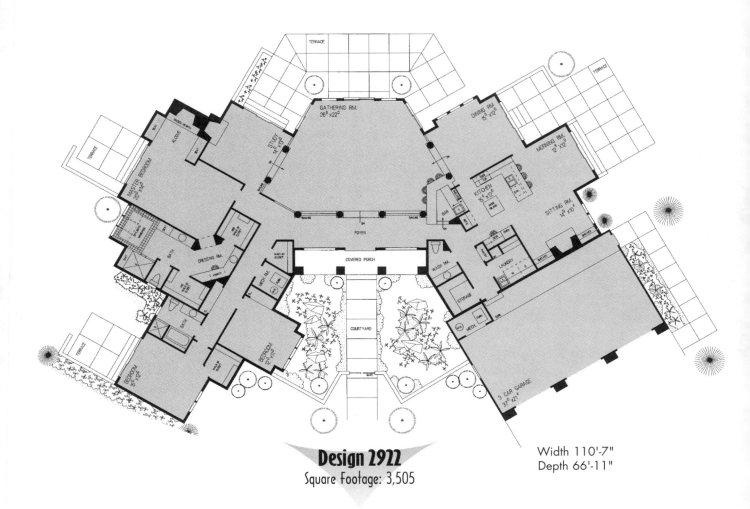

Design 2922
Square Footage: 3,505

Width 110'-7"
Depth 66'-11"

◆ Loaded with custom features, this plan seems to have everything imaginable. It's the perfect home for entertaining—there's an enormous sunken gathering room and cozy study. A full-sized bar is fashioned to serve the gathering room. The country-style kitchen contains an effi-cient work area, as well as space for relaxing in the morning room and fireside chats in the sitting room. Two nice-sized bedrooms share a hall bath. The luxurious master suite has a fireplace alcove, and an amenity-rich bath complete with twin walk-in closets, a dressing area and spa-style tub.

Cost to build? See page 436 to order complete cost estimate to build this house in your area!

—DESIGN BY—
HOME PLANNERS

Design 3630
Square Footage: 3,034

L

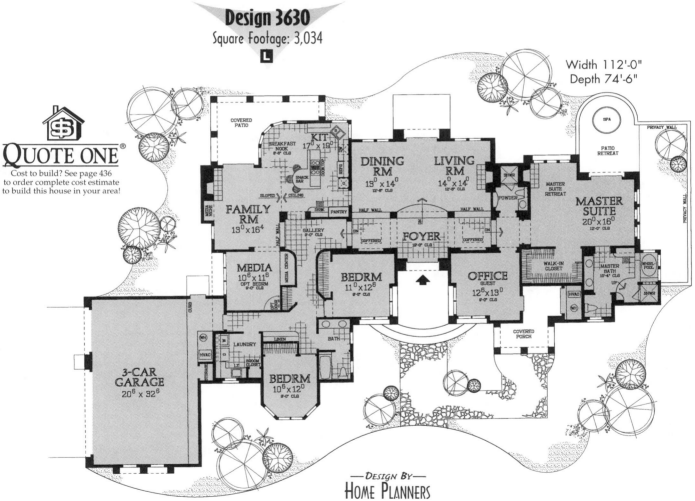

Width 112'-0"
Depth 74'-6"

Quote One®

Cost to build? See page 436
to order complete cost estimate
to build this house in your area!

COVERED PATIO

KIT 17⁰ x 19⁰

BREAKFAST NOOK 9'-6" CLG

SNACK BAR

DINING RM 13⁰ x 14⁰ 12'-6" CLG

LIVING RM 14⁰ x 14⁰ 12'-6" CLG

SLOPED CEILING

FAMILY RM 13⁰ x 16⁴ 9'-0" CLG

DESK

PANTRY

HALF WALL

HALF WALL

POWDER

MASTER SUITE RETREAT

MASTER SUITE 20⁰ x 16⁰ 12'-0" CLG

MEDIA 10⁶ x 11⁶ OPT BEDRM 9'-0" CLG

GALLERY 9'-0" CLG

COFFERED

FOYER 12'-6" CLG

COFFERED

BEDRM 11⁰ x 12⁶ 9'-0" CLG

OFFICE GUEST 12⁶ x 13⁰ 9'-0" CLG

WALK-IN CLOSET

MASTER BATH 10'-4" CLG

WHIRL POOL

HVAC

3-CAR GARAGE 20⁶ x 32⁶

LAUNDRY

LINEN

BATH

BROOM CLOSET

BEDRM 10⁶ x 12⁰ 9'-0" CLG

COVERED PORCH

SPA

PATIO RETREAT

PRIVACY WALL

PRIVACY WALL

— DESIGN BY —
Home Planners

◆ A grand entry enhances the exterior of this elegant stucco home. The foyer leads to an open formal area that will invite planned occasions. The corner kitchen with bayed breakfast area serves casual meals with a snack-bar counter, and more traditional and festive events with the formal dining room, defined by a decorative half-wall. The private master suite boasts an indoor retreat by a cozy fireplace, as well as access to a private patio with a spa, secluded by a privacy wall. Two family bedrooms on the opposite side of the plan share a full bath and a gallery hall that leads to the casual living area and to a media room.

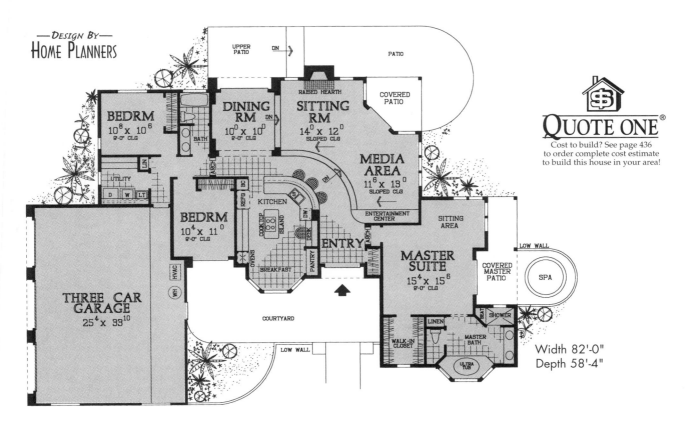

QUOTE ONE®

Cost to build? See page 436
to order complete cost estimate
to build this house in your area!

Width 82'-0"
Depth 58'-4"

◆ This home exhibits wonderful dual-use space in the sunken living room and media area. Anchoring each end of this spacious living zone is the raised-hearth fireplace and the entertainment center. The outstanding kitchen has an informal breakfast bay and looks over the snack bar to the family area. Through a graceful archway, a gallery hall leads to two family bedrooms. At the opposite end of the plan, a master suite features a sitting area filled with natural light, and French doors to the covered patio.

Design 3660
Square Footage: 2,086
L

Width 74'-0"
Depth 66'-10"

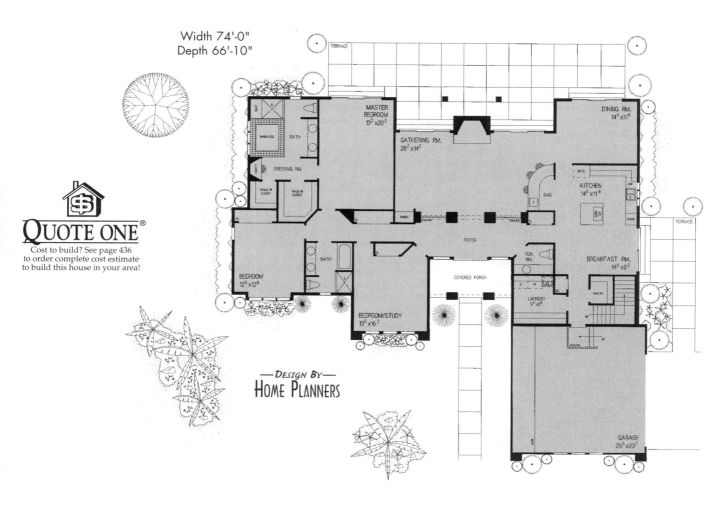

TERRACE

MASTER
BEDROOM
13² x20²

GATHERING RM.
28² x14²

DINING RM.
14⁴ x11⁶

BATH

DRESSING RM.

WALK-IN
CLOSET

WALK-IN
CLOSET

BAR

KITCHEN
14⁶ x11⁴

TERRACE

FOYER

BEDROOM
12⁶ x12⁸

BATH

FAM.
RM.

BREAKFAST RM.
14⁶ x9⁶

COVERED PORCH

LAUNDRY
9⁴ x6⁸

PANTRY

BEDROOM/STUDY
13⁰ x16²

GARAGE
23⁶ x23²

Quote One®
Cost to build? See page 436
to order complete cost estimate
to build this house in your area!

— DESIGN BY —
HOME PLANNERS

Design 2950
Square Footage: 2,559

◆ A natural desert dweller, this stucco, tile-roofed beauty is equally comfortable in any clime. Inside, there's a well-planned design. Common living areas—gathering room, formal dining room and breakfast room—are offset by a quiet study that could be used as a bedroom or guest room. A master suite features two walk-in closets, a double vanity and whirlpool spa. The two-car garage provides a service entrance; close by is an adequate laundry area and a pantry. A lovely hearth warms the gathering room and complements the snack bar area.

◆ A low, walled courtyard and exposed viga beams add Southwestern flair to this extraordinary Santa Fe pueblo home. Formal living and dining rooms are complemented by a large casual area containing a family room, morning room and kitchen. These are warmed by a circular hearth that extends outside to the patio. Three family bedrooms are found on the right side of the plan, as is a bonus room—perfect for hobbies, games or an additional bedroom. Two family bedrooms share a private bath, with whirlpool tub, while the other bedroom has private access to a hall bath. The master suite, with lush bath and huge walk-in closet, is on the left side of the plan, adjacent to a handy home office. A covered patio extends the entire length of the home—a welcome invitation to outdoor living.

—DESIGN BY—
HOME PLANNERS

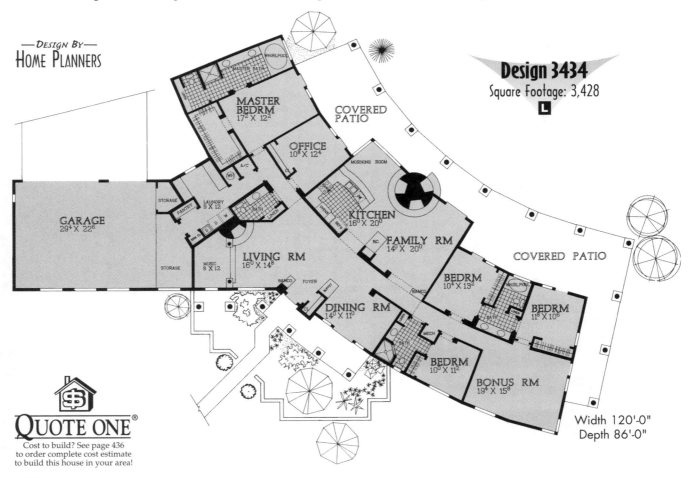

Design 3434
Square Footage: 3,428
L

Width 120'-0"
Depth 86'-0"

400

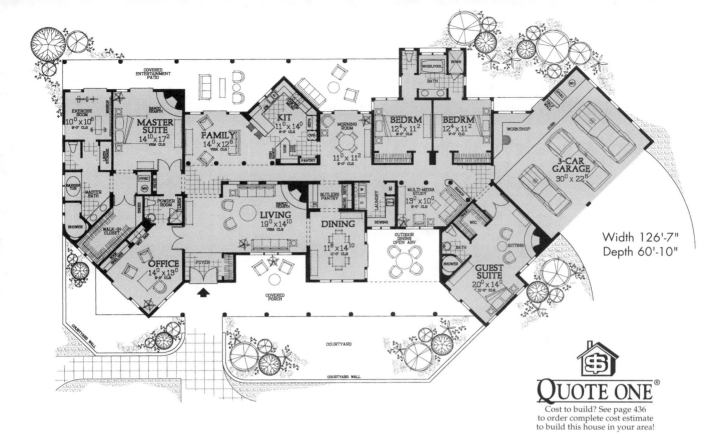

Width 126'-7"
Depth 60'-10"

Design 3693
Square Footage: 3,838

◆ This diamond in the desert gives new meaning to old style. Though reminiscent of old Pueblo-type dwellings of the Southwest, the floor plan is anything but ancient history. A cozy courtyard gives way to a long covered porch with nooks for sitting and open-air dining at the front. The double-door entry opens on the right to a gracious living room highlighted by a corner fireplace. Just beyond is the formal dining room with adjacent butler's pantry and access to the porch dining area. To the left of the foyer is a private office with convenient built-ins and attached powder room. The kitchen, family room and morning room separate family bedrooms from the master suite. Both sleeping areas are luxurious with whirlpool spas and separate showers. The master suite also boasts its own exercise room. Though connected to the main house, the guest suite has a private entrance as well, and includes another corner fireplace. Maintain the family fleet in the spacious three-car garage.

—DESIGN BY—
HOME PLANNERS

◆ Here's a rambling ranch with a unique configuration. Massive double doors at the front entrance are sheltered by a covered porch. This well-zoned plan offers exceptional one-story livability for the active family. The central foyer routes traffic effectively while featuring a feeling of spaciousness. Note the dramatic columns that accentuate the big living room with its high 17'-8" ceiling. This interesting, angular room has a commanding corner fireplace with a raised hearth, a wall of windows, a doorway to the huge rear covered porch and a pass-through to the kitchen. The informal family room has direct access to the rear porch and is handy to the three children's bedrooms. At the opposite end of the plan, and guaranteed its full measure of privacy, is the master suite. The master bedroom, with its high ceiling, is large and enjoys direct access to the rear porch.

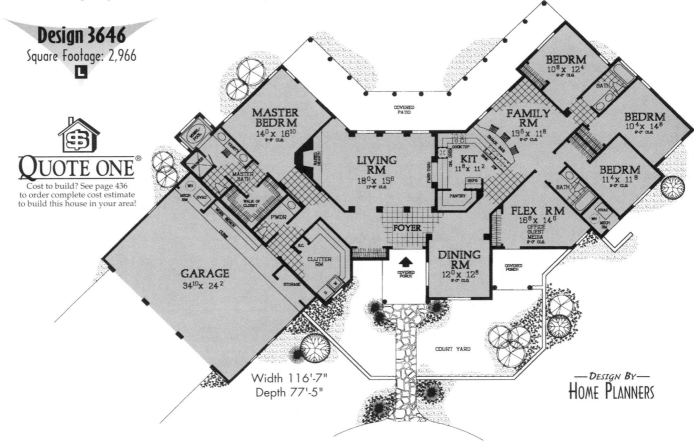

Design 3646
Square Footage: 2,966
L

Quote One
Cost to build? See page 436 to order complete cost estimate to build this house in your area!

Width 116'-7"
Depth 77'-5"

— DESIGN BY —
HOME PLANNERS

◆ The impressive, double-door entry to the walled courtyard sets the tone for this Santa Fe masterpiece home. The expansive great room shows off its casual style with a centerpiece fireplace and abundant windows overlooking the patio. Joining the great room is the formal dining room, again graced with windows and patio doors. The large gourmet kitchen has an eat-in snack bar and joins the family room to create a warm atmosphere for casual entertaining. Family room extras include a fireplace, entertainment built-ins and double doors to the front courtyard. Just off the family room are the two large family bedrooms, which share a private bath. The relaxing master suite is privately located off the great room and has double doors to the back patio.

Design 3694
Square Footage: 2,226
L

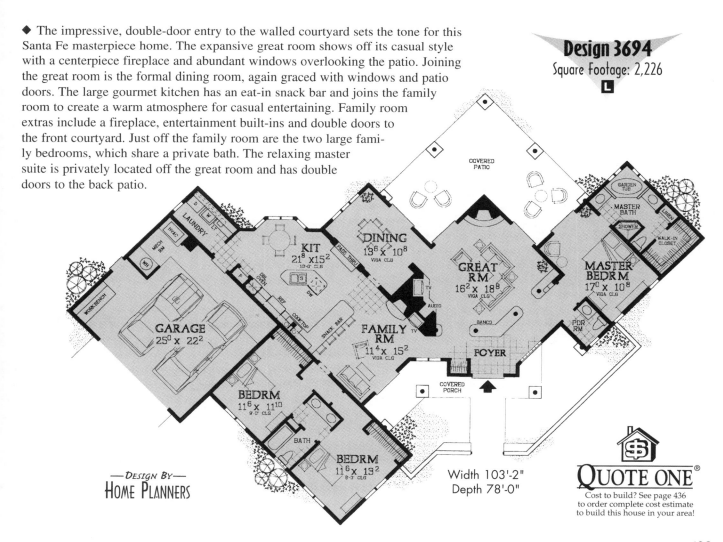

Width 103'-2"
Depth 78'-0"

— DESIGN BY —
HOME PLANNERS

Design 3642
Square Footage: 2,945

◆ Flat roofs, soft, curved wall lines, masses of stucco, exposed rafter tails, an arched privacy wall, carriage lamps and a courtyard are the distinguishing factors of this ranch house. Inside, twin archways provide access to the beam-ceilinged family room. The modified U-shaped kitchen and its breakfast area are open to the family room. The kitchen will be a delight in which to work with its island, pantry and fine counter space. Down the hall are four bedrooms and two baths. Each of the three bedrooms for the children is sizable and handy to the main bath with its double lavatories. The master suite is outstanding. The master bedroom has fine blank wall areas for flexible furniture placement. It has a view of the patio as well as direct access to it.

— Design By —
Home Planners

Width 73'-0"
Depth 68'-10"

Quote One®
Cost to build? See page 436
to order complete cost estimate
to build this house in your area!

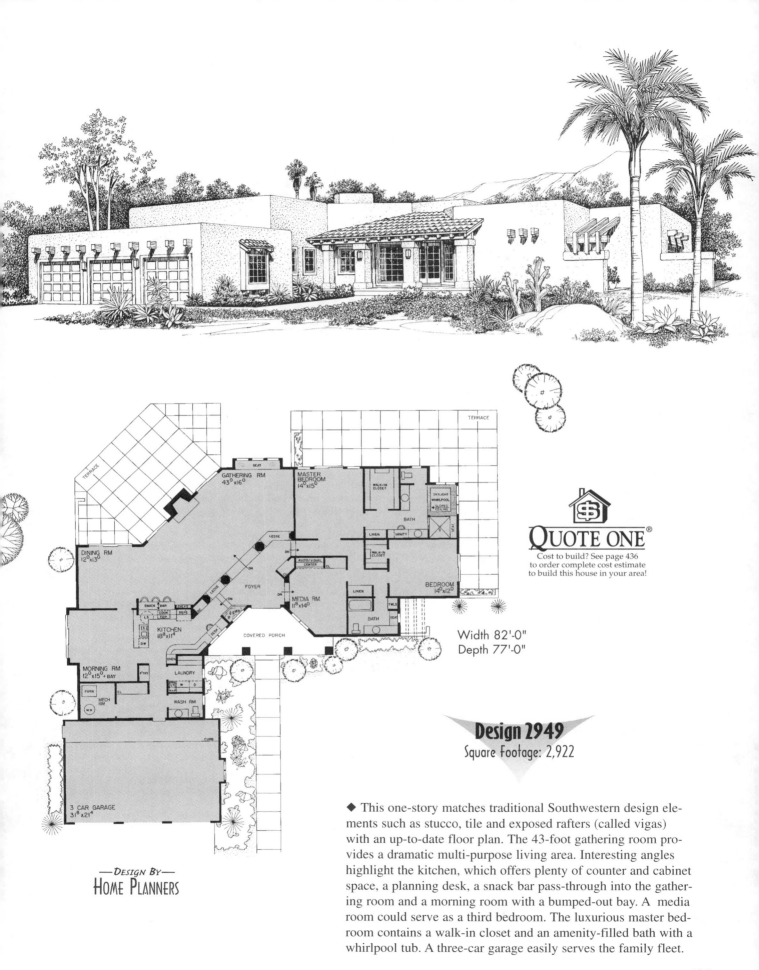

Quote One®

Cost to build? See page 436
to order complete cost estimate
to build this house in your area!

Width 82'-0"
Depth 77'-0"

Design 2949
Square Footage: 2,922

—DESIGN BY—
HOME PLANNERS

◆ This one-story matches traditional Southwestern design elements such as stucco, tile and exposed rafters (called vigas) with an up-to-date floor plan. The 43-foot gathering room provides a dramatic multi-purpose living area. Interesting angles highlight the kitchen, which offers plenty of counter and cabinet space, a planning desk, a snack bar pass-through into the gathering room and a morning room with a bumped-out bay. A media room could serve as a third bedroom. The luxurious master bedroom contains a walk-in closet and an amenity-filled bath with a whirlpool tub. A three-car garage easily serves the family fleet.

Design 3486
Square Footage: 2,000

—DESIGN BY—
HOME PLANNERS

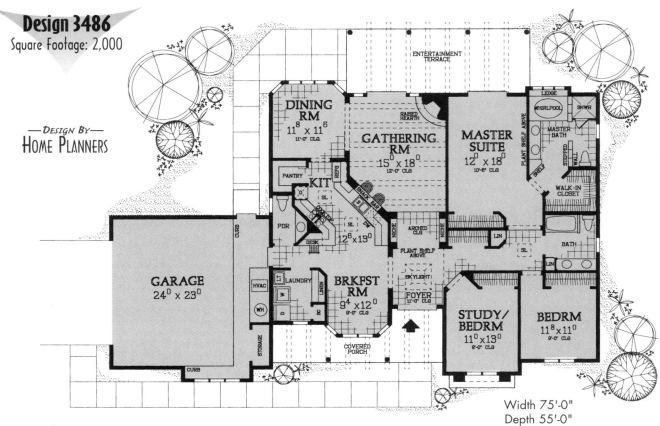

Width 75'-0"
Depth 55'-0"

◆ This classic stucco design provides a cool retreat in any climate. From the covered porch, enter the skylit foyer to find an arched ceiling leading to the central gathering room with its raised-hearth fireplace and terrace access. A connecting corner dining room is conveniently located near the amenity-filled kitchen that features an abundant pantry, a snack bar and a separate breakfast area. The large master bedroom includes terrace access and a master bath with a whirlpool tub, a separate shower and plenty of closet space. A second bedroom and a study that can be converted to a bedroom complete this wonderful plan.

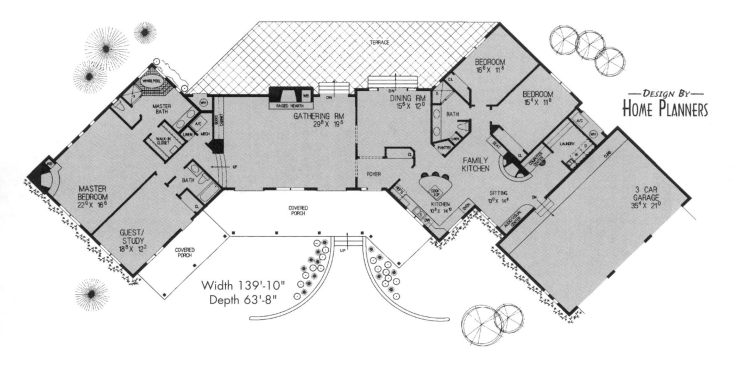

—DESIGN BY—
HOME PLANNERS

Width 139'-10"
Depth 63'-8"

Design 3405
Square Footage: 3,144
L

◆ In classic Santa Fe style, this home strikes a beautiful combination of historic exterior detailing and open floor planning on the inside. A covered porch running the width of the facade leads to an entry foyer that connects to a huge gathering room with a fireplace and a formal dining room. The family kitchen allows special space for casual gatherings. The right wing of the home holds two family bedrooms and a full bath. The left wing is devoted to the master suite and a guest room or a study.

Quote One®
Cost to build? See page 436 to order complete cost estimate to build this house in your area!

This home, as shown in the photograph, may differ from the actual blueprints. For more detailed information, please check the floor plans carefully.

Photo by Allen Maertz Photography

Width 94'-6"
Depth 79'-11"

COVERED PATIO

COVERED REAR PORCH

PRIVATE PATIO

TRELLIS ABOVE

SEAT

TUB

MBA

LINEN

SEAT

SHWR

— DESIGN BY —
HOME PLANNERS

TRELLIS ABOVE

TRELLIS ABOVE

FAMILY ENTERTAINMENT PATIO

KIT
11⁰ x 10⁸
10'-0" CLG.

PANTRY

REFG

WET BAR

LIVING RM
15⁰ x 15⁸
11'-6" CLG.

STUDY
11⁶ x 11⁰

MASTER BEDRM
16⁸ x 14²
10'-0" CLG.

WALK-IN CLOSET

NOOK
8⁸ x 9²
10'-0" CLG.

LAUNDRY

FAMILY RM
12⁷ x 14⁰
10'-0" CLG.

DINING RM
15⁰ x 11⁰
11'-6" CLG.

SLOPED CEILING

FOYER

PDR.

BEDRM
13² x 12⁶
10'-0" CLG.

STORAGE ROOM

WORK SHOP

HVAC

COVERED PATIO

COVERED PORCH

LINEN

WALK-IN CLOSET

BATH

WALK-IN CLOSET

HVAC

QUOTE ONE®
Cost to build? See page 436
to order complete cost estimate
to build this house in your area!

GARAGE
21⁹ x 29⁰

CURB

PRIVACY WALL

BEDRM
15² x 10¹⁰
10'-0" CLG.

PRIVATE PATIO

Design 3436
Square Footage: 2,573
L

◆ Oversized, double wood doors and an elegant tile foyer set the impressive tone of this Southwestern classic. The grand living room and adjoining dining room are the perfect backdrop for entertaining, with a fireplace and access to both the front and rear covered patios. Casual living is just as inviting in the family room with a snack bar and its own fireplace with an extended bench. The large, gourmet kitchen has a breakfast nook that opens onto the family entertainment patio. The sleeping zone features two family bedrooms with walk-in closets and private entrances to the compartmented bath. The master suite has a private patio, huge walk-in closet and a master bath with luxe appointments such as a spa tub, dual vanity and an oversized, walk-in shower.

Width 85'-8"
Depth 47'-0"

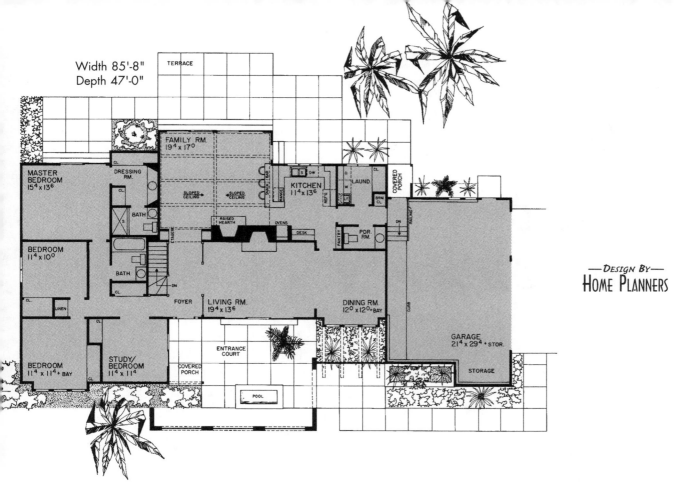

TERRACE

FAMILY RM.
19⁴ x 17⁰

MASTER
BEDROOM
15⁴ x 13⁶

DRESSING
RM.

KITCHEN
11⁴ x 13⁶

LAUND.

COVERED
PORCH

SLOPED
CEILING

SLOPED
CEILING

BATH

CL.

RAISED
HEARTH

OVENS

DESK

PANTRY

PDR.
RM.

BEDROOM
11⁴ x 10⁰

BATH

FOYER

LIVING RM.
19⁴ x 13⁶

DINING RM.
12⁰ x 12⁰ + BAY

GARAGE
21⁴ x 29⁴ + STOR.

LINEN

ENTRANCE
COURT

BEDROOM
11⁴ x 11⁴ + BAY

STUDY/
BEDROOM
11⁴ x 11⁴

COVERED
PORCH

STORAGE

POOL

—DESIGN BY—
HOME PLANNERS

Design 2820
Square Footage: 2,261
L D

◆ A privacy wall around the courtyard with pool and trellised planter area makes a gracious area by which to enter this one-story design. The Spanish flavor is accented by the grillework and the tiled roof. The front living room has sliding glass doors, which open to the entrance court. The adjacent dining room features a bay window. Informal activities will be enjoyed in the rear family room with a sloped, beamed ceiling, a raised-hearth fireplace, sliding glass doors to the terrace and a snack bar. The sleeping wing can remain quiet away from the plan's activity centers. Notice the three-car garage with extra storage space.

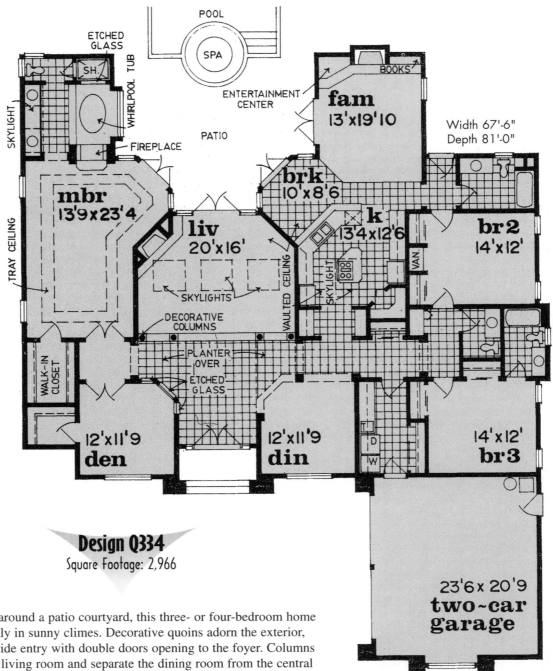

PUL

SPA

ETCHED
GLASS

SH

WHIRLPOOL TUB

SKYLIGHT

FIREPLACE

mbr
13'9 x 23'4

TRAY CEILING

WALK-IN CLOSET

12'x11'9
den

ENTERTAINMENT
CENTER

PATIO

liv
20'x16'

SKYLIGHTS

DECORATIVE
COLUMNS

PLANTER
OVER

ETCHED
GLASS

brk
10'x8'6

VAULTED CEILING

BOOKS

fam
13'x19'10

Width 67'-6"
Depth 81'-0"

k
13'4x12'6

SKYLIGHT

VAN.

br2
14'x12'

12'x11'9
din

W
D
T

14'x12'
br3

23'6 x 20'9
two-car
garage

Design Q334
Square Footage: 2,966

◆ Wrapping around a patio courtyard, this three- or four-bedroom home works perfectly in sunny climes. Decorative quoins adorn the exterior, including a wide entry with double doors opening to the foyer. Columns introduce the living room and separate the dining room from the central hall. The living room is further enhanced by skylights, a vaulted ceiling, a fireplace and French doors to the patio beyond. An island kitchen features a peninsular counter overlooking the breakfast room and a roomy pantry. The breakfast room also has double doors to the patio. A nearby family room sports built-ins, another fireplace and more patio access. Bedrooms are split with the family bedrooms—each with its own bath— on the right and the master suite on the left. The master bedroom has a tray ceiling, walk-in closet, patio access and a through-fireplace to the master bath. Look for a spa tub and separate shower here. A cozy den opens through double doors in the master suite entry. The two-car garage is accessed through the service entrance. Plans include details for both a basement and a crawlspace foundation. Details for both elevations are also included.

—DESIGN BY—
SELECT HOME DESIGNS

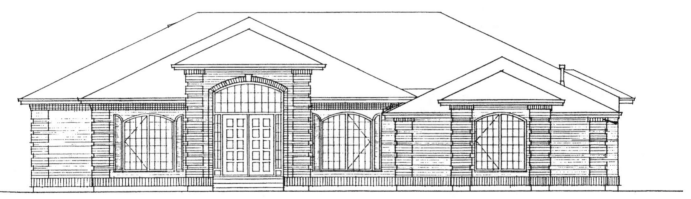

Alternate Elevation

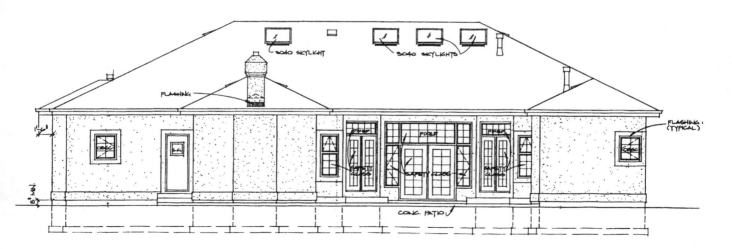

Rear Elevation

411

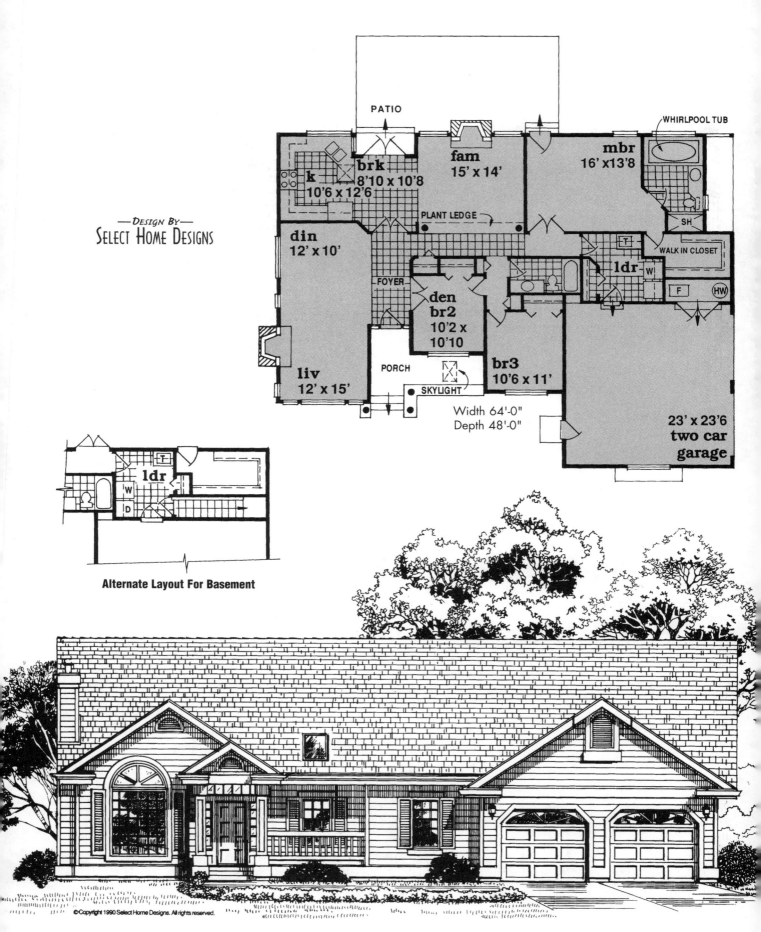

PATIO

fam
15' x 14'

WHIRLPOOL TUB

brk
8'10 x 10'8

mbr
16' x13'8

k
10'6 x 12'6

DESIGN BY
SELECT HOME DESIGNS

PLANT LEDGE

SH

din
12' x 10'

WALK IN CLOSET

FOYER

ldr

den
br2
10'2 x
10'10

W

F

HW

liv
12' x 15'

PORCH

br3
10'6 x 11'

SKYLIGHT

Width 64'-0"
Depth 48'-0"

23' x 23'6
two car
garage

ldr

W
D

Alternate Layout For Basement

© Copyright 1990 Select Home Designs. All rights reserved.

Alternate Elevation

Design Q372
Square Footage: 1,883

◆ Finish this home in either California stucco or horizontal siding, with the garage opening to the front or the side of the home. Rooflines vary depending on your choice. The interior retains the same great floor plan. From a skylit, covered porch, the plan begins with a large entry opening to the living room with fireplace and den—or Bedroom 2—which can be accessed through double doors in the entry or a single door in the hall. Decorative columns line the hall and define the family room space. A fireplace, flanked by windows, is a focal point in this casual living area. The nearby breakfast room opens to the patio and connects the family room to the U-shaped kitchen. The master bedroom is huge—and amenity filled. It also has patio access and features a bath with whirlpool tub and separate shower. An additional bedroom is served by a full bath. A large laundry room connects the two-car garage to the main house. Plans include details for both a basement and a crawlspace foundation.

View of Family Room from Breakfast

Design 3422
Square Footage: 1,932

L

COVERED PORCH

MASTER BATH

WHIRLPOOL

S

WALK-IN CLOSET

MASTER BEDROOM
13⁰ x 13⁸
SLOPED CEILING

FAMILY RM
12⁸ x 18⁶
SLOPED CEILING

BREAKFAST
7⁶ x 9⁴

KIT.
9⁴ x 13⁴
SNACK BAR
DW
OVENS
COOK TOP
REF
PANTRY
SLOPED CEILING

BEDROOM
9⁸ x 9¹⁰

CL

BATH

PDR RM

HALF WALL

DINING
13⁴ x 9⁶
SLOPED CEILING

S
BAR

LINEN

LT

BEDROOM
12⁰ x 10⁰

LAUND
W
D

STUDY
9⁸ x 9⁶

DN

SLOPED CEILING

WH
FURN
CL

CURB

FOYER

HALF WALL

LIVING RM
13⁴ x 13⁴

COVERED PORCH

GARAGE
21⁴ x 19⁸

Width 50'-0"
Depth 68'-0"

◆ An enclosed entry garden greets visitors to this charming Southwestern home. Inside, the foyer is flanked by formal and informal living areas—a living room and dining room to the right and a cozy study to the left. To the rear, a large family room, breakfast room and open kitchen have access to a covered porch and overlook the back yard. Notice the fireplace and bay window. The three-bedroom sleeping area includes a master with a spacious bath with whirlpool.

—DESIGN BY—
HOME PLANNERS

Quote One®
Cost to build? See page 436 to order complete cost estimate to build this house in your area!

Design 3419
Square Footage 1,965

L

BRKFST RM 11⁸ X 7⁸

COVERED PORCH

KITCHEN 11⁸ X 11⁸

DW

REF'G

RANGE

S

DINING 7⁸ X 10⁰

LIVING RM 12² X 15⁸

WHIRLPOOL

S

UP

BATH

MASTER BEDROOM 14⁸ X 15¹⁰

WALK-IN CLOSET

BEDROOM 10⁶ X 10⁰

SNACK BAR

BATH

LEDGE

FAMILY RM 19⁴ X 13⁰

PORCH

CURB

CL

FOYER

CL

L'IN

CL

CL

BEDROOM 9¹⁰ X 10¹⁰

BEDROOM 10⁶ X 11⁴

WASH RM

COVERED PORCH

W

D

LAUND/ MECH

WH

FURN

GARAGE 19⁴ X 20⁰

Width 56'-0"
Depth 56'-0"

◆ By combining the well-defined look of Floridian styling with just a hint of Tudor detailing, we've created a truly unique exterior that works well in any area—but was designed for the Florida lifestyle. Brick accents and wood detailing make the difference in this plan. The day-to-day living spaces in this home are kept to the left of the plan: large family room with fireplace, hard-working kitchen and dandy breakfast room. Formal areas are focused at the center of the plan and overlook the rear covered porch. Four bedrooms (in such a modest square footage!) are all to the right of the home. The master suite has a hexagonal bath with a compartmented shower and toilet and a whirlpool tub. The walk-in closet means easy access for the owner. The family bedrooms have access to a good-sized bath in the hall.

—DESIGN BY—
Home Planners

QUOTE ONE®

Cost to build? See page 436
to order complete cost estimate
to build this house in your area!

415

—DESIGN BY—
SELECT HOME DESIGNS

◆ Choose either the California stucco option or the version with horizontal siding and brick for the facade of this home. Details for both are included in the plans. An interesting floor plan awaits inside. A kitchen and breakfast room reside just beyond the entry and are open to a long living room/dining room combination. This area has a vaulted ceiling, a fireplace and access to the rear patio. A plant ledge decorates the hall entry and is lit by a centered skylight. Three bedrooms line the right side of the plan. Family bedrooms share a full hall bath. The master suite is to the rear and has an plant ledge at its entry, a vaulted ceiling and a bath with whirlpool tub. A door to the rear yard brightens the master bedroom. A laundry alcove sits in a service entrance to the two-car garage. If you choose, you may build this plan with a basement that can be expanded at a later time.

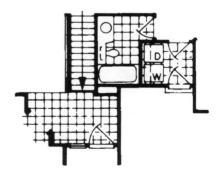

Basement Stair Location

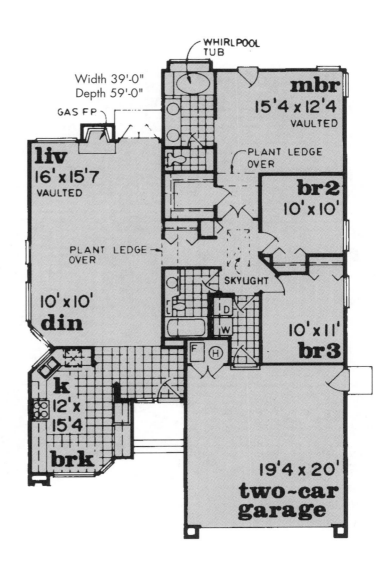

Width 39'-0"
Depth 59'-0"

GAS FP

WHIRLPOOL
TUB

liv
16' x 15'7
VAULTED

mbr
15'4 x 12'4
VAULTED

PLANT LEDGE
OVER

br2
10' x 10'

PLANT LEDGE
OVER

SKYLIGHT

10' x 10'
din

10' x 11'
br3

k
12' x
15'4

brk

19'4 x 20'
**two-car
garage**

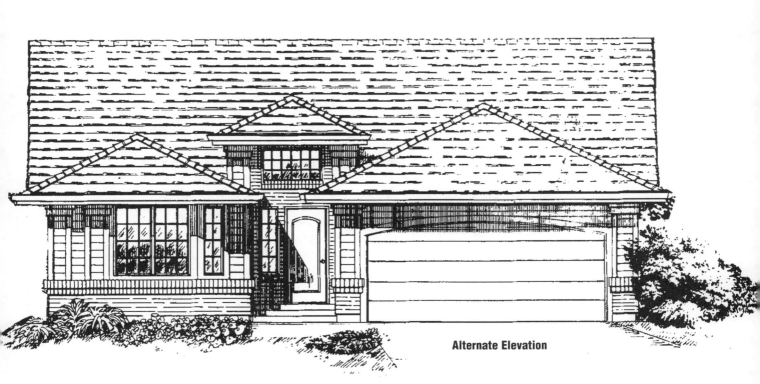

Alternate Elevation

Design Q314
Square Footage: 1,365

—DESIGN BY—
SELECT HOME DESIGNS

◆ This design offers the option of a traditional wood-sided plan or a cool, stucco version. Details for both facades are included in the plans. The interior offers a very comfortable floor plan in a smaller foot print. The off-set entry is covered and opens to a vaulted foyer with coat closet. Decorative columns and a three-foot high wall mark the boundary of the living room, which is vaulted and warmed by a gas fireplace. The dining area is nearby and connects to a U-shaped kitchen with peninsular counter. Both have cathedral ceilings. A den in the hall might be used as a third bedroom, if you choose. An additional family bedroom has a walk-in closet and full bath nearby. A vaulted ceiling highlights the master bedroom. Additional features here include a walk-in closet and a fully appointed bath. A two-car garage remains in the front of the plan and acts as a shield for the bedrooms. Plans include details for both a basement and a crawlspace foundation.

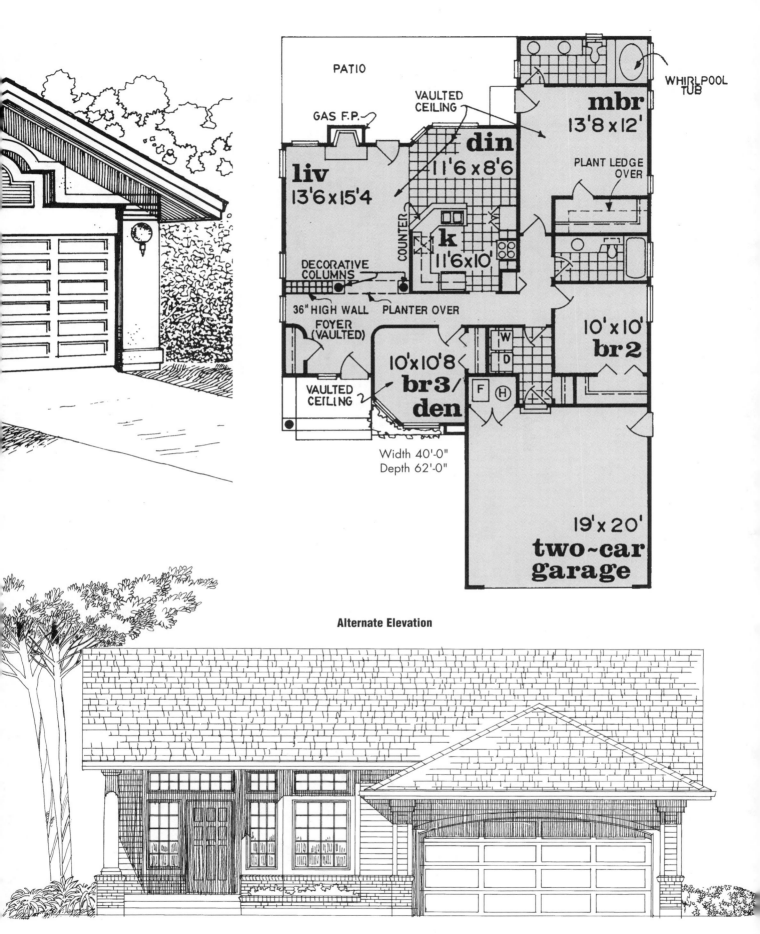

PATIO

GAS F.P.

VAULTED
CEILING

liv
13'6 x 15'4

din
11'6 x 8'6

COUNTER

k
11'6 x 10'

mbr
13'8 x 12'

WHIRLPOOL
TUB

PLANT LEDGE
OVER

DECORATIVE
COLUMNS

36" HIGH WALL   PLANTER OVER

FOYER
(VAULTED)

10' x 10'8
**br3/
den**

VAULTED
CEILING

W
D

F   H

10' x 10'
br2

Width 40'-0"
Depth 62'-0"

19' x 20'
**two~car
garage**

Alternate Elevation

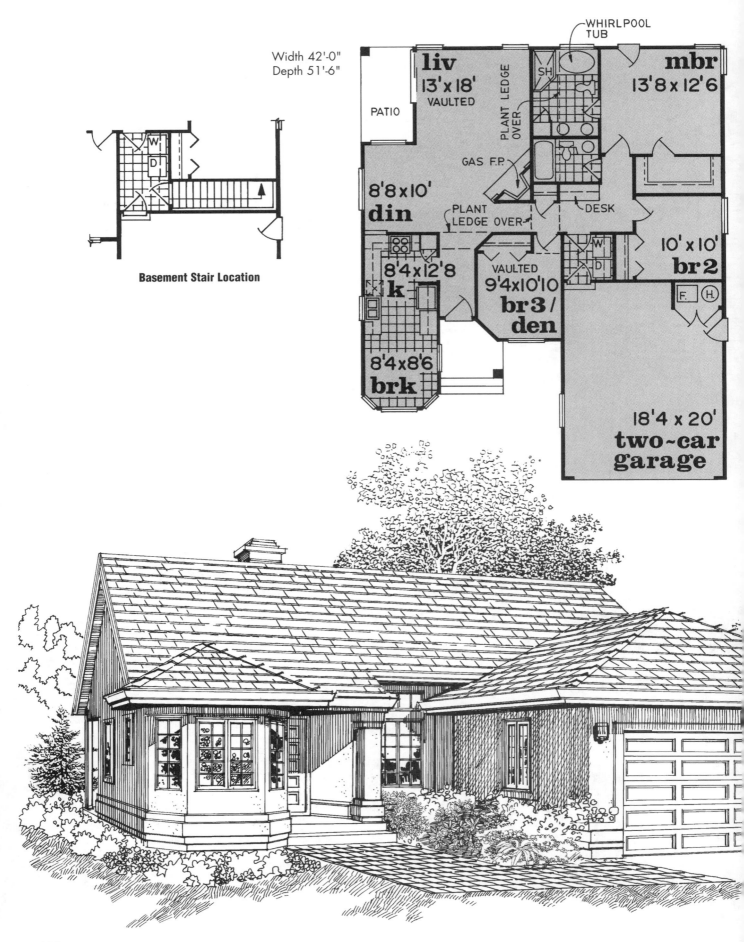

Width 42'-0"
Depth 51'-6"

WHIRLPOOL TUB

liv
13' x 18'
VAULTED

PATIO

PLANT LEDGE OVER

SH

mbr
13'8 x 12'6

GAS F.P.

8'8 x 10'
din

PLANT LEDGE OVER

DESK

VAULTED
9'4 x 10'10
**br3/
den**

8'4 x 12'8
k

W
D

10' x 10'
br2

F.   H.

8'4 x 8'6
brk

18'4 x 20'
**two~car
garage**

W
D

Basement Stair Location

Alternate Elevation

Design Q316
Square Footage: 1,328

◆ The choice is yours: California stucco or horizontal wood siding. Both are appealing and true to their classic traditions. Plans include details for both. The floor plan is designed for living areas to the rear of the plan, to capture views and take advantage of a rear patio. The living room is vaulted and has a corner fireplace and sliding glass doors. The L-shaped kitchen and breakfast room sit to the front. The kitchen has abundant counter space and a pass-through to the dining room. A vaulted ceiling graces the den (or third bedroom) which is also brightened by a transom window. A handy hall desk can serve the student in the family or work as a planning desk. A great master retreat awaits at the back of the plan. It holds a walk-in closet, rear access and a bath with whirlpool tub, separate shower and double vanities. The additional family bedroom has use of a full bath in the hall. A laundry alcove leads the way through a service entrance to the two-car garage. Plans include details for both a basement and a crawlspace foundation.

—DESIGN BY—
SELECT HOME DESIGNS

Design Q272
Square Footage: 1,375

—Design By—
Select Home Designs

Alternate Elevation

◆ This compact, affordable plan offers a choice of exteriors. The stucco version has box windows and a weather-protected entry. The heritage version offers a covered veranda and circle-top window. Plans include details for both. Off the foyer, the living room boasts a vaulted ceiling and a wood-burning fireplace with wood bin. The dining room has an optional buffet nook and sliding glass doors to the patio. The kitchen and attached breakfast room enjoy views of the garden and are directly in line with the entry hall. A master bedroom and two family bedrooms sit to the left of the plan. The family bedrooms share a full hall bath, while the master has a private bath. A stairway just off the breakfast room leads to a basement which can be developed into living or sleeping space at a later time.

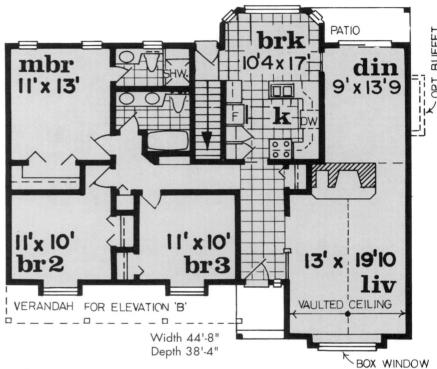

mbr 11' x 13'

brk 10'4 x 17'

PATIO

din 9' x 13'9

OPT BUFFET

SHW.

k

DW

F

11' x 10' br2

11' x 10' br3

13' x 19'10 liv

VAULTED CEILING

VERANDAH FOR ELEVATION 'B'

Width 44'-8"
Depth 38'-4"

BOX WINDOW

verandah
58'-0" x 12'-0"

recreation
25'-0" x 35'-0"

storage

garage
23'-4" x 24'-0"

up

up

One-Story Vacation And Second Homes

Design 6622
Square Footage: 2,190

—DESIGN BY—
THE SATER
DESIGN COLLECTION

QUOTE ONE®

Cost to build? See page 436
to order complete cost estimate
to build this house in your area!

©The Sater Group, Inc.

lanai
58'-0" x 10'-8"

master
suite
13'-0" x 15'-0"
9'-4" stepped clg.

built ins

fireplace

built ins

opt. aquarium

grand room
20'-0" x 18'-0" avg.
tray ceiling

kitchen
11' x 11'

arch

nook
11'-0" x 9'-4"

br. 2
12'-0" x 11'-4"
9'-4" flat clg.

utility

study
11'-0" x 11'-0"
9'-4" flat clg.

foyer

down

dining
10'-10" x 15'-0"
9'-4" flat clg.

br. 3
12'-0" x 11'-0"
9'-4" flat clg.

down

entry porch

planter

Width 58'-0"
Depth 54'-0"

◆ A strikingly simple staircase leads to the dramatic entry of this contemporary design. The foyer opens to an expansive grand room with a fireplace and a built-in entertainment center. An expansive lanai opens from the living area and offers good inside/outside relationships. For more traditional occasions and planned events, a front-facing dining room offers a place for quiet, elegant entertaining. The master suite features a lavish bath with two sizable walk-in closets, a windowed whirlpool tub, twin lavatories and a compartmented toilet. Double doors open from the gallery hall to a secluded study that is convenient to the master bedroom. Two additional bedrooms share a private hall and a full bath on the opposite side of the plan.

This home, as shown in the photograph, may differ from the actual blueprints.
For more detailed information, please check the floor plans carefully.

Photo by Oscar Thompson

— DESIGN BY —
SELECT HOME DESIGNS

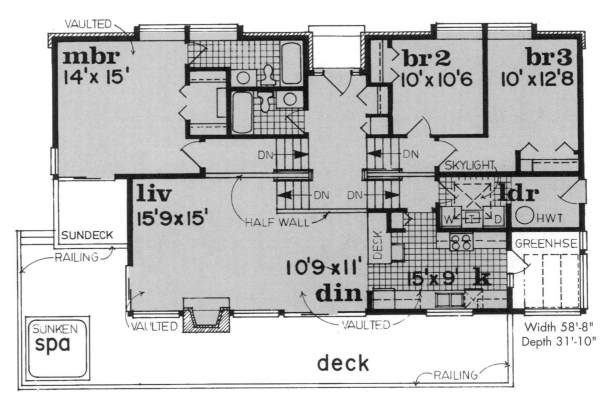

VAULTED

mbr
14' x 15'

br 2
10' x 10'6"

br 3
10' x 12'8"

DN

DN

DN

DN

SKYLIGHT

ldr

W | D | W/D | HWT

SUNDECK

RAILING

liv
15'9 x 15'

HALF WALL

DECK

GREENHSE

din
10'9 x 11'

k
15' x 9'

SUNKEN
spa

VAULTED

VAULTED

Width 58'-8"
Depth 31'-10"

deck

RAILING

Design Q283
Square Footage: 1,679

◆ Sided in horizontal wood with a large stone fireplace, this country retreat is the image of a rustic hideaway. A recessed entry opens to a central hall with bedrooms flanking it. A few steps down, the living areas are positioned to take advantage of outdoor views and the long deck with sunken spa that wraps two sides of the design. The living room, dining room and kitchen are all vault-ed. The living room is further enhanced by a fireplace. A greenhouse just beyond the kitchen can serve as a breakfast room, if desired. Two family bedrooms share the use of a skylit bath and also have box-bay windows. The master suite has double box-bays, a walk-in closet, vaulted ceiling and a private sundeck. Clerestory windows illuminate the main entry and hallway.

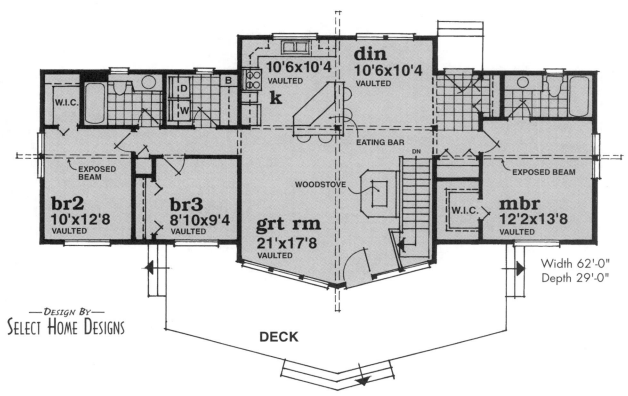

din
10'6x10'4
VAULTED

10'6x10'4
VAULTED

k

W.I.C.

D
W

B

EATING BAR

DN

EXPOSED
BEAM

WOODSTOVE

EXPOSED BEAM

br2
10'x12'8
VAULTED

br3
8'10x9'4
VAULTED

grt rm
21'x17'8
VAULTED

W.I.C.

mbr
12'2x13'8
VAULTED

Width 62'-0"
Depth 29'-0"

—DESIGN BY—
SELECT HOME DESIGNS

DECK

◆ This three-bedroom leisure home is perfect for the family that spends casual time out of doors. An expansive wall of glass gives a spectacular view to the great room and accentuates the high vaulted ceilings throughout the design. The great room is also warmed by a hearth and is open to the dining room and L-shaped kitchen. A triangular snack bar graces the kitchen and provides space for casual meals. Bedrooms are split, with the master bedroom on the right side of the plan and family bedrooms on the left. The master has an exposed beam in the ceiling, a walk-in closet and a full bath with soaking tub. Family bedrooms share a full bath. Plans include both basement and crawlspace foundations.

Design Q516
Square Footage: 1,405

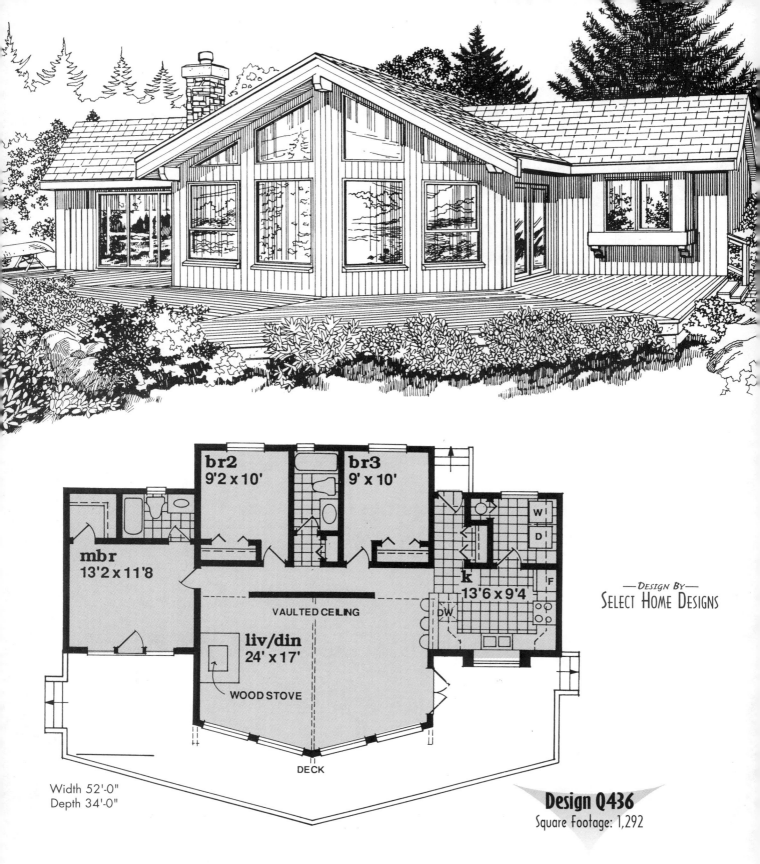

br2
9'2 x 10'

br3
9' x 10'

mbr
13'2 x 11'8

k
13'6 x 9'4

W

D

F

DW

VAULTED CEILING

liv/din
24' x 17'

WOOD STOVE

DECK

Width 52'-0"
Depth 34'-0"

DESIGN BY
SELECT HOME DESIGNS

Design Q436
Square Footage: 1,292

◆ This three-bedroom cottage is cozy and comfortable, yet room enough for the whole family. Its vertical wood siding and massive chimney stack grace the facade. Inside, a wall of windows in the living area allows for wonderful views; a vaulted ceiling and a wood stove further enhance its appeal. Double glass doors lead to a full-width deck that surrounds the living/dining area. The U-shaped kitchen features a box-bay window over the double sink and a pass-through counter to the dining area. Just beyond is the laundry. The master bedroom leaves nothing to chance, with deck access, a walk-in closet and full private bath. Family bedrooms share a full bath that separates them.

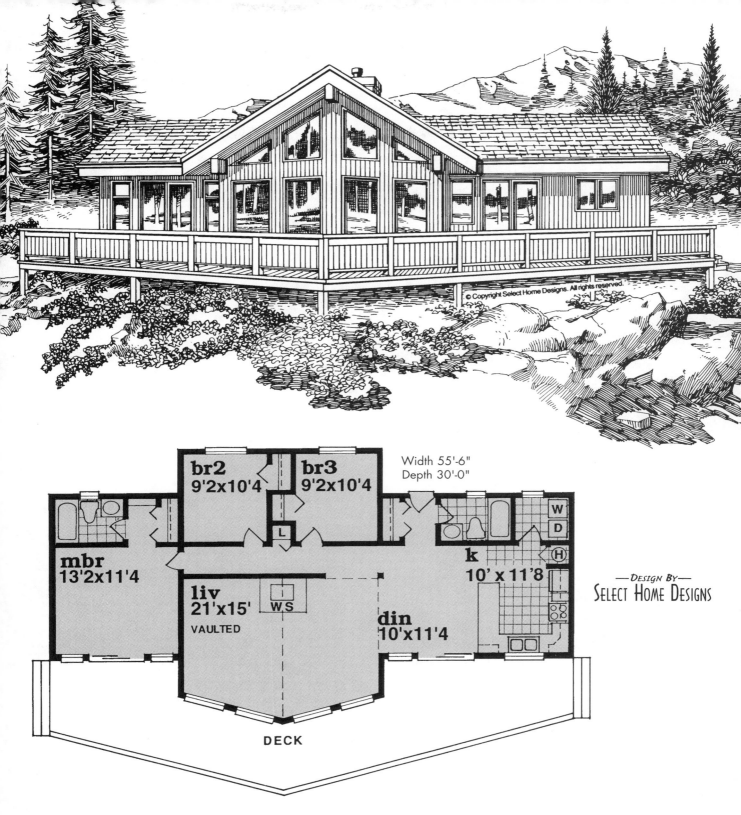

Width 55'-6"
Depth 30'-0"

br2
9'2x10'4

br3
9'2x10'4

mbr
13'2x11'4

liv
21'x15'
VAULTED

din
10'x11'4

k
10' x 11'8

W
D
H

L

W S

DECK

— DESIGN BY —
SELECT HOME DESIGNS

Design Q429
Square Footage: 1,230

◆ This is a grand vacation or retirement home, designed for views and the outdoor lifestyle. The full-width deck complements the abundant windows in rooms facing its way. The living room is made for gathering. It features a vaulted ceiling, a fireplace and full-height windows overlooking the deck. Open to this living space is the dining room with sliding glass doors to the outdoors and a pass-through counter to the U-shaped kitchen. The kitchen connects to a laundry area and has a window over the sink for more outdoor views. Two family bedrooms sit in the middle of the plan. They share a full bath. The master suite has a private bath and deck views. The basement option for this plan adds 1,296 square feet to its total and extends the depth to 33'.

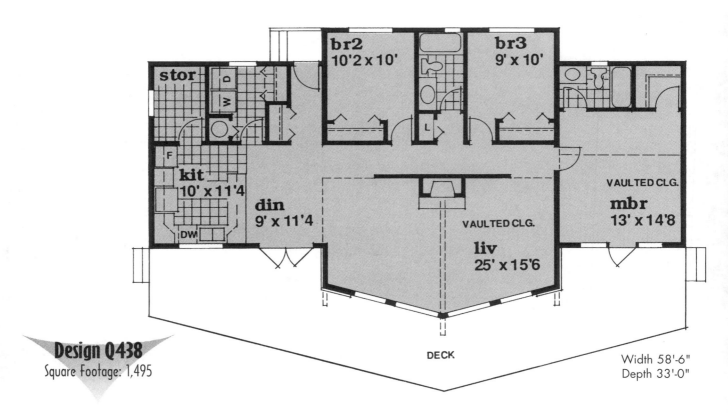

stor

br2
10'2 x 10'

br3
9' x 10'

kit
10' x 11'4

din
9' x 11'4

VAULTED CLG.

mbr
13' x 14'8

VAULTED CLG.

liv
25' x 15'6

DW

Design Q438
Square Footage: 1,495

DECK

Width 58'-6"
Depth 33'-0"

◆ This three-bedroom cottage has just the right rustic mix of vertical wood siding and stone accents. Inside, the living is pure resort-style comfort. High vaulted ceilings are featured throughout the living room and master bedroom. The living room also has a fireplace and full-height windows overlooking the deck. The dining room has double door access to the deck; the master bedroom has a single door that opens to the deck. A convenient kitchen has a U-shaped work area with a large storage space beyond. A laundry room with closet is also nearby. Two family bedrooms share a bath that is situated between them. The master suite features a walk-in closet and private bath.

— DESIGN BY —
SELECT HOME DESIGNS

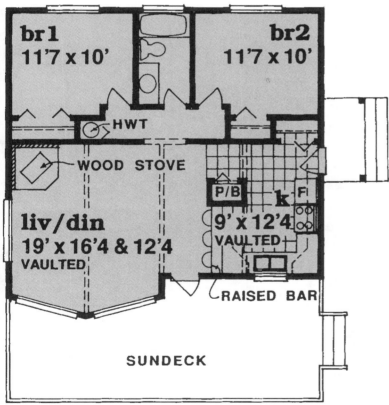

br1
11'7 x 10'

br2
11'7 x 10'

HWT

WOOD STOVE

P/B **k** **F**

liv/din
19' x 16'4 & 12'4
VAULTED

9' x 12'4
VAULTED

RAISED BAR

SUNDECK

Width 30'-0"
Depth 30'-0"

Design Q422
Square Footage: 825

◆ Compact and economical to build, this vacation home is nonetheless quite comfortable. It will fit easily into just about any vacation setting, from seaside to mountainside. A sundeck to the front stretches the width of the home and opens to a vaulted living room/dining room area with corner wood stove and full-height window wall. The kitchen has a raised bar with seating space open to the living area and also features a U-shaped workspace, a window over the sink and a large pantry or broom closet. Two bedrooms are to the back. They have wall closets and share a full bath with soaking tub.

—DESIGN BY—
SELECT HOME DESIGNS

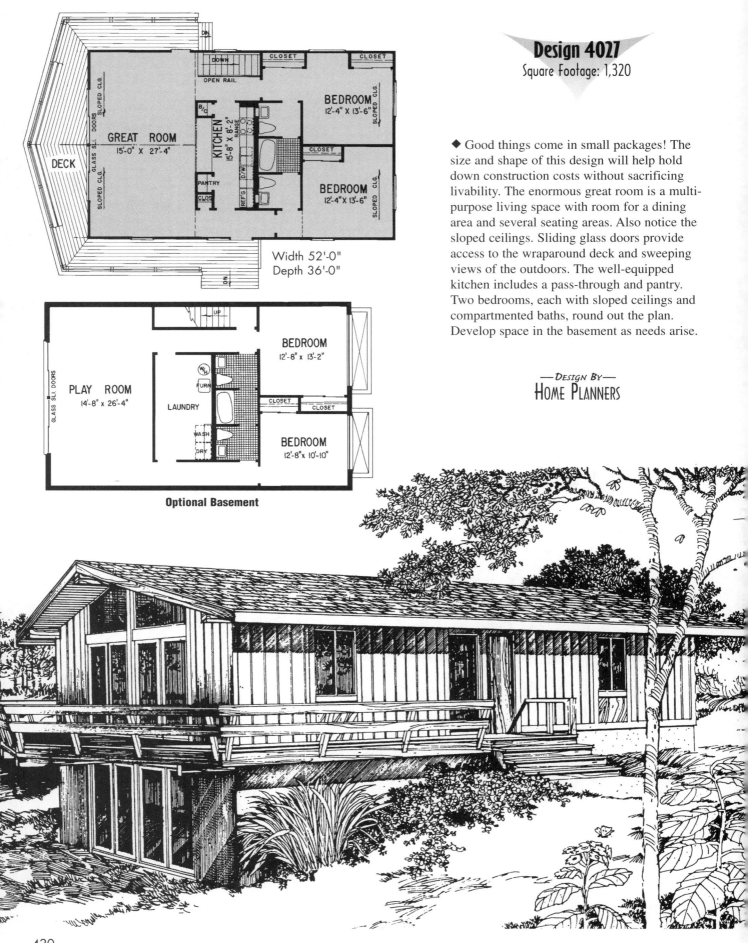

Design 4027
Square Footage: 1,320

DECK

GREAT ROOM
15'-0" X 27'-4"

KITCHEN
15'-8" X 8'-2"

DOWN

OPEN RAIL

CLOSET   CLOSET

BEDROOM
12'-4" X 13'-6"

CLOSET

BEDROOM
12'-4" X 13'-6"

B/C

RANGE

PANTRY

REF'G   D/W

CLOS

SLOPED CLG.   GLASS SLI. DOORS   SLOPED CLG.   SLOPED CLG.   SLOPED CLG.

Width 52'-0"
Depth 36'-0"

PLAY ROOM
14'-8" x 26'-4"

BEDROOM
12'-8" x 13'-2"

UP

W/H

FURN

LAUNDRY

CLOSET   CLOSET

WASH   DRY

BEDROOM
12'-8" x 10'-10"

GLASS SLI. DOORS

Optional Basement

◆ Good things come in small packages! The size and shape of this design will help hold down construction costs without sacrificing livability. The enormous great room is a multi-purpose living space with room for a dining area and several seating areas. Also notice the sloped ceilings. Sliding glass doors provide access to the wraparound deck and sweeping views of the outdoors. The well-equipped kitchen includes a pass-through and pantry. Two bedrooms, each with sloped ceilings and compartmented baths, round out the plan. Develop space in the basement as needs arise.

—Design By—
HOME PLANNERS

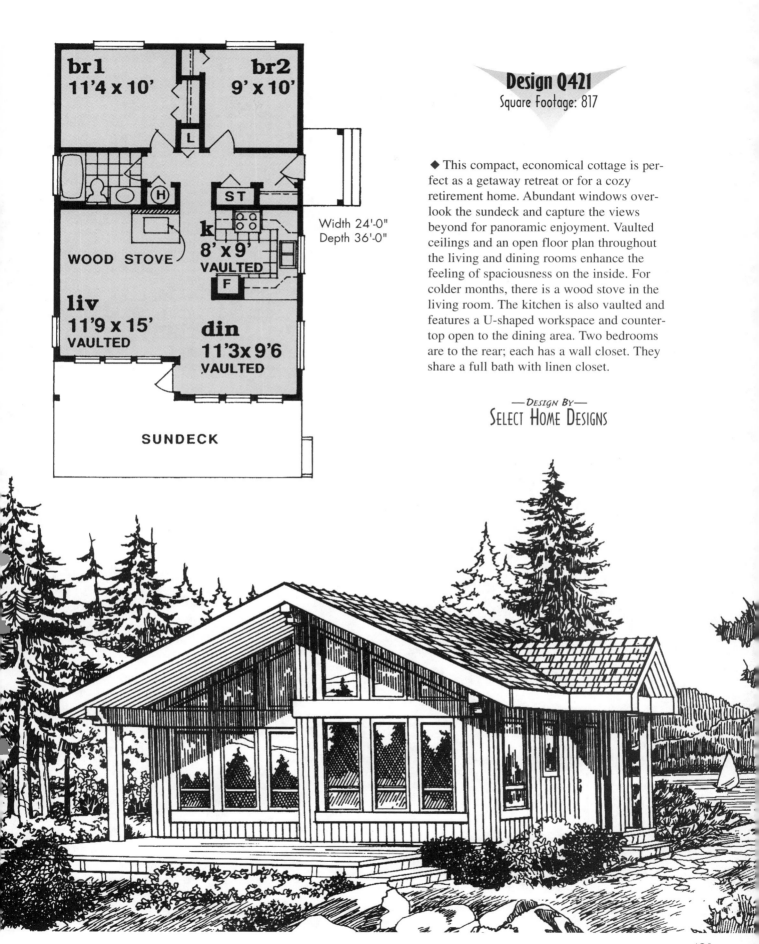

br1
11'4 x 10'

br2
9' x 10'

L

H

ST

k
8' x 9'
VAULTED

WOOD STOVE

F

liv
11'9 x 15'
VAULTED

din
11'3 x 9'6
VAULTED

SUNDECK

Width 24'-0"
Depth 36'-0"

Design Q421
Square Footage: 817

◆ This compact, economical cottage is perfect as a getaway retreat or for a cozy retirement home. Abundant windows overlook the sundeck and capture the views beyond for panoramic enjoyment. Vaulted ceilings and an open floor plan throughout the living and dining rooms enhance the feeling of spaciousness on the inside. For colder months, there is a wood stove in the living room. The kitchen is also vaulted and features a U-shaped workspace and countertop open to the dining area. Two bedrooms are to the rear; each has a wall closet. They share a full bath with linen closet.

— DESIGN BY —
SELECT HOME DESIGNS

431

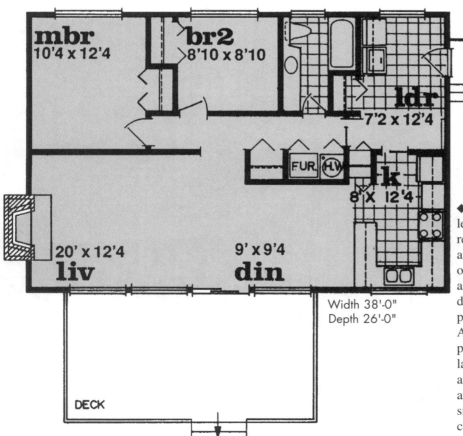

mbr
10'4 x 12'4

br2
8'10 x 8'10

ldr
7'2 x 12'4

FUR. HW

k
8' X 12'4

liv
20' x 12'4

din
9' x 9'4

Width 38'-0"
Depth 26'-0"

DECK

—DESIGN BY—
HOME PLANNERS

Design Q206
Square Footage: 988

◆ This cozy design serves nicely as a leisure home for vacations, or as a full-time retirement residence. Horizontal siding and a solid-stone chimney stack are a reminder of a rustic retreat. A spacious living/dining area has a full wall of glass overlooking a deck with views beyond. A masonry fireplace warms the space in the cold months. A U-shaped kitchen is nearby and has a pass-through counter to the dining room. A large laundry/mud room is across the hall and holds storage space. Sleeping quarters are comprised of a large master suite and smaller family bedroom, both with hall closets. A full bath serves both bedrooms.

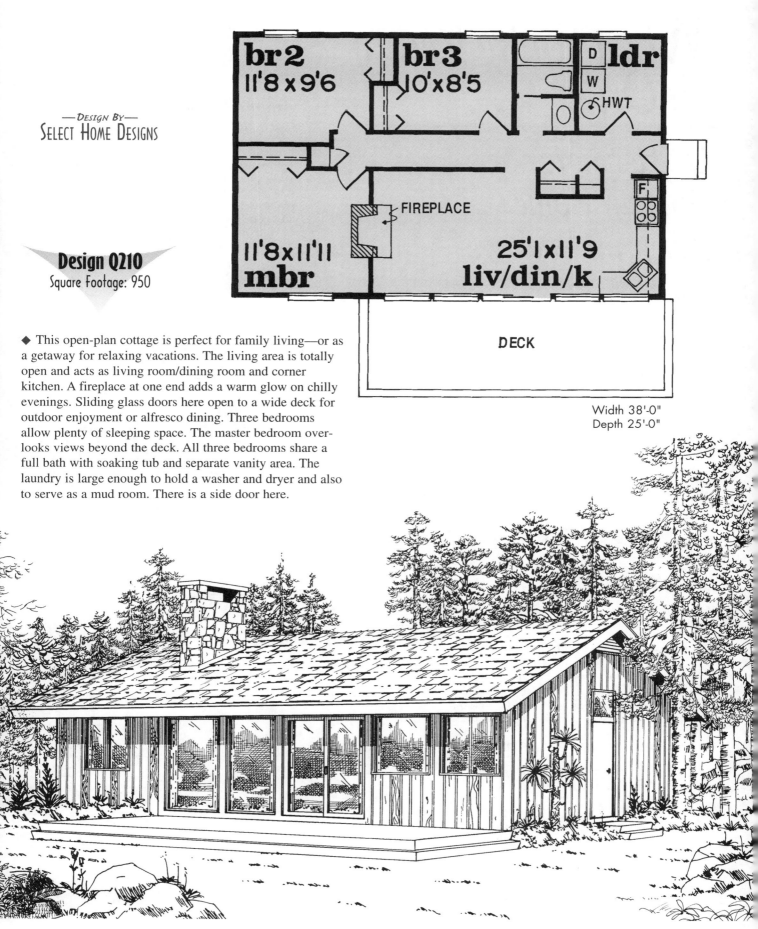

br2
11'8 x 9'6

br3
10' x 8'5

ldr

D

W

HWT

FIREPLACE

11'8 x 11'11
mbr

25'1 x 11'9
liv/din/k

F

DECK

Width 38'-0"
Depth 25'-0"

—Design By—
SELECT HOME DESIGNS

Design Q210
Square Footage: 950

◆ This open-plan cottage is perfect for family living—or as a getaway for relaxing vacations. The living area is totally open and acts as living room/dining room and corner kitchen. A fireplace at one end adds a warm glow on chilly evenings. Sliding glass doors here open to a wide deck for outdoor enjoyment or alfresco dining. Three bedrooms allow plenty of sleeping space. The master bedroom over-looks views beyond the deck. All three bedrooms share a full bath with soaking tub and separate vanity area. The laundry is large enough to hold a washer and dryer and also to serve as a mud room. There is a side door here.

When You're Ready To Order . . .

Let Us Show You Our Home Blueprint Package.

Building a home? Planning a home? Our Blueprint Package has nearly everything you need to get the job done right, whether you're working on your own or with help from an architect, designer, builder or subcontractors. Each Blueprint Package is the result of many hours of work by licensed architects or professional designers.

QUALITY

Hundreds of hours of painstaking effort have gone into the development of your blueprint set. Each home has been quality-checked by professionals to insure accuracy and buildability.

VALUE

Because we sell in volume, you can buy professional-quality blueprints at a fraction of their development cost. With our plans, your dream home design costs only a few hundred dollars, not the thousands of dollars that custom architects charge.

SERVICE

Once you've chosen your favorite home plan, you'll receive fast, efficient service whether you choose to mail or fax your order to us or call us toll free at 1-800-521-6797. For customer service, call toll free 1-888-690-1116.

SATISFACTION

Over 50 years of service to satisfied home plan buyers provide us unparalleled experience and knowledge in producing quality blueprints. What this means to you is satisfaction with our product and performance.

ORDER TOLL FREE 1-800-521-6797

After you've looked over our Blueprint Package and Important Extras on the following pages, simply mail the order form on page 445 or call toll free on our Blueprint Hotline: 1-800-521-6797. We're ready and eager to serve you. For customer service, call toll free 1-888-690-1116.

Each set of blueprints is an interrelated collection of detail sheets which includes components such as floor plans, interior and exterior elevations, dimensions, cross-sections, diagrams and notations. These sheets show exactly how your house is to be built.

Among the sheets included may be:

Frontal Sheet
This artist's sketch of the exterior of the house gives you an idea of how the house will look when built and landscaped. Large ink-line floor plans show all levels of the house and provide an overview of your new home's livability, as well as a handy reference for deciding on furniture placement.

Foundation Plan
This sheet shows the foundation layout includ-

SAMPLE PACKAGE

ing support walls, excavated and unexcavated areas, if any, and foundation notes. If slab construction rather than basement, the plan shows footings and details for a monolithic slab. This page, or another in the set, may include a sample plot plan for locating your house on a building site.

Detailed Floor Plans
These plans show the layout of each floor of the house. Rooms and interior spaces are carefully dimensioned and keys are given for cross-section details provided later in the plans. The positions of electrical outlets and switches are shown.

House Cross-Sections
Large-scale views show sections or cut-aways of the foundation, interior walls, exterior walls, floors, stairways and roof details. Additional cross-sections may show important changes in floor, ceiling or roof heights or the relationship of one level to another. Extremely valuable for construction, these sections show exactly how the various parts of the house fit together.

Interior Elevations
Many of our drawings show the design and placement of kitchen and bathroom cabinets, laundry areas, fireplaces, bookcases and other built-ins. Little "extras," such as mantelpiece and wainscoting drawings, plus moulding sections, provide details that give your home that custom touch.

Exterior Elevations
These drawings show the front, rear and sides of your house and give necessary notes on exterior materials and finishes. Particular attention is given to cornice detail, brick and stone accents or other finish items that make your home unique.

Note: Because of the diversity of local building codes, our blueprints may not include Electrical, Plumbing and Mechanical plans or Layouts.

Frontal Sheet

Foundation Plans

Detailed Floor Plans

Exterior Elevations

Interior Elevations

House Cross-Sections

*I*mportant Extras To Do The Job Right!

Introducing eight important planning and construction aids developed by our professionals to help you succeed in your home-building project.

MATERIALS LIST

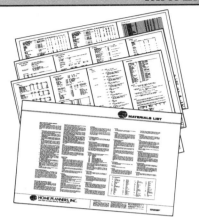

(Note: Because of the diversity of local building codes, our Materials List does not include mechanical materials.)

For many of the designs in our portfolio, we offer a customized materials take-off that is invaluable in planning and estimating the cost of your new home. This Materials List outlines the quantity, type and size of materials needed to build your house (with the exception of mechanical system items). Included are framing lumber, windows and doors, kitchen and bath cabinetry, rough and finish hardware, and much more. This handy list helps you or your builder cost out materials and serves as a reference sheet when you're compiling bids. A Materials List cannot be ordered before blueprints are ordered.

SPECIFICATION OUTLINE

This valuable 16-page document is critical to building your house correctly. Designed to be filled in by you or your builder, this book lists 166 stages or items crucial to the building process. It provides a comprehensive review of the construction process and helps in making choices of materials. When combined with the blueprints, a signed contract, and a schedule, it becomes a legal document and record for the building of your home.

QUOTE ONE®

Summary Cost Report / Materials Cost Report

A new service for estimating the cost of building select designs, the Quote One® system is available in two separate stages: The Summary Cost Report and the Materials Cost Report.

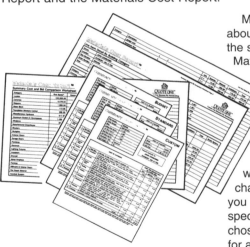

The Summary Cost Report is the first stage in the package and shows the total cost per square foot for your chosen home in your zip-code area and then breaks that cost down into various categories showing the costs for building materials, labor and installation. The total cost for the report (which includes three grades: Budget, Standard and Custom) is just $19.95 for one home, and additionals are only $14.95. These reports allow you to evaluate your building budget and compare the costs of building a variety of homes in your area.

Make even more informed decisions about your home-building project with the second phase of our package, our Materials Cost Report. This tool is invaluable in planning and estimating the cost of your new home. The material and installation (labor and equipment) cost is shown for each of over 1,000 line items provided in the Materials List (Standard grade) which is included when you purchase this estimating tool. It allows you to determine building costs for your specific zip-code area and for your chosen home design. Space is allowed for additional estimates from contractors and subcontractors. This invaluable tool is available for a price of $110 ($120 for a Schedule E plan) which includes a Materials List. A Materials Cost Report cannot be ordered before blueprints are ordered.

The Quote One® program is continually updated with new plans. If you are interested in a plan that is not indicated as Quote One®, please call and ask our sales reps, they will be happy to verify the status for you. To order these invalu- able reports, use the order form on page 445 or call 1-800-521-6797.

Plan-A-Home®

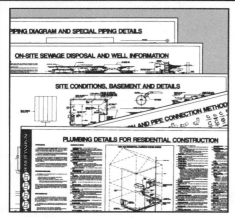

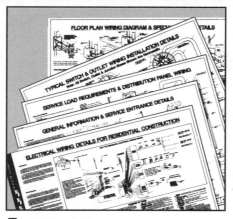

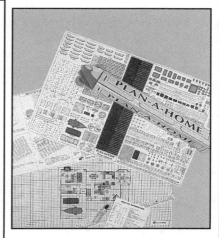

PLUMBING

The Blueprint Package includes locations for all the plumbing fixtures in your new house, including sinks, lavatories, tubs, showers, toilets, laundry trays and water heaters. However, if you want to know more about the complete plumbing system, these 24x36-inch detail sheets will prove very useful. Prepared to meet requirements of the National Plumbing Code, these six fact-filled sheets give general information on pipe schedules, fittings, sump-pump details, water-softener hookups, septic system details and much more. Color-coded sheets in-clude a glossary of terms.

ELECTRICAL

The locations for every electrical switch, plug and outlet are shown in your Blueprint Package. However, these Electrical Details go further to take the mystery out of household electrical systems. Prepared to meet requirements of the National Electrical Code, these comprehensive 24x36-inch drawings come packed with helpful information, including wire sizing, switch-installation schematics, cable-routing details, appliance wattage, door-bell hookups, typical service panel circuitry and much more. Six sheets are bound together and color-coded for easy reference. A glossary of terms is also included.

Plan-A-Home® is an easy-to-use tool that helps you design a new home, arrange furniture in a new or existing home, or plan a remodeling project. Each package contains:

- **More than 700 reusable peel-off planning symbols** on a self-stick vinyl sheet, including walls, windows, doors, all types of furniture, kitchen components, bath fixtures and many more.

- **A reusable, transparent, 1/4-inch scale planning grid** that matches the scale of actual working drawings (1/4-inch equals 1 foot). This grid provides the basis for house layouts of up to 140x92 feet.

- **Tracing paper** and a protective sheet for copying or transferring your completed plan.

- **A felt-tip pen,** with water-soluble ink that wipes away quickly.

Plan-A-Home® lets you lay out areas as large as a 7,500 square foot, six-bedroom, seven-bath house.

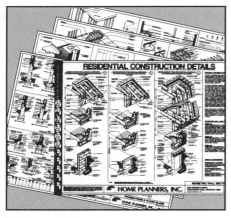

CONSTRUCTION

The Blueprint Package contains everything an experienced builder needs to construct a particular house. However, it doesn't show all the ways that houses can be built, nor does it explain alternate construction methods. To help you understand how your house will be built—and offer additional techniques—this set of drawings depicts the materials and methods used to build foundations, fireplaces, walls, floors and roofs. Where appropriate, the drawings show acceptable alternatives. These six sheets will answer questions for the advanced do-it-yourselfer or home planner.

MECHANICAL

This package contains fundamental principles and useful data that will help you make informed decisions and communicate with subcontractors about heating and cooling systems. The 24x36-inch drawings contain instructions and samples that allow you to make simple load calculations and preliminary sizing and costing analysis. Covered are today's most commonly used systems from heat pumps to solar fuel systems. The package is packed full of illustrations and diagrams to help you visualize components and how they relate to one an-other.

To Order, Call Toll Free 1-800-521-6797

To add these important extras to your Blueprint Package, simply indicate your choices on the order form on page 445 or call us Toll Free 1-800-521-6797 and we'll tell you more about these exciting products. For customer service, call toll free 1-888-690-1116.

◨ The Deck Blueprint Package

Many of the homes in this book can be enhanced with a professionally designed Home Planners' Deck Plan. Those home plans highlighted with a ◨ have a matching or corresponding deck plan available which includes a Deck Plan Frontal Sheet, Deck Framing and Floor Plans, Deck Elevations and a Deck Materials List. A Standard Deck Details Package, also available, provides all the how-to information necessary for building *any* deck. Our Complete Deck Building Package contains 1 set of Custom Deck Plans of your choice, plus 1 set of Standard Deck Building Details all for one low price. Our plans and details are carefully prepared in an easy-to-understand format that will guide you through every stage of your deck-building project. This page contains a sampling of 12 of the 25 different Deck layouts to match your favorite house. See page 440 for prices and ordering information.

SPLIT-LEVEL SUN DECK
Deck Plan D100

BI-LEVEL DECK WITH COVERED DINING
Deck Plan D101

WRAP-AROUND FAMILY DECK
Deck Plan D104

DECK FOR DINING AND VIEWS
Deck Plan D107

TREND SETTER DECK
Deck Plan D110

TURN-OF-THE-CENTURY DECK
Deck Plan D111

WEEKEND ENTERTAINER DECK
Deck Plan D112

CENTER-VIEW DECK
Deck Plan D114

KITCHEN-EXTENDER DECK
Deck Plan D115

SPLIT-LEVEL ACTIVITY DECK
Deck Plan D117

TRI-LEVEL DECK WITH GRILL
Deck Plan D119

CONTEMPORARY LEISURE DECK
Deck Plan D120

L *The Landscape Blueprint Package*

For the homes marked with an L in this book, Home Planners has created a front-yard landscape plan that matches or is complementary in design to the house plan. These comprehensive blueprint packages include a Frontal Sheet, Plan View, Regionalized Plant & Materials List, a sheet on Planting and Maintaining Your Landscape, Zone Maps and Plant Size and Description Guide. These plans will help you achieve professional results, adding value and enjoyment to your property for years to come. Each set of blueprints is a full 18" x 24" in size with clear, complete instructions and easy-to-read type. Six of the forty front yard Landscape Plans to match your favorite house are shown below.

Regional Order Map

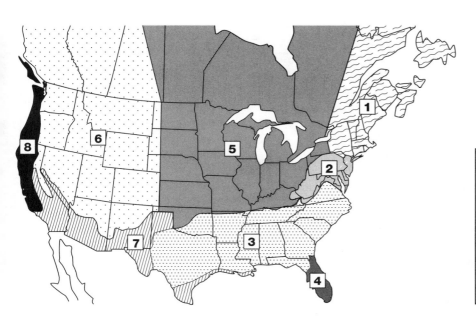

Most of the Landscape Plans shown on these pages are available with a Plant & Materials List adapted by horticultural experts to 8 different regions of the country. Please specify Geographic Region when ordering your plan. See page 440 for prices, ordering information and regional availability.

Region	1	Northeast
Region	2	Mid-Atlantic
Region	3	Deep South
Region	4	Florida & Gulf Coast
Region	5	Midwest
Region	6	Rocky Mountains
Region	7	Southern California & Desert Southwest
Region	8	Northern California & Pacific Northwest

CAPE COD COTTAGE
Landscape Plan L202

GAMBREL-ROOF COLONIAL
Landscape Plan L203

CENTER-HALL COLONIAL
Landscape Plan L204

CLASSIC NEW ENGLAND COLONIAL
Landscape Plan L205

COUNTRY-STYLE FARMHOUSE
Landscape Plan L207

TRADITIONAL SPLIT-LEVEL
Landscape Plan L228

Price Schedule & Plans Index

House Blueprint Price Schedule
(Prices guaranteed through December 31, 1999)

Tier	1-set Study Package	4-set Building Package	8-set Building Package	1-set Reproducible Sepias	Home Customizer® Package
A	$390	$435	$495	$595	$645
B	$430	$475	$535	$655	$705
C	$470	$515	$575	$715	$765
D	$510	$555	$615	$775	$825
E	$630	$675	$735	$835	$885

Prices for 4- or 8-set Building Packages honored only at time of original order.
Additional Identical Blueprints in same order ....$50 per set
Reverse Blueprints (mirror image)..................................$50 per set
Specification Outlines ....$10 each
Materials Lists (available only from those designers listed below):
▲ Home Planners Designs...$50
● The Sater Design Collection $50
✳ Larry Garnett Designs $50
≠ Larry Belk Designs $50
† Design Basics Designs $75
◆ Donald Gardner Designs $50
■ Design Traditions Designs...$50
✱ Alan Mascord Designs $50

Materials Lists for "E" price plans are an additional $10.

Deck Plans Price Schedule

CUSTOM DECK PLANS

Price Group	Q	R	S
1 Set Custom Plans	$25	$30	$35
Additional identical sets	$10 each		
Reverse sets (mirror image)	$10 each		

STANDARD DECK DETAILS
1 Set Generic Construction Details....................$14.95 each

COMPLETE DECK BUILDING PACKAGE

Price Group	Q	R	S
1 Set Custom Plans, plus 1 Set Standard Deck Details	$35	$40	$45

Landscape Plans Price Schedule

Price Group	X	Y	Z
1 set	$35	$45	$55
3 sets	$50	$60	$70
6 sets	$65	$75	$85

Additional Identical Sets ....$10 each
Reverse Sets (mirror image) ....$10 each

Index

To use the Index below, refer to the design number listed in numerical order (a helpful page reference is also given). Note the price index letter and refer to the House Blueprint Price Schedule above for the cost of one, four or eight sets of blueprints or the cost of a reproducible sepia. Additional prices are shown for identical and reverse blueprint sets, as well as a very useful Materials List for some of the plans. Also note in the Index below those plans that have matching or complementary Deck Plans or Landscape Plans. Refer to the schedules above for prices of these plans. All Home Planners' plans can be customized with Home Planners' Home Customizer® Package. These plans are indicated below with this symbol: 🏠. See page 445 for information. Some plans are also part of our Quote One® estimating service and are indicated by this symbol: 🏠. See page 436 for more information.

To Order: Fill in and send the order form on page 445—or call toll free 1-800-521-6797 or 520-297-8200.

DESIGN	PRICE	PAGE	CUSTOMIZABLE	QUOTE ONE®	DECK	DECK PRICE	LANDSCAPE	LANDSCAPE PRICE	REGIONS
▲1021	A	168	🏠						
▲1025	A	39	🏠						
▲1075	A	41	🏠		D114	R	L225	X	1-3,5,6,8
▲1107	A	38	🏠		D112	R	L225	X	1-3,5,6,8
▲1113	A	281	🏠	🏠	D113	R	L202	X	1-3,5,6,8
▲1186	B	72	🏠						
▲1191	A	285	🏠		D114	R	L225	X	1-3,5,6,8
▲1228	D	334	🏠		D124	S	L217	Y	1-8
▲1305	A	40	🏠		D106	S			
▲1311	A	44	🏠				L225	X	1-3,5,6,8
▲1323	A	34	🏠	🏠	D117	S	L225	X	1-3,5,6,8
▲1325	B	77	🏠		D106	S	L225	X	1-3,5,6,8
▲1346	B	71	🏠						
▲1364	A	292	🏠		D117	S			
▲1367	A	42	🏠						
▲1372	A	304	🏠						
▲1373	A	11	🏠						
▲1394	A	303	🏠		D105	R	L202	X	1-3,5,6,8
▲1761	C	138	🏠		D117	S	L217	Y	1-8
▲1788	C	116	🏠		D101	R	L206	Z	1-6,8
▲1829	B	287	🏠		D113	R	L226	X	1-8
▲1890	B	69	🏠						
▲1892	B	117	🏠		D106	S	L225	X	1-3,5,6,8
▲1896	B	70	🏠						
▲1911	D	340	🏠						
▲1920	B	284	🏠	🏠			L225	X	1-3,5,6,8
▲1939	A	43	🏠		D117	S	L225	X	1-3,5,6,8
▲1989	C	224	🏠		D100	Q	L220	Y	1-3,5,6,8
▲1993	D	335	🏠				L213	Z	1-8
▲2153	A	306	🏠		D114	R			
▲2165	A	10	🏠						
▲2170	B	229	🏠				L221	X	1-3,5,6,8
▲2181	C	136	🏠		D100	Q	L226	X	1-8
▲2204	B	115	🏠						
▲2206	B	228	🏠	🏠			L220	Y	1-3,5,6,8
▲2220	C	222	🏠		D114	R	L217	Y	1-8
▲2236	C	393	🏠						
▲2343	D	180	🏠						

DESIGN	PRICE	PAGE	CUSTOMIZABLE	QUOTE ONE®	DECK	DECK PRICE	LANDSCAPE	LANDSCAPE PRICE	REGIONS
▲ 2351	B	164	🏠						
▲ 2505	A	36	🏠	🏠	D113	R	L226	X	1-8
▲ 2528	B	177	🏠		D100	Q			
▲ 2534	D	339	🏠	🏠			L227	Z	1-8
▲ 2544	C	140	🏠		D124	S			
▲ 2550	B	114	🏠		D112	R			
▲ 2565	B	64	🏠		D101	R	L225	X	1-3,5,6,8
▲ 2573	C	238	🏠		D114	R	L220	Y	1-3,5,6,8
▲ 2597	B	288	🏠		D114	R	L226	X	1-8
▲ 2603	B	57	🏠	🏠	D106	S	L220	Y	1-3,5,6,8
▲ 2606	A	225	🏠				L221	X	1-3,5,6,8
▲ 2607	A	237	🏠				L220	Y	1-3,5,6,8
▲ 2611	B	74	🏠		D112	R	L225	X	1-3,5,6,8
▲ 2612	B	75	🏠		D112	R	L226	X	1-8
▲ 2615	D	344	🏠	🏠	D106	S	L211	Y	1-8
▲ 2670	D	348	🏠	🏠			L236	Z	3,4,7
▲ 2671	B	163	🏠	🏠	D114	R	L234	Y	1-8
▲ 2672	B	286	🏠	🏠	D112	R	L226	X	1-8
▲ 2675	C	137	🏠		D106	S			
▲ 2678	B	231	🏠		D117	S	L220	Y	1-3,5,6,8
▲ 2693	D	329	🏠						
▲ 2707	A	299	🏠	🏠	D117	S	L226	X	1-8
▲ 2728	B	230	🏠		D112	R	L221	X	1-3,5,6,8
▲ 2730	C	154	🏠		D124	S			
▲ 2737	B	226	🏠				L220	Y	1-3,5,6,8
▲ 2738	B	60	🏠						
▲ 2746	C	240	🏠		D101	R			
▲ 2756	C	172	🏠		D101	R	L234	Y	1-8
▲ 2768	D	341	🏠						
▲ 2777	B	111	🏠		D101	R	L221	X	1-3,5,6,8
▲ 2778	C	139	🏠		D120	R			
▲ 2779	D	330	🏠	🏠	D100	Q	L217	Y	1-8
▲ 2785	C	239	🏠		D100	Q	L220	Y	1-3,5,6,8
▲ 2789	C	158	🏠		D117	S	L228	Y	1-8
▲ 2790	B	170	🏠						
▲ 2802	B	58	🏠		D118	R	L220	Y	1-3,5,6,8
▲ 2803	B	58	🏠		D118	R	L225	X	1-3,5,6,8
▲ 2804	B	59	🏠		D118	R	L232	Y	4,7
▲ 2805	B	61	🏠	🏠	D113	R	L220	Y	1-3,5,6,8
▲ 2806	B	61	🏠		D113	R	L220	Y	1-3,5,6,8
▲ 2810	B	68	🏠	🏠	D112	R	L204	Y	1-3,5,6,8
▲ 2817	B	162	🏠		D112	R	L204	Y	1-3,5,6,8
▲ 2818	B	166	🏠	🏠	D101	R	L234	Y	1-8
▲ 2819	C	171	🏠		D113	R			
▲ 2820	C	409	🏠		D124	S	L236	Z	3,4,7
▲ 2832	C	143	🏠		D113	R			
▲ 2847	C	234	🏠				L220	Y	1-3,5,6,8
▲ 2851	C	133	🏠	🏠			L217	Y	1-8
▲ 2858	C	145	🏠						
▲ 2862	C	144	🏠						
▲ 2864	A	151	🏠	🏠	D100	Q	L225	X	1-3,5,6,8
▲ 2866	C	173	🏠						
▲ 2867	C	120	🏠				L220	Y	1-3,5,6,8
▲ 2871	B	174	🏠	🏠	D117	S			
▲ 2875	B	392	🏠	🏠	D113	R	L236	Z	3,4,7
▲ 2877	C	176	🏠		D114	R	L220	Y	1-3,5,6,8
▲ 2878	B	66	🏠	🏠	D112	R	L200	X	1-3,5,6,8
▲ 2879	D	338	🏠	🏠					
▲ 2880	C	142	🏠		D114	R	L212	Z	1-8
▲ 2888	D	342	🏠				L211	Y	1-8
▲ 2902	B	148	🏠	🏠			L234	Y	1-8
▲ 2911	A	24	🏠						
▲ 2912	B	381	🏠	🏠					
▲ 2913	B	155	🏠		D124	S			
▲ 2915	C	161	🏠		D114	R	L212	Z	1-8
▲ 2916	B	121	🏠				L221	X	1-3,5,6,8
▲ 2918	B	175	🏠		D124	S			
▲ 2920	D	345	🏠	🏠	D104	S	L212	Z	1-8
▲ 2921	D	343	🏠	🏠	D104	S	L212	Z	1-8
▲ 2922	D	396	🏠	🏠					
▲ 2929	B	227	🏠						
▲ 2931	B	118	🏠						
▲ 2941	B	78	🏠		D112	R			
▲ 2943	B	79	🏠	🏠	D112	R			
▲ 2947	B	259	🏠	🏠	D112	R	L200	X	1-3,5,6,8
▲ 2948	B	394	🏠	🏠					
▲ 2949	C	405	🏠	🏠					
▲ 2950	C	399	🏠						
▲ 2961	D	236	🏠						
▲ 2962	B	235	🏠	🏠					
▲ 3144	B	73	🏠						
▲ 3163	B	169	🏠						
▲ 3189	A	302	🏠		D113	R			
▲ 3314	B	62	🏠	🏠			L200	X	1-3,5,6,8
▲ 3327	C	125	🏠	🏠	D110	R	L217	Y	1-8
▲ 3329	C	347	🏠	🏠			L233	Y	3,4,7
▲ 3332	B	119	🏠	🏠			L200	X	1-3,5,6,8
▲ 3336	B	124	🏠	🏠			L200	X	1-3,5,6,8
▲ 3340	C	67	🏠	🏠			L224	Y	1-3,5,6,8
▲ 3344	D	388	🏠	🏠			L211	Y	1-8
▲ 3346	B	232	🏠	🏠			L204	Y	1-3,5,6,8
▲ 3348	C	293	🏠	🏠			L200	X	1-3,5,6,8
▲ 3355	A	18	🏠	🏠	D117	S	L220	Y	1-3,5,6,8
▲ 3357	D	167	🏠	🏠	D115	Q	L211	Y	1-8
▲ 3359	C	159	🏠	🏠	D124	S	L221	X	1-3,5,6,8
▲ 3368	C	165	🏠	🏠	D104	S	L220	Y	1-3,5,6,8
▲ 3376	B	56	🏠	🏠	D114	R	L205	Y	1-3,5,6,8
▲ 3377	C	233	🏠	🏠	D110	R	L203	Y	1-3,5,6,8
▲ 3405	D	407	🏠	🏠			L236	Z	3,4,7
▲ 3413	C	390	🏠	🏠			L238	Y	3,4,7,8
▲ 3416	A	300	🏠	🏠			L239	Z	1-8
▲ 3419	B	415	🏠	🏠			L239	Z	1-8
▲ 3421	B	384	🏠	🏠			L238	Y	3,4,7,8
▲ 3422	B	414	🏠	🏠			L239	Z	1-8
▲ 3423	C	349	🏠	🏠					
▲ 3434	D	400	🏠	🏠			L233	Y	3,4,7
▲ 3436	C	408	🏠	🏠			L227	Z	1-8
▲ 3440	C	352	🏠	🏠			L233	Y	3,4,7
▲ 3442	A	326	🏠	🏠	D115	Q	L200	X	1-3,5,6,8
▲ 3454	B	147	🏠	🏠	D110	R	L220	Y	1-3,5,6,8
▲ 3466	B	289	🏠	🏠	D110	R	L207	Z	1-6,8
▲ 3486	D	406	🏠	🏠					
▲ 3559	C	146	🏠	🏠	D111	S	L217	Y	1-8
▲ 3560	B	149	🏠	🏠			L234	Y	1-8
▲ 3600	C	93	🏠	🏠			L200	X	1-3,5,6,8
▲ 3601	C	94	🏠	🏠			L200	X	1-3,5,6,8
▲ 3603	C	369	🏠	🏠			L220	Y	1-3,5,6,8
▲ 3612	C	332	🏠	🏠			L206	Z	1-3,5,6,8
▲ 3613	C	95	🏠	🏠			L209	Y	1-6,8
▲ 3630	C	397	🏠	🏠			L209	Y	1-6,8
▲ 3631	C	379	🏠	🏠			L214	Z	1-3,5,6,8
▲ 3632	C	389	🏠	🏠			L237	Y	7
▲ 3633	C	382	🏠	🏠			L237	Y	7
▲ 3636	C	178	🏠	🏠			L238	Y	3,4,7,8
▲ 3637	D	179	🏠	🏠			L235	Z	1-3,5,6,8
▲ 3640	C	391	🏠	🏠			L286	Z	1-8
▲ 3642	C	404	🏠	🏠					
▲ 3646	C	402	🏠	🏠			L237	Y	7
▲ 3652	B	123	🏠	🏠	D105	R	L220	Y	1-3,5,6,8
▲ 3655	B	318	🏠	🏠			L205	Y	1-3,5,6,8
▲ 3656	A	318	🏠	🏠			L205	Y	1-3,5,6,8
▲ 3657	B	378	🏠						
▲ 3659	B	260	🏠	🏠			L290	Y	1-8
▲ 3660	B	398	🏠	🏠			L236	Z	3,4,7
▲ 3661	C	358	🏠	🏠			L288	Z	1-8
▲ 3662	B	251	🏠	🏠			L287	Z	1-8
▲ 3664	C	336	🏠	🏠			L287	Z	1-8
▲ 3665	C	359	🏠	🏠			L288	Z	1-8
▲ 3669	D	346	🏠						
▲ 3672	B	244	🏠		D111	S	L209	Y	1-6,8
▲ 3685	C	262	🏠	🏠					
▲ 3689	A	320	🏠	🏠	D124	S	L284	Y	1-8

441

Before You Order . . .

Before filling out the coupon at right or calling us on our Toll-Free Blueprint Hotline, you may want to learn more about our services and products. Here's some information you will find helpful.

Quick Turnaround

We process and ship every blueprint order from our office within two business days. Because of this quick turnaround, we won't send a formal notice acknowledging receipt of your order.

Our Exchange Policy

Since blueprints are printed in response to your order, we cannot honor requests for refunds. However, we will exchange your entire first order for an equal number of blueprints at a price of $50 for the first set and $10 for each additional set; $70 total exchange fee for 4 sets; $100 total exchange fee for 8 sets . . . *plus* the difference in cost if exchanging for a design in a higher price bracket or *less* the difference in cost if exchanging for a design in lower price bracket. One exchange is allowed within a year of purchase date. **(Sepias are not exchangeable.)** All sets from the first order must be returned before the exchange can take place. Please add $18 for postage and handling via Regular Service; $30 via Priority Service; $40 via Express Service.

About Reverse Blueprints

If you want to build in reverse of the plan as shown, we will include an extra set of reverse blueprints (mirror image) for an additional fee of $50. Although lettering and dimensions will appear backward, reverses will be a useful aid if you decide to flop the plan.

Revising, Modifying and Customizing Plans

The wide variety of designs available in this publication allows you to select ideas and concepts for a home to fit your building site and match your family's needs, wants and budget. Like many homeowners who buy these plans, you and your builder, architect or engineer may want to make changes to them. Some minor changes may be made by your builder, but we recommend that most changes be made by a licensed architect or engineer. If you need to make alterations to a design that is customizable, you need only order our Home Customizer® Package to get you started. As set forth below, we cannot assume any responsibility for blueprints which have been changed, whether by you, your builder or by professionals selected by you or referred to you by us, because such individuals are outside our supervision and control.

Architectural and Engineering Seals

Some cities and states are now requiring that a licensed architect or engineer review and "seal" a blueprint, or officially approve it, prior to construction due to concerns over energy costs, safety and other factors. Prior to application for a building permit or the start of actual construction, we strongly advise that you consult your local building official who can tell you if such a review is required.

About the Designers

The architects and designers whose work appears in this publication are among America's leading residential designers. Each plan was designed to meet the requirements of a nationally recognized model building code in effect at the time and place the plan was drawn. Because national building codes change from time to time, plans may not comply with any such code at the time they are sold to a customer. In addition, building officials may not accept these plans as final construction documents of record as the plans may need to be modified and additional drawings and details added to suit local conditions and requirements. We strongly advise that purchasers consult a licensed architect or engineer, and their local building official, before starting any construction related to these plans.

Local Building Codes and Zoning Requirements

At the time of creation, our plans are drawn to specifications published by the Building Officials and Code Administrators (BOCA) International, Inc.; the Southern Building Code Congress (SBCCI) International, Inc.; the International Conference of Building Officials; or the Council of American Building Officials (CABO). Our plans are designed to meet or exceed national building standards. Because of the great differences in geography and climate throughout the United States and Canada, each state, county and municipality has its own building codes, zone requirements, ordinances and building regulations. Your plan may need to be modified to comply with local requirements regarding snow loads, energy codes, soil and seismic conditions and a wide range of other matters. In addition, you may need to obtain permits or inspections from local governments before and in the course of construction. Prior to using blueprints ordered from us, we strongly advise that you consult a licensed architect or engineer—and speak with your local building official—before applying for any permit or beginning construction. We authorize the use of our blueprints on the express condition that you strictly comply with all local building codes, zoning requirements and other applicable laws, regulations, ordinances and requirements. **Notice:** Plans for homes to be built in Nevada must be re-drawn by a Nevada-registered professional. Consult your building official for more information on this subject.

Foundation and Exterior Wall Changes

Most of our plans are drawn with either a full or partial basement foundation. Depending on your specific climate or regional building practices, you may wish to change this basement to a slab or crawlspace. Most professional contractors and builders can easily adapt your plans to alternate foundation types. Likewise, most can easily change 2x4 wall construction to 2x6, or vice versa.

Disclaimer

We and the designers we work with have put substantial care and effort into the creation of our blueprints. However, because we cannot provide on-site consultation, supervision and control over actual construction, and because of the great variance in local building requirements, building practices and soil, seismic, weather and other conditions, WE CANNOT MAKE ANY WARRANTY, EXPRESS OR IMPLIED, WITH RESPECT TO THE CONTENT OR USE OF OUR BLUEPRINTS, INCLUDING BUT NOT LIMITED TO ANY WARRANTY OF MERCHANTABILITY OR OF FITNESS FOR A PARTICULAR PURPOSE.

Terms and Conditions

These designs are protected under the terms of United States Copyright Law and may not be copied or reproduced in any way, by any means, unless you have purchased Sepias or Reproducibles which clearly indicate your right to copy or reproduce. We authorize the use of your chosen design as an aid in the construction of one single family home only. You may not use this design to build a second or multiple dwellings without purchasing another blueprint or blueprints or paying additional design fees.

How Many Blueprints Do You Need?

A single set of blueprints is sufficient to study a home in greater detail. However, if you are planning to obtain cost estimates from a contractor or subcontractors—or if you are planning to build immediately—you will need more sets. Because additional sets are cheaper when ordered in quantity with the original order, make sure you order enough blueprints to satisfy all requirements. The following checklist will help you determine how many you need:

____ Owner

____ Builder (generally requires at least three sets; one as a legal document, one to use during inspections, and at least one to give to subcontractors)

____ Local Building Department (often requires two sets)

____ Mortgage Lender (usually one set for a conventional loan; three sets for FHA or VA loans)

____ TOTAL NUMBER OF SETS

Have You Seen Our Newest Designs?

Home Planners is one of the country's most active home design firms, creating nearly 100 new plans each year. At least 50 of our latest creations are featured in each edition of our NewDesign Portfolio. You may have received a copy with your latest purchase by mail. If not, or if you purchased this book from a local retailer, just return the coupon below for your FREE copy. Make sure you consider the very latest of what Home Planners has to offer.

Yes! Please send my FREE copy of your latest New Design Portfolio.

Offer good to U.S. shipping address only.

Name _____

Address _____

City _____ State _____ Zip _____

HOME PLANNERS, LLC
Wholly owned by Hanley-Wood, Inc.
3275 WEST INA ROAD, SUITE 110
TUCSON, ARIZONA 85741

Order Form Key

| OS |

444

Toll Free 1-800-521-6797

Regular Office Hours:
8:00 a.m. to 8:00 p.m. Eastern Time, Monday through Friday
Our staff will gladly answer any questions during regular office hours. Our answering service can place orders after hours or on weekends.

If we receive your order by 4:00 p.m. Eastern Time, Monday through Friday, we'll process it and ship within two business days. When ordering by phone, please have your charge card ready. We'll also ask you for the Order Form Key Number at the bottom of the coupon.

By FAX: Copy the Order Form on the next page and send it on our FAX line: 1-800-224-6699 or 1-520-544-3086.

Canadian Customers
Order Toll-Free 1-800-561-4169

For faster service and plans that are modified for building in Canada, customers may now call in orders directly to our Canadian supplier of plans and charge the purchase to a charge card. Or, you may complete the order form at right, adding 40% to all prices and mail in Canadian funds to:

The Plan Centre 60 Baffin Place
Unit 5
Waterloo, Ontario N2V 1Z7

OR: Copy the Order Form and send it via our Canadian FAX line: 1-800-719-3291.

The Home Customizer®

"This house is perfect...if only the family room were two feet wider." Sound familiar? In response to the numerous requests for this type of modification, Home Planners has developed **The Home Customizer® Package**. This exclusive package offers our top-of-the-line materials to make it easy for anyone, anywhere to customize any Home Planners design to fit their needs. Check the index on page 440-443 for those plans which are customizable.

Some of the changes you can make to any of our plans include:

- exterior elevation changes
- kitchen and bath modifications
- roof, wall and foundation changes
- room additions and more!

The Home Customizer® Package includes everything you'll need to make the necessary changes to your favorite Home Planners design. The package includes:

- instruction book with examples
- architectural scale and clear work film
- erasable red marker and removable correction tape
- ¼"-scale furniture cutouts
- 1 set reproducible, erasable Sepias
- 1 set study blueprints for communicating changes to your design professional
- a copyright release letter so you can make copies as you need them
- referral letter with the name, address and telephone number of the professional in your region who is trained in modifying Home Planners designs efficiently and inexpensively.

The price of the **Home Customizer® Package** ranges from $645 to $885, depending on the price schedule of the design you have chosen. **The Home Customizer® Package** will not only save you 25% to 75% of the cost of drawing the plans from scratch with a custom architect or engineer, it will also give you the flexibility to have your changes and modifications made by our referral network or by the professional of your choice. Now it's even easier and more affordable to have the custom home you've always wanted.

 **ORDER TOLL FREE!**
1-800-521-6797 or 520-297-8200

BLUEPRINTS ARE NOT RETURNABLE

**For Customer Service,
call toll free 1-888-690-1116.**

ORDER FORM

HOME PLANNERS, LLC
Wholly owned by Hanley-Wood, Inc.
3275 WEST INA ROAD, SUITE 110
TUCSON, ARIZONA 85741

THE BASIC BLUEPRINT PACKAGE
Rush me the following (please refer to the Plans Index and Price Schedule in this section):

_____	Set(s) of blueprints for plan number(s) _____.	$_____
_____	Set(s) of sepias for plan number(s) _____.	$_____
_____	Home Customizer® Package for plan(s)_____.	$_____
_____	Additional identical blueprints in same order @ $50 per set.	$_____
_____	Reverse blueprints @ $50 per set.	$_____

IMPORTANT EXTRAS
Rush me the following:

_____ Materials List: $50 (Must be purchased with Blueprint set.)
$75 Design Basics. Add $10 for a Schedule E plan Materials List. $_____
_____ **Quote One®** Summary Cost Report @ $19.95 for 1, $14.95 for
each additional, for plans _____ $_____
Building location: City _____ Zip Code _____
_____ **Quote One®** Materials Cost Report @ $110 Schedule A-D; $120
Schedule E for plan_____ $_____
(Must be purchased with Blueprints set.)
Building location: City _____ Zip Code _____
_____ Specification Outlines @ $10 each. $_____
_____ Detail Sets @ $14.95 each; any two for $22.95; any three
for $29.95; all four for $39.95 (save $19.85). $_____
❏ Plumbing ❏ Electrical ❏ Construction ❏ Mechanical
(These helpful details provide general construction
advice and are not specific to any single plan.)
_____ Plan-A-Home® @ $29.95 each. $_____

DECK BLUEPRINTS
_____ Set(s) of Deck Plan _____. $_____
_____ Additional identical blueprints in same order @ $10 per set. $_____
_____ Reverse blueprints @ $10 per set. $_____
_____ Set of Standard Deck Details @ $14.95 per set. $_____
_____ Set of Complete Building Package (Best Buy!)
Includes Custom Deck Plan _____
(See Index and Price Schedule)
Plus Standard Deck Details $_____

LANDSCAPE BLUEPRINTS
_____ Set(s) of Landscape Plan _____. $_____
_____ Additional identical blueprints in same order @ $10 per set. $_____
_____ Reverse blueprints @ $10 per set. $_____
Please indicate the appropriate region of the country for
Plant & Material List. (See Map on page 439): Region _____

POSTAGE AND HANDLING	1-3 sets	4+ sets
Signature is required for all deliveries.		
DELIVERY (Requires street address - No P.O. Boxes)		
• Regular Service (Allow 7-10 business days delivery)	❏ $15.00	❏ $18.00
• Priority (Allow 4-5 business days delivery)	❏ $20.00	❏ $30.00
• Express (Allow 3 business days delivery)	❏ $30.00	❏ $40.00
CERTIFIED MAIL	❏ $20.00	❏ $30.00
If no street address available. (Allow 7-10 days delivery)		
OVERSEAS DELIVERY		fax, phone or mail
Note: All delivery times are from date Blueprint Package is shipped.		for quote

POSTAGE (From box above) $_____
SUB-TOTAL $_____
SALES TAX (AZ, CA, DC, IL, MI, MN, NY & WA residents,
please add appropriate state and local sales tax.) $_____
TOTAL (Sub-total and tax) $_____

YOUR ADDRESS (please print)
Name _____
Street _____
City _____ State_____ Zip _____
Daytime telephone number (_____) _____

FOR CREDIT CARD ORDERS ONLY
Please fill in the information below:
Credit card number _____
Exp. Date: Month/Year _____
Check one ❏ Visa ❏ MasterCard ❏ Discover Card ❏ American Express
Signature _____
Please check appropriate box: ❏ Licensed Builder-Contractor
❏ Homeowner

 **ORDER TOLL FREE!**
1-800-521-6797 or 520-297-8200

Order Form Key
OS

Helpful Books & Software

Home Planners wants your building experience to be as pleasant and trouble-free as possible. That's why we've expanded our library of Do-It-Yourself titles to help you along. In addition to our beautiful plans books, we've added books to guide you through specific projects as well as the construction process. In fact, these are titles that will be as useful after your dream home is built as they are right now.

ONE-STORY

1 448 designs for all lifestyles. 860 to 5,400 square feet. 384 pages $9.95

TWO-STORY

2 460 designs for one-and-a-half and two stories. 1,245 to 7,275 square feet. 384 pages $9.95

VACATION

3 345 designs for recreation, retirement and leisure. 312 pages $8.95

MULTI-LEVEL

4 214 designs for split-levels, bi-levels, multi-levels and walkouts. 224 pages $8.95

COUNTRY

5 200 country designs from classic to contemporary by 7 winning designers. 224 pages $8.95

MOVE-UP
6 200 stylish designs for today's growing families from 9 hot designers. 224 pages $8.95

NARROW-LOT

7 200 unique homes less than 60' wide from 7 designers. Up to 3,000 square feet. 224 pages $8.95

SMALL HOUSE
8 200 beautiful designs chosen for versatility and affordability. 224 pages $8.95

BUDGET-SMART

9 200 efficient plans from 7 top designers, that you can really afford to build! 224 pages $8.95

EXPANDABLES

10 200 flexible plans that expand with your needs from 7 top designers. 240 pages $8.95

ENCYCLOPEDIA

11 500 exceptional plans for all styles and budgets—the best book of its kind! 352 pages $9.95

AFFORDABLE

12 Completely revised and updated, featuring 300 designs for modest budgets. 256 pages $9.95

ENCYCLOPEDIA 2

13 500 Completely new plans. Spacious and stylish designs for every budget and taste. 352 pages $9.95

VICTORIAN

14 160 striking Victorian and Farmhouse designs from three leading designers. 192 pages $12.95

ESTATE

15 Dream big! Twenty-one designers showcase their biggest and best plans. 208 pages. $15.95

LUXURY
16 154 fine luxury plans-loaded with luscious amenities! 192 pages $14.95

COTTAGES

17 25 fresh new designs that are as warm as a tropical breeze. A blend of the best aspects of many coastal styles. 64 pages. $19.95

BEST SELLERS

18 Our 50th Anniversary book with 200 of our very best designs in full color! 224 pages $12.95

SPECIAL COLLECTION

19 70 Romantic house plans that capture the classic tradition of home design. 160 pages $17.95

COUNTRY HOUSES

20 208 Unique home plans that combine traditional style and modern livability. 224 pages $9.95

CLASSIC

21 Timeless, elegant designs that always feel like home. Gorgeous plans that are as flexible and up-to-date as their occupants. 240 pages. $9.95

CONTEMPORARY

22 The most complete and imaginative collection of contemporary designs available anywhere. 240 pages. $9.95

EASY-LIVING

23 200 Efficient and sophisticated plans that are small in size, but big on livability. 224 pages $8.95

SOUTHERN

24 207 homes rich in Southern styling and comfort. 240 pages $8.95

SUNBELT

25 215 Designs that capture the spirit of the Southwest. 208 pages $10.95

WESTERN

26 215 designs that capture the spirit and diversity of the Western lifestyle. 208 pages $9.95

ENERGY GUIDE

27 The most comprehensive energy efficiency and conservation guide available. 280 pages $35.00

Design Software

BOOK & CD ROM

28 Both the Home Planners Gold book and matching Windows™ CD ROM with 3D floorplans. $24.95

3D DESIGN SUITE

29 Home design made easy! View designs in 3D, take a virtual reality tour, add decorating details and more. $59.95

Outdoor Projects

OUTDOOR

30 42 unique outdoor projects. Gazebos, strombellas, bridges, sheds, playsets and more! 96 pages $7.95

GARAGES & MORE

31 101 Multi-use garages and outdoor structures to enhance any home. 96 pages $7.95

DECKS

32 25 outstanding single-, double- and multi-level decks you can build. 112 pages $7.95

Landscape Designs

| EASY CARE | FRONT & BACK | BACKYARDS | BEDS & BORDERS | BATHROOMS | KITCHENS | HOUSE CONTRACTING | WINDOWS & DOORS |

  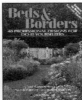    

33 41 special landscapes designed for beauty and low maintenance. 160 pages $14.95

34 The first book of do-it-yourself landscapes. 40 front, 15 backyards. 208 pages $14.95

35 40 designs focused solely on creating your own specially themed backyard oasis. 160 pages $14.95

36 Practical advice and maintenance techniques for a wide variety of yard projects. 160 pages. $14.95

37 An innovative guide to organizing, remodeling and decorating your bathroom. 96 pages $9.95

38 An imaginative guide to designing the perfect kitchen. Chock full of bright ideas to make your job easier. 176 pages $14 .95

39 Everything you need to know to act as your own general contractor...and save up to 25% off building costs. 134 pages $14.95

40 Installation techniques and tips that make your project easier and more professional looking. 80 pages $7.95

| ROOFING | FRAMING | VISUAL HANDBOOK | BASIC WIRING | PATIOS & WALKS | TILE | TRIM & MOLDING |

41 Information on the latest tools, materials and techniques for roof installation or repair. 80 pages $7.95

42 For those who want to take a more-hands on approach to their dream. 319 pages $19.95

43 A plain-talk guide to the construction process; financing to final walk-through, this book covers it all. 498 pages $19.95

44 A straight forward guide to one of the most misunderstood systems in the home. 160 pages $12.95

45 Clear step-by-step instructions take you from the basic design stages to the finished project. 80 pages $7.95

46 Every kind of tile for every kind of application. Includes tips on use installation and repair. 176 pages $12.95

47 Step-by-step instructions for installing baseboards, window and door casings and more. 80 pages $7.95

Additional Books Order Form

To order your books, just check the box of the book numbered below and complete the coupon. We will process your order and ship it from our office within 48 hours. Send coupon and check (in U.S. funds).

YES! Please send me the books I've indicated:

☐ 1:OS	$9.95	☐ 25:SW	$10.95
☐ 2:TS	$9.95	☐ 26:WH	$9.95
☐ 3:VSH	$8.95	☐ 27:RES	$35.00
☐ 4:HH	$8.95	☐ 28:HPGC	$24.95
☐ 5:FH	$8.95	☐ 29:PLANSUITE	$59.95
☐ 6:MU	$8.95	☐ 30:YG	$7.95
☐ 7:NL	$8.95	☐ 31:GG	$7.95
☐ 8:SM	$8.95	☐ 32:DP	$7.95
☐ 9:BS	$8.95	☐ 33:ECL	$14.95
☐ 10:EX	$8.95	☐ 34:HL	$14.95
☐ 11:EN	$9.95	☐ 35:BYL	$14.95
☐ 12:AF	$9.95	☐ 36:BB	$14.95
☐ 13:E2	$9.95	☐ 37:CDB	$9.95
☐ 14:VDH	$12.95	☐ 38:CKI	$14.95
☐ 15:EDH	$15.95	☐ 39:SBC	$14.95
☐ 16:LD2	$14.95	☐ 40:CGD	$7.95
☐ 17:CTG	$19.95	☐ 41:CGR	$7.95
☐ 18:HPG	$12.95	☐ 42:SRF	$19.95
☐ 19:WEP	$17.95	☐ 43:RVH	$19.95
☐ 20:CN	$9.95	☐ 44:CBW	$12.95
☐ 21:CS	$9.95	☐ 45:CGW	$7.95
☐ 22:CM	$9.95	☐ 46:CWT	$12.95
☐ 23:EL	$8.95	☐ 47:CGT	$7.95
☐ 24:SH	$8.95		

Canadian Customers
Order Toll-Free 1-800-561-4169

Additional Books Sub-Total $_____

ADD Postage and Handling $ 3.00

Sales Tax: (AZ, CA, DC, IL, MI, MN, NY & WA residents, please add appropriate state and local sales tax.) $_____

YOUR TOTAL (Sub-Total, Postage/Handling, Tax) $_____

YOUR ADDRESS (Please print)

Name _____

Street _____

City _____State_____Zip _____

Phone (_____) _____—_____

YOUR PAYMENT
Check one: ☐ Check ☐ Visa ☐ MasterCard ☐ Discover Card
☐ American Express
Required credit card information:

Credit Card Number_____

Expiration Date (Month/Year)_____/ _____

Signature Required _____

Home Planners, LLC
Wholly owned by Hanley-Wood, Inc.
3275 W. Ina Road, Suite 110, Dept. BK, Tucson, AZ 85741

OS

Design 3612, page 332

OVER 3 MILLION BLUEPRINTS SOLD

"We instructed our builder to follow the plans including all of the many details which make this house so elegant…Our home is a fine example of the results one can achieve by purchasing and following the plans which you offer…Everyone who has seen it has assured us that it belongs in 'a picture book.' I truly mean it when I say that my home 'is a DREAM HOUSE.'"

S.P.
Anderson, SC

"We have had a steady stream of visitors, many of whom tell us this is the most beautiful home they've seen. Everyone is amazed at the layout and remarks on how unique it is. Our real estate attorney, who is a Chicago dweller and who deals with highly valued properties, told me this is the only suburban home he has seen that he would want to live in."

W. & P.S.
Flossmoor, IL

"Your blueprints saved us a great deal of money. I acted as the general contractor and we did a lot of the work ourselves. We probably built it for half the cost! We are thinking about more plans for another home. I purchased a competitor's book but my husband wants only your plans!"

K.M.
Grovetown, GA

"We are very happy with the product of our efforts. The neighbors and passersby appreciate what we have created. We have had many people stop by to discuss our house and kindly praise it as being the nicest house in our area of new construction. We have even had one person stop and make us an unsolicited offer to buy the house for much more than we have invested in it."

K. & L.S.
Bolingbrook, IL

"The traffic going past our house is unbelievable. On several occasions, we have heard that it is the 'prettiest house in Batavia.' Also, when meeting someone new and mentioning what street we live on, quite often we're told, 'Oh, you're the one in the yellow house with the wrap-around porch! I love it!'"

A.W.
Batavia, NY

"I have been involved in the building trades my entire life…Since building our home we have built two other homes for other families. Their plans from local professional architects were not nearly as good as yours. For that reason we are ordering additional plan books from you."

T.F.
Kingston, WA

"The blueprints we received from you were of excellent quality and provided us with exactly what we needed to get our successful home-building project underway. We appreciate your invaluable role in our home-building effort."

T.A.
Concord, TN